Lecture Notes in Computer Science 4658

Commenced Publication in 1973
Founding and Former Series Editors:
Gerhard Goos, Juris Hartmanis, and Jan van Leeuwen

Tomoya Enokido Leonard Barolli
Makoto Takizawa (Eds.)

Network-Based Information Systems

First International Conference, NBiS 2007
Regensburg, Germany, September 3-7, 2007
Proceedings

Volume Editors

Tomoya Enokido
Rissho University
Faculty of Business Administration
4-2-16 Osaki, Shinagawa, Tokyo, 141-8602, Japan
E-mail: eno@ris.ac.jp

Leonard Barolli
Fukuoka Institute of Technology
Department of Information and Communication Engineering
3-30-1 Wajiro-Higashi, Higashi-ku, Fukuoka, 811-0214 Japan
E-mail: barolli@fit.ac.jp

Makoto Takizawa
Tokyo Denki University
Department of Computers and Systems Engineering
Ishizaka, Hatoyama, Saitama 350-0394, Japan
E-mail: makoto.takizawa@computer.org

Library of Congress Control Number: 2007933416

CR Subject Classification (1998): C.2.4, C.2.5, H.2.8, H.5.1, I.2.9, K.3.1, K.4.4

LNCS Sublibrary: SL 3 – Information Systems and Application, incl. Internet/Web and HCI

ISSN 0302-9743
ISBN-10 3-540-74572-6 Springer Berlin Heidelberg New York
ISBN-13 978-3-540-74572-3 Springer Berlin Heidelberg New York

Springer is a part of Springer Science+Business Media

springer.com

Printed in Germany

Typesetting: Camera-ready by author, data conversion by Scientific Publishing Services, Chennai, India
Printed on acid-free paper SPIN: 12115211 06/3180 5 4 3 2 1 0

Preface

Welcome to the proceedings of the 1st International Conference on Network-Based Information Systems (NBiS-2007), in conjunction with the 18th International Conference on Database and Expert Systems Applications DEXA-2007, which was held in Regensburg, Germany, September 3–4, 2007.

The main objective of NBiS-2007 was to bring together scientists, engineers, and researchers from both network systems and information systems with the aim of encouraging the exchange of ideas, opinions, and experience between these two communities.

NBiS started as a workshop and for 9 years it was held together with DEXA International Conference and is the oldest among DEXA Workshops. The workshop has been very successful in quantity and quality. We received many paper submissions every year, but as a workshop we could accept only a limited number of papers. This was the first year that NBiS was run as an international conference together with DEXA.

We received 122 research papers from all over the world. The submitted papers were carefully reviewed by at least two reviewers. Based on the review results, the Program Committee members selected 55 high-quality papers to be presented during the NBiS-2007 conference.

Many volunteers kindly helped us to prepare and organize the NBiS-2007 International Conference. First of all, we would like to thank all the authors for submitting their papers, Program Committee members, and reviewers who carried out the most difficult task of evaluating the submitted papers. We would like to thank the DEXA Association for giving us the chance to organize the conference. We would like to express our special thanks to Gabriela Wagner for her kind support and help, and also for dealing with conference registration. We would like to thank Kenichi Watanabe and other students of Takizawa Laboratory, Tokyo Denki University, Japan for their hard and timely work to maintain the Web system, distributing of CFP, dealing with the paper submissions, the paper reviewing process, and sending the notification letters to the authors. In addition, we extend our appreciation to the University of Regensburg as Local Organizers. Finally, we would like to thank all the participants of the conference.

June 2007

Tomoya Enokido
Leonard Barolli
Makoto Takizawa

Organization Committee

General Co-chairs

Makoto Takizawa, Tokyo Denki University, Japan
Leonard Barolli, Fukuoka Institute of Technology, Japan

Program Chair

Tomoya Enokido, Rissho University, Japan

Program Committee

Markus Aleksy, University of Mannheim, Germany
Irfan Awan, University of Bradford, UK
Bhed Bahadur Bista, Iwate Prefectural University, Japan
Goutam Chakraborty, Iwate Prefectural University, Japan
Kuo-Ming Chao, Coventry University, UK
Been-Chian Chien, National University of Tainan, Taiwan
S. Misbah Deen, Keele University, England, UK
Alex Delis, Polytechnic University, USA
Andrei Doncesku, University Paul Sabatier, France
Arjan Durresi, Louisiana State University, USA
Thomas Grill, University of Linz, Austria
Lin Guan, Loughborough University, UK
Takahiro Hara, Osaka University, Japan
Naohiro Hayashibara, Tokyo Denki University, Japan
Yoshiaki Hori, Kyushu University, Japan
Hui-huang Hsu, Tamkang University, Taiwan
Ismail Khalil Ibrahim, Johannes Kepler University Linz, Austria
Hiroaki Kikuchi, Tokai University, Japan
Akio Koyama, Yamagata University, Japan
Vincent Lee, Monash University, Australia
Kuan-Ching Li, Providence University, Taiwan
Yinsheng Li, Fudan University, China
Wen-Yang Lin, National University of Kaohsiung, Taiwan
Giuseppe De Marco, Fukuoka Institute of Technology, Japan
Wenny Rahayu, La Trobe University, Australia
Michel Raynal, IRISA-INRIA, France
Fumiaki Sato, Toho University, Japan
Nobuyoshi Sato, Toyo University, Japan
Elhadi Shakshuki, Acadia Univiversity, Canada

Yoshitaka Shibata, Iwate Prefectural University, Japan
Kuei-Ping Shih, Tamkang University, Taiwan
Timothy K. Shih, Tamkang University, Taiwan
Takuo Suganuma, Tohoku University, Japan
Kaoru Sugita, Fukuoka Institute of Technology, Japan
David Taniar, Monash University, Australia
Nguyen Manh Tho, Vienna University of Technology, Austria
Minoru Uehara, Toyo University, Japan
Fatos Xhafa, Polytechnic University of Catalonia, Spain
Chu-Sing Yang, National Su Yut-Sen University, Taiwan
Muhammed Younas, Oxford Brookes University, UK

Table of Contents

Sensor and Ad-Hoc Networks

Network Security

Secure System Applications

Web Technologies and Middleware Systems

Distributed Systems and Applications

Scheduling

Network Analysis

P2P Systems and Applications

Pervasive and Ubiquitous Systems

Network Applications and Protocols

Embedded Systems

Fuzzy Systems and Their Applications

A Simple Statistical Methodology for Testing Ad Hoc Networks

Makoto Ikeda[1], Giuseppe De Marco[2], and Leonard Barolli[1]

[1] Department of Information and Communication Engineering,
Fukuoka Institute of Technology (FIT)
3-30-1 Wajiro-Higashi-ku, Fukuoka 811-0295, Japan
mgm05001@ws.ipc.fit.ac.jp, barolli@fit.ac.jp
[2] Toyota Technological Institute,
2-12-1 Hisakata, Tenpaku-Ku, Nagoya 468-8511, Japan
demarco@toyota-ti.ac.jp

Abstract. Real-life tests of ad hoc networks are invaluable in order to assess models used in simulation. However, the number of factors affecting the performance of an ad hoc network is high. There are, for example, system factors, such as routing protocols, MAC and physical layer protocols, as well as environment factors, such as the presence of walls, foliage and moving objects. In this regard, it is important to design repeatable experiments of the network, in order to identify the parameters which really affect the system behavior. Here, we leverage methods of statistical testing theory to identify these parameters in a compact manner. In particular, we use OLSR as a routing protocol. Results from real experiments confirm the horizon effect of ad hoc multi-hop networks and shown that there is a treatment effect caused by the window size of OLSR.

1 Introduction

Ad hoc networks are infrastructureless networks, where a number of nodes can interconnect to each other in a decentralized manner. Applications of such networks range from emergence or spontaneous networking to space extension of Internet connections, which is commonly known as mesh networking. So far we can count a lot of simulation results on the performance of ad hoc networks, e.g. in terms of end-to-end throughput, delay and packet loss. However, in order to assess the simulation results, real-world experiments are needed and a lot of testbeds have been built to date [1]. The baseline criteria usually used in real-world experiments is guaranteeing the repeatability of tests. This requirement is very stringent, because in ad hoc networks there are a lot of uncontrollable parameters. Let us think at the wireless channel only. It might happen that in some days the channel is "better" than in other days. Also, effects such as multipath fading may vary along the experiment. Various solutions have been proposed in order to overcome these difficulties. One of the most active project on experimental analysis of ad hoc networks is that of the group at Uppsala University, which implemented a large testbed of 30 nodes [2,3]. They presented

T. Enokido, L. Barolli, and M. Takizawa (Eds.): NBiS 2007, LNCS 4658, pp. 1–10, 2007.

an automatic software called APE which can set and run measurements in an ad hoc network with a particular routing protocol, e.g. AODV, OLSR or LUNAR. The authors of the experiments suggested to use a particular metric to solve the repeatability problem. Here, we propose to use another way to solve this problem which does not need in principle additional metrics. This solution take advantage of the hypothesis test theory, which is often used whenever the experimenter wishes to identify true difference in performance of the system when tested under different scenarios. A scenario in a statistical parlance is a treatment. The results presented here are taken from a real-world testbed of five ad hoc nodes, which was run both in indoor and outdoor scenario. In particular, we used the Open Link State Routing (OLSR) as routing protocol, because it is the most evolving protocol worldwide, especially from the point of view of its software implementation [4,5].

The rest of paper is structured as follows. In Section 2, we review the basic properties of OLSR. In Section 3, we describe the components of our testbed and the methodology used to analyze the data. The application of this methodology is given in Section 4. Conclusions are presented in Section 5.

2 Routing: OLSR

By means of dedicated control messages, OLSR modifies the routing tables of the node it runs on. Its main tasks are neighbors sensing, Multi-Point Relaying (MPR) calculation and Topology Control (TC) messages dissemination. Neighbor sensing is performed by sending periodic broadcast HELLO messages with rate T_{HELLO}^{-1}. In OLSR, there are cross-layer operations to some extent. For example, in order to check the presence of a neighbor, OLSR has to compute a quality metric of all links towards neighboring nodes. According to the value of this metric for both directions of links, OLSR can judge upon the symmetry of links. Asymmetric links are discarded. It is well known [6] that hop-cont based metrics do not result in high throughput, because the routing protocol could choose a worse path (e.g. high delay) even if it has the minimum hop-count. A better metric is based on the Expected Transmission Count (ETX). Every node computes the forward and backward packet loss rate for every neighbor link. The backward packet loss rate is the packet loss "seen" by the neighbor. Then, the ETX is computed as $ETX = \frac{1}{p_f p_r}$ where p_f is the estimate of the forward packet loss rate and p_r is the reverse packet loss rate. This quantity is the mean number of re-transmissions per packet we have to wait for successful transmission over a particular link. The latter quantities are computed within a normalized time window whose default value is $w = 10$. For example, if $T_{\text{HELLO}} = 0.5$s, we have to wait 20s in order to compute a sample of ETX. Since we used single-radio NICs, we did not use more advanced metrics, like the Weight Cumulative Expected Transmission Time (WCETT) [7]. For instance, WCETT is conceived for multi-radio mesh networking.

There are several implementation of OLSR. However, the most known and update open project is OLSRd [4], originally implemented by Andreas Tønnesen.

In our opinion, the true strength of OLSRd is its flexibility. In fact, its plug-in based structure allows to easily implement user-defined functionality, like new control messages and additional routing services.

3 Testbed

The testbed was composed by five laptop computers and one desktop machine acting as gateway. Every machine ran Linux OS with kernel 2.6.17.x. The gateway was always located inside an office room and it served as coordination point of all measurements campaign. The indoor experiments have been carried out by interspersing laptops within a departmental floor near our lab. The total length of the floor was about 20m. The outdoor experiments have been performed in an open area, where moving cars, moving people and parking lots were present. Along the presentation, we use the following definitions.

Definition 1. *We refer to hop-distance between two nodes as the absolute difference in their IP addresses.*

Definition 2. *We refer to connection horizon as the maximum hop-distance for which there are not core performance differences or rather performance degradations.*

For example, the hop-distance between *.*.*.1 host and *.*.*.5 host is 4. Actually, the hop-distance might be different from the hop-count of the route selected by OLSR, because high quality direct links can exist. For example, the hop-distance from 1 to 5 is 4, but if there is a direct link between 1 and 5 with high LQ, the hop-count is 1. This depends on the type of topology. The traffic generation has been carried out by means of the open source Distributed Internet Traffic Generator (D-ITG) [8]. The constant bit rate of the generated traffic was set to 122pkt/sec, i.e 499.712Kbps. A web interface was provided in order to let the system acquiring all these and other settings, such as the duration of an experiment, the type of network protocol, as shown in Fig. 1-a.

3.1 IEEE 802.11 MAC

As MAC protocol, we used IEEE 802.11b. The transmission power was set in order to guarantee a coverage radius equal to the maximum allowed geographical distance in the network, especially for the outdoor experiments. For instance, by considering also shadowing phenomena, a value of 250m was fairly enough. Accordingly, the transmission power was set to 20dbm. Since we were interested mainly in the performance of the routing protocol, we kept unchanged all MAC parameters. In regard of the interference, it is worth noting that, during our tests, almost all the IEEE 802.11 spectrum had been used by other access points disseminated within the campus. In general, the interference from other access points is a non controllable parameter. We used wireless USB NICs, which were equipped with an external omnidirectional antenna. During the first trials of

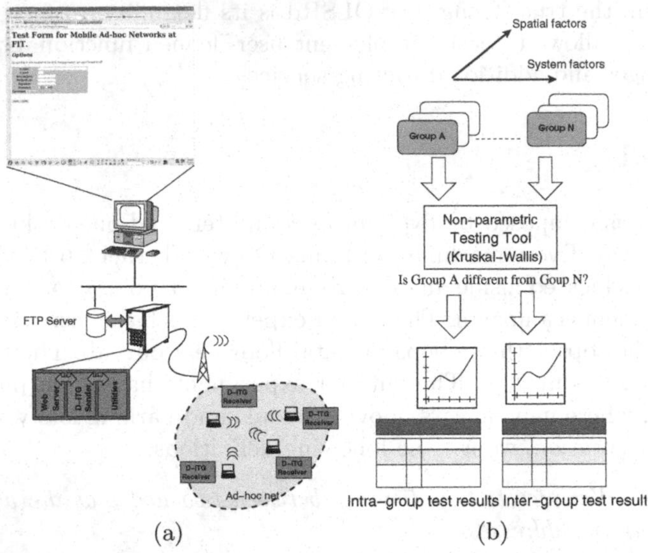

(a) (b)

Fig. 1. Schematic illustration of (a) the testbed and (b) the methodology of analysis

the experiments, we used on-board wireless cards and PCMCIA cards as well. However, we experienced an unpredictable loss of the signal strength which motivated us to turn-off the built-in cards and to use an external antenna-based NIC.

3.2 Topology

Other testbeds [9] used hardware artifacts to control the physical topology of the network, e.g. masking the wireless cards by means of copper plates. Although this procedure can fairly build the desired physical topology, it requires a try-and-test approach, which complicate the setup of the network, especially in the outdoor scenarios. We selected a suboptimal technique, by using the logical topology instead of the physical one. In fact, by means of MAC address filtering, it is possible to quickly build the desired topology[3]. The penalty of this technique is that some residual self-induced interference remains, because the transmitted signal can reach more nodes than those required by the logical topology. We used two kind of topologies, the Linear Topology (LT) and the Meshed Topology (MT). In LT, hop-distance equals the hop-count.

3.3 Methodology

The experimenter shall choose a set of independent parameters, which will be varied during the measurement campaign. The objective of the experimenter is testing whether core differences are present in the system when one of the independent parameters is changed. In statistical parlance, these parameters are

[3] In UNIX-like systems, this is readily done by the `iptables` command.

referred to as *factors.* A *treatment* is determined by a particular choice of factors. In this work, we assumed as factors: the hop-distance between two hosts, the environment (Indoor or Outdoor), the type of topology (LT or MT) and the window size w. As additional factors, we used the transport protocol type, i.e. TCP and UDP. The methodology consists in finding whether these factors impact on the communication performance of the ad hoc network. Precisely, let consider A_N groups of experiments or treatments, where for every A_k and A_j, $k \neq j$, at least one factor value is different. Every A_i is a collection of measurements, i.e. a sample, taken from the testbed. For example, in our testbed, a sample is the collection of 10s measurements of a particular metric. The question is: Do the factor differences really impact on the performance? Usually, many experiments we found in literature used just the mean value of some metric, such as the throughput and the delay. But it is very difficult to see the difference of a group of mean values by inspecting graphical plots. Even numerical data could say nothing about this difference, because data are taken from experimental data. Moreover, outliers and spurious values may arise, as well as different length of the samples. Consequently, the metrics depends on the size of the sample. One could perform long measurements in order to get a "big" sample. But how big? Another more elegant solution is to use a non-parametric hypothesis test among groups, see Fig. 1-b. By loosely speaking, given $1 \leq i \leq N$, the hypothesis test $\mathbf{Y}$ can be formulated as follows:

$$\mathbf{Y} \begin{cases} \mathcal{H}_0 : A_i\text{'s have different means} \\ \mathcal{H}_1 : \text{all } A_i\text{'s have equal means.} \end{cases}$$

The hypothesis $\mathcal{H}_1$ states that there is no difference in the mean of the samples (i.e. samples can be considered as extracted from the same population). On the other hand, if the null hypothesis is true, then we have discovered a core dependence on the factors used in the test. Every method used to perform the test is associated with some probability of error, which is the probability of rejecting the null hypothesis while it is true. The error probability is given in term of the significance level of the test, α. We use the Kruskal-Wallis (KW) test. The null hypothesis of the KW test is that the medians among samples are different. The test formula is not explained here and can be found in [10]. For the KW test, we use the common value of $\alpha = 0.05$. If the KW returns a value smaller than α then the sample medians can be considered different, otherwise we can declare that there is no "treatment effect".

We assume that there are two kind of factors: system factors and spatial factors, as shown in Fig. 1-b. System factors depend on the settings of networking protocol parameters, while spatial factors depends on the physical position of nodes. By incorporating the hop-distance in the spatial factors, we can analyze to which extent the hop-distance impacts on the performance. For sake of clarity and simplicity, the treatments presented in this work have been arranged as shown in Table 1. The testing procedure is performed as follows:

1. By means of Web interface, we set the parameters of the experiments, in particular its duration, the logical topology and the type of transport protocol.

2. At the gateway machine, we collect the samples for: throughput/goodput (T), Round-Trip Time (RTT) and packet loss (P_L)[4].
3. A MATLAB script picks the samples and executes the KW test. The outcomes of the scripts are: the medians of the metrics along with their box plots, and α.

Table 1. Treatments. I=Indoor; O=Outdoor, LT=linear topology; MT=meshed topology.

Treatments	Factor values $w = 10$	$w = 20$
A	(UDP, I, LT)	(UDP, I, LT)
B	(UDP, I, MT)	(UDP, I, MT)
C	(UDP, O, LT)	(UDP, O, LT)
D	(UDP, O, MT)	(UDP, O, MT)
E	(TCP, I, LT)	(TCP, I, LT)
F	(TCP, I, MT)	(TCP, I, MT)
G	(TCP, O, LT)	(TCP, O, LT)
H	(TCP, O, MT)	(TCP, O, MT)

Table 2. Intra-group significance levels for $w = 10$

Treatments	α		
	Goodput	Delay	Loss
A	0.00	0.00	0.0047
B	0.00	0.00	0.00
C	0.00	0.00	0.00
D	0.0099	0.00	0.00
E	0.00	0.00	0.00
F	0.0607	0.00	0.00
G	0.00	0.00	0.00
H	0.00	0.00	0.00

4 Measurement Results

Every experiment lasted 10s and it has been repeated 50 times. OLSR is continuously active during the experiment. Therefore, OLSR has enough estimates of packet losses to compute LQ values. In fact,

$$wT_{\text{HELLO}} < T_{\text{Exp}} \,,$$

where T_{Exp} is the total duration of the experiment, i.e., in our case, $T_{\text{Exp}} =$ 500s. However, the testbed was turned on even in the absence of measurement traffic. Therefore, the effective T_{Exp} was much greater. We run the experiments

[4] Excepting the case of TCP, where obviously the packet loss is always 0.

Table 3. Results of measurements for $w = 10$. For groups E-H, the packet loss is always 0.

	Hop-distance = 1			Hop-distance = 2		
Treatments	Goodput(Kbps)	RTT(s)	Loss	Goodput(Kbps)	RTT(s)	Loss
A	499.712	0.04077	0.002459	499.712	0.0732	0.2257
B	499.712	0.0425	0.00082	499.712	499.712	0.0008
C	499.712	0.0173	0.0307	499.712	0.476751	0.0939
D	499.712	0.0244	0.2357	499.712	1.8318	0.2576
α	0.0437	0.00	0.00	0.00	0.00	0.00
E	499.712	0.0462		499.712	0.056817	
F	499.712	0.0462		499.712	0.056817	
G	499.712	0.0256		336.914	0.060238	
H	499.712	0.0445		478.1933	0.073095	
α	0.43501	0.1202		0.00	0.003613	

	Hop-distance = 3			Hop-distance = 4		
Treatments	Goodput(Kbps)	RTT(s)	Loss	Goodput(Kbps)	RTT(s)	Loss
A	499.712	0.10161	0.0025	434.2437	2.6475	0.2257
B	499.712	0.10813	0.001639	498.6434	3.1523	0.1041
C	494.9924	10.346	0.45339	319.7056	10.2926	0.4883
D	499.712	2.0859	0.1993	499.712	0.0870	0.0016
α	0.00	0.00	0.00	0.00	0.00	0.00
E	499.712	0.0796		499.712	0.1051	
F	499.712	0.1149		499.712	0.1051	
G	179.0759	0.0842		241.9341	0.6382	
H	499.712	1.5961		455.526	0.1096	
α	0.00	0.00		0.00	0.00	

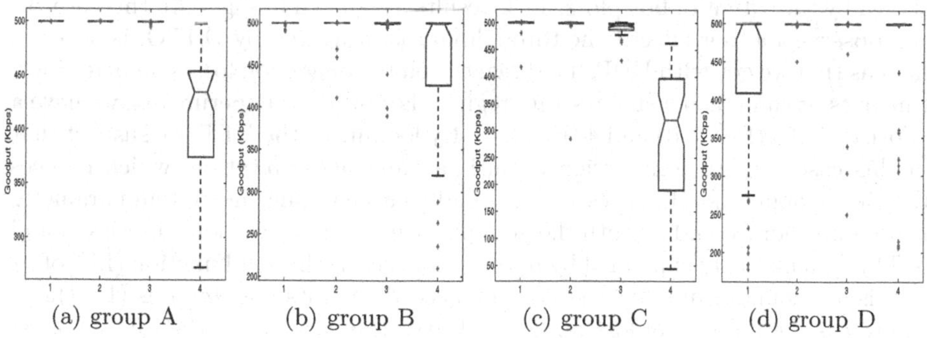

(a) group A (b) group B (c) group C (d) group D

Fig. 2. Goodput results

with one flow only. In order to vary the hop-distance, we changed only the flow destination, while the flow source was always located at the gateway. The

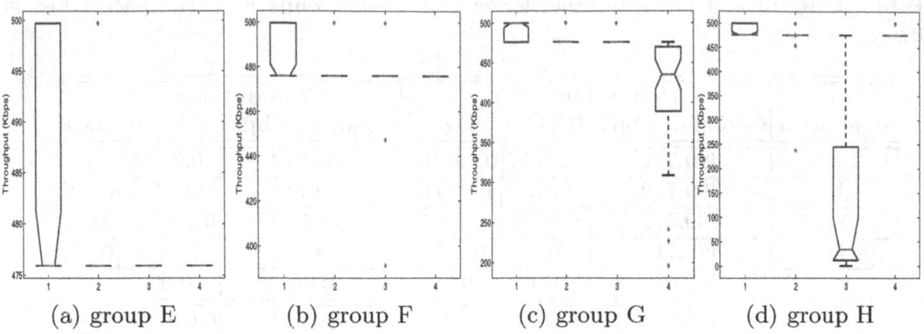

(a) group E (b) group F (c) group G (d) group H

Fig. 3. Throughput results for TCP

intra-group significance levels α for $w = 10$ are shown in Table 2. In Table 3, we show the results of the hypothesis test for $w = 10$, along with the inter-group significance level. For every experiment or treatment, we report the medians $(\widehat{T}, \widehat{RTT}, \widehat{P_L})$. Goodput is in Kbps, while delays are in seconds. With an abuse of notation, we inherently assume that for groups E-H the word goodput means throughput. We report for convenience also the box plots of $\widehat{T}$ in Figs. 2-3. By inspecting Tables 2 and 3, it seems that the test fails only for throughputs of group E, where the values are identical. For MT, i.e. without MAC filtering, in the case of groups A-D, we can observe two facts: 1) there are more spurious values than in the case of LT topologies; 2) the goodput decreases after a hop distance of 4, and, similarly, the RTT increases. For groups B and D, things can be different because line-of-sight links can exist, e.g. from host 1 to 5. We can observe the well-known "horizon" in the RTT (similar results hold for the other metrics). This visual discrimination of plots ca be assessed by inspection of Table 3. Let us note that at the horizon, the goodput is also more oscillatory, as shown by the extent of box plots. TCP results are shown in Fig. 3. In this case, we can observe another effect. The throughput, as measured by D-ITG, is never as high as that we get with UDP. TCP reacts well to congestion losses, and after few timeouts, it can reach a steady-state regime. For outdoor experiments, we have a "horizon" of 3 (Fig. 3-d) and 4 (Fig. 3-c). By looking at the RTT, we suspect that in this case wireless losses trigger spurious timeouts expiration, which reduces the throughput. As a final result, we found that changing the system parameter w does ameliorate and smooth the goodput/throughput, as shown in Figs. 4 and 5. This can be easily explained by noting that the Likelihood Function (LF) of p_f (p_r) is a binomial random variable, and, accordingly, its maximum is $(1-t)w^{-1}$ where t is the number of lost packets. Clearly, the variance of the LF is $\propto w^{-2}$. Then, the higher is w the lower is the index of variation of the ETX and the more stable are the routes computed by OLSR.

Based on the results of the statistical test, we can draw some simple conclusions. There is a "treatment effect" due to the environment, i.e. the performance in outdoor is different from that in indoor. Consequently, some applications may

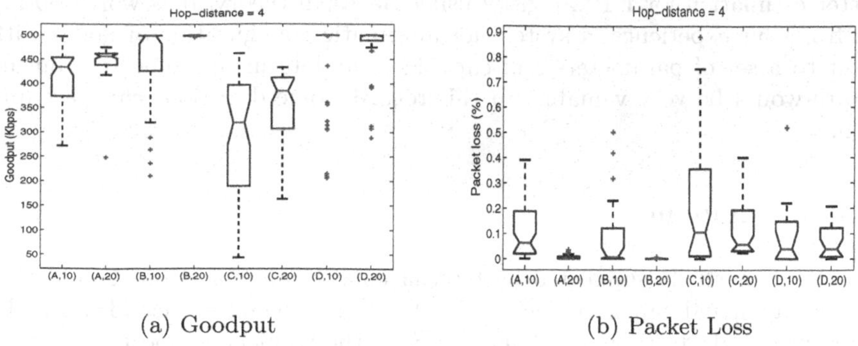

(a) Goodput (b) Packet Loss

Fig. 4. Comparison for groups A-B, with $w = 10$ and $w = 20$

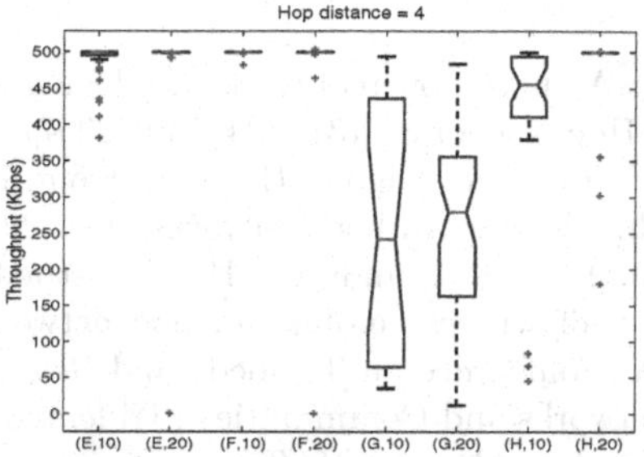

Fig. 5. Comparison for groups E-F

work well in indoor environment but not work in outdoor environment. This can be caused mainly by the interference and multipath footprints. In particular, outdoor environment seems to be more hostile. The index of variation of the goodput decreases as w increases. Therefore, varying w has a treatment effect. Although not shown for page limit constraints, the horizon seems to be independent of w and it has to be rooted in other causes, such as the interference due to the MAC [2].

5 Conclusions

In this work, we proposed a technique which can complement the analysis of measurement data taken from real-world ad hoc networks. In our opinion, when the number of parameters is high, the statistical test is a must in order to assess in a comprehensive way the real dependence of performance on system parameters. As example, we analyzed the performance of UDP and TCP over the ad hoc testbed, and we confirmed the presence of the connection horizon even in the case of UDP. This horizon surely depends on the MAC protocol, while the oscillatory behavior of metrics, such as the goodput, decreases to some extent if we change the window of OLSR. This fact can be exploited to construct a better estimation for ETX, e.g. by using Bayesian theory. It is worth noting that, from our experience, a system for automatic configuration of nodes with respect to a set of parameters and capable to update in real-time the routing software would be very valuable. In this regard, some directions can be found in [11].

Acknowledgment

This work is partially supported by International Communications Foundation (ICF) of Japan and Japanese Society for the Promotion of Science (JSPS). The authors would like to thank ICF and JSPS for the financial support.

References

1. Kiess, W., Mauve, M.: A survey on real-world implementation of mobile ad-hoc networks. Elsevier Ad Hoc Networks 5(3), 324–339 (2007)
2. Tschudin, C., Gunningberg, P., Lundgren, H., Nordström, E.: Lessons from experimental manet research. Elsevier Ad hoc Networks 3(2), 221–233 (2005)
3. Nordström, E., Gunningberg, P., Lundgren, H.: A testbed and methodology for experimental evaluation of wireless mobile ad hoc networks. In: Proceedings of the IEEE International Conference on Testbeds and Research Infrastructures for the Development of Networks and Communities (Tridentcom), pp. 100–109. IEEE Computer Society Press, Los Alamitos (2005)
4. Tønnesen, A.: Olsrd: Implementation code of the olsr (2006), `http://www.olsrd.org`
5. BATMAN: The better approach to mobile ad hoc networking (BATMAN) protocol (2007), Available online at `http://open-mesh.net/batman`
6. De Couto, D.S.J., Aguayo, D., Bicket, J., Morris, R.: A high-throughput path metric for multi-hop wireless routing. In: Proceedings of ACM MobiCom'03, pp. 134–146. ACM Press, New York (2003)
7. Draves, R., Padhye, J., Zill, B.: Routing in multi-radio, multi-hop wireless mesh networks. In: MobiCom '04. Proceedings of the 10th annual international conference on Mobile computing and networking, pp. 114–128. ACM Press, New York (2004)
8. D-ITG, Distributed Internet Traffic Generator: `http://www.grid.unina.it/software/`
9. Kawadia, V., Kumar, P.R.: Experimental investigations into tcp performance over wireless multihop networks. In: E-WIND '05. Proceeding of the 2005 ACM SIGCOMM workshop on Experimental approaches to wireless network design and analysis, pp. 29–34. ACM Press, New York (2005)
10. Gibbons, J.D.: Nonparametric Statistical Inference. Marcel Dekker Ltd. (December 1985)
11. Wiedemann, B.: Development of a software distribution platform for the berlin roof net. Technical report, Computer Science Department at Humboldt University of Berlin (January 2006),`http://sar.informatik.hu-berlin.de/research/publications/SAR-PR-2006-01/`

Sensor-Actuator Communication Protocols in Wireless Networks

Kiyohiro Morita[1], Keiji Ozaki[1], Kenichi Watanabe[1], Naohiro Hayashibara[1], Tomoya Enokido[2], and Makoto Takizawa[1]

[1]Tokyo Denki University, Japan
{kiyo,kei,nabe,haya}@takilab.k.dendai.ac.jp,
makoto.takizawa@computer.org
[2]Rissho University, Japan
eno@ris.ac.jp

Abstract. A wireless sensor-actuator network (WSAN) is composed of sensor and actuator nodes interconnected in a wireless channel. Sensor nodes can deliver messages to only nearer nodes due to weak radio and messages are forwarded by sensor nodes to an actuator node. Messages sent by nodes might be lost due to collision and noise. We discuss the redundant data transmission (RT) protocol to reduce the loss of sensed values sent to an actuator node even if messages are lost. In the RT protocol, a sensor node sends a message with not only its sensed value but also sensed values received from other sensor nodes. Even if a message with a sensed value v from a sensor node is lost, an actuator node can take the value v from other messages. We evaluate the RT protocol compared with the CSMA protocol in terms of how much sensed values an actuator node can receive in presence of message loss.

1 Introduction

A wireless sensor-actuator network (WSAN) [1,2,7] is composed of sensor nodes and actuator nodes interconnected in a wireless network. A sensor node sends sensed values to actuator nodes. An actuator node performs methods on actuation devices. If multiple nodes simultaneously send messages, the messages are lost due to collision. Synchronization mechanisms [3,8,9] are discussed to reduce message loss. However, only simple mechanisms like CSMA [3] are used in sensor nodes. In addition, the farther a destination node is from a source node, the more number of messages are lost due to noise in a wireless channel. Since sensor nodes can send only week radio, the more number of messages are lost due to noise the IEEE 802.11 [10].

In this paper, we discuss the *redundant data transmission* (RT) protocol to reduce the loss of sensed values where sensed values and control information in a message from a sensor node are redundantly transmitted in other messages. In the RT protocol, sensed values can be delivered to an actuator node even if a message with the sensed values is lost. We evaluate the RT protocol in terms of the number of sensed values delivered to an actuator node in presence of message

T. Enokido, L. Barolli, and M. Takizawa (Eds.): NBiS 2007, LNCS 4658, pp. 11–19, 2007.

loss caused in the traditional CSMA [3] based data transmission. The loss ratio of sensed values can be reduced to about 70% even if messages are lost.

In section 2, we discuss the RT protocol. In section 3, we evaluate the RT protocol in terms of data loss ratio.

2 Redundant Data Transmission (RT) Protocol

2.1 Message Format

We consider a wireless sensor-actuator network (WSAN) [4] which is composed of multiple *sensor* nodes $s_1, \cdots, s_n$ and one *actuator* node a which are interconnected in wireless channel. A sensor node gathers information in the physical world and then sends the sensed values to actuator nodes. Then, an actuator node a performs action from the sensed values on actuation devices. Typically, a sensor node can deliver messages to nodes in at longest 5 [m] while an actuator node can deliver to nodes in 100 [m] [11]. Every sensor node may not directly deliver a message to an actuator node. A sensor node forwards a message to other nodes in multi-hop communication. Each node transmits messages with the CSMA [3] transmission-scheme. Here, a node first listens to the channel. If it is idle, the node starts transmitting a message. Otherwise, the node waits for some time units.

Let us consider three nodes s_1, s_2, and s_3. Suppose the node s_1 sends a message m_1 and s_2 receives m_1. Suppose, s_3 does not receive m_1 due to noise and collision as shown in Figure 1. Suppose s_2 sends a message m_2 after receiving m_1 and s_3 receives m_2. Here, if the message m_2 carries data d_1 in m_1 to s_3, s_3 receives not only m_2 but also the data d_1 of the lost message m_1. Data of another message carried by a message is referred to as *backup data*. A sensor node s_i obtains a sensed value v and then sends a message m of the following format:

[Sensor message m**]**
- $m.src$ = source sensor node s_i of the message m.
- $m.seq$ = sequence number of the message m.
- $m.val$ = value v sensed by the sensor node s_i.
- $m.state$ = ON if the sensor node s_i knows that $m.val$ is received by an actuator node a, else OFF.
- $m.data$ = *backup* data $\langle data_1, \cdots, data_K\rangle$.
- $m.data_j$ = *backup* tuple $\langle sid, seq, val, state\rangle$ ($j = 1, \cdots, K$).

If a sensor node s_i sends a message m after sending another m_1, $m.seq = m_1.seq + 1$. In addition to sending the sensed value $m.val$, m carries *backup* data in $m.data$ which are sensed values which s_i has received from other sensor nodes. $m.data$ include the number K of *backup* tuples. For each *backup* tuple $d = \langle sid, seq, val, state\rangle$ in $m.data$, $d.state = ON$ if s_i receives the confirmation of the sensed value $d.val$, which is sent by $s_j(= d.sid)$ from an actuator node a. Here, the message m sent by s_i is referred to as *backup* message of m_j sent by another sensor node $s_j(= d.src)$ if $m_j.seq = d.seq$ and $d \in m.data$. If a node

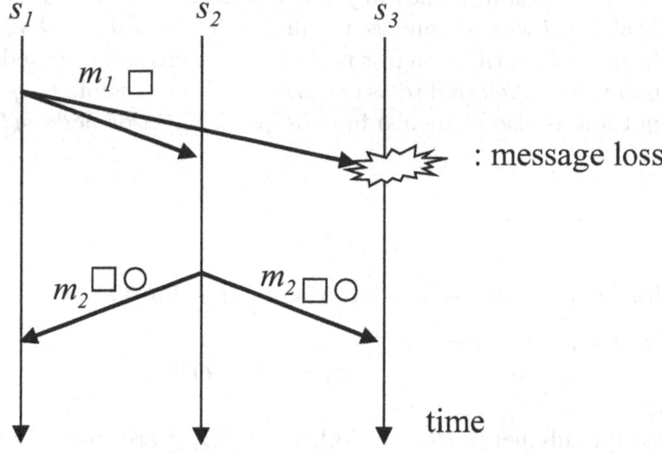

Fig. 1. Message loss

receives a *backup* message m_1 of a message m_2, the node can also take the sensed value $m_2.val$ in the *backup* tuple data of $m.data$.

An actuator node a sends a following confirmation message m to sensor nodes:

[Actuator message m**]**

- $m.src$ = source actuator node a of the message m.
- $m.seq$ = sequence number of the message m.
- $m.ack = \langle m.ack_1, \cdots, m.ack_A \rangle$ = receipt confirmation of sensed values.
- $m.ack_i$ = confirmation tuple $\langle sid, seq \rangle$ showing that the actuator node a receives every message m' sent by a sensor node sid, where $m'.seq \leq seq$.

2.2 Data Transmission of a Sensor Node

Each node c broadcasts a message by the function $send(c, m)$. If the sensor node s_i had received a message m_j from a sensor node s_j, m_j is buffered in the receipt subqueue RQ_{ij}. The sensor node s_i marks a message m_j in RQ_{ij} if m_j is confirmed in s_i. A receipt queue RQ_i is composed of receipt subqueues $\langle RQ_{i1}, \cdots, RQ_{in} \rangle$ in a sensor node s_i. For a queue Q, the functions $enque(Q, m)$: a tuple m is enqueued into a queue Q, $m = deque(Q)$: a top tuple m is dequeued from Q and $remove(Q, m)$: a tuple m is removed from Q are used. Each sensor node s_i manipulates a variable SEQ. Each time the sensor node s_i sends a message, SEQ is incremented by one.

A tuple of attributes $\langle seq, val, c.state, t.state \rangle$ showing a message sent by a sensor node s_j is stored in each subqueue RQ_{ij}. On receipt of a message m from a sensor node s_j, a tuple $\langle m.seq, m.val, OFF \rangle$ is enqueued into RQ_{ij}. "$state = OFF$" means that the message m is not yet confirmed by the actuator node a. In addition to the sensed value $m.val$, m carries the *backup* data $m.data = \langle data_1, \cdots, data_K \rangle$. Each *backup* tuple $m.data_k$ includes values of attributes $\langle sid, seq, val, state\rangle$, showing that a sensor node sid sends a message with a sensed value val whose sequence number is seq. If $state = ON$, the source node of m informs s_i that the actuator node a has received the sensed value val. Here, the sensed value is referred to as $confirmed$. Here, a tuple $\langle seq, val, state\rangle$ for the *backup* tuple is also enqueued into RQ_{ik} for a sensor node $s_k(= sid)$.

B. Transmission

A sensor node s_i sends and receives a message m with the sensed value v as follows:

[Transmission of a message m with a sensed value v]

{ $SEQ := SEQ + 1$; $m.seq := SEQ$;
$m.src := s_i$; $m.val := v$; $m.state := OFF$;
$copy(RQ_i, m)$;
/*tuples in receipt subqueues $RQ_i = \langle RQ_{i1}, \cdots, RQ_{in}\rangle$ are stored in the *backup* data $m.data$ of a message m. */
$enqueue(RQ_{ij}, \langle m.seq, m.val, m.state\rangle)$; $send(s_i, m)$;
}

[Receipt of a message m from a sensor node s_j]
{ $enqueue(RQ_{ij}, \langle m.src, m.seq, m.val, OFF\rangle)$;
for each *backup* tuple d **in** $m.data$ {
$s_k := d.sid$; $end := False$;
for every tuple t **in** RQ_{ik} **where** $t.seq \leq d.seq$ {
$t.state := ON$ **if** $d.state = ON$;
$end := True$; }
if $end = False$,
$enqueue(RQ_{ik}, \langle d.seq, d.val, OFF\rangle)$;
}
}

If a sensor node s_i receives the receipt confirmation message m from the actuator node a, the following receipt procedure is performed in s_i:

[Receipt of a confirmation m from an actuator node a]
for $i = 1, \cdots, A$, {
$b := m.ack_i$;
for every tuple t **in** RQ_{ik} **where** $s_k = b.sid$,
if $t.seq \leq b.seq$, $t.state := ON$;
}

2.3 Data Transmission of an Actuator Node

There are the following variables to send a confirmation message in the actuator node a $(i = 1, \cdots, m)$;

- CT = *total counter*, initially 0, showing how many messages the actuator node a has received from sensor nodes.

- CT_i = *local counter* for each sensor node s_i, showing the CT value of a message which the actuator node a has most recently received from s_i.
- SEQ_i = sequence number of a message which a expects to receive next from s_i.
- V_i = value sensed by a sensor node s_i.
- $S_i = ON$ if a had sent the *confirmation* for the sensed value in V_i, else OFF.

An actuator node a receives a message m from a sensor node s_i and sends a confirmation message m of received sensor messages to sensor nodes as follows:

[Receipt of a message m from a sensor node s_i]
if $SEQ_i = m.seq$ **and** $s_k = d.sid, \{$
$SEQ_i := SEQ_i + 1;\quad V_i := m.val;\quad S_i := OFF;$
$CT_i := CT;\quad CT := CT + 1;$
for each *backup* tuple d **in** $m.data$,
if $SEQ_k = d.seq, \{$
$SEQ_k = SEQ_k + 1;\quad V_k := d.val;$
$S_k := OFF;\quad CT := CT + 1; \}$
$CT_k := CT;$
}

[Transmission of a message m to sensors]
{ $h := 0;$
for $i = 1, \cdots, A\{$
if there is a sensor node s_j such that CT_j is the minimum where $CT_j \geq h$ and $S_j = OFF, \{$
$S_j := ON;\quad m.ack_i := \langle s_j, SEQ_j \rangle;\quad h := CT_j; \}$
else{*send*(a, m); **return;**}
send(a, m);
}

3 Evaluation

3.1 Noise and Collision

We evaluate the redundant data transmission (RT) protocol in terms of data loss ratio, i.e. how many sensed values are lost in an actuator node in presence of messages lost. Messages are lost due to noise and collision in a wireless channel. In the RT protocol, a message m sent by a sensor node s_i carries not only its sensed value but also sensed values and confirmation data in other messages which the sensor node s_i has received before sending the message m. Even if a node loses a message m, the node can receive sensed values in the lost message m if the node receives a *backup* message of m from another node.

We make the following assumptions on the evaluation:

1. There are n nodes, one actuator node c_0 and sensor nodes $c_1, \cdots, c_{n-1} (n > 1)$. The nodes are interconnected in a wireless channel. A sensor node is realized in an MICA mote [11].

2. The transmission interval of each sensor node c_i follows the normal distribution of average τ [msec] and variance σ^2, i.e. $N(\tau, \sigma^2)$.
3. Each message m sent by a sensor node c_i includes the number K of *backup* tuples ($K \geq 0$). A sensed value is two bytes long and the sensor identifier is also two bytes long. The length of one backup tuple is four bytes.
4. Every node takes the CSMA synchronization scheme against message collision in a wireless channel. Each MICA message [11] has a header of 13 bytes. Each sensor message carries 4 bytes for its sensed value and additional K backup tuples. Here, the length of a sensor message is $17 + 4K$ ($K \geq 0$).

The RT protocol is simulated in the simulator TOSSIM [6] which takes usage of the CSMA scheme [3] as the basic message transmission of a wireless channel.

A sensor node sends messages with weak radio due to the limited amount of battery charge. Messages are more lost due to noise in a wireless channel. First, we measure how many messages are lost for the distance among a pair of MICA sensor nodes [11] due to noise.

Suppose a node c_i sends a message m in a wireless channel. The farther the node c_j is from c_i, the higher probability c_j loses m due to noise. Figures 2 shows the message loss ratios for distance which are measured in actual sensor nodes and in the simulation. If a sensor node c_i sends a messages to another sensor node c_j which is one meter from the node c_i, about 2.0 % of the messages are lost due to noise. If the distance between nodes is longer than 5 $[m]$, the message loss ratio is drastically increased. For example, at the destination node c_j which is 6 $[m]$ from the sender node c_i, about 60 % of the messages are lost in the simulation and 95 % in the actual environment. Compared with the Ethernet 802.11, the message loss ratio in the sensor network is much larger as shown in Figure 2.

Next, we measure how many messages are lost in the CSMA protocol [3] of MICA [11] due to not only noise but also collision. Suppose nodes are interconnected in a wireless channel so that distance d $[m]$ between every pair of nodes is the same in the simulation. Here, one node c_1 sends messages to another node c_2. Each messages is 17 bytes long, i.e. thirteen bytes for header, two bytes for sensor id and two bytes for a sensed value. We consider two cases that 1)only one node c_1 sends messages and 2)every node of 50 nodes sends messages where transmission interval is given in the normal distribution $N(\tau, \sigma^2)$ where $\tau = 500$ [msec] and $\sigma^2 = 7500$. For example, a sensor node sends 1,000 messages. Here, 0.114 %, 46.07 % and 0.00107 % of the 1,000 messages are sent on 200 [msec], 500 [msec] and 900 [msec] after transmitting each message, respectively. We measure how many messages sent by the node c_1 are received by the node c_2 in the cases 1 and 2. Figures 3 shows the message loss ratios for two cases. The first case that only c_1 sends messages is the same as the simulation result in Figure 2. In case 2 that not only c_1 but also other 49 nodes, totally 50 nodes send messages. The difference between the message loss ratio of the case 1 and the case 2 indicates the message loss ratio due to collision. About 15-20 % of the messages are lost due to collision if the message loss ratio due to noise is smaller than 10 %.

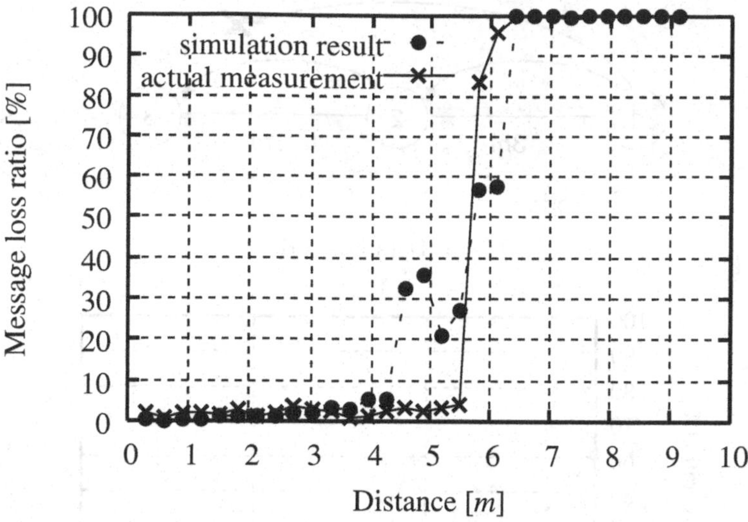

Fig. 2. Message loss ratio due to noise

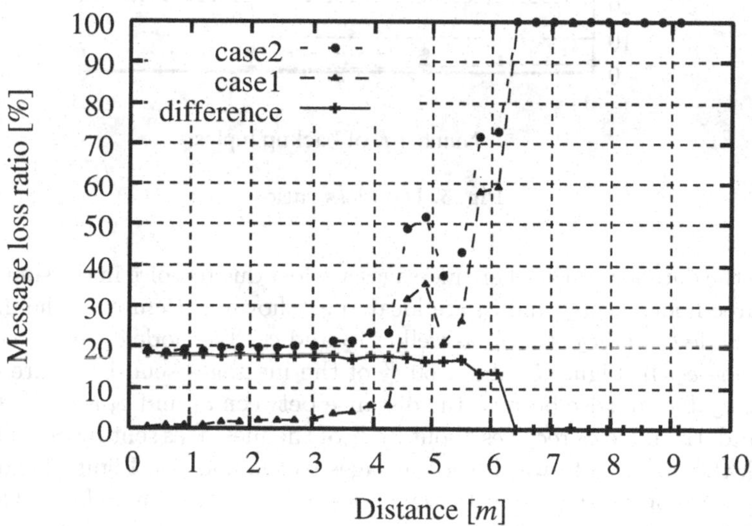

Fig. 3. Massage loss ratio

3.2 RT Protocol

In the RT protocol, each message m carries K backup tuples, i.e. sensed values included in K messages which the sender node has received before the message m is sent. ($K = 0, 1, 2, 3$). Even if a message m is lost, sensed values in the message m can be received by the actuator node c_1 if other messages carrying the sensed values are received. The *data loss ratio* shows the ratio of the number of sensed values which an actuator node c_0 receives to the total number of sensed values. We

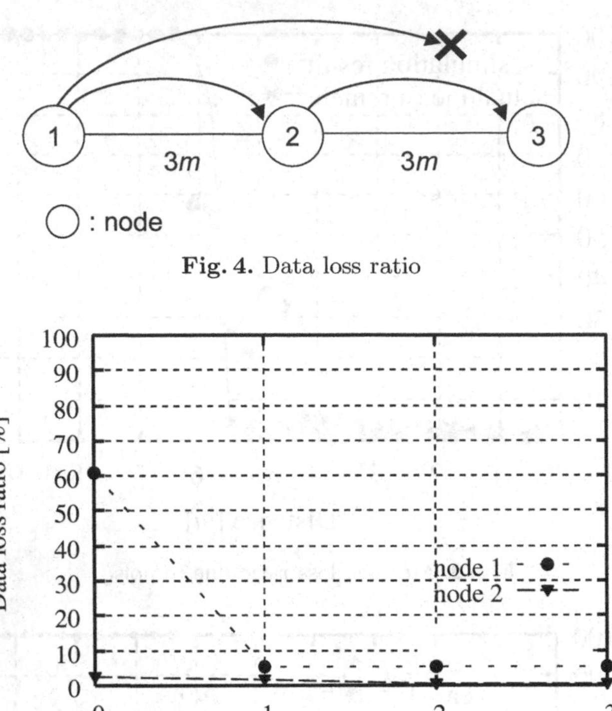

Fig. 4. Data loss ratio

Fig. 5. Data loss ratio

measure the data loss ratio where messages are lost due to noise in the simulation. First, three nodes c_1, c_2, and c_3 are located as shown in Figure 4. The distance between node c_1 and c_2 is 3 $[m]$ as well as c_2 and c_3. The node c_1 sends messages to the node c_3. In Figure 5, about 60 % of the messages send by c_1 are lost by the node c_3 due to noise because the distance between c_1 and c_3 is 6 $[m]$. On the other hand, the node c_2 receives about 97 % of the messages sent by c_1. In the RT protocol, the nodes c_2 forwards the messages to the node c_3. Figure 5 shows the data loss ratio of messages sent by the nodes c_1 and c_2 in the node c_3. The data loss ratio for the node c_2 is almost the same as the message loss ratio shown in Figure 2. If sensed values of c_1 are carried by messages sent by the node c_2 to c_3, about 95 % of the sensed values of c_1 can be delivered to the node c_3 in the RT protocol.

4 Concluding Remarks

We discussed and evaluated the redundant data transmission (RT) protocol in a wireless sensor-actuator network (WSAN). Messages sent by sensor nodes are lost in a wireless channel due to noise and collision. A message received by a sensor node is redundantly forwarded in another message sent by the sensor node in the RT protocol. Hence, even if some message is lost, an actuator node can receive sensed values in the message if the actuator node receives other backup messages carrying the sensed value. Thus, in the RT protocol, sensed values are redundantly in multiple messages.

We evaluated the RT protocol discussed in this paper by using the simulator TOSSIM of Mica [11]. We showed that the loss ratio of sensed values can be reduced to about 5 % without retransmission of lost messages in the RT protocol.

Acknowledgment

This research is partially supported by Research Institute for Science and Technology [Q06J-07] and Frontier Research and Development Center [18-J-6], Tokyo Denki University.

References

1. Akyildiz, I.F., Kasimoglu, I.H.: Wireless sensor and actor networks: research challenges. Ad Hoc Networks journal 2, 351–367 (2004)
2. Akyildiz, I.F., Su, W., Sankarasubramaniam, Y., Cayirci, E.: Wireless sensor networks: a survey. Computer Networks journal 38, 393–422 (2002)
3. Joe, I., Batsell, S.G.: Reservation CSMA/CA for multimedia traffic over mobile ad-hoc networks. In: IEEE International Conference on Communications, vol. 3, pp. 1714–1718. IEEE Computer Society Press, Los Alamitos (2000)
4. Ozaki, K., Watanabe, K., Itaya, S., Hayashibara, N., Enokido, T., Takizawa, M.: A Fault-Tolerant Model of Wireless Sensor-Actor Network. In: Proceedings of the Ninth IEEE International Symposium on Object and Component-Oriented Real-Time Distributed computing (ISORC'06), pp. 186–193. IEEE, Los Alamitos (2006)
5. Hayashibara, N., Défago, X., Yared, R., Katayama, T.: The φ Accrual Failure Detector. In: Proc. of the 23rd IEEE International Symposium on Reliable Distributed Systems (SRDS-23), vol. 1, pp. 68–78. IEEE Computer Society Press, Los Alamitos (2004)
6. Levis, P., Lee, N., Welsh, W., Culler, D.: TOSSIM: accurate and scalable simulation of entire tinyOS applications. In: Proceedings of the 1st international conference on Embedded networked sensor systems, pp. 126–137 (2003)
7. Paruchuri, V., Durresi, A., Barolli, L.: Energy Aware Routing Protocol for Heterogeneous Wireless Sensor Networks. In: Proc. of 16th International Workshop on Network-Based Information Systems (NBiS2005), pp. 133–137 (2005)
8. Chang, Y.-L., Shen, S.: Design of priority schemes in CSMA/CD local are networks. In: Proceedings of the 20th annual symposium on Simulation (ANSS'87), pp. 45–64 (1987)
9. Yao, Z., Fan, P., Cao, Z.: An enhanced CSMA-CA mechanism for multihop ad hoc networks. In: Communications, 2004 and the 5th International Symposium on Multi-Dimensional Mobile Communications Proceedings, vol. 2, pp. 966–970 (2004)
10. Chen, Y., Smavatkul, N., Emeott, S.: Power Management for VoIP over IEEE 802.11 WLAN. In: IEEE Wireless Communications and Networking Conference, vol. 3, pp. 1646–1653. IEEE Computer Society Press, Los Alamitos (2004)
11. MPR2400J/420/520 MIB User's Manual,Crossbow Technology, Inc. (2006)

The Effect of Routing Protocol Dynamics on TCP Performance in Mobile Ad Hoc Networks

C. Mbarushimana, A. Shahrabi, and H. Larijani

School of Computing and Mathematical Sciences
Glasgow Caledonian University
Glasgow G4 0BA, U.K.
{Consolee.Mbarushimana,A.Shahrabi,H.Larijani}@gcal.ac.uk

Abstract. TCP, the transport protocol used to carry the major portion of the internet traffic, performs poorly in Mobile Ad Hoc Networks (MANETs) as broadly reported in the literature. This is mainly due to the interactions between TCP and lower layers protocols. Among these, routing protocols have perhaps the greatest impact on the performance of TCP. In this paper, by extensive simulation, we evaluate how TCP interacts with some of the IETF standardised reactive (AODV, DSR) and proactive (OLSR) routing protocols under varying network conditions such as load, size and mobility. In contrast to most of previously reported studies, which have relied solely on TCP traffic, we consider a more realistic traffic carrying a mixture of Constant Bit Rate (CBR) and TCP. We also show how appropriate tuning of route expiry parameters in reactive protocols can improves TCP performance considerably while still generating less routing overhead.

Keywords: TCP, MANET, Routing Protocol, Performance.

1 Introduction

MANETs are future wireless networks consisting of nodes that communicate in the absence of any centralized support. Nodes in these networks both generate user and application traffic and carry out network control and routing duties. The poor performance of TCP in MANETs is attributed to the fact that it is unable to differentiate packet loss due to congestion and unavailability of routes, the later being the most common in MANETs. This calls for a routing protocol capable of constantly presenting valid routes to TCP. Routing protocols in MANETs has received wide interest in the past due to the fact that existing internet routing protocols were designed to support fixed infrastructure and their properties are unsuitable for MANETs. The current standardised protocols are classified into reactive (AODV [12], DSR [8]), and proactive protocols (OLSR [4], DSDV [11]).

Over the past few years, some studies [3], [5], [6] have been reported to evaluate the performance of the proposed routing algorithms. A detailed packet simulation using CBR traffic was reported in [3], and it was shown that DSR and AODV achieve good performance at all mobility rates and speeds whereas DSDV and TORA perform

T. Enokido, L. Barolli, and M. Takizawa (Eds.): NBiS 2007, LNCS 4658, pp. 20–29, 2007.

poorly under high speeds and high loads conditions respectively. In contrast to this study, Das *et al.* [6] conducted a performance evaluation of more routing protocols and showed that proactive protocols have the best delay and packets delivery fraction but at the cost of higher routing load. In [7] three routing protocols (AODV, DSR and FSR) were evaluated in a city traffic and it was shown that AODV outperforms both DSR and the proactive protocol FSR.

In some other studies, TCP performance was assessed over different routing protocols. Ahuja *et al.* [1] conducted a simulation study of TCP performance over DSR, AODV, DSDV and SSA; however limited conditions were used as the study was conducted with a single TCP connection. A similar study was conducted using TCP Vegas in [10] with reactive protocols outperforming DSDV over a single FTP connection. Different results were presented by Boppana *et al.* [2] who compared the performance of TCP over adaptive proactive (ADV) protocol, AODV and DSR. A limited simulation study of AODV, DSR and OLSR was conducted in [5] and it was shown that OLSR outperforms AODV and DSR by varying the number of TCP connections. Similarly, OLSR outperforms AODV irrespective of the TCP variation by varying the speed in the study conducted in [9].

The proactive protocols used in the above studies were not given further attention by IETF. Instead, IETF has standardised TBRPF and OLSR as proactive routing protocols. Since then, little work has been done to evaluate how the standardised proactive protocols interact with TCP compared to reactive routing protocols. Furthermore, the above named studies used either CBR or TCP; but although multimedia traffic has increased over the past few years, TCP still accounts for more than 90% of the internet traffic. It is therefore crucial to find a routing protocol that performs fairly well in networks where both TCP and UDP traffics coexist. In this paper, by means of OPNET simulations, we conduct a study to evaluate the performance of TCP over AODV, DSR and OLSR, while considering a mixture of TCP and UDP traffic, by varying the network load, network size and the speed of nodes. In addition, the different parameters used by the protocols play an important role in their performances [13]. This paper demonstrates how appropriate tuning of cache parameters in AODV can yield better results in routing TCP traffic while generating less routing overhead than OLSR.

Section 2 of this paper describes the protocols used in this study; section 3 presents the simulation environment, while the results and analysis are presented in section 4. Finally, some concluding remarks are given in section 5.

2 Routing Protocols and TCP Variant Used in the Study

2.1 Ad Hoc On-Demand Distance Vector Protocol (AODV)

AODV minimizes the number of broadcasts by creating routes on-demand. A route request packet (RREQ) is broadcasted by the source till it reaches an intermediate node that has recent route information about the destination or till it reaches the destination. When a node forwards a RREQ to its neighbours, it also records in its tables the node from which the first copy of the request came. This information is used to construct the reverse path for the route reply packet (RREP). AODV uses only symmetric links because the RREP follows the reverse path of the RREQ. If one of the intermediate nodes moves then the moved node's neighbour sends a link failure notification to its upstream neighbours and so on till it reaches the source upon which the source can reinitiate route discovery if needed.

2.2 Dynamic Source Routing Protocol (DSR)

DSR is a source-routed on-demand protocol. A node maintains caches containing the source routes that it is aware of and updates entries in the cache as and when it learns about new ones. The route discovery process is initiated when the source node doesn't have a route to the destination in cache or if the route has expired, it then broadcasts a RREQ. A RREP is generated when either the destination or an intermediate node with current information about the destination receives the RREQ. Each node transmitting the packet is responsible for confirming that the packet has been received by the next hop along the source route. If no receipt confirmation is received, the node returns a route error message to the original sender of the packet which can send the packet using another existing route or perform a new route discovery.

2.3 Optimized Link State Routing Protocol (OLSR)

OLSR is an optimization of pure link state algorithm in ad hoc network by use of Multipoint Relay (MPR). The routes are always immediately available when needed due to its proactive nature. Hop by hop routing is used in forwarding packets. Only nodes selected as MPRs periodically forward control traffic to their MPR selectors, reducing the size of control message. MPRs are also used to form a route from a given node to any destination in route calculation. Every MPR periodically broadcasts a list of its selectors instead of the whole list of neighbours. In order to exchange the topological information, the Topology Control (TC) message is broadcasted throughout the network. Each node maintains the routing table in which routes for all available destination nodes are kept.

2.4 TCP Reno with SACK and Delayed ACK

TCP Reno is the most widely used TCP variant. A lost packet is detected and retransmitted when triple duplicate ACKs are received or a timeout event occurs at the sender. The SACK option can be used with any TCP version, but it uses Reno mechanisms with minor modifications. The information in the SACKs blocks is used to estimate the number of packets in the network and to send a new segment with each ACK that acknowledge the reception of new data. In addition, the SACK information is used to selectively retransmit lost data. Delayed ACKs are expected to help by reducing the volume of ACK traffic in normal network conditions. In the case of a broken route, delayed ACKs allow the TCP sender to increase its send window in increments larger than one.

3 Simulation Environment

In order to conduct our comparative performance study, we used OPNET 11.0 network modelling environment from OPNET technology. The simulations were run for 1000 seconds. The Mobile Ad Hoc network simulated consists of nodes moving in a 1000m x 1000m area following the random waypoint model. The 802.11b in the distributed coordinated function (DCF) mode was used at the WLAN MAC layer.

The AODV simulation parameters are the same as in [2], but two values of Active Route Timeout (ART) were given; first a high value of 50 seconds was considered as in [2], then a more proactive approach to expire inactive routes quickly by having an ART value of 5 seconds was used. The DSR parameters we used are similar to those in [3], and as in AODV case two values of Route Expiry Timer (RET) was set to 30 seconds then 300 seconds. The Hello Interval and the TC Interval of OLSR were set to 2 and 5 seconds respectively. The link expiry time or Neighbour Hold Time (typically set to 3 times hello interval) was 6 seconds, and entries in topology table expire after 15 seconds.

TCP traffic was used as the main network traffic. In this study, FTP connections were established between mobile FTP clients and an FTP server. We also used ten CBR connections generating 50 Kbps as background traffic using UDP as the transport protocol.

4 Simulation Results

The performance of TCP over the different routing protocols was assessed under different network stresses, size and to topology change. Four important metrics were used; TCP goodput, retransmission count, delay and routing load. Goodput accounts for successfully delivered TCP packets collected at the transport layer. And retransmission count accounts for the average number of total TCP retransmissions in the whole network per second. The TCP delay expressed is a measure of average time is taken by all packets to be transmitted from source to destination including queuing and processing delay. The routing overhead produced by each routing protocol as number of bits of routing data generated per second at the IP layer was also measured.

4.1 The Effect of Workload

Ten TCP connections were established in which FTP clients upload a file varying from 10 Kbytes to 50 Kbytes every 20 seconds to an FTP server. We initially considered the case where AODV and DSR behave like typical reactive protocols and set the ART and RET to 50 and 300 seconds respectively. The nodes' speed is uniformly distributed between 0 and 20 m/s with a 5 seconds pause time.

An increase in TCP goodput is observed when the file size is increased (Figure 1(a)), but it is very low over AODV compared to the other two. This poor performance over AODV is attributed to the fact that the routes in the routing table are found invalid more often resulting in more packets being dropped following use of a broken route with a valid ART; this was also highlighted in [13]. TCP performs comparably over DSR and OLSR at lower loads, but DSR use of source routing results in more routing traffic being sent as the load increases, resulting in lower goodput at high loads. The TCP retransmissions (Figure 1(b)) increase with the file size, AODV has the highest retransmissions, due to the fact that more packets are dropped hence resulting in more retransmissions need. DSR has the lowest at lower load but again becomes more that of OLSR at higher loads.

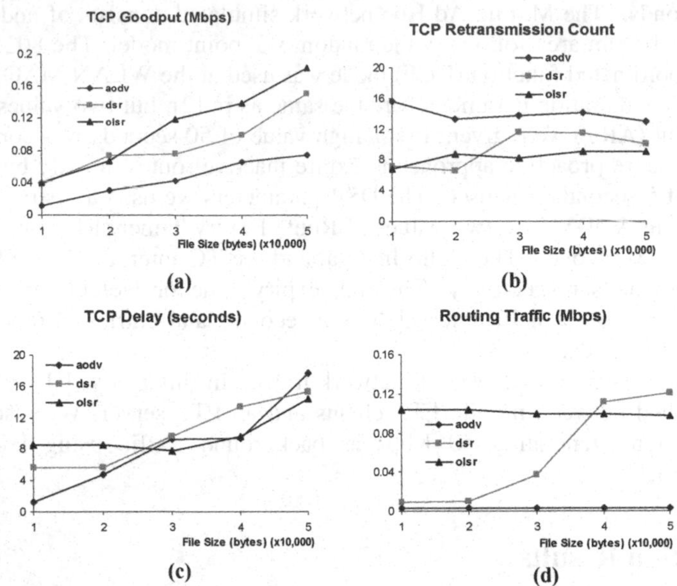

Fig. 1. Effect of Load on: TCP (a) Goodput, (b) Retransmissions (c) Delay and (e) Routing (AODV ART=50sec, DSR RET=300 sec)

The delay experienced by TCP packets is shown Figure 1(c). The reactive protocols show the smaller delay at low loads, but as the load increases OLSR shows the lowest. DSR delay is higher than AODV's because its route discovery takes longer, which results in more delay for TCP packets. The total routing load generated by all nodes is shown in Figure 1(d). OLSR, being a link state protocol shows the highest routing as expected. However, due to source routing, DSR routing load increases tremendously with load and becomes even higher than OLSR's at high loads. The routing load is almost insensitive to load variation in OLSR, but we observe a soft increase in proactive protocols' routing load with increase in network load.

The negative effect of stale routes over routing protocols has been discussed in some previous studies [3], [13]. To make the reactive protocols flush the routes in their routing tables and caches more frequently, we considered AODV ART and DSR RET values of 5 and 30 seconds respectively. As shown in Figure 2(a), the AODV goodput is the highest in this case outperforming even OLSR. DSR performance however is highly affected by setting a low value RET. This is due to the increased routing load produced by DSR as shown in Figure 2(d), which is 15 times more than in the previous case. The routing load is increased in AODV as well but on a smaller extent (5 times), however, it's still far lesser than the routing load generated by OLSR. AODV also has the smallest TCP retransmissions count and delay as shown in Figure 2(b) and 2(c) respectively. This being attributed to the fact that valid routes are constantly available in the routing table; therefore a lesser number of packets needs to be retransmitted following a packet drop or timeout.

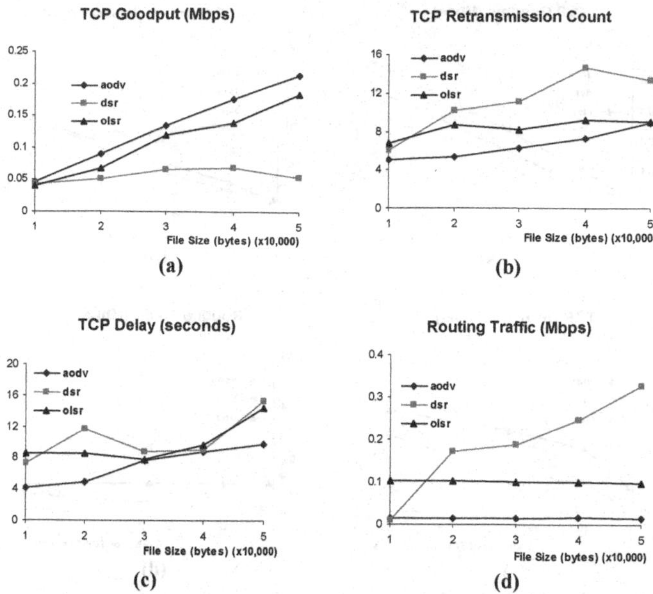

Fig. 2. Effect of Load on: TCP (a) Goodput, (b) Retransmissions (c) Delay and (e) Routing (AODV ART=5sec, DSR RET=30 sec)

4.2 The Effect of Number of Connections

The network workload was also varied by varying the number of TCP connections from 1 to 50. TCP goodput over the three protocols increases with the number of connections, but saturates early for DSR (Figure 3(a)). DSR behaviour is the result of source routing resulting in increased routing load (as seen in Figure 3(d)); therefore the network contention becomes higher which results in more timeouts hence the poor performance. Due to its use of routing tables, AODV performs better in higher number of connections, moreover, the routing tables contain more fresher routes as they are updated more regularly, decreasing timeouts drops and TCP retransmissions. In reactive protocols, packets are stored in the buffer while waiting for a route to be discovered. In CBR traffic transfer, it results in buffer overflows and packets drops, whereas in TCP, flow control reduces buffer overflows hence the better performance compared to CBR cases [5], [6].

The biggest variation is observed in the number of TCP retransmissions per file, where the average is less than one for one TCP connection, and increases to around 50 retransmissions for the 50 TCP connections network. This is due to the increased medium contention, and most are retransmissions due to timeouts. DSR shows the highest number of retransmissions after 10 TCP connections. The TCP delay also increases in the same order, with DSR showing the highest for a large number of TCP

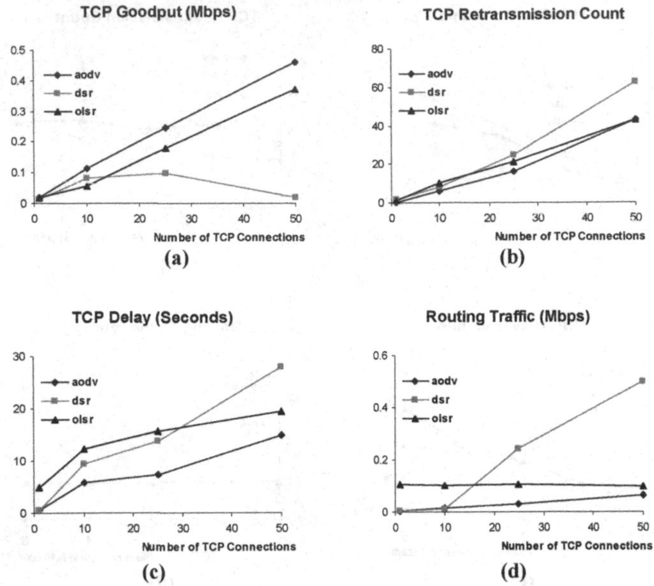

Fig. 3. Effect of Connections on: TCP (a) Goodput, (b) Retransmissions (c) Delay and (e) Routing (AODV ART=50sec, DSR RET=300 sec)

connections, i.e. it takes almost 30 seconds for DSR to deliver a packet in the scenario where every node is uploading a file to the FTP server. The other two protocols delay is also high with OLSR at disadvantage due to the higher routing load. The routing traffic generated increases for the reactive protocols as the number of traffic sources increases as seen on Figure 1(d).

4.3 The Effect of Network Size

The number of nodes is varied between 25 and 100. As seen in Figure 4(a), TCP goodput is almost insensitive to the increase in network size. In large networks, user s may communicate mostly with physically nearby nodes, path lengths could remain nearly constant as the network grows, leading to almost constant per node available goodput, hence the small degradation in overall network goodput. The major changes are observed in the amount of routing traffic generated especially by OLSR (Figure 4(d) due to its link state nature, more routing updates produced due to link states updates are produced and propagated regularly to more nodes. The TCP retransmission count increases softly due to the fact that the medium contention increased by having more routing load. OLSR producing the highest routing load, also shows the highest retransmissions (Figure 4(b)). Similarly, the TCP delay is increased softly with the highest delay in OLSR networks (Figure 4(c)).

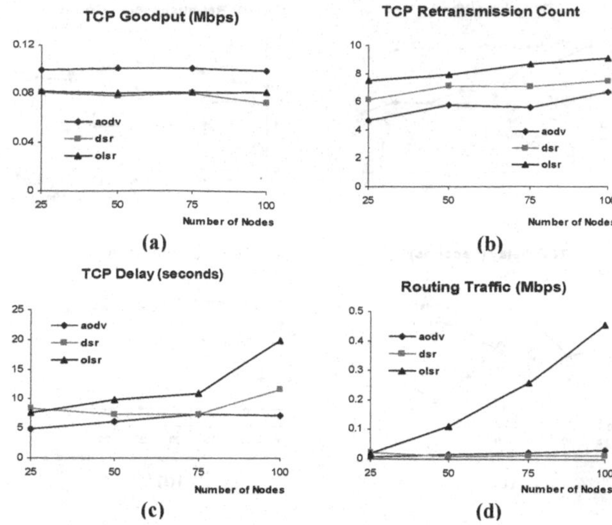

Fig. 4. Effect of Network Size on: TCP (a) Goodput, (b) Retransmissions (c) Delay and (e) Routing (AODV ART=5sec, DSR RET=300sec)

4.4 The Effect of Mobility

The scenarios considered in this case consists of 50 nodes moving with a speed varied between 0 and 40m/s, following a random waypoint mobility pattern with a 5 seconds pause time. Ten TCP connections are established in which a 25Kbytes FTP file is uploaded every 20 seconds.

As expected, the TCP goodput is negatively affected by increase in speed but differently for the three routing protocols (Figure 5(a)). The three protocols perform very well at low speeds; even for DSR where the route caching is useful as the routes in caches are constantly good and useful. AODV is the least affected by the speed increase, the routing tables are updated more frequently, and therefore fewer packets are dropped due to unavailability of routes. DSR and OLSR show a comparable performance, the drop in DSR being attributed to the use of routes in cache which are more likely to be stale at higher speeds. OLSR routes are updated regularly as in AODV, but there is no provision for packets buffering in proactive protocols, which puts OLSR at disadvantage. The number of TCP retransmissions increases for all the protocols as seen in Figure 5(b), due to packet losses due to frequent unavailability of routes. The TCP delay variation with speed is shown in Figure 5(c). At low speeds, AODV shows the lowest delay among the three protocols, but increases with speed. The routing load generated is almost insensitive to the change in speed (Figure 5(d)). OLSR still shows the highest routing load generated due to its proactive nature, but even if OLSR is a link state protocol and MPR periodically broadcast topology information to node across the network, it doesn't explicitly react to link changes.

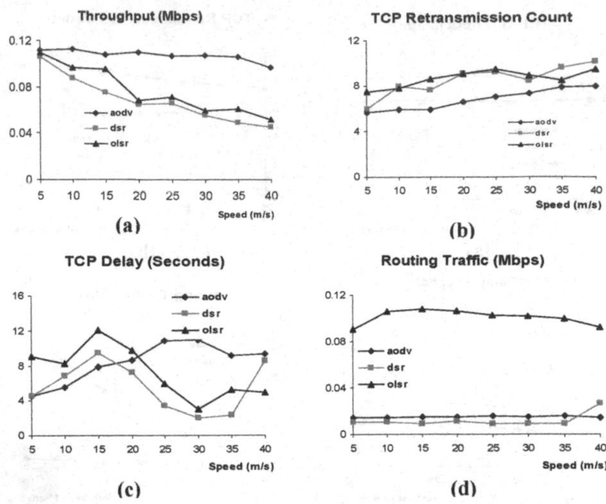

Fig. 5. Effect of Mobility on: TCP (a) Goodput, (b) Retransmissions (c) Delay and (e) Routing (AODV ART=5sec, DSR RET=300sec)

5 Conclusion

In this paper, we conducted a performance study of TCP over AODV and DSR, both reactive routing protocols but which have different routing mechanics and OLSR a proactive link state routing protocol. We simulated different scenarios, varying the network load, network size and the nodes speed.

Similar previous studies reported favoured the proactive protocols [2], [5], [9] based on the grounds that they are able to provide routes as they are needed therefore resulting in less packets drop. In this study, we forced AODV to update its routing tables more frequently, and it turns out to be the best choice outperforming OLSR and still produce lower routing load. The procedure of flushing DSR cache routes more frequently, however, has not been beneficial as it produces enormously high routing load, hence exacerbating TCP performance. The good performance of TCP over AODV is attributed to the fact that with TCP traffic, there is less possibility that the network layer drop packets while the routing protocol is still computing the route to destination because it provides a buffering capability unavailable in OLSR.

We also showed that TCP performance over DSR is poor in more stressful scenarios. DSR is based on source routing, which means that the byte overhead in each packet can affect the total byte overhead in the network quite drastically at high loads. Also, in highly mobile networks, frequent changes of network topology makes the routes in routing cache more and more obsolete. We also showed that, as opposed to some results reported in [5], proactive protocols depict the highest routing load. The reason for this being the exchange of periodical routing updates between nodes even in the cases that there is no data to transmit or when there is no topology change.

References

[1] Ahuja, A., Agarwal, S., Singh, J.P., Shorey, R.: Performance of TCP over Different Routing Protocols in Mobile Ad-Hoc Networks. In: Proc. of Vehicular Technology Conference (VTC 2000), vol. 3, pp. 2315–2319 (May 2000)

[2] Boppana, R., Dyer, T.D.: A Comparison of TCP Performance over Three Routing Protocols for Mobile Ad Hoc Networks. In: Symposium on Mobile Ad Hoc Networking & Computing (Mobihoc01) (October 2001)

[3] Broch, J., Maltz, D., Johnson, D., Hu, Y.C., Jetcheva, J.: A performance comparison of multi-hop wireless ad hoc network routing protocols. In: Proc. of MOBICOM '98, pp. 85–97 (October 1998)

[4] Clausen, T., Jacquet, P.: Optimized link state routing protocol (OLSR). Request for Comments 3626, MANET Working Group, Work in progress (2003), http://www.ietf.org/rfc/rfc3626.txt

[5] Clausen, T., Jacket, P., Viennot, L.: Comparative Study of Routing Protocols for Mobile Ad Hoc Networks. In: The First Annual Mediterranean Ad Hoc Networking Workshop (September 2002)

[6] Das, S.R., Castañeda, R., Yan, J., Sengupta, R.: Comparative Performance Evaluation of Routing Protocols for Mobile Ad hoc Networks. In: Proc. of the International Conference on Computer Communications and Networks (ICCCN 1998), pp. 153–161 (1998)

[7] Jaap, S., Bechler, M., Wolf, L.: Evaluation of Routing Protocols for Vehicular Ad Hoc Networks in City Traffic Scenarios. In: International Conference on ITS Telecommunications, France (2005)

[8] Johnson, D.B., Maltz, D.A., Hu, Y.-C., Jetcheva, J.G.: The dynamic source routing protocol for mobile ad hoc networks. Internet Draft, MANET Working Group, draft-ietf-manet-dsr-07.txt, Work in progress (February 2002)

[9] Kim, D., Bae, H., Song, J., Cano, J.C.: Analysis of the interaction between TCP variants and routing protocols in MANETs. In: Proc. of International Conference Workshops on Parallel Processing, ICPP, pp. 380–386 (June 2005)

[10] Papanastasiou, S., Ould-Khaoua, M.: Exploring the performance of TCP Vegas in Mobile Ad hoc Networks. Journal of Communication Systems 17(2), 163–177 (2004)

[11] Perkins, C.E., Bhagwat, P.: Highly Dynamic Destination-Sequenced Distance-Vector Routing (DSDV) for Mobile Computers. In: ACM SIGCOMM, ACM, New York (1994)

[12] Perkins, C.E., Royer, E.M., Chakeres, I.D.: Ad hoc On-Demand Distance Vector (AODV) Routing Protocol. Internet draft, draft-perkins-manet-aodvbis-00.txt (October 2003)

[13] Richard, C., Perkins, C.E., Westphal, C.: Defining an Optimal Active Route Timeout for AODV Routing Protocol. In: Proc. of International Conference on Sensor and Ad Hoc Communications and Networks IEEE SECON 2005. IEEE, Los Alamitos (2005)

Battery and Power Aware Routing in Mobile Ad Hoc Networks

Fumiaki Sato and Sumito Iijima

Department of Information Science, Toho University
2-2-1 Miyama, Funabashi 274-8510, Japan
fsato@is.sci.toho-u.ac.jp

Abstract. Ad hoc wireless networks are power constrained since nodes operate with limited battery. In this paper, it proposes the ad hoc network routing which considers both of power consumption and the amount of the battery remainder. To improve the availability of ad hoc networks, routing which considers both at the same time is needed though power consumption and the amount of the battery remainder have been separately examined in the research so far. We propose BPA-DSR (Battery and Power Aware enhancement to Dynamic Source Routing) which searches for the route by the flooding of two times. The path with large amount of the battery remainder is detected by the first flooding, and the location of the neighboring nodes of the route is computed from the received radio power at the same time. Each link of the route is divided into the power saving link and tuned up by the flooding of the second. Simulation results show that the amount of the battery remainder of the proposed method is better than other method (LP-DSR) which is aware of the power consumption. Power consumption of the proposed method is better than that of DSR though it is a little inferior to LP-DSR which detects the route of minimum power consumption. The number of hops of the detected route is suppressed to about 60% of LP-DSR.

Keywords: Ad hoc networks, power aware routing, battery aware routing, dynamic source routing.

1 Introduction

A Mobile ad hoc Network (MANET) is composed of a group of mobile wireless nodes that form a network independently of any centralized administration, while forwarding packets to each other in a multi-hop fashion. Since those mobile devices are battery-operated and extending the battery life has become as important objective, researchers and practitioners have recently started to consider power-aware design of network protocols for the Ad hoc networking environment. As each mobile node in a MANET perform the routing function for establishing communication among different nodes the “death” of even a few of the nodes due to energy exhaustion might cause disruption of service in the entire network.

In a conventional routing algorithm [1-5], which is unaware of energy consumption, connections between two nodes are established between nodes through

T. Enokido, L. Barolli, and M. Takizawa (Eds.): NBiS 2007, LNCS 4658, pp. 30–39, 2007.

the shortest path routes. This algorithm may however result in a quick depletion of the battery energy of the nodes along the most heavily used routes in the network. Recently a large volume of research has been conducted on the issue of energy efficiency for wireless networks [6-10]. Power aware routing protocols [6-8] are based on the metric that minimizes the total transmit power. Battery aware routing protocols [9-10] are based on the battery remainder. However, the research of the routing protocol which considered both of power consumption and the amount of the battery remainder was very few.

In this paper, we propose the ad hoc network routing which considers both of power consumption and the amount of the battery remainder. To improve the availability of ad hoc networks, routing which considers both at the same time is needed though power consumption and the amount of the battery remainder have been separately examined in the research so far. We propose BPA-DSR (Battery and Power Aware Dynamic Source Routing) which searches for the route by the flooding of two times. The path with large amount of the battery remainder is detected by the first flooding, and the location of the neighboring nodes of the route is computed from the received radio power at the same time. Each link of the route is divided into the power saving link and tuned up by the flooding of the second.

The rest of the paper is organized as follows. Section 2 reviews the related work. Section 3 presents an overview of our power aware routing. Section 4 describes our simulation model and discusses the simulation results. Section 5 concludes the paper.

2 Related Works

2.1 Power Aware Routing

Some routing protocols which focus to the power saving have been proposed. In general, the overall transmission power of the route is decreased by increasing the number of hops and decreasing the distance of one hop because transmission radio power is proportional to n (>2) power of the distance. PCDC (Power Control Dual Channel) [6] achieves high electric power efficiency by constructing the route by using only the power saving link. The power saving link of the node is direct link to the vicinity which is low power than the link with an indirect communication. And, the route is constructed only with the recognized power saving link. However, PCDC has the problem to need location information to recognize the power saving link and a lot of control traffic.

DPER (Directionality-based Power Efficient Routing) [7] is a protocol to decrease power consumption, which divides the space between the source and the destination into some areas, and select the node which can transmit the lowest power as the next hop from an adjacent area where it approaches to the destination. In DPER, the next hop which certainly approaches the destination is selected based on location information on the destination. However, the power efficiency might degrade according to the topology. Moreover, there is a problem which cannot be used if location information on all terminals is not already-known.

LP-DSR [8] is a routing method to enhance DSR. It floods putting power consumption information on the message of RREQ (Route Request). The sum of the received radio power and the power consumption information which has been described to the received RREQ is computed, and it is assumed the power consumption of the route. If the power consumption computed from RREQ received now is smaller than the power consumption computed from RREQ which has already been received, power consumption information on the RREQ is rewritten and own node ID is added, and it floods. Otherwise, the RREQ is not forwarded. The route with the smallest power consumption can be discovered by this method. However, it is necessary to wait for the RREQ packet which passes various paths to decide the route of the lowest power consumption, and a lot of time is needed. Moreover, the hop increases, and this becomes a delay of the communication and an unstable factor for the link.

2.2 Buttery Aware Routing

There is a problem that the battery of the specific node is consumed and the node stops even if power saving route is used. The stop of some nodes is a serious problem for the availability and lifetime of the entire ad hoc network. The routing method considering the amount of the battery remainder is proposed so that the battery life is maximized.

PA-DSR [9] is a routing protocol which enhanced DSR and considers the amount of the battery remainder. Battery information of the node that RREQ passes is attached to the RREQ, and the node learns the amount of the battery remainder of a surrounding node from the information. The average of a surrounding amount of the battery remainder is also added to RREQ. If the amount of the battery remainder of the node is smaller than the average in the RREQ, it drops without relaying it. Otherwise, the average of the amount of the battery remainder including the node is added to the RREQ and the RREQ is flood. The difference is only a method of forwarding RREQ, and the remainder follows DSR. In PA-DSR, lower node than the average of the amount of the battery remainder of a surrounding node is not selected, and the route with the node with large amount of the battery remainder is searched. However, there is the case where the route to the destination is not found when surrounding nodes of destination have the battery less than the average.

CMMBER (Conditional Max-Min Battery Capacity Routing) [10] is routing to maximize the battery life by avoiding the node with low amount of the battery remainder. In CMMBER, the route will be avoided when the node below the threshold is in the route from the source to the destination. And, the route where power consumption is the smallest in the route is selected when there are two or more routes with an enough amount of the battery remainder. In this method, the route might not be still found by the threshold.

3 Battery and Power Aware Routing

At first, the proposal protocol assumes that the transmission power of physical layer is controllable and signal strength of the received packet is available in the network layer. It is also assumed that the distance between nodes is able to calculate based on the radio propagation model, transmission power and signal strength of the received packet.

The proposal protocol is enhancing DSR, and basic operation follows DSR. Greatly differing from usual DSR is a point to search the route by flooding two times. The flooding of the first time makes the route by using the node whose amount of the battery remainder is larger than that of surroundings. In the flooding of the second times, the link in the route detected in the first flooding is divided into some links and tuned up to power saving route. Because the amount of the battery remainder is considered at the tuning, the route considering not only making to the power saving but also the amount of the battery remainder can be constructed. However, it takes time to the path discovery to do repeating the flooding twice. Details of the protocol are described as follows.

3.1 Estimation of the Distance Between Nodes

The distance between nodes is computed from the received power of RREQ/RREP (Route Request / Route Reply), and each node preserves the distance in cash so that the proposal protocol may use the transmission power control. It is assumed that each node uses the maximum power to transmit the control packet such as RREQ to calculate the distance between nodes correctly. If the node is not the destination in RREP, it receives RREP in the promiscuous mode. The distance information of each link is used for tuning in the second flooding.

In this paper, the two-lay model is used as the radio propagation model.

3.2 Routing Based on the Battery Remainder (First Flooding)

The flooding of the first time makes the route by using the node whose amount of the battery remainder is larger than that of surroundings. After some standby time passes, the node which receives RREQ relays RREQ. The standby time becomes long as the amount of the battery remainder decreases. On the other hand, the node with large amount of the battery remainder relays RREQ without the standby time. Therefore, the routes composed of the node with large amount of the battery remainder will be discovered earlier than routes which contain the node with a little amount of the battery remainder. At this time, it is necessary to consider the threshold (*T1*) of the amount of the battery remainder to set the standby time that is the delay of the relay of RREQ. If the threshold is too small, the possibility that the node with small amount of the battery remainder is included in the route increases. Oppositely, if the threshold is too large, the delay of the first flooding increases.

Another purpose of the flooding of the first time is to limit the node which participates in the flooding of the second times. The node which was not able to hear RREP by the flooding of the first time does not participate in the flooding of the second times. This contributes to the saving of the control packets.

3.3 Routing Based on the Power Consumption (Second Flooding)

The route which is discovered in the flooding of the first time is a route which composes of the node with large amount of the battery remainder. However, the transmission power consumed for the communication is large in this route. So, the route is tuned up in the second flooding.

The tuning is applied to the route discovered at first. The process of the second flooding starts from the transmission of ReRREQ (Reroute Request) from the source node first of all. If the node which receives ReRREQ is in the route discovered in the first flooding, the ReRREQ is relayed to the node of the next hop. If the node is not in the route of the first flooding, it works as a candidate with the relay node in case of the node which met the requirement of the distance with the both ends node of the link of the tuning

Figure 1 explains the spread of ReRREQ. It is assumed that the route discovered by the flooding of the first time is A-B-C. ReRREQ that node A transmitted is relayed by node B and reaches node C. If node P or Q which is not in the route A-B-C receives the ReRREQ, it decides whether it is the candidate node of the link. In the Figure 1, node P is the candidate with the intermediate node of the link A-B, and node Q is not. Therefore, node P transmits ReRREQ to node B but node Q does not.

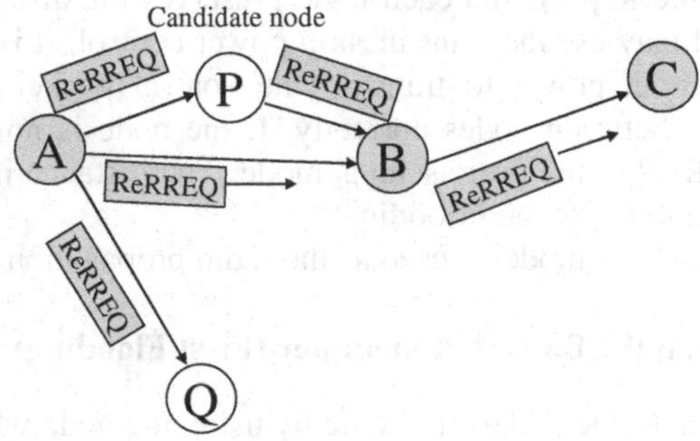

Fig. 1. Flooding of ReRREQ

3.4 Condition for Intermediate Node

There is a condition to be an intermediate node at the tuning. The requirement of the node that becomes an intermediate node is that the power consuming becomes lower than before. The power consuming depends on the distance between nodes. Therefore, the following two conditions are assumed to be an intermediate node. The node which cleared the following conditions is a candidate node.

Assumption: Link A-B is in the route discovered by the first flooding. Node P is a candidate with intermediate node. Hereafter, the condition concerning the location of node P, node A, and node B is as follows.

Condition 1: Distance of A-P < Distance of A-B and
Distance of B-P < Distance of A-B

Condition 2: Distance of A-P + Distance of B-P < Distance of A-B + constant
(P is in the ellipse which has focus A and B)

Moreover, to avoid candidate nodes are approaching too much, the threshold (*T2*) of the distance between candidate nodes is set.

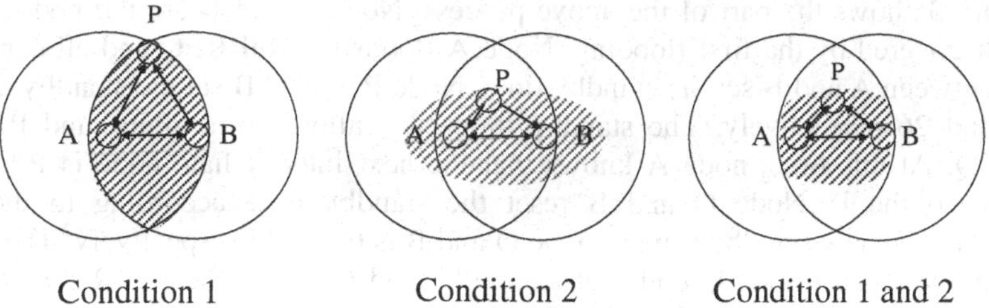

Fig. 2. Conditions of intermediate node

3.5 Action of Candidate Nodes

The candidate node operates as follows. At first, ReRREQ is sent from the source node to the next hop of the route discovered at the first flooding. The all candidate nodes between nodes in the route set the standby time according to the received power of ReRREQ. The larger power of ReRREQ is, the more short time is set. Therefore, the closest node to the sender of ReRREQ wakes up early. When the standby time ends, the node relays ReRREQ. At this time, the relay node keeps the sender node of the ReRREQ and the distance to the sender node. In the same way, the sender of ReRREQ also keeps the next relay node and the distance to the node, because the relay of ReRREQ is received by the sender. If the node receives another ReRREQ before the standby time ends, the node cancels the standby time and sets the new standby time according to the new ReRREQ. If the standby time of the next hop node ends, the node transmits the ReRREQ to the next link of the route. This process is repeated to the last link. If the standby time of the last node of the route ends, the last node transmits ReRREP (Reroute Reply) to the previous intermediate node that discovered by ReRREQ. The ReRREP is relayed by all intermediate nodes and returns to the source node. Then the new route is detected.

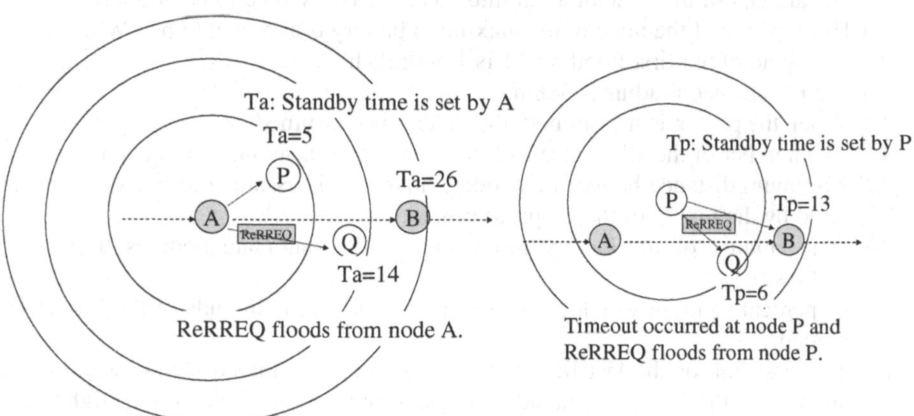

Fig. 3. Action of candidate nodes

Figure 3 shows the part of the above process. Node A and B are the nodes in the route discovered by the first flooding. Node A floods the ReRREQ and all candidate nodes between A and B set the standby time. Node P, Q and B set the standby time as 5, 14 and 26 respectively. The standby time ends after 5 time units, and P relays ReRREQ. At this time, node A knows that the next intermediate node is P and the distance to the P. Node Q and B reset the standby time according to the new ReRREQ. The new standby time of node Q and B is 6 and 13 respectively. Therefore, the standby time of node Q ends subsequently, and Q relays the ReRREQ. Node Q keeps the node P as the sender of ReRREQ and the distance to the P. At the same time, Node P knows that the next intermediate node is Q. At last of this link, the standby time of node B ends and relays the ReRREQ to the next link. At this time, the node Q knows that the last intermediate node of this link is Q and distance to B.

4 Simulation

We conducted simulations by using GloMoSim which is the network simulator supports a wireless communication. The proposal protocol is evaluated from the experiment result with the simulator.

4.1 Simulation Model

The environment used by the simulation is as follows.

1) Each node is arranged on the plane of two dimensions.
2) The node is arranged in the field of 500m×500m.
3) 32 nodes are arranged in the field.
4) The transmission node arranges at the location (50, 50), the destination node at the location (450, 450).
5) The nodes do not move in Figure 4 to 7. In figure 8, each node moves based on the Random Way Point model. Pause time is 30 sec.
6) The amount of the node of a minimum battery is assumed to be 500mWh.
7) The capacity of the node of the maximum battery is assumed to be 2Wh.
8) Threshold of the first flooding T1 is 1,500mWh.
9) The transmission radius is 388m.
10) When the packet is transmitted, the battery is consumed.
11) The number of the allowance and maximum hops is assumed to be ten.
12) Minimum distance between candidate nodes T2 is assumed to be 30m. This is used by the tuning of the proposal protocol.
13) The amount of the battery remainder of the candidate node is limited as follows.

(a) 80 percent or more which is the lower node among both ends of the link to be divided.
(b) The first link or the last link of the route is out of this condition because the amount of the battery remainder of the source or the destination might be a little.

4.2 Simulation Results

The protocols to be compared are DSR and LP-DSR. First of all, the data packet transmission frequency is changed and transmission powers consumed on the network are compared (figure 4). Because the transmission power consumed on the entire network is measured, not only the power for the data transmission but also the route discovery is included.

Next, the amounts of the average battery remainder of the route after the communicated are compared (figure 5). Because different protocols are compared, the number of hops is different. Therefore, the amounts of the average of the battery remainder are computed and compared. At the same time, the numbers of hops of paths used to communicate (figure 6) and time to discover the route (figure 7) are compared. Finally, arrival rate of packets is measured, and compared (figure 8).

4.3 Evaluation

LP-DSR is a protocol which discovers the route with the least power consumption according to the communication. It is thought that the reason why the amount of power consumption of the proposal protocol is less is that extra traffic is a little when the transmission frequency is a little. The amount of power consumption of LP-DSR decreases when the transmission frequency increases. The proposal protocol became the power consumption of 1/3 compared with DSR. Moreover, the amount of the battery remainder of the node of the proposal protocol is the best result of three protocols. And, the number of hops has decreased compared with LP-DSR. The number of hops of the detected route is suppressed to about 60% of LP-DSR.

However, the time which takes to the route discovery is about ten times in the proposal protocol compared with DSR. The arrival rate for the node speed is also the worst. The reason is thought to do the flooding twice. This seems an improvement point in the future. One of the most simple improvement methods is to use the route of the first flooding. And, this route is changed to the route by the flooding of the second. This improvement will make the time to construct the route short and the arrival rate better.

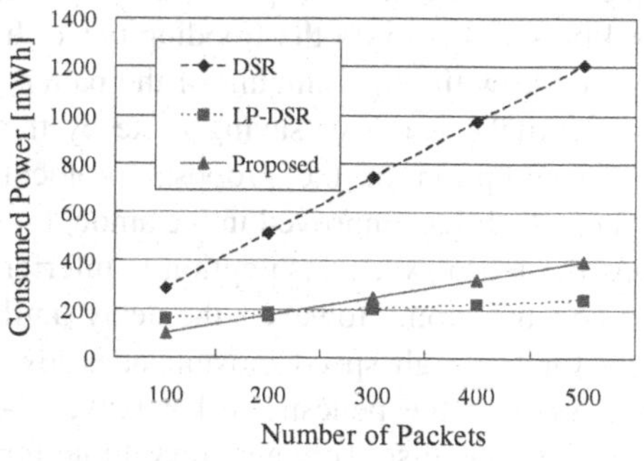

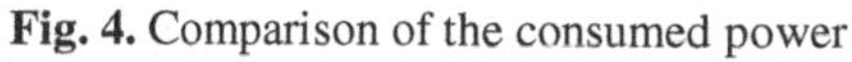

Fig. 4. Comparison of the consumed power

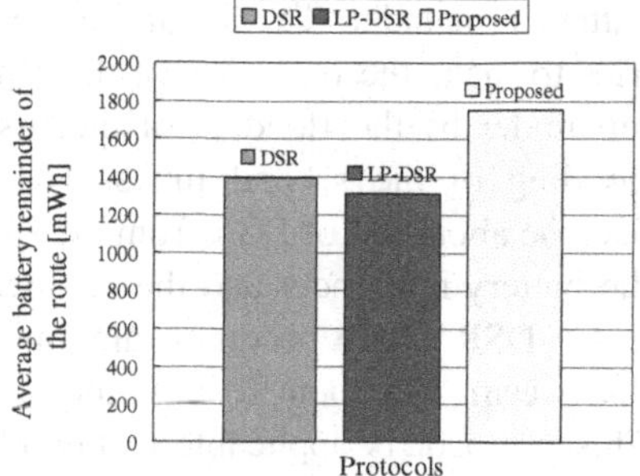

Fig. 5. Comparison of the average battery remainder of the route

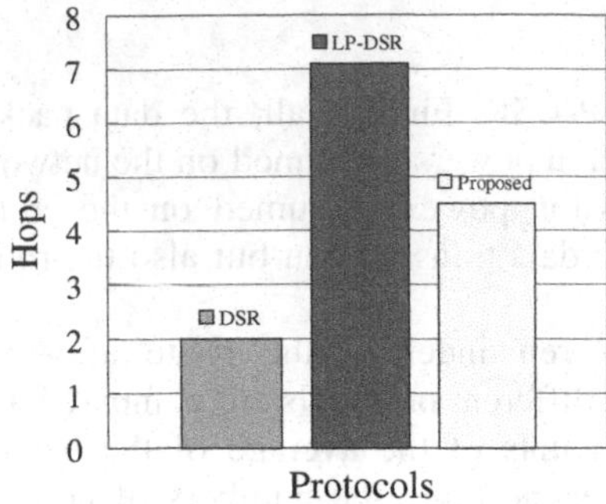

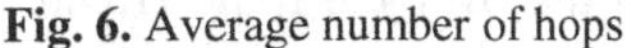

Fig. 6. Average number of hops

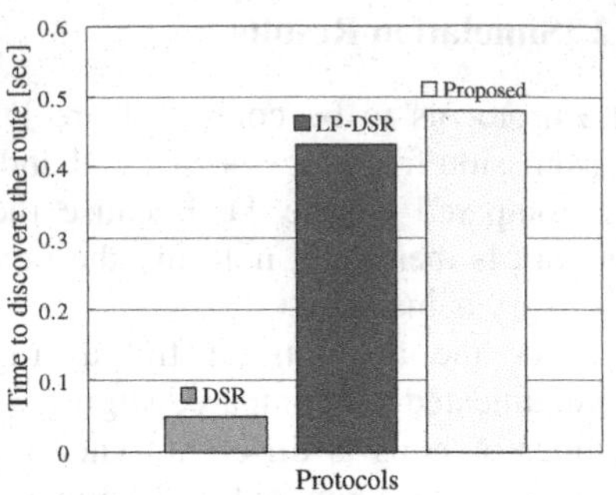

Fig. 7. Time to discover the route

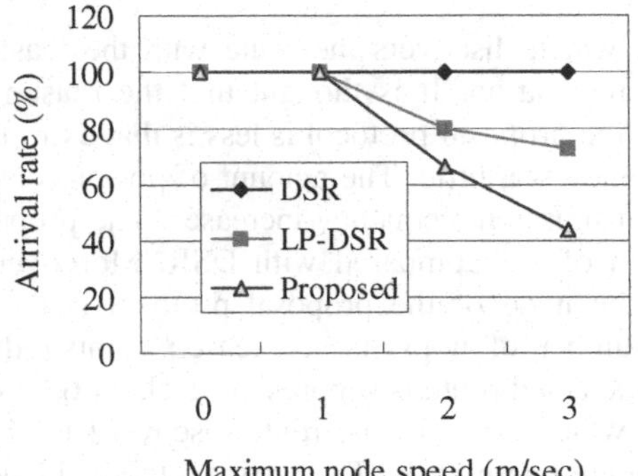

Fig. 8. Arrival rate for node speed

5 Conclusions

In this paper, we proposed the routing protocol considering both power saving and battery remainder. The feature of the proposal protocol is to do the flooding twice. It tries to make the backbone of the route of the node with large amount of the battery remainder by the flooding of the first time, and make it power saving route by the flooding of the second times. The power consumption of the proposal protocol became about 1/3 of DSR from the simulation result. It has improved in the amount of the battery remainder and the number of hops though power consumption is inferior to LP-DSR which becomes minimum power consumption. However, the delay until discovering the route is large and arrival rate for the high speed movement is low. This protocol is applicable to the ad-hoc networks of the pedestrian that moves 1-2m/sec. Future work is to improve the delay of the route discovery and arrival rate for the high speed movement.

References

1. Johnson, D.B.: Routing in Ad Hoc Networks of Mobile Hosts. In: Proceedings of the Workshop on Mobile Computing Systems and Applications, pp. 158–163. IEEE Computer Society, Santa Cruz, CA (1994)
2. Perkins, C.E., Royer, E.M.: Ad hoc On-Demand Distance Vector Routing. In: Proceedings of the 2nd IEEE Workshop on Mobile Computing Systems and Applications, New Orleans, LA, pp. 90–100. IEEE, Los Alamitos (1999)
3. Clausen, T., Jacquet, P., Laouiti, A., Muhlethaler, P., Viennot, Q.L., et al.: Optimized Link State Routing Protocol IEEE INMIC Pakistan (2001)
4. Perkins, C.E., Bhagwat, P.: Highly dynamic Destination-Sequenced Distance-Vector routing (DSDV) for mobile computers. In: Proceedings of the SIGCOMM '94 Conference on Communications Architectures, Protocols and Applications, pp. 234–244 (1994)
5. Park, V.D., Corson, M.S.: A highly adaptive distributed routing algorithm for mobile wireless networks. In: Proceedings of INFOCOM'97, pp. 1405–1413 (1997)
6. Muqattash, A., Krunz, M.: Power Controlled Dual Channel (PCDC) Medium Access Protocol for Wireless Ad Hoc Networks. In: Proc. IEEE INFOCOM, IEEE Computer Society Press, Los Alamitos (2003)
7. Choi, J.M., Ko, Y.B., Kim, J.H.: Utilizing Directionality Information for Power-Efficient Routing in Ad Hoc Networks. In: Proc. of the IEEE/IEE 3rd International Conference on Networking, IEEE, Los Alamitos (2004)
8. Sawada, K., Nakanishi, T., Fukuda, A.: Evaluation of Low Power Dynamic Ad Hoc Network Routing. IPSJ SIG Technical Report 2001-MBL-18/2001-ITS-6, pp. 91–98 (2001)
9. Ikeda, T., Kitasuka, T., Nakanishi, T., Fukuda, A.: Power Aware Dynamic Source Routing and Its Preliminary Evaluation. IPSJ SIG Technical Report 2002-EVA-3, pp.13-18 (2002)
10. Toh, C.K.: Maximum Battery Life Routing to Support Ubiquitous Mobile Computing in Wireless Ad hoc Networks. IEEE Communication Magazine (June 2001)

Wireless Balloon Network for Disaster Information System

Yoshitaka Shibata[1], Yosuke Sato[1], Kazuya Sakakibara[2], and Kazuo Takahata[3]

[1] Faculty of Software and Information Science, Iwate Prefectural University
[2] Nortel Co. Ltd. Japan
[3] Faculty of Human and Social Studies, Saitama Institute of Technology

Abstract. In this paper, in order to quickly recover communication network where the communication facility was seriously damaged and to collect the information with evacuated residents and disaster areas, we propose a balloon wireless network which is realized by combining balloons and wireless LANs and organizing into an adhoc network in the air. Using this balloon network, the damaged communication line can be quickly recovered. By combining with balloon wireless network and wired Internet overlay network, more robust, flexible and large scale disaster information network system can be realized even though some of the network lines and nodes are damaged and destroyed. In order to verify the usefulness of the suggested balloon network, a prototype system was constructed and made performance evaluation.

Keywords: Disaster Information, Wireless Network, Reliability.

1 Introduction

Recently, large scale sizes of natural disasters, such as earth quick, mountain explosion, seismic sea wave, frequently happened in addition to ordinal disasters, such as typhoon, hurricane, rain flooding and snow-slide are occurring in many countries in the world. Many residents by those disasters are loosing their lives. However, in many cases of disaster occurrences, the resident lives can be saved if the disaster information network system could effectively work just after disaster happened. In order to save our lives from those disasters, more reliable and robust information network for disaster prevention purpose than the conventional information network.

As for the safety confirmation with the residents in the stricken area, it is very important to quickly process the frequent inquiries from the people outside of the disaster area whether the residents could be safely evacuated or injured. Furthermore, in order to quickly manage and distribute foods and life supplies to evacuated residents, and register and assign volunteers, information and communication network system in the evacuation places is also important. However, When a disaster happened, various wire-based communication networks around the disaster area seriously damaged and disconnected and cannot perform their functions as communication means. Therefore, more reliable and usable communication network is required even just after the disaster happened.

As advent of Internet and high-seed wireless LAN technologies, various information and communication networks have been used as disaster information

T. Enokido, L. Barolli, and M. Takizawa (Eds.): NBiS 2007, LNCS 4658, pp. 40–48, 2007.

transmission means without any restriction for individuals in bi-directional ways. Moreover, most of the people using mobile terminal such as VoIP and PDAs can interactively communicate each other even though the public communication lines are out of order.

So far, we have developed Disaster Prevention Information Network based on wireless LANs and various application systems for disaster including Resident safety information system", Resource management system and Bi-directional video communication system[1][2][3].

However, due to failure of communication devices and disconnection of communication lines there are many cases where the communication means cannot function and the evacuated residents are isolated. Therefore, it is required to quickly establish the communication means effective on emergency.

In this paper, in order to quickly recover communication network where the communication facility was seriously damaged and to collect the information with evacuated residents and disaster areas, we propose a balloon wireless network which is realized by combining balloons and wireless LANs and organizing into an adhoc network in the air. Using this balloon network, the damaged communication line can be quickly recovered. By combining with balloon wireless network and wired Internet overlay network, more robust and flexible, and large scale disaster information network system can be realized provide even some of network lines and nodes are damaged and destroyed when the disaster happened.

2 System Configuration

Fig. 1 shows our proposed large scale disaster information network based on a combination of overlay network such as Internet and Mobile Adhoc Networks (MANET). In this paper, we newly propose a balloon wireless network as one of MANET.

As shown in Fig. 2, a balloon wireless network is organized by multiple balloons with wireless LANs. Since the wireless LAN has auto-configuration function, which

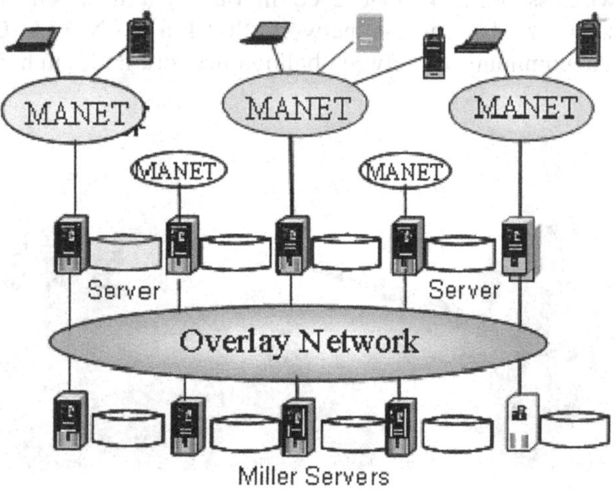

Fig. 1. System Configuration

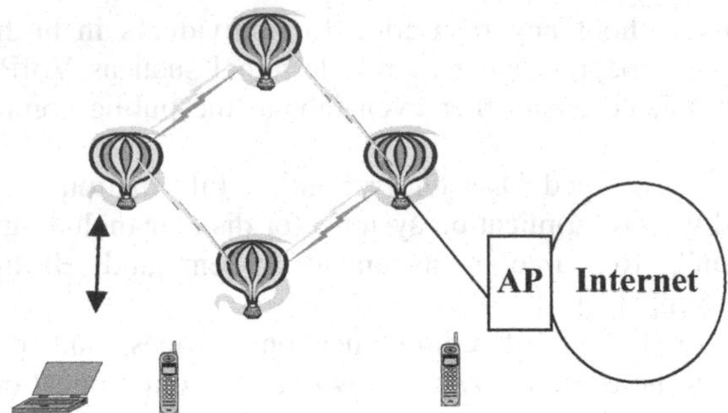

Fig. 2. Balloon Wireless Network as MANET

the network connection can be dynamically and automatically realized into a large adhoc network in the air. User can ensure the communication path from the disaster areas and evaluation places to the nearest access point to Internet by multi-hopping the balloon wireless nodes.

3 Wireless Balloon Network

A commercially available balloon which is made by vinyl chloride is used in this system as shown in Fig. 3 because of its simple structure and low price. The volume and weight of the balloon are about 3.5 m^3 and 8 Kg respectively. By injecting helium gas in the balloon, the buoyant can be attained about 20Kg. By considering 50 % merging the buoyant, total 10 Kg weight of wireless LAN device can be moored in the air around 40~100m high on the ground.

3.1 Wireless Network

Fig. 3 shows wireless network node used in our system which consists of two different LANs. A wireless access network 802.11a LAN (4.9 GHz, 54Mbps, 250mW) is used to communicate between balloon network nodes in horizontal.

Fig. 3. Balloon and Wireless Network Node

A ordinal wireless 802.11b/g LAN (2.4GHz, 54Mbps, 10mW) between balloon network node and mobile terminal such as mobile PCs, wireless mobile IP telephone, PDAs in vertical. The maximum distance to be able to communicate between wireless balloon network nodes is about 600m using plain antenna. On the other hand, the maximum area distance for mobile terminals on the ground to be able to receive the signal from wireless balloon network node is 100m. When the multiple wireless balloon nodes are launched from the ground, those nodes can automatically construct an wireless adhoc network in the air by their auto-configuration functions by which each node can establish communication path to the node with the strongest wave power density among the neighbor node. Also, when the wireless balloon network nodes moves each other or some nodes are out of order, the wireless adhoc network are automatically re-configured

The evacuation places in each city are interconnected by those MANET and wireless LANs and lead to the central disaster center. Each evacuation places and central disaster center include safety information database servers and disaster information Web servers including disaster information as well as ordinal life information. The advantages of using MANET and wireless LAN are to be able to achieve relatively high-speed and cost-effective network and to realize robust and reliable physical connection even though the disaster happened [3]. In addition, even though the disaster provided serious damage to the information network, network function recovery from the damage can be relatively quickly and simply attained by compensating the damaged line by MANET and temporal wireless LAN which is installed on the relied vehicle[4][5]. In addition, by combining wireless LANs, MANET and mobile terminals such as mobile PCs, PDAs or wireless VoIPs, more flexible and effective safety information system is realized [1][2].

This is said that the disaster information to be offered to the residents, volunteers, personnel in disaster area varies depending on the time to time. There are mainly three different applications and services, including are required, particularly just after disasters happened. Those including Disaster information, evacuation information, resident safety information, Wireless mobile IP telephone service, High-definition video transmission system.

4 Wide-Area Disaster Information and Sharing Network

It is predicted that not only traffic congestion on the information network by many inquiries for safety information regarding with the evacuated residents but also failure and disorder of information servers and networks derive the fatal whole system failure just after disaster happened. Therefore, in order to minimize the influence to the whole system functions by the system failure or disorder, distributed disaster information system is more suitable than central system.

In general, the evacuation places such as community centers or schools perform a very important role for residents to register his/her safety information whether they safely evacuated or injured and need medical treatment. Therefore, in our system, the safety information database server and web server with the disaster are distributed to the pre-assigned evacuation places. Thus, the safety information with residents is first collected on the safety information database servers on every evacuation place and then sent to the central disaster information center to totally integrate into unified safety information.

4.1 Local Server at Evacuation Place

The local server is organized by registration module, presentation module and database. The registration module receives a query with safety information from the client and retrieves from database and returns the retrieved results to the client through the network. The registration module newly registers the safety information from the client. The presentation module provides menu so that client can select registration, retrieving, presentation of detail information by HTML format. The database based on the RDB stores and manages the safety information to attain the high-speed database retrieving. The database manages the safety information with the evacuated residents including evacuation place, current health condition and locational data by GPS when the resident is on the way of evacuation.

4.2 Integration Server at Disaster Information Center

The integration server also includes the same function modules as the local server. In addition, the integration server performs a gateway function to the other local servers by showing the evacuation places by inquiring to the status management module on all of the local servers and showing a list of status of the local servers.

The status management module checks whether the local servers have failures or not and whether the daemon processes in the web servers at the each evacuation place are alive or not. When those servers are out of order, this integrated server performs backup functions. In addition, the integrated server also integrates all of the safety information by issuing inquiry to the local server. When the central server has failure, the remote backup server performs backup function by mirroring the information through high-speed network.

4.3 Backup Server at Remote Place

The backup server is always standing by to respond to the failure on the central server by mirroring all of the safety information. The backup server consists of the same modules and performs the function as integration server at the central disaster center. When the central server incidentally occurred into a failure, the backup server immediately substitutes. Since the multiple backup servers are allocated at the remote place far from the disaster area, the probability that both the central server and back up servers failed at the same can reduce as small as possible.

4.4 Network Environment

In order to realize more reliable and robust large scale disaster information system as network environment, interconnection of both wired and wireless network is introduced. Internet services are directly taken from the wireless network while the communication between the clients and local servers can be attained on wireless network based on IP protocol. The data communication between the client and server applications such as safety information is implemented using HTTP protocol to directly develop the web based service. Furthermore, the integrated servers on each central disaster centers are connected to the reliable high-speed network such as Japan Gigabit Network which is a nation-wide area testbed network across the Japan island. Thus, by combining the nationwide ultra high-speed network, conventional wired network and wireless network, the any residents can access to the disaster information system using mobile terminals, such as mobile note PCs, PDA, mobile phone as well as desktop PC through Internet environment.

5 Prototype System

In order to confirm the effectiveness of the suggested system in our research, a prototype system is constructed as shown in Fig. 4 and its functional and performance evaluations were carried out. In this system, a number of web servers and the database servers were set as local servers around the Mt. Iwate at the center of Iwate prefecture. On the other hand, the central server was set in Iwate Prefectural University as the disasters information center. Furthermore, 4 remote servers were set up at the remote places, such as Saitama, Shizuoka, Hokuriku and Kita-kyusyu.

Those places are mutually apart from each other but connected through Japan Gigabit Network II as the high-speed backbone network in our system is shown Figure 11 in addition to Internet. Moreover, as client terminals, mobile PCs, PDAs and mobile IP phones were used through wireless LAN, mobile network and Internet.

As development of this disaster information system, we used Apache1.3.27 for a web server and used PostgreSQL 7.4.6 and MySQL as the database system (RDBMS). We also used CGI (ActivePerl 5.6.1) for information extraction from the database server. Linux (Kernel 2.4.27) as operating system because of its popularity and free domain source. Currently its function and performance are evaluating by testing the experiment on "Wide area Disaster Information sharing system (WIDIS System)" which is collaborative research testbed by universities and public research institutes.

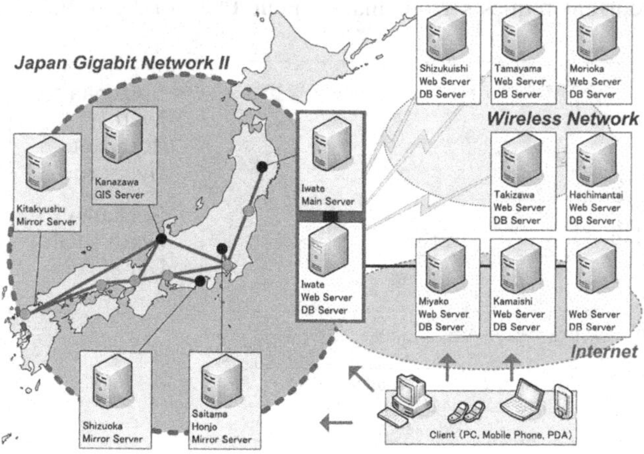

Fig. 4. Prototype System over JGNII

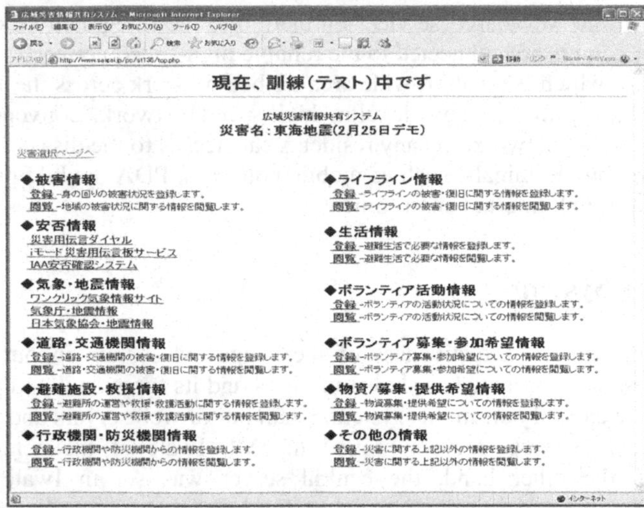

Fig. 5. Top of WIDIS

The top page of WIDIS is shown in Fig. 5. Various Disaster information, such as disaster locations information using GIS so called Denshi-Kokudo, resident safety information, weather information, life-line information, foods and materials salvation information, load traffic information, volunteers information, are is registered and maintained by the disaster volunteers at anytime and anywhere through Internet. Those registered information is also opened to all of the residents. We also evaluated the performance of our suggested system to initially analyze how many number of requests to WIDIS in a seconds can be processed in this network system prototype. The performance of distributed disaster servers 3 were observed using OLACLE bench mark for both static page access and dynamic database access cases.

Fig. 6 shows the result of the succeeded requests to dynamic database access to WIDIS servers at Iwate (Higher processing power server) by changing the total number of concurrent requests from many client PCs for both JGN2 and Internet

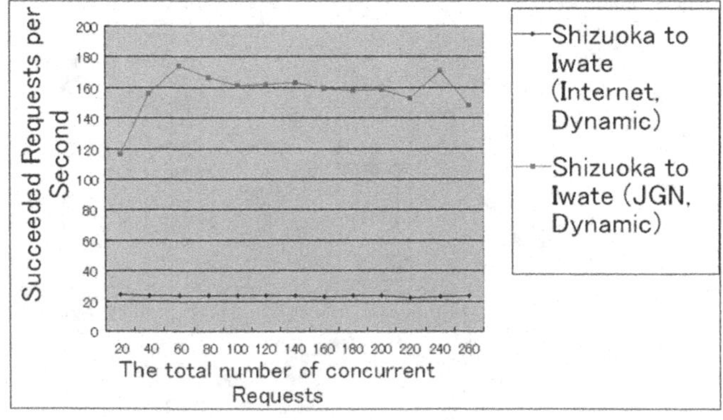

Fig. 6. Performance for Higher Performance Server

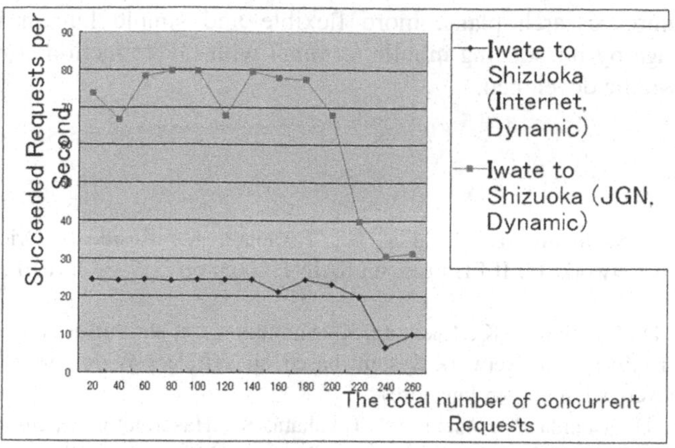

Fig. 7. Performance for Lower Performance Server

cases. It is clear that the succeeded requests of the WIDIS server through JGN2 is about 160 per second and 8 times larger than through Internet. Thus higher-speed network can provide higher processing the requests for a WIDIS server.

Fig. 7 shows the result of the succeeded requests to dynamic database access to WIDIS servers at Shizuoka (Lower processing power server) for both JGN2 and Internet cases. Since the WIDIS server at Shizuoka is a half in processing power than that of Iwate, the succeeded requests in a second is limited to about 80 and even worse when the number of the concurrent requests are increased. This is due to the lack of the processing power of the WIDIS server at Shizuoka. Therefore, we could estimate the required network speed and the number of the WIDIS servers if the number of the concurrent requests in a second is given.

6 Conclusions

In this paper, we introduced a large scale distributed resident-oriented safety information system constructed over Japan Gigabit Network II. The safety information with residents is registered to the local database in the evacuated area and integrated into a central database server at the disaster information center in the district area. Those local databases are mutually covered when the some of the databases are destroyed or disordered. On the other hand, the central database servers are located to mutually different locations with long distance to isolate the influence to the same disaster. The backup servers are also mirrored to support when the some of the central database servers are out of order. Thus, by introducing two levels of redundancy and backup functions, more robust and large scale safety information database system can be realized. We actually designed and implemented a prototype system using our suggested method over Japan Gigabit Network II to evaluate whether our suggested method is useful or not.

As our future research plans, more flexible and simple human interface for children, old age by introducing mobile terminal with GPS function combining with electric map will be developed.

References

[1] Shibata, Y., Nakamura, D., Uchida, N., Takahata, K.: Residents Oriented Disaster Information Network. In: IEEE Proc. on SAINT'2003, pp. 317–322. IEEE, Los Alamitos (2003)

[2] Sakamoto, D., Hashimoto, K., Takahata, K., Shibata, Y., et al.: Performance Evaluation of Evacuation information Network System based on Wireless Wide Area Network, DPS, 100-12 (November 2000) (in Japanese)

[3] Nakamura, D., Uchida, N., Asahi, H., Takahata, K., Hashimoto, K., Shibata, Y.: Wide Area Disaster Information Network and Its Resource Management System. In: AINA'03 (2003)

[4] Uchida, N., Asahi, H., Shibata, Y.: Disaster Information System and Its Wireless Recovery. In: IEEE Proc. on SAINT'04, pp. 317–322. IEEE, Los Alamitos (2004)

[5] Asahi, H., Takahata, K., Shibata, Y.: Recovery Protocol for Dynamic Network Reconstruction on Disaster Information System. In: IEEE Proc. on AINA'04, pp. 87–90. IEEE, Los Alamitos (2004)

Wireless Networks as an Infrastructure for Mission-Critical Business Applications

Krzysztof Gierłowski and Krzysztof Nowicki

Department of Computer Communications, Technical University of Gdańsk
ul. Gabriela Narutowicza 11/12, 80-952 Gdańsk
{krzysztof.gierlowski,krzysztof.nowicki}@eti.pg.gda.pl

Abstract. Despite the dynamic growth of wireless network systems, their presence in business-support infrastructure has been limited. In the article we provide an overview of generic corporate network architecture and examine usefulness of available wireless network solutions in such systems. Following this overview we analyze new wireless network architecture which currently undergoes standardization process – wireless mesh. It can result in significant increase in both bandwidth and reliability of complex wireless systems, even to a level suitable for mission-critical business applications. In conclusion we point out research directions and topics which are critical for integration of wireless solutions into business-support network infrastructure as they differ from currently followed main line of standardization works on the subject.

Keywords: e-business, corporate networks, wireless networks, WiFi, WiMAX, wireless mesh.

1 Introduction

Wireless network systems are amongst the most dynamically expanding computer technologies today. This growth is most observable in case of Wireless Local Area (WLAN) and Metropolitan Area Networks (WMAN). They are widely used in many scenarios, starting from simple two-computer ad-hoc setups through private home and SOHO networks to large, public Internet access systems.

With such economically viable and widely supported wireless network technologies as WiFi (IEEE 802.11) [1] and WiMAX (IEEE 802.16) [2], it would seem that we should be eager to integrate wireless solutions into corporate networks, to support various classical business and e-business activities. Their low deployments costs and obvious benefits of unwired access should make them a solution of choice. In reality it is not the case, and apart from last-mile Internet access networks, wireless solutions trend to stay out of business support infrastructure.

In the article we offer our analysis of this state of affairs and point out its possible causes, based on both our theoretic research concerning 802.11/802.16 standards [3-6] verified by extensive practical experience in designing and deploying such installations [7-10]. We would also like to present a new emerging type of wireless network architecture, which in our opinion, is able to remove the limitations which currently

T. Enokido, L. Barolli, and M. Takizawa (Eds.): NBiS 2007, LNCS 4658, pp. 49–58, 2007.

makes them unfit to provide ample support for business applications – especially high-availability mission-critical tasks.

2 Network System Architecture

To decide if currently available wireless technologies are adequate for building production-grade enterprise networks suitable to support mission-critical business applications (services requiring highest possible availability including precise level of QoS), we are going to analyze overall architecture of such networks. Then we will present sets of qualities for each network type, which are necessary for efficient support of business environment.

We can partition most currently operating enterprise grade computer networks into two basic building blocks: backbone and access networks.

Backbone network system is responsible connecting all separate elements of corporate network, which requires transporting large amounts of assorted network traffic, needed to support all kinds of applications present in enterprise. There are relatively few endpoints in such a network, each responsible for handling whole network system instead of a single workstation, and the amount of network traffic is very high. There is also a limited set of different traffic types present, each requiring different QoS parameters. The setup of backbone network is relatively static and resource requirements possible to predicate, so such networks are often statically managed, with limited need for dynamic management and configuration protocols.

Access networks, in contrast, consist of a considerable number of networked workstations and a single (or in some cases redundant) point of contact with backbone network. A considerable number of traffic flows exists between workstations and backbone network, but there also exist numerous direct flows between workstations in such network. They carry substantial amounts information and are most often short-lived and highly unpredictable. QoS parameters required for such diverse traffic are hard to predicate and often impossible to fulfill due to limited network resources.
In such environment there is a dire need for efficient monitoring, dynamic management and configuration mechanisms, especially if we aim to provide QoS guarantees for our users and applications. Moreover, users often retain significant control over their workstation's configuration, which leads to even more unpredictable network setup and highly possible misconfiguration. That makes such mechanisms even more crucial, but unfortunately they trend to drastically raise hardware costs, so frequently administrators of access networks depend on drastically extended bandwidth as means to offset potential problems.

Many requirements needed to support business applications are the same in both backbone and access networks. The main difference between these network type is dynamically changing nature of access networks, number of devices and the fact that most of these devices are under control of end-users.

From our research and experience with *corporate backbone network systems* [3,4,8] we believe that the list below covers most important characteristics of such networks. We present them here in order of importance: *Reliability, Resources and efficiency, Quality of Service, Security, Range.*

Reliability is the main requirement of backbone network, as failure here will segment our system into separate LAN segments and in most cases, deny users the access to most system resources.

As backbone connects whole systems instead of single workstation, it needs sufficient network resources and should be able to provide QoS mechanisms required to support variety of applications present in corporate environments. These tasks are also important, but backbone network characteristics make them relatively easy to provide.

Most of business data will be passing through the backbone network, so providing adequate security is highly advisable, but is also a relatively simple tasks for the reasons described above. Correctly chosen security mechanisms will also raise reliability of our system.

As the final of major requirements, backbone is likely to connect systems in a number of remote locations, so it should be able to provide its services over long distances.

A similar list of key requirements can be created for *access networks*: *Security, Reliability, Auto configuration and management, Quality of Service, Resources.* As we can see they share most of their requirements with backbone installations, but order of priorities differs considerably.

Access network is a point of contact between corporate system and end-user, so there is a critical need for strong security mechanisms: user/device authentication, authorization to specific network and system resources, transmission confidentiality and integrity. Always desirable reliability is a difficult task here, as access network administrators do not have control over all participating devices. Correctly designed automatic configuration mechanisms can provide enormous help in this task, as they both allow users to gain access to system resources more easily and eliminate threat of misconfigured end-user devices – one of the most common causes of network problems. Access network structure often dynamically changes and that makes efficient monitoring and management mechanisms essential.

Large number of participating devices, variety of dynamic support mechanisms and their lesser efficiency makes high resource level a desirable quality and QoS requirements much harder to fulfill.

3 Wireless Networks in Corporate Environment

Having defined usage scenarios and their requirements we should be able to assess if currently available wireless technologies are prepared to function in corporate environment and support modern business applications.

About two years ago, the answer would be easy – they are not. There were no economical solution in the area of WMAN networks, and WLAN solutions were still suffering from immature and faulty mechanisms – there were no QoS support, no automatic configuration, no efficient wireless domain management mechanisms, and security mechanisms suffered from multiple basic design errors (recovery of secret encryption key was possible in under 5 minutes of traffic capture and analysis). As a result these solutions were unreliable, difficult to manage and offered the worst security level possible – a false one [4].

Today however, with the lessons learned, wireless LAN technologies matured sufficiently to consider their use in business environment, even as elements of primary network infrastructure. Also economically viable wireless MAN solutions emerged allowing us to take them into consideration. In this situation we selected an 802.11 family (WiFi) WLAN and 802.16 (WiMAX) WMAN solutions for further analysis.

3.1 WiFi

WiFi is inexpensive, popular and widely supported technology and as such, an attractive solution for many kinds of commercial systems.

We have tested this technology in a variety of test setups and production installations ranging from simple, single access-point hotspots (by providing consulting services), through complex corporate networks (consulting services and our own campus networks) to an agglomeration-wide installation [7-10], counting tenths of access points over 150 km^2 metropolitan area.

WiFi supports two basic modes of operation: infrastructure and ad-hoc. The first requires an access point – a device which will control and organize the network, and take part in all transmissions. The second (ad-hoc) allows us to create a network without such device, by connecting many peer devices in range of mutual transmission range, as data forwarding in multi-hop networks is neither described by the standard nor supported by vendors. Also system management, limited in infrastructure mode is next to nonexistent in ad-hoc. In such situation we will limit our analysis to infrastructure mode, as ad-hoc in its current standardized state instantly and completely fail most of our requirements and trend to be highly unpredictable setup.

Security. Current state of development of security mechanisms in WiFi networks enable us to provide decent security level and all serious problems discovered to date were corrected. With WPA2 (Wireless Protected Access 2) security mechanisms we have at our disposal dependable and easily extensible authentication mechanisms based on 802.1x and Extensible Authentication Protocol (EAP), strong confidentiality and integrity protection with modern AES block cipher. All these mechanisms are assisted by decent key management mechanisms.

Of course transmission can still be relatively easily intercepted due to open nature of wireless transmission, but limited range of WLANs here works in our favor, as with proper design unwanted availability of the signal can be limited, especially in case of system employed indoors.

Such characteristics and security mechanisms make 802.11 networks suitable for both backbone and access networks in terms of security.

Reliability. WiFi networks work in unlicensed ISM band ant that fact severely impacts their reliability, which remains a serious problem of these networks, but at short ranges (25-40 m.) it remains at sufficiently high level. At short ranges and inside buildings the threat of interference with outside installations is limited and the main sources of problems are rouge transmitters (foreign laptops, palmtops etc.) and our own improperly configured devices. Proper network design and external management mechanisms will bring reliability of 802.11 systems to a level suitable for mission-critical access networks, but for critical backbone systems we would have to provide massive redundancy to fulfill reliability requirements.

Resources and efficiency. Currently available WiFi devices allow us to transmit up to 54 Mbits/s with well-known 802.11g standard and the emerging 802.11n standard promises speeds over 500 Mbits/s. These are considerable values, sufficient for any business application we could require including real time multimedia (with correct QoS support). The problem lies with inefficient usage of this bandwidth, as the access methods are mainly based on contention access, leading to collisions. Another problem originates in popular point-to-multipoint configuration of such networks which prevents direct communication between wireless stations and requires access point to retransmit such traffic, halving available bandwidth.
Despite these problems, transmission capabilities offered by these wireless solutions make them viable solution for both access and backbone networks.

Quality of Service. With introduction of 802.11e amendment [11] to basic standard, WiFi networks are able to support different priorities of network traffic, but the differentiation is only statistical, so we still cannot <u>guarantee</u> certain level of QoS. There is also a controlled access mode in 802.11e which would allow such guarantees, but as yet it is very rarely implemented and so far seems to share the fate of forgotten controlled access method of 802.11 base standard – Point Coordination Function.
Currently implemented mechanisms are sufficient for creating QoS aware access networks, but without controlled access method lack of QoS guarantees makes them unfit for use as corporate backbone systems.

Range. Hardware manufacturers specify up to 300-500 meters in the open and up to 50 m inside buildings. A real-world communication range is even shorter and from our own measurements in dense urban areas it would not exceed 80 m outside and 40 m indoors due to small signal strength and interference with neighboring systems.
Proper use of directional antennas can extend this range significantly, but line of sight (LOS) between both antennas is strictly required.
Range of reliable operation remains the main concern of 802.11 based systems. It results in large number of access points (relaying on wired backbone) which need to be employed to build an access network covering a given area. In case of backbones such lack of reliable long range transmission capability is even greater hindrance.

Management. While with extended security support in WiFi networks, we can maintain some control over network security, but there are no other significant management mechanisms and we have no control whatsoever over client hardware.
Some vendors offer Wireless Management Systems (Cisco, HP) which employ Lightweight Access Points – a setup where majority of network mechanisms reside on a central controller, to provide better, centralized management functionality.
Efficient monitoring and management mechanisms remain the key to successfully employing WiFi network in any kind of business environment. While such mechanisms are not yes included in 802.11 standard, there are stable solutions available on the market. Corresponding standardization process is also currently underway in IEEE 802.11 Task Group v [12].

With proper management capabilities 802.11 networks are now suitable as mission-critical *access networks*. They are cheaper in both initial deployment and later maintenance that their wired counterparts, adapt well to topology changes, and provide added benefits such as easy user access and even user mobility. In case of *backbone scenario* their insufficient range, questionable reliability at longer ranges, lack of strict QoS guarantees and contention based access methods make them unadvisable.

3.2 WiMAX

The new WiMAX wireless MAN still undergoes dynamic development and extension, but in its present state it can be considered mature solution, incorporating all necessary functionality to support business environment network systems. Its design allows manufacturers to easily incorporate new elements in their hardware as they became standardized, without losing compatibility with existing devices.

We were able to thoroughly test the available WiMAX hardware, starting with early (802.16-2004 compliant) models, due to cooperation with Intel Technology Poland and Alvarion Ltd. in "Wireless City Gdansk" initiative [7-10]. It includes extensive tests of WiMAX hardware and its deployment in heterogeneous environment as a metropolitan area network working in both backbone and access role.

Security. IEEE 802.16 standard has been created with security matters in mind from the very beginning. We have at our disposal a comprehensive security solution, providing mutual base and subscriber station authentication, authorization, data confidentiality and integrity, cryptographic key management mechanisms and protection against theft of service (accessing resources outside users contract). WiMAX security suite is also easily extensible, as it provides methods of auto negotiation of mutually supported security mechanisms set.

A comprehensive suite of security mechanisms present in 802.16 standard fulfills all requirements of both backbone and access networks, covering all key aspects of network security: authentication, access control and transmission safety.

Reliability. WiMAX networks support multiple physical layer type, allowing us to choose from different radio bands, both unlicensed and licensed – this allows us to reduce costs or avoid unorganized free frequencies. We also do not have to worry about incorrectly configured WiMAX terminals, because standard forbids them to transmit anything until they are synchronized with base station so they would not disrupt ongoing communications.

The combination of dynamic adaptation of the best transmission profiles, comprehensive monitoring and management mechanisms and ability to function in licensed frequency bands makes WiMAX a wireless technology of choice when it comes to a reliable corporate networking.

Resources and efficiency. The standard currently allows transmission speeds up to 75 Mbits/s. This is maximum bandwidth under perfect conditions at relatively short range. In practice, currently available hardware allows about 18 Mbits/s in a few kilometers range. This is substantially less than WLAN offer but the efficiency of transfer is much higher as the access to medium is reserved and controlled, not contention based, and medium usage efficiency reaches levels in excess of 90%, compared to about 30% in contention based WLANs.

Even with speeds offered by currently available hardware implementations WiMAX remains a cost-effective solution (yet a bit slow for a high-speed corporate backbone) and the efficiency of transmission and QoS mechanisms helps to improve service.

Quality of Service. Support for QoS is one of the strongest point of WiMAX technology. With DAMA (Demand Assigned Multiple Access) method of medium control, where stations signal their QoS needs to base station and are granted medium access for transmission, we are able to *guarantee* QoS parameters for connections.
Supported set of over ten QoS parameters enable us to satisfy needs of any QoS sensitive application.

Range. In case of WiMAX technology, we are able to choose between maximum available bandwidth and transmission range. The maximum range reaches about 50 km in with line of sight (LOS) between base station and user terminal. In case of urban environment, WiMAX network has unique ability to function without LOS, relaying only on signal reflections from buildings, terrain etc. In such case the maximum range depends on particular conditions and varies from 1 to 5 km.

Management. WiMAX features one of the best wireless network management systems available, which allows administrator to prepare terminals for use with almost no on site configuration. The system also permits remote monitoring of all vital network functions, such as network traffic statistics, noise to signal ratio, transmission modulation and coding used etc. Full control over QoS parameters is also provided, complete with ability to monitor if network is able to fulfill currently active QoS contracts.
All these management function utilize standardized mechanisms such as SNMP, DHCP, TFTP – the use of these well tested solutions promises stable management system and allows administrator to use third-party utilities for WiMAX network management instead of tying him to software suite provided by hardware manufacturer.

Functionality provided by WiMAX technology makes it a very good choice for corporate environment. It has all the necessary properties: reliability, security, high efficiency, superb QoS support, decent range, easy deployment and low cost for a wireless MAN. The only potential drawback is limited maximum transmission speed of currently available hardware. Despite this limitation, WiMAX technology is a very good choice for creating efficient, cost-effective and reliable, medium-range backbone networks and large-area access networks.

In *backbone role*, WiMAX is extremely useful in providing connectivity between separate locations in the same metropolitan area. Here its range and unique non-LOS capability are invaluable. As an *access network* WiMAX can provide support for local access networks created with use of WLAN technologies, by covering area outside their range to create comprehensive access system or to provide redundancy in case of local WLAN system malfunction. Ability to deploy WiMAX network almost on demand and at low cost, especially compared to wired solutions, is yet another vast advantage, and comprehensive management system allows this technology to be successfully deployed even as provider network for external clients.

4 Wireless Mesh Technologies

In the above chapters we analyzed the most popular wireless solutions today in their native (meaning: most popular) mode of operation: point-to-multipoint. In both cases it meant existence of one unique device (base station or access point) which coordinated the network and took part in all transmissions. This is hardly the most effective architecture but it allows a significant simplification of network mechanisms as there is only one, central network control entity.

In case of wireless mesh network, one of leading topics of our current research, we abandon this setup and allow a set of wireless capable devices to communicate directly with each other. There is no central entity controlling access of stations to the network which results in completely different approach to access protocols and their higher complexity.

There is also no need for all devices in the network (nodes) to be in range with each other – if transmission is addressed to remote network node a path is chosen going through a number of immediate devices which will forward data do its destination.

Mesh architecture creates environment, where we have at our disposal a multiple possible paths to a single destination and where network topology can be a subject of dynamic change as new nodes connect, existing disappear and transmission environment changes. Such characteristics create multiple implementation challenges, which delayed deployment of such networks in production environment.

For a wireless mesh network to function, a set of additional mechanisms is required:

- Network discovery and autoconfiguration – new devices should be able to detect occupied and free frequency channels, available mesh networks, acquire their basic properties and employed mechanisms, to decide if they are able to participate.
- Neighborhood discovery – a node must be able to discover its neighbors and create connections with all or a selected set of them. Due to dynamic nature of wireless network, this process must be carried on continuously.
- Path discovery and selection – as multiple paths to a given destination are possible, a node must be able to discover possible paths and select a most advantageous one. All of these in dynamically changing environment.

Wireless mesh network are *self organizing,* allowing new nodes to integrate themselves automatically in existing network architecture, which additionally adapts itself automatically to environment conditions changes. This coupled with the fact, that many alternative paths can be chosen to transmit data in case of basic path malfunction, results in high level of reliability. Mandatory inclusion of autoconfiguration mechanisms also results in drastic reduction of misconfigured wireless nodes that could impair functionality of our network.

Multiple possible paths between communicating nodes can be chosen dynamically and in real time with various properties in mind: bandwidth, reliability, low delay, small network resources consumption, etc.

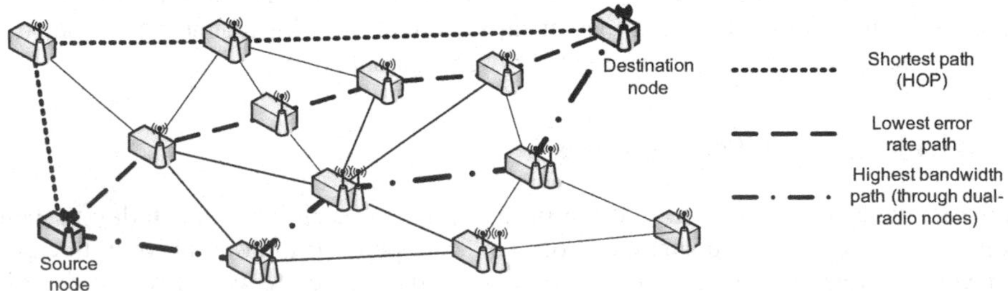

Fig. 1. Wireless mesh muli-path capability

In case of more stable network layouts and conditions, mesh can form multiple virtual backbones selected with different any of these characteristics in mind, or disperse traffic through the whole system, to maximize available bandwidth by employing as many independent paths to destination as possible. Of course mixing these dynamic and static path selection methods is also possible.

These abilities eliminate the need for wired short-range backbone to connect wireless access points to, as mesh network can carry all traffic internally, from node to node, over long distances. Such functionality can allow the lack of all but long range backbone connections, as the virtual ones formed by mesh can be faster, more reliable and able to automatically reconfigure in case of malfunction. Our experiments show that WLAN mesh is a preferable solution for intra-building connectivity.

For the mesh to be effective it should sufficiently dense, which means high number of participating stations in given area, compared to stable network range.

A standard addressing mesh networking employing 802.11 wireless local area network is currently under development as 802.11s [13].

In case of WMAN networks the advantage of mesh architecture will not be so big because of relatively lower number of more expensive network devices, but in case of more complex WMAN systems it could also provide significant improvement. IEEE 802.16 standard (a foundation of WiMAX technology), already incorporates elements of optional mesh mode, but so far it is not supported by currently available hardware.

5 Conclusions

From both our research and extensive practical experience from multiple commercial projects that we used to verify theoretical claims, we conclude, that wireless network finally reached the stage where they are practical in corporate environment, in support of business applications. They can provide sufficient reliability, security, bandwidth, quality of service and range to support any application and task, with exception of mission-critical applications and high-speed backbone networks. Of course, careful design of the system, backed up by knowledge and practical experience is required to a higher degree that in case of classical cable networks.

Of two wireless technologies leading the market of cost-effective wireless networks WiMAX seems ready for deployment in corporate networks [7], but WiFi technology requires additional support, lacking standardization of key elements: efficient monitoring and management mechanisms [4,5,8]. In light of our analysis a rapid creation of IEEE 802.11v (management) standard is of critical importance [12].

Greatly disconcerting is continuing lack of interest in WiFi controlled access mode (PDC and HCCA) exhibited by hardware vendors – without such mode of operation, WiFi usefulness in anything more complicated than simple Internet access network would be limited.

The emergence of wireless mesh networks [13] opens up completely new possibilities as such solutions could offset literally all drawbacks of wireless technologies in high-reliability environment required for support of e-business, retaining their unique advantages. Wireless mesh can accommodate even the most requiring applications with sufficient level of service to support mission-critical processes.

While 802.16 standard describes rudimentary mechanisms of an optional mesh mode but their definitions are too generic to be implemented by hardware manufacturers.

Unfortunately their exact specification seems a low priority task for the standard creators, which our analysis shows as a serious mistake.

The 802.11s (WiFi mesh) standard is still under early development, but the standardization process here is proceeding fast in this case and with attention and support of hardware manufacturers. Unfortunately the current scope of this standard does not cover all necessary aspects of wireless corporate networking – from our practical experience we conclude that topics concerning *reliability, virtual backbone creation, monitoring, management and methods of ensuring cooperation of nodes participating in a wireless mesh* [5,6], are subjects crucial for creating dependable production-grade wireless network systems, fit to support business applications.

We can conclude that wireless networks reached the point where there are already suitable for business deployment, but the direction of their development will decide whatever all their undisputed advantages will be available in complex business systems or will be limited research test setups and Internet access networks. WLAN mesh mode our current research concentrates on, promises not only to drastically raise their reliability in classical setups (access networks) but also allow their deployment as dynamically configured, short and medium range, high-speed backbone networks.

References

1. IEEE Information technology - Telecommunications and information exchange between systems - Local and metropolitan area networks - Specific req. Part 11: Wireless LAN MAC and PHY Specifications, IEEE Standards Library
2. IEEE Standard for Local and Metropolitan Area Networks, Part 16: Air Interface for Fixed Broadband Wireless Access Systems, IEEE Standards Library
3. Matusz P., Woźniak J., Gierołwski K., et al: Heterogeneous wireless networks - selected operational aspects. Telecommunication Review and Telecommunication News No 8-9/2005.
4. Woźniak, J., Gierłowski, K., Gierszewski, T., Nowicki, K.: Secure Wireless Networks in Medical Appliances. In: 3rd International Conference on Telemedicine and Multimedia Communication, Kajetany (2005)
5. Gierszewski, T., Gierłowski, K., Nowicki, K.: Interference issues in high-density wireless networks. Scientific Bulletin of the Faculty of Electronics, Gdansk (2006)
6. Konorski, J.: A game-theoretic study of CSMA/CA under a backoff attack. IEEE/ACM Trans. on Networking 14(6) (2006)
7. Gierłowski, K., Nowicki, K.: Test Installation of WiMAX Network on Gdansk University of Technology. Multimedia in Commerce Organizations and Education, Warszawa (2006)
8. Woźniak, J., Gierłowski K., et al.: Wireless Network Design Guidelines in Wireless City Gdansk Project. In: 13th Conference on Information Networks and Systems, Lodz (2005)
9. eCitizenship for All - European Benchmark Report 2005, EUROCITIES Knowledge Society Forum - TeleCities & Deloitte (November 2005)
10. Citizen, content and connect: inclusion through technology. The Concluding Report of the Urbact Information Society Network (May 2006)
11. IEEE Information technology - Telecommunications and information exchange between systems - Local and metropolitan area networks - Specific req. Part 11: Wireless LAN MAC and PHY Specifications, Amendment 8: MAC QoS Enhancements, IEEE Standards Library
12. Working Documents of IEEE 802.11 Task Group v: Wireless Network Management
13. Working Documents of IEEE 802.11 Task Group s: Mesh Networking

The DecoyPort: Redirecting Hackers to Honeypots

Iksu Kim and Myungho Kim

School of Computing, Soongsil University,
1-1 Sangdo-dong, Dongjak-gu, Seoul 156-743, South Korea
skycolor@ss.ssu.ac.kr, kmh@ssu.ac.kr

Abstract. Most of computer security systems use the signatures of well-known attacks to detect hackers' attacks. For these systems, it is very important to get the accurate signatures of new attacks as soon as possible. For this reason, there have been several researches on honeypots. However, honeypots can not collect information about hackers attacking active computers except themselves. In this paper, we propose the DecoyPort system to redirect hackers toward honeypots. The DecoyPort system creates the DecoyPorts on active computers. All interactions with the DecoyPorts are considered as suspect because the ports are not those for real services. Accordingly, every request sent to the DecoyPorts is redirected to honeypots by the DecoyPort system. Consequently, our system enables honeypots to collect information about hackers attacking active computers except themselves.

1 Introduction

As the need for computer security increases, so does the need for computer security systems to be developed to provide adequate protection to all users. These may include Intrusion Detection Systems(IDS)[1,2], Intrusion Protection Systems(IPS), and others. Most IDS and IPS use the signatures of well-known attacks to detect hackers' attacks. Accordingly, it is important and necessary to collect data regarding the attack strategies and tools of hackers. For this reason, there have been several researches on honeypots[3,4,5,6].

Honeypots are security resources which are intended to get compromised. They aim at collecting data regarding the attack strategies and tools of hackers. The data can be analyzed with analysis tools so that security systems can be updated to respond to new types of attacks. The more honeypots deloyed, the greater the chance of tracking hackers activities. Unfortunately, the more honeypots are deployed, the more IP addresses and computer hardware are required.

In this paper, we propose the DecoyPort system to redirect hackers toward honeypots. The DecoyPort is a port which is not used for a service but is used to lure hackers. The DecoyPort system creates the DecoyPorts on active computers. All interactions with the DecoyPorts are considered as suspect because the ports are not those for real services. Accordingly, every request sent to the DecoyPorts is redirected to honeypots by the DecoyPort system. Consequently,

T. Enokido, L. Barolli, and M. Takizawa (Eds.): NBiS 2007, LNCS 4658, pp. 59–68, 2007.

our system can complement the problem that honeypots can not collect information about hackers attacking active computers except themselves. First of all, the DecoyPort system can increase the chance of capturing and tracking hackers activities without wasting additional IP addresses and computer hardware. Unlike existing port-forwarders, the DecoyPort system can control the network traffic load caused by hackers, and prevent them from recognizing existence of a honeypot.

The rest of this paper is structured as follows. Section 2 gives an overview of the honeypot and honeytrap for collecting data regarding the attack strategies and tools of hackers. Section 3 and 4 describe the design and implementation of the DecoyPort system respectively. The DecoyPort system is evaluated in Section 5. Lastly, we conclude this paper in Section 6.

2 Background

2.1 Hacker and Internet Worm

When a hacker attacks a server, he generally start with OS fingerprinting and port scanning to identify the type of OS and the set of services in it. After that, he exploits vulnerabilities in a service daemon to run a root shell. He also install a keystroke logger on the server to gain more users IDs and passwords.

Internet worms are designed to exploit vulnerabilities found on many computers. They can find vulnerable computers by sending some packets. For example, Linux Slapper worm uses an OpenSSL buffer overflow exploit to run a shell on a remote computer. When the Linux Slapper worm finds vulnerable servers, it attempts to connect on port 80. It also sends an invalid GET request to the server to identify the Apache system. After the worm finds an Apache system, it tries to connect on port 443 to send the exploit code to the SSL service that is listening on the remote computer. Internet worms harm the computers and consume the bandwidth of networks.

2.2 Honeypot

The time delay involved in resolving new types of attacks makes it important and necessary to collect and analyze data regarding the attack strategies and tools in the most efficient and effective manner possible.

A honeypot is a security resource whose value lies in being proved, attacked, or compromised[7]. It aims to collect information regarding the attack strategies and tools of hackers. All activities within a honeypot are suspicious because it is not a production system. The information collected by honeypots are highly valuable and provide white hats a much fuller understanding of the intent, knowledge level, and modes of operation of hackers. Moreover, honeypots do not produce vast amounts of logs. On the other hand, traditional security systems, including firewalls, IDSs and others, collect vast amounts of data every day. These data make it difficult to find out new types of attacks. A honeypot is normally located at a single point and the probability can be quite small that attackers will attack it. The more honeypots deployed, the greater the chance of identifying, capturing, and tracking hackers activities. Unfortunately, the more honeypots are deployed, the more IP addresses and computer hardware are required.

Honeypot farms are consolidated environments in which a large number of honeypots reside[8]. Instead of having individuals all over the world build, customize, deploy, and maintain a separate honeypot for every network, we can build and deploy a single, centralized honeypot farm. This centralization then makes maintaining, standardizing, and analyzing the honeypots far simpler. When hackers interact with unused and predetermined IP addresses in a network, they are redirected to a honeypot in the honeypot farm by a reflector in the network. The hackers think they are interacting with a victim computer, when in reality they have been redirected to the honeypot farm.

Honeypots and honeypot farms can effectively collect information regarding Internet worms' attacks because they tend to scan vulnerable servers over several networks. However, honeypots and honeypot farms can only collect a small amount of information because they are systems based on unused and predetermined IP addresses.

2.3 Honeytrap

Honeytrap is a network security tool written to observe attacks against TCP services[9]. As a low-interactive honeypot, it collects information regarding known or unknown network-based attacks and thus can provide early-warning information. When the honeytrap daemon detects a request to an unbound TCP port, it considers the request as suspect. Honeytrap can relay incoming connections to a different host or service and at the same time record the whole communication. If it were installed on many computers and relayed incoming connections to honeypots, information regarding attacks could be analyzed effectively. However, the honeypot is easy to be fingerprinted when a hacker relayed by the honeytrap runs ifconfig or netstat. For instance, when the hacker runs ifconfig on the honeypot, it reports the status of a honeypot, but not that of a honeytrap-installed computer. Moreover, honeytrap can not control the network traffic load caused by relaying.

3 Design of DecoyPort System

3.1 Idea of DecoyPort System

Port numbers are divided into three ranges. The well-known ports are those from 0 through 1023, the registered ports are those from 1024 through 49151, and the dynamic ports are those from 49152 through 65535. Hackers generally attack the well-known ports or registered ports which are used by server programs.

The DecoyPort system creates the DecoyPorts on active computers. The DecoyPort is a port which is not used for a service but is used to lure hackers. All interactions with the DecoyPorts are considered as suspect because the ports are not those for real services. The DecoyPort system uses closed ports from 0

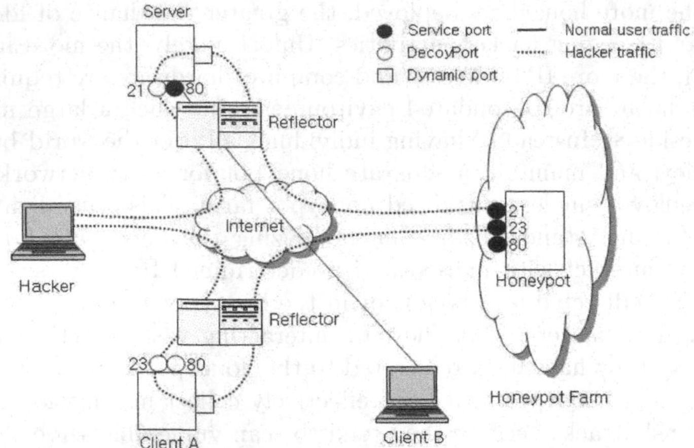

Fig. 1. DecoyPort system redirecting a hacker to a honeypot

through 49151 as DecoyPorts. When a hacker interacts with a DecoyPort, he is redirected to a honeypot by the DecoyPort system as shown in Fig. 1.

A reflector can not redirect a hacker who accesses active computers to a honeypot. However, the DecoyPort system can redirect the hacker to the honeypot. In Fig. 1, the server has opened port 21 for a DecoyPort and port 80 for a service, while the client A has opened ports 23 and 80 for DecoyPorts. If needs be, they can open more DecoyPorts. The honeypot has opened ports 21, 23, and 80 to receive requests redirected from DecoyPorts. The hacker thinks that the server and client A have opened ports 21, 80 and 23, 80 for services respectively. When the hacker sends a request to port 23 or 80 of client A, or port 21 of the server, the request is redirected to a honeypot through a dynamic port.

3.2 Architecture of DecoyPort System

The DecoyPort system is installed on active computers. Fig. 2 illustrates the architecture of the DecoyPort system. The arrows indicate packet flows, and the dotted-arrows indicate data and control flows between modules. Requests arriving via service port 80 are processed by the web service daemon and those arriving via DecoyPorts are processed by the packet forwarding module. The DecoyPort system has four modules as follows: port scan module(PSM), DecoyPort management module(DMM), packet forwarding module(PFM), and access control module(ACM).

- PSM: The DecoyPorts have to be created from closed ports, but not open ports. PSM creates a list of open ports on a computer and sends the list to DMM.
- DMM: Sometimes servers have to start a new service daemon or stop a running service daemon. For instance, the DecoyPort system has to close port 23 which has been used as a DecoyPort on a server, before the server

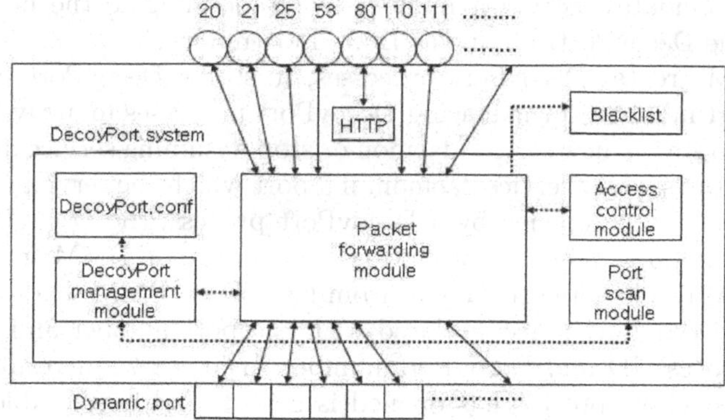

Fig. 2. Architecture of DecoyPort system

can start TELNET service daemon. The DecoyPort system also has to open port 23 as a DecoyPort, after the server stops TELNET service daemon. DMM manages DecoyPorts.
- PFM: PFM forwards packets arriving via the DecoyPorts to a honeypot and logs hackers' IP addresses. When hackers redirected by the DecoyPorts run ifconfig or netstat, the honeypot is easy to be fingerprinted. Accordingly, the DecoyPort system has to prevent them from recognizing existence of a honeypot.
- ACM: The DecoyPort system has to minimize loads caused by the DecoyPorts. ACM monitors and controls network traffics arriving via the DecoyPorts.

4 Implementation of DecoyPort System

4.1 PSM

Hackers attack a vulnerable service daemon listening on an open port which is one of the well-known ports or registered ports. For this reason, PSM scans a client or server computer for open ports from 0 through 49151 ports. This module creates a list of open ports from 0 through 49151 by running netstat and sends the list to DMM because DMM has to create DecoyPorts from unused ports, but not open ports. Here all ports which are not included in the list are candidate DecoyPorts.

4.2 DMM

DMM creates and destroys DecoyPort processes. Every DecoyPort processes opens a DecoyPort and forwards packets arriving via the port to a honeypot. This module uses information received from PSM and the DecoyPort.conf file's contents to create DecoyPort processes. The DecoyPort.conf file includes port numbers for popular services, including FTP, HTTP, SMTP, DNS, and etc.

DMM uses candidate DecoyPort numbers corresponding to the port numbers included in the DecoyPort.conf file as DecoyPort numbers.

After DMM creates DecoyPort processes, it stores DecoyPort process IDs and DecoyPort numbers for managing DecoyPort processes in array. Sometimes servers have to start a new service daemon or stop a running service daemon. Before a server starts a new service daemon, if a port which the service daemon will open has already been opened by a DecoyPort process, the DecoyPort system has to close the port. When an administrator commands DMM to close a DecoyPort, DMM receives a port number from him. Then DMM sends a SIGKILL signal to the DecoyPort process related with the port number and deletes the DecoyPort process ID and DecoyPort number in array. As a result, the port which the DecoyPort process has opened is closed, and it is usable as a port for a new service daemon. If the server stops a running service daemon, DMM creates a new DecoyPort process using the port opened by the daemon.

4.3 PFM

This module forwards packets arriving via the DecoyPorts to a honeypot and logs hackers IP addresses. Every DecoyPort processes created by DMM runs PFM. The source codes of PFM are as follows:

```
PFM() {
   create_decoyport();
   notify_pid();
   while(1) {
      usleep();
      recv();
      alter_IP();
      send();
      notify_total_bits();
      add_hacker();
   }
}
```

PFM creates a DecoyPort by calling the function create_decoyport() and sends process ID to DMM by calling the function notify_pid(). Therefore, DMM can store the DecoyPort process IDs for managing DecoyPort processes in array. After a hacker is redirected to a honeypot by the DecoyPort system and succeeds in attacking it, if he executes ifconfig or netstat, the honeypot is easy to be fingerprinted. The function alter_IP() alters the honeypot's IP address included in payload into the victim computer's IP address. The function notify_total_bits() notifies the total number of bits received on the DecoyPort to ACM. The function add_hacker() adds IP addresses of hackers accessing the DecoyPort to blacklist. All interaction with DecoyPorts are treated as attacks because those ports are not ports for real service. To consult the problem, a server administrator can contact a domain administrator who is responsible for an IP address used by a hacker. If the DecoyPort system is installed on client computers, the function add_hacker() also creates rules as follows:

```
iptables -A INPUT -p TCP -s hacker_IP --dport service_ports -j
DROP
```

Accordingly, IPtables can prevent hackers from accessing open ports except the DecoyPorts. The function recv() strips off the header of a packet received from a honeypot or hacker, and the function send() adds a new header to the packet. The regenerated packet is sent to the honeypot or hacker.

4.4 ACM

ACM monitors and controls network traffic arriving via DecoyPorts. The DecoyPort system has to minimize loads caused by DecoyPorts. The source codes which control network traffics arriving via DecoyPorts are as follows:

```
ACM() {
   if(bps_on_decoyports > THRESHOLD)
      interval += 100000;
   else if((bps_on_decoyports < THRESHOLD) && (interval != 0))
      interval -= 100000;
}
```

ACM controls the total number of bits received on DecoyPorts per second. The variable bps_on_decoyports indicates the total number of bits received on DecoyPorts per second and the constant value THRESHOLD does the maximum permissible number of bits arriving via DecoyPorts per second from hackers. The interval variable indicates times when the functions recv() and send() of PFM are suspended from execution for forwarding data. At first, the initial value of interval variable is set to be zero.

5 Evaluations

Table 1 shows an experiment environment for testing the DecoyPort system. We installed DecoyPort system on three client computers. The reflector uses one unused and predetermined IP address for lack of the IPv4 address space.

After hackers generally probe the available services of a server, they exploit vulnerabilities in a service daemon to run a root shell. However, it's impossible for us to predict the victim IP address. For this reason, we implemented a packet sender which sends packets to the victim. It randomly selects a well-known port and an IP address between xxx.xxx.xxx.1 to xxx.xxx.xxx.254. We executed the

Table 1. Experiment environment

	Computers running DP system	Honeypot	Predetermined IP
Host ID	55, 63, 79	31	234
OS	Red Hat Linux	Red Hat Linux	no
DecoyPort	21, 22, 23, 25	no	no
Service port	no	21, 22, 23, 25, 80, 443	no

Table 2. Total number of packets arrived to a honeypot

Honeypot	Honeypot Farm	Honeypot Farm One DP System	Honeypot Farm Two DP Systems	Honeypot Farm Three DP Systems
28	60	80	103	117
33	62	79	93	106
23	44	52	74	89
26	44	58	73	85
32	61	79	87	94

packet sender five times, and measured the total number of packets arrived to a honeypot as shown in Table 2. The honeypot can collect only data about hackers attacking it. On the other hand, the honeypot farm can collect not only data about hackers attacking honeypots in it, but also data about hackers interacting with predetermined IP addresses. In our experiments, the honeypot farm could collect 91% more packets than the honeypot. When deploying a DecoyPort system, the possibility that hackers may attack the honeypot farm could be increased by about 28%. The more the DecoyPort system deployed, the greater the chance of capturing and tracking hackers activities.

Table 3. Comparison of system resource consumption between the proposed system and the honeytrap

System Resource	Proposed system	Honeytrap
CPU	0.0%	1%
Memory	0.1%	3.2% increases every 10 seconds
Network	11KiB/s	1.9MiB/s

Table 3 shows the amounts of system resource consumption when the proposed system and the honeytrap forward a 700MB file. In the proposed system, the amounts of system resource consumption were measured in every 10 seconds, and threshold for protecting system overloads was set to 10KB. As shown in Table 3, the honeytrap does not control transmission speed during packet forwarding. Therefore, huge overloads occurred to the clients. Especially, memory consumption had been increased by 3.2% every 10 seconds, and finally the total memory was exhausted within a short time and the system became slow. On the other hand, the proposed system minimized system overloads through transmission speed control by delay time.

Fig. 3 shows the activities of a hacker redirected by DecoyPort system. When the hacker runs ifconfig, it reports the status of a honeypot, but not that of the victim computer as shown on the left side of Fig. 3. In other words, the IP address reported by ifconfig is not xxx.xxx.xxx.79 but xxx.xxx.xxx.31. Because we have implemented the function alter_IP(), hackers can not recognize existence of the honeypot as shown on the right side of Fig. 3.

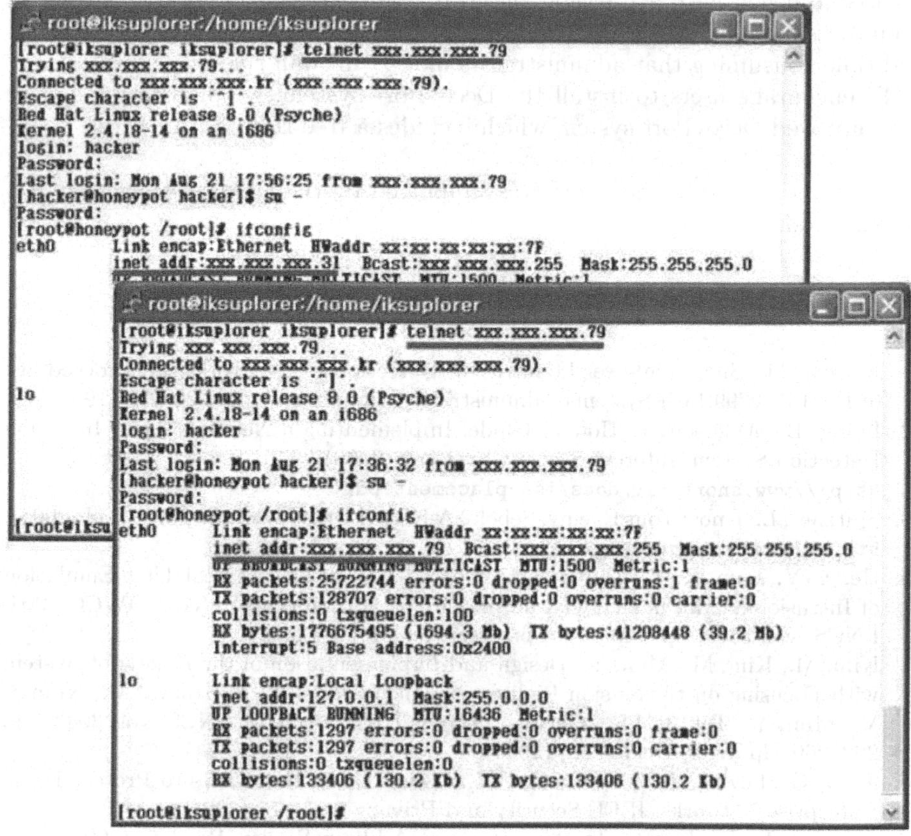

Fig. 3. Altering a honeypot IP address into a victim IP address

6 Conclusion

In this paper, we proposed the DecoyPort system to redirect hackers toward honeypots. Our system can complement the problem that honeypots can not collect information about hackers attacking active computers except themselves. In our experiments, when deploying a DecoyPort system, the possibility that hackers may attack the honeypot farm could be increased by about 28%. Moreover, the DecoyPort system can increase the chance of capturing and tracking hackers activities without wasting additional IP addresses and computer hardware. Unlike existing port-forwarders, the DecoyPort system controls the network traffic load caused by hackers, and prevents them from recognizing existence of a honeypot.

Server administrators can contact a domain administrator who is responsible for an IP address used by a hacker because the DecoyPort system adds IP addresses of hackers accessing the DecoyPorts to blacklist. When the DecoyPort system is installed on client computers, it prevents hackers from accessing open ports except the DecoyPorts. The DecoyPort concept is a technique that can be accomplished with a firewall, router, or switch technology. However, active computers open or close ports from time to time. Accordingly, it is very difficult and time consuming that administrators modify firewall ruleset periodically.

To encourage users to install the DecoyPort system, we plan to implement the improved DecoyPort system which includes a free IDS or Anti-Virus.

Acknowledgments. This work was supported by the Soongsil University Research Fund.

References

1. Roesch, M.: Snort-Lightweight Intrusion Detection for Networks. In: Proceedings of the LISA '99:13th Systems Administration Conference, pp. 229–238 (1999)
2. Laing, B., Alderson, J.: How to Guide: Implementing a Network Based Intrusion Detection System. Internet Security Systems (2000), `http://www.snort.org/docs/iss-placement.pdf`
3. Spitzner, L.: Know Your Enemy: Sebek2 A Kernel Based Data Capture Tool (2003), `http://www.honeynet.org/`
4. He, X.-Y., Lam, K.-Y., Chung, S.-L., Chi, C.-H., Sun, J.-G.: Real-Time Emulation of Intrusion Victim in HoneyFarm. In: Chi, C.-H., Lam, K.-Y. (eds.) AWCC 2004. LNCS, vol. 3309, pp. 143–154. Springer, Heidelberg (2004)
5. Kim, M., Kim, M., Mun, Y.: Design and Implementation of the HoneyPot System with Focusing on the Session Redirection. In: Laganà, A., Gavrilova, M., Kumar, V., Mun, Y., Tan, C.J.K., Gervasi, O. (eds.) ICCSA 2004. LNCS, vol. 3043, pp. 262–269. Springer, Heidelberg (2004)
6. John, G., Levine, J.B., Grizzard, H.L.: Owen: Using Honeynets to Protect Large Enterprise Networks. IEEE Security and Privacy 2, 74–75 (2004)
7. Spitzner, L.: Honeypots: Tracking Hackers. Addison-Wesley, Reading (2003)
8. Spitzner, L.: Honeypot Farms (2003), `http://www.securityfocus.com/infocus/1720`
9. Werner, T.: honeytrap - trap attacks against tcp services, `http://honeytrap.sourceforge.net/start.html`
10. Fyodor: The Art of Port Scanning. Phrack Magazine 7(51) Article 11 (1997)

Network Security Improvement with Isolation Implementation Based on ISO-17799 Standard

Yeu-Pong Lai and Jui-Heng Tai

Department of Computer Science and Information Engineering,
Chung Cheng Institute of Technology,
National Defense University, Taoyuan, Taiwan, 33509, R.O.C.
Tel.: 886-3-3805249-212
Fax: 886-3-3894770
{lai,g961201}@ccit.edu.tw

Abstract. In these years, many researchers proposed the way — to isolate the computers with sensitive information from outside attackers or unauthorized users. The Taiwan government has ruled the importance of network isolation in several policies, such as "The Handling Implementation Program of Information Security Emergency Incidents for government departments" and "The Responding Protocol of Notifying Information Security Events in Executive Yuan and its Departments." However, there are few materials available for implementing network isolation. In ISO-17799, there is no implementation guidance for practicing network isolation but auditing network physical isolation. This paper provides the implementation guidance of network isolation with some logical isolation techniques and management polices.

Keywords: Network isolation, Physical and environmental security, Security network control, Segregation in networks, Sensitive system isolation, ISO-17799.

1 Introduction

That becomes more important to prevent secrets from being stolen, since attackers have gradually organized into a union and developed more complex and more devastating attacks in multi-combination styles. Network attacks aim at specific targets.[1] The spend in information security has grown 17% to US$25.7 billion from 2004 to 2005. Expectedly, it may be US$40.7 billion in 2008.[2] Unfortunately, the increasing budgets and labors might not reduce network security events.

In Taiwan, the regulation, "The Practical Plan to Eliminate Crisis Events in Information Security for Departments," announced by Executive Yuan in October 2004, demands departments have to encrypt "the most important" and "important sensitive" documents, data, and files.[3] Intranets should be physically isolated for preventing information from being revealed, modified, or accessed by unauthorized people. The "handling procedure", in the responding procedures, mentions that "Each department should establish an environment for protecting the security of information in communication systems and networks. ... Physical isolation may be applied and

T. Enokido, L. Barolli, and M. Takizawa (Eds.): NBiS 2007, LNCS 4658, pp. 69–78, 2007.

practiced."[4] The network isolation is one selection to protect these important information and systems in networks.

Network isolation techniques are different from other network security devices, such as firewall, virus wall, and Intrusion Detection System. They consist of two aspects, management procedures and technique equipment, to carry out physical isolation or logical isolation. Physical isolation means that network devices are exactly disconnected to other networks. It should be audited frequently with proper policies and procedures from information security management. Logical isolation allows a connected node in each network system to exchange data. The connections between networks, however, are via these interfaces, "network separate equipment". The equipment switches the connection to one network at a time.

In 1997, Mark Joseph Edward proposed the ways for "Physical Isolation" and "Protocol Isolation".[5] E. NYONI defined and illustrated isolation schemes in many different ways.[6] Faithfully, both schemes, "Physical Isolation" and "Protocol Isolation" expatiated by Mark Joseph Edwards and E. NYON, are not "real" isolation in our views with referring to our national policies. Besides, the company, CISCO, proposed the Network Admission Control (NAC) architecture that is a combination of CTA (Cisco Trust Agent), ACS (Cisco Secure Access Control Server), and network access devices. These devices verify the statuses of hosts in intranet for quarantining those disqualified hosts from others.[7] Microsoft in 2004 presented Network Access Protection (NAP) architecture. That consists of IPSec internal network isolation, VPN remote connection, IEEE802.1X authentication, enforced DHCP, and CM (Connection Manager) to check whether hosts have installed security measures, such as personal firewall, anti-virus system, system vulnerability repairing program, and virus code update program. These, not fitting the requirement of security, would be isolated. In fact, both NAC and NAP are mechanisms for the network access management. They do not achieve the intra-network disconnected.

Section 2 describes the definitions "logical isolation" that satisfies the isolation requirement in our national policies with the property of network disconnection. Section 3 depicts the logical isolation techniques, products, and architecture. The implementation of network isolation in ISO-17799 is then discussed in Section 4. These implementation outlines of logical isolation can be devoted to establishing network security standards for our nation.

2 The Concept of Network Isolation

Differing from the network quarantine by CISCO NAC and Microsoft NAP, in practicing network isolation, the network disconnection mechanisms are required, which can prevent intra-systems from outside attacks. In this section, the definitions of network isolation are provided. Section 2.1 is for the physical isolation. Logical isolation is defined in Section 2.2.

2.1 The Concept of Network Physical Isolation

The physical isolation network implies an independent network without any connection or data transforming with outside services. For implementing two physical isolated networks, all devices and systems should be duplicated. That means higher cost is required. The physical isolated networks are only applied for protecting high value information properties or preventing unexpected threats, for example, the defense strategic network, financial network, police network, and R&D network. These physical isolation networks are closed networks that users can not access to other networks and servers do not provide for public services. Network physical isolation is not only at a high cost, but also uneasy to implement. The audit procedures for connections should be performed regularly and frequently. The alternative selection, the network logical isolation, allows an indirect connection between networks if necessary. These techniques would be discussed in the following section.

2.2 Network Logical Isolation

Preventing from the high cost of physical isolation and the insecure shortcomings of protocol isolation, the concept of logical isolation is designed and proposed. Network logical isolation allows one connection between network systems at a time. In other words, hosts in the logically isolated network can still exchange data with these hosts in other networks. The systems in a logical isolation network cannot connect to those in other network system directly, which is performed with these separate network devices, for example, separate NIC, separate Hub, separate switch, and separate router. These devices switch connection between two logically isolated networks. Hosts in different logical isolation network cannot exchange data directly. Logical isolation can not only protect highly sensitive information, but also exchange and share information to users in different networks. Next section will discuss the network logical isolation techniques and devices.

3 Implementation of Network Logical Isolation

This section introduces the way to organize the network logical isolation. Several segregate devices are introduced in Section 3.1. Besides, a simple topology is also illustrated. Section 3.2 provides the properties of the logical isolation network.

3.1 Devices for Network Logical Isolation

The separate devices for logical isolation disconnect the physical links of the threatening session. Differing from hosts in both NAC and NAP, the hosts in logical isolation network can not connect to other network directly. The separate devices switch connection to one realm at a time. In NAC and NAP, the physical links are actually still connected. If the vulnerabilities on the NAC and NAP devices are explored, these hosts will be still in danger.

In logical isolation network, these segregate devices of every variety have the same property of disconnection. The link disconnection stands for the security of the "physical layer" in OSI network model. These network systems and devices, such as firewall, IDS, and anti-virus wall, are for the secure properties in "network layer" and "application layer". For advanced some of separate devices are designed with similar functions for securing layer 2 to layer 7, through analyzing protocols and striping protocol.[9] These devices can strip all TCP/IP, so some vulnerabilities in TCP/IP protocol can be eliminated. [10]

GAPs are a kind of separate devices for network logical isolation. They consist of three systems, the internal network system, the transforming system, and the external network system. The transforming system can only connect with either internal network system or external network system at a time. The internal network system and the external network system are two isolated interfaces connected to two distinct networks for logical isolation. When data taped in each of these two systems, the operating modules perform for data security in the virus detection, the content filtration, and the malicious code detection.[11][12] When hosts connecting with external network interface are attacked and affected, because of GAP's network isolation mechanism, those in the internal network would remain normal.

Except placing GAPs, there are alternative ways with separate NICs installed in hosts and separate Hubs/Switches located in network for network logical isolation. When users need to connect with two different networks, they can install separate NIC and separate Hub (or Switch). For instance, the separate NIC controls two hard disks. Each hard disk is for data while the host communicates with hosts in one network. When the connection to one network established, there is only one hard disk powered on. The network isolation is then ensured, since there is no data transmitted between networks.[13] Separate Hubs/Switches switch hosts having separate NICs into different networks. The control processors of separate switches connect switching modules. Two different network systems connect with different switching modules in switch, respectively. [14] The use of separate NICs and separate Hubs/Switches then practice the network isolation methods.

3.2 The Topology of Network Logical Isolation

In organizing the network security of a department, the topology for isolating information security is then shown in Figure 1. The red links are for communications with these servers in the sensitive networks. Those in blue are then for accessing public services. When the personal computer communicates with sensitive service servers, the data are isolated in a certain hard disk. If the personal computer connects with public service servers, the different hard disk driver is powered on to manipulate information. This hard disk with sensitive data is powered off.

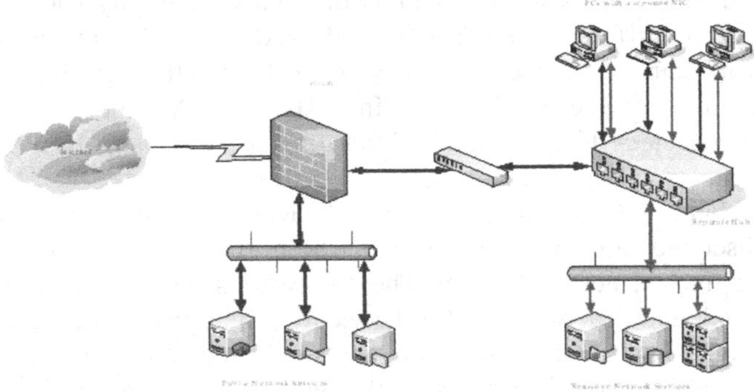

Fig. 1. Implementation of two isolated networks with separate NICs/ Hubs /Switches

Though network isolation techniques and products can make up the inadequacy of firewall, IDS, it is impossible to defeat all risks in network. The management and audit policies should be employed and continually refine according to the progressive techniques and transforming department.

4 Review and Revise the Material of Network Isolation in ISO-17799:2005

ISO-17799 is a well-known standard for information security management practices. Referring to ISO-17799, Taiwan establishes it own security standard, CNS-17799, in September 2000. Although in this standard there are many management schemes presented, the materials in network isolation are not sufficient. Section 4.1 reviews the related materials of the network isolation in ISO-17799:2005. This materials are about "Physical and environmental security," "Network control," "Security of network services," "Segregation in networks" and "Sensitive system isolation." Actually, the material does not include network logical isolation among network isolation. Section 4.2 proposes the adaptive revision of implementation guidance for segregation.

4.1 Network Isolation in ISO-17799

There is no specific chapter for network isolation in ISO-17799:2005. Scatters of network isolation materials are in these chapters of "Physical and environmental Security", "Network control", "Security of network services", "Segregation in networks", and "Sensitive system isolation".[15]

1. Physical and environmental security

In ISO-17799: 2005, Chapter 9 describes the principle that the important or sensitive information processing devices should be set in a secure environment. That includes taking proper security control measures, such as in protecting buildings and equipment from physical damage, unauthorized entrance, and some other unexpected behaviors. The consideration and guidance are tabulated in Table 1, for two objectives, "Secure Areas" and "Equipment Security".

Table 1. The consideration and guidance for physical security

Topic \ Objective	Secure Areas	Equipment Security
Control and Implementation guidance	Physical security perimeter	Equipment sitting and protection
	Physical entry control	Supporting utilities
	Securing offices, rooms, and facilities	Cabling security
	Protecting against external and environmental threats	Equipment maintenance
	Working in secure areas	Security of equipment off - premises
	Public accessing, delivering, and loading areas	Secure disposal or re-use of equipment

2. Network control
Network control, in Chapter 10.6.1 of ISO17799, is for the network security management that determines what information is authorized with referring to network security control.

3. Security of network services
Security of network services, in Chapter 10.6.2 of ISO 17799, is for the network security management. No matter the services are for interior or exterior users, these should be explicit, the security properties of services, the authentication mechanisms of services and the managerial procedures of services. Network services include providing connection, personalized services, and managing procedures.

4. Segregation in networks
In Chapter 11.4, "Network access control", the segregation procedures are presented in Chapter 11.4.5 for classifying the network services to each group, users and other systems. The methods for organizing segregated networks are as follows.

(1) Establish the firewalls (or the security gateways) and insert the package filtration systems to prevent illegal accesses, due to the department policies
(2) Apply cryptography systems, establish authentication schemes, and secure transmission tunnels for the communications between different networks.
(3) Elevate functions of network devices via making one MAC address directly mapped with a fixed IP address, and cooperate transmissions of packet routing via referring to the IP addresses with the consideration to security policies

5. Sensitive system isolation
In Chapter 11.6, the "Application of information access control", the subsection "Sensitive system isolation", Chapter 11.6.2, shows that these sensitive systems within a department should set and operate in an independent environment. When sensitive application services are operated in a public environment, the person in charge should confirm the sharing resources and evaluate possible risks in the system. For some Special /High sensitive applications, the procedures in "segregation in networks" should be employed. Otherwise, the systems can only be executed on specific computers in an independent environment.

In ISO-17799, the network security measures and isolation methods with the above controls and implementation guidance mention the methods of "segregation in networks." These methods employ security facilities and protection techniques to ensure network security of departments. Actually, these facilities and techniques secure the data from the layer 2 to the layer 7 of the OSI network protocols. The physical link connections between networks are not considered. That is different from network isolation techniques by which the physical links are disconnected until authorized transmission requests for connections. These network isolation techniques should be also considered in the network separation applications for network security. The following section presents the revised implementation guidance for segregating networks, with referring to the format of ISO 17799. The reversion consists of these technologies for network isolation methods that are separation and quarantine techniques.

4.2 The Revised Implementation Guidance for "Segregation in Networks"

The access and isolation facilities in ISO-17799 are packet filters, cryptography schemes, and access control in software or hardware. However, these techniques for network logical isolation are not considered, although they can also provide the properties of network segregation. The following revision presents the management control with separate techniques for implementing physical isolation, network logical isolation, and protocol isolation.

1. Implementation guidance

(1) For the highly sensitive data or systems, the physical isolation policy should be implemented.

a. Network system prohibits any access from external network
b. No physical cable connection is allowed
c. Ensure network system working in a secure and independent environment
d. Removable/mobile access media are restricted
e. The hosts within the network should be set with schemes for access authority and protection control

(2) Based on department's policies in the access to external networks, the network logical isolation techniques can provide a secure way to exchange data between networks. The considerations are in the following:

a. Using GAP techniques or products ensures the disconnection mechanism between isolated networks
b. Exchanging data between devices and hosts in different networks is not allowed, except through the GAP mechanism
c. Employing the following techniques ensures the security of data transmission between or in networks.
   (a) Anti-virus system
   (b) Content filter
   (c) Malicious code detection
d. Applying separate NICs, Hubs, and Switches enhances the security in networks

(3) For the secure in isolation networks, the following protection mechanisms must be employed.

a. Establishing firewall or secure gateway to eliminate illegal accesses via configuring the rules on packet filtering, according to the policies of departments
b. Applying cryptography schemes to establish authenticated and secure transmission tunnels for communications
c. Adopting verification functions on network devices to make one MAC address directly map to an IP address

2. Other implementation guidance

(1) For the departments processing with lower sensitive data, the departments can apply the methods proposed in "segregation in networks" to divide the internal network into smaller domains.

(2) For the servers processing with non-sensitive data or for inner users only, the departments can use the protocol isolation scheme to reduce the invasion risks from external network. The selected protocol should be not routed out of this domain.
(3) For improving the protection on hosts, second defense system, NAC or NAP, can be employed in isolated networks.

3. Management and Audit
To ascertain the techniques and procedures of separate networks do be practiced, the followings check-list controls should be are confirmed at least. Departments can rule out their own controls for security audit surely.

(1) The authentication schemes are not only performed as outsiders or new-comers request these internal services, but also as the insiders request these services to external servers.
(2) The removable storage should be restricted by department policies. If the removable storages are requisite, they should be restrained by classified persons. No private removable storage is allowed in departments.
(3) Before data transmitted to outbound areas, administrators are able to identify the sensitiveness and confidentiality of data to prevent the unauthorized transmission.
(4) The staffs for network management should monitor and log the outbound connections and transmitted information.
(5) The configuration and the parameter of network devices and service systems should be logged fully and be audited regularly.
(6) The operating system and application software on hosts and servers should be updated and patched regularly.

In Section 4.1, the concept of isolation in ISO-17799 is introduced. Section 4.2 then provides the revised implementation guidance of these segregation methods upon the requirements of sensitive classes. With referring to the implementation guidance in ISO 17799, our government has established a Security Plan of "The Implementation Plan for Information Security Level in Government Departments". In the Plan, departments are classified into several protection levels for their information systems.

5 Conclusions and Future Works

As known, the bigger the departments are, the more difficult the physical isolation can be practiced. If the department has branches in districts, or even nations, for instance the Foreign Office or the Ministry of Foreign Affairs, it is almost impossible to build the physically isolated infrastructure. They always employ the VPN schemes to communicate with branches, which may be the dial-up VPN, LAN-to-LAN VPN, or others. Nevertheless, the split tunnel techniques in VPN might spread the disasters from one network to others. The cost to establish networks in physical isolation however are so expensive that the alternative method, the logical isolation, is developed and introduced. The fulfillment of this network isolation technique can be with a set of hardware devices, or a combination of hardware and software. These isolation models are introduced in Section 2, which have the property in directly or indirectly disconnecting to other network.

In 2005, our government adopts the security plan, "The Practical Plan to Eliminate Crisis Events in Information Security for Departments,"[3] and "The Notifying and Responding Procedures for Offense against Information Security in Executive Yuan and its Departments." [4] Both mentioned that the implementation of network isolation techniques is one of the essential requirements for information security. In this paper, we rule the disconnection concept in network isolation, where "directly disconnection" is for the network physical isolation and "indirectly disconnection" is for network logical isolation schemes. According to the concept, we examined the international standard ISO-17799 :2005 for practicing network isolation. We organized some related materials in the standard with our network isolation definitions to rule the implementation guidance and managerial procedure.

Acknowledgement. This project has been sponsored by Taiwan National Science Council with the reference number of NSC95-3114-P-014-001-Y. Thanks for the consultants in the *i*Cast project providing useful information to complete this project.

References

1. Information security: emerging cyber-security issues threaten federal information systems' United States Government Accountability Office, Report to Congressional Requesters (May 2005)
2. Ho, S.-Y.: The thread and situation of global information security market, Market Intelligence Center in Industrial Development Bureau Ministry of Economic Affairs, Technical Reports (July 7, 2006)
3. The practical plan to eliminate crisis events in information security for departments, National Information and Communication Security Taskforce, Programs (October 21, 2004)
4. The notifying and responding procedures for offense against information security in Executive Yuan and its departments. Researching, Developing and Evaluating Commission of Executive Yuan, Programs, (November 2, 2005)
5. Edwards, M.J.: Understanding network security (December 1997) Available at: http://www.windowsitlibrary.com/Content/121/02/1.html Accessed (May 1, 2006)
6. Nyoni, E.: Technical options oF computerized world, Accessed (May 1, 2006) (2000), Available at: http://www.wmo.ch/web /www/reports /nyoni.html
7. CISCO, Network admission control, Accessed (October 10, 2006) Available at http://www.cisco.com/en/US/netsol/ns466/networking_ solutions_package.html
8. Microsoft, Network access protection Accessed (October 10, 2006) Available at http://www.microsoft.com/technet /itsolutions /network/nap/default.mspx
9. Whale Communications, Air gap architecture Accessed (May 1, 2006) Available at http://www. whalecommunications.com/site/whale/corporate/homepage.html
10. Farn, K.-J., Lin, S.-K., Cheng, T.-S.: First Step in the Definition of Network Segregation for Security. In: Proceedings of Information Security Conference 2005, Kau-Shong, Taiwan (June 2005)
11. Lee, Z.-P.: The secure isolation gap, China Pattern: CN2588677 (November 26, 2003)

12. Chen, X.: Feature and application of GAP technique. Ningxia Engineering Technology 4(3), 244–246 (2005)
13. He, H.-J., Zhang, Y.-J., Jiao, X.-G., Hou, F.-Y.: The network security control device based on monitoring data exchange for the physical isolation, China Pattern: CN1421794 (June 4, 2003)
14. Wang, Z.-H., Han, D.-W.: The physical isolation switches: introduction and practice, China Pattern:CN1464403 (December 31, 2003)
15. ISO/IEC, Information technology - Code of practice for information security management, ISO/IEC 17799 (2005)

Positive and Negative Authorizations to Access Protected Web Resources

Sylvia Encheva[1] and Sharil Tumin[2]

[1] Stord/Haugesund University College, Bjørnsonsg. 45, 5528 Haugesund, Norway
sbe@hsh.no

[2] University of Bergen, IT-Dept., P.O. Box 7800, 5020 Bergen, Norway
edpst@it.uib.no

Abstract. In this paper we present a model that can prevent conflict situations caused by applying both positive and negative authorizations for access to a resource. Such conflict situations may occur if an organization has decentralized administration, and/or several collaborating organizations have access to one resource and some of them apply positive authorizations while others apply negative authorizations. The proposed solution involves Belnap's logic.

Keywords: Collaboration, positive and negative authorization.

1 Introduction

A number of computer-based access control systems apply positive authorizations. Such authorizations define those accesses that are going to be allowed [1]. Authorization models supporting positive authorization apply closed policy, i.e. access is allowed to a few users only.

A serious problem with this approach is that a particular user without a given authorization from this closed policy can obtain an authorization from a different resource manager. Suppose a resource at an educational institution is accessible by lecturers and students. This institution has decentralized administration, i.e. lecturers and students are managed by different resource managers. Then a user, who is a student in one subject and a lecturer in another one, can lack authorization to access a resource as a student but might be able to obtain the desired authorization as a lecturer.

Authorization models supporting negative authorization apply open policy, i.e. accesses are to be allowed to all but a few users. Examples of negative authorizations are an approval of a bank card transaction in which the customer's account number is compared against a list of cancelled accounts numbers and verification systems in which only poor credit risks are noted in the credit check. A credit that is not negatively reported is assumed to be verified. Other applications are discussed in [2], [4], and [9].

Negative authorizations are often used because they give opportunities to include exceptions [7]. Without involvement of exceptions one should considerably increase the number of authorizations, and thus make the management of authorizations more complicated. Following the example with lecturers and students

T. Enokido, L. Barolli, and M. Takizawa (Eds.): NBiS 2007, LNCS 4658, pp. 79–87, 2007.

we consider a case where all lecturers are granted an authorization to a resource with the exception of the one who is also a student. Without negative authorizations, one should satisfy the requirement by giving a positive authorization to each lecturer except one. With help of negative authorizations, this situation can be resolved by granting a positive authorization to the group of lecturers and a negative authorization to the one who is a also student.

We present a model that prevents conflicts generated by applying positive and negative authorizations to users accessing resources in a large networked system.

The rest of the paper is organized as follows. Related work, basic terms and concepts are presented in Section 2. The management model is described in Section 3. The system architecture is discussed in Sections 4, 5. The paper ends with a description of the system implementation in Section 6 and a conclusion in Section 7.

2 Background

A formal model of role based access control (RBAC) is presented in [12]. Permissions in RBAC are associated with roles, and users are made members of appropriate roles, thereby acquiring the roles' permissions. The RBAC model defines three kinds of separation of duties - static, dynamic, and operational. Separation of duties was discussed in [7], [13] and [17]. A framework for modeling the delegation of roles from one user to another is proposed in [3]. A multiple-leveled RBAC model is presented in [10]. The design and implementation of an integrated approach to engineering and enforcing context constraints in RBAC environments is described in [18] and [19].

While RBAC provides a formal implementation model, Shibboleth [16] defines standards for implementation, based on OASIS Security Assertion Markup Language (SAML). Shibboleth defines a standard set of instructions between an identity provider (Origin site) and a service provider (Target site) to facilitate browser single sign-on and attribute exchange.

The semantic characterization of a four-valued logic for expressing practical deductive processes is presented in [6]. In most information systems the management of databases is not considered to include neither explicit nor hidden inconsistencies. In real life situation information often come from different contradicting sources. Thus different sources can provide inconsistent data while deductive reasoning may result in hidden inconsistencies. The idea in Belnap's approach is to develop a logic that is not that dependable of inconsistencies. The Belnap's logic has four truth values 'T, F, Both, None'. The meaning of these values can be described as follows: an atomic sentence is stated to be true only (T), an atomic sentence is stated to be false only (F), an atomic sentence is stated to be both true and false, for instance, by different sources, or in different points of time (Both), and an atomic sentences status is unknown. That is, neither true, nor false (None).

A user is defined as a valid domain identity at a particular organization O_i. A group is a set of users. A resource defines a set of protected Web objects.

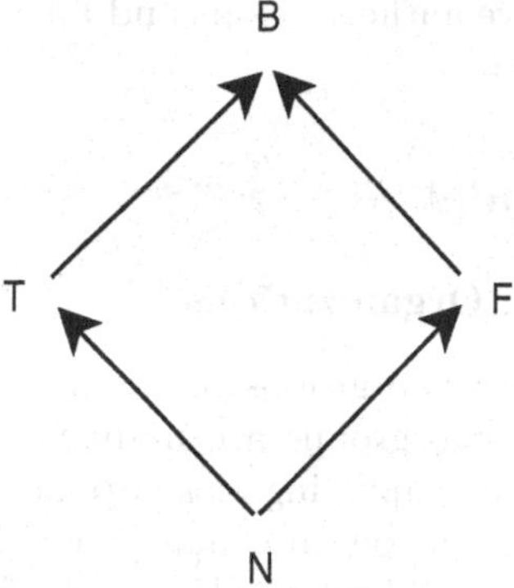

Fig. 1. Approximation lattice

A permission defines a right of a user to perform an action on a resource. An authorization gives a set of permissions to a user to execute a set of operations on a specific set of resources.

A billatice is a set equipped with two partial orderings $\leq_t$ and $\leq_k$. The t partial ordering $\leq_t$ means that if two truth values a, b are related as $a \leq_t b$ then b is at least as true as a. The k partial ordering $\leq_k$ means that if two truth values a, b are related as $a \leq_k b$ then b labels a sentence about which we have more knowledge than a sentence labeled with a.

The four truth values in Belnap's logic are elements of an approximation lattice [6] (see Fig. 1). The information about the truth-value of a sentence can have values from None to Both.

The four truth values are arranged in a logical lattice [6] in Fig. 2. A logical conjunction and logical disjunction are related to the meet operation and to the join operation respectively.

A *closed policy* permits specification of only positive authorizations and allows only those accesses that are explicitly authorized. An *open policy* permits

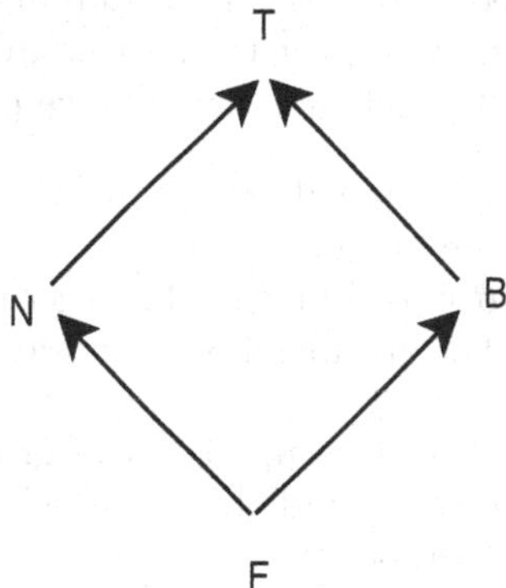

Fig. 2. Logical lattice

specification of only negative authorizations and allows only those accesses that are not explicitly denied [8].

3 Management Model

3.1 Two Collaborating Organizations

Suppose an organization has two groups of users who are interested to access a particular resource. The two groups are managed by two different resource managers where one of them is applying closed policy and the other is applying open policy. Conflicts of access permits may occur if a user belongs to both groups (see Section 3.2). Such conflicts can be avoid if four-valued logic is applied.

If two collaborating organizations have groups described as above and wish to avoid conflicts related to access permits than sexteen-valued logic should be applied. Obviously further increase of the number of collaborating organizations would lead to higher number for the many-valued logic needed. In Section 3.2 we propose a possible solution that needs only four-valued logic.

3.2 Several Collaborating Organizations

This management model refers to collaborating organizations using resources hosted by some of these organizations (see Fig. 3). Suppose a resource at one organization can be accessed by two groups A_1 and B_1 of members of organization O_1 and two groups A_2 and B_2 of members of another organization O_2. Suppose these four groups are administered by four resource managers, two at organization O_1 and two at organization O_2. Assume the resource managers of groups A_1 and A_2 apply closed policy and the resource managers of groups B_1 and B_2 apply open policy.

Some of the conflict situations that may occur are - a user belongs to group A_1 or group A_2 and at the same time belongs to group B_1 or group B_2, or another user may be affiliated with two organizations and belong to three or four groups. In order to avoid such conflicts we propose use of four valued logic. All groups $A_i, i = 1, ..., n$ are considered as one group A and all groups $B_i, i = 1, ..., n$ are considered as one group B with respect to the resource.

Based on the truth table for Belnap's logic [6] we propose the following:

- A user belongs to group A and does not belong to group B. The user is authorized to access the resource.
- A user belongs to both groups A and B. The user is not authorized to access the resource before his/her membership is considered by the corresponding resource managers.
- A user is neither a member of group A nor of group B. The user is authorized to access the resource, provided he/she belongs to at least one of the organizations applying open policy.
- A user does not belong to in group A and belongs to group B. The user is not authorized to access the resource.

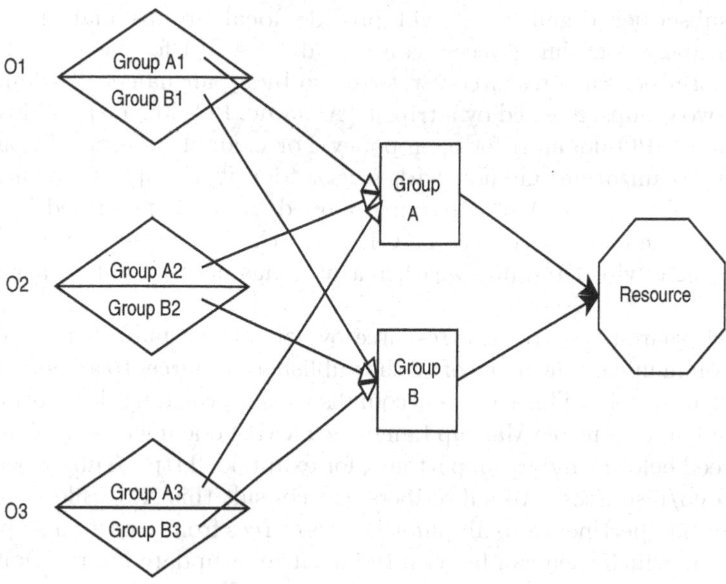

Fig. 3. Positive and negative authorizations for users at organizations O_1, O_2, O_3

4 System Model

Let signify the resource owner organization as the publisher organization (PO) and an organization that uses the shared resources as a subscriber organization (SO).

Each subscriber organization administers its own domain users group membership for a particular subscribed resource. Two groups provide access control to each subscribed resource, namely, group A that applies close policy and group B that apples open policy to that particular resource.

To a publisher organization, the two groups defined at the subscriber organizations, will be referred to as a list of pairs {SO-domain, URI}. The domains are the subscriber organizations' domain names of the Domain Name System (DNS), for example 'uib.no' and 'hsh.no'. The Uniform Resource Identifiers (URIs) are the subscriber organizations' Web application addresses from which the publisher organization's access controller can do queries about group membership and thus access rights to a particular resource, of a user from a particular subscriber organization.

The resource owner needs to maintain a database containing subscriber organization table (SOT) for each subscriber organization subscribing to his/her resources. A particular SOT entry can be for example, ['uib.no', 'http://gatekeeper:letmein@siam.uib.no/groups']. In addition to SOT, the publisher organization also needs to maintain a resource names and resource policies table (RPT). For example a resource 'math-1' with a default closed policy will have an entry in the RPT as ['math-1', 'A'].

Each subscriber organization will provide local groups management and groups database containing access control table (ACT) for each resource they wish to subscribe. Each resource is referred to by a pair name, PO-domain and will have two groups, referred by a triplet {A, name, PO-domain} for close policy and {B, name, PO-domain} for open policy. For example, a user at a particular subscriber organization 'uib.no', with a user identifier 'edpst' is a member of the closed policy group A of a resource named 'math-1' published by domain 'hsh.no', will then have an entry in ACT, ['edpst', 'A', 'math-1', 'hsh.no']. Data entries in ACT will determine weather a user has access right to a particular resource.

For each shared resource the resource owner, at the publisher organization needs to communicate the name of all the published resources to all potential subscriber organizations. This can be accomplished by providing descriptions of all resources in an Extensible Markup Language (XML) document at an URI collectively agreed before hand by all partners, for example, 'http://subscriber:gogetit @mat.hsh.no/resources'. All subscribers can consult this XML file at any time for information pertinence to all published resources from a particular publisher organization, which then can be used to initialize or update information in subscriber organizations' databases represented in ACT.

Within this model, both the publisher organizations and the subscriber organizations need to provide Web services for each other in order to communicate user identities and authorizations to control access on shared Web resources. There are many ways of providing these services, where among most common ones are, Java based remote method invocation (RMI), XML remote procedure (XML-RPC) and Simple Object Access Protocol (SOAP). We propose a simpler mechanism inspired by Representational State Transfer (REST).

Compare to the other mechanism, REST is much simpler because REST does not define its own transport protocol. REST depends on generic Web interface of HTTP GET, POST, PUT and DELETE. In order to provide and utilize Web services one needs only to deploy Web server and client that support XML documents formatting and parsing.

5 System Architecture

To support REST type Web services participating organizations need to install and maintain a so-called three-tier architecture of

1. Presentation Tier,
2. Application Tier, and
3. Data Tier.

The presentation tier provides interfaces to the system. These interfaces are referred to by applications' clients using some published URIs. A client can query a service of an application by addressing its URI and using HTTP GET parameters, for example, 'http://gatekeeper:letmein@siam.uib.no/groups?user=edpst& resource=math-1'. We propose using Apache Web server for implementing the presentation tier.

The application tier implements system processing logic. Data submitted by client queries trigger processing events in the application tier. Depending on URI, programs or scripts in the application tier will be executed. The GET parameters will be used as input parameters to these programs that will provide a responce or an error message. We propose using 'mod_python' to the Apache Web server. The application server will be programmed using Python scripting language. The module 'mod_python' supports the Apache capabilities by incorporating Python runtime interpreter within the Web server itself. All the Apache's application programming interfaces (API) are directly connected to the Python runtime environment, which makes Web application programming simpler.

The data tier implements data store for the system. Information is stored and retrieved from a relational database management system (RDBMS). We propose using Oracle XE, a free small RDBMS from Oracle. It will then be easy to upgrade the database to enterprise level, if that need arises. The RDBMS is chosen since it should support Structured Query Language (SQL) standard. The database stores long-term persistence information about users, groups, resources and applications states. Data stored in the database will affect the behavior of the whole system. Applications initialize and modify information in the database. Data is written, replaced and deleted by application programs. There are many Python Oracle modules that integrate the application tier to the data tier in the system. We propose using DCOracle2 module.

By providing Web services architecture using simple REST style we believe that the system will be easy to implement and maintain. Any Web tools can be used, if they collectively support HTTP, XML and SQL.

We propose using the basic authentication scheme when a client connects to a server. The simple mechanism is a part security measure to the system. The basic authentication is implemented by the Web server and it is easy to deploy. In addition of host address access control, this provides us with good enough security measure for the system described in this paper. Thus, any client that knows the basic authentication parameters and belongs to a clients-list of a server can make use of the services provided by the server.

6 System Implementation

The subscriber organizations provide a portal to their local users. By using cookies and redirect, an authenticated user can be transferred from local portal to a shared Web resource. The central issue in implementing the system is on how the XML responses from the server look like. We propose providing XML response containing security information together with the reply. Our proposal is based on this request/response scenario:

1. A client uses basic authentication to send query of a particular service to a server.
2. A server parses GET parameters and executes appropriate program if parameters are valid and the client belongs to the list of valid clients.

3. A server formats the reply block in XML containing message identifier, timestamp and data blocks. The server then calculates a hash value for this reply block. The hash is then encrypted applying a symmetric key encryption using a shared secret key that both the server and the client know. A complete XML is sent back to the client.
4. The client collects the reply blocks and verifies that the hash is valid. The client parses the XML and executes appropriate program with the reply provided by the server.

A typical example of XML reply document is as follows:


```
<?xml version="1.0" encoding="utf-8"?>
<zebra rows="2" reply="user\# hash="537851618991316fae7bd23b0b03adc4"
cipher="blowfish">
    <id>Ver2.06 GetAgent@mat.hsh.no \#12</id>
    <ts>20070304170853</ts>
    <user>
        <id>edpst</id>
        <domain>uib.no</domain>
        <resource>math-1</resource>
        <group>A</group>
    </user>
    <user>
        <id>sbe</id>
        <domain>uib.no</domain>
        <resource>alg-2</resource>
        <group>A</group>
    </user>
</zebra>
```


The client needs to trust that the response reply comes from the server and that the XML message has not been tempered with during transit. Hash functions and symmetric key encryptions provide this trust.

7 Conclusion

A problem arises if a user is affiliated with an organization applying both positive and negative authorization managed by different resource managers or with several organizations at the same time. This problem is difficult to solve and may not be a major issue if a conflict of access rights can be resolved applying many-valued logic. We propose a model that simplifies user access to resources in a large networked system.

References

1. Al-Kahtani, M., Sandhu, R.: Rule-based RBAC with negative authorization. In: 20th Annual Computer Security Applications Conference, Arizona (2004)
2. Andress, M.: Access control. Information security magazine (2001)

3. Barka, E., Sandhu, R.: Role-based delegation model/ hierarchical roles. In: 20th Annual Computer Security Applications Conference, Arizona (2004)
4. Barkley, Beznosov, Uppal: Supporting relationships in access control using Role Based Access Control. In: Fourth ACM Workshop on Role-Based Access Control, ACM, New York (1999)
5. Belnap, N.J.: How a computer should think. In Contemporary Aspects of Philosophy. In: Proceedings of the Oxford International Symposia, Oxford, GB, pp. 30–56 (1975)
6. Belnap, N.J.: A useful four valued logic. In: Dunn, J.M., Epstain, G. (eds.) Modern uses of multiple-valued logic, pp. 8–37. D. Reidel Publishing Co., Dordrecht (1977)
7. Bertino, E., Bonatti, P.A., Ferrari, E.: TRBAC: A temporal Role-Based Access Control model. ACM Tr. on ISS 3(3), 191–223 (2001)
8. Bertino, E., Jajodia, S., Samarati, P.A.: A Flexible Authorization Mechanism for Relational Data Management System. ACM Transactions on Information Systems 17(2), 101–140 (1999)
9. Bhatti, R., Bertino, E., Ghafoor, A., Joshi, J.B.D.: XML-based specification for Web services document security. IEEE Computer 37(4) (2004)
10. Chou, S-C.: L^nRBAC: A multiple-levelled Role-Based Access Control model for protecting privacy in object-oriented systems. J. of Object Technology 3(3), 91–120 (2004)
11. Davey, B.A., Priestley, H.A.: Introduction to lattices and order. Cambridge University Press, Cambridge (2005)
12. Ferraiolo, D., Cugini, J., Kuhn, D.R.: Role-Based Access Control (RBAC): Features and motivations. In: 1995 Computer Security Applications Conference, pp. 241–248 (1995)
13. Ferraiolo, D., Sandhu, R., Gavrila, S., Kuhn, R.D., Chandramouli, R.: Proposed NIST standard for Role-Based Access Control. ACM Transactions on Information and System Security (TISSEC) 4(3), 224–274 (2001)
14. Ferraiolo, D., Kuhn, D.R., Chandramouli, R.: Role-Based Access Control. Artech House, Computer Security Series (2003)
15. Schwoon, S., Jha, S., Reps, T., Stubblebine, S.: On generalized authorization problems. In: Proc. 16th IEEE Computer Security Foundations Workshop, Asilomar, Pacific Grove, CA, June 30 - July 2, 2003, pp. 202–218. IEEE Computer Society Press, Los Alamitos (2003)
16. `http://shibbolethinternet2.edu`
17. Simon, R., Zurko, M.: Separation of duty in role-based environments. In: Proceedings of 10th IEEE Computer Security Foundations Workshop, Rockport, Mass, pp. 183–194 (1997)
18. Strembeck, M.: Conflict checking of separation of duty constraints in RBAC-implementation experiences. `http://wi.wu-wien.ac.at/home/mark/publications/se2004.pdf`
19. Strembeck, M., Neumann, G.: An integrated approach to engineer and enforce context constraints in RBAC environments. ACM Transactions on Information and System Security 7(3), 392–427 (2004)

An Analysis of Mobile WiMAX Security: Vulnerabilities and Solutions

Taeshik Shon and Wook Choi

IP Lab, Telecommunication R&D Center, Samsung Electronics
Dong Suwon, P.O. BOX 105, 416, Maetan-3dong, Suswon-si, Gyeonggi-do, 442-600, Korea
{ts.shon,to.choi}@samsung.com

Abstract. The IEEE 802.16 Working Group on Broadband Wireless Access Standards released IEEE 802.16-2004 which is a standardized technology for supporting broadband and wireless communication with fixed and nomadic Access. The standard has a security sublayer in the MAC layer called, Privacy Key Management, which aims to provide authentication and confidentiality. However, several researches have been published to address the security vulnerabilities of 802.16-2004. After the IEEE 802.16-2004 standard, a new advanced and revised standard was released as the IEEE 802.16e-2005 amendment which is foundation of Mobile WiMAX network supporting handoffs and roaming capabilities. In the area of security aspects, Mobile WiMAX adopts improved security architecture, PKMv2, including Extensible Authentication Protocol (EAP) authentication, AES-CCM-based authenticated encryption, and CMAC or HMAC based message protection. However, there is no guarantee that PKMv2-based Mobile WiMAX network will not have security flaws. In this paper, we first describe an overview of security architecture of IEEE 802.16e-based Mobile WiMAX and its vulnerabilities. Based on the related background research, we focus on finding new security vulnerabilities such as a disclosure of security context in initial entry and a lack of secure communication in network domain. We propose possible solutions to prevent these security vulnerabilities.

1 Introduction

More and more, our life is closely related to a variety of networking environments for using Internet-based services and applications. The ever-changing trends of our lifestyle require faster speed, lower cost, and more broadband capacity as well as nomadic and mobility support. Due to these reasons and demands, the Institute of Electrical and Electronics Engineers (IEEE) 802.16 working group on broadband wireless metropolitan area networks has created new standards with mobility Access called the IEEE 802.16e-2005 amendment. It has also been developed by many working groups of the Worldwide Interoperability for Microwave Access (WiMAX) Forum, similar to Wi-Fi in IEEE 802.11 standards. The WiMAX Forum tries to coordinate the interoperability and compatibility of various company products as a field standard. Mobile WiMAX means system profiles and network architectures from WiMAX Forum based on IEEE 802.16e-2005 standards. Specifically, Mobile WiMAX technology is

T. Enokido, L. Barolli, and M. Takizawa (Eds.): NBiS 2007, LNCS 4658, pp. 88–97, 2007.

considered as one of the best next-generation wireless technologies because it can support high-speed, broadband data transmission, fully-supported mobility, and wide coverage and high capacity. Of these, Mobile WiMAX has many advantages and unique characteristics such as superior performance (multiple handoff mechanisms, power-saving mechanisms, advanced Quality of Service and low latency, advanced Authentication, Authorization, Accounting functionality), flexibility (global roaming, deployment from the edge infrastructure to overlay/complement networks, various spectrum usage), advanced IP-based architecture (fully support Internet Multimedia Subsystem, 3GPP2, and Multichannel Multipoint Distribution), attractive economics (open standards, mass adoption of subscriber units, attractive Intellectual property rights structure) [1-4]. From a security viewpoint, the Mobile WiMAX system based on the IEEE 802.16e-2005 amendment has more enhanced security features than the existing IEEE 802.16-based WiMAX network system. The improved core part of the security architecture in Mobile WiMAX, called Privacy Key Management version 2 (PKMv2), is operated as a security sublayer in a Medium Access Control (MAC) layer like PKMv1 in IEEE 802.16-2004. The PKMv2 in a security sublayer provides a message authentication scheme using HMAC/CMAC (Hash-based Message Authentication Code/Cipher-based Message Authentication Code), device/user authentication using Extensible Authentication Protocol (EAP) methods, and confidentiality using AES-CCM (Advanced Encryption Standard – Counter with CBC Mode) encryption algorithm. Moreover, user credentials exist including: Username/Password, SIM/USIM (Subscriber Identity Module/Universal SIM) Cards, Smart Cards, Universal Integrated Circuit Card (UICC), Removable User Identity Module (RUIM), and Digital Certificate [3-4]. Even though Mobile WiMAX uses more enhanced security schemes supported by PKMv2, it can not guarantee the reliability of the whole Mobile WiMAX systems and network architectures. In addition, open architecture and various applications of Mobile WiMAX could cause much more risks to try to compromise Mobile WiMAX network than existing systems.

Among many potential risks in Mobile WiMAX network, this paper focuses on two security vulnerabilities according to security requirements of each Mobile WiMAX network domain. Mobile WiMAX network has a link range domain(access network) and network domain. Therefore, in order to deal with the security vulnerabilities from the various network domains, we propose enhanced security approaches applying well-known cryptographic methods such as Diffie-Hellman (DH) key agreement [5] and Public Key Infrastructure (PKI).

The rest of this paper is organized as follows. In section 2, we study an overview of Mobile WiMAX security and analyze known security vulnerabilities and attacks. In section 3, new security threats in Mobile WiMAX network are examined. In section 4, we propose possible solutions in order to cope with the new threats we mention in section 3. In section 5, we describe a reliable Mobile WiMAX architecture including our proposed solutions. In the last section, we conclude with a summary and discussion of future work.

2 Background: Known Vulnerabilities and Attacks

The security architecture of Mobile WiMAX is partially originated from wireless networks based on IEEE 802.11. In the case of IEEE 802.11-based wireless networks, a great deal of security-related research has already been studied and a few vulnerabilities have been known as [7-9]. Among a lot of interesting research, John Bellardo and Stefan Savage's research [7] showed a possibility of Denial of Service (DoS) attacks using identity vulnerability and Media Access Control (MAC) vulnerability in MAC layer of IEEE 802.11 at the USENIX conference. In this section, we investigate well-known vulnerabilities based on the IEEE 802.16 network architecture from the existing research [10-11]. These former researches mainly analyzed the following vulnerabilities: Ranging Response (RNG-RSP) vulnerability, Auth Request and Invalid vulnerability, and Rogue BS.

First, in the case of the vulnerability of using a RNG-RSP message, the message belongs to a Ranging procedure in the first part of Mobile WiMAX network initialization. According to IEEE 802.16-2004 standard, the Ranging is a process of acquiring the correcting timing offset and power adjustments such that the SS's transmissions are aligned to a symbol that marks the beginning of a minislot boundary in physical layer. When SS first tries to join Mobile WiMAX network, it sends a Ranging Request (RNG-REQ) message to the BS including the following information: SS requests transmission timing, power, frequency and burst profile information. After receiving the RNG-REQ message from the SS, the BS sends a RNG-RSP message to the SS. At this time, the problem is that the RNG-RSP message can do more than merely fine-tune SS transmission times, and BS can use the RNG-RSP message to distinguish SS to change Timing, Power Level, Offset Frequency, Ranging Status, and other Ranging parameters. It means that the RNG-RSP message can be used to cause lots of abnormal cases using the information in a RNG-RSP message. The RNG-RSP message has a variety of encoded contents such as Timing Adjust for Tx timing offset adjustment, Power Level Adjustment for Tx power offset adjustment, Offset Frequency Adjust for Tx frequency offset adjustment, and Ranging Status for indicating whether uplink messages are received. Moreover, in the case of IEEE 802.16-2004 standard (not IEEE 802.16e-2005), Ranging messages is not encrypted, authenticated, and the messages are stateless. Thus, malicious attackers can easily modify ranging messages to try to attack or interrupt regular network activities. For instance, the most popular exploitation is to spoof unsolicited RNG-RSP messages with Ranging Status field set to a value of 2, it means "abort." If SS receives this RNG-RSP message during a Ranging procedure, the Ranging request will be finished without returning an initial state of a Ranging status. Thus, this vulnerability can cause a kind of Denial of Service attack which is interrupting normal SS's Ranging Request.

Moreover, attacks using Auth Request message is originated from a vulnerability of authorization state machine in PKM. In the case of Auth Request attack, the message is sent at the beginning of a process of Authorization Key (AK) exchange and includes various security-related contents such as SS-certificate, Security Capabilities, Security Capabilities Digest, and SAID (Security Association IDentification). The aim of Auth Request is to negotiate cryptographic suites and request AK to BS. If the sharing security capabilities are not the same between SS and BS after sending an Auth Request message, BS notifies a Perm Auth Reject to SS. The SS which receives a Perm Auth Reject message goes into a silent state of authorization state machine.

Thus, if malicious attackers can modify Security-Capabilities attributes in Auth Request message, BS may understand SS can not provide appropriate cryptographic suites, and then BS causes a permanent error condition with Perm Auth Reject message. In order to solve such a security vulnerability using an Auth Request message, BS requires a verification method with message authentication and confidentiality function when receiving an Auth Request message from SS. Fortunately, in Mobile WiMAX based on IEEE 802.16e-2005, all PKM messages are to be protected using message authentication schemes with HMAC/CMAC tuple.

Finally, in a security vulnerability known as a Rogue BS attack, SS can be compromised by a forged BS. At this time, SS maybe believe he is connected to real the BS. Thus, the forged BS can intercept SS's whole information. In other words, the rogue BS attack is a kind of Man-In-The-Middle (MITM) attack which is one of the well-known attacks in wireless networks. In IEEE 802.16 using PKMv1, Auth Request message includes only the contents for SS authentication itself without correspondent BS's authentication. When SS tries to establish a connection to BS, there is no way to confirm whether the BS is authorized or not. The authorization process based on RSA authentication protocol allows only BS to authenticate SS in PKMv1. Thus, it is possible to masquerade as a Rogue BS after sniffing Auth-related message from SS. However, in the case of Mobile WiMAX using PKMv2, it is difficult to use the Rogue BS vulnerability because mutual authentication function between SS and BS is mandatory during authorization process. In authorization state of PKMv2, the mutual authentication has two modes. In one mode, RSA-based mutual authentication is used for only mutual authentication. In the other mode, mutual authentication is followed by EAP authentication during initial entry process.

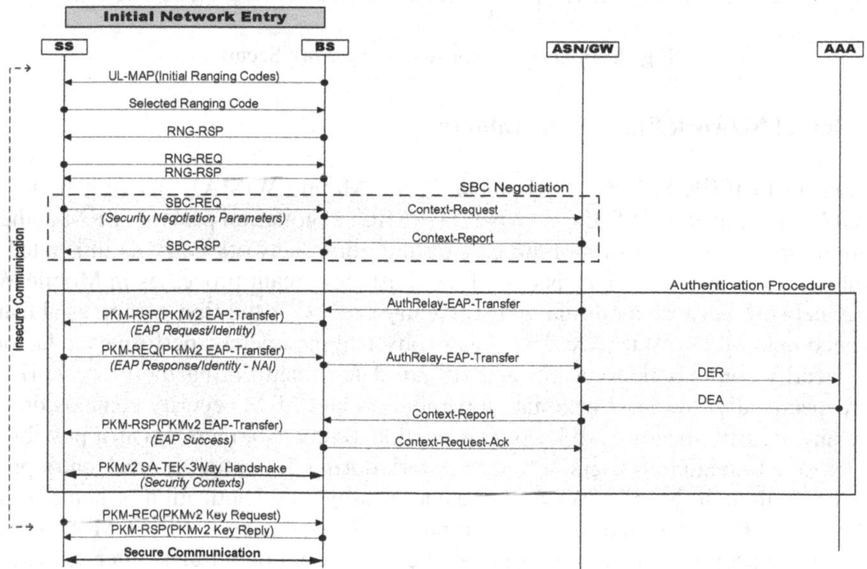

Fig. 1. An Overview of Initial Network Entry Procedure

3 New Security Threats

Even though great deals of advanced security features are applied to IEEE 802.16e-2005 based Mobile WiMAX, it still has a few vulnerabilities: a disclosure of security context in network entry, a lack of secure communication in Access network, and a necessity of efficient handover supporting security capability. In this section, we examine the security vulnerabilities of Mobile WiMAX within a framework of the following two security requirements we studied in chapter 2: Initial Network Entry Security and Access Network Security.

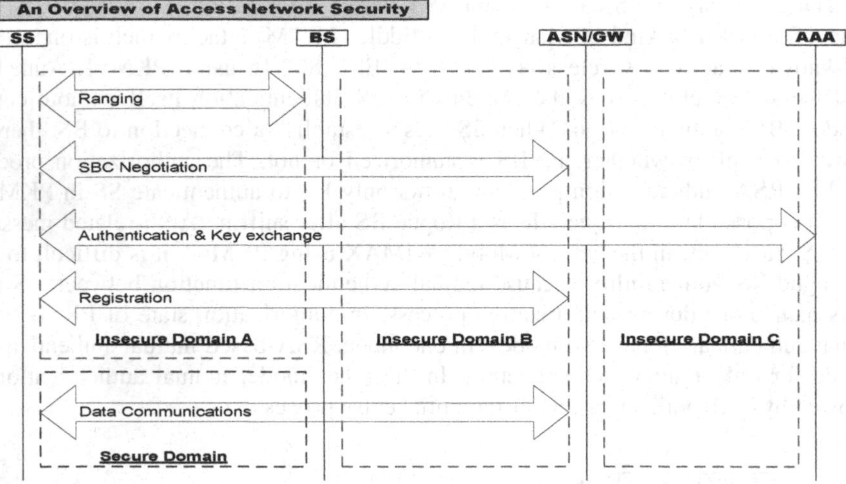

Fig. 2. An Overview of Access Network Security

3.1 Initial Network Entry Vulnerability

According to IEEE 802.16e-2005 standard, the Mobile WiMAX network performs initial Ranging process, SS Basic Capability (SBC) negotiation process, PKM authentication process, and registration process during initial network entry as illustrated in Figure 1. Initial network entry is one of the most significant processes in Mobile WiMAX network because the initial network entry process is the first gate to establish a connection to Mobile WiMAX. Thus, many physical parameters, performance factors, and security contexts between SS and BS are determined during the process. However, specifically, the SBC negotiation parameters and PKM security contexts do not have any security measures to keep their confidentiality. So, there exists a possibility of exposure to malicious users or outer network during the initial network entry process. Even though Mobile WiMAX has a message authentication scheme using HMAC/CMAC codes and traffic encryption scheme using AES-CCM based on PKMv2, the security schemes are only applied to normal data traffic after initial network entry process not to control messages during initial network entry. Therefore, it is necessary to prepare a solution to protect important messages such as security negotiation parameters in SBC messages and security contexts in PKM messages during initial network entry.

3.2 Access Network Vulnerability

The WiMAX Forum defined Network Reference Model (NRM) which can accommodate the requirements of WiMAX End-to-End Network Systems Architecture [6] for Mobile WiMAX network. The NRM is a logical representation of Mobile WiMAX architecture consisting of the following entities: Subscriber Station (SS), Access Service Network (ASN), and Connectivity Service Network (CSN). SS means one of the mobile devices that would like to join Mobile WiMAX network. ASN is a complete set of network functions needed to provide radio Access to Mobile WiMAX subscribers. ASN consists of at least one BS and one ASN Gateway (ASN/GW). Also, CSN is a set of network functions that provide IP connectivity services to the WiMAX subscribers. CSN consists of AAA Proxy/Server, Policy, Billing, and Roaming Entities. Basically, Mobile WiMAX architecture originated from the IEEE 802.16 standards. At the view point of NRM, IEEE 802.16 standards only define a set of functions between SS and BS. It means the security architecture given by IEEE 802.16 standards does not cover intra ASN and ASN-to-CSN. From the figure 2, we are able to distinguish a secure domain covered by IEEE 802.16 standard and insecure domains required additional security services. In the case of communication range between SS and BS, the exchange of messages during network entry process (by the end of registration process) is belonging to insecure domain A. The security threat of insecure domain A is already mentioned in the previous section, 3.1, and a possible solution will be described in chapter 4. On the other hand, the communication range after network entry (at the beginning of normal data traffic) belongs in the secure domain because it can be protected by TEK encryption scheme and message authentication function using HMAC/CMAC. Thus, there remain two insecure domains: insecure domain B between BS and ASN/GW and insecure domain C between ASN and CSN. The reason we called the areas insecure domains is because Network Working Group (NWG) in WiMAX Forum just assumes the insecure domain B as illustrated in Figure 2 is a trusted network without suggesting any security function [6]. Moreover, in the case of insecure domain C, they just mention a possibility of applying an IPSec tunnel between ASN and AAA (in CSN) [6]. Therefore, in order to make a more robust Mobile WiMAX network, more concrete and efficient countermeasures are required.

4 Possible Countermeasures

Based on the security vulnerabilities of Mobile WiMAX network mentioned in the previous chapter, we propose possible solutions to prevent the security vulnerabilities in this chapter. In the case of the initial network entry vulnerability, Diffie-Hellman key agreement scheme [7] is used as an essential point to protect security contexts during initial network entry. In order to provide secure Access network communication, a simple key exchange method using Public Key Infrastructure (PKI) is applied to ASN and CSN in Mobile WiMAX.

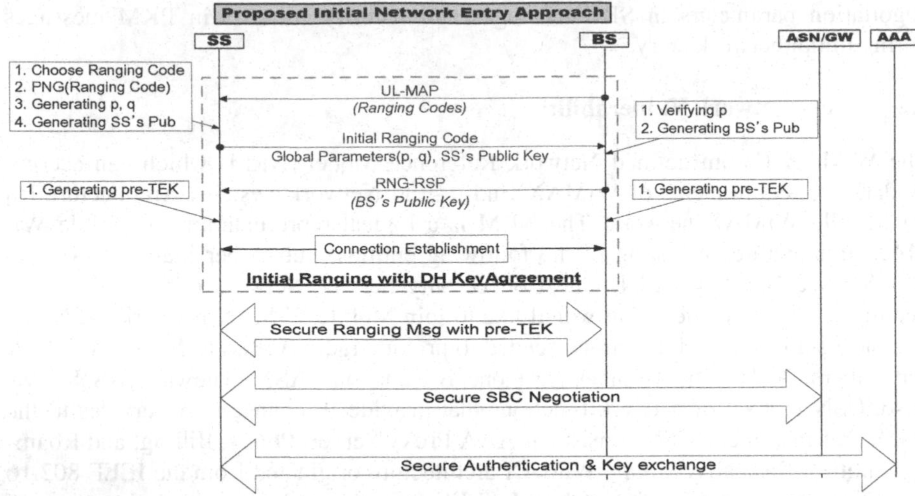

Fig. 3. Proposed Network Initial Entry Approach

4.1 Approach to Initial Network Entry Vulnerability

Although much significant information is exchanged during initial network entry, there are not appropriate methods to protect the exchanged control messages. In order to eliminate the security vulnerability during initial network entry, this paper applies DH (Diffie-Hellman) key agreement scheme to initial ranging procedure as shown in figure 3. DH key agreement is a kind of key management method to share an encryption key with global variables known as prime number 'p' and 'q' a primitive root of p. Initial ranging procedure is started when SS receives UL-MAP message including ranging codes. Among the received ranging codes from BS, SS selects a ranging code and sends the selected code to BS. At this time, BS notifies that the ranging code is accepted with an RNG-RSP message. From the proposed security approach in initial network entry as illustrated in figure 4, a selected ranging code is not only Mobile WiMAX communication, but also used for generating a prime number 'p' as one of global variables in order to apply DH key agreement method to network entry procedure. At the same time, SS generates the other global variable 'q' and public/private key pair, and then sends them to BS. BS receives a public key of SS and global variables (prime number and its primitive root). If the received key and variables are verified, BS also sends his public key to SS. Thus, BS and SS can share DH global variables and public key each other through initial ranging process. Of these, they can generate a shared common key called "pre-TEK" separately and establish secret communication channels. Therefore, the proposed approach can protect SBC security parameters and PKM security contexts using the shared session encryption key (pre-TEK) during initial network entry procedure.

4.2 Approach to Access Network Vulnerability

PKM which is main security architecture in Mobile WiMAX only covers wireless traffic between SS and BS because the other connection ranges needed a security function is beyond IEEE 802.16e-2005 standard. Moreover, Technical documents of Network Working Group (NWG) in WiMAX Forum assume ASN network is trusted and AAA connections between ASN and CSN may be protected with IPSec tunnel. Thus, we have studied concrete countermeasure which is required to make Access network more secure domain in chapter 3. In this paper, a simple and efficient key exchange method based on Public Key Infrastructure (PKI) is proposed to provide Access network security. The PKI structure is a base architecture to solve Access network vulnerability as a way to obtain correspondent's public keys and verify the certificates. Therefore, in the proposed security scheme for secure Access network communication, we assume devices in Mobile WiMAX are certified from public authority and they can verify certificates. From figure 5, all network devices in Mobile WiMAX network have their own certificate and a certificate chain for verification. If BS would like to exchange important messages with ASN/GW, BS needs to generate a session encryption key for secure communication between BS and ASN/GW. In this case, BS first searches for an appropriate certificate (including correspondent's public key) to verify ASN/GW's identity and obtain public key. After getting public key, BS generates "asn-TEK" as a session encryption key for secure communication with ASN/GW. Using the "asn-TEK", BS encrypts a message and sends the encrypted message together with the encrypted "asn-TEK" key using ASN/GW's public key, Timestamp, and Authority's certificate to ASN/GW. When ASN/GW receives the messages from BS, ASN/GW first tries to verify the authority's certificate and checks the validation time from Timestamp. If the verification process is success, ASN/GW decrypts the "asn-TEK" key and the original message. Thus, a problem of insecure communication between BS and ASN/GW can be solved by using "asn-TEK" key as a encryption key between BS and ASN/GW. In the case of ASN-to-CSN, the proposed method generates a common encryption key called "asn-csn-TEK" using the same method as a way to BS-to-ASN/GW for establishing secure connection. From figure 4, we can show an example using "asn-csn-TEK".

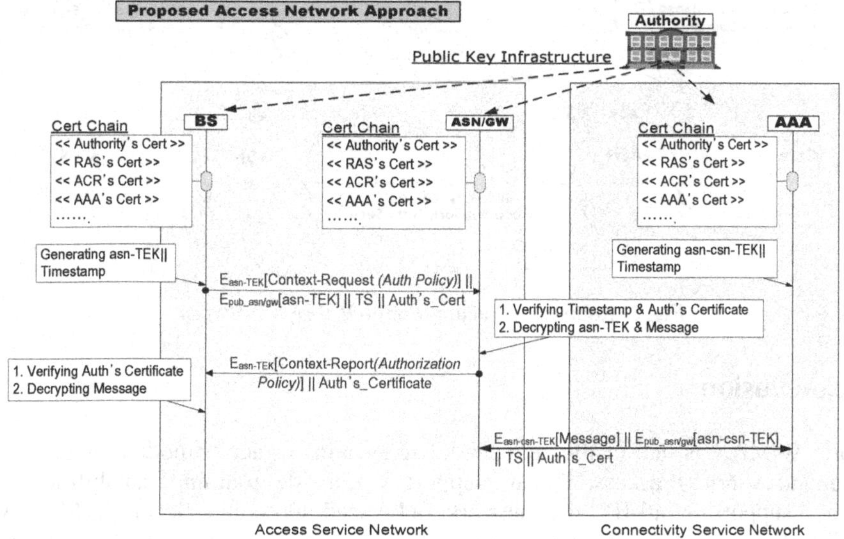

Fig. 4. Proposed Access Network Approach

5 Discussion of Robust Mobile WiMAX Network

This paper proposed novel approaches to minimize security risks in Mobile WiMAX network. We showed a reliable Mobile WiMAX architecture applying the security approaches called **RO**bust **S**ecure **M**obil**E** WiMA**X** (ROSMEX) as illustrated in figure 5. In ROSMEX, the enhanced network entry process has a modified initial ranging process with DH key agreement. The approach assigns a temporary Security Association (e.g. pre-TEK and pre-defined cryptographic suites) to prevent a primary management connections between SS and BS. Thus, ROSMEX can give confidential communications to whole wireless range because our proposed approach generates and uses temporary traffic encryption key before SBC negotiation. Moreover, ROSMEX supports secure communications in all Access network. Any two entities in Mobile WiMAX can establish a secure channel using PKI-based simple key exchange. The approach eliminates all possibilities of disguising as a valid entity in Mobile WiMAX. It is also a more efficient method than an approach using IPSec in [6].

Therefore, ROSMEX architecture which has the enhanced security countermeasures can satisfy not only the security requirements but also performance requirements during Initial Network Entry and Access Network Communication in Mobile WiMAX.

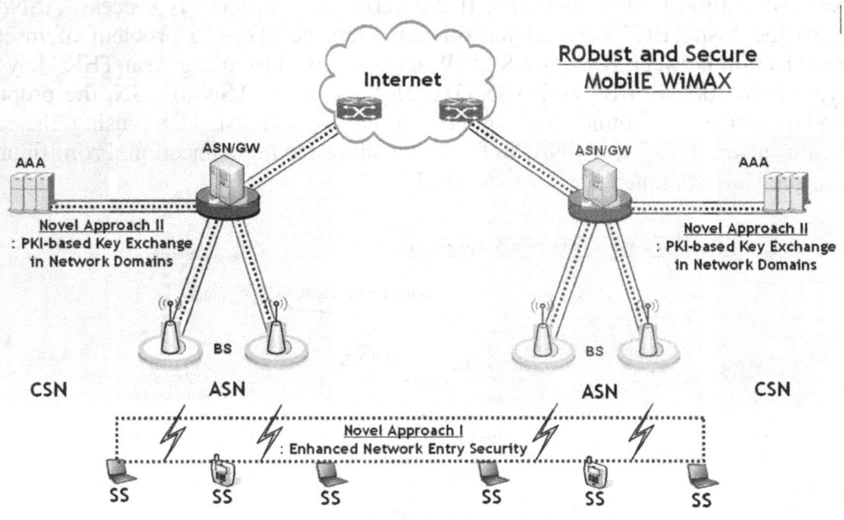

Fig. 5. Robust and Secure Mobile WiMAX Network

6 Conclusion

Mobile WiMAX is one of the best candidate systems to accommodate demands for broadband wireless access. It can support worldwide roaming capabilities, low latency, supporting all-IP core network, advanced QoS and Security. Moreover, Mobile WiMAX can cooperate with existing and emerging networks. However, Mobile WiMAX technology is not perfect and is not an ultimate solution for beyond

3G networks, but a kind of bridging system toward 4G networks. In the case of security aspects in Mobile WiMAX, it still has a potential possibility of a few security related vulnerabilities.

In this paper, we investigated new security vulnerabilities such as a disclosure of secret contexts during initial entry procedure and a lack of a protection mechanism in network domain. Therefore, in order to eliminate the security vulnerabilities, we proposed possible countermeasures. In the case of an initial entry process threat, DH key agreement is applied to initial ranging process to generate session encryption key. Using the encryption key, the messages including security contexts can be protected during initial entry procedure. Secondly, a simple key exchange scheme based on PKI was proposed as a solution to settle the vulnerability of the access network. Thus, each network component in ASN and CSN can generate session encryption keys and the correspondents also can verify them.

Based on the proposed approaches, ROSMEX architecture was presented. We believe that our ROSMEX architecture will contribute to make an enhanced Mobile WiMAX. In future work, we have to consider handover security between mobility domains. Moreover, a lot of research to simulate our possible solutions is needed.

References

[1] The Institute of Electrical and Electronics Engineers: IEEE Standard for Local and Metropolitan Area Networks Part 16: Air Interface for Fixed Broadband Wireless Access Systems, IEEE Std 802.16-2004. IEEE (2004)

[2] The Institute of Electrical and Electronics Engineers. IEEE Standard for Local and Metropolitan Area Networks Part 16: Air Interface for Fixed Broadband Wireless Access Systems, Amendment 2: Physical and Medium Access Control Layers for Combined Fixed and Mobile Operation in Licensed Bands and Corrigendum, IEEE Std 802.16e-2005. IEEE (2005)

[3] WiMAX Forum: Mobile WiMAX: The Best Personal Broadband Experience! (2006), Available at http://www.wimaxforum.org

[4] WiMAX Forum: Mobile WiMAX – Part I: A Technical Overview and Performance Evaluation (2006) Available at http://www.wimaxforum.org

[5] Diffie, W., Hellman, M.: New directions in cryptography. IEEE Transactions on Information Theory 22, 644–654 (1976)

[6] WiMAX Forum: WiMAX End-to-End Network Systems Architecture (Stage 3: Detailed Protocols and Procedures) (2006) Available at http://www.wimaxforum.org

[7] Bellardo, J., Savage, S.: 802.11 Denial-of-Service Attacks: Real Vulnerabilities and Practical Solutions. In: Presented at 11th USENIX Security Symposium (2003)

[8] Boshonek, R.: Advanced Denial of Service Techniques in IEEE 802.11b Wireless Local Area Networks. Naval Postgraduate School Master's Thesis (June 2002)

[9] Meyers, W.: Exploitation of an IEEE 802.11 Standard Wireless Local Area Network through the Medium Access Control (MAC) Layer. Naval Postgraduate School, Master's Thesis (June 2001)

[10] Boom, D.D.: Denial Of Service Vulnerabilitie In IEEE 802.16 Wireless Networks, Thesis at Naval Postgraduate School Monterey, California

[11] Johnston, D., Walker, J.: Overview of the 802.16 Security. IEEE computer society, Los Alamitos (2004)

An Automatic Meta-revised Mechanism for Anti-malicious Injection

Jin-Cherng Lin[1], Jan-Min Chen[1,2], and Hsing-Kuo Wong[3]

[1] The Dept. of Computer Sci & Eng, Tatung University, Taipei 10451, Taiwan
[2] The Dept. of Information Management, Yu Da College of Business Miaoli 36143, Taiwan
[3] Chung-shan Institute of Science *and* Technology, Taiwan
`jclin@ttu.edu.tw, ydjames@ydu.edu.tw, davidwong1536@gmail.com`

Abstract. "Invalidated Input" is Top One Critical Web Application Security Vulnerabilities according to have been released by Open Web Applications Security Project (OWASP) on July 14, 2004. Many web application security vulnerabilities result from generic input validation problems. Some sites attempt to protect themselves by filtering malicious input, but it may not be viable to modify the source of such components. We have tried to develop an automatic defense mechanism that can produce a proper input validation function on security gateway to filter malicious injection. To verify the efficiency of the tool, we picked the websites made up of some Web applications often contain third-party vulnerable components which was shipped in binary form. Among our experiments, the defense mechanism can automatically organize validation functions to avoid malicious injection attack. *abstract* environment.

Keywords: Black box testing, Malicious injection, Input validation, Security gateway.

1 Introduction

Many web application security vulnerabilities result from generic input validation problems. Some sites attempt to protect themselves by filtering malicious input, but a surprising number of web applications have no validation mechanisms. Many tools have been developed to detect Web application vulnerabilities but hackers are still successfully exploiting Web applications. A possible reason is that most tools just scan Web application vulnerabilities, but few tools can automatically revise these vulnerabilities. An advanced tool producing a proper input validation function depending on the database server and the application framework has been developed and verified its efficiency [2], but source code needed for inserting input validation function to revise injection vulnerabilities. If we can't modify the source of such components (either because the code was shipped in binary form or because the license agreement is prohibitive), above method can't be used.

In this paper, we present an advanced proposal adopting concept of application-level security gateway and more effectively resolving the problem than similar

T. Enokido, L. Barolli, and M. Takizawa (Eds.): NBiS 2007, LNCS 4658, pp. 98–107, 2007.

gateways or proxies. Our system consists of black box testing, validation functions and redirection mechanism. Black box testing can find all entry pointers and produce vulnerability lists. Validation functions can be dynamically organized and filter HTTP requests / responses to avoid malicious injection attacks. Redirection mechanism can avoid attack requests propagated to the web-server and return an error page to the user.

The remainder of the paper is structured as follows: Section 2 surveys a number of web application vulnerabilities and discusses related works have be proposed. In Section 3 we describe the technical details of our system for anti-malicious injection. Our system implementation is discussed in Section 4. The efficiency of our implementation is evaluated in Section 5, finally, Section 6 concludes.

2 Web Application Vulnerabilities and Related Work

Of all vulnerabilities identified in Web applications, problems caused by unchecked input are recognized as being the most common [1]. Static analysis can be used to analyze Web application code, for instance, ASP or PHP scripts. However, this technique fails to adequately consider the runtime behavior of Web applications and we must get source code. Recently, Y.W. Huang, S.K. Huang, T.P. Lin, and C.H. Tsai have developed a tool called WebSSARI (Web application Security Analysis and Runtime Inspection) [4,5]. The tool can be successfully used for automated Web application security assessment.

Another method called a black-box approach is adopted to analyze Web applications externally without the aid of source code. A black-box security analysis tool can perform an assessment very quickly and produce a useful report identifying vulnerable sites. Y.W. Huang, S.K. Huang, T.P. Lin, and C.H. Tsai have developed a remote, black-box security testing tool for Web applications is also called the Web Application Vulnerability and Error Scanner (WAVES) [6]. It can be used to analyze the design of Web application security assessment mechanisms in order to identify poor coding practices that render Web applications vulnerable to attacks such as SQL injection and cross-site scripting. The Open Web Application Security Project (OWASP) [7] has launched a WebScarab project. Two other available commercial scanners include SPI Dynamics' WebInspect [8] and Kavado's ScanDo [9].

Above works just only focus on detection, they seldom propose efficient method to automatically fix program's vulnerabilities. An advanced tool producing a proper input validation function depending on the database server and the application framework has been developed and verified its efficiency by us [2], but program or component's source code needed for inserting input validation function to revise injection vulnerabilities. Scott and Sharp [3] take the programmatic approach of specifying a security policy explicitly to provide a web application input validation mechanism-a rule-based security gateway- to protect against common application-level attacks. However, to enforce a security policy across a large web-application is difficult and adapt this mechanism requires that rules be defined for every single data entry point since they often contain some complex structures with little documents. Sanctum Inc. provides a plug-and-play tool called AppShield which adopts Security Gateway to inspect HTTP messages in an attempt to prevent application-level attacks, but it only can provide a limited degree of protection for existing websites with application level security problems [10]. Based on similar strategies, some advanced firewalls now also incorporate deep packet inspection technologies [11] for filtering application-level traffic to provide immediate assurance. However, using predicted behavior to produce general patterns without investigating the actual vulnerabilities may reduce compromise quality.

3 Anti-malicious Injection

The methods having been used to inject malicious data into Web applications are common and can cause great losses, we focus our research on this topic. Although the majority of web vulnerabilities are easy to understand and avoid, many web developers are not security-aware. Testing Web applications for security defects is now considered a necessary part of the development process. However, none of the traditional methods of automated security testing provides comprehensive security coverage and accurate results for Web applications. While source code analysis is capable of finding insecure programming practices that have potentially rendered the code vulnerable to malicious attacks, it can be limited by the types of languages that have been utilized in crafting the Web application and can only find potential vulnerabilities rather than actionable results.

Black box testing analyzes the application from the actual view of the user (and also a potential hacker), and not the developer of the application. Wherever there is an opportunity to inject malicious user input, the black box testing application injects it and analyzes the response to take further action. While black box testing techniques are beneficial because they eliminate language dependency and the need for parsing the source or binary code into an analyzable form, they are also limited by the fact that do not have access to the source code, and if unable to "guess" where some pages or files are located, can provide a false sense of security by producing numerous "false negatives".

Only an approach that combines the strengths of both source code analysis and black box testing can be used to produce secure Web applications. This hybrid analysis approach can provide broad code coverage, identify all entry points of input to an application, track data as it moves through an application, and then validate the vulnerabilities it does find, ultimately resulting in more accurate results [12]. Hybrid analysis method combines the depth of source code analysis with the accuracy of black box testing.

We try to develop an advanced proposal adopting concept of application-level security gateway. Our system consists of some techniques, such as black box testing, validation functions and redirection mechanism. Black box testing can been used not only to find entry pointer in a Web site that contain HTML forms but also to get name of variables, cookie or parameter and types of script language. According to these data have been gotten, vulnerability lists have been produced. Validation functions can be dynamically organized and filter HTTP requests / responses to avoid malicious injection attacks. Redirection mechanism can avoid attack requests propagated to the web-server and return an error page to the user.

3.1 Application-Level Security Gateway

Fig. 1 shows the tasks performed by the Security Gateway on receipt of an HTTP request. First, the URL is extracted from the HTTP header. Having identified a valid URL, the security gateway proceeds to check the names of all parameters and cookies passed in the HTTP request. Errors are generated if any of the parameters present precisely match those specified in deny_list (included some characters have been proved to high risky attack patterns). If any violations occur at this stage then a descriptive error message is returned to the client.

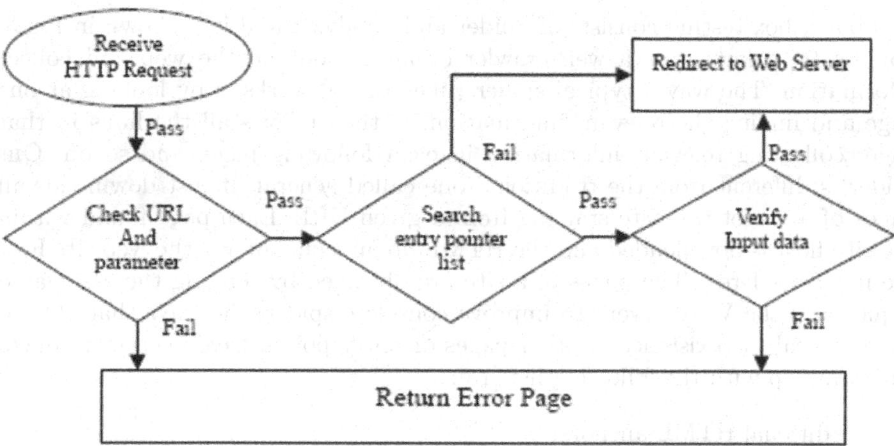

Fig. 1. The tasks performed by the Security Gateway

After previous black box testing, we can create an entry pointer list having written all records needed to be validated. Once we are sure that the HTTP message contains a valid combination of cookies and GET / POST parameters, we'll search entry pointer list. If we can find a record from the list, we'll continue to validate input data. Otherwise the redirection mechanism will be applied.

Next the proper validation functions are applied to verify input data. Section 3.2 and 3.3 will describe this process in detail. Finally, if all of the validation functions evaluate to true then the redirection mechanism will be used to process tasks forwarding HTTP request to the web-server and HTTP responses returned from the web-server. Section 3.4 will describe this process in detail. Fig.2 shows how the security gateway works.

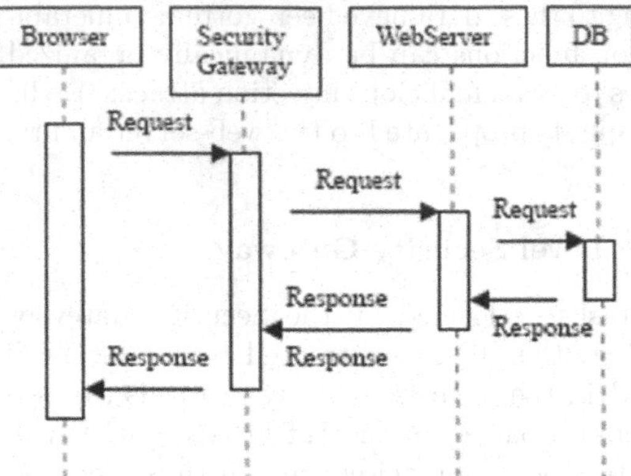

Fig. 2. Show how the security gateway work

3.2 Black Box Testing

Our black box testing consists of Spider and Analyzer and it is shown in Fig.3. Spiders (also known as a web crawler or ant)go out on the web and collect information. The way a typical spider (like google) works is by looking at one page and finding the relevant information. It then follows all the links in that page, collecting relevant information in each following page, and so on. Our spider is different from the traditional one called general. It just downloads all pages of a target web site starting from a given URL. Each page found within the site host is downloaded and the HTML documents outside the web site host are not considered. The pages of a site are obtained by sending the associated requests to the Web server. To improve complete spider, the ways that HTML pages reveal the existence of other pages or entry points have been mentioned, and came up with the following list [13]:

1. Traditional HTML anchors.
   Ex: <href = "http://www.google.com">Google </a>
2. Framesets.
   Ex: <frame src = "http://www.google.com/top frame.htm">

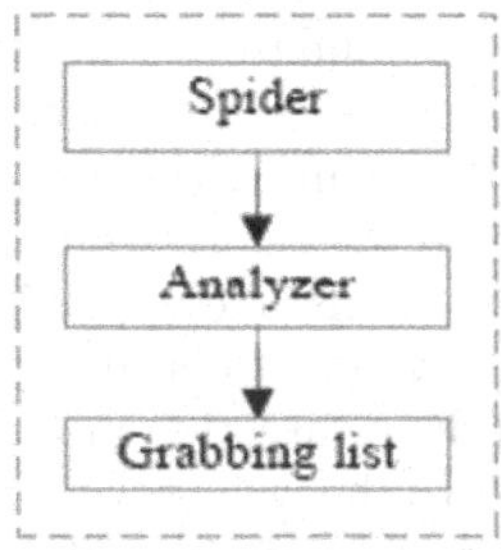

Fig. 3. A diagrammatic view of black box testing

3. Meta refresh redirections.
   Ex: <meta http-equiv = "refresh" content = "0; URL = http://www.google.com">
4. Client-side image maps.
   Ex: <area shape = "rect" href = "http://www. google.com">
5. Form submissions

Our spider grabs only some variables in web page having been traversed. To achieve the goal, we should know what HTML tags delimit the information we want to find. A typical example of HTML form source code is presented in Fig. 4.

```
<form method="post" action="verify.exe">
 <input type="text" name="struser" />
 <input type="password" name="strpass" />
 <input type="submit" value="Login" />
</form>
```

Fig. 4. A typical example of HTML form source code

The <Form> tag implies the existence of entry pointer, and the <input> tag reveal input process. Our spider scans the HTML for <form> tags and extracts the destination URL from the form action attribute. We also have to look at the form's method attribute to determine whether the fields will be sent as GET or POST parameters. The second step was to grab parameters named "struser" and "strpass" from the input name attribute. Upon completion of finding variables process, we can get a list as follow. A typical example of list is presented in Table 1:

Table 1. A typical example of grabbing result list

Result Field	Value
URL for testing	verify.exe
Form Method	post
Parameter1	struser
Parameter2	strpass

3.3 Validation Functions

Meta program will be automatically organized by means of grabbing record and include proper validation function to process the form's input. We referenced the existing literature on malicious injection techniques to create a set of malicious

```
(1) Input Validation Function:
    function anti_injection($sql)
    {   //injection patterns
    $sql = preg_replace(sql_regcase("/(from|select|insert|delete|where|drop
    table|show tables|#|\*|--|\\\\)/"),"",$sql);
    $sql = trim($sql);
    $sql = strip_tags($sql);
    $sql = addslashes($sql);
    return $sql; }
(2) meta program (verify.php) segment:
    $struser= anti_injection($_POST["struser "]) ;
    $strpass= anti_injection($_POST["strpass "]) ;
```

Fig. 5. Validation function and meta program

injection patterns. Our input validation function can filter malicious Characteristics by means of malicious injection patterns. A typical example of input validation function about SQL Injection source code and meta program are presented in Fig. 5. Note that the Italic words should be replaced by variables grabbed at black box testing step.

4 System Overview

We have described the technical details of our system in Section 3. Fig. 6 shows a diagrammatic view of the components of our system and interactions between them. By means of testing result, we can create a testing web site on security gateway. The testing web site consists of all web programs needed to verify their input data. For example, if there is a real program named "verify.exe" on web server, our system can automatically produce a meta program named "verify.php" on security gateway to validate input data. Meta program will be automatically organized by means of grabbing record from testing result and include proper validation function to processthe form's input. By means of meta program, the web programs may not being viable to modify their vulnerable source code (either because the code was shipped in binary form or because the license agreement is prohibitive) can filter input malicious data to avoid injection attack. It is our system's great contribution to web security.

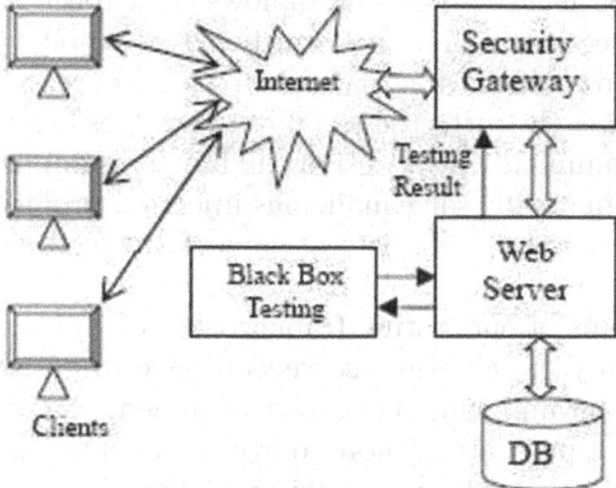

Fig. 6. A diagrammatic view of our system

5 System Evaluation

We create the framework for event driven security testing. The testing framework's diagrammatic view of the components is shown in Fig. 7. It consists of Tester, Monitor, Verifier and reporter. The Tester is similar to general malicious injection tools, such as Web Scarab's Parameter fuzzer [7], to expose incomplete parameter validation, leading to vulnerabilities like Cross Site Scripting (XSS)

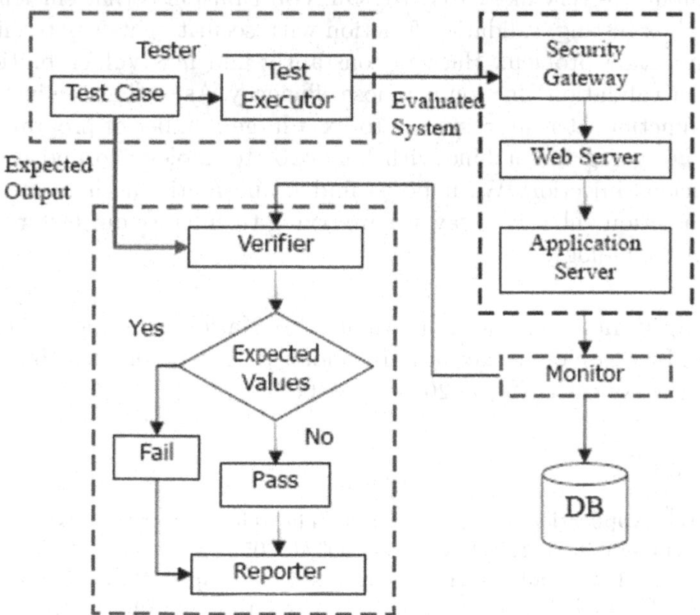

Fig. 7. A diagrammatic view of the components of our testing framework

and SQL Injection. It generates tests and knows the expected output. The Verifier compares the expected output or previously stored output to the actual output received by the Monitor. If the security gateway can successfully filter malicious input, and if it validates the correctness of input variables before constructing and executing the SQL command, the injection will fail. This implies our meta-revised mechanism can automatically solve malicious injection problem.

We try to create a website consists of some form feed web pages, example programs having some security problems and general web pages having no entry pointers. By means of our testing framework, our Spider can correctly find entry point, and Analyzer can also resolve web page to grab variables we need. The proper meta program including correct arguments has included validation function to validate input data. Among our experiments, the security gateway can be in accord with expectation to avoid malicious injection attack. Because our security gateway must be in front of web server, the mechanism can not be experimented on a large number of internet websites.

6 Conclusions and Future Works

In this paper, we present an advanced proposal adopting concept of application-level security gateway to solve the problem as we can't modify the source code (either because the code was shipped in binary form or because the license agreement is prohibitive).

Unless a web application has a strong, centralized mechanism for validating all input from HTTP requests (and any other sources), vulnerabilities based on malicious input are very likely to exist. Our contribution is that efficiently combines black box testing, validation function with security gateway to eliminated malicious injection problem. Hackers constantly find new vulnerabilities to attack, so older validation function may lose efficiency. As to that, we just enhance validation function. It is an easy way to fix a large number of programs. In the future, we are going to combine with honeypot technology to find new attack about malicious injection. We hope to find a automatic mechanism adjusting validation function. That is to say, we are trying to enhance our tester by means of honeypot technology.

Acknowledgments. The authors thanks to National Science Council *and* Chung-shan Institute of Science *and* Technology, Taiwan for their financial support under the contract NSC96-2623-7-036-002-D.

References

1. Open Web Application Security Project. The ten most critical Web application security vulnerabilities (2004) visit on 2005/10/05, `http://umn.dl.sourceforge.net/sourceforge/owasp/OWASPTopTen2004.pdf`
2. Lin, J.-C., Chen, J.-M.: An Automatic Revised Tool for Anti-malicious Injection. In: Proceedings of The Sixth IEEE International Conference on Computer and Information Technology (CIT'06), IEEE, Los Alamitos (2006)

3. Scott, D., Sharp, R.: Abstracting Application-Level Web Security. In: The 11th International Conference on the World Wide Web (Honolulu, Hawaii, May 2002), pp. 396–407 (2002)
4. Huang, Y.W., Huang, S.K., Lin, T.P., Tsai, C.H.: Securing Web application code by static analysis and runtime protection. In: Proceedings of the 13th International World Wide Web Conference, New York (May 17-22, 2004)
5. Huang, Y.W., Yu, F., Hang, C., Tsai, C.H., Lee, D.T., Kuo, S.Y.: Verifying Web applications using bounded model checking. In: Proceedings of the 2004 International Conference Dependable Systems and Networks (DSN2004), Florence, Italy (June 28-July 1, 2004)
6. Huang, Y.W., Huang, S.K., Lin, T.P., Tsai, C.H.: Web Application Security Assessment by Fault Injection and Behavior Monitoring. In: Proc. 12th Int'l. World Wide Web Conference, pp.148–159, Budapest, Hungary (2003)
7. OWASP. WebScarab Project. visit on 2005/10/08, `http://www.owasp.org/webscarab/`
8. SPI Dynamics. Web Application Security Assessment. SPI Dynamics Whitepaper (2003)
9. KaVaDo. Application-Layer Security: InterDo 3.0. KaVaDo Whitepaper (2003) Available from `http://www.kavado.com/`
10. Sanctum Inc. AppShield. white paper (March 2003) Available from `http://www.sanctuminc.com/`
11. Dharmapurikar, S., Krishnamurthy, P., Sproull, T., Lockwood, J.: Deep Packet Inspection Using Parallel Bloom Filters. In: Proc. 11th Symp. High Performance Interconnects (HOTI'03), Stanford, California, pp. 44–51 (2003)
12. SPI Labs, Hybrid Analysis- An Approach to Testing Web Application Security, visit on 2006/3/05 Available from: `http://www.spidynamics.com/assets/documents/hybrid_analysis.pdf`
13. Chen, D.-J., Hwang, C.-C., Huang, S.-K., Chen, D.T.K.: A Testing Framework for Web Application Security Assessment. Journal of Computer Networks 48(5), 739–761 (2005)

SKEMON: A Simple Certificate-Less Method for Key Exchange by Using Mobile Network

C. Sakamoto[1], G. De Marco[1], R. Yaegashi[2], M. Tadauchi[1], and L. Barolli[3]

[1] Toyota Technological Institute, Tenpaku-Hisakata 2-12-1, Nagoya 468-8511, Japan
{demarco,tadauchi}@toyota-ti.ac.jp
[2] Shibaura Institute of Technology, 3-7-5 Toyosu, Toto-ku, Tokyo 135-8543, Japan
rihito@sic.shibaura-it.ac.jp
[3] Department of Information and Communication Engineering,
Fukuoka Institute of Technology (FIT)
3-30-1 Wajiro-Higashi, Higashi-ku, Fukuoka 811-0295, Japan
Tel.: +81-92-606-4970
barolli@fit.ac.jp

Abstract. Secure communications requires the exchange of keying material, which in general is not trivial problem. A simple solution is to use alternative communication channels to exchange the cryptographic keys, like standard mail services or reciprocal visual inspection of text strings. Here, we propose to use the standard Public Mobile Network (PMN) as an alternative channel, because the use of mobile phones has become pervasive and affordable for most of users. The basic assumption is that the PMN is more secure than other wireless and wired networks. We envision a system for subscribers who wish to exchange their cryptographic keys, which can be used afterwards for sending encrypted messages over other (insecure) communication channels, like Internet. We assume that every user or its mobile phone is able 1) to generate a public/private key pair, and 2) to store it inside his/her mobile phone rubric. The public key is exchanged by sending special requests by means of standard PMN services, like the text messaging system. We analyze the scalability of such a system, by assuming that the subscribers can send group queries, i.e. queries which request the whole (public) keys stored in the rubrics of a subset of the closest neighbors of an user. The performance of such an approach depends on the properties of the graph model of interactions among people. By means of simulations, we show that it is preferable to send few group queries instead of many single requests. This result can be used to dimension the service provided by the PMN.

1 Introduction

Nowdays, we can count a lot of solutions to tackle the security concerns of network based information systems. Perhaps, the most famous solution is the Public Key Infrastructure (PKI) which uses asymmetric cryptography, in order to provide confidentiality, privacy and perfect forward secrecy[1]. As representative public key cryptosystem, we cite S/MIME (Secure Multipurpose Internet

[1] For example, by using Ephemeral Diffie-Hellman.

T. Enokido, L. Barolli, and M. Takizawa (Eds.): NBiS 2007, LNCS 4658, pp. 108–117, 2007.

Mail Extensions) used to secure e-mails, IPSec (Internet Protocol Security)[10] used for establishing VPN connections (Virtual Private Network) [8] and TLS (Transport Layer Security)/SSL (Secure Socket Layer) [6] aimed at secure transactions on the Web. One of the problem of PKI is the distribution of keys [12]. The standard solution is providing users with signed certificates distributed by trusted Certificate Authorities (CA). However, CAs are single point of failure and deploying a lightweight PKI infrastructure even for simple and daily communications can be difficult. Furthermore, anonymity is not always guaranteed in PKI. In fact, the public keys must be known to both parties of the communication. If one of the party does not know the correspondent's public key, he/she must require a certificate. Sending a certificate over an insecure channel allows attackers to know the participants of the communication.

Here, we propose Simple Key Exchange by using MObile Network (SKEMON), a certificate-less system to distribute the encryption keys by using the Public Mobile Network (PMN). The invaluable advantage offered by the PMN with respect to the Internet is that the spoofing and/or the attacks are relatively difficult. In fact, wiretapping a communication over the PMN is very hard or at least costly, while it is very easy sniffing, analyzing and forging packets flowing through an IP network . For example, in wireless Ethernet as the IEEE 802.11, the `aircrack` tool can easily recover the keys used for encryption of the communication; in wired Ethernet, the `etthercap` tool can easily mount Man in the Middle (MiM) attacks [1]. Here, we assume that users trust one another, or rather their public keys are implicitly signed, as in the scheme of Günther. This self-certification is given by the reciprocal knowledge of cell phone numbers. Accordingly, the exchange of public keys can be executed by using cell phone themself. In this way, users inherently signed their public keys and a certificate server is not needed. The system uses only two messages and it is like a messaging system. We leverage the security of the PMN in order to exchange the encryption keys. We analyze pros and cons of the proposed architecture in case of one-to-one and one-to-many communications.

The rest of the paper is organized as follows. In Section 2, we briefly review related works about key exchange proposals. In Section 3, we discuss our proposal and in Section 4, we analyze the system both from the point of view of the security and the scalability. In Section 5, we give our simulation results, by comparing single queries against group queries, and we conclude the paper in Section 6.

2 Related Works

A classical way to exchange the key of two parties is the Diffie-Hellman (DH) protocol which requires two messages only. The DH protocol is vulnerable to MiM, and it is a point-to-point protocol which does not scale as the number of users increases. Other solutions propose the use of a Key Distribution Server (KDS), which pre-distributes symmetric keys to every user. Although this solution can be optimized with respect to the scalability, e.g. by using the Blom's

KDS system, it requires a centralized server. In this regard, it resembles the Identity Based Encryption (IBE)[4,9,3]. In IBE, every user has a public key derived from some unique information about his/her identity, e.g. the user's E-mail address. A trusted third party, called the Private Key Generator (PKG), generates the corresponding private keys. For example, if Alice wants to send a secure message to Bob, she encrypts messages by using Bob's E-mail as public key. Bob obtains his private key by contacting the PKG. However, there is not mutual authentication and we still need a server.

A famous key agreement scheme based on the PKI with digital signatures is OpenPGP [5], which uses the concept of "web of trust". The certificates can be digitally signed by other users. The scheme is flexible, unlike most PKI designs, and it leaves trust decision in the hands of individual users. However, if the web is large, the certificates of the public keys could not be reliable.

The simplest way to distribute keys is to use alternative channels. For example, in [13] the authors note that a sort of perfect security can be reached whenever the exchange of secret material, such as the keys, is done by visual inspection. For example, when two users meet each other, they could safely read and check the exchanged keys on the screen of a portable device. It is assumed that the communication is short-range and then secure. However, the scheme requires physical contact of the users, and the request group of keys at the same time could be problematic.

Our idea follows the footprints of [13], but it uses the PMN as alternative channel. Basically, it is a modification of the Needhman-Schroeder (NS) public-key protocol [11], which provides mutual entity authentication and mutual entity transport.

3 SKEMON System

Definitions

$[M]_{\mathrm{A}}$	Message M decrypted or signed with A(lice)'s private key
$\{M\}_{\mathrm{A}}$	Message M encrypted with A's public key
$E(M, K)$	Message M encrypted with key K
Pk_{A}	Public key of A
S	Request message of a key (single query)
S_M	Request message of a group of keys (group query)
$\mathrm{A} \Rightarrow \mathrm{B} : S$	A sends to B(ob) a message S
$\mathcal{P}_{\mathrm{A}}$	Set of keys stored by A
G_{A}	Contacts group or contacts list of A
T_{A}	Telephone number of A
ID_{A}	Identity of A

3.1 Assumptions

The assumptions of our proposal are as follows. The wireless channel is a secure channel. This is a reasonable assumption given that attacks on the PMN, although not impossible, are costly and harder than those in wired IP networks. Therefore, in this context we assume that the IP network is the insecure channel.

1. The parties know one another. In particular, the intended peers know the telephone numbers of the others. That is, every $v \in G_{\mathrm{A}}$ knows T_{A}.
2. Every party has a mobile phone which is equipped with a rubric of keys. That is, every contact is assigned a public key. For the management of the rubric key and the key generation a dedicated software runs on the mobile phone.
3. The parties can save the public key of contacts in a particular file of their PC.
4. The SKEMON system is used whenever a party wishes to send an e-mail message in a secure way.

The cell phone should also implement a dedicated software in order to process the delivery and the reception of S messages. To this aim, the MN phone could implement a particular user-space application, e.g. by means of Mobile Java, or a particular module embedded in the operating system. The underlying hypothesis is that when a peer receives a request message S he/she can or cannot accept it.

3.2 SKEMON Procedures

The steps taken by the SKEMON protocol are shown in Fig. 1. First, whenever Alice (A) wants to send a secure message to Bob (B), she sends a request message

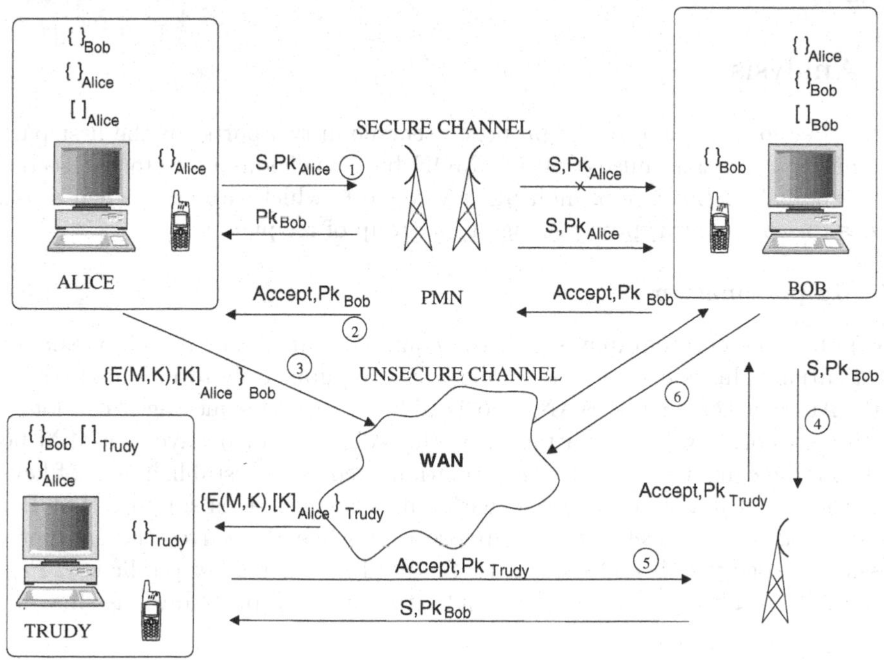

Fig. 1. SKEMON messages

1. if $T_B \in G_A$	: $A \Rightarrow B : S, Pk_A$
2. if B is not available	: $PMN \Rightarrow B : S, Pk_A$
3. if B accepts	: $B \Rightarrow A : Pk_B$
4.	$\mathcal{P}_A \leftarrow \mathcal{P}_A \cup Pk_B$
5. else	: do nothing
6. $A \Rightarrow B : \{E(M, K), [K]_A\}_B$	

Fig. 2. Basic SKEMON

S along with her public key[2], Pk_A to the B's cell phone (step 1). If B is available, and if he accepts to share its public key with A, he sends an ACCEPT message, along with his public key, Pk_B (step 2). In the NS scheme, the originator A uses the recipient's publick key, Pk_B, to encrypt a session key along with his/her identity. In our scheme, this simple classical procedure is supported by the PMN. By this way, we have solved the problem of distributing the public keys to intended parties. In fact, in ordinary Internet or enterprise networks sniffing the content of packets [1], and then the public keys, is very simple. It is worth noting that we want authentication among group G and not a universal authentication. This is something like what happens in messaging systems, where the user is allowed to deny or accept new requests of joining the user contact list. After that A has received B's public key, she can encrypt the message M, along with a signed session key K. The resulting message is $\{E(M, K), [K]_A\}_{\text{Bob}}$, as shown in Fig. 2

4 Analysis

In this Section, we analyze the proposed scheme in two parts. In the first part, we analyze a possible misuse of SKEMON by a malicious user. In the second part, we analyze the case of multiple key requests which can arise when a user wishes to send an encrypted message to a group of recipients.

4.1 Impersonation

The public key cryptography solves the confidentiality issue as well as the authentication. This is because the public keys are public only to intended parties in G. An attacker on the WAN who is able to read A's messages cannot do anything. In other words, an attacker on the WAN cannot behave as a MiM because she/he cannot see sensitive information such as the establishment of keys. But, there is still a subtle problem with this system. Let us suppose that B is behaving as an incorrect party[3]. Suppose that when B receives the encrypted message, he decrypts it and sends it to Trudy (T), by using her public key, Pk_T. In fact, B can always retrieves T's key by the previous procedure, as shown in

[2] If she has not yet Bob's public key, Pk_B.

[3] In this context, an incorrect party is not an attacker as intended in the usual way. The incorrect party has not in mind to destroy the system.

steps 4 and 5 of Fig. 1. At this point, T can decrypt the message sent by B, by using her private key, and since she knows Pk_{A} she could decrypt the message originally intended for B. In other words, B could re-send the messages sent from Alice (number 3 in Fig. 1) to another party. The latter could in turn assume to have received a (private) message from A. At a first look, it seems that this fact jeopardizes the protocol. However, there are some shortcomings which refrain B to launch such an impersonation attack. First of all, the cost. In fact, sending S message in step 4 is billed by the PMN. Secondly, if we suppose the public keys do not change, T does decrypt the B's message, but she will find a message encrypted with the A's key. Since T receives a message from B which contains a message wrote by Alice, she can turn reasonably suspicious. To add more privacy, we can simply add the identity of the user in the request message, e.g. the e-mail message will be composed as $\{E(M, K), [ID_{\mathrm{B}}, K]_{\mathrm{A}}\}_{\mathrm{B}}$. In this case, the key K is signed by A along with the recipient's identity. Even if B can open the message, he/she cannot re-sign it on behalf of A.

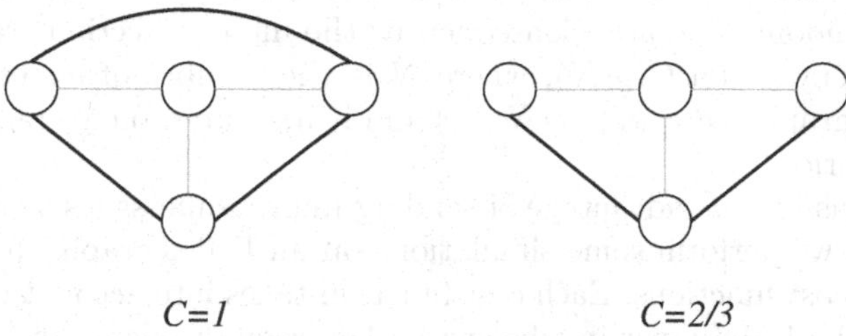

Fig. 3. Cluster coefficient

4.2 Multiple Queries

In this case, we assume that A wishes to send an e-mail to a group of recipients. In this section, we model the relations among people by means of a graph $G(V, E)$, where V is the vertexes set and E is the links set. A link or arc between two $u, v \in V$ means that u is in the cell phone rubric of v and vice versa. We analyze the worst case only, i.e. A performs this operation for the first time or when all her contacts changed their keys. We refer to *complete* rubric key as a rubric where every contact is assigned its public key. In general, the rubric is not complete, because some contacts might have not performed the key request operation with their respective neighbors. Alice has two choices: 1) send all S messages to her neighbors, or 2) send S_M messages[4] to a subset of $R \subset G_A$. Which is the best choice? It is clear that, in the latter case, by assuming that A's neighbors have a complete rubric, A hopes to reach all her neighborhood in one key-request operation. The more A's rubric is "large", the more she will have high success probability of getting all public keys. This probability depends

[4] An S_M message is request message of the content of the rubric. For example, if B receives an S_M messages, and if B accepts it, the content of B's rubric is sent back.

on the type of interconnection among people, i.e. the cluster coefficient of the graph. The cluster coefficient C_i of a node $i \in V$ is the ratio between the number of links among neighbors of i and the number of all possible links which could exist among them. For example, in Fig. 3, there is a vertex with $C = 1$ and $C = \frac{2}{3}$. The more people are connected, at least from the point of view of their cell phone rubrics, the higher the cluster coefficient is. If $C = 1$, A is very lucky, because by making just one request, she can retrieves all keys.

This kind of relations graph has been studied only for particular associations of people. For example, relations among actors, citations of papers, and so on. It has been shown that when people tend to organize in community groups, within the group everyone knows everyone, while there are few people who connect these community to one another. This is the famous small-world effect. However, for friendship relations it is not clear if the small-world effect holds. We assume that the relations among users rubrics can be taught as a friendship relations, and, accordingly, assume that the correspondent graph is not a small-world graph [7]. For instance, we assume that every user's rubric has an entry toward another user with probability p. The connection or links among people are assumed i.i.d Bernoullian random variables. Consequently, the interconnection graph $G(V, E)$ is an Erdös-Rény graph $G(p, N)$, where N is the number of nodes. The mean degree of this graph is $d = \overline{k_i} = p(N-1)$ and it measures, on average, how large is the keys rubric.

In order to assess the advantage of sending many S messages against few S_M group queries, we perform some simulations on an Erdös graph. In this regard, we define two cost functions. Each cost function takes into account the overhead the user and the PMN incur in whenever a key request operation is performed. Let U_S be the cost function in the case of sending S messages only, and U_M the cost function in the case the user chooses to send few S_M messages. We assume also that the maximum size of a message allowed by the PMN is T_h units. The threshold T_h is normalized with respect to size of one message. It is straightforward to define the following cost functions:

$$U_M^i(k_i) = \gamma_i p_S + \sum_{j \in \mathcal{N}_\gamma^i} \left\lceil \frac{k_j}{T_h} \right\rceil + (1 - p_S)(2k_i - \gamma_i) \tag{1}$$

$$U_S^i(k_i) = 2k_i\,, \tag{2}$$

where $\gamma_i \triangleq \lceil \frac{k_i}{k} \rceil$ is the number of messages S_M that a node decides to send to a subset of neighbors, p_S is the success probability and k_j is the degree of the neighbors of i. If we choose to send messages S_M, the neighborhood of i is the set $\mathcal{N}_\gamma^i$ which contains all selected neighbors. Obviously, $|\mathcal{N}_\gamma^i| = \gamma_i$. The probability p_S is the probability of reaching all neighbors by means of S_M messages. For example, if A chooses to send γ_A queries of type S_M, A succeeds if she can retrieve all the required keys. Otherwise, she has to send additional messages to the missing neighbors. It is clear that if A fails, she has to pay the cost for the first γ_A messages plus the cost for the additional S messages. This cost is the

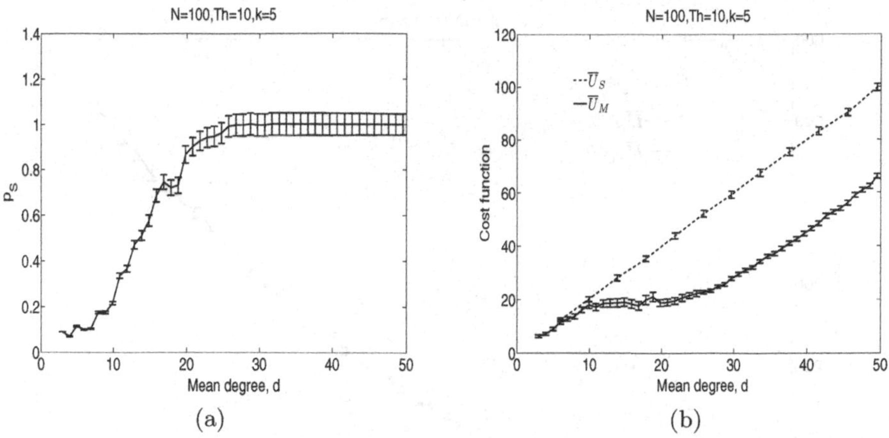

Fig. 4. Simulation results. Connection probability p ranges from 0.03 to 0.5, and the mean degree is $d = p(N-1)$.

third term in (1). If we take the average over all nodes in the graph, by using Jensen's inequality and random sums theorem, we have:

$$\overline{U}_M(d) \leq \gamma p_S + \frac{\gamma d}{T_h} + 2(d-\gamma)(1-p_S) \tag{3}$$

$$\overline{U}_S(d) = 2d\,, \tag{4}$$

where γk. As pointed out by equation (1), U_M^i is a non-linear but monotone function of the node degree: since the number of S_M messages, γ, decreases with k_i, the cost due to S_M messages decreases, as indicated by the middle term in (1). On the other hand, p_S increases with d. The trade-off between p_S and the cost depends on the threshold T_h. In the following section, we perform some simulations in order to assess this trade-off.

5 Simulations

We performed some Monte-Carlo simulations in order to compute the cost functions in (3)(4). In MATLAB, we generated synthetic graphs, $G(p, N)$, with the number of users, $N = |V| = 100$. We can imagine that N users make use of the system. The average rubric size is representative of the relations with other people and it is simply the average degree, $d = p(N-1)$, where p is the connection probability [2]. We let the probability p ranges from 0.03 to 0.5. For every p, we compute the sample averages of cost functions and the sample success probability, p_S, for 200 generated graphs, along with their respective 95% confidence intervals. In order to compute these metrics, we choose one generic node i and randomly select γ_i of its links. Since the value of $k = 5$, the number of S_M messages is greater than 1 iff $d \leq 5$. In Fig. 4-(a)(b), we show p_S, $\overline{U}_M$ and $\overline{U}_S$, respectively. First, note that when a node has $d < 10$, sending messages

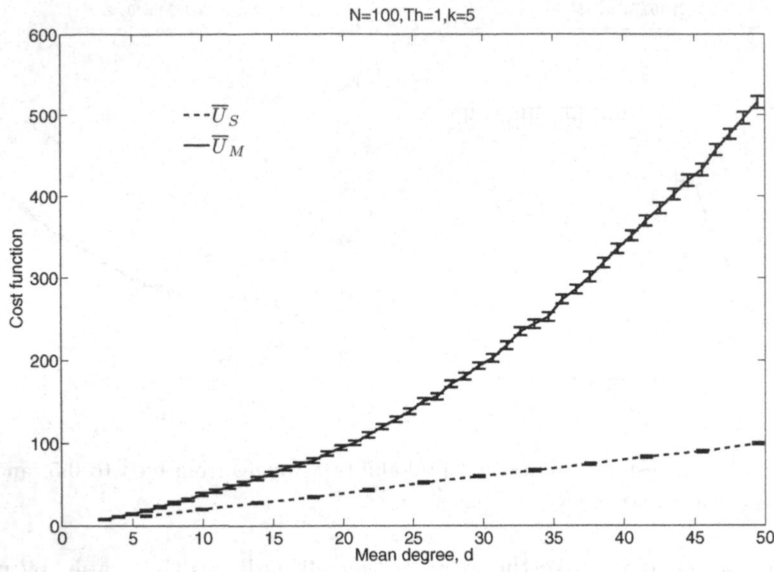

Fig. 5. Case of $T_h = 1$

of type S_M is, on average, equivalent to send messages of type S. Although not immediately intuitive, the results of cost functions were expected. In fact, despite the fact that success probability converges to 1 for $d > 25$, $\overline{U}_M < \overline{U}_S$, for $d > 10$, because of the polynomial dependence of $\overline{U}_M$ on d. This first result says that for rubrics of average size greater than 10 contacts, from the point of view of the number of transmitted messages, it is more convenient to send messages S_M than S. This result can be easily explained by noting that in an Erdös random graph, the cluster coefficient $C = p$. Thus, the higher is p, the higher will be the probability that the neighbors of a user belong to the same cluster. Consequently, until the relations of people in terms of entries in the cell phone rubrics can be modelled by means of random graph, sending group queries is better than sending single queries. This advantage persists if $d < T_h k$, as it can be easily derived by solving $(U_M(d) < U_S(d))\,|_{P_S=0.5}$.

For example, in Fig. 5, we show the results for $T_h = 1$. As expected, in this case the cost due to the PMN is to high, and it is better to send single query message.

6 Conclusion

In this paper, we proposed a simple mechanism to exchange encryption public keys by using the PMN as an alternate communication channel. The system results in a certificate-less server, if one assumes that users of the PMN are implicitly trusted. By this way, i.e. the combination of this reciprocal acquaintance and the strong security of the PMN, we can encrypt and send messages over other insecure channel, as IP networks, where MiM attacks and identity spoofing can be launched. More interestingly, we analyzed also the scalability of the system, e.g. in the case of multiple requests of public keys. By exploiting results from random graph theory, we have shown that, from the point of view of the number of transmitted messages, it is better to use group queries. A group query is a message which requests all keys known by a subset of contacts of the user. In this way, by envisioning a dedicated software running in the cell phone, the user can retrieve the necessary keys. This procedure can arise also when the user begins the procedure for the first time, or when she/he decides to initiate an updating of stored keys. Studying SKEMON by assuming other kind of relationships among users, such as the power law graph and the availability of a simple prototype are on going works.

References

1. http://www.insecure.org
2. Bollobás, B.: Random Graphs. Number 73 in Cambridge Studies in Advanced Mathematics. Cambridge
3. Boneh, D., Boyen, X.: Secure identity-based encryption without random oracles. In: Franklin, M. (ed.) CRYPTO 2004. LNCS, vol. 3152, pp. 443–459. Springer, Heidelberg (2004)
4. Boneh, D., Franklin, M.: Identity based encryption from the weil pairin. SIAM Journal of Computing 32(3), 586–615 (2003)
5. Callas, J., Donnerhacke, L., Finney, H., Thayer, R.: RFC 2440 OpenPGP message format, November
6. Dierks, T., Allen, C.: RFC 2246: The tls protocol (January 1999)
7. Dorogovtsev, S.N., Mendes, J.F.F.: Evolution of networks. Advances in Physics 51, 1079 (2002)
8. Gleeson, B., Lin, A., Heinanen, J., Armitage, G., Mlis, A.: RFC 2764 A Framework for IP Based Virtual Private Networks (February 2000)
9. Horwitz, J., Lynn, B.: Toward hierarchical identity-based encryption. In: Knudsen, L.R. (ed.) EUROCRYPT 2002. LNCS, vol. 2332, pp. 466–481. Springer, Heidelberg (2002)
10. Kent, S., Atkinson, R.: RFC 2401, Security Architecture for the Internet Protocol (November 1998)
11. Menezes, A., van Oorshot, P.C., Vanstone, S.A.: Handbook of Applied Cryptography. CRC Press (1997)
12. Stamp, M.: Information Security, Principles and Practice. Wiley, Chichester (2006)
13. Čagalj, M.,Čapkun, S., Hubaux, J.-P.: Key agreement in peer-to-peer wireless networks. IEEE Proceedings 94(2) 467–478 (2006)

A Secure Authentication Scheme for a Public Terminal Before a Transaction

Chin-Ling Chen[1], Yu-Yi Chen[2], and Jinn-Ke Jan[3]

[1] Department of Computer Science and Information Engineering, Chaoyang University of Technology, Taichung, Taiwan 413, ROC
clc@mail.cyut.edu.tw
[2] Department of Management Information Systems, National Chung Hsing University, Taichung, Taiwan 402, ROC
chenyuyi@nchu.edu.tw
[3] Department of Computer Science, National Chung Hsing University, Taichung, Taiwan 402, ROC
jkjan@cs.nchu.edu.tw

Abstract. Due to the fast progress of the Internet, and with the increasing numbers of public terminals spread everywhere, people can access personal sensitive data or perform transactions easily through these public terminals. Identifying these public terminals is therefore a most urgent topic. We propose an efficient and secure scheme that meets real environmental conditions for authenticating these public terminals before conducting a transaction.

Keywords: Cryptography, security, public terminal, kiosk.

1 Introduction

Today, people can access personal sensitive data or perform financial transactions through public Internet kiosks that are located at malls, airports, hospitals, government agencies, etc.. Unverified kiosks are problematic for secure Internet services, as all service data is available in unencrypted form to the kiosk. Before performing personal data access or a transaction, people are required to enter their password or PINs to reliably authenticate themselves to the backend service server. However, using a public Internet access terminal creates an opportunity for persons with criminal intent to use a fake-terminal to cheat users. Currently, a counterfeit public terminal can keep users completely in the dark. The fake-terminal usually reports some plausible error messages to the users after the sensitive information has been revealed.

In accordance with these problems, in 1999, Asokan et al. [1] proposed solutions for different scenarios that correspond to different situations where the users are equipped with devices of different capacity, such as a personal trusted device with its own display, a smart card without a display, or a memory card. The Asokan et al.'s working model is shown in Fig. 1. Asokan et al.'s solutions assume the use of suitable existing authentication protocols such as Secure Sockets Layer (SSL) [5], KryptoKnight [2],

T. Enokido, L. Barolli, and M. Takizawa (Eds.): NBiS 2007, LNCS 4658, pp. 118–126, 2007.

and Kerberos [8] Later, Cheng et al. [4] modified part of Asokan et al.'s work using the public key algorithm concept. However, in a general and comprehensive pre-view, these solutions are not perfect because many interactive steps are necessary.

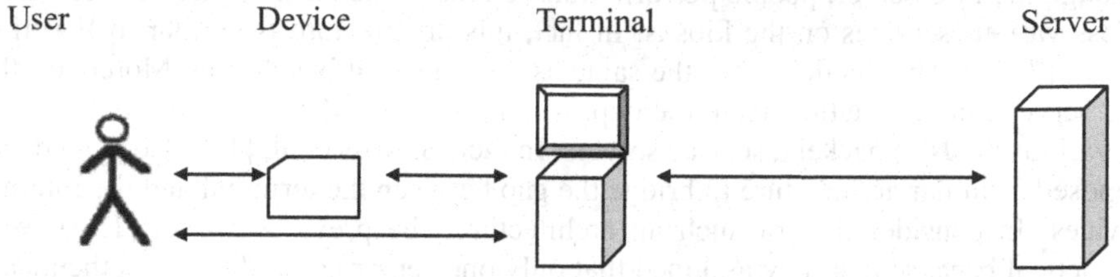

Fig. 1. Asokan et al.'s working model

In their proposals [1, 4], there were only four parties in their working model: the user, the personal trusted device, the public terminal and the server. Any public terminal can be activated by the user's trusted device to access various services from the server. These public terminals are susceptible to the fake-terminal attack: the attackers set up a fake terminal and steal the unsuspecting users' sensitive information, such as passwords, PINs or private e-mails, when the users attempt to use these fake terminals. Because unverified terminals are problematic for secure Internet service, all users will intend to authenticate the secure authenticated channel between the terminals and the server has already been set up before performing any transactions.

In consideration of the real environment, there should be a *PoC* (Point-of-Contact) server to handle all communications with kiosks [3, 6]. This concept was proposed by Laufmann [9] and the architecture was sketched as Fig. 2.

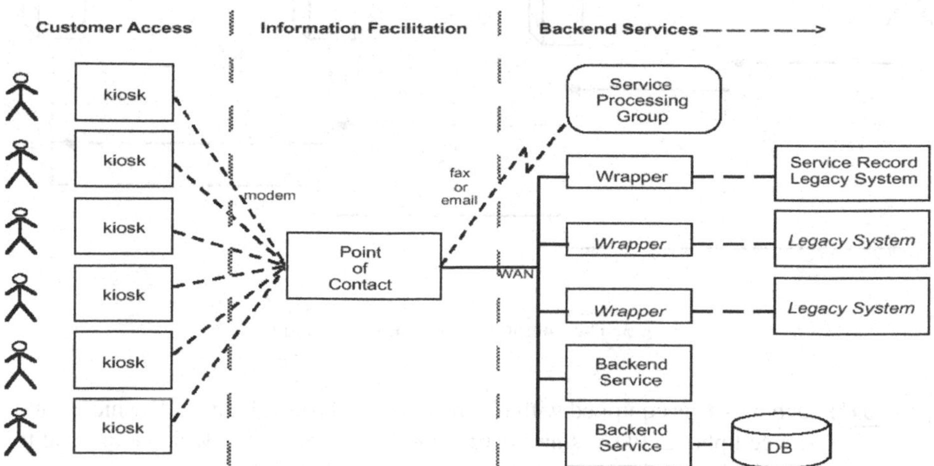

Fig. 2. Kiosk Support Service Architecture [9]

In Laufmann's proposal, the role of the PoC server is an agent to serve the deployed kiosks as a single point of contact, managing message traffic and performing service tasks between the kiosk request and the backend services. It isolates the kiosks, both physically and architecturally, from the backend service servers, and vice versa. Through the PoC server, people perform transactions to the backend service servers to access various services on the kiosks. In fact, this architecture is similar to E-voting system [7, 14]. This model is not the same as Asokan et al.'s solution. Moreover, the PoC server can only authenticate the deployed kiosk since the users' accounts are on the various kinds of backend service servers. In fact, S. Ross et al. [12] also agreed and proposed a similar architecture to bridge the gap between the terminal and the Internet services. In consideration of such an architecture, the previous works [1, 4] were impractical because that they assumed that only one server could directly authenticate both the users and the public terminals. We therefore propose a novel scheme based on Laufmann's model to meet the real environment.

2 Our Scheme

In this section, we propose an efficient and more competent secure method to meet the kiosk support service architecture. There are five entities in this system, each user ***U*** is equipped with his personal trusted device ***D*** which is used to connect the public terminal ***T*** to access the Internet service from the web-site server ***W*** through the PoC server ***P***. The following Fig. 3 will briefly sketch the interaction flow of our scheme.

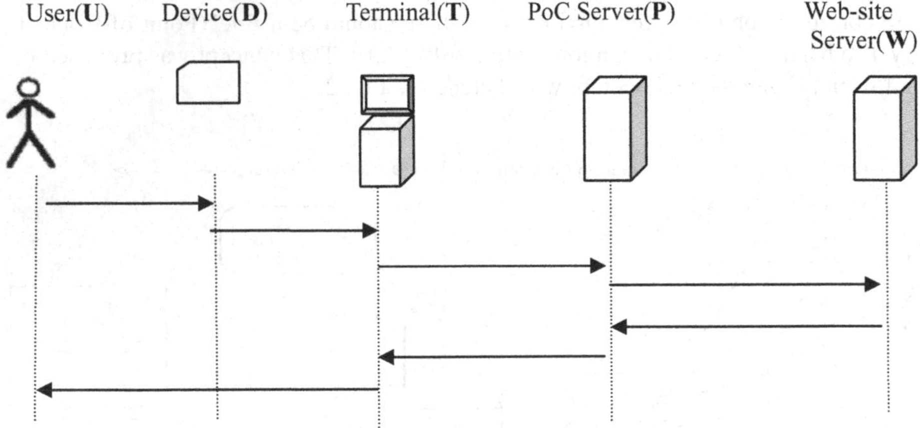

Fig. 3. The interaction flow of our scheme

$\boxed{U \rightarrow D}$: Each user ***U*** is equipped with his own personal trusted device ***D*** which could be a cell phone, PDA, smart card, or memory card. The device ***D*** is used to connect the public terminal ***T*** to access the Internet service.

$\boxed{D \rightarrow T}$: Before processing any transaction, the device ***D*** will request the terminal ***T*** to authenticate itself to the PoC server ***P***. At the mean time, the device ***D*** also prepares some information to ask the terminal to forward and acquire the evidence to prove that this terminal is not a fake terminal.

$\boxed{T \rightarrow P}$: Only a real terminal ***T*** deployed by the PoC server ***P*** can pass the authentication to forward the evidence-request information to the server ***P***.

$\boxed{P \rightarrow W}$: Under the public key system infrastructure, the PoC server ***P*** and the web-site server ***W*** can authenticate one another. The evidence-request information can be securely forwarded to the server ***W***.

$\boxed{W \rightarrow P}$: According to the user's account and the evidence-request information, the evidence, called ***authenticator,*** will be decrypted by the web-site server ***W*** and sent back to the PoC server ***P***.

$\boxed{P \rightarrow T}$: The PoC server ***P*** forwards the ***authenticator*** to the terminal ***T***.

$\boxed{T \rightarrow U}$: The terminal ***T*** shows the ***authenticator*** to the user ***U*** as evidence that it has passed the authentication series.

In addition to the above descriptions, we will use some notations to explain how to construct our scheme in the remaining part of this section.

ID_X	: the identification of ***X***.
SK_X	: the secret key of ***X***.
PK_X	: the public key of ***X***.
K_U	: the pre-defined share key between ***U*** and ***W***.
K_T	: the randomly selected session key between ***T*** and ***W***.
$h()$	: a secure and public one-way hash function. [10, 11]
$E_{PK_X}()$	: using the public key PK_X to encrypt some message.
$D_{SK_X}()$	: using the secret key SK_X to decrypt some message.
t, t', t''	: the timestamps.
ξ	: a reasonable constant time interval.

Our scheme is divided into two cases by the different types of user trusted devices: one is the device with a smart card; the other is the memory card.

2.1 The Scenario for a Smart Card

Step 1: $\boxed{U \rightarrow D}$

U selects a $authenticator_i$ on ***D*** and requests ***D*** to connect to ***T***. (The $authenticator_i$ should be displayed if there is a built-in display on ***D***.)

Step 2: $\boxed{D \rightarrow T}$

D requests ***T*** to authenticate itself to ***P***. ***D*** then selects a nonce *N* and sends to ***T*** the ID_U , $h(K_U \oplus N) \oplus authenticator_i$, $E_{PK_W}(N)$ data.

Step 3: $\boxed{T \rightarrow P}$

T runs a mutual authentication protocol to ***P***. If it succeeds; they set up an authenticated channel. At the same time, using *t* as the timestamp, ***T*** also forwards the ID_T , $E_{PK_W}(K_T,t)$, ID_U , $h(K_U \oplus N) \oplus authenticator_i$, $E_{PK_W}(N)$ data to ***P*** during the authentication.

Step 4: $\boxed{P \rightarrow W}$

All of the above data are hashed and signed by ***P***'s secret key SK_P as the *stamp* $= E_{SK_P}(h(ID_T, E_{PK_W}(K_T,t), ID_U, h(K_U \oplus N) \oplus authenticator_i, E_{PK_W}(N)))$, and ***P*** forwards all of the data with the *stamp* to ***W***.

Step 5: $\boxed{W \rightarrow P}$

W verifies that the *stamp* was really signed by ***P*** using $h(ID_T, E_{PK_W}(K_T,t), ID_U, h(K_U \oplus N) \oplus authenticator_i, E_{PK_W}(N)) \stackrel{?}{=} D_{PK_P}(stamp)$. If this is verified, ***W*** decrypts the encrypted data $E_{PK_W}(K_T,t)$ to get the session key K_T and to check the timestamp, which should be within a reasonable range $(t'-t<\xi)$ ***W*** then decrypts the encrypted data $E_{PK_W}(N)$ to get the nonce N. Therefore, ***W*** can use the pre-defined share key K_U, the nonce N, the hash function *h*( ), and the exclusive-or function to compute the $authenticator_i$ i.e. $authenticator_i = h(K_U \oplus N) \oplus (h(K_U \oplus N) \oplus authenticator_i)$. Thereafter, ***W*** sends back to ***P*** the encrypted data $E_{PK_P}(ID_T, E_{k_T}(authenticator_i, t'))$.

Step 6: $\boxed{P \rightarrow T}$

P uses SK_P to decrypt the encrypted data $E_{PK_P}(ID_T, E_{k_T}(authenticator_i, t'))$, and forward $E_{k_T}(authenticator_i, t')$ to ***T***.

Step 7: $\boxed{T \rightarrow U}$

T uses the session key K_T to decrypt the received data $E_{k_T}(authenticator_i, t')$ and to check the timestamp, which should be within a reasonable range $(t''-t'<\xi)$. Consequently, ***T*** displays the $authenticator_i$ to ***U***. Only if the displayed $authenticator_i$ is the same as the one selected by ***U***, can ***U*** trust that ***T*** has finished all of the verification procedures.

2.2 The Scenario for a Memory Card

Step 1: $\boxed{U \rightarrow T}$

U requests ***T*** to authenticate itself to ***P***. ***U*** also enters the index *i* of his random selected $E_{PK_W}(authenticator_i)$ which is stored in the memory card.

Step 2: $\boxed{T \rightarrow D}$

T reads the encrypted $E_{PK_W}(authenticator_i)$ from ***D***.

Step 3: $\boxed{T \rightarrow P}$

T runs a mutual authentication protocol to ***P***. If it succeeds, they set up an authenticated channel. At the same time, using *t* as the timestamp, ***T*** also forwards the ID_T , $E_{PK_W}(K_T,t)$, ID_U , $E_{PK_W}(authenticator_i)$ data to ***P*** during the authentication.

Step 4: $P \rightarrow W$

All of the above data are hashed and signed by ***P***'s secret key SK_P as the ***stamp*** $= E_{SK_P}(h(ID_T, E_{PK_W}(K_T,t), ID_U, E_{PK_W}(authenticator_i)))$, and ***P*** forwards all of the data with the ***stamp*** to ***W***.

Step 5: $W \rightarrow P$

W verifies if the *stamp* was really signed by ***P*** using $h(ID_T, E_{PK_W}(K_T,t), ID_U, E_{PK_W}(authenticator_i)) \overset{?}{=} D_{PK_P}(stamp)$. If this is verified , ***W*** decrypts the encrypted data $E_{PK_W}(K_T,t)$ to get the session key K_T and to check the timestamp that should be within a reasonable range ($t' - t < \xi$). ***W*** then decrypts the encrypted data $E_{PK_W}(authenticator_i)$ to get the $authenticator_i$. Thereafter, ***W*** sends back to ***P*** the $E_{PK_P}(ID_T, E_{k_T}(authenticator_i, t'))$.

Step 6: $P \rightarrow T$

P uses SK_P to decrypt the encrypted data $E_{PK_P}(ID_T, E_{k_T}(authenticator_i, t'))$, and forward $E_{k_T}(authenticator_i, t')$ to ***T***.

Step 7: $T \rightarrow U$

T uses the session key K_T to decrypt the received data $E_{k_T}(authenticator_i, t')$ and to check the timestamp, which should be within a reasonable range ($t'' - t' < \xi$). Consequently, ***T*** displays the $authenticator_i$ to ***U***. Only if the displayed $authenticator_i$ is the same as the one selected by ***U***, can ***U*** trust that ***T*** has finished all of the verification procedures.

3 Discussions

In this section, we will examine our scheme against the **"fake terminal attack"** and the **"fake-in-the-middle-attack"**. The *fake terminal attack* involves an attacker setting up a fake terminal to fool users into trusting it. The *fake-terminal-in-the-middle attack* involves a fake terminal connected to a legal terminal to fool users into trusting it.

3.1 The Smart Card Model

We know that the trustworthiness of ***T*** depends on the correctness of the displayed *authenticator*. In our solution for the smart card, only the legal terminal ***T*** can get the correct *authenticator* from ***W*** through ***P*** (in step 5 and step 6) under the situation that ***P*** is authenticated by ***W*** (in step 5) and ***T*** is authenticated by ***P*** (in step 3).

To speak in detail, in step 5, ***W*** authenticates ***P*** by verifying its signature as $h(ID_T, E_{PK_W}(K_T,t), ID_U, h(K_U \oplus N) \oplus authenticator_i, E_{PK_W}(N)) \overset{?}{=} D_{PK_P}(\textbf{stamp})$ under the public key system infrastructure. Thereafter, ***P*** will be a trusted intermediary between ***W*** and ***T***. Of course, ***W*** will also trust ***T*** since any fake terminal cannot pass the authentication to ***P*** in step 3. Using these authenticated channels between ***W*** and ***T***, the encrypted data of ID_U, $h(K_U \oplus N) \oplus authenticator_i$, and $E_{PK_W}(N)$ which are generated by ***D*** can be securely transferred to ***W*** in step 3 and step 4. Only ***W*** can decrypt $h(K_U \oplus N) \oplus (h(K_U \oplus N) \oplus authenticator_i) = authenticator_i$ since: (1) the nonce N can be only decrypted by ***W*** using its secret key SK_W; (2) the shared key K_U is only known to ***W*** and ***U***. In step 5, ***W*** sends back to ***T*** the encrypted data $E_{k_T}(authenticator_i, t')$ through ***P***. Finally, in step 7, only ***T*** can decrypt it to get the $authenticator_i$ using its selected session key K_T and then show it to ***U***. Clearly, a fake terminal cannot acquire the decrypted $authenticator_i$ even it gets $h(K_U \oplus N) \oplus authenticator_i$ from the smart card, because it cannot pass the authentication series. In this way, any user can make insure that ***T*** is legal before any transaction. Consequently, our scheme can stand against the "*fake terminal attack*".

Moreover, in the "*fake-terminal-in-the-middle-attack*", is there any real probability for a fake terminal to be connected to a legal terminal tries to foil users in trusting it? In fact, the displayed *authenticator* shows only on the monitor of the legal terminal without any other output channel. Suppose the attacker cannot capture the magnetic radiation from the legal terminal or there is no place to hide a video camera in front of the legal terminal, then there is no way to clone the displayed *authenticator*. Clearly, the "*fake-terminal-in-the-middle-attack*" will not occur if the hardware and software of the legal terminal are invulnerable.

3.2 The Memory Card Model

Similarly, in our solution for the memory card, only the legal terminal ***T*** can get the correct *authenticator* from ***W*** through ***P*** (in step 5 and step 6) under the situation when ***P*** is authenticated by ***W*** (in step 5) and ***T*** is authenticated by ***P*** (in step 3). In detail, ***W*** authenticates ***P*** in step 5 by verifying its signature as $h(ID_T, E_{PK_W}(K_T,t), ID_U, E_{PK_W}(authenticator_i)) \overset{?}{=} D_{PK_P}(stamp)$ under the public key system infrastructure. Thereafter, ***P*** will be a trusted intermediary between ***W*** and ***T***. Of course, ***W*** will also trust ***T*** since any fake terminal cannot pass the authentication to ***P*** in step 3. Using these authenticated channels between ***W*** and ***T***, the encrypted data of $E_{PK_W}(authenticator_i)$ which is stored in the memory card can be securely transferred to ***W*** in step 3 and step 4. Only ***W*** can decrypt it to get the $authenticator_i$ using its secret key SK_W. In step 5, ***W*** then sends back to ***T*** the encrypted data $E_{k_T}(authenticator_i, t')$ through ***P***. Finally, in step 7, only ***T*** can decrypt it to get the $authenticator_i$ using its selected session key K_T and then show it to U. Clearly, a fake terminal cannot acquire the decrypted $authenticator_i$ even it gets $E_{PK_W}(authenticator_i)$ from the memory card, because it cannot pass the authentication series. In this way, our scheme against the "*fake terminal attack*" and the "*fake-terminal-in-the-middle-attack*".

4 Conclusions

In this paper, a secure authentication models that guard against the fake terminal and fake-terminal-in-the-middle attacks for the public computer kiosk (public terminal) support service architecture. In our scheme, unverified terminals will not be the problematic terminals will be detected, and can not serve for secure Internet service because all users will authenticate the secure authenticated channel between the terminals and the server that has already been set up before performing any transactions. We believe that our work in this area will help bring more commerce applications to the public terminal support service architecture. For example, Smith and Pedersen [13] organized such electronic services into security taxonomies: K_0 (standalone), K_1 (networked), K_2 (private information), K_3 (transactional). According to these taxonomies, there are more security topics for further research such as:

1. How to provide private, remote information such as a user's query about current credit limits etc. via a networked kiosk system?
2. How to allow clients to change private, remote information such as electronic transaction via a networked kiosk system?

In the future, people will be accustomed to accessing various transactions through public terminals conveniently. Research on security problems should therefore receive more attention.

Acknowledgements. This research was supported by National Science Council, Taiwan, R.O.C., under contract number NSC94-2213-E-005-023.

References

1. Asokan, N., Debar, H., Steiner, M., Waidner, M.: Authenticating public terminates. Computer Networks 31, 861–970 (1999)
2. Bird, R., Gopal, I., Herzberg, A., Janson, P., Kutten, S., Molva, R., Yung, M.: Systematic design of a family of attack resistant authentications. IEEE Journal on Selected Areas in Communications 11(5), 679–693 (1993)
3. Burris, M.W., Pietrzyk, M.C.: Interactive Transportation Information Stations, Center for Urban Transportation Research, College of Engineering, University of South Florida (1997), http://citeseer.nj.nec.com/278953.html
4. Cheng, C.Y., Seman, K., Yunus, J.: Authentication public terminals with smart cards. In: Proc. TENCON 2000 pp. I-527-I-529 (2000)
5. Frier, A.O., Kariton, P., Kocher, P.C.: The SSL Protocol: Version 3.0, Technical Report, Internet Draft (1996)

6. Hochnerg, J., Smith, S.W., Murphy, M., Pedersen, P., Yantis, B.: Kiosk Security Handbook. Los Alamos Unclassified Release LA-UR-95-1657, Los Alamos National Laboratory (1995)
7. Jan, J.-K., Chen, Y.-Y., Chen, C.-L.: A Realistic Secure Anonymous E-Voting Protocol Based on the ElGamal Scheme. In: Proceedings of the International Conference on Communications & Broadband Networking, Bangalore, INDIA, Sect III 1-9 (2003)
8. Kohl, J.T., Neuman, B.C.: The Kerberos Network Authentication Service (V5), Internet Request for Comment RFC 1510 (1993)
9. Laufmann, S.C.: Toward Agent-Based Software Engineering for Information-Dependent Enterprise Applications. In: IEE Proceedings of Software Engineering (1997), http://citeseer.ist.psu.edu/laufmann96toward.html
10. NIST FIP PUB 180, Secure hash standard, National Institute of Standards and Technology, US department of Commerce, DRAFT (1993)
11. Rivest, R.L.: The MD5 message –digest algorithm, RFC 1231, Internet Activities Board, Internet Privacy Task Force (1992)
12. Ross, S., Hill, J., Mike, Y.C., Joseph, A.D., Culler, D.E., Brewer, E.A.: A Security Architecture for the Post-PC World, http://citeseer.ist.psu.edu/302477.html
13. Smith, S.: IBM Research Paul Pedersen, Los Alamos National Laborator, Organizing Electronic Services into Security Taxonomies. In: Proc. of the Second USENIX workshop on Electronic Commerce (1996), http://citeseer.ist.psu.edu/338966.html
14. Chen, Y.-Y., Jan, J.-K., Chen, C.-L.: The Design of a Securely Anonymous Internet Voting System. Computers & Security 23(4), 330–337 (2004)

Development and Evaluation of New User Interface for Security Scanner with Usability in Human Interface Study

Michitaka Yoshimoto, Takashi Katoh, Bhed Bahadur Bista, and Toyoo Takata

Iwate Prefectural University,
152-52 Takizawa-aza-sugo, Takizawa Iwate, Japan
g236d011@edu.soft.iwate-pu.ac.jp

Abstract. In this paper, we propose methodology for improving usability of security tools based on human interface study. Today, users in general cannot use or operate presently available security tools effectively because they lack interface with high usability making them difficult to use or operate. However, if the security tools are effectively used, it is possible to find potential vulnerability information of a client computer. Therefore, we consider security scanners, and develop an interface for them with high usability based on human interface study, so that even general users can use them to find and fix vulnerability of their computers. We perform usability evaluation based on human interface study to the interface we have developed and we show that high usability has been realized from an objective viewpoint.

Keywords: Usability, Security Scanner, Human Interface Study.

1 Introduction

Today, Internet users with constant connection are increasing explosively [1], and the hosts are becoming diverse. On the other hand, the number of illegal accesses are also increasing, and becoming tricky and wicked, and targets can be anybody, from an individual user to large corporations [2]. Recently, most users are connected to Internet by high-speed line with constant connection directly or via internal networks, but it is not always true that the users have sufficient knowledge of security.

As for the basis of our claim, in [3], corporate users which reply “We believe that we have taken sufficient security measures for organized cyber crime” are only 15 percents. It indicates how diffident even corporate users are about security. It is reasonable to suppose that individual user’s percentage is lower than that of corporate users. However, if the networks are not secure, users must protect their own computers, even though they do not have sufficient knowledge of security.

Additionally, about 50% users do not understand meaning of “vulnerability” at all [4]. Even if we provide them with presently available technology and information about security, almost all users cannot implement security measures properly.

Furnell, et al. in [5] have reported usability test on operation and configuration of security features for Microsoft Windows XP and three applications with 340 subjects.

T. Enokido, L. Barolli, and M. Takizawa (Eds.): NBiS 2007, LNCS 4658, pp. 127–136, 2007.

They have reported that almost all subjects have found it considerably difficult to operate and configure the security features for them.

To resolve the above mentioned problems that the users cannot use or operate security tools and implement security measures without sufficient knowledge of security, we investigate methodology of how to improve usability of currently available security tools for general users so that they can use or operate the security tools easily. To attain the goals, as a working example, we consider security scanners that can find vulnerability in end-user's client machine easily and develop a security scanner with enormous improvement in usability.

Almost all security tools are developed without considering users' ability to operate them, and thus users cannot use these tools exhaustively. The security scanner we developed is in accordance with User Centered Design (UCD) which was proposed by IBM in [6]. In UCD, software is designed from user's viewpoint, and frameworks of developing processes are followings:

1. Determining user's *availability*
2. Determining user's *needs* from availability
3. Making *solution* for fulfilling user's needs
4. *Evaluating* solution
5. Feeding back result of the evaluation, and *improving* the solution
6. *Alternating* between evaluation and improvement

We develop our security scanner by conducting usability evaluation based on human interface study, and finally compare it with the presently available security scanners. We demonstrate methodology for improvement of usability based on human interface study.

First, in order to grasp the problems related to usability that exist in presently available security scanners, we perform formative and summative evaluation on them. Based on the problems that we find, we propose and develop a user interface for a security scanner and conduct formative evaluation as we develop it. Finally we conduct summative evaluation on it to show the enormous improvement of usability of the security scanner from an objective viewpoint.

The paper is organized as follows. Section 2 shows process of formative evaluation and summative evaluation of presently available security scanners. Section 3 describes points for improvement of the user interface in response to the results of the evaluation. Section 4 describes the formative evaluation and summative evaluation of the proposed user interface, and also presents the evaluation results.

2 Formative Evaluation and Summative Evaluation of Existing Security Scanners

In this section, we conduct formative evaluation for receiving feedback in intermediate step of development, and conduct summative evaluation for numerical results to evaluate whether presently available security scanners fulfill user's requirements or not.

2.1 Context Interview

First, in order to grasp user's requirements, we conduct context interview to six subjects using context inquiry. Holzblatt, et al, developed a context inquiry in [7], and by using this interview, an interviewer can hear in-depth opinions of subjects compared to using traditional interview method because the subject is motivated to "teach" anything to the interviewer. In context interview, the questions are decided as the context interview progresses.

As an example of result of the interview, all subjects have their own computer; however they have not updated their operating systems or applications. They have not implemented security measures actively also, because they do not have sufficient knowledge of security and are afraid of their computer becoming unstable or inoperable.

From the interview, we could grasp how they use their computers and what their needs and requirements are.

2.2 Formative Evaluation

Next, we conduct usability evaluation for grasping user's ability to use presently available security scanners. For the evaluation, we adopted *think aloud method* that has been developed by Lewis, et al, in [8] as formative evaluation. In think aloud method, subjects say what they feel or think while they are operating the object in evaluation, and thus we can grasp the difficulties they encounter at any point of the evaluation process. We closely watch, record, and analyze every word and action of subjects, for example, what they display, their direction of eyes, and motion of hands and the mouse.

Table 1 shows experimental circumstances and tasks of formative evaluation. We adopt Nessus [9] as the security scanner because it is considered the best one among freely available security scanners. We adopt NessusWX, which is Windows client software for Nessus, as a user interface for the evaluation object. We installed Microsoft Windows 2000 with Service Pack 4 in the newly formatted Hard Disk of the experimental computer and connected Nessus server which found 12 vulnerabilities as of 14-19 November 2006.

Nielsen has proposed and given reasons in [10] that five subjects are enough for formative evaluation of an object. In our case, the number of subjects is six. In our formative evaluation, the supervisor of the examination gives an instruction on start and goal of the experiment, and gives minimum and necessary information to subjects. In the examination, we attach importance to three elements of usability

Table 1. Experimental circumstances and tasks of formative evaluation

Client OS	Microsoft Windows2000 Service Pack 4		
Security Scanner	Nessus	Interface	NessusWX
Number of vulnerabilities	12	Number of subjects	6
Task 1	Subjects check vulnerabilities in the client by NessusWX		
Task 2	Subjects fix a vulnerability by patch or Microsoft Update etc.		
Task 3	Subjects fix all vulnerabilities, and confirm no vulnerability in the client by NessusWX.		

explained in ISO 9241-11:1998 [11]. If there is any problem in any of the three elements, the system is considered to be "not usable". The elements are as follows:

1. Accuracy and completeness with which users achieve specified goals (effectiveness)
2. Resources expended in relation to the accuracy and completeness with which users achieve goals (efficiency)
3. Freedom from discomfort, and positive attitudes towards the use of the product (satisfaction)

In task 1, su bjects ran NessusWX, and connected it to server running Nessus daemon. However NessusWX gave a few and hardly understandable messages, icons, and menus and all subjects were confused. Then, they searched Web sites on how to operate NessusWX because they could not understand what they have to do in the next operation. In case of inputting client computer's IP address, five subjects could not grasp the IP address of their clients, and three subjects inputted wrong IP address.

In task 2, all the subjects could not understand computer terminology even if the results were displayed in their native language. They wasted time in understanding solutions of the vulnerabilities because the displayed results were huge and presented flatly in columns. In this case, almost all solutions of the vulnerabilities were pointed to Microsoft's Web site and patches. However, the site is hardly understandable also for all subjects because they do not have sufficient knowledge of security. They could not understand the information presented on the Web sites sufficiently to download suitable patches from the sites or by other means.

In task 3, the supervisor suggested taking a different approach for the subjects who applied patched in task 2, because in this case it takes a long time to fix 12 vulnerabilities. For example, if we use Microsoft Update, we can patch and update the system easily and smoothly and also exclude the updates or patches which user does not want. However, the information about Microsoft Update was written in hardly understandable place on the page and was not written sufficiently. Therefore even if subjects could read it out, they could not understand the benefit of Microsoft Update, and all subjects took a long time to bring it in use. Besides, Microsoft Update needs to be re-run again and again if all the updates and patches not completed in first run. However, there were no descriptions about it on the page of Microsoft Update. All subjects rescanned computer before fixing all vulnerabilities because they believed that they have patched completely. In this case, the supervisor could notice the situation that the subjects have not reached the goal. There is a possibility that the users run Microsoft Update only once and leave the system in critical condition without completely updating or patching it.

As it can be observed from the above experiment, NessusWX has critical problems not only on its operation, but also on presenting the solutions, which give only a Microsoft site that provides hardly understandable information for users. We concluded that NessusWX is not usable for all users.

2.3 Summative Evaluation

Next, we conduct performance measurement as summative evaluation. Effectiveness can be shown by achievement rate of a task. The evaluation was given 1-3 points with

Table 2. Result of Performance measurement on NessusWX (effectiveness)

	A	B	C	D	E	F
Task 1	2	2	2	2	2	1
Task 2	2	2	2	2	3	2
Task 3	2	2	2	2	2	2

3 being the highest point. If a subject pulls oneself up by his/her bootstraps smoothly she/he is marked 3, if not she/he is marked 2. If a subject cannot complete a task she/he is marked 1. Table 2 shows result of effectiveness.

All subjects could not perform almost all tasks smoothly. In task 1, three subjects inputted wrong IP address. This shows that users may wrongly judge their competence and leave the system in critical situation.

Efficiency can be measured by task performance time. We recorded which task subject dawdled away. Table 3 shows result of efficiency (counted in minutes). We did not count time for necessary operations such as scanning, downloading, installing, and rebooting, but counted time for unnecessary operation, e.g. scanning before patches are completely applied, scanning untargeted client by putting wrong IP address and so on.

Table 3. Result of Performance measurement on NessusWX (efficiency)

	A	B	C	D	E	F
Task 1	12	22	19	36	20	40
Task 2	18	6	19	17	3	25
Task 3	14	9	5	13	17	9
Total time	44	37	43	66	40	74

All subjects dawdled away in task 1, and they could not use or operate it exhaustively.

Satisfaction can be measured by subjective evaluation. We conduct satisfaction by following *web usability evaluation scale* (WUS) [12] developed by IID, Inc. and FUJITSU LIMITED. WUS has 21 questions, and we evaluate usability of Web sites by seven evaluating factors which are generated from the 21 questions. The WUS's seven evaluating factors are "easily understandable operation", "easily understandable structure", "easily viewable", "easily respondable", "likeability", "authenticity", and "serviceability", respectively. WUS is usually used on Web site and the satisfaction was evaluated by the results that were displayed by NessusWX (the result can be

Table 4. Result of performance measurement (satisfaction)

	A	B	C	D	E	F
Average of satisfaction	1.95	2.71	1.80	2.90	2.76	2.95

viewed on Web site), and Microsoft Web site that was pointed by NessusWX as solutions. Subjects were marked 1-5 points with 5 being the highest point. Table 4 shows result of satisfaction.

In the satisfaction evaluation, all subjects gave low points, because essential information was lacked and unnecessary information was flooded which caused confusion among the subjects. Especially, all subjects had dissatisfaction saying that "there are many understandable words", which lessen serviceability.

Based on the above experimental observation, we develop a security scanner that resolves detected problems from the evaluation.

3 Improvement of Interface of Proposed Security Scanner

We have already proposed and developed a user interfaces for security scanner in [13], [14], and [15]. In this section, we solve the detected problems of the proposed security scanner with heuristic evaluation.

3.1 10 heuristics

In [16], Nielsen analyzed many problems of usability, and as a result categorized the fundamental principle of usability underlying the problems called 10 heuristics. Table 5 shows the 10 heuristics.

Table 5. 10 heuristics

1	Visibility of system status	6	Recognition rather than recall
2	Match between system and the real world	7	Flexibility and efficiency of use
3	User control and freedom	8	Aesthetic and minimalist design
4	Consistency and standards	9	Help users recognize, diagnose, and recover from errors
5	Error prevention	10	Help and documentation

Based on the 10 heuristics, we improve solutions for problems of our proposed and developed user interface of security scanner with heuristic evaluation on usability inspection which is discussed by Nielsen in [17]. We conduct heuristic evaluation with three subjects four times.

3.2 XML Vulnerability Database

We develop XML vulnerability database to implement user's requirements. By conducting think aloud protocol on formative evaluation mentioned in Section 2.1, if we gave detailed information to a general user without sufficient knowledge, the user not only could not understand the contents but also was confused. The user could not read out necessary information. We proposed that the system gives "vulnerability name", "reference URL", "solution", and "postscript" for the user from XML database. Postscript is additional information to provide flexibility by the administrator of the system mainly to provide a postscript for the insufficient information. As an example, in case of vulnerability such as MS06-040 [18], we recommend Microsoft Update and display minimum and necessary usage of the update.

For expert users with sufficient knowledge of security, they might want other vender's information. The proposed system collects information provided by venders, which are referred in CVE [19], JVN [20], analyzes it, transforms it to XML which is then stored in the XML database. Thereby, we have also realized that expert users can obtain necessary information for detected vulnerabilities.

3.3 Solutions We Improved

Table 6 shows a part of critical problems and their solutions of the interface of the security scanner we are proposing to develop. Other than above, we detected other 20 problems and solved them also.

Table 6. A part of critical problems and solutions on proposed security scanner

Problems	Solutions we improved
There ware unfamiliar words in vulnerability information.	We replace it understandable words in postscript. (2, 7, 8 in 10 heuristics)
Risk of vulnerability was hardly understandable on the view	We add easy to understand icon about "Security hole" or "warning" (6)
The system might require over the remaining time.	The system display load average by numerical value and graph, and if load average is high, it display requiring time. (2)

3.4 Structure of Improved User Interface of Proposed Security Scanner

We adopt Nessus as the core of our proposed scanner and develop only the interface for the scanner because creating scan scripts, performing operation checks and maintenance entail huge costs. Besides, developing another scanner will be reinvention of the wheel, which should be avoided in open source community. The user interface communicates with Nessus directly. Therefore, the proposed security scanner makes sure that the reliability is maintained by executing the same instructions as Nessus.

We realized Web based security scanner and the interface that communicate with each other through CGI. We adopted Adobe Flash for developing user interface as it allows us to develop graphic interface with flexibility. Adobe Flash runs on almost all Internet clients. Moreover, almost all the clients are provided with Adobe Flash already installed. Even if a client does not have it, Adobe Flash can be installed easily. Thus, our improved scanner does not depend on operating systems. Moreover, the improved scanner can be operated by a mouse click only, and has a mechanism which cannot be operated beyond user's competence.

As an example, if a user cannot understand a text, the user interface displays detail explanation of the text if the mouse cursor is rolled on the text. Moreover, the user interface displays the progress of scanning dynamically.

To satisfy "Flexibility and efficiency of use" in 10 heuristics, the system needs to supply a demand for requirement of minimum and necessary information for general users without sufficient knowledge of security, and advanced information for expert users with sufficient knowledge of security dynamically. Our improved scanner provides minimum and necessary interface in default configuration. If a user needs more function, the system provides optional interface for configuration of functions.

4 Formative Evaluation and Summative Evaluation of Improved User Interface of the Proposed Security Scanner

We conduct usability evaluation of our improved user interface of the proposed security scanner.

4.1 Formative Evaluation of Improved Interface

We conduct formative evaluation, which is mentioned in Section 2.2, of the improved interface. Experimental description is the same as Table 3 except that the object of the evaluation is our improved scanner. The number of subjects is five in this evaluation as [7] states that five is sufficient for the number of subjects.

In task 1, first, connecting to the server is completed by only inputting URL on a Web browser. Next, the improved interface displays cautionary statement for subjects so that they do not operate the scanner beyond their competence. All subjects operate the task 1 smoothly because it was possible to operate it with several clicks just by reading the information (balloon help in the interface) that was provided.

In task 2, all subjects could grasp solutions swiftly as the improved interface has cut out all unnecessary description, and displays minimum and necessary information clearly. All subjects use Microsoft Update that was pointed by the postscript.

In task 3, almost all the subjects did not rescan the client before completely installing the patches, because the subjects were provided with message to perform Microsoft Update multiple times until the special message was stopped displaying in Postscript.

4.2 Summative Evaluation of Improved Interface

We conduct performance measurement as summative evaluation of the system as mentioned in Section 2.3. Table 7 shows results of effectiveness of improved interface. Method of evaluation is the same as that of Table 3.

Table 7. Result of Performance measurement on improved interface (effectiveness)

	A	B	C	D	E
Task 1	3	3	3	3	3
Task 2	3	3	3	3	3
Task 3	2	3	3	2	3

Table 8. Result of Performance measurement on improved interface (efficiency)

	A	B	C	D	E
Task 1	2	2	2	2	3
Task 2	3	3	2	2	2
Task 3	7	1	5	6	2
Total time	12	6	9	10	7

Almost all the subjects could operate all tasks smoothly.

Table 8 shows results of efficiency on improved interface (counted by minutes). Method of evaluation is the same as that of Table 4.

All subjects could reduce the time she/he took to perform all tasks compared to that of NessusWX. Especially, in task 1, all subjects could reduce the task performance time greatly. Therefore it is clear that subjects can perform a task effectively. Moreover, we can understand that subjects can perform tasks smoothly when they are provided with minimum and necessary operation results.

Table 9 shows result of satisfaction on improved interface. Method of evaluation is the same as that of Table 5.

Table 9. Result of Performance measurement on improved interface (satisfaction)

	A	B	C	D	E
Average of satisfaction	3.47	3.81	3.86	3.71	4.33

All subjects' average satisfaction marks are higher than those of NessusWX.

5 Conclusion

In this paper, we considered security scanners and showed by developing the user interface and XML database that, currently available security tools can be easily and exhaustively used by even general users. We showed high usability has been realized from an objective viewpoint by formative evaluation and summative evaluation. Thereby we concluded that the enhancement of usability based on human interface study has been achieved.

Our future work is to accomplish the methodology of enhancement of usability by importing the knowledge of human interface study.

References

1. comScore Networks, Inc. 694 Million People Currently Use the Internet Worldwide According to comScore Networks 2007/2/13, http://www.comscore.com/press/release.asp?id=849
2. Information-technology Promotion Agency (IPA) Japan, Status Report on Notification of Vulnerability (in Japanese) 2007/2/26, http://www.ipa.go.jp/security/vuln/report/press.html

3. ITmedia: Corporate Users Have Little Confidence in Security of Their System (in Japanese) 2007/2/27, http://www.atmarkit.co.jp/news/200605/02/ibm.html
4. Information-technology Promotion Agency (IPA) Japan, Attitude Survey Toward Threat on Information Security (in Japanese) 2007/2/27, http://www.ipa.go.jp/
5. Furnell, S.M., et al.: The Challenges of Understanding and Using Security: A Survey of End-users. Computers & Securities 25, 27–35 (2006)
6. IBM User Experience Design Center, User Centered Design http://www-6.ibm.com/jp/design/eou/2center/index.html
7. Holzblatt, K., et al.: Contextual Design. Morgan Kaufmann Pub., San Francisco (1999)
8. Lewis, C., et al.: Task-Centered User Interface Design 2007/02/27 http://hcibib.org/tcuid/
9. Nessus: The Nessus Project 2007/2/27, http://www.nessus.org/
10. Nielsen, J.: Sability Testing With 5 Users (Jakob Nielsen's Alertbox) 2007/2/27, http://www.useit.com/alertbox/20000319.html
11. ISO 9241-11:1998: ISO - International Organization for Standardization 2007/1/30, http://www.iso.org/iso/en/CatalogueDetailPage.CatalogueDetail?CSNUMBER=16883&ICS1=13&ICS2=180&ICS3=
12. Nakagawa, K., et al.: The Development of Questionnaire for Evaluating Web Usability. In: Proceedings of the Human Interface Symposium 2001 (2001)
13. Yoshimoto, M., et al.: Development of Security Scanner with High Usability. In: Proc. AINA2004, vol. 1, pp. 139–144 (2004)
14. Yoshimoto, M., et al.: Development of Security Scanner with High Portability and Usability. In: Proc. AINA2005, vol. 2, pp. 407–410 (2005)
15. Yoshimoto, M., et al.: Enhancement of Usability by Adding New Interface to Existing Security Products-For the Case of Security Scanner. In: CSS2006, pp. 67–72 (November 2006)
16. Nielsen, J.: Heuristics for User Interface Design 2007/2/27, http://www.useit.com/papers/heuristic/heuristic_list.html
17. Nielsen, J., et al.: Usability Inspection Method. John Wiley and Sons, Chichester (1994)
18. Microsoft Corporation: Microsoft Security Bulletin MS06-040: Vulnerability in Server Service Could Allow Remote Code Execution (921883) 2007/02/27, http://www.microsoft.com/technet/security/bulletin/MS06-040.mspx
19. The MITRE Corporation: CVE - Common Vulnerabilities and Exposures 2007/2/27, http://cve.mitre.org/
20. JVN, JP Vendor Status Notes 2007/2/27, http://jvn.jp/
21. Nielsen, J.: Usability Engineering. Morgan Kaufmann Pub., San Francisco (1994)
22. Tarumoto, T.: Usability Engineering, Ohmsha (October 2005) (in Japanese)

A Key Predistribution Scheme for Wireless Sensor Networks Using the Small-World Concept*

Yung-Tsung Hou, Chia-Mei Chen, and Bingchiang Jeng

Department of Information Management,
National Sun Yat-Sen University, Kaohsiung, Taiwan
{ythou,cmchen,jeng}@mis.nsysu.edu.tw

Abstract. Most of wireless sensor networks (WSNs) are deployed in an environment where communication between sensors may be monitored. For applications which require higher security, it is therefore necessary to employ some cryptographic scheme in the network. However, key management in WSNs is a challenging task due to the constrained resources. In this paper, based on the concept of small worlds, we present a group-based key predistribution scheme which enables any pair of sensors to establish a unique shared key. The key path establishment uses only local information with logarithmic memory overhead to the number of groups. Other performance, including communication and computing overhead, are evaluated also. The results show that the proposed key management method performs better than other known methods.

Keywords: Key predistribution, Small worlds, Wireless sensor networks.

1 Introduction

Wireless sensor networks (WSNs) are composed of small and inexpensive sensors with limited resources in battery power, memory, computation, and communication. Recent advances in computing and communication technologies have created a variety of such applications [12] including habitat monitoring, remote climate monitoring, and other commercial and military applications. In some applications like battlefield sensing or critical infrastructure protection, sensor nodes are deployed in a hostile environment under numerous threats including information eavesdropping, sensor compromising, sensor impersonating, and even denial-of-service attacks. Secure transmission therefore becomes an important issue in WSNs.

Key management in WSNs is not trivial. The approaches used for general computer networks are not applicable for WSNs due to resource limitations in sensors. Thus, symmetric cryptography which shares a key between two parties is considered, and several schemes for pair-wise shared key establishment are developed. Among them, the key predistribution scheme which distributes key information to sensors before the

* This work was supported in part by TWISC@NCKU, National Science Council under the Grants NSC 94-3114-P-006-001-Y and NSC 95-2221-E-110-083.

T. Enokido, L. Barolli, and M. Takizawa (Eds.): NBiS 2007, LNCS 4658, pp. 137–146, 2007.

deployment is viewed as an efficient approach to set up shared secret keys. An example is the full pair-wise approach in which each sensor node is preloaded with a set of unique keys and each of them is shared with another node in the network. Under such a scheme, a node will need to carry $n - 1$ secret keys for a network of n nodes. Hence, its memory overhead makes this scheme impractical as n goes larger.

Random key predistribution schemes [1, 2] were proposed as a remedy for the above situation. The basic idea is to preload each sensor node with a random subset of keys from a large key pool before deployment. Since the keys in different nodes are from the same pool, any two neighboring nodes will have a certain probability to share a common key and they could use it for communication. If such a key does not exist, they will instead establish a key path using intermediary nodes, and then use it to exchange a key to establish a direct link.

In this paper, we propose a group-based random key predistribution scheme for WSNs. Our scheme is based on the concept of small worlds [5, 8, 9]. A small-world network has the following properties: (1) the local neighborhood is preserved; and (2) the diameter of the network increases logarithmically with the number of nodes in the network. The network created by the proposed scheme will have pre-built secure links that satisfies the criterion of small worlds -- any two nodes in the network can be connected with just a few secure links. In the initial key preloading stage, each node is loaded with a set of keys shared with other nodes in the same group and additional keys shared with the nodes in distant groups based on a probability distribution. With the preloaded shared keys, any two nodes will be able to find efficiently a secure path connecting them in an average path length logarithmic to the number of sensor groups. This path length is shorter than others found in literature. A simulation later will demonstrate the performance.

1.1 Related Work

Eschenauer and Gligor [1] first proposed a random key predistribution scheme for key management in WSNs. The basic idea of their scheme is as described in the previous section. Several studies [2-4] later proposed new predistribution schemes. Their methods utilize the high connectivity property of a random graph when the average degree of its nodes exceeds a threshold. The performance of these schemes depends on the network's topology, which might degrade rapidly if the nodes are sparsely or non-uniformly distributed in the network.

PIKE [11] is a deterministic scheme for key predistribution. In the method, any pair of nodes in the network exists an intermediary node that has shared keys with each node. This intermediary node is used as a trusted peer to establish a key path. PIKE shows significantly improvement over random key predistribution schemes. However, PIKE might require network-wide communication to establish the key path. Its communication overhead makes it unsuitable for large sensor networks.

The small-world concept was first studied by Milgram [5-7] in the 1960's. His experiments in mail delivery using acquaintances resulted in an average of "six degrees of separation". After that, several network models have been proposed to study the phenomenon. Watts and Strogatz [8] proposed a refined network model and showed that the small world phenomenon is pervasive in a wide range of networks.

Based on statistical properties, small-world networks could be classified into three classes [9]: (a) scale-free networks: the connectivity distribution follows the power law; (b) broad-scale networks: the connectivity distribution has a power law regime followed by a sharp cutoff; and (c) single-scale networks: the distribution has a fast decaying tail. Since scale-free networks are not suitable for WSNs, our method will try to build a single-scale network with preloaded secure links.

In small-world networks, how to find a path connecting a pair of nodes is a critical searching problem. Kleinberg [10] solved it by defining a generalized network model that has an efficient decentralized algorithm capable of finding short paths with a high probability. Based on the characteristics of WSNs, our method will use and refine Kleinberg's model as a framework for key management in WSNs.

2 The Proposed Scheme

We assume that n sensors are deployed in a two-dimensional square field, which is partitioned into $m \times m$ square cells, and sensors located in a same cell belong to a same group. Let $G_{i,j}$, where $i = 1, \ldots, m$ and $j = 1, \ldots, m$, denote the sensor group deployed at the cell in row i and column j of the sensor field. The distribution of sensor locations in a cell depends on the sensor deploying method. Our scheme suits with different deploying methods, but for explaining simplicity, we assume that sensors could be deployed into the assigned cell in a precise way by robots. We assume that the probability of a sensor being deployed outside its cell is very small. Thus, the location of a sensor could be estimated from its group location and a variation of geographical routing method could be used as the underlying routing method. In the later section, we will discuss the situation in which the sensor groups are distributed randomly.

The distance between two groups is defined as the minimal number of other groups fall in between the two groups, and is calculated below:

$$Distance\ (G_{i1,j1}, G_{i2,j2}) = max\ (\ |i_1 - i_2|, |j_1 - j_2|\ ) \tag{1}$$

Each sensor node is identified by a unique sensor ID from 1 to n. Without loss of generality, we assume that the sensors in group $G_{i,j}$ have the sensor ID from $(i-1) \times (n/m) + (j-1) \times n/(m \times m) + 1$ to $(i-1) \times (n/m) + (j-1) \times n/(m \times m) + n/(m \times m)$. Therefore, the group of a sensor could be inferred according to its sensor ID.

2.1 The Proposed Key Predistribution

For intra-group sensors, each pair of them is preloaded with a unique shared key, and is treated as a trusted peer node to each other. This arrangement has memory overhead linear to the group size, and is acceptable if the group is kept small. For example, if a group is of size 50 and the key length is 64 bits, each sensor requires only 8*49 = 392 bytes to store the intra-group keys.

Additionally, each sensor needs to possess a few long-range shared keys with nodes in distant groups. These long-range shared keys have to be distributed nearly uniformly over all distance scales as shown in Fig. 1. Given a sensor node s in group $G_{i,j}$, for each non-diagonal neighboring group (at most 4 such groups), a shared key is established with a sensor node randomly chosen from that group. The rest of groups are partitioned into sets A_0, A_1, …,$A_{\log m}$, where A_k consists of the groups whose distance to $G_{i,j}$ is between 2^k to 2^{k+1}. Therefore, all groups in A_k are at approximately the same distance to group $G_{i,j}$. Within each set A_k, a group is selected arbitrarily and a shared key is generated for *s* and a node randomly chosen from the group. In total, each sensor node stores at most 4 + 2 *log m* additional keys for inter-group secure links and the memory for storing keys is logarithmic to the number of groups.

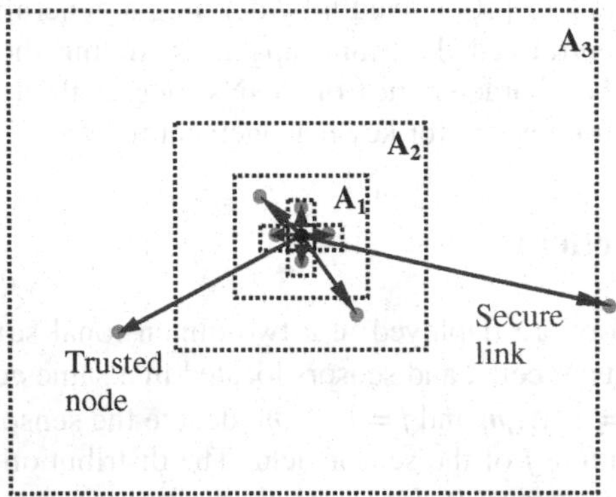

Fig. 1. A sensor node and its secure links to distant trusted peer nodes

2.2 Key Path Establishment

After the key predistribution stage, a key path establishment process is needed to build a secure link between any pair of sensors. So, we present two strategies in this section using only local information for key path establishment. Strategy 1 uses a sensor node's own information to set up a path, while strategy 2 uses not only the local information but also the information from its neighbors for path establishment.

2.2.1 Key Path Establishment by Strategy 1

Suppose a sensor node receives a key establishment requirement from another node which contains the destination sensor ID. It reads the content of the message after decrypting it. The node now needs to decide which sensor node is the next target to forward to, and processes it with a localized mechanism described as follows.

```
KEY ESTABLISHMENT STRATEGY 1
1.  Determine the group which the destination sensor
    belongs to from the destination sensor ID.
2.  S_next ← NULL
3.  if (the destination sensor is in the same group)
4.       S_next ← the destination sensor
5.  else
6.       S_next ← the trusted node that is nearest to the
         destination in the sense of group distance.
7.  Encrypt and delivery the message to the selected
    node, S_next, using the corresponding shared key.
```

2.2.2 Key Path Establishment by Strategy 2

Strategy 2 is motivated by real world experiences. When we look for something, we can search it ourselves or ask friends for help. This is what strategy 2 does, which uses its own and the neighbors' information for key path establishment. We define that a sensor is in phase j if the group distance between the sensor's group and the destination's group is greater than 2^j and no more to 2^{j+1}. When such a sensor receives a request for key path establishment, it will check its own information first. If it finds a trusted peer node that belongs to a phase less than j, it forwards the message to that peer. Otherwise, it broadcasts a message to its intra-group neighbors to acquire their nearest trusted peers, and choose the best one from the responses to forward to.

```
KEY ESTABLISHMENT STRATEGY 2
1.  Determine the group which the destination sensor
    belongs to from the destination sensor ID.
2.  j ← the phase number
3.  S_next ← NULL
4.  if (the destination sensor is in the same group)
5.  {    S_next ← the destination sensor        }
6.  else
7.  {   S_next ← the trusted node that is nearest to the
        destination.
8.      if (S_next can not enter the phase less than j)
9.      {   Send messages to its intra-group neighbors
            querying about their nearest trusted nodes
            to the destination.
10.         S_t ← the neighbor who has minimal result.
11.         S_r ← the nearest trusted peer node of S_t
12.         if (S_r can enter the phase less than j)
13.             S_next ← S_t
14.     }
15. }
16. Encrypt and deliver the message to S_next using the
    corresponding shared key.
```

3 Performance Metrics and Analysis

3.1 Memory Overhead

We estimate the number of keys that each node needs to preload for the key establishment scheme. This measure does not count the temporary storage that is needed during the execution of the scheme.

Suppose that a group has l sensors and there are m^2 groups in the network. Each sensor has shared keys with all other sensors in the same group. Hence a sensor needs to store $(l - 1)$ intra-group keys. For inter-group keys, a sensor needs to share keys with non-diagonal neighboring groups. Since there are at most 4 non-diagonal neighboring groups around it, at most 4 such inter-group keys are required. For distant groups, it has a distant shared key with a group in set A_k, where k is at most $log\ m$.

Hence it needs to keep at most $2\log m$ such keys. In total, the number of keys preloaded in a sensor is at most $(l-1)+4+2\log m = l+2\log m+3$.

3.2 Computing Overhead

During the key path establishment, the request messages are relayed to the destination sensor node through a set of intermediated trusted peer nodes, where messages are decrypted to read the content and encrypted again to relay to the next trusted node. Hence, the total number of the decrypt-encrypt operations for a key path establishment is considered as the computing overhead which is proportional to the number of the intermediated trusted peer nodes along the established path.

3.2.1 Performance Analysis of Strategy 1

We first analyze the upper bound of the expected total number of intermediate peer nodes in strategy 1. Suppose sensor *s* is the sensor that holds the message and is in phase *j*, i.e. the group distance to the destination is greater than 2^j and at most 2^{j+1}. The value of *j* is at most log *m*. If sensor *s* can find a trusted peer node *s'* which can enter a phase less than *j*, *s'* must be in a group whose group distance is at most 2^j to the destination. Let B_j be the set of groups whose distance is within 2^j to the target group and A_j be the set of groups whose distance to the group of the message holder, *s*, is greater than 2^j and at most 2^{j+1} as described in section 2.1. The number of groups in the set A_j is at most

$$|A_j| \le (2\times 2^{j+1}+1)^2-(2\times 2^j+1)^2 = 12\times 2^{2j}+4\times 2^j \tag{2}$$

Let I_j denote the intersection of B_j and A_j. Sensor *s* is in phase *j* and the group distance to the destination is at most 2^{j+1}. Therefore, I_j has at least $(2^j+1)^2-1$ groups as shown in Fig. 2. Since sensor *s* has a preloaded secure link to a randomly chosen group in A_j, the probability that this chosen group falls into I_j is

$$\frac{|B_j\cap A_j|}{|A_j|}=\frac{|I_j|}{|A_j|}\ge\frac{(2^j+1)^2-1}{12\times 2^{2j}+4\times 2^j}=\frac{2^{2j}+2\times 2^j}{12\times 2^{2j}+4\times 2^j}\ge\frac{2^{2j}+2^j}{12\times 2^{2j}+12\times 2^j}=\frac{1}{12} \tag{3}$$

Hence, the probability that sensor *s* has an intermediate peer *s'* which can enter into a phase less than *j* is at least 1/12, as shown in Fig. 2.

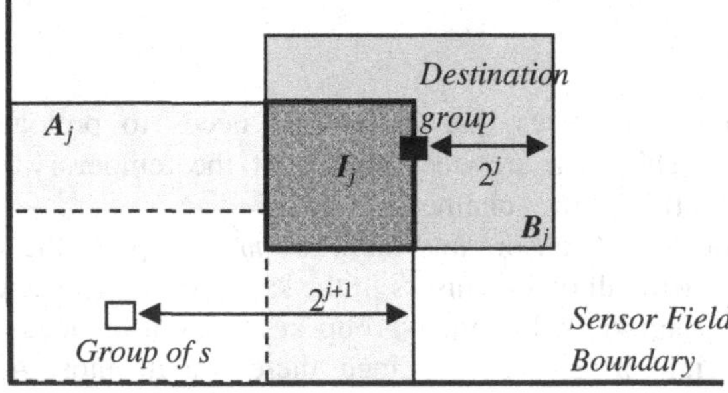

Fig. 2. As the group of s is near the corner, A_j has fewer groups but I_j still has at least $(2^j+1)^2-1$ groups. The probability that sensor *s'* locates in I_j is larger then 1/12.

Let X_j denote the total number of intermediate peer nodes that are in phase j. (X_0 is at most 1.) For $1 \le j \le \log m$, the expected number of X_j, is at most

$$EX_j \le \sum_{1}^{\infty}\left(\frac{1}{12}\right)\left(\frac{11}{12}\right)^{i-1} \times i = 12 \cdot \tag{4}$$

Let X be the total number of intermediate peer nodes, i.e.,

$$X = \sum_{j=0}^{\log m} X_j \tag{5}$$

The average number of X is

$$EX \le 1 + 12\log m \tag{6}$$

Therefore, the upper bound is logarithmic to the number of groups in the sensor network. This property makes the network a small world.

3.2.2 Performance Analysis of Strategy 2

Assume the node holding the message is in phase j and it has k intra-group neighbors. Let p be the probability that the neighbors have at least one trusted peer which can enter into a phase less than j. Then the value of p is

$$p \ge 1 - \left(\frac{11}{12}\right)^k \tag{7}$$

X_j denotes the total number of intermediate peer nodes that are in phase j. Therefore, the upper bound of the expected number of X_j is

$$\begin{aligned} EX_j \le\ & 1\times\frac{1}{12} + 2\times\frac{1}{12}\times p \\ & + 2\times\frac{1}{12}\times\frac{11}{12}(1-p) + 3\times p\times\left(\frac{11}{12}\right)^2\times(1-p) \\ & + 3\times\frac{1}{12}\times\left(\frac{11}{12}\right)^2(1-p)^2 + 4\times p\times\left(\frac{11}{12}\right)^3\times(1-p)^2 + \ldots \\ = & \sum_{i=1}^{\infty}\{i\left(\frac{1}{12}\right)\left(\frac{11}{12}\right)^{i-1}(1-p)^{i-1} + (i+1)p\left(\frac{11}{12}\right)^i(1-p)^{i-1}\} \end{aligned} \tag{8}$$

Let $r = \frac{11}{12}(1-p)$. We have

$$EX_j \le \frac{1}{12(1-r)^2} + \frac{11}{12}p\left(\frac{1}{r(1-r)^2} - \frac{1}{r}\right) \tag{9}$$

As the number of neighbors, k, is no smaller than 10, the expected number is smaller than 2.5, and the limit is 1.917 as k approaches infinity. When k is no smaller than 10, the average number of the total number of intermediate nodes is smaller than or equal to $1 + 2.5 \log m$, which is smaller than the result of strategy 1.

3.3 Communication Overhead

Similar to computing overhead, the communication overhead is proportional to the length of a communication path. Therefore, we define the communication overhead to be the total length of the secure links in the established key path.

Given two sensor nodes, the theoretical minimal communication overhead is the Euclidean distance between them. If sensor nodes are uniformly distributed into a square of area *A*, the average distance between two sensor nodes [13] is $0.52\sqrt{A}$. Therefore, the expected communication overhead is better if the value is closer to $0.52\sqrt{A}$. In our scheme, it is assumed that group $G_{i,j}$ is deployed into the cell in row *i* and column *j* in the field. Thus, the group distance is proportional to the Euclidean distance. As the key path establishment algorithm tries to find a closest next sensor node in the sense of group distance, it also try to find a short route to the destination.

3.4 Random Group Deployment

Our scheme also works well when groups are randomly deployed. In our scheme, both the key preloading and key path establishing do not involve the geography of the sensor field. The secure-link graph depicted in Fig. 1 could be viewed as a virtual group space and is not necessarily a real map for group deployment. The performance including memory overhead and computing overhead are the same. The differences are in the performance of communication overhead and the underlying routing support. With this random deployment, the scheme needs a globally addressable communication infrastructure such as GPSR [14].

4 Simulations

We also use simulations to verify the performance of the proposed key distribution scheme. The results are compared to the PIKE-2D scheme [11]. In the experiments, the networks were deployed in a two dimensional square field. The number of the sensor nodes varied from 10,000 to 250,000 and the number of sensors per group was set to 25. Sensors for a group were deployed uniformly in the corresponding group cell. The deployment density of sensors is 0.01 node/m^2. The default wireless communication range is 30*m*. Hence the number of neighbors in communication range is about $30^2\pi*0.01 \fallingdotseq 28$.

Fig. 3 shows the memory overhead of our scheme and PIKE-2D. Our method requires very low memory for key storage. For a sensor network of m^2 groups, with group size *l*, it needs to preload each sensor with $l + 3 + 2 \log m$ keys as described in the previous section. In contrast, the memory overhead of PIKE-2D is $\left|\sqrt{n}\right| + 1$, where *n* is the total number of sensors. Thus, our scheme has better performance on memory overhead than the latter, especially when the network size is large.

Fig. 4 shows the computing overhead of our scheme and PIKE-2D. The computing overhead of our method is logarithmic to the number of sensor groups. Hence the computing overhead increases very slowly with respect to the network size. The simulation result for strategy 1 shows that even when the network size is 250,000, the value is still smaller than 8. The result for strategy 2 is even better than strategy 1.

For the scheme of PIKE-2D, there is always an intermediate trusted node between any two nodes. Therefore, the average number of intermediate nodes for it is always 1. Although our results are worse than PIKE-2D's, they are nearly in the same order. This is a trade-off between memory overhead and computing overhead. Our method spends much less memory for keys with only a little increase in computing overhead.

For PIKE-2D, it has to consume much communication resource. The intermediate trusted node for communication could be located anywhere in the sensor field; hence it needs to route to the distant trusted node and makes the communication overhead very high. Fig. 5 shows both results of communication overhead in case of randomly selected pairs of nodes and in case of neighboring pairs of nodes.

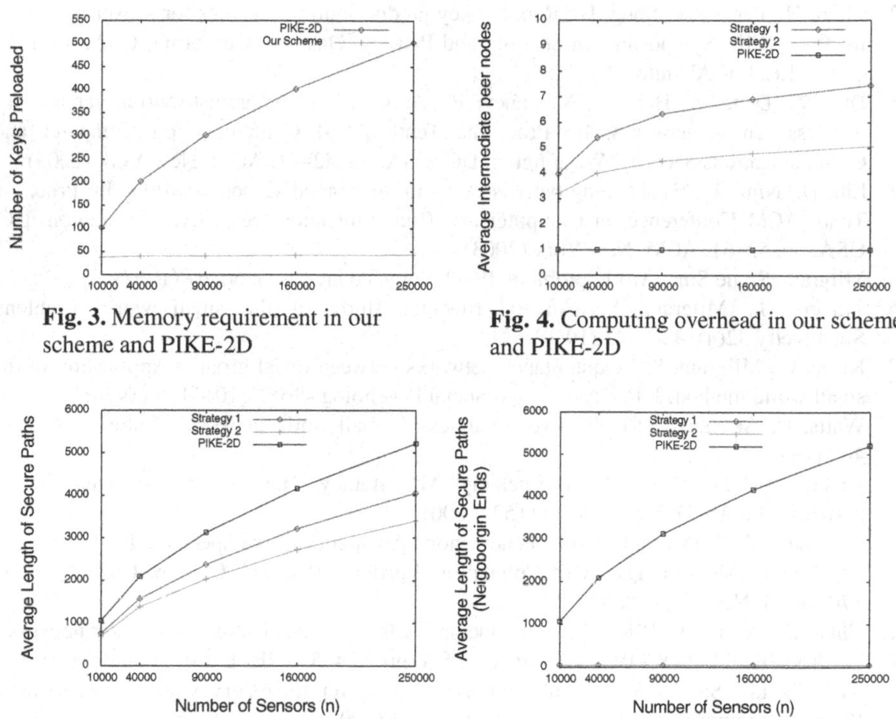

Fig. 3. Memory requirement in our scheme and PIKE-2D

Fig. 4. Computing overhead in our scheme and PIKE-2D

Fig. 5(a) Average communication overhead for random selected pairs

Fig. 5(b) Average communication overhead for neighboring pairs

5 Conclusions

We have proposed a group-based key predistribution scheme based on the concept of small worlds. With the proposed method, any two sensor nodes in the network can efficiently establish a secure transmission path. The memory overhead for key storage is logarithmic to the number of sensor groups; hence, each sensor node needs only to carry few keys even if the size of the sensor network is very large.

Two different strategies for the key path establishment are presented. Both strategies use only local information nearby sensors and hence are practical under the resource constraints in sensor networks. We evaluated the performance of our method both by analysis and by simulations. The results indicate that the presented scheme is superior to current methods.

References

1. Eschenauer, L., Gligor, V.: A key-management scheme for distributed sensor networks. In: Proc. the 9th ACM Conference on Computer and Communication Security, Washington, DC, USA, pp. 41–47. ACM, New York (2002)
2. Chan, H., Perrig, A., Song, D.: Random key predistribution schemes for sensor networks. In: Proc. IEEE Symposium on Security and Privacy, Oakland, California, USA, pp. 197–213. IEEE, Los Alamitos (2003)
3. Du, W., Deng, J., Han, Y., Varshney, P.: A pairwise key predistribution scheme for wireless sensor networks. In: Proc. the Tenth ACM Conference on Computer and Communications Security, Washington, DC, USA, pp. 42–51. ACM, New York (2003)
4. Liu, D., Ning, P.: Establishing pairwise keys in distributed sensor networks. In: Proc. the Tenth ACM Conference on Computer and Communications Security, Washington, DC, USA, pp. 52–61. ACM, New York (2003)
5. Milgram, S.: he Small world problem. Psychology Today 61(1), 60–67 (1967)
6. Travers, J., Milgram, S.: An experimental study of the small world problem. Sociometry 32(4), 425–443 (1969)
7. Korte, C., Milgram, S.: Acquaintance networks between racial groups: Application of the small world method. J. Personality and Social Psychology 15(2), 101–108 (1978)
8. Watts, D., Strogatz, S.: Collective dynamics of small-world networks. Nature 393, 440–442 (1998)
9. Amaral, L.A.N., Scala, A., Barthelemy, M., Stanley, H.E.: Classes of small world networks. PNAS 97(21), 11149–11152 (2000)
10. Kleinberg, J.: The small-world phenomenon: An algorithm perspective. In: Proc. 32nd ACM Symposium on Theory of Computing, Portland, Portland, Oregon, USA, pp. 163–170. ACM, New York (2000)
11. Chan, H., Perrig, A.: PIKE: Peer intermediaries for key establishment in sensor networks. In: Proc. IEEE INFOCOM 2005, Miami, USA, pp. 524–535. IEEE, Los Alamitos (2005)
12. Akyildiz, I.F., Su, W., Sankarasubramaniam, Y., Cayirci, E.: A survey on sensor networks. IEEE Communications Magazine 40(8), 102–114 (2002)
13. Ghosh, B.: Random Distances within a rectangle and between two rectangles. Bull. Calcutta Math. Soc. 43, 17–24 (1951)
14. Karp, B., Kung, H.T.: GPSR: greedy perimeter stateless routing for wireless networks. In: Proc. the Sixth International Conference on Mobile Computing and Networking (MobiCom 2000), Boston, Massachusetts, USA, pp. 243–254 (2000)

Multigroup Rekeying for a Wireless Network*

Kuang-Hui Chi[1], Ji-Han Jiang[2], and Yu-Ching Hsu[3]

[1] Department of Electrical Engineering, National Yunlin University of Science and Technology, Taiwan
chikh@yuntech.edu.tw
[2] Department of Computer Science and Information Engineering, National Formosa University, Taiwan
[3] Information and Communications Research Laboratories, Industrial Technology Research Institute, Taiwan

Abstract. In the context of secure group communication, a shared secret key is generated anew for data protection whenever group membership changes. This paper presents an approach to fast rekeying in a wireless network that is subject to time-varying channel conditions. We address a scenario where a station joins one group at a time, but may leave multiple groups at once for abrupt link failure or cascading application termination. In our architecture, each station is assigned a private number and a code, so as to exploit Fermat's Little Theorem and an orthogonal coding methodology, respectively. The former is used to protect the delivery of updated group keys, while the latter to encode keying material meant for different sites in an aggregate form as a payload for message distribution. Since rekeying messages are delivered via multicast, intended stations can decode information of interest at the same time. Therefore rekeying among multiple groups can still be carried out timely with $O(1)$ message complexity. Our design provides a complementary facility to current schemes for performance improvement. Pragmatic considerations of our approach are discussed as well.

1 Introduction

Secure group communication is generally accomplished by using a shared cryptographic key for data protection. For forward and backward secrecy, however, a rekeying process is performed whenever group membership changes. As far as a wireless network is concerned, group membership is likely to change over time due to link outage on account of radio signal characteristics or user's mobility. Such network dynamics may cause frequent group rekeyng, at the cost of repeated message exchanges taking nontrivial delay. This gives rise to an *out-of-sync* problem between keys and data [9] or disruptions of message delivery among communicating parties. In addition, group keys are generally meant for

* This work was supported by the National Science Council, ROC, under grants NSC 95-2221-E-224-016-MY2 and NSC 95-2622-E-150-035-CC3, and by the Ministry of Economics, ROC, under the grant 6301XS2430.

T. Enokido, L. Barolli, and M. Takizawa (Eds.): NBiS 2007, LNCS 4658, pp. 147–156, 2007.

temporal use, requiring updates from time to time. Therefore the development of a fast group rekeying procedure is essential.

There has been active research on group key management. For an expository survey, we refer the reader to [3,7]. A common treatment is to organize a group of nodes in a tree or in a logical key hierarchy (key graph [14].) Considering such a hierarchy, schemes like [11] reduced rekeying overhead by keeping the tree balanced. Another avenue to reduce the overhead results from batch rekeying, as opposed to individual rekeying after each join or leave (see [4,9] for example.) Group rekeying can also be approached by one-way hash functions, e.g. in [8,15], or the Group Diffie-Hellman contributory key agreement, e.g. in [2,13]. Though effective, these schemes incur communication or computational costs in some sense. Additional cost results from rekeying when a node belonging to multiple groups leaves the system or when periodic updates to different group temporal keys are required. In that event, the blackout period of disrupted traffic grows longer unless rekeying among multi-groups is properly designed.

As a remedy, we tackle above issues by exploiting Fermat's Little Theorem and an orthogonal coding technique. These two techniques enable stations of different groups to retrieve keying information of interest to respective sites parallelly from a single, scrambled message. In this fashion, multigroup rekeying can be completed sooner than would otherwise be possible. Our approach allows for the broadcast property of wireless media or network-level multicast where available. It is also feasible to incorporate our development in counterpart schemes for performance improvement. Our proposed approach is not a trivial extension of conventional group rekeying protocol in that we simplify an original procedure of repeated message exchanges and represent information for separate groups in a compact form in a single message. This saves overall rekeying delay and space overhead of separate rekeying messages per group like redundant message headers and trailers. Communication activities will thus become better streamlined to the user's benefit.

The rest of this paper is organized as follows. In Sect. 2, we shall first describe our system model and the rationale behind the proposed scheme. Then we discuss how the scheme operates upon a join or a leave. Next we avail ourselves of an orthogonal coding technique to achieve rekeying across multiple groups by means of a single message. Subsequently complexity results of some well-known group rekeying schemes are compared in Sect. 3. Sect. 4 summarizes this study. Lastly, how the proposed scheme is related to a pragmatic IEEE 802.11i network is given in the Appendix.

2 The Proposed Approach

Consider a network containing a group key controller (GKC) and n wireless stations (Fig. 1.) These stations communicate via some point of attachment to the system, referring to a base station or multicast-capable router at which the GKC may be colocated. The GKC maintains a secure communication channel with the point of attachment to transport security information specific to stations. We

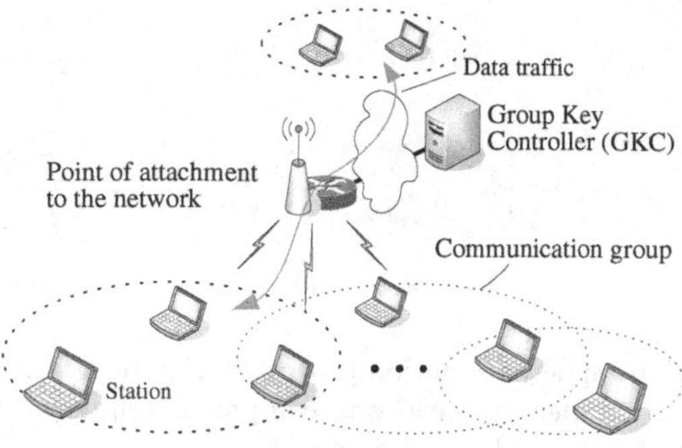

Fig. 1. An architecture of n wireless stations under common management of some GKC. Stations enclosed by dashed lines represent participants of a same group.

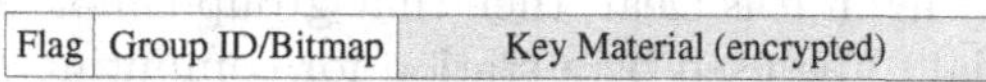

Fig. 2. Format of group rekeying information

are mainly concerned with regional communication activities such as in a local area network or on a campus. The local network, however, can be part of group communication that spans on the Internet.

2.1 Preliminaries

In our architecture, the GKC maintains a large prime p_i for each station $i \in \{1, 2, \cdots, n\}$. Such a prime is unique, i.e., $p_i \neq p_j$ if $i \neq j$. To join a group, each station i authenticates with the GKC for admission whereby p_i can be derived from mutual authentication methods, say, over the IEEE 802.1X Extensible Authentication Protocol (see the appendix.) As can be seen shortly, p_i specific to a station i is used to compute shared secret keys for groups to which i belongs. Besides, the GKC needs to detect departures of stations per group somehow, probably through explicit notifications by stations or timeout of periodic reauthentications. Hence the GKC is assumed knowledgeable about each station in its administrative domain involved in which group(s).

Since two or more stations can form a group, a station may participate in multiple groups. We address a common scenario where a station joins one group at a time, but may leave several groups at once (possibly out of abrupt link failure or cascading application terminations.) Whenever group membership changes, the GKC generates rekeying information as in Fig. 2 toward intended stations via multicast or link-scoped broadcast. The first field (Flag) valued either 0 or 1 indicates whether to interpret the second field as a group identity or a bitmap. The former is used when a station joins some group, whereas the latter relates to simultaneous departures of a station from multiple groups. A bitmap keeps track of which groups require rekeying. Each group is indicated by a bit in the

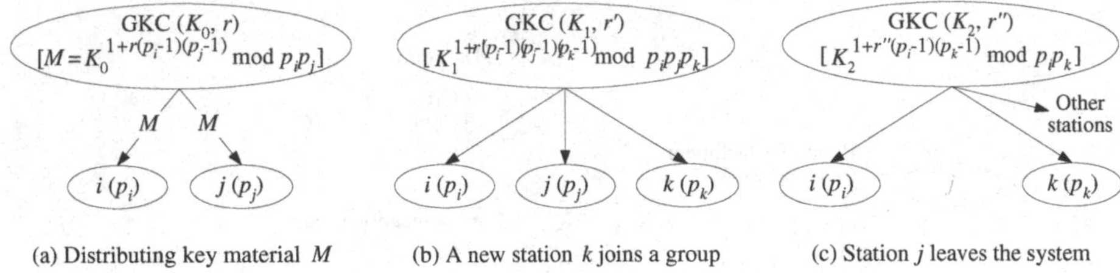

(a) Distributing key material M (b) A new station k joins a group (c) Station j leaves the system

Fig. 3. An example of group key formation processes. Parenthetical numbers represent private numbers used by respective entities to compute group keys. Numbers in square brackets are carried in the Key Material field of Fig. 2.

map and its index in the bitmap corresponds to some group that a station joins in chronological oder during its lifetime. If the bit is set, the corresponding group should undergo rekeying; if it is clear, then that group is not affected. The third field contains material to be used by a station for computing new group keys.

New group keys are computed mainly using Fermat's Little Theorem in following lines. As exemplified in Fig. 3(a), a group consisting of stations i and j will derive the shared secret key K_0 from the received Key Material. K_0 is encrypted by the GKC in ciphertext $M = K_0^{1+r(p_i-1)(p_j-1)} \bmod p_ip_j$ before transmission. Here r is a nonce generated for temporary use. K_0 is selected as an integer smaller than $\min\{p_i, p_j\}$ whose value is relatively prime to p_i and p_j. A receiving station, say i, decrypts M using arithmetic mod p_i to find K_0:

$$\begin{aligned} M \bmod p_i &\equiv K_0(K_0^{p_i-1})^{r(p_j-1)} \bmod p_i \\ &= K_0(1)^{r(p_j-1)} \bmod p_i \\ &= K_0 \bmod p_i \\ &= K_0 \end{aligned} \quad (1)$$

Similarly, station j does arithmetic mod p_j to find a common K_0. In our architecture, key material involves the GKC that determines the group key, raises it to some random power for scrambling purpose, and performs modular arithmetic using private numbers of respective stations. Upon receipt, destination stations are able to extract the correct group key using their associated private numbers.

2.2 Joining a Group

Fig. 3(b) illustrates how a concerned group key is updated when a new station joins. Suppose that originally stations i and j comprise a group. Upon receiving a join request from a new station k, the GKC and k perform mutual authentication to agree on a private number p_k. Then the GKC selects a new pair of group key K_1 and nonce r', and prepares ciphertext $M = K_1^{1+r'(p_i-1)(p_j-1)(p_k-1)} \bmod p_ip_jp_k$. Note that K_1 is chosen smaller than $\min\{p_i, p_j, p_k\}$ and relatively prime to p_i, p_j, and p_k. Subsequently a rekeying message is sent to intended group members, with the Flag field set to 0 and the Key Material field set to M. The provision of M

allows correct stations to extract K_1 by using arithmetic modulo their respective private numbers as in (1). Stations without holding correct private numbers can hardly decrypt M because factoring a big number is hard.

As a note, the rekeying message in the join protocol can grow in proportion to group size. For instance, for a group involving all the n stations, the length of Key Material amounts to $|p_1 p_2 \cdots p_n| \leq |p_1| + |p_2| + \cdots + |p_n|$, where $|p_t|$ denotes the number of bits in use to represent the integer $p_t, t = 1, 2, \cdots, n$. However, as far as a local area network is concerned, its accommodated membership of a group is generally not large. This implies that our protocol does not suffer such potential limit in most cases. Alternatively, the problem can be dealt with by selecting group keys and private numbers associated with new stations properly. In words, when a station k is about to join the group (K_0 being the original group key), the GKC resolves a new group key K_1 and a nonce r' such that K_1 is smaller than and relatively prime to both K_0^α and p_k. The integer exponent α ($\alpha > 1$) is introduced here to generate a larger value K_0^α to expand the range of choosing K_1. Letting α be 2, the GKC sets $M = K_1^{1+r'(K_0^2-1)(p_k-1)} \bmod K_0^2 p_k$ for distribution. All stations of the original group holding the key K_0 will thus be able to decrypt M to find K_1 by performing $M \bmod K_0^2$ similarly to (1). Meanwhile, station k performs $M \bmod p_k$. In this manner, the rekeying message carries ciphertext M encoded by the original group key and another new private number, keeping modulo operations irrespective of group size. Therefore, even though there are n stations to rekey, the rekeying message is restricted to an order of $2|K_0| + |p_k|$ in length.

2.3 Leaving Multiple Groups

When a station, say j, with membership of more than one group departs from the system, immediate departures from multiple groups occur. Suppose that j participated in a set $\mathcal{G}_j$ of groups. Upon detecting such a leave, the GKC generates a new pair of K_2 and r'', and instructs affected groups to change their secret keys. Considering stations belonging to any group in $\mathcal{G}_j$, K_2 is selected to be smaller than and relatively prime to private numbers of these stations, whereas r'' is not a multiple of $(p_j - 1)$. The GKC proceeds to send a rekeying message carrying 1 in the Flag field, a suitable Bitmap field (see the next subsection), and $M = K_2^{1+r''\Pi(p_t-1)} \bmod \Pi p_t$ in the Key Material field, where p_t denotes the private number of each station other than j participating in some group(s) of $\mathcal{G}_j$. This enables each intended station (ruling out j) to decrypt M as in (1), and then uses the received Bitmap to locate which group(s) in its membership requires rekeying by means of the obtained K_2.

As an example shown in Fig. 3(c), let i and k be such stations involved in different groups of $\mathcal{G}_j$. Provided a group key K_1 in use by i, the station computes its new key for that group as $K_1 \oplus K_2$ (exclusive OR operations of K_1 with K_2.)[1]

[1] In general, a one-way hash function f can be employed that yields the new group key as $f(K_1, K_2)$. This ensures that only a member in possession of K_2 can obtain the updated group key.

Given the secret key K_1' used by k for another group, station k computes the new group key as $K_1' \oplus K_2$. Note that we take K_2 for a random bit stream to settle on new keys of different groups. In the meantime, computations for new group keys are carried out by each station with membership in $\mathcal{G}_j$. Thus, if there exist other stations of the same group as i or k in $\mathcal{G}_j$, similar calculations are performed to derive concerned group keys. In that event, M should be set accordingly to accommodate private numbers of all intended stations. In the way of using K_2, stations of a same group still reach to a common, new secret key.

2.4 Preparation of Bitmap

A bitmap is referenced on per-station basis. To amalgamate bitmaps for different stations into one Bitmap field, we exploit an orthogonal coding methodology whereby each receiving station can retrieve its bitmap from the field. For this, each station i is assigned a unique code $\tilde{c_i}$, a binary vector, in which the xth bit is denoted by $c_i[x]$. The code $\tilde{c_i}$ may assume the private number p_i. However, a number occupying fewer bits generally suffices $\tilde{c_i}$ which needs not be secret. All the codes assigned to stations are of identical length $\mathcal{L}$ and pairwise orthogonal. That is, the inner product of any two distinct codes $\tilde{c_i}$ and $\tilde{c_j}$ (written as $\tilde{c_i} \bullet \tilde{c_j}$) is zero, whereas the inner product of any $\tilde{c_i}$ with itself equals $\|\tilde{c_i}\|^2 > 0$. Namely,

$$\tilde{c_i} \bullet \tilde{c_j} = \sum_{x=1}^{\mathcal{L}} c_i[x] c_j[x] = \begin{cases} 0 & \text{if } i \neq j \\ \|\tilde{c_i}\|^2 & \text{otherwise} \end{cases}$$

Observe that bitwise AND and OR operations are sufficient to evaluate inner products. Example codes are $\tilde{c_i} = \langle 1, 0, 1 \rangle$ and $\tilde{c_j} = \langle 0, 1, 0 \rangle$.

Given the orthogonality property, the Bitmap field is prepared in following lines. Suppose that the GKC shall notify station 1 of bitmap b_1, station 2 of b_2, and so forth. (Here a bitmap forming a bit string of all zeros is regarded *null.*) Viewing these bitmaps as scalars, we encode them in a vectored format $b_1\tilde{c_1} + b_2\tilde{c_2} + \cdots + b_n\tilde{c_n}$ using scalar multiplications. The encoded sum of vectors is then delivered in the Bitmap field of a rekeying message to wireless stations. Upon receipt, a correct station i using $\tilde{c_i}$ computes

$$(b_1\tilde{c_1} + b_2\tilde{c_2} + \cdots + b_n\tilde{c_n}) \bullet \tilde{c_i} = b_i \|\tilde{c_i}\|^2.$$

Dividing the decoded result by $\|\tilde{c_i}\|^2$ restores b_i. Any other station j can perform likewise to acquire its corresponding b_j. However, if station j decodes to null, it is deduced that the current rekeying procedure does not involve j and is thereby ignorable. As a consequence, stations can extract information of interest from an ensemble of bitmaps at the same time and act accordingly. This facilitates to complete rekeying processes for multi-groups faster that would otherwise be required for separate rekeying per group.

3 Complexity Results

Since it is easier to rekey after a join than a leave [9], let us next concentrate on complexities of group rekeying schemes at a leave, in terms of communication

Table 1. Complexity results of selected schemes (in the case of $|b|$ groups involved)

	Communication	Computational
Chang *et al.*'s scheme [4]	$O(\|b\| \log n)$	$O(\|b\| \log n)$
Mittra's scheme [10]	$O(\|b\|n)$	$O(\|b\|)$
Wong *et al.*'s scheme [14]	$O(\|b\|n)$	$O(\|b\|n)$
Our scheme	$O(1)$	$O(1)$

and computational aspects. The former measurement index refers to how many rekeying messages are generated, while the latter the number of key encryptions/decryptions during transmission. Table 1 compares corresponding results in the case of $|b|$ groups. To gain a fairer basis for comparisons, our GKC is likened to the group controller in Chang *et al*'s scheme [4], a group security intermediary in Mittra's scheme [10], or the key server of a star key graph in Wong *et al*'s scheme under the group-oriented rekeying paradigm [14]. (Another paradigm—a tree key graph—in Wong *et al*'s scheme has similar complexities to Chang *et al.*'s scheme.) Note that conventional rekeying schemes operate mostly on per-group basis, so their incurred costs can grow linearly with the involvement of more groups. In contrast, the proposed scheme allows for multigroup rekeying with $O(1)$ message complexity, such as to complete rekeying faster.

A side effect of our scheme is that a rekeying message might appear lengthy due to carrying excess bitmaps or key material indicative of a large number of stations to rekey. However, the side effect will arguably become less prominent if the bitmap length $|b|$ or the number n', $1 \leq n' \leq n$, of stations involved in rekeying can be maintained. To see this, observe that our Bitmap field contains $b_1\tilde{c_1}+b_2\tilde{c_2}+\cdots+b_n\tilde{c_n} = \langle\sum_{i=1}^{n} b_ic_i[1], \sum_{i=1}^{n} b_ic_i[2], \cdots, \sum_{i=1}^{n} b_ic_i[\mathcal{L}]\rangle$. Since each b_i ranges from 0 to $2^{|b|}-1$, every element of the $\mathcal{L}$-tuple sums up to $n(2^{|b|}-1)$, which can be represented using $|b|+\log n$ bits. Thus, the Bitmap field occupies at most $\mathcal{L}(|b|+\log n)$ bits. Concerning the best-known counterpart scheme whose rekeying message containing per-group identity and key material is delivered to stations, in the event that a group identity indicates a 128-bit IPv6 address (as defined by RFC 4291), there will totally require $|b|(|H|+128+|M|\log n)$ bits in a message, where $|H|$ and $|M|$ denote the number of bits in the message header (plus message trailer) and key material M, respectively. Relating the bit count of our rekeying message to that of the counterpart scheme, we find that the inequality $|H|+1+\mathcal{L}(|b|+\log n) + n'|M| \leq |b|(|H| + 128 + |M| \log n)$ holds if $|b| \geq (|H|+1+\mathcal{L}\log n+n'|M|)/(|H|+128+|M|\log n-\mathcal{L})$. The condition implies that maintaining the bitmap length $|b|$ or n' can ensure our approach to incur comparatively less message space, although our key material is n' times the size of key material in the counterpart scheme.

For example, given that $|H|$ is 224 in an IEEE 802.11 network, $\mathcal{L}=n$, $|M|=128$, $n'=n/2$ on average, and $n=10$, we have $|b|\geq 1.86$. In other words, when a station belonging to more than two groups departs from the system, our proposed approach would outperform counterpart schemes in terms of communication complexity as well. Under the prescribed parametric setting, it is further deduced that $|b| \geq 3.22$ at worst (in case $n' = n$.) In that case, our approach saves message space if more than 3 groups of stations should rekey at a leave.

4 Conclusion

This paper developed a means of fast multigroup rekeying in wireless networks. Our objective is to improve timeliness over conventional schemes that rekey mainly for respective groups. To this end, we assign each station a private number with pairwise orthogonality to protect the delivery of keying material and for information encoding. Multicast capability of wireless media is exploited so that multigroup rekeying can be accomplished using a single message without introducing undue overhead. This reduces overall rekeying delay and workload at the GKC and receiving station sites. It is apropos to incorporate our development in counterpart schemes that operate in a logical key hierarchy, while using the proposed approach to deal with regional rekeying activities. Qualitative discussions (Sect. 3) have delimited the usefulness of the proposed scheme. Our design lends itself to applications such as Digital Rights Management in streaming media services like IP/TV.

Concerning future work, since a group service is one of network-based applications, the withstanding or resilience to network merging and partitioning is generally required. A network partitioning splits the communication environment into two or more disjoint parts, a common occurrence in wireless networks containing mobile nodes. Note that our treatment in Sections 2.3 and 2.4 applies to the scenario where more than one station depart from the system on account of network partitioning. (Other rekeying schemes dealing with batch joins or leaves may also operate in this case.) However, the application of our scheme in this scenario gives rise to some additional considerations. On the contrary, network merging will cause issues on changes in coalition membership or on reconciling the effects of partitioned group communication. These issues require further investigation in the future.

References

1. Aboba, B., Blunk, L., Vollbrecht, J., Carlson, J., Levkowetz, H.: Extensible Authentication Protocol (EAP), RFC 3748, IETF Network Working Group (2004)
2. Amir, Y., Kim, Y., Nita-Rotaru, C., Schultz, J., Stanton, J., Tsudik, G.: Secure group communication using robust contributory key agreement. IEEE Trans. Parallel and Distributed Syst. 15, 468–480 (2004)
3. Canetti, R., Garay, J., Itkis, G., Micciancio, D., Naor, M., Pinkas, B.: Multicast security: A taxonomy and some efficient constructions. In: Proc. 18th Ann. Joint Conf. IEEE Comp. and Comm. Societies, vol. 2, pp. 708–716. IEEE, Los Alamitos (1999)
4. Chang, I., Engel, R., Kandlur, D., Pendarakis, D., Saha, D.: Key management for secure Internet multicast using boolean function minimization techniques. In: Proc. 18th Ann. Joint Conf. IEEE Comp. and Comm. Societies, vol. 2, pp. 689–698. IEEE, Los Alamitos (1999)

5. Eronen, P., Hiller, T., Zorn, G. (eds.): Diameter Extensible Authentication Protocol (EAP) application, RFC 4072, IETF Network Working Group (2005)
6. IEEE Std 802.11i, IEEE Standard for Telecommunications and Information Exchange between Systems—LAN/MAN Specific Requirements—Part 11: Wireless Medium Access Control (MAC) and Physical layer (PHY) specifications. Amendment 6: Medium Access Control (MAC) security enhancements (2004)
7. Kim, Y.: Group key agreement—theory and practice, Ph.D. Thesis, Department of Computer Science, University of Southern California, USA (2002)
8. Kim, H., Hong, S.-M., Yoon, H., Cho, J.W.: Secure group communication with multiplicative one-way functions. In: Proc. Int'l Conf. Info. Technology, pp. 685–690 (2005)
9. Li, X.S., Yang, Y.R., Gouda, M., Lam, S.S.: Batch rekeying for secure group communications. In: Proc. Int'l World Wide Web Conf. pp. 525–534 (2001)
10. Mittra, S.: Iolus: A framework for scalable secure multicasting. In: Proc. ACM Conf. Applications, Technologies, Architectures, and Protocols for Computer Commun. pp. 277–288. ACM, New York (1997)
11. Moharrum, M., Mukkamala, R., Eltoweissy, M.: Efficient secure multicast with well-populated multicast Key trees. In: Proc. 10th Int'l Conf. Parallel and Distributed Systems, pp. 215–222 (2004)
12. Rigney, C., Willens, S., Rubens, A., Simpson, W.: Remote Authentication Dial-In User Service (RADIUS), RFC 2865, IETF Network Working Group (2000)
13. Steiner, M., Tsudik, G., Waidner, M.: CLIQUES: A new approach to group key agreement. In: Proc. 18th Int'l Conf. Distributed Computing Syst. pp. 380–387 (1998)
14. Wong, C.K., Gouda, M., Lam, S.S.: Secure group communications using key graphs. IEEE/ACM Trans. Networking 8, 16–30 (2000)
15. Yang, C., Li, C.: Access control in a hierarchy using one-way hash functions. Computers & Security 23, 659–664 (2004)

A Appendix

As mentioned in Sect. 2, each station i shares a unique prime p_i with the GKC. This appendix exemplifies the provision of such primes in an IEEE 802.11i network. IEEE 802.11i specifying security enhancements to an IEEE 802.11 network, can be viewed to consist of two levels. On the lower level are encryption protocols known as the temporal key integrity protocol (TKIP) and the counter mode with CBC-MAC protocol (CCMP.) (CBC-MAC stands for cipher-block chaining with message authentication code.) Overlying TKIP and CCMP is IEEE 802.1X—a framework for authentication and key material distribution.

IEEE 802.1X allowing for various authentication methods over the Extensible Authentication Protocol (EAP) [1], entails mutual authentication between a station and a backend Authentication Server. As illustrated in Fig. 4, EAP messages carrying upper-layer authentication information are encapsulated in EAP over LAN (EAPOL) frames for wireless transport and in the Diameter protocol on the wired side, respectively. Here the AP (access point) acts as a transit entity to relay authentication messages. Diameter operates using a general-purpose message header plus an extensible collection of Attribute Value Pairs indicating application-specific commands. For synergy use of Diameter

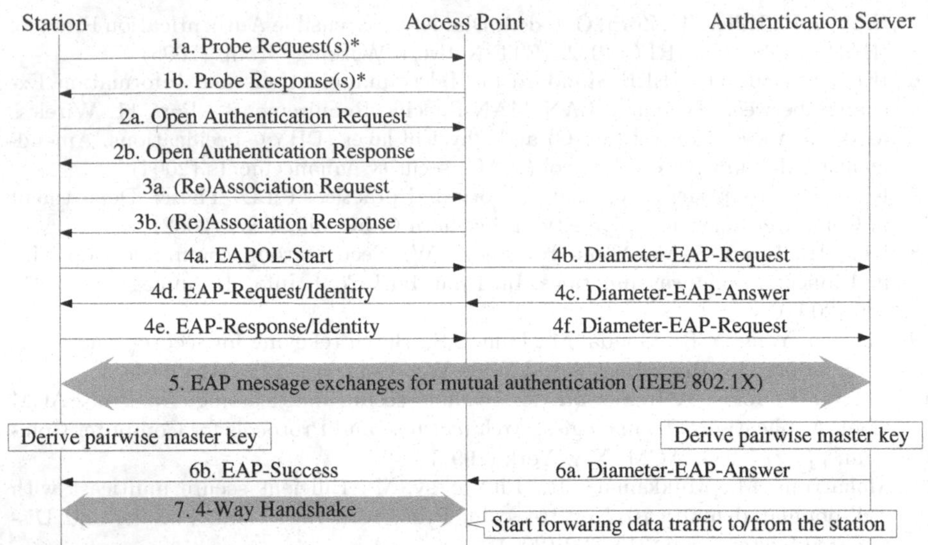

Fig. 4. Message flow in an IEEE 802.11i network (message marked with '∗' may be not always present.) Messages between an AP and its backend Authentication Server are exchanged over a secure channel.

and EAP, we refer the reader to [5]. A counterpart to Diameter is the RADIUS (Remote Authentication Dial-In User Service) protocol that conveys messages over UDP (User Datagram Protocol.)

IEEE 802.1X authentication is initiated with an EAPOL session start-up (Step 4a of Fig. 4), followed by challenge-response interactions between the station and the Authentication Server (Step 5). Interactions terminate successfully when these two parties share a 256-bit pairwise master key. Subsequently the Authentication Server sends the station's local AP a Diameter-EAP-Answer message with a result code and a payload containing the pairwise master key (Step 6a.) Accordingly the AP issues a corresponding EAP-Success message toward the station (Step 6b), whereupon a 4-Way Handshake derives a pairwise transient key (PTK) (Step 7.) The pairwise transient key is then used by TKIP or CCMP for protecting traffic over the wireless medium.

In our architecture, the GKC can be co-situated at an IEEE 802.1X Authentication Server or at an AP. In the former case, we let p_i for each station i be the prime smaller than but closest to the pairwise master key (taking the pairwise master key as an integer.) In case that the GKC is configured at the AP, p_i may take the prime smaller than but closest to the pairwise transient key.

Rich Internet Architectures for Browser-Based Multiplayer Real-Time Games – Design and Implementation Issues of virtual-kicker.com

Matthias Häsel

Institute for Computer Science and Business Information Systems,
University of Duisburg-Essen, Germany

Abstract. With the ongoing evolvement of Rich Internet Application (RIA) technology, browser-based game development has reached a point where exciting real-time applications with remote players can be produced and distributed quickly and easily. However, as the browser is a very different operating environment and interactive experience from that of classical game software, browser-based real-time multiplayer games involve gaming architectures that are distinct from their classical counterparts. Elaborating on the case of an online tabletop soccer game with two remote players, this paper presents the design and implementation of two distinct architectural models that RIA developers can fall back on when implementing distributed, browser-based real-time applications.

1 Introduction

Due to advances in game design and the availability of broadband Internet access to the end-user, multiplayer online games with real-time interaction have come into wide use [1,2,3] and many researchers regard multiplayer online games as the future of the interactive entertainment industry [4,5,6]. The majority of these games are made up by classic software titles that need to be installed on the players' machines [6]. Browser-based multiplayer games, on the contrary, can be run instantly from a web site, but have, due to technical limitations, long been round-based, strategy-focused games. However, with the ongoing evolvement of Rich Internet Application (RIA) technology [7] such as Adobe Flash and Java, browser-based game development has reached a point where also *real-time* games can be produced and distributed to a large audience quickly and easily. Browser-based games can be integrated in e-business environments in a very simple way and hold a number of exciting possibilities for new online business models, new markets, and new growth [8,5]. However, the browser is a very different operating environment and interactive experience from that of classical game software [9]. Browser-based real-time multiplayer games therefore involve software architectures that are distinct from their classical counterparts. A major challenge when designing and implementing such architectures is that multiplayer games are highly vulnerable to propagation delays resulting from redundant communication, bottlenecks, single points of failure and poor reactivity to changing

T. Enokido, L. Barolli, and M. Takizawa (Eds.): NBiS 2007, LNCS 4658, pp. 157–166, 2007.

network conditions [10]. As latency from input of information to its output determines gameplay and fairness [4], architectures have to be designed in a way that it mitigates latency effects and meets the expectations of the players [3].

Elaborating on the case of *virtual-kicker.com*, an online tabletop soccer game with two remote players, this paper presents design and implementation issues for such Rich Internet architectures. More specifically, after giving a short background information on the abovementioned case and an overview on multiplayer gaming architectures in general, it introduces two architectural models that can be applied to implement browser-based multiplayer real-time games, gives practical implications for RIA developers that intend to create similar application concepts, and it points out future research work required in the area.

2 Background: Tabletop Soccer at virtual-kicker.com

As one of the first browser-based multiplayer real-time games that have become available in the German-speaking Web, virtual-kicker.com was launched in August 2006. In collaboration with the 18 clubs of the German Soccer League ('Bundesliga'), virtual-kicker.com was developed with the idea to create a portal website for German soccer fans that would allow them to register for their favourite club and compete against each other in an online tabletop soccer game. Paralleling the official schedule of the German Soccer League, virtual-kicker.com features virtual matches of the respective opponents.

More than 60,000 players had registered to the game until May 2007. Via the web-based hosting and matchmaking portal, they can communicate with each other and gain access to services such as player profiles, league tables and high scores. The player-side RIA is implemented in Adobe Flash. As the amount of players is likely to differ between the clubs, players competing for the team with the superior number of players have to queue until an opponent is available. This time can be bridged in a club-specific chatroom featuring a score ticker, allowing teammates to discuss current results and strategies.

3 Multiplayer Online Gaming Architectures

Online games that give the player the ability to compete against other players over a network emerged strongly in the mid of the last decade. Traditionally, multiplayer online games have been implemented using client-server architectures [11,12]. However, to address various problems associated with client-server architectures, many authors and game designers have developed fully distributed peer-to-peer (P2P) architectures [6,11].

3.1 Client-Server vs. Peer-to-Peer

In a client-server architecture, the player-side game software connects to a central authoritative server designed to handle game logic [6,3,13]. The server deals out information individually to each client as it is requested and keeps all the players up to date with the current state of the game [6]. Whenever a client performs an action, the data is sent to the server, which calculates the effects of that action and sends the updated game state to the clients [6]. Client-server architectures have the advantage that a single decision point orders the clients' actions, resolves conflicts between these actions and holds the global game state [11]. Unfortunately, they have the disadvantage that they introduce delay because messages between players are always forwarded through the server [11]. This adds additional latency over the minimum cost of sending commands directly to other clients [14]. Moreover, traffic and CPU load at the server increases with the number of players, creating localized congestion and limiting the architecture by the computational power of the server [11].

In a P2P architecture, in contrast, players send their actions to each other and react on the received action. In opposite to client-server, each player communicates with every other player [13]. Each peer acts as a decision point that has exactly the same responsibilities as every other peer [6]. P2P architectures have a lot of advantages. Firstly, there is neither a single point of failure nor an expensive server infrastructure. Moreover, the amount of bandwidth required is reduced dramatically as there is a direct communication between two peers. This also reduces latency on the network, as the bottleneck caused by a server is eliminated [6]. Consequently, many authors regard P2P architectures to provide a better, cheaper, more flexible, robust, and scalable technology solution for multiplayer online games than client-server architectures [6,14]. However, unlike games using a client-server architecture, where there is a single authoritative copy of the game state kept at a central server, P2P architectures require an up-to-date copy of the entire game state to be kept at each peer. Consequently, these architectures require some form of distributed agreement protocols between the peers that prevents the peers' game states from diverging over time and becoming inconsistent [13,14].

3.2 Latency, Playability and Fairness

Although most online games have low bit-rate requirements sending frequent but small packets typically well within the capacity of broadband connections [4], deploying these applications over a large-scale infrastructure presents a significant technological challenge. In both client-server and P2P architectures, an increase in the geographical distances among participating clients and/or servers results in an unavoidable end-to-end delay that may render the game "unresponsive and sluggish even when abundant processing and network resources are available" [4, p. 46]. It can be attributed to many network components, such as time needed to transmit and receive an IP packet, the time for the packet to propagate from one link to another, the time spent waiting in a router queue during network congestion, and the 'last-mile' access network of game players at home [3]. Moreover, differences in game responsiveness to user input may give some players an unfair advantage [1,4]. If the latency between a client and the server (or between two peers) is large enough, the responsiveness of the game to a player's action decreases, and the player's performance is likely to degrade [3]. The game can be regarded as playable if the players find its performance acceptable in terms of the perceptual effect of its inevitable inconsistencies, whereas fairness is concerned with relative playability among all players [4].

4 Real-Time Gaming in a Rich Internet Environment

While the last section primarily reviewed existing literature on architectural concepts and issues of traditional multiplayer online games, the remainder of this paper will examine to what extent these concepts and issues hold for browser-based real-time multiplayer games and, in particular, implementing an online tabletop soccer game. For virtual-kicker.com, Adobe Flash has been chosen as the player-side RIA technology since its common runtime environment across operating systems, browsers and chip architectures enables easy deployment on multiple platforms and devices [7]. In contrast to Java as a possible alternative, Flash has a much higher diffusion rate and can be updated by the player in a very easy way. Moreover, Flash is very efficient in rendering vector graphics and thus provides an optimal runtime for fast-paced games. Another advantage of Flash is that it supports developers to partition the application into components that can be loaded at runtime [7]. This application modularity allows loading club-specific MP3 and JPEG files of well-known fan singings and the logos of a club's sponsors, and dynamically managing these files via a custom-made content management system.

With respect to real-time and multiplayer functionality, Flash applications are able to integrate socket-based, two-way communications and keep live connections to servers for building applications with persistent connectivity [7]. However, a major limitation of Flash is the fact that these live connections are inevitably based on TCP. At first sight, this seems to be fairly advantageous, since TCP enables an error-free, ordered data transfer and a retransmission of lost packets, rendering built-in mechanisms to deal with message loss unnecessary [15]. In the context of real-time games, however, TCP connections are unfortunate since a client cannot receive the packets coming after a lost packet until the retransmitted copy of the lost packet is received [15]. In fact, for real-time multiplayer game clients it would be more useful to get most of the data in a timely fashion (as it would be the case for UDP) than it is to get all of the data in succession, as the resulting effects of packet loss can be mitigated by frequent game-state updates and techniques such as dead reckoning [13,1] and client-side prediction [4]. Though packet loss and latency resulting from applied packet loss mitigation techniques is zero, latency in connection with TCP results from the data transmission itself.

Researchers agree that it is almost impossible to exchange the current player actions and game states continuously or at some very small time unit [1]. However, whether or not game playing experience is affected by these natural limitations of the Internet depends on the type of game, as not all player interactions are equally sensitive to latency. To explain this variable effect, [3] offers a categorization of the effects of latency on different player actions based on the precision required to complete an action successfully as well as the deadline by which an action must be completed. Actions with greater precision and tighter deadlines are sensitive to even modest latencies, while actions with less precision and loose deadlines are more impervious to Internet latencies [3]. In the case of virtual-kicker.com, precision is concerned with the exact position of the ball or the opponent's goalkeeper. Deadline is the time required to achieve the final outcome of the action, i.e. the time to target the opponent's goal before the ball moves out of range or the time the goalkeeper moves in between the striker and the goal. With network latency between the player action and the game server recording that action, the goalkeeper may have moved in between the striker and the goal, preventing the striker to score a goal and thus degrading fairness.

Besides precision and deadline demands of the action, the effect of latency on gameplay degradation also depends on the player's perspective [3]. In that sense, authors argue that the degradation is most notable for games with a first-person perspective [14,3]. One could argue, however, that a tabletop soccer game has even higher latency requirements, as besides the abovementioned issues of precision and deadline, there are two more specifics to such fast-paced games. Firstly, the update vectors representing the movement of the player's stakes as well as the vector representing the ball movement are in a continuous change as the players are continuously and unforeseeably changing stake positions. Secondly, the top view (with the players' eyes constantly focusing on the moving ball) makes the players highly sensitive for inaccuracies in the ball movement. As the difference in network latency becomes larger, the position of the ball displayed at one player diverges more largely from that at another player, bringing inconsistency among the players [2].

In particular, there are two kinds of inconsistencies [4] that may occur during an online tabletop soccer session: First, the increased response time, i.e. the delay between the time of the player's input (i.e. the stake movement) and the rendering of the respective results on the player's screen (i.e. the ball movement), may frustrate players and make the game unplayable. Second, a presentation inconsistency may occur due to the fact that the game-state update reaching a RIA is already outdated to some degree because the real game state may have varied while the update packet was on its way. This would mean, for instance, that the player's perception of the current ball position is slightly inconsistent with the real ball position at the server, respectively, the opponent's RIA. Such inconsistencies can lead to unfairness and player frustration, especially in the highly competitive game environment of an online soccer league [13].

5 Architecture Design and Implementation

When implementing an appropriate gaming architecture for virtual-kicker.com, the sandbox principle (which both Flash applications and Java applets are subject to) turned out as a major limitation, as it renders a direct data exchange (i.e. P2P communication) between two RIAs impossible. Consequently, browser-based multiplayer games must inevitably be based on a physical client-server architecture.

With respect to the logical nature of virtual-kicker.com, however, two distinct alternatives have been designed and implemented: client-server and hybrid peer-to-peer. The main difference between these two approaches lies within the distribution of the game's decision points. In the former, the current game state is calculated by the server, whereas in the latter, calculation of the game states is performed by the clients, while the game server is simply relaying P2P communication. In the following, these two approaches will be discussed in more detail, including the advantages and drawbacks resulting from each alternative.

5.1 Hybrid Peer-to-Peer Architecture

In order to prevent the game server from becoming the main bottleneck for both network traffic and CPU capacity, a first version of the tabletop soccer game was designed as a hybrid P2P architecture, i.e. an architecture where communication between two peers is relayed via a *non-authoritative* game server. This game server was implemented in Java, using its TCP socket API for exchanging real-time data with the Flash clients. The server enables players to join the game and manages the club-specific player queues for assigning opponents to each other. While the client-server model guarantees event ordering because messages from all the players are only delivered at a central decision point [13], P2P games introduce discrepancies among decision points that can cause some decision points to evaluate events out of order, possibly violating causality and prompting incompatible decisions [4]. Event consistency in P2P architectures has been well studied in the online gaming literature devised to guarantee a uniform view of the game state, using causality control techniques such as bucket synchronization [16,15], trailing state synchronization [14], delta-causality control [2], and time warp synchronization [17]. However, these techniques have been mainly designed for real-time games with high consistency requirements, but *low* latency requirements [14], and thus cannot be used in conjunction with highly fast-paced games such as the tabletop soccer. Moreover, implementing clock-based synchronization in Flash renders extremely difficult, as timing depends on the respective client machines and browsers. These limitations make a topology with multiple decision points unfeasible.

One solution for guaranteeing event consistency despite this limitation is to transfer causality control to one of the RIAs during the game session (Fig. 1). With respect to the game design, this is feasible since the game sessions on virtual-kicker.com are relatively short-lived (approx. 3 minutes), i.e. there is no global game state that needs to be preserved for several hours or days. However, with respect to playability and fairness, there are two main drawbacks of this approach: First, the player acting as the decision point is per se in advantage, as for this player, the propagation delay of the game state is zero, while, in comparison to the client-server architecture, the other player's response time has roughly *doubled.* As a fair game gives all users the same level of handicap [4], a possibility to reestablish fairness is to switch the decision point between the RIAs during the game session. In the tabletop soccer game, this is done after each goal and at halftime. Second, the fact that one of the RIAs takes over server functionality increases the amount of outgoing traffic for that client

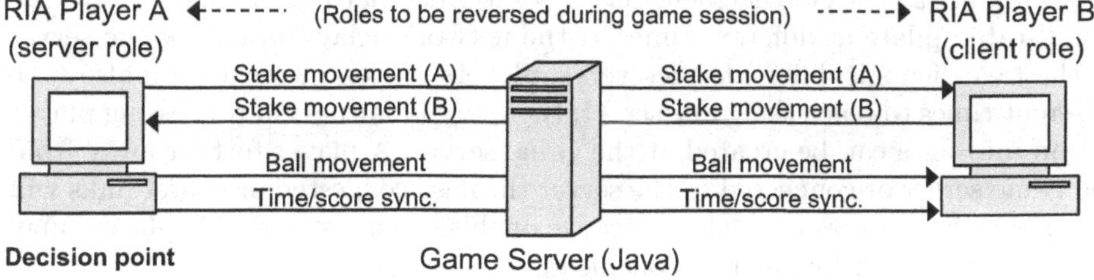

Fig. 1. State updates in the hybrid peer-to-peer architecture

to approximately 32kbps (instead of 8kbps for the other player). As the *upload* speed of bandwidth lines such as ADSL is relatively low, this may introduce an additional bottleneck at the respective decision point.

5.2 Client-Server Architecture

A second version of the game was designed as a client-server architecture. This time, the game server was implemented using Adobe Flash Media Server [18], a server-side RIA solution providing a framework with a number of ready-made server-side components for building Flash-based client-server applications with real-time capabilities. The server acts as a central decision point that calculates and simulates the game states based on the players' actions (Fig. 2). The Flash clients, in contrast, simply render and present the game states to the players and send the players' inputs to the server. In the context of virtual-kicker.com, each player sends update vectors representing the stakes he controls, including each stake's current position and rotation. These vectors are relayed to the opposing client. In contrast to hybrid P2P, though, the server uses these vectors to calculate an update vector representing the current ball position and trajectory, and sends it to the clients. Again, total server bandwidth required for each client is approximately 32kbps. Clients themselves do not (and cannot) communicate with each other, neither do they play any active role in deciding the ordering of actions in the game. Moreover, the server sends synchronization updates relating to the current score and time. This is necessary because the local timing of the Flash clients, depending on the application's frame rate, the local CPU speed and type of browser, is highly inaccurate.

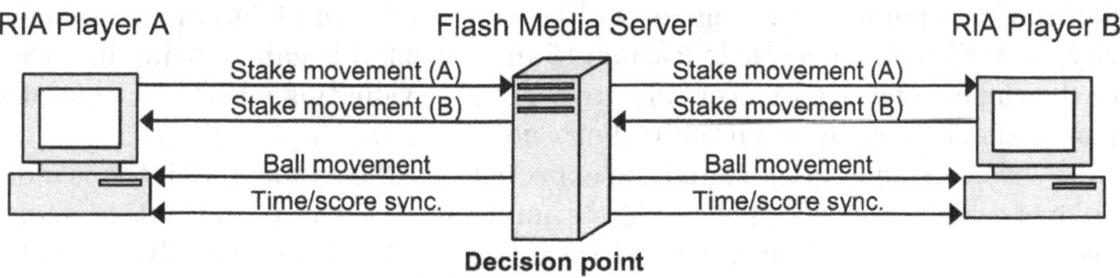

Fig. 2. State updates in the client-server architecture

A major drawback of the client-server solution is that players may receive the same state update at different times as the network delay from the game server to the two clients is different. Vice versa, players' action messages can also take different times to reach the game server, therefore unfairness in processing player action messages can be created at the game server. A player further away from the game server or connected to the server through congested or slower links will experience longer message delay. Because of this, even fast reacting players may not be given credit for their actions, leading to an unfair advantage for players with small message delays [13]. For instance, a player with a large delay would always see the ball later than the other player and, therefore, this player's action on the ball would be delayed even if the player reacted instantaneously after the ball position was rendered [1]. Despite these drawbacks, playability and fairness of the client-server solution turned out to be considerably improved with respect to the issues experienced in the hybrid P2P version. However, depending on the number of concurrent players, this solution incurs significant cost in the form of more CPU capacity and server software licences (which typically depend on the total bandwidth requirements).

6 Future Work

It will be interesting to see which architectural model and what kind of technology will prevail in the realm of browser-based multiplayer real-time games. Although current RIAs still entail some limitations with respect to real-time communication, this is likely to change in the future. Researchers will have to further explore what combination of gaming architecture and technology is best-suited for what kind of browser-based game. To do so, the respective impact for the players (in terms of playability and fairness) has to be evaluated in detail and related to measures such as bandwidth and latency. It also has to be explored to what extent the two architectural models presented in this paper can be applied to implement browser-based real-time games featuring *more* than two remote players in a single game session, as well as distributed real-time applications in domains apart from gaming.

With respect to online gaming portals with several thousand concurrent players, the architectural concepts presented in this paper have to be enhanced. As Flash Media Server uses a scripting language for server-side logic, its computational capacity is likely to be overloaded with an increasing number of players. This may be avoided by shifting the computationally intensive game state calculation to a separate game engine. As Flash Media Server allows direct connectivity to J2EE containers, it is feasible to implement this game engine in Java. The developers of virtual-kicker.com are currently evaluating whether a separate game engine is actually required in their specific case.

Moreover, a single server cannot be expected to suffice to deal with thousands of players synchronously. This suggests implementing the authoritative game server as cluster of machines with dedicated responsibilities that dynamically share resources and are consistent with each other [19]. Using a concept of origin and edge servers, Flash Media Server technology already features such clustering techniques. Future research has to explore how such concepts can be optimally applied in connection with real-time multiplayer games.

Besides that, multiple server clusters can theoretically be located at different places in the real world, allowing players to use the clusters located near to them geographically and thus reducing the effect of network latency [4,12]. Such approaches need to consider the selection of the best performing server, depending on a player's current location. This is relatively easy for a single player. However, if fixtures of opposing players are defined a priori in a competitive environment such as an online soccer league, intelligent methods are required to dynamically select the best-suited game server for a group of geographically dispersed players [20]. Similarly, such game server selection processes need to be re-evaluated concerning their applicability in connection with browser-based games.

7 Conclusion

With the advent of RIA technology, browser-based multiplayer gaming has finally reached a point that deserves the attention of serious game designers and online gaming researchers. The vast possibilities connected with technologies such as Adobe Flash and Java include producing many engaging and sought-after types of multiplayer real-time games. When implementing such games, the main challenge lies within guaranteeing playability and fairness despite synchronization issues that are connected with the current best-effort Internet. These issues need to be solved by designing appropriate game architectures and trading off inconsistencies between players depending on their perceptual impact. This paper introduced two architectural models that can be used to implement browser-based real-time multiplayer games. Both models rely on a central server, as a direct P2P communication cannot be realized with current RIA technology. However, this server can either form a global decision point that is calculating the current game state (client-server architecture) or simply relay game data between the clients, while one of the clients takes over decision point functionality (hybrid P2P architecture). While the former approach makes the game server a major bottleneck and incurs significant cost, the latter approach has major drawbacks resulting from the two different roles that clients can play.

Whether a browser-based real-time multiplayer gaming architecture is implemented using the client-server or the hybrid P2P model, fairly depends on the type of game as well as the availability of technology and financial means. A client-server architecture using server-side RIA technology currently seems to be the choice delivering the highest performance with respect to playability and fairness in highly fast-paced browser-based games. Slower games, on the contrary, may rather be implemented using a less cost-intensive hybrid P2P architecture.

References

1. Aggarwal, S., Banavar, H., Mukherjee, S., Rangarajan, S.: Fairness in Dead-Reckoning based Distributed Multi-Player Games. In: Proceedings of 4th ACM SIGCOMM workshop on Network and system support for games, pp. 1–10. ACM Press, New York (2005)

2. Yasui, T., Yutaka, I., Ikedo, T.: Influences of Network Latency and Packet Loss on Consistency in Networked Racing Games. In: Proceedings of 4th ACM SIGCOMM workshop on Network and system support for games, pp. 1–8. ACM Press, New York (2005)
3. Claypool, M., Claypool, K.: Latency and Player Actions in Online Games. Communications of the ACM 49(11), 40–45 (2006)
4. Brun, J., Safaei, F., Boustead, P.: Managing Latency and Fairness in Networked Games. Communications of the ACM 49(11), 46–51 (2006)
5. Sharp, C., Rowe, M.: Online games and e-business: Architecture for integrating business models and services into online games. IBM Systems Journal 45(1), 161–179 (2006)
6. El Rhalibi, A., Merabti, M.: Agents-Based Modeling for a Peer-to-Peer MMOG Architecture. Computers in Entertainment 3(2) Article 3B (2005)
7. Allaire, J.: Macromedia Flash MX – A next-generation rich client (white paper) (2002), `http://download.macromedia.com/pub/flash/whitepapers/richclient.pdf`
8. Kollmann, T., Häsel, M.: Cross-Channel Cooperation – The Bundling of Online and Offline Business Models. DUV, Wiesbaden (2006)
9. Silver, M.: Browser-based applications: popular but flawed? Information Systems and E-Business Management 4(4), 361–393 (2006)
10. Ramakrishna, V., Robinson, M., Eustice, K., Reiher, P.: An active self-optimizing multiplayer gaming architecture. Cluster Computing 9(2), 201–205 (2006)
11. GauthierDickey, C., Zappala, D., Lo, V., Marr, J.: Low Latency and Cheat-proof Event Ordering for Peer-to-Peer Games. In: Proceedings of NOSSDAV '04, pp. 134–139 (2004)
12. Smed, K., Hakonen, H.: Aspects of networking in multiplayer computer games. The Electronic Library 20(2), 87–97 (2002)
13. Guo, K., Mukherjee, S., Rangarajan, S., Paul, S.: A Fair Message Exchange Framework for Distributed Multi-Player Games. In: Proceedings of 2nd ACM SIGCOMM workshop on Network and system support for games, pp. 29–41. ACM Press, New York (2003)
14. Cronin, E., Kurc, A., Filstrup, B., Jamin, S.: An Efficient Synchronization Mechanism for Mirrored Game Architectures. Multimedia Tools and Applications 23(1), 7–30 (2004)
15. Pantel, L., Wolf, L.: On the Impact of Delay on Real-Time Multiplayer Games. In: Proceedings of NOSSDAV '02, pp. 23–29 (2002)
16. Diot, C., Gautier, L.: A distributed architecture for multiplayer interactive application on the Internet. IEEE Network Magazine 13(4), 6–15 (1999)
17. Mauve, M., Vogel, J., Hilt, V., Effelsberg, W.: Local-lag and time-warp: Providing consistency for replicated continous applications. IEEE Transactions on Multimedia 6(1), 47–57 (2004)
18. Lesser, B., Guilizzoni, G., Reinhardt, R., Lott, J., Watkins, J.: Programming Flash Communication Server. O'Reilly, Cambridge (2005)
19. Wang, T., Wang, C.L., Lau, F.: Grid-enabled multi-server network game architecture. In: Proceedings of the 3rd International Conference on Application and Development of Computer Games (2004)
20. Lee, K.W., Ko, B.J., Calo, S.: Adaptive Server Selection for Large Scale Interactive Online Games. Journal of Computer Networks 49(1), 84–102 (2004)

Distribution of Lecture Concepts and Relations in Digital Contents

Po Jen Chuang[1], Chu-Sing Yang[2], and Ming-Chao Chiang[1]

[1] Department of Computer Science and Engineering,
National Sun Yat-sen University, Kaohsiung, Taiwan, R.O.C.
[2] Department of Electrical Engineering,
National Cheng Kung University, Tainan, Taiwan, R.O.C.
{chuangpj,mcchiang}@cse.nsysu.edu.tw
csyang@mail.ee.ncku.edu.tw

Abstract. Digital contents contains a large number of learning concepts most of which contribute to the main learning ideas. How to focus on the learning faults and improve the learning process is important. In this paper, we propose a novel approach to retrieving the main ideas from, as well as to constructing a domain tree to represent, the contents of materials. The nodes of the domain tree consist of meaningful texts. We collect the meaningful texts by segmenting words of the digital contents and then recombining these texts to form a binary number. We define a scoring method for the digital contents by assigning a sequence of 0's and 1's to the texts. These binary numbers can then be easily calculated by a function of sequence with power n and base 2, where $n \in N$. Each sequence can get a unit score which indicates the location in the context. An expression of digital contents represents a unit, a chapter, a section, or a paragraph. This expression can be provided as a feedback to teachers or students. Based on the feedback, teachers can make questions in the exam sheet more evenly distributed while students can improve the way they learn.

Keywords: Learning, Knowledge-based, Word Segmentation, Feedback.

1 Introduction

We bring up an idea to score the concepts of learning materials and to establish a domain tree to represent the concepts [1]. Each concept has a unique score to represent the location of the learning materials [2]. In the new century of knowledge economics, the key to touch the future is by e-learning. Digital learning can leap learning across space and hours. To provide personalization support is an important e-learning research called adaptive learning in the Learning Management System (LMS) [3], [4], [5]. Adaptive learning mentions that personal learning situation can be caught [6], [7]. One way to catch learner's situation is by testing. In LMS, the first step is to establish testing banks to support a great deal of testing. Teachers get the learning condition of leaner's by means of the result of the testings in LMS [9], [10].

T. Enokido, L. Barolli, and M. Takizawa (Eds.): NBiS 2007, LNCS 4658, pp. 167–176, 2007.

Most of the learning management systems only support online testing or exam. The score is the result. In terms of testing, learning management system catches students' testing and calculates scores, but not in terms of learning [11], [12], [13]. In this paper, we use elementary school, grade 4, second semester textbook for experiment. There are many publishers for grade 4 textbooks. We choose two popular editions to compare the difference. They are "KANG HSUAN Educational Publishing Group" [14] and "HAN LIN Educational Publishing Group" [15].

In the textbook, each chapter is divided into several sections, and each section consists of several paragraphs. Given a binary expression, a paragraph can be broken into a set of texts. We use "The CKIP (Chinese Knowledge and Information Processing) group" [16] to provide Chinese Texts. Besides, the CKIP helps us break up contents into text sets. We set a paragraph of contents into a binary sentence, i.e., the combination of 0's and 1's. Finally, two different binary sentences can unite together and become a larger binary set. A concept tree is built to represent a chapter [17], [18]. In the same way, we check the questions of exam and break up the sentence into a binary expression. A question can be classified to a paragraph of context [20], [21]. Afterwards, we can locate the wrong answer from the exam and help in learning.

There is a modern method Vector Space Model(VSM) for counting the ranks among all the documents [19], [8]. VSM uses the frequency of each term as a coordinate. Each document can be treated as a vector, even the questions. VSM can exactly calculate the relation ratio between any arbitrary documents, which is computation intensive. Our method has short cut from the terms to mark the location, because we only need to take the relations between questions and contents.

The remainder of the paper is organized as follows. Section 2 introduces the proposed method to construct a domain tree. The feedback from the domain tree to teachers and students is discussed in Section 3. Section 4 provides an instance of real learning material, and Section 5 concludes the paper.

2 Lecture Distribution

Testing by itself can not lead to good learning. Instead, it just lets you get acquainted with computers. On the other hand, testing system provided in the Learning Management System by itself will not be a complete system. We believe that digital learning will promote learning speed and enhance learning achievement. In fact, an item bank combined with testing system can certainly promote learning process. However, what is the difference between online testing and paper testing?

In general, the correct and effective learning will lead to a good score for learners. Extracting context of learning material is the first step. Academia Sinica [22] has developed a Chinese Texts System. With this environment and technology now well established, we are focusing on knowledge-based information processing. It is a web service. Sending the format data to the web service and then, the service return the set of terms.

```
Main Context:

家鄉的機構可以分為民間和政府兩類。
民間機構包括:
銀行、醫療診所及各種性質的團體組織,
例如: 各類民間保育團體、紅十字會、救難協會等。

Chinese Texts:

家鄉(Nc) 機構(Na) 分為(VG) 民間(Nc) 政府(Na)
民間(Nc) 機構(Na) 包括(VK)
銀行(Nc) 醫療(VC) 診所(Nc) 性質(Na) 團體(Na) 組織(Na)
民間(Nc) 保育(VC) 團體(Na) 紅十字會(Nc) 救難(VA) 協會(Nc)

Result Texts:

家鄉 機構 分為 民間 政府 包括 銀行 醫療
診所 性質 團體 組織 保育 紅十字會 救難 協會
```

Fig. 1. CKIP Chinese Texts. The main context is a paragraph of the contents of learning material. The Chinese Texts consists of four lines which correspond to the main context. The result texts is the result after segmentation.

2.1 Chinese Texts

The word which can be freely used is the minimum and meaningful language unit. It is necessary to segment words of text in any language processing system. Then, the words can be processed, say, machine translation, analysis of the language, and information mining. Because the number of Chinese word segmented is a large scale, there does not exist a dictionary or method that contains all. Chinese Text System returns various nouns, verbs, adverbs and prepositions. We eliminate pronouns, adverbs, symbols and conjunctions which are not the main ideas among the contents. The meaningful texts for us are the nouns and verbs.

The main text in Figure 1 is just a paragraph of context. After the conjunctions are eliminated, we got 20 different texts shown in result texts. The returned Chinese Texts have morphology tags attached. The attached tag `Nc` is an address noun, `Na` is a normal noun, and `VA, VC, VG, VL, VK, VJ` are verbs. The others are as shown in `CKIP`.

2.2 Determination of Context

Determination of the context can be the feedback of creating sheet or study suggestion. Combining Chinese texts sets is the first step. The text items of a set are in a particular order. A binary expression form can be intuitively established, and a method of scoring is created.

Domain Tree. A Domain Tree of a context is a representation of the largest texts' union. Each paragraph supplies a set of texts, and two sets make a tree. Several sets can be established as a tree by recursively applying the union operation. The largest set of the text items are arranged in a certain order. We will establish a domain tree to represent the learning material. The operation we adopt is the union of all of the paragraphs.

Consider a learning material that is composed of two paragraphs which are denoted $\boldsymbol{Par_a}$ and $\boldsymbol{Par_b}$. Let's assume that the set $P_a = \{A, B, C, D, E\}$ represents the text items for $\boldsymbol{Par_a}$, and the set $P_b = \{B, E, F, G, I, K\}$ represents the text items for $\boldsymbol{Par_b}$. The union of these two sets can be computed as $P_r = P_a \cup P_b = \{A, C, D, B, E, F, G, I, K\}$.

Definition 1. *The root P_r of a domain tree is defined as the union of all of its children.*

$$P_r = P_1 \cup P_2 \cup \ldots \cup P_n. \tag{1}$$

where P_1, $P_2, \ldots, P_n$ are sets themselves.

Binary Numbers. After being united together, a score can be assigned to each of the two sets P_a and P_b. This score can determine what the degree of set in the largest set. To reach the step, a binary number will first be set. All the text items in a set are assigned the value 1; otherwise, the value is 0. To simplify the computation of the scores, the sets P_a, P_b, and P_r can be represented as binary numbers the length of which are exactly the same as the number of elements in P_r. Also, the location of the elements in P_r must be fixed, as follows:

Sequence from the union of two sets

```
 Algorithm Concat (S, T)
 {The input is the two sets S and T, and the output is a sequence W,
   which is a concatenation of the sets S − H, H, and T − H.}
begin
  Step 1  Find the intersection H of sets S and T.
  Step 2  Let the sequence be W  =  seq(S − H) · seq(H) · seq(T − H).
  Step 3  Return W.
end.
```

(Compute the union of two sets and then convert the result into a sequence so that the order of all the elements are *fixed*. Note that *seq*(A) is a conversion operator, which converts the elements of A into a sequence, and $\cdot$ is a concatenation operator, which concatenates all the sequences together.)

The binary number corresponding to the set P_a can be computed as follows:

1. Let b be a binary number with all the bits set equal to 1 and the length of which is exactly the same as the number of elements in the set P_r.
2. Reset all the bits in b representing a member in the set $P_r - P_a$ to 0.

P_b can be computed similarly.

Then, the set P_a can be denoted the binary number b, as follows:

$$\mathcal{B}(P_a, P_r) = (b_{a_{n-1}}, b_{a_{n-2}}, \ldots, b_{a_0}). \tag{2}$$

where $b_{a_i} \in \{0, 1\}$.

At a result, the largest set will be $P_r = \{A, C, D, B, E, F, G, I, K\}$, the binary number assigned to $\mathcal{B}(P_a, P_r)$ will be 111110000, and the binary number assigned to $\mathcal{B}(P_b, P_r)$ will be 000111111.

Scoring. Let a calculation Λ be the sum of the power function based 2 denoted as follows:

$$\Lambda(\mathcal{B}(P_a, P_r)) = \sum_{i=0}^{n-1} 2^i b_{a_i} \tag{3}$$

Then, the score of the sequence of P_a can be calculated as follows:

$$\Lambda(\mathcal{B}(P_a, P_r)) = 1\times2^8+1\times2^7+1\times2^6+1\times2^5+1\times2^4+0\times2^3+0\times2^2+0\times2^1+0\times2^0.$$

The score of paragraph $\boldsymbol{Par_a}$ is $\Lambda(\mathcal{B}(P_a, P_r)) = 496$ and the score of $\boldsymbol{Par_b}$ is $\Lambda(\mathcal{B}(P_b, P_r)) = 63$. Besides, the boundary is about 48. It means that the context belongs to paragraph $\boldsymbol{Par_a}$ if the score is between 48 and 496 while the context belongs to paragraph $\boldsymbol{Par_b}$ if the score is smaller than 48. It belongs to both of paragraph $\boldsymbol{Par_a}$ and $\boldsymbol{Par_b}$ if the score is 16, 32 or 48.

A domain tree for learning material is established. In fact, learning material usually consists of two or three units. Each unit is about two to four sections, and each section contains several paragraphs. The example of real material will be shown later.

2.3 Discussion

The Victor Space Model spends much time to calculate, the term frequency tf_i, where all the terms in all the documents are collected. The summary of each term's frequency in all documents is denoted as df_i. Let D be the total number of documents. VSM then calculates the logarithm of the quotient for D/df_i. The final step of VSM is comparing the distance between the query and the document weights and the relation rates in all the documents.

Figure 2, we compare VSM and our approach. First, we establish a domain tree using the segmented terms. Second, we use the binary numbers instead of IDF_i. The binary number is the expression of the interaction between the query and the domain tree. Finally, the scoring of the binary numbers can be used to indicate the location of the relation in the domain tree, where the location implies the paragraph of the document.

Our approach outperforms VSM in terms of the running time, because of the way the distance is calculated. We only find the location where the query is related in the document. In this case, the ranks, between documents, can be computed as the ration of the terms in the paragraph.

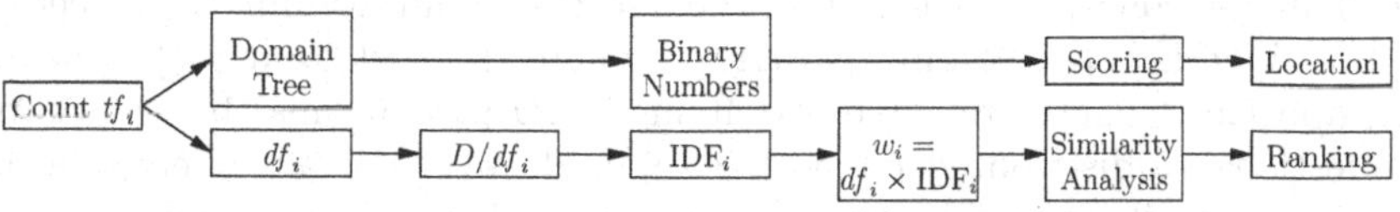

Fig. 2. The computing sequences of VSM and BUS for the purpose of comparison

3 Feedback to the Users

The value of an intelligent Learning Management System is on the feedback to the users. There are two faces to the feedback in the learning system. For the teachers, its main purpose is how to maintain an examination paper. For the students, it is how to get a high score in testing. Nevertheless, to get a high score is to learn well in the learning material. After a testing, teachers can analyze the questions which most people answer correct or wrong. Teachers can then modify the questions to increase or decrease the number of text items. On the other hand, for the students, the questions with wrong answers derive an awkward learning.

3.1 Creating Examination Sheet

Examination sheet is used for students to get acquainted with learning materials. The range of questions must include most of the context. There are two important things to be concerned. The first is that each section contents should be covered. Besides, more questions should be given to a section if that section is more important. Secondly, it should be a guide of remedial course.

Consider a question Q in an examination sheet that contains the text items A, C, D, G, H. That is, $Q = \{A, C, D, G, H\}$. Translating Q into a binary number by the operation $\mathcal{B}$. The binary expression $\mathcal{B}(Q, P_r) = 111000100$ and the score $\Lambda(\mathcal{B}(Q, P_r))$ is 452. The text item $\{H\}$ which appears neither in Par_a nor in Par_b will be erased. The text items of all questions in a examination sheet can be collected together. If the score of the text items of an examination sheet is high, then this exam is more closed to the content. Clearly, the question consists more parts of paragraph Par_a.

3.2 Learning Adjustment

To receive a high score in testing, it means that students understood what the books say. First, students need to understand the context of materials. Then, students must construct a structure of the concepts of a paragraph in mind. Finally, students must make the structures recalling rapidly. In the examination sheet, the questions with wrong answers will be collected, analyzed, and then locating the paragraphs. As a result of the operation Λ, it is clearly whether the students did understand the meaning of concepts.

Usually, a question is a mixture with more than one paragraph mingled, even more than one concept. For instance, the question of an examination sheet consists of $\{A, D, E, G\}$. The only paragraph where the text item $\{G\}$ appears is paragraph Par_b. There are three text items in Par_a. It means that concepts of the question are distributed on both Par_a and Par_b. For a student, the best choice is to read it again. The smallest unit we set is paragraph, and we propose to read the whole paragraph again. Clause of the concept is not only a key word but also a statement. If someone gets wrong answers in questions, it is better to review the statement.

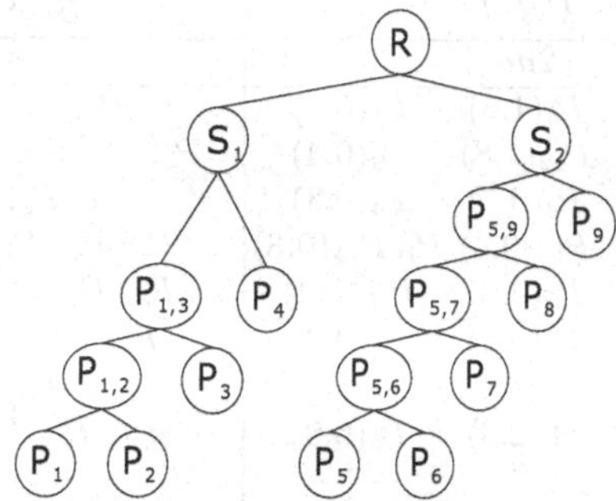

R:地表 高低 起伏 狀態 地形 山地 丘陵 臺地 盆地 平原
觀察 家鄉 地圖 景觀 特色 鄉民 聚居 型態 生活 方式
地區 種植 作物 農村 建築 高樓大廈 人口 密集 商業 活動
發達 都市 限制 土地 開發 困難 居住 稀疏 聚落 平緩
山坡地 茶園 果樹 坡度 森林 保育 自然 生態 氣候 氣溫
雨量 風向 天氣 溫度 變化 溫度計 測量 降雨 多寡 雨量計
風吹 方向 風向儀 記錄 降雨量 幫助 深入 認識 特徵 寒流
來襲 農漁業 災害 用水 缺乏 不便 颱風 挾帶 強風 豪雨
生命 財產 損失 解決 危機 生物 生長 適應 條件 多雨
地方 騎樓 方便 人們 雨天 行走 農民 季節 農作物

S_1:地表 高低 起伏 狀態 地形 山地 丘陵 臺地 盆地 平原
觀察 家鄉 地圖 景觀 特色 鄉民 聚居 型態 生活 方式
地區 種植 作物 農村 建築 高樓大廈 人口 密集 商業 活動
發達 都市 限制 土地 開發 困難 居住 稀疏 聚落 平緩 山坡地
茶園 果樹 坡度 森林 保育 自然 生態

S_2:家鄉 氣候 氣溫 雨量 風向 天氣 溫度 變化 溫度計 測量
降雨 多寡 雨量計 觀察 風吹 方向 風向儀 記錄 降雨量 幫助
深入 認識 特徵 鄉民 生活 寒流 來襲 農漁業 災害 雨量
用水 缺乏 不便 颱風 挾帶 強風 豪雨 生命 財產 損失
解決 危機 自然 景觀 生物 生長 適應 條件 方式 多雨
地方 建築 騎樓 方便 人們 雨天 行走 農民 季節 種植
農作物

P_1:地表 高低 起伏 狀態 地形 山地 丘陵 臺地 盆地 平原
觀察 家鄉 地圖 景觀 特色

P_2:家鄉 地形 鄉民 聚居 型態 生活 方式

P_3:平原 地區 種植 作物 農村 建築 高樓大廈 人口 密集 商業
活動 發達 都市

P_4:山地 地區 地形 限制 土地 開發 困難 居住 人口 較少
稀疏 山地 聚落 平緩 山坡地 茶園 種植 果樹 坡度 地區
森林 保育 維護 自然 生態

P_5:家鄉 氣候 受到 氣溫 雨量 風向

P_6:氣溫 天氣 溫度 變化 溫度計 測量 雨量 降雨 多寡 雨量計
觀察 風向 風吹 方向 風向儀

P_7:觀察 記錄 氣溫 變化 降雨量 幫助 深入 認識 家鄉 氣候
特徵

P_8:天氣 鄉民 生活 寒流 來襲 氣溫 造成 農漁業 災害 雨量
用水 缺乏 不便 颱風 挾帶 強風 豪雨 造成 生命 財產
損失 解決 危機

P_9:氣候 自然 景觀 生物 生長 鄉民 適應 條件 生活 方式
多雨 地方 建築 騎樓 方便 人們 雨天 行走 農民 季節
種植 農作物

Fig. 3. Domain Tree of learning material. The root R, which is the union of section 1 and section 2, contains 99 text items. S_1 and S_2 are sections and P_n, $1 \leq n \leq 9$, are paragraphs. $P_{i,j}$ means the TextUnion from paragraph P_i to P_j.

	VSM			BUS
	1st	2nd	3rd	
Q_1	$P_4(4.3)$	$P_3(1.5)$	$P_1(0.7)$	P_1, P_3, P_4
Q_2	$P_2(8.5)$	$P_{12}(2.8)$	$P_9(0.4)$	P_2, P_5, P_7, P_9, P_{12}
Q_3	$P_1(1.4)$	$P_2(0.7)$	$P_4(0.3)$	P_1, P_2, P_4
Q_4	$P_1(5.5)$	$P_{13}(0.4)$	$P_4, P_{14}(0.3)$	P_1, P_4, P_{13}, P_{14}
Q_5	$P_4(2.4)$	$P_9(2.3)$	$P_{13}(0.4)$	P_3, P_4, P_{13}, P_{14}
Q_6	$P_6(7.1)$	$P_7(0.4)$	$P_1(0.3)$	P_1, P_2, P_6, P_7
Q_7	$P_8(7.6)$			P_8
Q_8	$P_7(7.9)$	$P_6(2.3)$	$P_5(0.9)$	P_1, P_5, P_6, P_7
Q_9	$P_6(7.2)$			P_6
Q_{10}	$P_9(4.3)$	$P_{14}(2.1)$	$P_2(1.1)$	P_2, P_5, P_7, P_9
Q_{11}	*	*	*	*
Q_{12}	$P_{10}(1.9)$	$P_{11}(1.7)$	$P_{12}(0.2)$	P_{10}, P_{11}, P_{12}, P_{13}, P_{14}
Q_{13}	$P_{14}(3.2)$	$P_{10}(1.3)$	$P_{13}(0.3)$	P_1, P_2, P_5, P_7, P_8, P_{10}
Q_{14}	$P_{12}(4.4)$	$P_1(1)$	$P_9(0.8)$	P_1, P_9, P_{12}
Q_{15}	$P_{14}(4.2)$			P_{14}

Fig. 4. Vector Space Model vs Binary Union Structure. Binary Union Structure (BUS), a variant of Vector Space Model (VSM). The symbol $*$ is meant not found.

4 Experimental Results

The following example demonstrates how a decision-maker (teacher or student) chooses a solution. Optimization depends on different user. The basic procedure is to find the text items set in learning material. The next step is to determine whether the binary number can provide suggestion. The final step is to use the formulation to get the goal and to allow the decision-maker to choose a preferred solution. This experiment uses a program written in Visual Basic 6.0 in Windows XP to count the results.

Step 1. we set the paragraphs of material to Chinese Text System and get the text items. The main text is the context of a subject Society of grade four.

Step 2. construct a domain tree by paragraphs united. According to the result of Chinese Text, we establish a domain tree to represent the main text.

The domain tree has six layers, the root $R = S_1 \cup S_2$, the section layers $S_1 = P_1 \cup P_2 \cup P_3 \cup P_4$, $S_2 = P_5 \cup P_6 \cup P_7 \cup P_8 \cup P_9$, and the paragraph layer P_n, for $1 \leq n \leq 9$. $P_{i,j} = P_i \cup P_{i+1} \cup \ldots \cup P_j$. The root R of the domain tree contains ninety nine unique text items. The other nodes of the domain tree are as shown in Figure 3.

After constructing a domain tree, we choose questions from the examination sheet and compute the score $\Lambda(\mathcal{B}(question, R))$. The text item sets are computed by the operation $Q_i \wedge R$, where $i \in \{1, 2, 3\}$. The items marked by 1 indicate the text items existing in S_1. We can find that Q_1 and Q_2 belong to S_1, and Q_3 belongs to most parts of S_1. A teacher can get the feedback and create more questions derived from S_2. For students, there is no doubt that section S_1 must be paid more attention.

Figure 4 illustrates the result of locating the questions from 14 paragraphs in a content. Compared with VSM, BUS gives the same resulted except ranking. It seems that BUS can locate where the questions come from in a content by the simple comparison.

5 Conclusion and Future Works

As our experimental result shows, each question of the examination sheet can be derived from one paragraph. A teacher makes the amount of questions equally from different part of context. It is a good uniform distribution where questions distribute among the context. And teacher can certainly determine which part of context is more than the others. On the other hand, student gets a realization that some of the context is needed to study again.

Furthermore, we can compare two different sections which have the same title. There are many publishers who publish books for elementary schools. So many topics have the same title but the contexts are different. In this method, comparing paragraph and section, we can determine whether those books are similar. When a teacher creates a examination sheet, this information can provide a wide context to use.

Acknowledgments. This work was supported in part by a sub-plan of "National IPv6 Development and Promotion Project for NICI IPv6 Backbone Division" (I-0600) from Ministry of Transportation and Communications and in part by National Science Council, R.O.C. under contract number 95-2221-E-006-509-MY2. We would like to take this opportunity to thank both organizations for their financial support.

References

1. Billings, D.M.: A conceptual model of correspondence course completion. In: Moore, M.G., Clark, G.C. (eds.) Readings in Distance Learning and Instruction, 2. University Park, PA:ACSDE (1989)
2. Brusilovsky, P.: Adaptive hypermedia. User Modeling and User Adapted Interaction. In: Kobsa, A. (ed.) Ten Year Anniversary Issue, vol. 11 (1/2), pp. 87–110 (2001)
3. Bark, C.C., Geoffrey, I.W.: Dual-Model: An Architecture for Utilizing Temporal Information in Student Modeling. In: 7th International Conference on Computers in Education, pp. 111–118 (1999)
4. Brusilovsky, P.: Methods and Techniques of Adaptive Hypermedia. User Modeling and User Adapted Interaction 6(2-3), 87–129 (1996)
5. Ball, R.: Where are we and where are we going. ADL Library (2001), `http://www.adlnet.org/library/library_details.cfm?Repo_Id=555`
6. Borgatti, S.P.: @ What Is Social Network Analysis? `http://www.analytictech.com/networks/whatis.htm`

7. Carro, R.M., Pulido, E., Rodriguez, P.: Dynamic generation of adaptive Internet-based courses. Journal of Network and Computer Applications 22, 249–257 (1999)
8. Dik Lun, L., Kent, E.S., Huei, C.: Document Ranking and the Vector Space Model. IEEE Software 14(2), 67–75 (1997)
9. Feng, T., Fionn, M.: Towards Knowledge Discovery from WWW Log Data. In: Proceedings of the The International Conference on Information Technology:Coding and Computing (2000)
10. Hewitt, G.: A portfolio primer: Teaching, collecting and assessing student writing. Portsmouth, NH:Heinemann (1995)
11. ADL Technical Team. Sharable Content Object Reference Model (SCORMTM) Version 1.2. (2001)
12. AICC CMI subcommittee AICC/CMI Guideline For Interoperability Version 3.5 (2001)
13. Agarwal, R., Prasad, J.: Are Individual Differences Germane to the Acceptance of New Information Technologies? Decision Sciences 30(2), 361–391 (1999)
14. KANG HSUAN Educational Publishing Group `http://www.knsh.com.tw`
15. HAN LIN Educational Publishing Group `http://www.hle.com.tw`
16. Chinese Knowledge and Information Processing group `http://ckipsvr.iis.sinica.edu.tw/`
17. Chuang, P.J., Yang, C.-S., Lee, H.-T.: Visualizing the Multi-Direction of Portfolio. In: Conference on Information Technology and Applications in Qutlying Islands June 2-3, Kinman (2006)
18. Chuang, P.J., Yang, C.-S., Chiang, M.-C.: Visualizing The Learning Portfolio. In: IADIS International Conference Cognition and Exploratory Learning in Digital. Barcelona Spain (2006)
19. Salton, G., McGill, M.J.: Introduction to Modern Information Retrieval. McGraw Hill Book Co., New York (1983)
20. Liao, S.-J.: Constructing Decision Tree Using Leaners' Portfolio for supporting e-Learning. master thesis, National Sun Yat-sen University. Kaohsiung City, Taiwan (2003)
21. Chen, Y.-P.: Dynamic Constructing Decision Rules from Learning Portfolio to support Adaptive Instruction. master thesis, National Sun Yat-sen University. Kaohsiung City, Taiwan (2004)
22. Academia Sinica: `http://www.sinica.edu.tw`

Design of the Middleware Enabling Context Awareness and Energy Optimizing for Smart Environment*

Yuebin Bai[1], Haixing Ji[1], Huabin Lu[2], Chao Li[1], Qi Zou[1], and Peng Lv[1]

[1] School of Computer Science and Engineering, Beihang University, China
[2] Communication Telemetry & Telecontrol Research Institute,CETC, China
yuebinb@163.com

Abstract. Context-aware computing is a class of new conceptual pervasive computing system, which spring up and develop rapidly recently. In order to screen heterogeneity of ubiquitous networks and support rapid development of applications in context-awareness, the idea of middleware is widely adopted. In this paper, the middleware is proposed to support the application development of context-awareness under the wireless sensor networks environment. It applies the updated service-oriented and light-weight structure with excellent expansibility and efficiency in the running process. The runtime structure of the middleware is presented. During the process of context-awareness, the new method of awareness synchronization is designed to ensure the sensitivity to context switch. The algorithm of the energy efficiency during the context-awareness process is designed and evaluated. At the end of the paper, a healthcare scenario is used to validate the design methodology and demonstrate the supporting function of middleware.

Keywords: Context Awareness, Energy Efficiency, Middleware, Smart Environment, Pervasive Computing.

1 Introduction

Context-aware computing is a class of new conceptual pervasive computing system, which spring up and develop rapidly recently. context-aware applications are more and more widely used.[1, 2]. Recent research on context-awareness mainly focuses on two aspects: the methodology of modeling and the mechanism of awareness process. Since context-awareness applications are usually characterized by "one scenario, one development", the tools which support context-awareness application development are extensively studied and implemented. Dey [1] put forward a collection of context-awareness tools, some of which are reusable so as to support rapid development of context-awareness prototype. Also, Dey leveraged idea of middleware [3, 4, 5, 6, 7] is also employed. By defining the runtime architecture to co-support the development of

* This research work is supported by the National Natural Science Foundation of China (granted Nos. 90612004, 90412011, 60673180 and 90104022), and the Co-Funding Project of Beijing Municipal Commission of Education under granted No.SYS100060412.

T. Enokido, L. Barolli, and M. Takizawa (Eds.): NBiS 2007, LNCS 4658, pp. 177–186, 2007.

application, it usually turns the common process into an abstract one and encapsulates all kinds of operation into interfaces.

In this paper, we initially propose middleware enabling context awareness and energy optimizing for smart environment, with the purpose to give a service-oriented middleware to bridge the gap between the programmable application layer consisting of different scenarios and the hardware layer consisting of extremely heterogeneity devices. In this process, the middleware utilizes a service-oriented, distributed-extensible architecture to achieve the service in each awareness service domain, and the aware process is achieved by applying rule-based reasoning. In context-awareness, how to perceive scenario switching remains to be an open issue. An agent-based method could solve this problem.

The rest of the paper is organized as follows: section 2 describes the design principles of the middleware. Section 3 analyzes its runtime mechanism, especially the context-awareness process and energy optimizing approach. The application of the middleware in healthcare scenario and energy efficient evaluation is demonstrated in section 4. Section 5 summarizes the paper.

2 Design Principles of the Middleware

The middleware plays the supporting role in smart environment and its application development. On one hand, it could make bottom hardware transparent. On the other hand, it supports kinds of scenarios to release the expenses, which is achieved by supplying reusable application programming interface or criteria in development. Main design considerations include as following.

A. Service Oriented Approach in Middleware

Most of the context-awareness application system works under certain type of phenomenon and flows in a certain limited region. Actually, context-awareness usually is a process in which many factors interact with each other. It is common that one process depends on the status feature of another one. The traditional context-awareness system could not deal with this situation for lack of communication when obtaining contexts. The service oriented methodology in the paper aims to resolve the problem.

The service receives, manages, stores, and distributes context information. It is designed as a light-weight multi-thread running model, and only includes the necessary resources for a context-awareness process, such as the related awareness facts and rules. This model represents the customize process.

B. Smart Context-awareness

As a branch of expert system, rule based reasoning has its certain requirements. Firstly, in context-awareness, rule based reasoning is an event stimulated execution based on enough condition rather than a fixed logical workflow. The rule based reasoning in context-awareness shields the change of logical workflow efficiently and reduces the expenses of development. Furthermore, as the rules of runtime are customized, the programmer could load many rules into rule engine dynamically to carry out the process of customized awareness and reasoning.

When rule engine runs, entities' attributes will produce facts. Programmers analyze the scenario and abstract rules within the scenario, then import them to rule engine. When the imported facts meet the demand of some rule, the rule will be inspired. This process is called reasoning the rule and the production of result. The result will react with physical world through application presentation layer.

C. Energy efficiency and Rule-based Reasoning

Through rule-based reasoning as well as last state and recent state of entity, the part of monitoring object which should pay attention would be forecasted on application layer. This part of object is likely to engender some expectancy event or abnormal incident to make certain nodes which monitor it working, while, other nodes could hibernate at the same time in order to achieve energy-efficient.

The function of application layer straightly reflects the task of wireless sensor networks, that means these function explicitly express "what to do" for the network. For this reason, it can control every node's working condition according to function of network. Meanwhile, function of application layer usually runs on the powerful sink node, from which it can obtain classified information of every sensor node. Application layer can judge network status comprehensively via this way, and achieve energy-efficient on top layer. Through this process, we can realize the best practice in energy saving in the whole network; contemporarily avoid blindness energy saving on lower network layer .This energy efficient principle can ensure effectiveness of smart environment.

D. Extensibility of middleware architecture

The architecture of middleware must meet the extensive demands of context-awareness scale and the distribution character of the awareness objects. Generally, it is a kind of on-demand model which requires no time order but fixed regulation in the services communication.

The running system of middleware is displayed as a hybrid Peer-to-Peer fashion [6]. After registration, every service starts running independently and communicates with the another.

3 Runtime Structure of the Middleware

The middleware is expected to have excellent software runtime structure and efficiency. The runtime structure of the middleware is shown in Figure 1. Services are deployed in accordance with the form of "one scenario, one service, one reasoning and awareness process".

As is the shown in figure 1, the dynamic rule loading system in middleware makes it convenient for the users to add their own rules into the rule engine. The feedback function of context-awareness requires middleware to offer a reflection system, which could ensure proper feedback function or control of awareness and reasoning over relative physical devices and apparatuses. The *context agents* bridge up the entity in context-awareness service and devices in physical world. The feedback function is

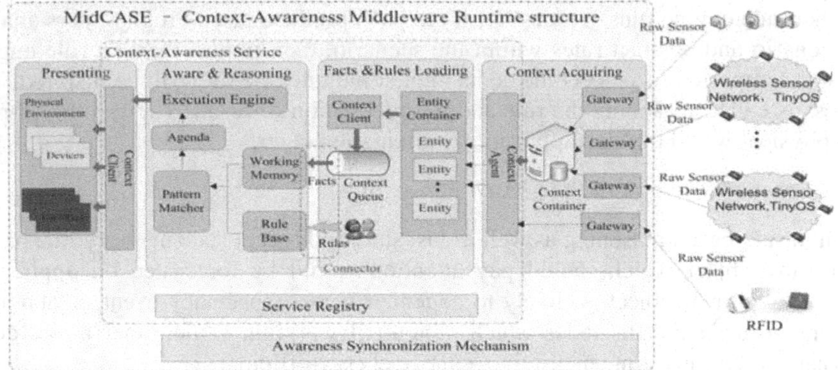

Fig. 1. Runtime Structure of the Middleware

implemented through the status change of relative physical device after visiting the status information of the changing entity in the service.

3.1 Context Modeling

Context modeling mechanism aims to supply context model tools to redisplay the physical world in computer. Generally speaking, it is achieved by *entity*. An entity models something that you want to manage information for, that is to say the variable entity produced in the process symbols the existed objects in the real world. Taken a nurse, a patient and a monitor as entities for examples, the status and capability of the objects refers to the attribute and methods of the entities. The selection of entities and their attribute, and the methods is critical in the model building process. Context service domain composed of *Context Agent* and *Context Tuple Space* and *Context Rule Engine* refers to the application of context awareness. The tuple space includes all the needed resources such as entities in one awareness process. The awareness process is implemented by rule engine, which manifests the smartness of the system.

The interfaces and methods are defined in the process, which shows the three effects of middleware: to define the interface method to supply model tool; to establish the model workflow by using the inherited relation between interface and class; to display the model building process by defining the call relation among methods.

3.2 Context Switch Perception and Awareness Synchronization

When the context service starts to work, the sensor network or other devices get data from physical world and then input them into the stored entities as their attribute value. An event-driven synchronized model is used to implement the process. In particularly, varieties of context agent are designed according to the diversity of ubiquitous network environment. The workflow is showed below:

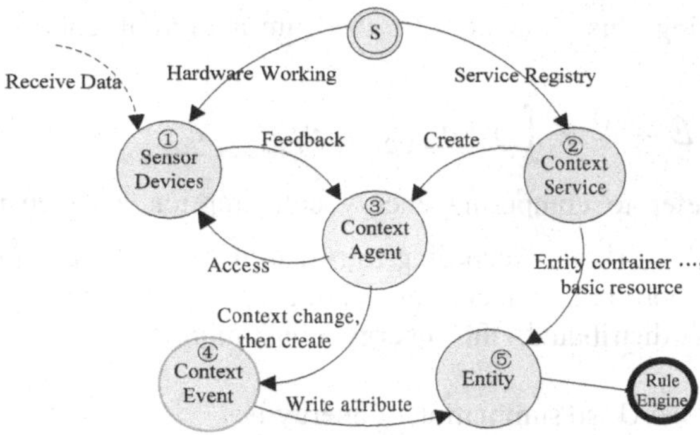

Fig. 2. Aware Synchronizing Process

Context agents constantly access the related sensor devices to get data. The data is then compared with previous data that was stored a moment ago. The differences between the two groups of data will originate context event, which means the switching of scenario. The attribute of the relative entities could be changed through context event and be input into rule engine as facts. When the facts occur and satisfy some rule, rule engine start working and produce some results. During the process, the synchronization of awareness depends on the regular polling of context agent's hardware devices. The more frequent the polling is, the better the efficiency of synchronization and the awareness to the switching of scenario is.

3.3 Design of Energy Efficient Approaches

A. Analyzing the Energy Consumption of the Environment

Energy effectiveness in wireless sensor networks is analyzed in the perspective of information redundancy. Suppose during the time slot t, one *sink* node have received the N packets which contains the monitor data produced by the sensor nodes. Among these packets, $N^{'}$ packets are included for available information and available information means that network must react with it, and entity monitoring or entity behavior may not be influenced by other information.

We assume e_{tran} refers to average energy consumption of one data packet, and e_{tran} can represent a data packet energy consumption of transmission from the sensor node to gateway. e_{tran} is given by

$$e_{tran} = \int_{t} f\left(n_1, n_2, \ldots, n_l\right) dt \tag{1}$$

in this expression ,we define $f\left(n_1, n_2, \ldots, n_l\right)$ as energy consumption function for single data packet, and this function is a multi-variable function which is co-related with network congestion, quality of service of network and node work station ,and so on.

Therefore, during this time slot t, the summation of energy consumption is expressed by

$$E = N * \int_t f(n_1, n_2, ..., n_l)dt + e_{comp} + e_{sens} \circ \quad (2)$$

e_{comp} and e_{sens} refer to computing energy consumption and sensing consumption during the network working. According to research work, the computing energy and sensing energy is more less than communication energy, particularly, in the condition of the large-scale distributed, this energy consumption status can be express as $\lim_{n\to\infty} \frac{e_{comp} + e_{sens}}{e_{tran}} \to 0$, so summation of energy is

$$E = N * \int_t f(n_1, n_2, ..., n_l)dt = N * e_{tran} \quad (3)$$

Similarly, energy of transmitting available information is

$$E^{'} = N^{'} * \int_t f(n_1, n_2, ..., n_l)dt = N^{'} * e_{tran} \quad (4)$$

We define the *energy efficiency* of wireless sensor network as:

$$\eta = \frac{E^{'}}{E} = \frac{N^{'} * \int_t f(n_1, n_2, ..., n_l)dt}{N * \int_t f(n_1, n_2, ..., n_l)dt} = \frac{N^{'}}{N} \quad (5)$$

And energy consumption of redundant data packets which exist in the process of network working can be given by

$$E_{waste} = E - E^{'} = (N - N^{'}) * e_{tran} \quad (6)$$

The recent research mainly focus on how to reduce the e_{tran}, and this can be achieved by designing energy efficient protocol or mechanism on physical layer, MAC layer and routing layer which reduce single packet energy consumption. However, few researches pay attention to how to reduce E_{waste}, which means reducing amount of redundant packets.

From the expressions 6, for certain application scenarios, there is lots of potential energy efficient work to do to reduce the redundant packets. Additionally, we suppose that energy consumption of single packet transmitting is the same in the condition of transmitting $N^{'}$ packets and N packets during the time slot t. However, in the real situation of network working course, the possibility of collisions and errors as well as re-transmitting packets will rapidly increase with the data packet increasing in the networks. Consequently, the single packet transmission energy when transmitting $N^{'}$ packets during time slot t is larger than transmitting N packets, that is $e_{tran} > e^{'}_{tran}$. Specially, when $N \gg N^{'}$, e_{tran} is not equals to $e^{'}_{tran}$, indeed larger. All this performance explains that e_{tran} is increasing with N in an exponential relation, so the practical energy efficiency of the network running is given by

$$\eta_r = \frac{E'}{E} = \frac{N' * \int_t f(n_1, n_2, ..., n_l)dt}{N * \int_t f(n_1, n_2, ..., n_l)dt} < \frac{N'}{N} \quad (7)$$

The practical redundant energy is

$$E_{waste,r} = E - E' = (N - N') * e_{tran} > (N - N') * e'_{tran} \quad (8)$$

Thus it can be seen, the redundant energy consumption does not increase according to linear relation but speedup. By this it is important to reduce redundant packets, nevertheless, this is just an aspect to improve on recently.

B. Energy Efficient Algorithm Design on Application Layer

The core thinking of Intelligent Energy Management (IEM) is to only allow critical node set working and non-critical node hibernate after entering into the normal status. Non-critical node set hibernates represent the all the nodes belong to that cluster should hibernate. So does critical node set.

The key of the algorithm is status judgment and it can be achieved by rule engine. Rule engine contains plenty of rules in rule base. The left side of rule is the value of a status and rule engine match the sampling data with rule which in rule base, meanwhile, the right side of the rule is critical node set of this status. If one status is known-status, the rule engine will find matching rule and together with correlated critical node set. Otherwise, if this status is fresh status, then a judgment will be made whether it is normal status or alert status. When the status is normal status, then a corresponding rule will be added to rule base. This rule form should be like this: the left side is value of this status and the right side is null or certain critical node which is appointed. When this status is alert status, the new critical nodes which change sharply should be founded through comparing current status to last status, then modify right side of the rule which represent last status. Additionally, the new rule which corresponds to this alert status will be added to rule base. The right side of this rule may be appointed to? The entire node to critical node or some certain nodes which is designated.

4 Implementation, Evaluation and Performance Study

4.1 Application Scenario and Test Bed Implementation

The prototype of the middleware has been implemented. Moreover, the iterating development method enables the perfection of middleware. The well-framed feedback system ensures the simultaneous reflection on physical environment. At present, the prototype of middleware could support the development of context-awareness in many scenarios. The healthcare scenario has been used to demonstrate the application of middleware. In Figure 3, Berkeley's MOTE-Kit 2400CB is used as the wireless sensor networks.

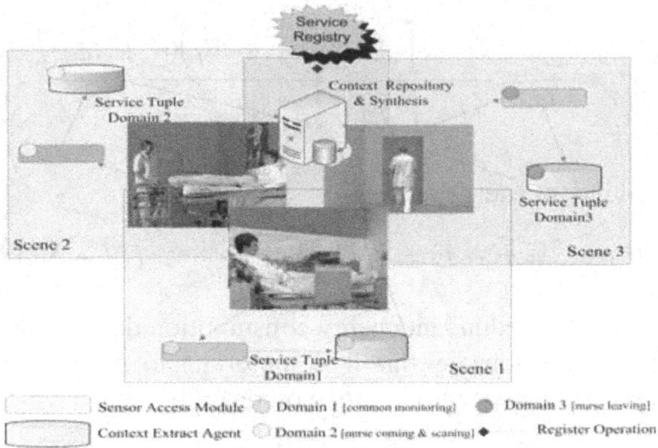

Fig. 3. The Context-Awareness in Healthcare

The above figure shows three scenes:

- *Scene 1*- The context-awareness service around patient. This service includes the collection of the monitor status information of patient such as temperature, blood pressure, cardio rate and other physiological parameters, and the storing of the data into database as the attribute value of patient. The monitor will go through the whole process and shows the program chosen by patient.
- *Scene 2* - Entering the service domain. In this scene the nurse enters the domain by using RFID tag to acknowledge her identification. After the identification, the monitor stops the program chosen by patient and begins showing the physiological information of the patient, as well as the basic personal information and medicine plan of the patient. This information could prevent medical accidents and enable nurses to have a direct view of the health condition of the patient.
- *Scene 3* - Leaving the context service domain. The last scene shows the leaving of the nurse from the domain. Subsequently, the monitor will restart the patient's program.

During the realization of scenario, after nurse enter the room the scenario changes. The content on the screen could inform the nurse of the current condition instantly. In addition, if any abnormal things happen, the awareness device could inform the monitor center immediately, which is managed efficiently through the synchronization mechanism. The whole process of context-awareness demonstrates the interacting model of man-machine. By adapting rule-based reasoning, the application of context-awareness could act automatically after the changes of environment without the interference of human being.

4.2 Energy-Efficient Algorithm: Simulation and Evaluation

We use *Matlab*7.2 to verify the algorithm. By combining the scenario of the middleware test-bed, a healthcare instance is adopted. The monitoring object is third day physical condition of a patient after operation. The monitoring time started from

0:00 time and lasted for 24 hours. This male patient is 28 years old and is in good condition .Some ailment is cardiac rate different, specified that when inspiration the rate increase and exhalation the rate decrease.

There are two group of wireless sensor network system in the process of simulation, and every group has sensor which can monitor cardiac rate, temperature, inspiration/exhalation, and blood pressure (see figure 3). *STEM* algorithm is used for group and *IEM* for another, then monitoring data and energy consumption is record to make comparisons with *Matlab*. The figure 4 shows this energy comparison:

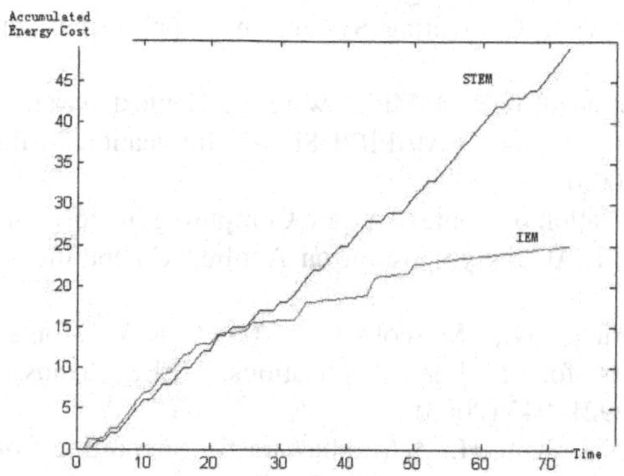

Fig. 4. The Context-Awareness Energy Consumption Comparison

Figure 4 explains the energy consumption with different energy-efficient algorithm. as the figure shows, because of the cardiac rate is changed greatly, the group which use *STEM* will report this change to gateway at high frequency, but the group which use *IEM* have the ability to reason that rate change corresponds with inspiration/exhalation, then sensor node will not report to gateway. For this reason the energy consumption of IEM is much lower.

5 Conclusions

The tendency of current research suggests the power of middleware to simplify the application development task in complex environments. The middleware, supporting context-awareness and energy optimizing based on wireless sensor networks, is proposed in this paper. A service oriented methodology is adapted to meet the demands of scenario customizing in concrete application development. The service is deployed in peer way which could adapt to the increasing extent of application scale. Meanwhile, the awareness synchronization mechanism and event-driven model in the running of middleware enable the process reflect environment instantly. Moreover, the rule based reasoning in the process brings up a good man-machine interacting environment. To validate design principals and make an experiment on the middleware prototype, the scenario of healthcare has been employed to demonstrate the vital supporting function of middleware.

References

[1] Dey, A.K., Salber, D., Abowd, G.D.: A Conceptual Framework and a Toolkit for Supporting the Rapid Prototyping of Context-Aware Applications? Human-Computer Interaction (HCI) Journal 16(2-4), 97–166 (2001)

[2] Mostéfaoui, G.K., Pasquier-Rocha, J., Brézillon, P.: Context-Aware Computing: A Guide for the Pervasive Computing Community. In: Proceedings of the IEEE/ACS International Conference on Pervasive Services, IEEE, Los Alamitos (2004)

[3] Kiani, S.L., et al.: A Distributed Middleware Solution for Context Awareness in Ubiquitous System. In: Proceedings of the 11th IEEE International Conference on Embedded and Real-Time Computing System and Applications, pp. 1533–2306. IEEE, Los Alamitos (2005)

[4] Ranganathan, A., Cambell, R.H: A Middleware for Context-Aware Agents in Ubiquitous Computing Environments. In: ACM/IFIP/USENIX International Middleware Conference, ACM, New York (2003)

[5] Bardram, J.E.: Application of Context-Aware Computing in Hospital Work - Example and Design Principles? In: ACM Symposium on Applied Computing, ACM Press, Bardram (2004)

[6] Capra, L., Emmerich, W., Mascolo, C.: CARISMA: Context-Aware Reflective mIddleware System for Mobile Applications. IEEE Transactions on Software Engineering 29(10), 921–945 (2003)

[7] Park, N.-S., Lee, K.-W., Kim, H.: A Middleware for Supporting Context-Aware Services in Mobile and Ubiquitous Environment. In: Proceedings of the International Conference on Mobile Business (2005)

[8] Kubisch, M., Karl, H., Wolisz, A., Zhong, L.C., Rabey, J.M.: Distributed algorithm for transmission power control in wireless networks. In: IEEE Wireless Communications and Networking Conference (WCNC'2003), March 16-20, 2003. IEEE Computer Society Press, Los Alamitos (2003)

Multilayer Quality and Grade of Service Support for High Speed GMPLS IP/DWDM Networks

Walter Colitti, Kris Steenhaut, Ann Nowé, and Jan Lemeire

Vrije Universiteit Brussel, ETRO Dept., COMO Lab., Pleinlaan 2, 1050, Brussels,
Erasmushogeschool Brussel - IWT
{wcolitti,ksteenha,asnowe,jlemeire}@etro.vub.ac.be

Abstract. IP over optical networks controlled by the GMPLS control plane have become the common infrastructure for a variety of services, such as triple play and grid applications. The traffic aggregation requires the services to be differentiated in a multilayer fashion, so as to guarantee higher levels of GoS and QoS to 'gold' traffic. This means that the traditional DiffServ technology needs to be combined with differentiation mechanisms in the optical domain. This paper proposes a framework for multilayer QoS and GoS support in GMPLS based IP/WDM networks. The scheme is based on a multilayer strategy which combines two routing policies that optimize the resource utilization. The system also provides a lightpath differentiation which allows the operator to accommodate sensitive traffic on lightpaths able to guarantee a certain level of transmission quality. The benefits of the scheme are illustrated by a simulation study, discussing blocking probability and resource utilization.

Keywords: GMPLS, DiffServ, QoS, GoS, Multilayer Traffic Engineering, routing, grooming.

1 Introduction

Over the last few years the telecommunications world has considerably evolved towards new challenging scenarios. The increased adoption of broadband access technologies such as Digital Subscriber Line (DSL), cable modem and Ethernet passive optical networks, has lead to the migration of most services towards the Internet Protocol (IP).

Based on the type of application supported, Internet traffic can be roughly divided into two large groups. On the one hand, there is the so called triple play, being the bundle of voice, video, and data services [1, 12]. Due to the fast advance in Voice over IP (VoIP), video on demand, IPTV (IP television) and Web 2.0 technologies, triple play applications have become omnipresent in our daily lives. The second group is the set of the large-scale grid computing services such as e-science applications emerging on a variety of scientific fronts, including geosciences, biomedical informatics and nuclear physics [4]. These applications enhance the understanding of complex systems that share and process data distributed in geographically dispersed locations.

T. Enokido, L. Barolli, and M. Takizawa (Eds.): NBiS 2007, LNCS 4658, pp. 187–196, 2007.

The traffic change has given rise two phenomena that change the scenario of the telecommunication networks: the massive increase of the bandwidth needs and the migration of the traffic patterns from the predictable and stable behavior of the traditional voice traffic to a self-similar and asymmetric nature of data flows. Consequently, dynamic allocation of resources has become extremely important for the cost effectiveness of a network. In order to satisfy traffic's quantity and quality, network operators have to replace the traditional expensive and statically provisioned networks with dynamic and self adaptive infrastructures. Such networks provide traffic with time-depended application-driven communications paths established by means of near real time signaling.

The fast progress in optical networking and Dense Wavelength Division Multiplexing (DWDM) technologies has made available a huge amount of bandwidth at a lower cost and with predictable performance. DWDM mesh networks provide clients with all-optical high speed channels (i.e. lightpaths) up to 10 Gbps (OC-192) and 40Gbps (OC-768) rates. Lightpaths bypass the electronic switching at intermediate IP routers and improve the communication performance in terms of end-to-end delay, jitter and packet loss. In addition, there has been an effort in providing optical components with a certain grade of automation in order to facilitate intra/inter domain communication by means of an intelligent control plane – called Generalized Multi Protocol Label Switching (GMPLS) [5, 9, 10]. GMPLS eliminates the burden of the human manual intervention b erators need technologies for guaranteeing communications quality and increasing the Return on Investment (ROI). The preferred technology for scalable IP Quality of Service (QoS) deployments is Differentiation Service (DiffServ). DiffServ supports differentiated and assured delay, jitter and loss commitments on the same IP network for different Classes of Service (CoS). However, the massive traffic increase and the flexibility introduced by GMPLS and IP/DWDM networks have made IP layer QoS control mechanisms insufficient. Operators are required to implement new integrated techniques able to satisfy the communication quality on both IP and DWDM layer. The communication quality in IP/DWDM networks encloses two concepts: QoS and Grade of Service (QoS) [6]. The QoS concerns the transmission performance during the data communication phase, such as delay, jitter, Bit Error Rate (BER) and packet loss. The GoS is the set of parameters related to y using sophisticated signaling and routing mechanisms to set up on-demand high speed end-to-end connections in the order of milliseconds. In such a dynamic scenario, the network nodes become intelligent agents able to automatically react to the traffic changes in a multilayer way. This can be thought of as a cooperation between the IP layer (by means of traffic grooming) and the optical layer (by means of dynamic lightpath establishment) in traffic engineering the network and called Multilayer Traffic Engineering (MTE).

When aggregating different traffic types with different Service Level Agreements (SLAs) on the same infrastructure, op the connection establishment, such as blocking probability. Both aspects need to be considered by a network operator to guarantee higher quality communication to high priority sensitive traffic.

This paper proposes and analyzes a framework for multilayer QoS and GoS support in GMPLS based IP/WDM networks. In order to address both QoS and GoS issues, the system differentiates the traffic in two steps. In the first, the traffic differentiation is based on the required bandwidth. High bandwidth applications – likely grid computing services – are routed according to a policy preferring the installation of new lightpaths in order not to overload existing connections. Low bandwidth applications – likely triple play services – are first attempted to be groomed on existing lightpaths in order to optimize the bandwidth utilization while keeping physical resources available for high bandwidth connection requests. In the second step, the traffic differentiation is based on the priority assigned by the DiffServ domain and on an admission control accepting sensitive traffic only in case it can be accommodated on lightpaths providing a sufficient level of QoS. The simulation results show the improvements obtained by the proposed scheme in terms of resource utilization and blocking probability.

The paper is organized as follows. Section 2 describes the motivation and the related work. In Section 3 we give a detailed explanation of the proposed framework. In Section 4 the simulation results and their discussion are presented. Section 5 draws some conclusions.

2 Motivation and Related Work

In this section we first describe the related work found in the literature and then we present the twofold contribution of this paper.

The work in [6] focuses on the importance of the GoS in optical networks. The authors present three mechanisms for GoS differentiation in a DWDM network. The first policy is based on the resource preservation for high priority requests. The authors introduce a threshold that is used to decide on the amount of resources that should remain available for high priority requests at the expenses of low priority. The second mechanism is based on routing algorithms which assign a higher number of routes to high priority traffic. This policy results in a lower blocking probability for high priority requests but in a higher set up time due to the higher number of attempts the systems executes among the available paths. The last proposed GoS method is based on the preemption of low priority requests when the system is unable to find sufficient resources for high priority traffic.

The work presented in [1] proposes a multilayer routing solution based on a hybrid on-line/off-line approach. High priority traffic is accommodated by means of an off-line system that optimizes the route calculation based on a foreseen traffic matrix. Low priority traffic is routed in a real time fashion with an on-demand route computation based on the network state. The system needs to be equipped with a preemption module in order to guarantee a lower blocking probability to gold requests at the expense of the low priority traffic. According to our point of view, this system has several weaknesses. Firstly, it requires a high implementation complexity due to the need for an on-line and an off-line routing modules and a preemption module. Secondly, it relies on the assumption that high priority traffic is predictable.

In [4], an approach for service differentiation in a GMPLS grid infrastructure is proposed. The scheme is based on a mapping between thc MPLS label and the lightpaths' quality. When traffic enters an optical network, the incoming label determines the received QoS treatment: high priority traffic is routed over lightpaths offering a lower signal degradation. This framework achieves a lower packet loss for high priority traffic with a slight increase of the total blocking probability. However, the GoS is not considered and therefore the author cannot guarantee lower blocking probability to high priority traffic.

In [10] and in [16] the authors propose two routing strategies. Either the system accommodates new traffic preferably on the existing virtual topology or it first tries to set up one or more lightpaths. The weakness of these schemes is that the system can only statically apply one routing policy therefore causing a non-optimal resource utilization level.

The analysis of the aforementioned studies suggests two considerations: GoS and QoS are typically considered individually and the routing/grooming strategies are always statically decided.

The contribution of this paper is twofold. Firstly, we propose a control scheme that differentiates the traffic considering both GoS and QoS. Secondly, the system accommodates requests according to bandwidth-depended multilayer routing policies.

3 A Scheme for Multilayer QoS and GoS in GMPLS Networks

In this section, we first recall some background information needed to understand the rest of the paper and then we describe (in paragraphs 3.1 and 3.2) the main building blocks.

In MPLS a connection is usually called Label Switched Path (LSP), indicating that a path between source and destination MPLS routers – called Label Edge Routers (LER) – is a set of links represented by a set of labels. The core routers along the LSP are called Label Switching Routers (LSRs). LSRs switch packets according to a forwarding table which associates an incoming link and label with an outgoing link and label. The counterpart of the LSP in GMPLS is called Optical LSP (OLSP), meaning that a source-destination connection is a set of wavelengths traversing one or more OXCs. Due to the non-packet nature of optical networks, the OXCs forward traffic by mapping an incoming fiber and wavelength on an outgoing fiber and wavelength.

In a DiffServ domain, IP packets are aggregated and marked using the DiffServ Code Point (DSCP) field in the packet, in order to identify the class of service. To guarantee the QoS to high priority traffic, the DiffServ paradigm defines three forwarding per-hop behaviors (PHB) to be applied to the traffic at each hop depending on the traffic classes: high sensitive traffic, bandwidth guaranteed traffic and best-effort traffic. These classes are respectively represented by the Expedited Forwarding (EF), the Assured Forwarding (AF) and the Default PHBs.

We suppose that a DiffServ/MPLS connection requires accommodation on a GMPLS optical network.

The scheme's architecture is described in figure 1. The modules implemented to build the proposed scheme are the GoS and the QoS modules. They are described in paragraph 3.1 and 3.2 respectively.

3.1 GoS Module

The GoS module gets input from the User Network Interface (UNI) module. The UNI is a set of protocols allowing the client network – in this case an MPLS/DiffServ domain – and the server domain (e.g. optical network) to communicate with each other. More precisely, by sending UNI request messages, the LSPs requests invoke the optical domain for the OLSPs setup, while the optical layer acknowledges the success or the failure of the OLSP establishment by sending UNI reply messages. The parameter passed by the UNI to the GoS module is the bandwidth required by the LSP. By looking at the required bandwidth, the GoS module decides on which multilayer routing policy to apply

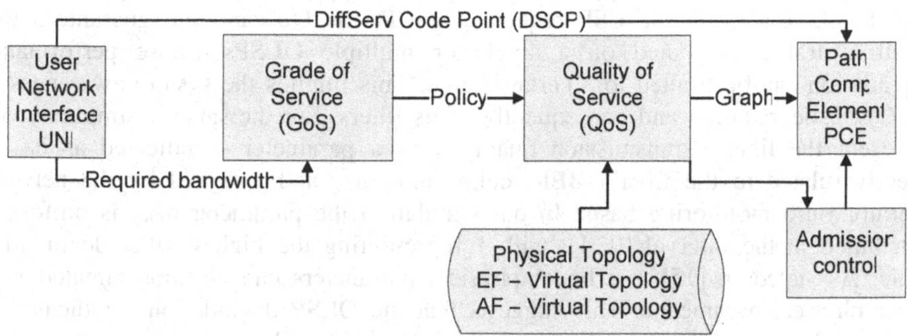

Fig. 1. Architecture of the proposed control scheme

The policy decision is taken by comparing the required bandwidth value with a fixed threshold: a high bandwidth LSP request is accommodated with the New Lightpath First (NLF) policy, while a low bandwidth LSP request is routed with the Grooming First (GF) policy. The two policies are described as follows:

- *NLF policy*. The system first attempts to establish a new direct OLSP between source and destination LERs. If a new OLSP cannot be established due to physical resource shortage (i.e. available wavelengths and ports) the system tries to aggregate the traffic over the existing virtual topology.
- *GF policy*. The system first attempts to groom the LSP request over the existing virtual topology. If there is not sufficient bandwidth and a path is not found, a new OLSP establishment is triggered.

The rationale for routing LSPs according to two different policies originates from empirical assessments and conceptual considerations concerning blocking probability and resource usage. On the one side, the NLF policy achieves a lower blocking probability at the expenses of a low bandwidth utilization level. The GF policy achieves a better bandwidth utilization level when the average LSP's required bandwidth is relatively low.

The previous considerations suggest that neither NLF nor GF are valid candidates as unique multilayer routing policy and that a higher grade of optimality can be achieved if the system suitably applies both strategies. In the system we propose, applications with massive bandwidth requirements (e.g. grid computations) are accommodated according to the NLF policy. Such applications likely have higher priority than low bandwidth applications and therefore require a lower blocking probability. Low bandwidth LSPs are routed according to the GF policy in order to improve the bandwidth utilization level at the expenses of a slightly higher blocking probability.

3.2 QoS Module

The output of the GoS module is a multilayer routing policy which is passed to the QoS block. Based on the LSP request's DSCP, the QoS module guarantees that sensitive traffic is routed on a single or multiple OLSPs whose performance degradation can be limited to a certain value. This implies the system awareness of the OLSP degradation and consequently of its fibers. For the sake of simplicity, we represent the fiber's transmission quality with a parameter – indicated as α_{fiber} - directly related to the fiber's BER, delay and jitter and assigned by the network operator on a monitoring basis. In our simulation the parameter α_{fiber} is uniformly distributed in the interval [0, 1], with 1 representing the highest fiber degradation value. As stated in [15] non linear physical parameters can be approximated with linear physical parameters. This suggests that the OLSP degradation – indicated as α_{OLSP} – is the sum of the degradation of all its constituent fibers.

The GoS module differentiates the created OLSPs according to a threshold – indicated as α_{max} – representing the maximum signal degradation an OLSP can support to provide a certain grade of transmission quality. Consequently, an OLSP is considered to be a high quality OLSP (HQ-LSP) if its signal degradation α_{OLSP} is lower than the threshold α_{max}, while an OLSP is considered to be a low quality OLSP (LQ-LSP) if its signal degradation α_{OLSP} is higher than α_{max}. By differentiating the OLSPs an operator can transmit sensitive traffic (EF-LSPs) by using only connections able to guarantee a deterministic performance in terms of BER, delay and jitter. In order to keep the HQ-OLSPs available in case sensitive traffic need to be transmitted, traffic requiring less tight QoS commitments (AF-LSPs) is accommodated on LQ-OLSPs.

4 Performance Evaluation and Results Analysis

The performance of the proposed multilayer QoS and GoS control scheme for IP/DWDM networks has been evaluated by means of simulation experiments under the OMNET++ simulation tool [16]. OMNET++ is an open source discrete event simulation system providing a component architecture based on reusable modules. The model topology is specified using the NED language while the modules are written in C++ programming language. We provided extensions for the basic OMNET++ package in order to model a GMPLS based IP over optical network.

The network under test is illustrated in figure 2. It consists of 21 nodes and 36 bidirectional optical fibers with the value of the signal degradation (α) uniformly distributed in the interval [0, 1]. The threshold for the OLSP differentiation – the maximum signal degradation α_{max} – has been chosen according to the formula $\alpha_{max} = (D + 1)\alpha_{av}$. D represents the network diameter, defined as the average minimum

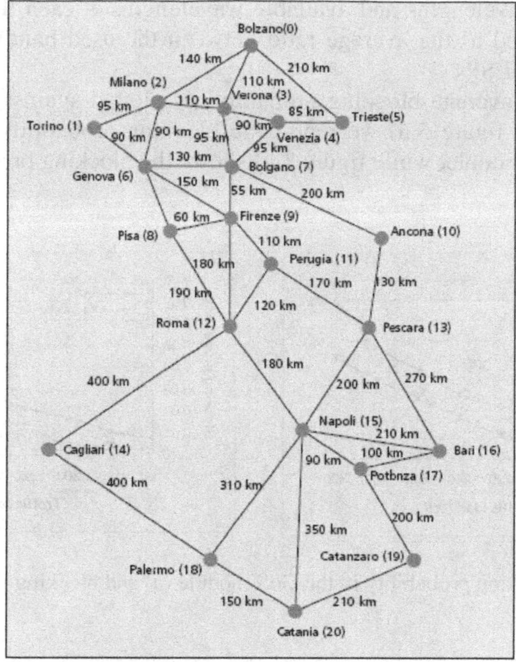

Fig. 2. Network topology under test

distance between any two nodes in the network. α_{av} is the mean value in the interval where α is generated. In our experiments $\alpha_{av} = 0.5$ and D = 2.78, therefore $\alpha_{max} = 1.89$.

Every fiber is equipped with 16 wavelengths each one supporting capacity values from 51.84 Mbps (OC-1) to 40 Gbps (OC-768).

The traffic sources are modeled with a Poisson process with an average rate λ and connection holding time exponentially distributed with mean $1/\mu$. The network load is given by $\gamma = \lambda/\mu$ Erlangs. The generators are set to generate 40% of Expedited Forwarding (EF) requests and 60% of Assured Forwarding (AF) requests. The connection requests have a bandwidth demand uniformly distributed among all the supported values, namely in the interval [OC-1, OC-768]. The threshold to differentiate a high bandwidth LSP (HB–LSP) from a low bandwidth LSP (LB-LSP) is set to OC-24. This means that all the connection requests with a bandwidth requirement lower than the threshold are considered as LB-LSP and are accommodated with the GF policy while connection from OC-24 till OC-768 are considered to be HB-LSP and are routed according to the NLF policy.

Each simulation run generates 10^6 requests with source and destination uniformly distributed among the entire set of nodes. In all the experiments the plotted results are the average values calculated over 10 outcomes for each value of the X-axis.

The performance is evaluated in terms of blocking probability, optical network resource utilization and bandwidth utilization. The blocking probability is defined as the average ratio between the number of rejected requests and generated requests. The optical network wavelength utilization is defined as the average ratio between the number of used wavelengths and available wavelengths at each link. The bandwidth utilization is defined as the average ratio between the used bandwidth and the total bandwidth of the OLSPs.

In figure 3, the average blocking probability is plotted against different values of the traffic load. In figure 3.a) we report the blocking probability undergone by the traffic in the GoS module, while figure 3.b) shows the blocking probability in the QoS module.

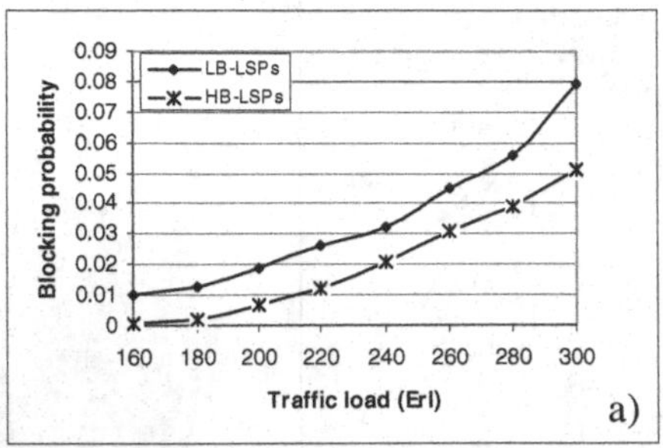

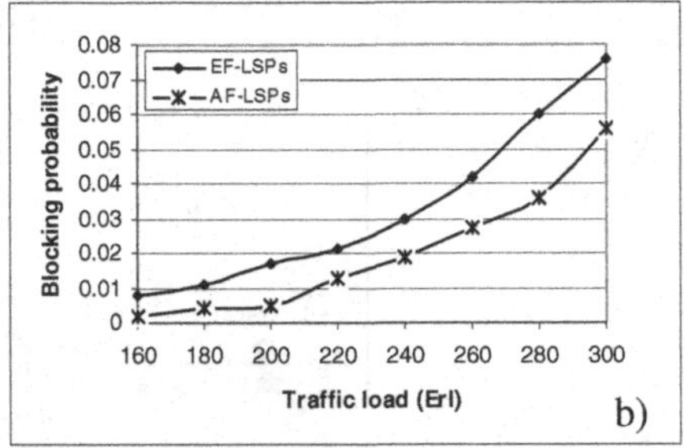

Fig. 3. Average blocking probability in the GoS module (a) and blocking probability in the QoS model (b)

As reported in figure 3.a), the combination of the NLF and GF policies gives rise to different values for the blocking probability suffered by high bandwidth and low bandwidth traffic. The number of blocked HB-LSPs is constantly lower than the one measured for LP-LSPs for every value of the traffic load. This is due to the fact that in the chosen network model, the system has more chances to find available wavelengths and ports to accommodate HB-LSPs on a new OLSP than to find available bandwidth to groom LB-LSPs on the existing virtual topology. Such a choice originates from the fact that only HB-LSPs have to undergo the QoS admission control because they imply a new OLSP establishment. However, the network operator can directly influence the performance by deploying a lower number of wavelengths and ports.

As shown in figure 3.b), sensitive traffic is penalized with a higher blocking probability for every traffic load condition. This is due to the QoS admission control that blocks EF-LSPs if the OLSPs do not provide a sufficiently low value of the signal degradation. It is straightforward that the threshold α_{max} directly affects the HP-LSP blocking probability. Consequently, the network operator can vary the network performance by changing the value of α_{max} according to the SLAs.

In figure 4, the resource utilization level is reported. In figure 4.a) we show the wavelengths utilization (optical layer), while figure 4.b) illustrates the bandwidth utilization (IP layer). In order to demonstrate the benefits of using a combination of the NLF and GF policies as multilayer routing strategy, the results obtained from the simulation of the proposed system are compared with the two cases in which either the NLF policy or the GF policy is used.

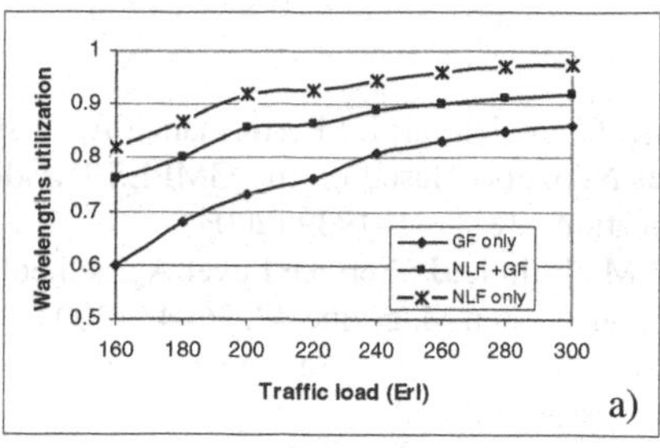

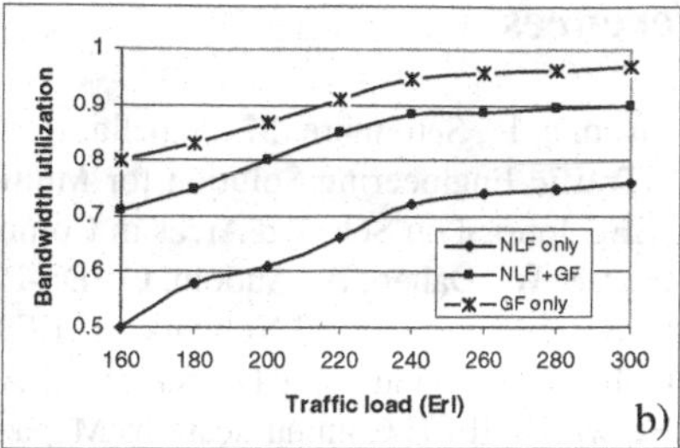

Fig. 4. Wavelength utilization (a) and bandwidth utilization level (b)

As expected, the use of only a static single policy as routing strategy leads to resource underutilization. The GF policy has a significantly low wavelengths usage (figure 4.a) while the NLF policy results in a very low bandwidth utilization level (figure 4.b). In both cases the curve representing the results obtained when using the proposed scheme (NLF + GF in the figure 4) is closer to the curve with the best performance. This explains that the combination of the two policies leads to a resource utilization compromise that combines the advantages of both policies.

5 Conclusions

Due to the migration of most services over the IP protocol, the service differentiation has become important not only in the IP layer, but also in the optical layer.

In this paper we proposed a framework for multilayer QoS and GoS support in GMPLS based IP/WDM networks. The system differentiates the traffic according to the required bandwidth and to the QoS needed. Under a first differentiation, high bandwidth connections are accommodated according to a routing policy that first tries to accommodate the request on a new direct lightpath and then tries to groom it on the existing virtual topology. Low bandwidth traffic is groomed on the existing virtual topology if possible, otherwise the systems considers a new lightpath set up. The second differentiation is based on the lightpath quality. Sensitive traffic is accommodated only on lightpaths with a signal degradation under a certain threshold. This admission control is not provided when accommodating traffic with less strict QoS requirements.

The benefits of the proposed system have been shown in terms of blocking probability and resource utilization level. The combination of the two multilayer routing policy leads to a compromise between optical resources utilization level and bandwidth utilization level.

Acknowledgements

This research work has been funded by the Fonds voor Wetenschappelijk Onderzoek (FWO) Vlaanderen (Research Foundation Flanders).

References

1. Iovanna, P., Settembre, M., Sabella, R., Conte, G., Valentini, L.: Performance Analysis of a Traffic Engineering Solution for Multilayer Networks Based on the GMPLS Paradigm. IEEE Journal on Selected Areas in Communications 22, 1731–1739 (2004)
2. Fawaz, W., Daheb, B., Audoin, O., Du-Pond, M., Pujolle, J.: Service Level Agreement and Provisioning in Optical Networks. IEEE Communication Magazine 42, 36–43 (2004)
3. Golmie, N., Ndousse, T.D., Su, D.H.: A Differentiated Optical Service Model for WDM Networks. IEEE Communications Magazine 38, 68–73 (2000)
4. Palmieri, F.: GMPLS-based service differentiation for scalable QoS support in all-optical Grid applications. Future Generation Computer Systems 22, 688–698 (2006)
5. Sabella, R., Iovanna, P.: Self Adaptation in Next-Generation Internet Networks: How to react to Traffic Changes While Respecting QoS? IEEE Transactions on Systems, Man, and Cybernetics 36, 1218–1229 (2006)
6. Szymanski, A., Lason, A., Rzasa, J., Jajszczyk, A.: Grade-of-Service-Based Routing in Optical Networks. IEEE Communications Magazine 45, 82–87 (2007)
7. Sato, K., Yamanaka, N., Takigawa, Y., Koga, M., Okamoto, S., Shiomoto, K., Oki, E., Imajuku, W.: GMPLS-based photonic multilayer router (Hikari router) architecture: an overview of traffic engineering and signaling technology. IEEE Communications Magazine 40, 96–101 (2002)
8. Daheb, B., Pujolle, G.: Quality of Service Routing for Service Level Agreement Conformance in Optical Networks. In: Proc. of GLOBECOM, St. Louis, Missouri (2005)
9. Pasqualini, S., Kirstadter, A., Iselt, A., Chahine, R., Verbrugge, S., Colle, D., Pickavet, M., Demeester, P.: Influence of GMPLS on Network Providers' Operational Expenditures: A Quantitative Study. IEEE Communications Magazine 43, 28–38 (2005)
10. Oki, E., Shiomoto, K., Shimazaki, D., Imajuku, W., Takigawa, Y.: Dynamic Multilayer Routing Schemes in GMPLS-Based IP + Optical Networks. IEEE Communications Magazine 43, 108–114 (2005)
11. Bosco, A., Manconi, E., Sabella, R., Valentini, L.: An Innovative Solution for Dynamic Bandwidth Engineering in IP/MPLS Networks with QoS support. Photonic Network Communications 7, 37–42 (2004)
12. Evans, J., Filsfils, C.: Deploying Diffserv at the Network Edge for Tight SLAs, Part I. IEEE Internet Computing 8, 61–65 (2004)
13. Lobo, J.F., Jimenez, F.J.: Impact of GMPLS on an Integrated operator. In: proc. WGN5, V Workshop in G/MPLS Networks, Girona, Spain (2006)
14. Strand, J., Chiu, A.L., Tkach, R.: Issues for routing in the optical layer. IEEE Communications Magazine 39, 81–87 (2001)
15. Cugini, F., Andriolli, N., Valcarenghi, L., Castoldi, P.: Physical Impairment Aware Signalling for Dynamic Lightpath Set Up. In: proc. ECOC 2005, Glasgow, Scotland (2005)
16. Salvadori, E., Battiti, R.: A Traffic Engineering Scheme for QoS Routing in G-MPLS Networks based on transmission Quality. In: proc. ONDM 2004, Gent, Belgium (2004)
17. http://www.omnetpp.org

Implementing Range Queries with a Decentralized Balanced Tree over Distributed Hash Tables

Nuno Lopes* and Carlos Baquero

CCTC-Department of Informatics
University of Minho
Braga, Portugal

Abstract. Range queries, retrieving all keys within a given range, is an important add-on for Distributed Hash Tables (DHTs), as they rely only on exact key matching lookup. In this paper we support range queries through a balanced tree algorithm, Decentralized Balanced Tree, that runs over any DHT system.

Our algorithm is based on the B^+-tree design that efficiently stores clustered data while maintaining a balanced load on hosts. The internal structure of the balanced tree is suited for range queries operations over many data distributions since it easily handles clustered data without losing performance.

We analyzed, and evaluated our algorithm under a simulated environment, to show it's operation scalability for both insertions and queries. We will show that the system design imposes a fixed penalty over the DHT access cost, and thus inherits the scalability properties of the chosen underlying DHT.

1 Introduction

Distributed Hash Table (DHT) systems [1,2,3,4] are used as efficient distributed dictionary implementations, offering a scalable and robust P2P framework that efficiently locates objects given a key [5,6]. However, such efficiency is achieved by an exact key matching lookup interface. The discrete key lookup interface uses an hash function on the key value to locate objects. This hash function removes locality properties from keys which restricts it's use for range queries. A range query consists in retrieving all keys that fall within a specific range interval. Range query is a desired feature when using data that is indexed by contiguous values (consider for example, numeric spatial coordinates).

Previous systems have offered range queries by either using specially designed structures [7,8,9] or building on top of generic DHTs [10,11,12]. Because the first class of systems is bound to some particular basic storage structure, it offers a limited solution that may not be as efficient as some DHT systems are. This

* Supported by a Ph.D. Scholarship from FCT-Foundation of Science and Technology, the Portuguese Research Agency.

T. Enokido, L. Barolli, and M. Takizawa (Eds.): NBiS 2007, LNCS 4658, pp. 197–206, 2007.

makes the second class of systems, building a tree structure over a generic DHT, the most flexible choice. By building on a generic DHT, one can choose the best DHT implementation available for the system, while maintaining the range query functionality. However, recent structures available in the literature: Prefix Hash Tree (PHT) [10] and Distributed Segment Tree (DST) [12], are sensitive to clustered data.

Clustered data is common on real data sets, in particular when data depicts geographical placement of items that are tied to human activity. For instance, the concentration of WiFi access points is clustered around cities and along roads [10], so that sharing access point locations and querying for nearby access points will yield a response depicting clustered data.

This steams from population concentration patterns, where clustered data typically follows a power-law distribution, or a combination of power-laws centered on several focus points [13]. This common setting depicts a few higher density key regions while most of the data is sparsely distributed across the key domain.

In this paper we show that the Decentralize Balance tree (DEB tree) algorithm, an algorithm based on the B^+-tree design [14], offers a structure suitable for storing clustered data on block oriented storage (in this case a DHT) while supporting range queries without loss of performance.

The algorithm is capable of running on top of any generic DHT without incurring in a significant overhead. Insertions can be reduced to O(1) complexity in terms of DHT operation requests, if caching is used at clients. Each DHT request cost depends on the DHT implementation selected. In this sense, the scalability of the tree design closely follows the scalability properties of the used DHT.

Query cost depends on the data stored on the index rather than on the range size. Additionally, it is possible to parallelize the query operation, reducing latency to a logarithmic factor on the stored data size in terms of DHT operations.

2 Related Work

Related work can be divided into two groups: range query systems with specific underlying structures and range query systems using a tree structure over a generic DHT interface. Due to space restrictions we will focus on the later group and only provide a brief mention to some systems in the first group.

Mercury [7] supports multi-attribute range queries using a circular overlay, similar to Chord, but without key hashing, so that locality is preserved. Skip graphs [8] are a generalization of skip lists in which nodes are part of distributed linked lists that form a distributed binary tree. Baton [15] builds a binary balanced tree structure where each tree node is mapped into a peer host and maintains connections to the peers containing tree node neighbours.

All previous systems maintain a specific routing algorithm that offers logarithmic cost in terms of network hops to access data. Our DEB-tree algorithm assumes a generic DHT implementation is used. Such assumption enables the use of one-hop DHTs [5,6] or the use of specific DHTs to handle churn efficiently [4] or efficient load-balancing extensions.

Chawathe et al. proposed the use of a Prefix Hash Tree (PHT) for building a trie-based structure over a generic DHT [10]. The main difference between the PHT and DEB tree is that our structure is not sensible to clustered data. The PHT, in order to adapt to clustered data places leaves at different tree levels, causing an irregular tree structure that has impact on the query performance. Data is placed on tree nodes according to a prefix value, which is also used as the block identification scheme. Since the identification scheme is independent from the data itself, it is possible to access any tree block directly without knowing the tree structure in advance. On the other hand, this independence between data and block ids can create overloaded blocks storing a large number of objects that share a common prefix value. Our algorithm adapts efficiently to clustered data distributions, creating a balanced tree with bounded block sizes, but cannot directly access any block without an initial tree traversal.

Zheng et al. presented a Distributed Segment Tree (DST) algorithm, also running over a generic DHT [12]. This binary tree structure is static, where all tree nodes have a pre-defined range limit. Static range limits are incapable of handling clustered data properly, possibly generating either empty or overfull nodes depending on the key distribution. Just like on the PHT, the block identification does not depend on the data, allowing direct access to any tree node. This algorithm allows access to any block directly, a feature that is used on queries to reduce the number of accesses by replicating data on additional tree nodes. This design is very efficient for small queries, at the cost of using more storage. However, when using clustered data, even queries for a small range can produce large results, requiring additional accesses.

Our tree algorithm assigns node ranges dynamically according to the data distribution, which tends to create a good storage distribution for data even in presence of strong clustering. Furthermore, queries do not make redundant accesses to the tree but instead access only the minimum amount of nodes necessary to retrieve the (complete) answer.

3 Decentralized Balanced Tree

In this section, we will review the DEB tree algorithm, which was described in [16], and show how it can be adapted under a generic DHT to support range queries.

3.1 Tree Structure

The tree structure, following the B^+-tree design, is made from *leaf* and *internal* blocks. Leaf blocks contain data items stored on the tree while internal blocks contain only references to children blocks. All leaf blocks are at the same tree level, that is, all leaf blocks are at the same distance from the root. This feature creates a logarithmic bound on the number of block accesses to reach any leaf block.

To maintain high availability even during tree structure maintenance, each block keeps a *next* block reference, that points to the consecutive block at the same tree level [17]. The block size is bounded by the block's maximum size parameter s. Every block must have at least $s/2$ items and at most s items, except the root block which only has the maximum bound [14]. Additionally, each block contains a limit interval (minimum and maximum values) that specifies the range of data the block is responsible for.

3.2 DHT Mapping

We use a single DEB tree to store the entire index data. The support for multiple spaces or dimensions can be obtained using one of two methods: 1) using multiple trees or 2) using a space-filling curve function. The support for multiple trees requires the capability to distinguish blocks of different trees on the same DHT key domain. A single tree can only store and compare values (or range intervals) on a linear space. Storing n-dimensional data on the system is possible by mapping the n-dimensional space into a single-dimension space with a space-filling curve [10].

Each tree block is stored on the DHT host responsible for the hash value of the block id. Although block ids are generated dynamically, they must be globally unique (on the DHT key domain) and not collide or force the change of an already existing identification. This would require moving the block's data on the DHT and updating all the references on other blocks pointing to it.

The block identification is defined as the tuple: $\langle level, minlimit\rangle$, where the *level* field identifies the tree level this block is and the *minlimit* distinguishes the block inside the level.

3.3 Operation Request Model

Access to block data uses the typical *put* and *get* DHT interface. The modification of a block's content requires a three cycle procedure at the caller: *get*–execute–*put* operations. For each block access, a *get* operation must be issued to retrieve the block's data from the DHT to the caller. If the data is modified, an additional *put* operation must also be issued to store the new data on the DHT. This design was used by both PHT and DST to implement a tree structure on top of a generic DHT, like the OpenDHT system [18]. However, unlike the previous structures, the DEB algorithm does not support concurrency on some operations. To operate correctly, the algorithm requires some mechanism to detect concurrent modifications of the same object, in this case the block's content.

We propose a simple extension to the *get* and *put* semantics: to include a logical time stamp parameter, so that concurrent puts can be detected and prevented from happening. This extension would work as follows. When a *get* is made, the current time stamp, an integer, is returned together with the data. When a put is made, the caller sends an increased time stamp value, indicating a modification. If another caller has, in the meantime, already putted a new value for that key, the DHT host receiving the put request can detect that both puts are concurrent and abort the second.

4 Index User Interface

In this section we will describe the two index operations available to the user: insertions (or removals) and range queries. The user calls these operations to store or retrieve data items from the system. Each client host must explicitly store data in the system so that it can be later retrieved by range queries.

4.1 Insertion and Removal

The insertion operation stores a data item into the index. Data items consist on two fields: 1) the location key, which places the item on the space and 2) the data item value, that will be fetched if it's location is contained inside range queries. In order to insert a data item into the tree, the insertion operation must first locate the correct leaf block by performing a top-down traversal of the tree and then adding the new data to the leaf content's. The removal of an item from the tree is identical to the insertion except for the removal of the item on the leaf block. When leaf blocks get full, the caller must also perform a split operation on the block by transferring half of the data to a new block. We omit here the details of the split operation.

Both insertion and removal operations are bound by the cost of vertically traversing the tree, the tree height, which is $O(\log I)$ for I stored items in the tree. Each tree access is equivalent to a *get* DHT call except for the leaf block that requires both *get* and *put* calls. Any DHT call complexity depends on the DHT implementation, ranging from $O(\log N)$ to $O(1)$ for N hosts. Overall, the insertion is bound either by $O(\log I \log N)$ or $O(\log I)$, respectively.

4.2 Range Queries

A range query for the $[s, t]$ interval consists in retrieving all the items on the tree whose locations are contained in the interval. Since items are stored on leaf blocks, the operation is divided in two steps: 1) locate the leaf blocks whose range limits intersect $[s, t]$ and 2) retrieve such blocks. The first step is identical to the location step in the insertion case. This step complexity grows logarithmically with the number of items inserted on the tree, which corresponds to the tree height, $O(\log I)$. The second step involves *get*ing the targeted leaves. The number of *get*s used to retrieve the answer depends directly on the number of stored items whose location keys are contained in the range interval ($I_{[s,t]}$) and not on the size of the query range itself. The size of $I_{[s,t]}$ depends on the distribution of data and will be analyzed in more detail in the Simulation section.

The retrieval of all leaves can be made by following the *next* pointer at each leaf starting at the first ordered leaf that contains s. The downside of this approach is increasing the query latency. Recall that each block access requires a

DHT *get* call, whose complexity depends on the DHT implementation. To reduce the query latency, it is possible to parallelize the block accesses by having the client retrieve simultaneously all tree blocks of the same tree level that intersect the range interval. This procedure reduces the latency to the tree height ($O(\log I)$), at the cost of additional concurrent block accesses. The number of *gets* on leaves remain the same.

4.3 Internal Block Caching

User oriented operations, insertions and queries, always require a tree top-down traversal from the root block to reach the target leaf block. We eliminate the bottleneck on upper level blocks by caching internal blocks at the callers. Caching reduces the top-down traversal cost while maintaining the operation's correctness as internal blocks serve only for location purposes. Furthermore, even if stale cached versions are used, the caller either succeeds in finding the correct block or detects it is using a stale cache entry. To reduce cache update overhead, caching uses a passive update mechanism in which clients only refresh block data after detecting tree inconsistencies.

Caching can reduce the cost of a vertical tree traversal from $O(\log I)$ to $O(1)$ when all internal blocks except leaves are already present at the client. In the worst case, it incurs in constant overhead for the client to update it's entire local cache.

5 Simulation

We implemented the DEB tree algorithm over a custom-made simulator in Python. The basic DHT functionality was simulated using a local storage. However, using a real DHT platform like OpenDHT would be quite straightforward except for the concurrency issue already described.

The simulation data was synthetically generated using either uniform and power-law distributions in order to determine the impact of clustered data on the algorithm. In the clustered case we considered a small number of focus points of clustering chosen uniformly at random.

Points are randomly allocated to the left and right of the focus points under a Pareto distribution with density $f(x) = \frac{kb^k}{x^{k+1}}$. We used a shape parameter $k = 0.5$ and set the minimum x to be 1 by making $b = 1$. Each random value obtained from the distribution was decremented by 1 (transforming the range from $[1, +\infty[$ to $[0, +\infty[$) and either added, or subtracted, to the position of a focus point. The resulting data set mimics the usual distribution of population in a geographic linear space.

5.1 Insertion

The insertion simulation consisted in placing 2^{16} points within a 2^{20} linear space ($\approx 10^6$) into the system sequentially and determine the adaptation of the algorithm to clustered and uniform data. We used two data distributions

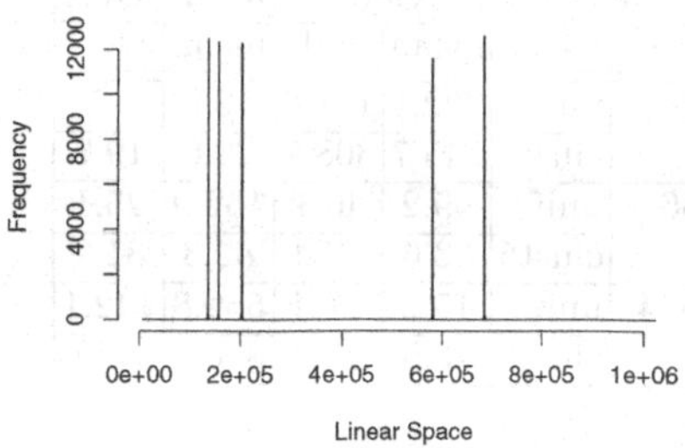

Fig. 1. The data point distribution for a five cluster configuration

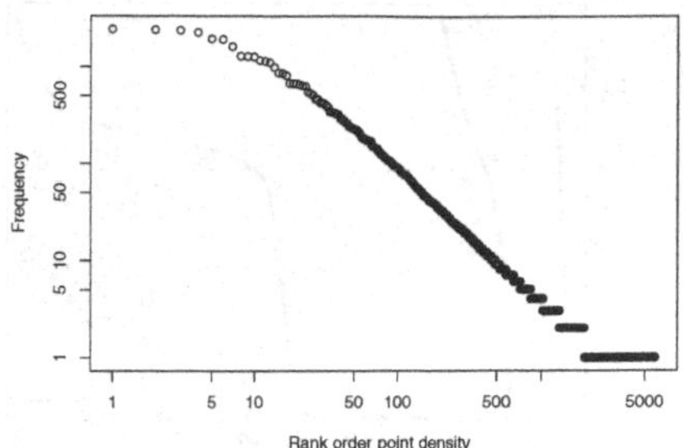

Fig. 2. Log-log rank order

for the insertion points: an uniform distribution and a five cluster distribution. Figures 1 and 2 show some details of an actual five cluster sample. The first Figure shows the concentration of points in the linear space and the second shows rank ordered point densities. Here we can observe the five clusters and the expected linear decrease of point densities in a log-log scale, the graphical signature of power-laws.

We ran the simulations for three maximum block sizes: 64, 256 and 1024 items, and repeated each experiment 50 times to exclude random variations. The DHT is simulated and we assume that the DHT hash function uniformly distributes blocks across the system hosts.

Figure 3 shows the ECDF on the (average) number of stored items per block. The tree algorithm balances data perfectly, as we can see that simulations using the same block size but with different data distributions, whether uniform or clustered, tend to create identical ECDF's. The block usage, the number of stored items per block, varies between 50% and 100% of the block size with the single exception of the root block. The largest block size case, 1024, shows two clusters: one around half the block size and the other around the full block size. This clustering is due to the number of inserted points being large enough to split blocks but small enough to fill them completely. A greater number of points ($\approx 2^{16}$) would make the 1024 line more similar in shape to the 256 and 64 lines.

To insert a single item on the tree, a vertical tree traversal is made, requiring the access to one block for each level. The cost of insertions is therefore equal to the tree height. The tree height h is defined by the expression $h \leq \log_t \frac{n+1}{2}$ where $2t$ is the block size and n is the number of stored items. We measured the tree heights for all simulations, resulting in 3 levels for trees with block sizes of 64 and 256 items, and 2 levels for the 1024 item block size case.

5.2 Range Query

We generated a set of 500 range queries using a middle point and a range size around that middle point. The middle points were generated from an uniform distribution on the linear space. The range size was generated from a normal distribution with 0 mean and a standard deviation of 5% of the space length.

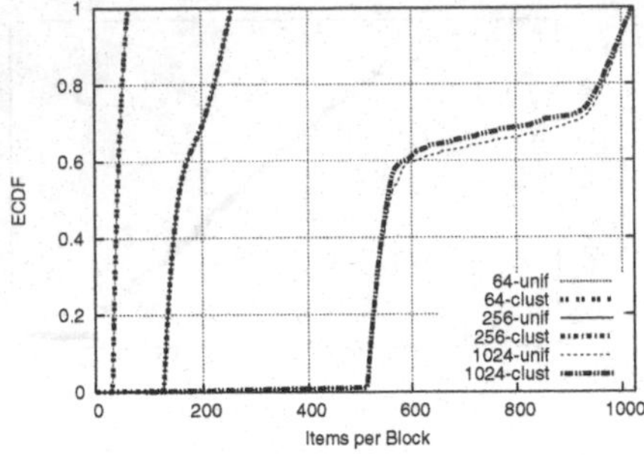

Fig. 3. ECDF (Empirical Cumulative Distribution Function) on the number of stored items per block

Block Size	Data Dist.	Gets mean	Gets s-d	Items/Gets mean	Items/Gets s-d
64	unif	222.1	171.6	42.9	3.5
	clust5	245.7	308.7	23.6	19.7
256	unif	59.2	46.1	152.9	25.1
	clust5	63.6	77.4	82.3	81.2
1024	unif	15.2	11.4	559.8	142.1
	clust5	16.9	20.2	306.2	314.0

Fig. 4. The simulation of a query set over different storage distributions (uniform and five clusters) and different block sizes

We measured query performance as the number of leaf blocks that had to be retrieved in order to obtain a complete answer. We did not take into account internal blocks since their cost is constant for all queries, equal to $h - 1$ DHT accesses. Clients can cache internal blocks locally, removing the height traversal cost. Furthermore, queries can be parallelized for each tree level, reducing query latency to the tree height in the number of hops at the cost of increased bandwidth.

Figure 4 shows the results of simulations with two different insertion point distributions (uniform distribution and five cluster distribution) and three maximum block sizes: 64, 256 and 1024 items.

We used the same query set for all simulations. Measured the mean and standard deviation of the number of DHT *get* calls (on leaf blocks) and the ratio between items retrieved and gets made per query. Since we used the same insertion set for simulations with the same insertion data distribution, these simulations returned the same results no matter what the block size was (an average of 9855 items for the uniform case and 10913 average items for the clustered case).

As the block size increases, we see that the mean number of DHT gets necessary to reply the query decreases, along with it's standard deviation, since larger blocks are capable of returning more data. The mean ratio also increases because of the greater block capacity, where each get request returns more items. However, the ratio's standard deviation also increases, meaning that queries obtain increasingly different amounts of items per get on each query. This can be explained by the larger block capacity storage distribution, where the size of blocks is distributed between half and full maximum size. Larger block capacities will generate blocks spawning a wider load variation, which is reflected on the different number of items each block returns and consequently on the ratio's standard deviation.

Figure 4 also compares the algorithm efficiency when running a query set on point data created by an uniform distribution or a five cluster distribution. As expected, the number of gets per query were about the same for both distributions. However, the standard deviation was greater in the clustered case. An uniform distribution is likely to return the same approximate number of items for queries across all the linear space, whilst the same queries on a clustered distribution are likely to have more disparity on the number of items returned depending on the density of stored data at the query range area, hence the higher standard deviation.

The item/get ratio mean is higher for the uniform case across all block sizes. The standard deviation, on the contrary, is always significantly smaller. These results show that the algorithm adapts perfectly to the storage data distribution. When running over uniform data, the standard deviation is low because all queries tend to receive the same amount of results. When running over clustered data, the higher standard deviation shows that the algorithm returns different amounts of data for the same query set, which is in accordance to the clustered distribution of data with many sparse regions and a few highly dense regions.

6 Conclusion

In this paper we show how our DEB tree algorithm, which is based on balanced trees, can easily provide a scalable range query implementation over generic DHT systems.

The solution induces an even distribution of items per DHT block and consequently balances the storage and network load on the hosts that support the DHT. We have considered two opposite data sets, one with data uniformly distributed in space and another exhibiting highly clustered data. These two scenarios induce almost indistinguishable patterns of data allocation in the DHT, depicting similar ECDFs.

Finally, we considered the effects of a typical range query scenario. Users query for items (e.g. WiFi access points) within a given spatial distance of their current location. The choice of maximum block size is the driving factor that dictates the number of DHTs requests that are needed for a given usage pattern. An optimal size must take into account not only the expected usage pattern, but also the number of stored items and the combined effects of caching and concurrent DHT gets.

This approach presents a clear advance over previous systems by providing a design that is mostly insensitive to the presence of clustered data, while building on of-the-shelf DHT middleware.

References

1. Stoica, I., Morris, R., Karger, D., Kaashoek, F., Balakrishnan, H.: Chord: A scalable Peer-To-Peer lookup service for internet applications. In: Proceedings of the ACM SIGCOMM'01 Conference, pp. 149–160. ACM Press, New York (2001)
2. Rowstron, A., Druschel, P.: Pastry: Scalable, decentralized object location, and routing for large-scale peer-to-peer systems. In: Proceedings of the 18th IFIP/ACM International Conf. on Distributed Systems Platforms, Germany, pp. 329–350. ACM Press, New York (2001)

3. Ratnasamy, S., Francis, P., Handley, M., Karp, R., Shenker, S.: A scalable content addressable network. In: Proceedings of the ACM SIGCOMM'01 Conference, pp. 161–172. ACM Press, New York (2001)
4. Rhea, S., Geels, D., Roscoe, T., Kubiatowicz, J.: Handling churn in a dht. In: Proceedings of the USENIX Annual Technical Conference, pp. 127–140 (2004)
5. Gupta, A., Liskov, B., Rodrigues, R.: Efficient routing for peer-to-peer overlays. In: Proceedings of the 1st Symposium on Networked Systems Design and Implementation (NSDI'04), pp. 113–126 (2004)
6. Ramasubramanian, V., Sirer, E.G.: Beehive: O(1) lookup performance for power-law query distributions in peer-to-peer overlays. In: Proceedings of the 1st Symposium on Networked Systems Design and Implementation (NSDI'04), pp. 99–112 (2004)
7. Bharambe, A., Agrawal, M., Seshan, S.: Mercury: Supporting scalable multi-attribute range queries. In: Proceedings of SIGCOMM 2004, pp. 353–366 (2004)
8. Aspnes, J., Shah, G.: Skip graphs. In: Fourteenth Annual ACM-SIAM Symposium on Discrete Algorithms, pp. 384–393. ACM, New York (2003)
9. Zhang, C., Krishnamurthy, A., Wang, R.: Brushwood: Distributed trees in peer-to-peer systems. In: Castro, M., van Renesse, R. (eds.) IPTPS 2005. LNCS, vol. 3640, pp. 47–57. Springer, Heidelberg (2005)
10. Chawathe, Y., Ramabhadran, S., Ratnasamy, S., LaMarca, A., Hellerstein, J., Shenker, S.: A case study in building layered dht applications. In: Proceedings of the ACM SIGCOMM'05 Conference, pp. 97–108. ACM Press, New York (2005)
11. Gao, J., Steenkiste, P.: An adaptative protocol for efficient support of range queries in dht-based systems. In: Proceedings of the 12th IEEE Int. Conference on Network Protocols (ICNP'04), pp. 239–250. IEEE Computer Society Press, Los Alamitos (2004)
12. Zheng, C., Shen, G., Li, S., Shenker, S.: Distributed segment tree: Support of range query and cover query over dht. In: Electronic publications of the 5th International Workshop on Peer-to-Peer Systems (IPTPS'06), California, USA (2006)
13. Zipf, G.: Human Behaviour and the Principle of Least Effort. Addison-Wesley, Reading (1949)
14. Cormen, T., Leiserson, C., Rivest, R.: Introduction to Algorithms. MIT Press, Cambridge (1989)
15. Jagadish, H., Ooi, B.C., Vu, Q.H.: Baton: A balanced tree structure for peer-to-peer networks. In: Proceedings of the 31st International Conference on Very Large Data Bases, Trondheim, Norway, pp. 661–672 (2005)
16. Lopes, N., Baquero, C.: Using distributed balanced trees over dhts for building large-scale indexes. Technical report, University of Minho (October 2006)
17. Johnson, T., Krishna, P.: Lazy updates for distributed data structures. In: Proceedings of the 1993 ACM SIGMOD Intl. Conf. on Management of data, pp. 337–346. ACM Press, New York (1993)
18. Sean Rhea, B.G., Karp, B., Kubiatowicz, J., Ratnasamy, S., Shenker, S., Stoica, I., Yu, H.: Opendht: A public dht service and its uses. In: Proceedings of SIGCOMM 2005, pp. 73–84 (August 2005)

Byzantine-Tolerant, Information Propagation in Untrustworthy and Unreliable Networks

Kai Han[1], Binoy Ravindran[1], and E. Douglas Jensen[2]

[1] ECE Dept., Virginia Tech, Blacksburg, VA, USA
{khan05,binoy}@vt.edu

[2] The MITRE Corporation, Bedford, MA, USA
jensen@mitre.org

Abstract. In a decentralized network system, an authenticated node is referred to as a Byzantine node, if it is fully controlled by a traitor or an adversary, and can perform destructive behavior to disrupt the system. Typically, Byzantine nodes together or individually attack point-to-point information propagation by denying or faking messages. In this paper, we assume that Byzantine nodes can protect themselves from being identified by authentication mechanisms. We present an authentication-free, gossip-based application-level propagation mechanism called LASIRC, in which "healthy" nodes utilize Byzantine features to defend against Byzantine attacks. We show that LASIRC is robust against message-denying and message-faking attacks. Our experimental studies verify LASIRC's effectiveness.

1 Introduction

In a decentralized, network-based information system, nodes communicate with each other through point-to-point information propagation (i.e., directly sending messages to destination nodes without receiving help from a server). The propagation may suffer attacks from malicious nodes hiding in the system. Attacks where a traitor or an adversary has full control of an authenticated device, and can perform destructive behaviors to disrupt the system are referred to as Byzantine attacks [1]. A node showing Byzantine behaviors is called a Byzantine node. Byzantine nodes are more difficult to deal with than other attackers [2].

We consider network systems where authentication mechanisms (including any kind of encryption) are unable to defend against Byzantine attacks [3]. Since Byzantine nodes are authenticated, in any authentication process, they act just like other nodes. Therefore, a "healthy" node cannot trust its peers — it does not know whether another node is a friend, a traitor, or an adversary. Further, we assume that Byzantine nodes are intelligent—i.e., if a Byzantine node cannot protect itself from being identified by others, it will not attack. For instance, it is less possible for an attacker to fake a reply message during a request message propagation process, because such an attack will finally be identified by the real reply node (we discuss this attack scenario in Section 2.2). In the rest of the paper, we use the terms "Byzantine nodes" and "Byzantine attackers", interchangeably.

T. Enokido, L. Barolli, and M. Takizawa (Eds.): NBiS 2007, LNCS 4658, pp. 207–216, 2007.

We focus on application-level Byzantine attacks in *request-reply* message propagation. A node initiates such a process by sending REQUEST (REQ) messages to others, trying to get a "YES"/"NO" answer from them (e.g., requesting a service that it cannot provide [4]). A knowing receiver responds by sending back REPLY (REP) messages, indicating its answer to the sender. Byzantine nodes may attack both processes by denying or faking messages (e.g., faking requested service ID in a REQ message, faking "NO" for an "YES" answer in a REP message, or directly faking REP messages). Furthermore, we consider information systems that use *unreliable networks* (e.g., those without a fixed network infrastructure, including mobile, ad hoc and wireless networks) with dynamically uncertain properties. These uncertain properties, which are application- and network-induced, include arbitrary node failures, transient and permanent network failures, and varying packet drop behaviors. Example such systems that motivate our work include US DoD's Network-Centric Warfare system [5].

In this paper, we present LASIRC, a Byzantine-tolerant, gossip-based, point-to-point application-level information propagation model/mechanism. Gossip mechanisms are well-known for their robustness to propagation uncertainties in unreliable networks [2,6]. A node initiates a gossip process by starting a series of synchronous gossip rounds. During each round, nodes holding REQ messages randomly select a set of neighbors and send REQ messages to them. The number of gossip rounds (or R), and the number of selected neighbors (i.e., the "fan-out" number, or F) are determined by the original sender. If a receiver knows the answer, it gossips REP messages back. Message losses and node failures may happen during a gossip process. However, gossip "fights" non-determinism (i.e., unpredictable message losses and node failures) with non-determinism (i.e., randomly selecting sending targets) — duplicated REQ and REP messages guarantee the normal information propagation. Our gossip-based LASIRC model/mechanism also features this same robustness, and makes LASIRC robust against Byzantine message-denying attacks, as these attacks can be regarded as message losses/node failures (Byzantine attackers receive, but do not forward messages). In addition to message-denying attacks, LASIRC also provides a set of mechanisms to detect and defend Byzantine message-faking attacks.

The rest of the paper is organized as follows: In Section 2, we discuss possible Byzantine attacks in the LASIRC model. We then present our Byzantine attacker detectors in Section 3. Sections 4 describe and analyze the LASIRC model and mechanism, respectively. In Section 5, we report on our experimental (simulation) studies. We conclude the paper in Section 6.

2 Byzantine Attacks

We describe the REQ and REP message structures, discuss Byzantine attack types (denying and faking messages), and possible Byzantine attacks in REQ and REP message propagation under gossip protocols.

Message Structures. A REQ message contains the original sender's (the request node) IP, the intermediate node's (message-transferring node in gossip protocol) IP, the requested service ID, the gossip fan-out number (F), and the number of gossip rounds (R). A REP message contains the original sender (the reply node)'s IP, the intermediate node's IP, the requested service ID, the answer ("YES" or "NO"), F, and R.

2.1 Byzantine Attack Types

A message-denying attack issued by an individual attacker is called a *Black Hole* attack. In addition, two or more attackers may collude together to form a larger "*Black Hole*". We call these two attacks as *Black Hole Class (BHC)* attacks [7]. BHC attacks become more serious if attackers participate in message propagation at early gossip rounds, or a large number of attackers collude together. Under such conditions, BHC attacks largely reduce the message number, and thus seriously slow or even cease message propagation.

A *Message-Faking (MF)* attack is more harmful than a BHC attack. Unlike BHC attackers that only deny messages, an MF attacker directly propagates incorrect information, misleading other nodes to make a wrong decision. For instance, a node may send a REQ message requesting a remote service. If an MF attacker replies with a "NO" instead of the correct answer "YES", the sender will incorrectly abort a waiting task. If the attacker replies with a "YES" for a "NO", the sender has to keep the ineligible task and hold all resources that the task needs, thereby delaying the execution of eligible tasks, which is undesirable if tasks have time constraints.

2.2 Byzantine Attacks in REQ Message Propagation

BHC attackers try to slow or even cease REQ message propagation, while MF attackers try to spread incorrect service ID or fake REP messages. Figure 1(a) shows BHC and MF attacks in REQ message propagation.

If an MF attacker spreads a fake requested service ID, it can activate an irrelevant receiver to gossip back, and thus increase the message overhead in the network. If the attacker directly spreads a fake REP message, it may tempt the sender to give wrong responses.

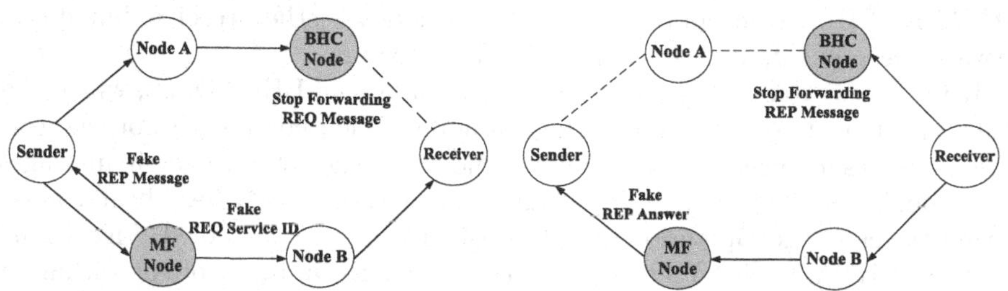

(a) Attacks in REQ Message Propagation (b) Attacks in REP Message Propagation

Fig. 1. Byzantine Attacks in REQ and REP Message Propagation

If a Byzantine node is "intelligent" as discussed in Section 1, it will not execute the second MF attack. An important feature of gossip is that every node will finally receive the (attacker's fake) messages, with a high probability [8]. If the original REQ sender receives a fake REQ message with an incorrect requested service ID, it cannot identify the attacker by comparing it with the real requested service ID. This is because the intermediate node IP in a REP message might only be a transferring node's IP, and not the original MF attacker's IP. However, if the real receiver gets a fake REP message, it may easily identify the attacker (by comparing it with the real answer). Therefore, "intelligent" Byzantine nodes will not execute such an MF attack in REQ message propagation.

2.3 Byzantine Attacks in REP Message Propagation

Figure 1(b) shows BHC and MF attacks in REP message propagation. BHC attacks stop forwarding REP messages, while MF attacks spread REP messages with fake answer (NO for a YES or vice versa).

Unlike in REQ message propagation, an "intelligent" attacker can execute MF attacks in REP message propagation without being identified by other nodes. Although the real receiver can finally get fake REP messages and can identify this attack by comparing the REP message answer with its own, it cannot identify the fake message initiator. This is because, it is quite possible that the sender in a REP message is only an intermediate node, and this node can be a victim cheated by a real MF attacker.

Note that MF attackers cannot mislead the real receiver by faking requested service ID in REQ message propagation. However, they can directly disturb REP message propagation. Therefore, MF attack on REP message propagation is more dangerous than that on REQ message propagation. Thus, we focus on how to guarantee a correct REP message propagation.

3 Byzantine Attacker Detection

In this section, we present BHC Attacker Detector (BHCAD) and MF Attacker Detectors (MFADs).

BHCAD. BHC attackers behave like failed nodes — they receive, but do not forward messages. BHCAD acts as a failure detector.

BHCAD operates as follows: Each node maintains a BHCAD list, which contains a heartbeat counter for each known node. When gossiping to others, each node increases its own heartbeat counter and sends the list with gossip messages. If the node does not receive any change in another node's heartbeat counter during the entire gossip period, it will consider that node as failed. Algorithm 1 describes BHCAD. The GOSSIP() procedure invoked in line 7 of Algorithm 1 is shown in Algorithm 2.

MFAD. MFAD utilizes MF attackers' feature of faking requested service ID in REQ messages, or faking the answer in REP messages. To execute MF attacker

Algorithm 1. BHC Attacker Detector

```
Each node i maintains a BHCAD list;
for each known node j do
    combine i.heartbeat_counter with i's address;
for each gossip round do
    i.heartbeat_counter++;
    combine i's list with gossip messages;
    GOSSIP(messages);
Upon receiving a message from node k:
    for each member j in BHCAD list do
        j.heartbeat_counter ← max{i's, k's};
    if j.heartbeat_counter does not change after gossip finishes then
        i considers j as failed;
```

detection, the first node that is not an MF attacker must initiate its own MFAD before others. (We call a node that is not an MF attacker as a "healthy node.")

Algorithm 2. Gossip Emission (GOSSIP() Function)

```
On gossiping a message msg:
    while R != 0 do
        Every gossip round Γ, randomly select F target nodes;
        for each m ∈ [1, ..., F ] do
            SEND(target_i, msg);
        R = R - 1;
```

To detect MF attackers faking requested service ID, the initiating MFAD broadcasts "REQ" messages in the system, but includes its own service ID in them and sets the gossip round R to 1. MF attackers will change this service ID. Since $R = 1$, an attacker must broadcast fake "REQ" messages to all other nodes in one gossip round. Therefore, the initiating MFAD can easily identify an MF attacker by checking the requested service ID in every received "REQ" message. For those activated MFADs located on other "healthy" nodes, since they receive the original "REQ" message from the initiating "healthy" node, they can also identify MF attackers by comparing every received "REQ" message with the original one. MFADs are described in Algorithms 3 and 4.

To detect MF attackers faking the answer in REP messages, the initiating MFAD broadcasts "REP" messages in the system, includes its preset answer (e.g. "YES") in them, and sets $R = 1$. MF attackers will reverse the answer (e.g. "NO"). Since $R = 1$, an attacker must broadcast fake "REP" messages to all other nodes in one gossip round. Similar to MFAD in REQ message propagation, both initiating and activated MFAD can easily identify an MF attacker. Since MFADs in REP message propagation behave similar to those in REQ message propagation, we do not separately show their algorithm descriptions.

Algorithm 3. Initiating MF Attacker Detector

Node i puts its own service ID in "REQ" messages;
Node i sets $R = 1$;
At the first gossip round: Broadcast "REQ" messages in the system;
After the second gossip round: Check service ID in every received "REQ" message;
if *the service ID is changed* **then**
  Identify this message sender as an MF attacker;

Algorithm 4. Activated MF Attacker Detector

At the first gossip round: Receive "REQ" messages from the initiating MFAD;
At the second gossip round: Broadcast "REQ" messages once;
After the second gossip round: Compare service ID in every received "REQ" message with the one in the original message;
if *the service ID is changed* **then**
  Identify this message sender as an MF attacker;

If an activated MFAD does not receive the original "REQ" or "REP" message from the initiating MFAD, it cannot identify any MF attacker later. If an MFAD does not receive the one-time broadcast "REQ" or "REP" message from a node, it cannot regard that node as an MF attacker. Therefore, the effectiveness of an MFAD depends on successful point-to-point message propagation.

4 LASIRC Model and Mechanism

BHCAD and MFADs cannot exhaust attackers if message loss rate is larger than zero, which is common in unreliable networks. Since gossip is robust to message losses and node failures, it is relatively easy to deal with hiding BHC attackers. However, gossip cannot handle hiding MF attackers, which is more dangerous. Therefore, it is necessary to design a gossip-based propagation model/mechanism to defend against MF attacks.

4.1 LASIRC Model

As stated in Section 2.2, due to the REQ message structure, it is difficult to identify an MF attacker that fakes service ID in REQ message propagation. In addition, though such an attack increases communication overhead, it does little harm to the real REQ message propagation process. Therefore, we focus on modeling node behaviors in REP message propagation.

We introduce terminations for nodes during REP message propagation:

1. **Healthy Node** A node that is not an MF attacker.
2. **Host (H)** A node that has received one or more REP messages.
3. **Launcher (L)** The initiating sender of the REP messages.
4. **Attacker (A)** An MF attacker that tries to spread a fake answer.

5. **Susceptible (S)** A healthy node that has not received any REP message.
6. **Infective (I)** A healthy host that has a fake answer.
7. **Removed (R)** A healthy host that knows its answer is correct, or always sends correct REP messages.
8. **Consumer (C)** The initiating sender of REQ messages.

We introduce terminations for REP messages:

9. **Agent** A fake REP message from an attacker.
10. **Virus** A fake REP message that possibly turns a susceptible into an infective.
11. **Antibiotic** An agent that turns a susceptible/infective into a removed.
12. **Berry** A correct REP message.
13. **Vaccine** A berry that possibly turns a susceptible into a removed.

We refer to this model as the LASIRC model. Note that we assume that every healthy node only checks the first received REP message, discarding all of the following messages with the same message ID, unless the message is an antibiotic, or contains a change defined in the REP message definitions.

A host is said to be immune to an attacker, if its MFAD has identified that attacker. A host gets immunized when its first received message is a vaccine.

4.2 LASIRC Mechanism

We now describe the LASIRC mechanism. Algorithm 5 shows how a launcher works. A launcher is the initiating sender of REP messages. It holds the correct answer, so it cannot be infected by an MF attacker.

Algorithm 5. Launcher

Initialize REP message `rep`;
GOSSIP(`rep`);

When an MF attacker receives a REP message, it is activated. If the sender is another attacker, it follows the sender's answer. Otherwise, it reverses the answer ("NO" for a "YES"). Algorithm 6 describes the MF attacker.

Algorithm 6. MF Attacker

On receiving a REP message `rep`:
  if *the sender is not an MF attacker* **then** reverse the answer in `rep`;
  GOSSIP(`rep`);

Algorithm 7 shows healthy node behaviors in the LASIRC mechanism. A susceptible turns into a removed if its first received message is a vaccine (from a removed), or turns into an infective if that message is a virus (from an infective or an MF attacker).

Consumer behavior in the LASIRC mechanism is shown in Algorithm 8. A consumer acts as other healthy nodes during gossip rounds. After gossip finishes, if it still cannot identify itself as a removed (knowing the correct answer), it

Algorithm 7. Susceptible, Infective and Removed

```
On receiving the first REP message rep:
  GOSSIP(rep);
On receiving another REP message with the same message ID:
  if the sender has sent REP message before then
    if the answer changes then
      adopt answer in new REP message; //Identify sender has changed
      from an infective to a removed
      reverse the answer in rep;
      GOSSIP(rep); //Change from an infective to a removed
  if the sender is an identified MF attacker then
    if the answer in the first rep is equal to this attacker's then
      reverse the answer in rep;
      GOSSIP(rep); //Change from an infective to a removed
```

will count the number of the same answers in received REP messages. If the consumer is optimistic, it believes MF attackers occupy less than half of the total number of nodes. Then, it will select the answer in most received REP messages. Otherwise, the consumer is pessimistic, and will select the answer in less received REP messages.

Algorithm 8. Consumer

```
In gossip: Act as other healthy nodes do in Algorithm 7
After gossip finishes:
  if the consumer has not identified itself as a removed then
    select the answer in most(less) received REP messages; //Optimistic
    (Pessimistic) consumer
```

5 Experimental Studies

We simulated the LASIRC mechanism in a 100-node system, in which every node is reachable to others. We considered a scenario where BHC attacks resulted in 15% of message loss during propagation, and compared LASIRC with the Susceptible-Infective (SI) mechanism, which is the gossip protocol without any MF attacker detection and protection methods. The number of gossip rounds (R) and the fan-out number (F) was 10.

Figure 2 shows the Detection Ratio (DR; the ratio of number of MF attackers detected by a node to the total number of MF attackers) along with the message loss ratio (MLR). We observe that DR on both the detection initiating detector and activated detectors decrease when MLR increases, because MFAD depends on received messages; thus its performance degrades when MLR increases. In addition, we observe that the initiating detector's DR is higher than that of activated detectors. This is because, the initiating detector knows the correct answer before the detection begins, and activated detectors need to receive messages (message transmissions may suffer message losses) from the initiating one to know the correct answer. We also observe that MFAD cannot detect all MF attackers if MLR is larger than 0. Therefore, we need LASIRC mechanism to deal with hiding MF attackers that survive this detection.

Figure 3 shows the consumer Correctness Ratio (CR; the number of times a consumer gets the correct answer after gossip finishes over the total simulation time) with an optimistic consumer. We also show CRs of SI, LASIRC without Consumer Decision Mechanism (CDM, Algorithm 8), LASIRC without CDM and Sender Identification Area Mechanism (SIM, part of Algorithm 7), as comparisons.

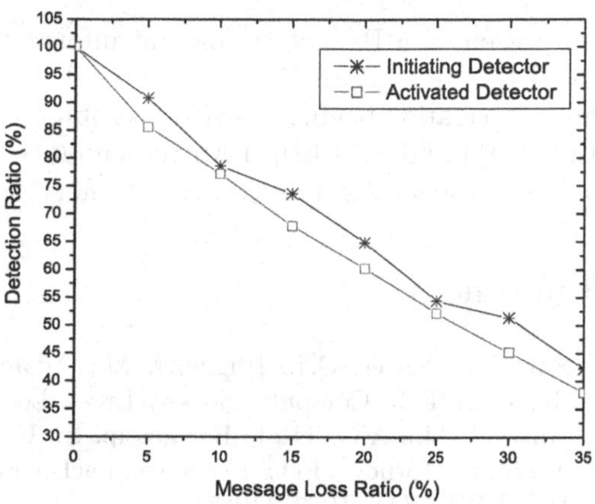

Fig. 2. LASIRC MF Attacker Detection

We observe that LASIRC gets a satisfactory result. With N increases, LASIRC's CR remains almost 100%, while SI's CR dramatically decreases to 4.97% ($N = 35$). With MFADs, CDM and SIM, LASIRC mechanism guarantees that the consumer can finally get the correct answer after gossip finishes. The other two curves indicate the function of each LASIRC method. We observe that the CR of LASIRC without CDM and SIM is much better than that of SI.

This comparison illustrates the importance of MFADs to LASIRC. MFADs help turn a virus message into an antibiotic message, which largely reduces the number of infectives.

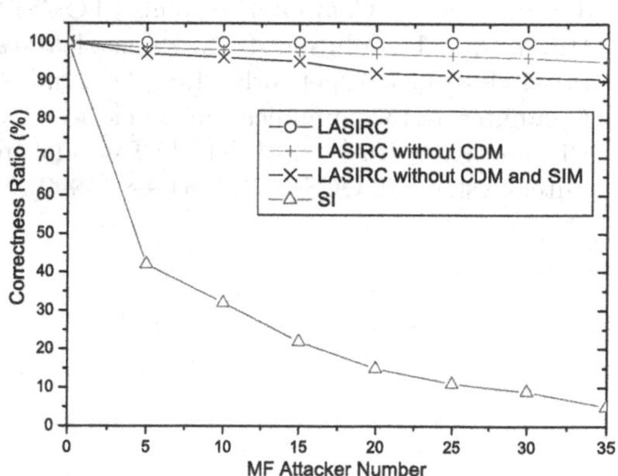

Fig. 3. Consumer Correctness Ratio

We also observe that LASIRC without CDM is better than LASIRC without CDM and SIM — this demonstrates that SIM helps to enhance the CR. Also, LASIRC is better than all the others. If other methods cannot help, CDM (Algorithm 8) finally determines the answer. To determine the final answer, we need to set a consumer to be optimistic or pessimistic. This setting depends on the attacker number. We conclude that MFADs provide major contribution to CR, and CDM and SIM improve CR to almost 100%.

6 Conclusions

We presented a Byzantine-tolerant information propagation model/mechanism called LASIRC. With BHCADs and MFADs, LASIRC can detect attackers before propagation begins. LASIRC is robust to BHC attacks for its gossip feature. And CDM and SIM help LASIRC enhance its performance under MF attacks. Our experimental studies verify the effectiveness of the LASIRC mechanism.

References

1. Suri, N., Walter, C.J., Hugue, M.M.: Advances in Ultra-Dependable Distributed Systems. IEEE Computer Society Press, Los Alamitos (1995)
2. Harry, C., Li, A.C., et al.: Bar gossip. In: USENIX OSDI, pp. 191–204 (2006)
3. Jubin, J., Tornow, J.D.: The darpa packet radio network protocols. Proceedings of the IEEE 75(1), 21–32 (1987)
4. Han, K., et al.: Exploiting slack for scheduling dependent, distributable real-time threads in mobile ad hoc networks. In: 15th International Conference on Real-Time and Network Systems (RTNS'07) (March (2007)
5. Freebersyser, J.A., Macker, J.P.: Realizing the network-centric warfare vision: network technology challenges and guidelines. In: IEEE Military Communications Conference (MILCOM), pp. 267–271. IEEE Computer Society Press, Los Alamitos (2001)
6. Van Renesse, R., Birman, K.P., Vogels, W.: Astrolabe: A robust and scalable technologyfor distributed system monitoring, management, and data mining. ACM Transactions on Computer Systems (TOCS) 21(3), 164–206 (2003)
7. Hu, Y.C., A.P., Johnson, D.B.: Packet leashes: A defense against wormhole attacks in wireless ad hoc networks. In: The 22nd Annual Joint Conference of the IEEE Computer and Communications Societies (INFOCOM 2003) (April 2003)
8. Birman, K.P., Hayden, M., et al.: Bimodal multicast. ACM Transactions on Computer Systems (TOCS) 17(2), 41–88 (1999)

COMICS: A Global Constraint Manager for Interactive Component Database Systems

Ludmila Himmelspach, Mehmet Kolac, Krasimir Kutsarov, Alexander Chernin, Christopher Popfinger, and Stefan Conrad

Institute of Computer Science
University of Düsseldorf
D-40225 Düsseldorf, Germany

Abstract. When several heterogeneous database systems are combined to a federation it is necessary to deal with the problem of maintaining the consistency of semantically interrelated data. The integrity constraints that are defined on the schemas of the federation's members must be monitored and ensured. In this paper we introduce the COMICS system, a global **C**onstraint **M**anager for **I**nteractive **C**omponent Database **S**ystems, that is able to ensure strict consistency in a collection of autonomous and heterogeneous databases. The system uses the functionality of enhanced active databases to trigger a global integrity check from a local update operation.

1 Introduction

In the modern industrial and scientific world large amounts of data are being manipulated daily. Although the sources of this data are established independently, it is often necessary to combine them into federations. Thereby one must ensure that a high degree of autonomy is preserved and that federated data remains consistent. During the last two decades, various systems that handle this problem have been developed, but to our knowledge none of them ensures strict consistency of data. In this paper we present COMICS, a system which interconnects a collection of autonomous and heterogeneous relational databases to ensure strict consistency among interdependent databases. COMICS is specifically designed for Enhanced Active Databases, which are able to detect immediately all changes on their data stock and to actively notify a constraint manager about the modifications. The constraint manager checks the global integrity constraints by querying affected remote component systems and returns a permission to commit or reject the corresponding local transaction. In this way we can be sure that strict consistency is preserved without the need of recovery mechanisms.

The paper is structured as follows. First we introduce Enhanced Active Databases as prerequisite for our system. Section 3 describes the architecture of COMICS. Section 4 gives a detailed explanation of the process of checking global integrity constraints and an application scenario, followed by evaluation results and optimizations in Section 5. Section 6 discusses related work, while Section 7 concludes and catches up future work.

T. Enokido, L. Barolli, and M. Takizawa (Eds.): NBiS 2007, LNCS 4658, pp. 217–226, 2007.

2 Enhanced Active Databases

The COMICS system is specifically designed for *Enhanced Active Databases (EADBS)* [1], which are a subclass of active databases. An EADBS is an active database system that is able to execute programs or methods from within its DBMS to interact with software or hardware components beyond its system border. The execution of a program or method in this context is called an *External Program Call* (EPC). External programs can be called during the execution of a trigger or as a stored procedure to add new functionalities to the database system. This allows a program call to be executed as part of a database transaction triggered by a certain local event. An EADBS that is integrated into a federated information system as an *Active Component Database System (ACDBS)* [1] can use this enhanced activity to interact with other components of the federation to coordinate their actions. In particular, the extended functionality can be used to ensure consistency of interdependent data and to enforce business rules in the form of global integrity constraints. Within recent commercial database systems a commonly supported programming language that meets this requirement is Java (e.g. Java Stored Procedures or Java UDFs [2]). Besides JDBC, as a database connectivity framework, it contains libraries for various communication channels, such as sockets and the Remote Method Invocation Framework (RMI). Although we cast our work in the context of relational databases using Java and RMI, the concept adapts to other types of Enhanced Active Databases supporting different languages that fulfill the requirement just mentioned.

3 The COMICS System

The paper [1] has already presented an architecture for global integrity checking in heterogeneous information systems using active component systems. Global integrity constraints are enforced using constraint checking mechanisms which are implemented directly on the ACDBSs. In this way, the integrity constraint checks are processed on each component system independently from the constraint checks on the remaining CDBSs. This approach works well as long as the number of interrelated component systems is small, however with an increasing number of components in the system the risk of deadlocks also increases if relations in the CDBSs are updated concurrently. To overcome this drawback, we introduce an external constraint manager component, which enables and controls the communication among the ACDBSs during the global integrity constraint checking. Furthermore, the management of schema mappings and interdependencies between the data sources is shifted from the ACDBSs to an external mapping repository. One advantage of this approach is that adding or removing of mapping information of CDBs can be done quickly at a single point, namely in the central mapping repository. In this section we outline the architecture of COMICS shown in Figure 1 and describe its functionality.

In the COMICS system, global constraints are checked by the constraint manager (CM). Each global constraint is decomposed into a set of *partial integrity constraints* for each affected component database. A partial constraint consists of a local check and a remote check on one or more interdependent databases. Triggered by a local transaction, the DBMS first evaluates the local constraint check and then, if the constraint is not already violated, evaluates the remote check by querying the remote databases. This remote check is implemented in the external constraint manager using *synchronous* external program calls to trigger the constraint evaluation process from within a local transaction. Communication between the database and the constraint manager is hereby established via channels set up by external notification programs (ENPs). Depending on the remote check, the ENP receives a message to commit or abort the corresponding local transaction.

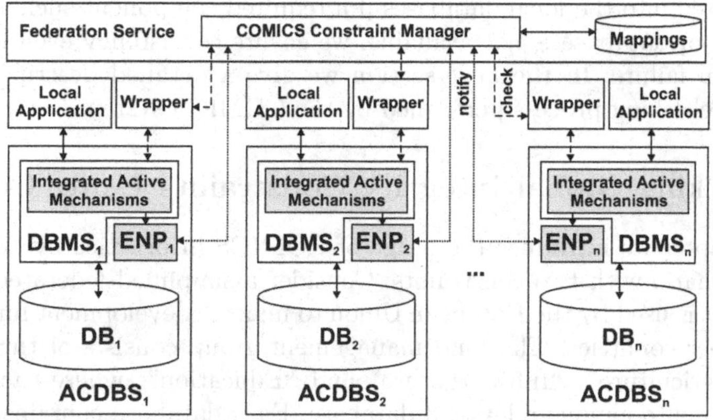

Fig. 1. Federated Information System with COMICS Constraint Manager

The checking of global integrity constraints on interrelated CDBSs is based on a wrapper/mediator architecture [3]. The constraint manager is a global component that communicates with the data sources via wrapper components. The wrappers provide a uniform interface to query and manipulate the encapsulated databases using specific connection information and database drivers. They minimize the heterogeneity and thus the CM does not need individual adjustment to different types of ACDBS. Therefore the system can be extended easily on additional ACDBSs.

Constraint Manager: The Constraint Manager (CM) is the heart of the COMICS system. If it fails, all transactions between interrelated CDBSs are cancelled. The CM enables and controls the communication between the ACDBSs by synchronising the transactions and inspects the global integrity constraints.

Mapping Repository: The repository stores the mappings between the local schemas of the ACDBSs. They are used by the CM to identify depending data in remote CDBSs. Mappings are created when a new component database is attached to the Constraint Manager for integrity maintenance. Each trigger which is stored in the repository has its own table and a designation that is pushed to the CM as a parameter. The table designation in the repository and the parameter designation are identical. An entry in the repository consists of the IP of the remote wrapper, the name of the schema, table, and attribute to check in the remote database, as well as the type of constraint, and, in case of an aggregate constraint, the threshold value to check.

The CM coordinates and serializes all constraint checks triggered by local transactions, which are blocked during a remote constraint check performed by the CM. The CM executes only one check at a time. Thus, the COMICS system is able to provide strict consistency of interrelated data. Although acting as a system bottleneck, we benefit from the strict consistency the CM ensures. Furthermore, by performing pessimistic constraint checks that do not allow data to be inserted into the local databases if a required component such as the CM, a wrapper, or database is not available, we ensure consistency even in the case of a system failure. In the next section we give a detailed description of the constraint checking process performed by the COMICS system.

4 Checking Global Integrity Constraints Using COMICS

In this chapter we introduce the usage of COMICS in practice by describing a sample scenario with two constraints. Consider a simplified federated database system that is used by the European Union to manage development funds for the new member countries. The fund management group consists of three departments: “Agriculture”, “Infrastructure” and “Education”, where each of them has its own autonomous relational database. Each database contains a relation with following information: project id, project title, budget. The overview of the system is listed in Table 1. Each project is identified by a unique id number, so that the values of id_A, id_I and id_E are globally unique. Furthermore, the fund management has a budget limit for all projects. That means that the sum of values in $budget_A$, $budget_I$ are $budget_E$ together can never exceed a certain value (i.e. 20.000.000 Euro).

Table 1. Example databases of a company

Department	Database	Relations
Agriculture (A)	DB_A	$project_A(\underline{id_A}, title_A, budget_A)$
Infrastructure (I)	DB_I	$project_I(\underline{id_I}, title_I, budget_I)$
Education (E)	DB_E	$project_E(\underline{id_E}, title_E, budget_E)$

According to [1], constraints can be defined as follows:

Key Constraint Key_G: $Key_{DB_A} \wedge Key_{DB_I} \wedge DB_E$
Aggregate Constraint $Aggr_G$: $Sum_{DB_A} \wedge Sum_{DB_I} \wedge Sum_{DB_E}$

Each global constraint is then decomposed into three partial constraints for each affected database.

4.1 Basic Process

For the constraint checking we implement the Local Test Transaction Protocol (LTT) presented by Grefen and Widom in [4]. The process consists of four basic steps:

1. A local modification on data is detected by a trigger component. It subsequently evaluates the corresponding partial constraint including one local check and one remote check. If the local check fails then the local transaction is aborted, otherwise the remote check is executed.
2. The remote check is performed by the Constraint Manager. The trigger uses an ENP to connect to the external CM via RMI to initiate the process. This call is executed synchronously, i.e. the local transaction is blocked until the call returns.
3. The CM receives the message from the ENP including the name of the database and relation that was modified. It looks up a set of schemas of remote component databases which the updated schema is related to and schedules the query of these databases.
4. After the interrelated schema items have been identified, the CM queries the remote databases to check if the constraint is violated. If a constraint violation occurs then the transaction on the database is rejected.

We will now take a closer look at the components performing the essential tasks: the trigger to react on local events, the ENP to connect to the CM, and the external CM that executes the remote part of the partial constraint check.

4.2 Trigger Definition

First, we consider the key constraint described above, which has to be checked whenever data is inserted or updated in the relation $project_A$. Analogous to the basic concept, we define a trigger as in Figure 2.

When a local transaction inserts or updates data items Δp in $project_A$, the trigger is executed for each single item in Δp *before* the transaction is completed. Corresponding to the partial integrity constraint, the trigger executes two integrity checks: first a local test on local data and after that a remote test on interrelated data on other component databases. To test if the new or updated project

```
CREATE TRIGGER key_project
BEFORE INSERT OR UPDATE ON projectA
REFERENCING NEW AS n
FOR EACH ROW
  DECLARE localtest, remotetest, notify INTEGER;
  SET localtest =
  (SELECT COUNT(ID_A) FROM projectA WHERE ID_A = n.ID_A);
  IF (localtest > 0) THEN
   RAISE LOCAL ERROR;
  SET remotetest = checkKey('CM_IP', 'key_project', n.ID_A);
  IF (remotetest != 1) THEN
  SET notify = notifyCM('CM_IP');
  RAISE REMOTE ERROR;
END
```

```
CREATE TRIGGER aggr_project
AFTER INSERT OR UPDATE ON projectA
FOR EACH STATEMENT
  DECLARE localsum, remotetest, notify INTEGER;
  SET localsum =
   (SELECT SUM(budget) FROM projectA);
  IF (localsum > 20000000) THEN
   SET notify = notifyCM('CM_IP');
   RAISE LOCAL ERROR;
  SET remotetest =
    checkAggr( 'CM_IP', 'aggr_project', localsum);
 IF (remotetest != 1) THEN
  SET notify = notifyCM('CM_IP');
  RAISE REMOTE ERROR;
 ELSE
  SET notify = notifyCM('CM_IP');
 END
```

Fig. 2. Definition of a key constraint trigger (left) and an aggregate constraint trigger (right)

number already exists in the local data stock, we execute a local query, which counts the number of tuples with the corresponding project number. If a project with this number already exists, then the transaction is rejected without executing the remote check. Otherwise, the trigger executes the remote check via the external program *checkKey* to check the existence of the project number in related databases. If the remote check fails, i.e. the project number already exists in one of the related databases or an error has occurred during the test, then the transaction is rejected and the CM is notified about the end of the check.

In most commercial database systems the before triggers can be defined only for each row. However, in our approach we also want to check statements which concern several tuples. Therefore we define an after trigger which is executed for the insert or update statements. In contrast to the `before` trigger, the `after` trigger has access to the temporary table that contains all tuples affected by the insert or update statement. Thus, if one tuple of the statement violates an integrity constraint, then the entire statement is revoked. During the key constraint checking, an `after` trigger is used simply to point at the end of the statement and to notify the CM about the end of the checking. The aggregate constraint is checked in the `after` trigger, because access to the whole statement is needed. Thus, we define additionally to the `before` trigger for the key constraint check an `after` trigger for the aggregate constraint (cp. Fig. 2).

Analogous to the `before` trigger, which checks the key constraint, the `after` trigger also executes two integrity checks: a local and a remote test. First, the trigger checks if the budget together with new or updated projects exceeds the limit. This can be done using a local query which sums the budgets of old and new (updated) projects together in the local table. If the budget limit is exceeded, then the transaction is rejected without executing the remote check. Otherwise, the trigger executes the remote test via the external function *checkAggr* to check if the total sum of related projects in both databases DB_I and DB_E and local projects including the new or updated projects does exceed the budget limit. If the remote check fails, then the transaction is rejected and the CM is notified about the end of the checking.

In many database systems the `after` trigger locks the local table during the checking. Thus, no other transaction can read the data from the local relation until the local transaction is completed. Thereby we can prevent the nonrepeatable read of the data by other transactions in the local relation. If the trigger does not lock the local relation, then the CM postpones the next check as long as the local transaction is not completed.

4.3 The External Notification Program

In our case, the ENP is a Java program, which must be installed as a stored procedure in the EADBS before it can be used in COMICS. It is executed by the trigger which is activated by a modification operation on the affected relation. The ENP operates as an RMI client and performs one of the following remote method calls to the Constraint Manager:

$$checkKey(CMAddr, triggerID, key\_value) = \begin{cases} 1, & \text{if key does not exist} \\ 0, & \text{if key exists} \\ -1, & \text{if exception occurs} \end{cases}$$

$$checkAggr(CMAddr, triggerID, budget\_value) = \begin{cases} 1, & \text{if limit is not exceeded} \\ 0, & \text{if limit is exceeded} \\ -1, & \text{if exception occurs} \end{cases}$$

$$notifyCM(CMAddr) = \begin{cases} 0, & \text{if release operation successful} \\ -1, & \text{if exception occurs} \end{cases}$$

Both methods *checkKey*() and *checkAggr*() have the same number of parameters: they need the IP address or DNS of the CM and the trigger id to identify the constraints in the repository. Furthermore, *checkKey*() requires the value of the modified project key(id_A) that has to be checked in the remote databases and *checkAggr*() needs the value of the bugdet required for the current project to check if the overall budget limit has not been exceeded. The method *notifyCM*() requires only the address of the Constraint Manager, since it is called by the after trigger and always refers to a unitary transaction. The actual use of the remote methods will be described in the next section.

4.4 The Constraint Manager

The Constraint Manager is the main component in the COMICS system that plans, initiates and monitors the execution of remote state queries among a set of interactive component databases. It receives synchronous notifications from the databases via RMI and thereupon executes queries on interdependent component databases. The synchronization is implemented with the help of a queue. While being checked for global integrity constraints by the CM, a second trigger can arrive at the CM, where it enters the queue and waits until the checking process is being completed.

Referring to our example, if a set of new projects is inserted into the relation $project_A$, we must ensure that the ID of the new projects has not already been used and the budget limit of 20.000.000 Euro is not exceeded. After the ENP has started the remote method *checkKey*(), it has to check if the CM is already busy with a transaction. In this case, the current transaction will be put into a queue. Otherwise, the CM checks the IP addresses, the schema information and constraint rules of the affected databases to control the key constraints from the repository. After that it queries the remote databases DB_E and DB_I to check if id_A already exists. If the value already exists in one of the data sources, then the method *checkKey*() returns 0 and the transaction on $project_A$ is rejected. Otherwise, it returns 1 so that the trigger can start the ENP again to control the aggregate constraint. The External Notification Program starts the remote method *checkAggr*() which operates in the same way as the method *checkKey*(). It controls if the global aggregation constraint (sum of all budgets > 20.000.000 Euro) is violated. If the limit is exceeded it returns 0 and the whole transaction is rejected. Otherwise it returns 1 and the transaction is committed. Subsequently (no matter if the transaction was committed or not) the trigger launches the method $notifyCM()$ which signals to the CM that the next transaction from the queue can be started.

The Constraint Manager is implemented as a centralised component in the architecture. Since all remote checks in the entire information system are performed by one centralised system, this builds a performance bottleneck. However, it guarantees global consistency, since updates on interrelated data that require partial constraint checks are globally serialized by the CM. Furthermore, it prevents global deadlocks and ensures atomic execution of partial constraint checks. Besides, semantic information is moved from the sources to the Constraint Manager, which makes it easier to add or remove interdependent sources or to maintain schema mappings. In COMICS the CM queries the databases using JDBC and SQL. Future implementations could include decentralised CMs that are assigned to only a subset of the data sources in the information system. They would be able to communicate with each other during partial constraint checks if a check requires access to multiple Constraint Managers.

5 Evaluation

In this section we present a worst-case performance outline of the COMICS system. The tests were made with three relational databases: two DB2 under Linux and one Oracle under Windows on machines with AMD Athlon XP2000 1.67 GHz. The Constraint Manager is implemented in Java and was in the same LAN as the databases. During the tests the system had to ensure that a global key constraint and an aggregated SUM constraint over the sum of a certain attribute were not violated. In both worst case scenarios we tested the system at full utilisation by inserting records in one and two of three dependent relational databases and measuring the time it takes to complete the insertion. To simulate a worst case, the records that were used were unique, so that a complete scan of the attached databases was ensured. The checking of the SUM constraint was also carried out completely over the entire record pool in the three databases. Each database had been populated with 1000 records that had to be scanned to check for global constraint violations. In Figure 3 the results of the tests in the worst case with one and two clients are shown. A single COMICS transaction takes therefore around 250 milliseconds in the worst case under our lab conditions

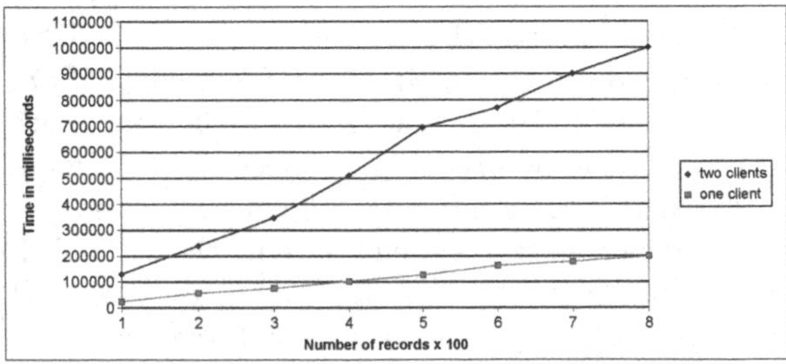

Fig. 3. Performance of the COMICS system in the worst case

when one client is active. It includes a local scan, four RMI calls to the remote databases, two remote scans and the local database update itself.

We already saw an application scenario of the system, where it could be used to manage constraints in an environment that does not contain time-critical processes, such as enterprise environments. Our tests showed that concurring access by more than one user is handled reliably by the system and no constraints were violated, because the system either allowed a transaction, queued it if the system was busy, or aborted it after a timeout.

The case when several clients try to execute updates deserves special attention because of the fairness that the system should guarantee to all participants. The COMICS Constraint Manager distributes transaction requests evenly, regardless of a client's priority. Depending on the system in which COMICS is used, however, requests of lower priority can be forced to wait in the queue while other critical transactions are being handled. Last but not least, the worst-case tests above give an overview of the limits of the system, but it is likely that in some cases a transaction is canceled due to a constraint violation. In such cases the order in which the remote checks are carried out is important for the performance, because if the system checks first the databases that return more update errors, there is a higher probability to cancel a transaction earlier and thus spare computing time. For that reason, one possible optimization would be to save statistics in the repository about the errors that were returned and let the system determine the scanning order.

6 Related Work

In the last years, research on integrity constraints in heterogeneous environments mainly considered the simplification, evolution, or reformulation of constraints rather then mechanisms or protocols for integrity checking. A closely related concept in terms of the rule structure and constraint types is presented in [5]. The authors use private and public global constraints to define dependencies between data in different databases, similar to the partial constraints presented in this paper. One of the main differences is the use of a layered approach to support the active functionality required for event detection and rule processing. A reactive middleware based on CORBA encapsulates active and passive sources and processes rules using an external remote rule processing mechanism. The disadvantage of this approach is that operations which are activated within the DBMS cannot be detected by the event monitoring component.

Further related architectures are described in the Hyperion project [6], the X^2TS prototype [7], the CORBA-based system presented in [8], or the database gateway solution as part of the REACH project [9]. A common characteristic of these architectures is the use of a layered approach with event monitoring to somehow notify a mediating component (e.g. a constraint manager, rule processor, or middleware component) about events occurring in the local database. If the source is not monitored, the notification mechanism is generally based on active capabilities of the underlaying database management system, but there is so far no detailed description of this interaction published. The most distinctive characteristic of our concept is the direct usage of existing active capabilities of modern database management systems without the need for monitoring components. Since a remote condition is evaluated during the execution of a trigger, it is irrelevant if the triggering transaction was a global or local update. We benefit from the active functionality of the DBMS in terms of transaction scheduling, locking, and atomicity, resulting in a synchronous integrity checking mechanism. Especially the ability to rollback updates depending on a remote state query makes corrective or compensative actions basically superfluous.

7 Conclusion and Future Work

In this paper we have presented the COMICS system, a prototype of a centralized environment based on the concept of constraint management in component database systems with enhanced active functionality. We have described the concept of EADBS, the prerequisite for a proper and reliable component interaction and outlined the architecture of COMICS. We also took a deeper look into the process of checking global integrity constraints by describing an interaction of system components in a real-world scenario. Subsequently, we analyzed the system's performance and mentioned some optimization options that could be implemented in the future.

References

1. Popfinger, C., Conrad, S.: Maintaining Global Integrity in Federated Relational Databases using Interactive Component Systems. In: Meersman, R., Tari, Z. (eds.) On the Move to Meaningful Internet Systems 2005: CoopIS, DOA, and ODBASE. LNCS, vol. 3760, pp. 539–556. Springer, Heidelberg (2005)
2. Loney, K., Koch, G.: Oracle8i: The Complete Reference. McGraw-Hill, New York (2000)
3. Popfinger, C., Conrad, S.: Tightly-coupled wrappers with event detection subsystem for heterogeneous information systems. In: DEXA Workshops, pp. 62–66 (2005)
4. Grefen, P.W.P.J., Widom, J.: Integrity constraint checking in federated databases. In: CoopIS, pp. 38–47 (1996)
5. Gomez, L.G.: An Active Approach to Constraint Maintenanc. In: A Multidatabase Environment. PhD thesis, Arizona State University (2002)
6. Kantere, V., Mylopoulos, J., Kiringa, I.: A distributed rule mechanism for multidatabase systems. In: Meersman, R., Tari, Z., Schmidt, D.C. (eds.) CoopIS 2003, DOA 2003, and ODBASE 2003. LNCS, vol. 2888, pp. 56–73. Springer, Heidelberg (2003)
7. Liebig, C., Malva, M., Buchmann, A.P.: Integrating Notifications and Transactions: Concepts and X^2TS Prototype. In: EDO, pp. 194–214 (2000)
8. Koschel, A., Kramer, R.: Configurable Event Triggered Services for CORBA-based Systems. In: EDOC, pp. 306–318 (1998)
9. Kudrass, T., Loew, A., Buchmann, A.P.: Active Object-Relational Mediators. In: Conference on Cooperative Information Systems (CoopIS), Brussels, pp. 228–239 (June 1996)

Guidelines for Network Service Pricing: An Extended Model Considering Increase of Network Users

Valbona Barolli[1], Heihachiro Fukuda[2], Leonard Barolli[3], and Makoto Takizawa[4]

[1] Graduate School of Science Engineering, Tokyo Denki University
Ishizaka, Hatoyama, Saitama 350-0394, Japan
barolli@mte.biglobe.ne.jp
[2] Department of System Management, Fukuoka Institute of Technology (FIT)
3-30-1 Wajiro-Higashi, Higashi-ku, Fukuoka 811-0295, Japan
fukuda@fit.ac.jp
[3] Department of Information and Communication Engineering,
Fukuoka Institute of Technology (FIT)
3-30-1 Wajiro-Higashi, Higashi-ku, Fukuoka 811-0295, Japan
barolli@fit.ac.jp
[4] Department of Computers and System Engineering, Tokyo Denki University
Ishizaka, Hatoyama, Saitama 350-0394, Japan
taki@takilab.k.dendai.ac.jp

Abstract. In this paper, we provide an evaluation model for marketable quality and profitability. We define the marketable quality as a qualitative aspect of profitability. We apply the real values of some leading manufacturing corporations in Japan to our proposed model to analyze its accuracy. From the analysis, we found that theoretical and real standard values of the marketable quality indicator were very close. This shows that the proposed model has a good approximation. From the fair relation of network service providers and users, we present the network pricing guidelines and extend our proposed network service pricing model considering network externalities.

1 Introduction

Now the economy society is shifting from the economies of scale to the quality enhancement. For this reason, the achieved standard profitability depends on the free competition between corporations. This is a very important concept that should be considered to evaluate the corporation profitability. The corporation profitability is conceptually considered to be a function of two variables: the qualitative and quantitative aspects. In fact, the quality and quantity are independent variables. But, for the profitability, there is a relation between them.

The Break-Even Point (BEP) ratio expressed in the following equation is used as an indicator related to profitability to measure the degree of safety against a risk of loss.

T. Enokido, L. Barolli, and M. Takizawa (Eds.): NBiS 2007, LNCS 4658, pp. 227–237, 2007.

Table 1. Annual relevant indicator values in the manufacturing industry

Item	Year												
	1986	1987	1988	1989	1990	1991	1992	1993	1994	1995	1996	1997	1998
r	1.128	1.159	1.207	1.214	1.198	1.154	1.109	1.087	1.100	1.127	1.146	1.135	1.098
Est. β	77.09	76.59	81.77	83.82	85.55	83.62	76.49	72.92	72.06	73.77	74.20	77.34	71.34
AGAV	28.37	29.41	32.78	35.19	37.49	33.58	32.45	31.30	32.12	33.56	35.08	34.51	31.15
AFC	37.49	38.93	41.73	45.08	49.14	45.92	46.38	45.30	47.82	48.40	50.10	50.63	48.63
β_0	0.606	0.574	0.561	0.569	0.596	0.628	0.622	0.617	0.596	0.581	0.565	0.600	0.592
$E(\beta)$	79.48	77.72	77.00	77.44	78.93	80.68	80.36	80.08	78.93	78.11	77.22	79.15	78.71

BEP Ratio = Sales at BEP / Sales = Fixed Costs / (Sales - Variable Costs)

This indicator is based on the profit graph presented by Knoeppel [1]. Another profitability indicator (relative annual profit) has been obtained from the rate of operation and the rate of operation at the BEP [2].

Relative Annual Profit = Rate of Operation / Rate of Operation at BEP = Marginal Profit / Fixed Costs.

We consider the relative annual profit as a profitability indicator in this study. We define the marketable quality based on the quality aspects of products and services provided by corporations. In order to define the quality, Garvin [3] considers five viewpoints, i.e., transcendent, product based, user based, manufacture based and value based as main approaches. We define the marketable quality as a qualitative aspect of profitability (value based).

In this work, we present an evaluation model for marketable quality and profitability and extend our model for network service pricing. Furthermore, we enhance our network service pricing model considering network externalities.

The paper is organized as follows. In the next section, we present a model to evaluate the marketable quality and profitability. In Section 3, we give the econometric methodology. In Section 4, we present network service pricing guidelines and the extended network service pricing model. Finally, in Section 5, we give some conclusions.

2 Proposed Model

2.1 Basic Variables

If a certain corporation consists of m kinds of processes or divisions for a certain period, we consider the capacity of process i be T_i^c, and its costs (fixed costs) be F_i, where $i = 1, \ldots, m$. The necessary capacity of process i is assumed to be T_i and the marginal profit which is calculated as the value of sales minus the variable costs is assumed to be M.

There is a minimum required level (minimum passing level) to purchase a product considering a sacrifice (price or fee) from the customers' side related to the quality of products or services given by a corporation. This means the minimum level to be achieved, even if the sacrifice is small. Therefore, we consider the minimum passing level as P_0 and the other levels as P.

2.2 Model Indicators

Rate of Operation Indicator. In our study, the rate of operation of a corporation β, is expressed in Eq. (1) as the average value of the rates β_i. The capacity cost values are used as weights for each process [2].

$$\beta = \frac{\sum_i \beta_i F_i}{\sum_i F_i} = \frac{\sum_i T_i f_i}{F} \tag{1}$$

Hence, $\beta_i = \frac{T_i}{T_i^c}$, $f_i = \frac{F_i}{T_i^c}$, $F = \sum_{i=1} F_i$.

Eq. (1) can be seen as a degree of used capacity costs.

In Refs. [4,5], the weighted average values are calculated by using added values of the rate of operation for each item which are considered as indicator of the rate of operation. Estimated values of the rate β of operation for each year are shown in Table 1. The corporation Average Gross Added Value (AGAV) and Average Fixed Costs (AFC) for each year [6] show that there is a high positive correlation (Correlation Coefficient (CC)= 0.721) between them. For this reason, we can apply the data of the rate of operation in Table 1 to the corporation rate of operation.

Profitability Indicator. The indicator representing relative annual profit only in the time dimension can be obtained as follows [2]. The ratio of marginal profit to necessary capacity costs (the amount of use of capacity costs) is defined as the following marginal profit rate:

$$\gamma = \frac{M}{\sum_i T_i f_i} \,. \tag{2}$$

The inverse number of γ is α, which is the minimum utilization rate of the capacity costs required to cover capacity costs F at the marginal profit rate γ. If the minimum capacity cost required to cover F is considered to be F_0,

$$\alpha = \frac{F_0}{F} = \frac{\sum_i T_i f_i}{M} \,. \tag{3}$$

This equation can be obtained by using this relation: $F_0 \frac{M}{\sum_i T_i f_i} = F$.

Therefore, the general relative profitability r can be measured by the ratio of β to α:

$$r = \frac{\beta}{\alpha} = \frac{M}{F} \,. \tag{4}$$

This parameter is considered as the relative annual profit.

Marketable Quality Indicator. The indicator P is impossible to be used as an evaluation indicator to compare the quality aspects of corporations. In order to build a quality indicator to compare product quality of corporations, we combine P with time and corresponding costs. The evaluation of the minimum passage level P_0 is based on the capacity costs as input and marginal profit as output for a certain rate of operation B ($0 < B \leq 1$) and capacity costs per rate of operation F/B [7]. The parameter B is the rate of operation of the BEP, when the production is made at the minimum passage level $P = P_0$.

The marginal profit $V(P_0, \beta)$ when the rate of operation differs from B in the minimum passage level $P = P_0$ is obtained by: $V(P_0, \beta) = \frac{F}{B}\beta$.

If marginal profit increases in proportion to the evaluated level P, the marginal profit $V(P, \beta)$ at the evaluated level P and the rate β of operation is computed by the following equation:

$$V(P, \beta) = P\frac{P}{P_0}\frac{\beta}{B}\,. \tag{5}$$

The marginal profit of Eq. (5) on the corporations' side plus the variable costs is considered as the price (fee) which the consumers should pay (sacrifice). By considering the input (costs) indicator corresponding to output of the evaluated level in Eq. (5), we obtain Eq. (6).

$$\text{Input (Cost) Indicator} = \frac{F}{B}\beta \tag{6}$$

Therefore, the relative value of P can be obtained by the ratio of output indicator Eq. (5) to the conditional input indicator Eq. (6) under the rate of B operation.

$$\text{Conditional Relative Value} = \frac{P}{P_0} \tag{7}$$

However, the relative value of Eq. (7) is possible only between corporations having the same B. Thus, it is impossible to make a relative evaluation by Eq. (7), because of different comparison conditions. For this reason, we carry out a more general comparable evaluation for the qualitative aspects of corporations.

For a certain corporation and for a certain period, a point (β, r) for each value of β and r is considered [8]. The price function $u(\beta)$ is expressed by the following equation:

$$r(\beta) = u(\beta)\beta\,. \tag{8}$$

The price function can be considered as a fair relationship when a rate of profit increases due to an increase in the rate β of operation ($\frac{dr(\beta)}{d\beta}$) (profit on the corporations' side) and the rate of reduction in the total price ($-\beta\frac{du(\beta)}{d\beta}$) (profit on the customer' side) are equal. This can be obtained by solving the following differential equation.

$$2\beta\frac{du(\beta)}{d\beta} + u(\beta) = 0 \tag{9}$$

$$u(\beta) = \frac{c}{\sqrt{\beta}}\,,\ c: \textit{integration constant}$$

There exist price functions when the rate of profit increase and the rate of price reduction are equal within a region where the integration constant c is a positive number. An incremental profit and a reduction in the total price on a reasonable price function at the rate β of operation are both expressed by the following equation.

$$r(\beta) = \int_0^\beta \frac{dr(\beta)}{d\beta}d\beta = \int_0^\beta -\beta\frac{du(\beta)}{d\beta}d\beta = c\sqrt{\beta} \tag{10}$$

Eq. (10) shows a fair relationship between the relative annual profit and the rate of operation. If the rate of operation at the BEP where fixed costs (capacity costs) can be just covered by an incremental profit is considered to be β_0, the integration constant c can be obtained by Eq. (10): $c\sqrt{\beta_0} = 1$. From this equation, we get: $c = \frac{1}{\sqrt{\beta_0}}$.

Therefore, from the Eq. (10) of relative annual profit, we obtain the following equations:

$$r(\beta) = \sqrt{\frac{\beta}{\beta_0}} \tag{11}$$

$$0 < \beta_0 \leq 1\,. \tag{12}$$

By Eq. (11), we classify the point $(\beta, r) \in R$ by considering β_0 as a relative profitability of the qualitative aspect from the viewpoint of fair relationship between β and r [9]. The value of β_0 is calculated by following equation by using Eq. (4) and Eq. (11).

$$\beta_0 = \frac{\alpha^2}{\beta} = \frac{\beta}{r^2} \tag{13}$$

The β_0 is related to variables: P, P_0, B, and β. From Eq. (5) and Eq. (13), we get the following equation.

$$\beta_0 = \frac{P_0^2 B^2}{P^2 \beta} \tag{14}$$

Because point $(\beta, r) \in R$ corresponds to point (β_0, β), it is possible to measure the following profitability function consisting of two variables: the generally comparable quality indicator β_0 and the rate β of operation.

$$r(\beta_0, \beta) = \sqrt{\frac{\beta}{\beta_0}} \tag{15}$$

3 Econometric Methodology

Let us look at Table 1 to see how our proposed marketable quality indicator β_0 approaches the real values. For the period from 1986 to 1998 from a total average viewpoint, β_0 shows major fluctuations. This period includes the period of the bubble economy of leading Japanese manufacturing corporations. The average value of β_0 for 13 years is 0.593.

To find the marketable quality indicator β_0, it is important to consider the difficulty of production on the producers' side and the sacrifice on the consumers' side [8]. The smaller is β_0 value (from 1 to 0) in Eq. (12), the greater is the incremental profit in Eq. (11). However, when β_0 is small, it is more difficult to realize the marketable quality on the producers' side. The sacrifice on the consumers' side is equal to the incremental profit on the producers' side.

In the case when β_0 is a value within the range of Eq. (12), its probability distribution is set independently from β in the following way. If the probability density function of β_0 is assumed to be $f(\beta_0)$, its value is obtained as Eq. (16) by using Eq. (11).

Table 2. Standard distribution of profitability r

r	β_0	$1-F(\beta_0)$	$P(r-0.1 \leq x < r)$
1.1	0.698	0.4168	0.4168
1.2	0.518	0.6272	0.2104
1.3	0.401	0.7461	0.1189
1.4	0.321	0.8181	0.0720
1.5	0.263	0.8651	0.0470
1.6	0.220	0.8968	0.0317
1.7	0.187	0.9191	0.0223
1.8	0.161	0.9354	0.0163
1.9	0.140	0.9476	0.0122
2.0	0.123	0.9569	0.0093
2.1	0.109	0.9640	0.0071
2.2	0.097	0.9698	0.0058
2.3	0.087	0.9743	0.0045
2.4	0.079	0.9778	0.0035
2.5	0.071	0.9811	0.0033
2.6	0.065	0.9834	0.0023
2.7	0.060	0.9853	0.0019
2.8	0.055	0.9871	0.0018
2.9	0.051	0.9885	0.0014
3.0	0.047	0.9898	0.0013
3.1	0.043	0.9911	0.0013

$$f(\beta_0) = \frac{\sqrt{\frac{\beta_0}{\beta}}}{\int_0^1 \sqrt{\frac{\beta_0}{\beta}}d\beta_0} = 1.5\sqrt{\beta}_0 \tag{16}$$

Therefore, the expectation of the marketable quality indicator β_0 is obtained by Eq. (17).

$$E(\beta_0) = \int_0^1 \beta_0 f(\beta_0)d\beta_0 = \int_0^1 \beta_0(1.5\sqrt{\beta_0})d\beta_0 = 0.6 \tag{17}$$

By this expectation, the standard value of β_0 can be set equal to 0.6. Such theoretical standard value of β_0 nearly agrees with the average 0.593 of β_0 in Table 1.

The difficulty degree to realize the rate β of operation for each β_0 in Eq. (11) exceeding the BEP (within the range of $\beta_0 \leq \beta \leq 1$) is in proportional relation to the size of the incremental profit in Eq. (11). The probability density function of β is obtained by Eq. (18).

$$f(\beta) = \frac{\sqrt{\frac{\beta_0}{\beta}}}{\int_{\beta_0}^1 \sqrt{\frac{\beta_0}{\beta}}d\beta} = \left\{2\left(1-\sqrt{\beta_0}\right)\sqrt{\beta}\right\}^{-1} \tag{18}$$

Therefore, the expectation of β is obtained by Eq. (19).

$$E(\beta) = \int_{\beta_0}^1 \beta f(\beta)d\beta = \frac{1}{3}(\beta_0 + \sqrt{\beta_0} + 1) \tag{19}$$

The $E(\beta)$ can be established as the theoretical standard value of β at β_0. Therefore, the standard relationship between the marketable quality indicator β_0 and relative annual profit r is derived by Eq. (20), where $E(\beta)$ is considered as a parameter. The r value can be obtained by putting Eq. (19) into Eq. (11).

$$r = \left\{ \frac{1 - \beta_0 \sqrt{\beta_0}}{3(1 - \sqrt{\beta_0})\beta_0} \right\}^{0.5} \tag{20}$$

The r value and its incremental rate increase with the decrease of β_0. This represents a gradual increase in profitability (returns) by improvement of marketable quality.

The standard value of marketable quality $\beta_0 = 0.6$ based on the standard operation rate gives a profitability value r. This value can be calculated from Eq. (20) and will be:

$$r = 1.1486. \tag{21}$$

In following, the distribution of r can be obtained as shown in Table 2, by transforming Eq. (20) to Eq. (22) and applying this value to the distribution of β_0 in Eq. (16) [10,11].

$$\beta_0 = \left\{ \frac{1 + \sqrt{12r^2 - 3}}{2(3r^2 - 1)} \right\}^2 \tag{22}$$

Then, the expectation of r is theoretically calculated as follows.

$$E(r) = \int_0^1 r(\beta_0) f(\beta_0) d\beta_0 = 1.2649 \tag{23}$$

Therefore, the effect in the standard value of the gradual increase of profitability due to improvement of marketable quality can be measured by the profitability of Eq. (23) minus profitability of Eq. (21), i.e. 0.116. The value of marketable quality for this effect is $\beta_0 = 0.437$.

4 Network Service Pricing Model

4.1 Network Service Pricing Guidelines

If a certain network provider has a network system for a certain period, we consider the total capacity of the network system to be T^c, its cost (fixed cost) F, and the necessary capacity of customers j in the given period t_j, $j = 1, \ldots, n$. We consider the fair relation between network service providers and consumers. Also considering the Eq.(11) and the relation between r and F ($r = M/F$), when r is equal to 1, the marginal profit M is the same with fixed costs F.

In Fig. 1 is shown the relation between β_0, β and r. If β_0 is constant and we increase β, then the r value is increased. Otherwise, if we consider β constant, the value of r is decreased with increase of β_0. However, when r is 1, the marginal profit M does not change when β is changed. In this case, the M can be considered the cost. Therefore, the network service provider costs (c_j) for customer j are computed as follows:

$$c_j = t_j f_0 + v_j \tag{24}$$

where, $f_0 = F / \sum_j t_j$ and v_j are variable service costs. The $t_j f_0$ value in Eq. (24) is the allocated capacity costs (fixed costs) for customer j when the marginal profit M is equal with fixed costs F and β_0 is equal to β.

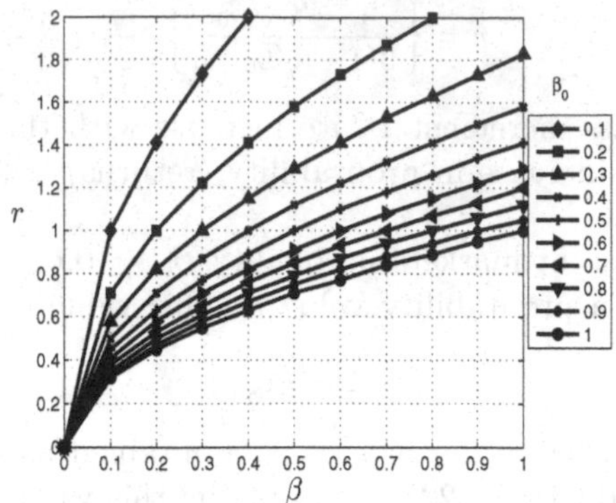

Fig. 1. Relationship between r, β and β_0

The network service price (P_j) for customer j is calculated as follows:

$$P_j = (t_j f)\gamma + v_j \tag{25}$$

where, $f = F/T^c$, $\gamma = (\beta\beta_0^*)^{-0.5}$, $\beta = \sum_j t_j/T^c$.

On the other hand, if the network service price P_j for a customer j is given for a network market, we can compute the marketable quality indicator value β_{0_j} for this customer j and the value β_0^* of a network service provider by using Eq. (26):

$$\beta_{0j} = \beta^{-1}\gamma_j^{-2} \tag{26}$$

where, $\gamma_j = M_j/t_j f_j$, $M_j = P_j - v_j$, $\beta_0^* = \beta^{-1}\gamma^{-2}$, $\gamma = \sum_j M_j / \sum_j t_j f$.

If the rate of operation β decreases, the network available capacity will increase. Thus, the network can serve a more larger number of users. Also, the quality of the network service can be improved by decreasing the total delay in sending information packets through the network. But, if the value of β is constant and the aggregate user demands increase more than the total network available capacity the delay will increase and the network quality of service will decrease, too.

A guideline of network pricing based on Eq. (20) can be given as follows. The relation between the marketable quality indicator β_0 and the theoretical standard value of the rate of operation β in Eq. (19) is transformed to the relation between β and γ (see Fig.2) using Eq. (13) and Eq. (19) as shown in Eq. (27).

$$\gamma = \frac{1 + \sqrt{3(4\beta - 1)}}{2(3\beta - 1)\sqrt{\beta}} \tag{27}$$

The maximum profitability point in Eq. (27) is when γ goes to infinite and β approaches to 1/3 from the infinite side. From the abovementioned considerations, we conclude that the network service pricing for a customer can be obtained from the fair relationship between network providers and consumers.

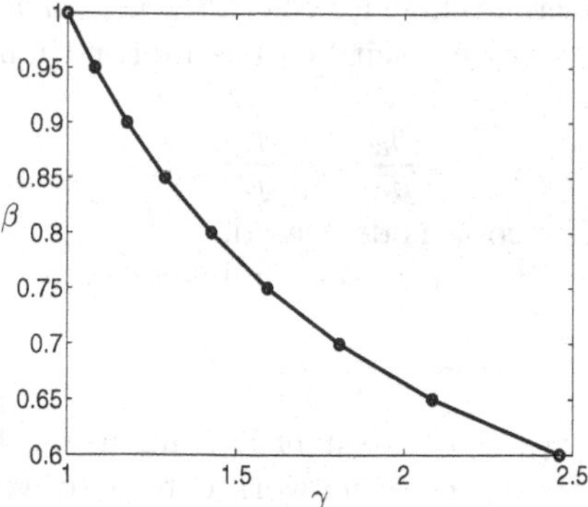

Fig. 2. Relationship between β and γ

4.2 Extended Network Service Pricing Model

We extend our work on network service pricing by considering the influence of network externalities. There are many network externalities, but we concentrate here on the increase of the number of network users.

Let us consider that we have m providers, which we denote as $prov_i$, where $i = 1, 2, \ldots, m$. We consider that the number of users for a provider is n_i. In the case when the number of users for a provider is increased from n_{i1} to n_{i2}: $\sum_i n_{i1} << \sum_i n_{i2}$, we consider the influence that the increase of number of users has on the network service pricing. Based on this increase the parameters of Eq.(26) change as follows: marketable quality indicator β_{0i} changes from β_{0i1} to β_{0i2}; rate of operation β_i changes from β_{i1} to β_{i2}; average marginal profit rate γ_i changes from γ_{i1} to γ_{i2}; average necessary capacity t_i changes from t_{i1} to t_{i2}; unit capacity cost f_i changes from f_{i1} to f_{i2}; average marginal profit M_i changes from M_{i1} to M_{i2}.

In this case, based on the effect of "mass production", the average necessary capacity cost $t_i f_i$ will be decreased ($t_{i1} f_{i1} > t_{i2} f_{i2}$). Because, in our model, we consider the fair relation between providers and users, both the providers and users have the same marginal profit. However, by considering the effect of the network externalities, the users can get the following additional profit increase.

1. One profit increase on the users side is by the decrease of the rate of operation β_i ($\beta_{i1} > \beta_{i2}$) based on the guideline model of Eq.(27) and the decrease of necessary capacity t_i ($t_{i1} > t_{i2}$) by the effect of "mass production". There are also some other effects from the increase of the quality of service.
2. Another profit increase on the users side is from the increase of information flow in the network. This is because, if the number of network users is increased, any user will get more information and the network resources will be used efficiently.

Let us consider the increase profit of Item 1 with x_i and increase profit of Item 2 with y. The x_i profit is a profit for each user, while profit y is a common profit.

Let us consider the average capacity cost $t_i f_i/\beta_i$ of $prov_i$. When the decrease rate of the average necessary capacity cost is higher than the decrease rate of the rate of operation, that is:

$$\frac{\beta_{i2}}{\beta_{i1}} > \frac{t_{i2} f_{i2}}{t_{i1} f_{i1}}, \tag{28}$$

then, the average capacity costs is decreased.

This partial decrease z_i for each user can be calculated as follows.

$$z_i = \frac{t_{i1} f_{i1}}{\beta_{i1}} - \frac{t_{i2} f_{i2}}{\beta_{i2}} \tag{29}$$

Assuming the fair relation between $prov_i$ and users, the average marginal profit M_{i2} considering the effect of network externalities can be calculated as follows.

$$M_{i2} = \frac{1}{2}(x_i + y) + M_{i1}(1 - \frac{\beta_{i1} z_i}{2 t_{i1} f_{i1}}) \tag{30}$$

If we consider that the profit increase by y is higher than z_i, then $M_{i2} > M_{i1}$. Therefore, the profitability r_i of $prov_i$ will be increased from $r_{i1} = M_{i1}/(t_{i1} f_{i1}/\beta_{i1})$ to $r_{i2} = M_{i2}/(t_{i2} f_{i2}/\beta_{i2})$. Also, from Eq.(13) $\beta_{0i1} > \beta_{0i2}$. From these results, we conclude that by the enhancement of the marketable quality, the profitability is increased.

5 Conclusions

In this paper, we proposed an evaluation model for marketable quality and profitability considering relation between service providers and consumers. We extended our model for network service pricing and presented a network pricing guideline, whic can be obtained considering the relation between marginal profit rate and rate of operation.

Considering the effect of the network externalities on network service pricing model, we conclude as follows: the users can get additional profit increase by the decrease of the rate of operation, the effect of "mass production" and the increase of information flow in the network; by decreasing the marketable quality indicator (increase of the marketable quality), the profitability is increased; the increase of the profitability by enhancement of marketable quality can be derived using the proposed model.

Acknowledgment

This work is supported by a scholarship from C&C Foundation of Japan. The authors would like to thank C&C Foundation for the financial support.

References

1. Knoeppel, C.E.: Profit Engineering, Applied Economics in Making Business Profitable. McGraw-Hill, New York (1933)
2. Fukuda, H.: An Economy Indicator for Process Capability and Capacity Planning. Journal of Japan Industrial Management Association 39(3), 139–145 (1988)

3. Garvin, D.A.: Managing Quality. The Free Press, New York (1988)
4. Miti and the Economic Planning Agency in Japan, `http://wp.cao.go.jp/zenbun/keizai/wp-je91/wp-je91bun-3-1-3z.html`
5. Ministry of Economy, Trade and Industry (METI): Explanation of Index of Industrial Production (2003)
6. The Industrial Policy Bureau of Ministry of International Trade and Industry in Japan (MITI): Business Analysis of Japanese Corporation - Industrial Classification Statistics Compilation. Printing of Bureau of Japanese Ministry of Finance (1992-1997-2000)
7. Nakata, T., Fukuda, H., Yang, Q.: Construction of an Indicator for Measuring White-collar Productivity. Journal of Japan Industrial Management Association 50(1), 20–26 (1999)
8. Fukuda, H.: A Standard Relationship Between Relative Annual Profit and Production Ratio in Process Capability and Capacity Planning. Journal of Japan Industrial Management Association 40(3), 171–176 (1989)
9. Koga, F., Fukuda, H., Matsuo, T.: Development of Quality Evaluation Technique for Service Enterprises. Journal of Japan Industrial Management Association 53(4), 282–291 (2002)
10. Barolli, V., Fukuda, H.: A Distributed Computing Approach for Marketable Quality and Profitability of Corporations. In: Proc. of IEEE DPNA-2005/ICPADS-2005, Fukuoka, Japan, pp. 659–663. IEEE Computer Society Press, Los Alamitos (2005)
11. Barolli, V., Fukuda, H.: A Distributed Computation Model for Marketable Quality and Profitability Considering Unfair Relationship. In: Proc. of NBiS-2005/DEXA-2005, Copenhagen, Denmark, pp. 15–21 (2005)

Role-Based Scheduling and Synchronization Algorithms to Prevent Illegal Information Flow

Tomoya Enokido[1], Valbona Barolli[2], and Makoto Takizawa[2]

[1] Rissho University, Japan
eno@ris.ac.jp
[2] Tokyo Denki University, Japan
valbona@takilab.k.dendai.ac.jp, makoto.takizawa@computer.org

Abstract. Information systems have to be consistent and secure in presence of multiple conflicting transactions. The role-based access control model is widely used to keep information systems secure. Here, a role is a set of access rights, i.e. permissions. A subject is granted a family of roles, i.e. one or more than one role. A subject s is allowed to issue a method op to an object o only if an access right $\langle o, op \rangle$ is included in the roles granted to the subject s. In the access control models, even if every access request satisfies the access rules, illegal information flow might occur as well known confinement problem. In this paper, we define a legal information flow relation ($R_1 \Rightarrow R_2$) among a pair of role families R_1 and R_2. This means, no illegal information flow occur if a transaction T_1 with a role family R_1 is performed prior to another transaction T_2 with R_2. In addition, we define which role families are more significant than others in terms of types of methods and security classes of objects. Conflicting methods from different transactions are totally ordered in the significancy of roles of the transactions. We discuss how to synchronize transactions so as to prevent illegal information flow and how to serialize conflicting methods from multiple transactions in terms of significancy and information flow relation of roles families.

1 Introduction

It is critical to discuss how to make information systems more consistent and secure in presence of various kinds of security attacks and conflicting accesses to resources. In the basic access control model [2], only a subject s, i.e. user and program is allowed to issue a method op to an object o like a database system [13,16] only if an access right (or permission) $\langle o, op \rangle$ is granted to the subject s. In an enterprise, each person plays one or more than one role. Here, a role shows a job function. In the role-based access control models [9,10,15,17], a role is specified in a collection of access rights, which shows what subjects playing the role can do on resources of an enterprise. While the access control models are widely used in information systems like database systems [13,16], illegal information flow among subjects through objects may occur even if each subject can safely manipulate objects according to the access rights. This is *confinement* problem [3,12]. In the lattice-based access control model is discussed [4,14], each

T. Enokido, L. Barolli, and M. Takizawa (Eds.): NBiS 2007, LNCS 4658, pp. 238–247, 2007.

entity, i.e. subject and object is classified into a security class. Information flow relation among security classes is defined. Access rules on read, write, and modify are defined according to the information flow relation.

In this paper, we newly discuss a concurrency control mechanism to synchronize conflicting transactions to achieve two objectives. First, a more significant method should be performed prior to others from the application point of view. Next, no illegal information flow should occur. First, we discuss how to prevent illegal information flow in the role-based access control model. A subject s issues a transaction T to manipulate objects. The transaction T is assigned a subfamily of the roles granted to the subject s. The subfamily of the roles is referred to as *purpose* of the subject s to perform T. First, we define a *legal information flow* relation $R_1 \Rightarrow R_2$ among purposes R_1 and R_2. This means that there occur no illegal information flow if a transaction T_1 with the purpose R_1 is performed prior to another T_2 with R_2. We also discuss which role family is more significant than another role family based on the significancy of methods [5,6,7]. For example, *write* is more significant than *read* since the object state is changed by *write* and *withdraw* is more significant than *deposit* in a bank application. The types of schedulers to perform a method from a more significant transaction prior to a less significant one are also discussed. We discuss how to serialize conflicting read and write methods from multiple transactions so that illegal information flow is prevented based on the legal information flow relation of the purposes.

In section 2, we overview the role-based access control models and briefly discuss what role family is more significant than another. In section 3, we define the legal information flow relation among roles. In section 4, we discuss the role-based scheduling and synchronization mechanisms of multiple transactions to prevent illegal information flow while serializing conflicting transactions.

2 Role-Based Access Control Models

2.1 Roles

In the access control models [2,4,9,10,14,15,17], a system is composed of two types of entities, subjects and objects. A subject is an entity who issues methods to objects like user. An object is an entity which performs methods from subjects like database. Only a subject s granted an access right (or permission) $\langle o, op\rangle$ is allowed to issue a method op to an object o.

In the role-based access control models [9,10,15,17], a role is given as a set of access rights and shows a job function in an enterprise. Let O be a set $\{o_1, ..., o_m\}$ of objects in the system. Each object o_i supports methods for manipulating data (i = 1, ..., m). Let R be a set of roles $\{r_1, ..., r_n\}$ in a system. Each role r_i is a collection $\{\alpha_{i1}, ..., \alpha_{il_i}\}$ of access rights. Each access right α_{ij} is a pair $\langle o_{ij}, op_{ij}\rangle$ of an object o_{ij} in O and a method op_{ij} for manipulating o_{ij}. A subject s is granted one or more than one role. Let $SR(s)$ ($\subseteq R$) be a family of roles granted to a subject s. A subject s is allowed to issue a method op to an object o only if an access right $\langle o, op\rangle$ is in the role family $SR(s)$.

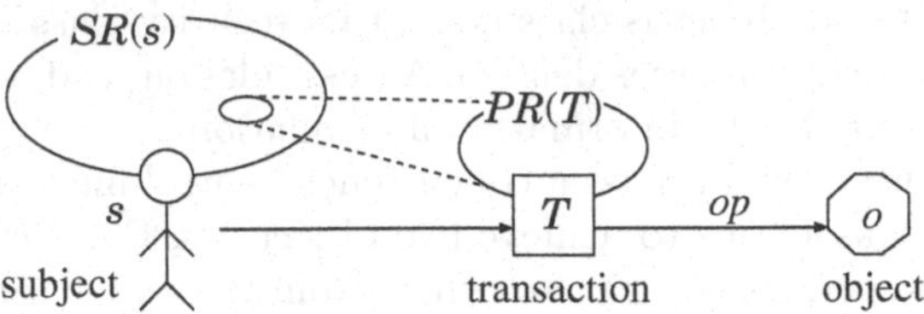

Fig. 1. Purpose

A subject s initiates a transaction T. Here, the transaction T is assigned a subfamily $PR(T)$ of the roles in the family $SR(s)$ of roles granted to the subject s ($PR(T) \subseteq SR(s)$) [Figure 1]. $PR(T)$ is referred to as *purpose* [5,6,7] of the subject s to issue the transaction T. The transaction T issues a method *op* to an object o for an access right $\langle o, op \rangle$ in the purpose $PR(T)$. A *write* method *conflicts* with *write* and *read* methods while *read* conflicts with *write* since the result obtained by performing the methods depends on the computation order. Conflicting transactions should be serializable to realize the mutual consistency of objects [8]. In the locking protocols [3,8,11,18], transactions arbitrarily hold objects based on the first-comer-winner principal. In the timestamp ordering (TO) schedulers [1], transactions are totally ordered in their timestamps. Objects are manipulated by conflicting transactions in the TO order.

The access control models imply the confinement problem [3,12]. For example, a subject s_1 is granted a pair of access rights $\langle f, read \rangle$ and $\langle g, write \rangle$ on file objects f and g while another subject s_2 is only granted an access right $\langle g, read \rangle$. Suppose the subject s_1 reads data x from the file f and then writes x to the file g. Here, the subject s_2 can read x from g although s_2 is not allowed to read the data x in f. Here, information x *illegally flows* to the subject s_2.

2.2 Significancy of Roles

The authors discuss which role family is more significant than another role family [5,6,7]. In the papers [5,6,7,18], various types of methods on objects are discussed. In this paper, we take only two types of methods *read* and *write* on each object for simplicity. The definition of the role significancy [5,6,7] is simplified as follows. Let α_1 and α_2 be access rights $\langle o_1, op_1 \rangle$ and $\langle o_2, op_2 \rangle$, respectively, where o_1 and o_2 are objects and op_1 and op_2 are methods. α_1 *significantly dominates* α_2 ($\alpha_2 \preceq^s \alpha_1$) if o_1 is more secure than o_2. Suppose that the objects o_1 and o_2 belong to the same security class. Here, α_1 significantly dominates α_2 ($\alpha_2 \preceq^s \alpha_1$) if op_1 is *write* and op_2 is *read*. Based on the significancy $\preceq^s$ of access rights, the significantly dominant relation $\preceq^s$ of roles is defined as follows:

Definition. A role r_1 is *significantly dominated* by a role r_2 ($r_1 \preceq^s r_2$) iff there is no access right β in r_2 such that $\alpha \preceq^s \beta$ for every access right α in r_1.

In Figure 2, a circle node indicates an access right and a directed edge $\alpha \rightarrow \beta$ shows that an access right α is significantly dominated by β ($\alpha \preceq^s \beta$). In Figure 2 (a), a role r_1 is *more significant* than another role r_2 ($r_1 \preceq^s r_2$) since there is no access right β in r_2 such that $\alpha \preceq^s \beta$ for every access right α in r_1. On the other hand, there are access rights α in r_1 and β in r_2 such that $\alpha \preceq^s \beta$ and $\beta \preceq^s \alpha$ in Figure 2 (*b*). Hence, $r_1 \not\preceq^s r_2$ and $r_2 \not\preceq^s r_1$.

Let r_1 and r_2 be roles in a role family R. The least upper bound (*lub*) $r_1 \sqcup^s r_2$ of r_1 and r_2 is defined to be a role r_3 in R such that $r_1 \preceq^s r_3$, $r_2 \preceq^s r_3$, but no role r_4 such that $r_1 \preceq^s r_4 \preceq^s r_3$ and $r_2 \preceq^s r_4 \preceq^s r_3$. The greatest lower bound (*glb*) $r_1 \sqcap^s r_2$ is also defined.

A subject s and a transaction T are assigned with role families $SR(s)$ and $PR(T)$, respectively. We define the significancy $\preceq^s$ among role families.

Definition. A role family R_i is *significantly dominated* by a role family R_j ($R_i \preceq^s R_j$) iff $\sqcup^s_{r \in R_i} r \preceq^s \sqcap^s_{r \in R_j} r$.

In Figure 3, a circle node r_i indicates a role r_i and a directed edge $r_i \rightarrow r_j$ shows that a role r_j significantly dominates a role r_i ($r_i \preceq^s r_j$). Suppose a role family $R_1 = \{r_1, r_2, r_3\}$ and $R_2 = \{r_3, r_4, r_5\}$. Here, $(r_1 \sqcup^s r_2 \sqcup^s r_3) = r_3$ since $r_1 \preceq^s r_3$, $r_2 \preceq^s r_3$ and there is no role r' such that $r_1 \preceq^s r' \preceq^s r_3$ and $r_2 \preceq^s r' \preceq^s r_3$. Since $(r_1 \sqcup^s r_2 \sqcup^s r_3) \preceq^s (r_3 \sqcap^s r_4 \sqcap^s r_5)$, $R_1 \preceq^s R_2$.

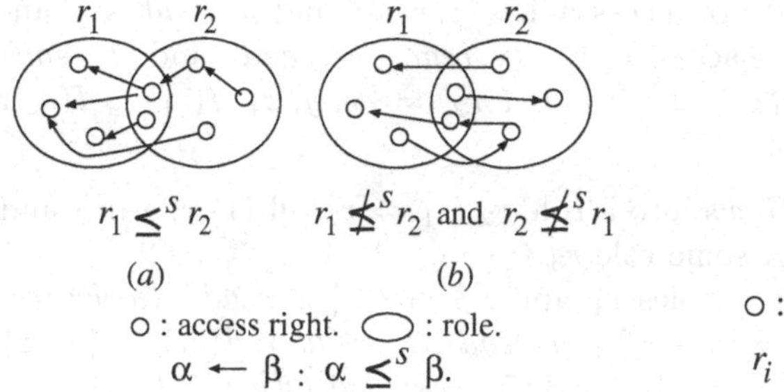

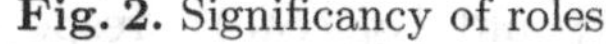

Fig. 2. Significancy of roles

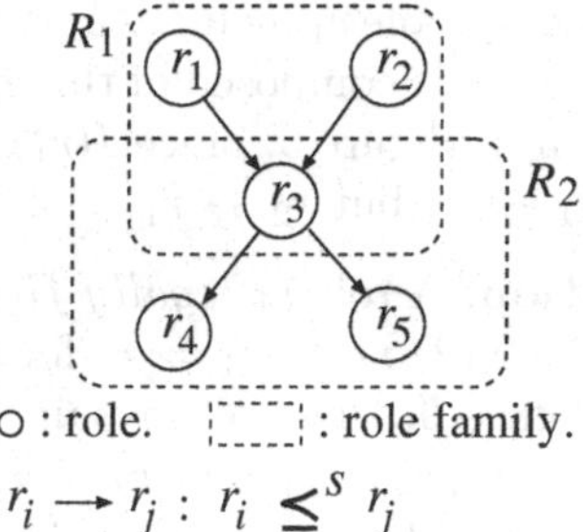

Fig. 3. Significancy of role families

3 Information Flow Relations

3.1 Information Flow on Roles

Let R be a set of roles and O be a set of objects in a system. We first introduce relations $r \mapsto o$ and $o \mapsto r$ for a role $r \in R$ and an object $o \in O$ showing that $\langle o, write \rangle \in r$ and $\langle o, read \rangle \in r$, respectively. $r \mapsto o$ and $o \mapsto r$ mean that a transaction with a role r is allowed to write and read an object o, respectively. Let $I(r)$ and $O(r)$ be *input* and *output* sets of objects $\{o \mid o \mapsto r\}$ and $\{o \mid r \mapsto o\}$ for a role r, respectively. A transaction granted a role r is allowed to read and write objects in $I(r)$ and $O(r)$, respectively.

Definition. A role r_1 *flows into* a role r_2 ($r_1 \mapsto r_2$) iff $r_1 \mapsto o$ and $o \mapsto r_2$ for some object o or $r_1 \mapsto r_3 \mapsto r_2$ for some role r_3, i.e. $O(r_1) \cap I(r_2) \neq \phi$.

Suppose a transaction T_1 is assigned with a role r_1 and another transaction T_2 with a role r_2. A flow relation $r_1 \mapsto r_2$ means that data written by T_1 might be

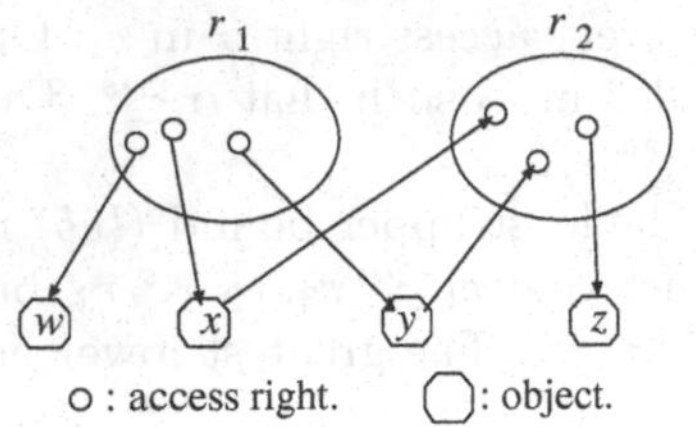

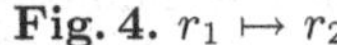

Fig. 4. $r_1 \mapsto r_2$

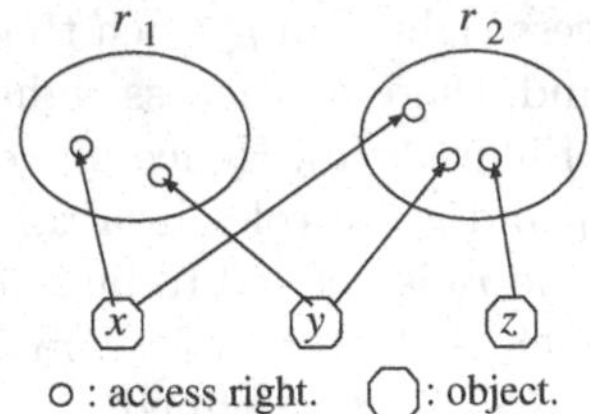

Fig. 5. $r_1 \rightarrow r_2$

read by T_2. That is, information might flow from T_1 to T_2. For example, suppose there are a pair of roles r_1 and r_2 where $r_1 = \{\langle x, write\rangle, \langle y, write\rangle, \langle w, write\rangle\}$ and $r_2 = \{\langle x, read\rangle, \langle y, read\rangle, \langle z, write\rangle\}$ where w, x, y, and z are objects as shown in Figure 4. Here, $O(r_1) = \{x, y, w\}$ and $I(r_2) = \{x, y\}$. $O(r_1) \cap I(r_2) = \{x, y\} \neq \phi$. Hence, $r_1 \mapsto r_2$.

Definition. A role r_2 *reads more* objects than a role r_1 ($r_1 \rightarrow r_2$) iff $o \mapsto r_2$ for every object o such that $r_1 \mapsto o$, i.e. $I(r_1) \subseteq I(r_2)$ or $r_1 \rightarrow r_3 \rightarrow r_2$ for some role r_3.

Suppose a role r_1 includes a pair of access rights $\langle x, read\rangle$ and $\langle y, read\rangle$ and another role r_2 is composed of three access rights $\langle x, read\rangle$, $\langle y, read\rangle$, and $\langle z, read\rangle$ as shown in Figure 5. Since $I(r_1) = \{x, y\}$ and $I(r_2) = \{x, y, z\}$, $I(r_1) \subseteq I(r_2)$. Here, $r_1 \rightarrow r_2$ but $r_2 \not\rightarrow r_1$.

Definition. A role r_1 *legally flows* into a role r_2 ($r_1 \Rightarrow r_2$) iff (1) $r_1 \mapsto r_2$ and $r_1 \rightarrow r_2$ or (2) $r_1 \Rightarrow r_3 \Rightarrow r_2$ for some role r_3.

In Figure 6, there are a pair of roles r_1 and r_2, $r_1 = \{\langle x, read\rangle, \langle y, write\rangle, \langle z, read\rangle, \langle v, write\rangle\}$ and $r_2 = \{\langle x, read\rangle, \langle y, read\rangle, \langle z, read\rangle\}$. $I(r_1) = \{x, z\}$ and $O(r_1) = \{y, v\}$. $I(r_2) = \{x, y, z\}$. $I(r_1) \subseteq I(r_2)$ and $O(r_1) \cap I(r_2) \neq \phi$. Hence, $r_1 \Rightarrow r_2$.

Let r_1 and r_2 be roles $\{\langle x, read\rangle, \langle y, write\rangle\}$ and $\{\langle y, read\rangle\}$, respectively. Let T_1 and T_2 be a pair of transactions where purposes $PR(T_1) = \{r_1\}$ and $PR(T_2) = \{r_2\}$ as shown in Figure 7. Suppose the transaction T_1 reads data v from an object x and writes the data v to another object y, i.e. $\langle x, read\rangle \in r_1$ and $\langle y, write\rangle \in r_1$. Then, suppose T_2 reads the object y since $\langle y, read\rangle \in r_2$. However, $\langle x, read\rangle \notin r_2$, i.e. T_2 is not allowed to read data in the object x. Here, illegal information flow occurs since T_2 reads x's data in the other object y although T_2 is not allowed to read x. On the other hand, if $\langle x, read\rangle \in r_2$, $r_1 \Rightarrow r_2$ from the definition. T_2 can read the value of the object x from the other object y since T_2 is allowed to read x. Thus, the legal flow relation $r_1 \Rightarrow r_2$ shows that no illegal information flow occur if T_1 is performed prior to T_2.

Definition. Let r_1 and r_2 be a pair of roles. The following relations between r_1 and r_2 are defined:

1. $r_1 \equiv^I r_2$ (r_1 and r_2 are *information-flow (I-) equivalent*) iff $r_1 \Rightarrow r_2$ and $r_2 \Rightarrow r_1$.
2. $r_1 \prec^I r_2$ (r_2 is more *I-significant* than r_1) iff $r_1 \Rightarrow r_2$ but $r_2 \not\Rightarrow r_1$.

3. $r_1 \preceq^I r_2$ (r_2 *I-dominates* r_1) iff $r_1 \Rightarrow r_2$ or $r_1 \equiv^I r_2$.
4. $r_1 \|^I r_2$ (r_1 and r_2 are *I-uncomparable*) iff neither $r_1 \preceq^I r_2$ nor $r_2 \preceq^I r_1$.

A least upper bound (*lub*) $r_1 \sqcup^I r_2$ of roles r_1 and r_2 is a role r_3 such that $r_1 \preceq^I r_3$, $r_2 \preceq^I r_3$, and no role r_4 such that $r_1 \preceq^I r_4 \preceq^I r_3$ and $r_2 \preceq^I r_4 \preceq^I r_3$. The greatest lower bound (*glb*) $r_1 \sqcap^I r_2$ is similarly defined. Thus, a lattice $\langle R, \preceq^s, \sqcup^I, \sqcap^I \rangle$ is defined for a set R of roles in a system. Here, the bottom $\bot$ is ϕ and the top $\top$ is R.

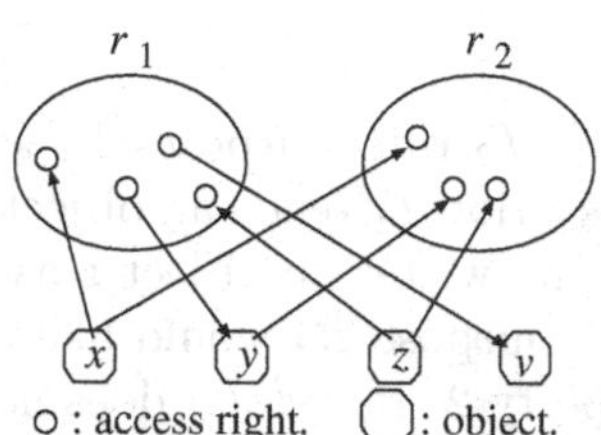

Fig. 6. $r_1 \Rightarrow r_2$

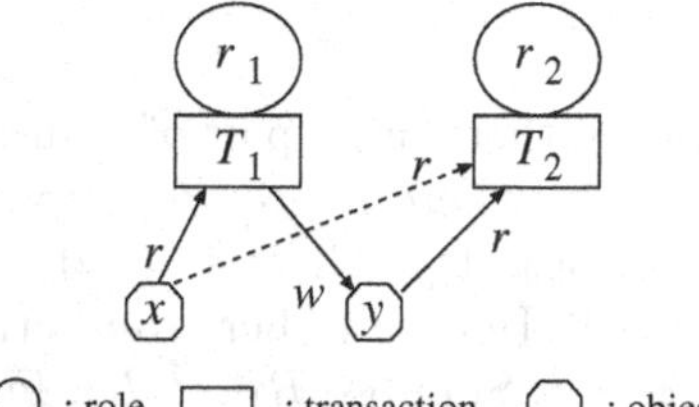

Fig. 7. $r_1 \Rightarrow r_2$

3.2 Information Flow on Role Families

A subject s is granted one or more than one role in a system. Let $SR(s)$ ($\subseteq R$) show a family of roles granted to a subject s. A transaction T issued by a subject s is assigned a purpose $PR(T)$ which is a subset of $SR(s)$. We discuss the legal information flow relation $\preceq^I$ among role families ($\preceq^I \subseteq 2^R \times 2^R$).

Definition. Let R_1 and R_2 be a pair of role families. R_2 $I(informationflow)$-*dominates* R_1 ($R_1 \preceq^I R_2$) iff $\sqcup^I_{r_1 \in R_1} r_1 \preceq^I \sqcap^I_{r_2 \in R_2} r_2$.

$R_1 \equiv^I R_2$, $R_1 \prec^I R_2$, and $R_1 \|^I R_2$ are defined in terms of the *I-dominant* relation $\preceq^I$ of roles. Suppose there are a pair of role families $R_1 = \{r_1, r_2\}$ and $R_2 = \{r_2, r_3\}$ as shown in Figure 8. Here, r_1, r_2, and r_3 are roles where $r_1 = \{\langle x, read\rangle, \langle y, write\rangle\}$, $r_2 = \{\langle x, read\rangle, \langle y, read\rangle, \langle z, write\rangle\}$, and $r_3 = \{\langle x, read\rangle, \langle y, read\rangle, \langle z, read\rangle\}$. According to the definitions, $r_1 \preceq^I r_2 \preceq^I r_3$ since $r_1 \Rightarrow r_2 \Rightarrow r_3$. Here, $\sqcup^I_{r \in R_1} r = r_1 \sqcup^I r_2 = r_2$ since $r_1 \preceq^I r_2$ and there is no role r' such that $r_1 \preceq^I r' \preceq^I r_2$. Similarly, $\sqcap^I_{r \in R_2} r = r_2 \sqcap^I r_3 = r_2$. Then, $R_1 \preceq^I R_2$ since $\sqcup^I_{r \in R_1} r \preceq^I \sqcap^I_{r \in R_2} r$.

The following properties hold on role families R_1, R_2, and R_3.

Property 1. $R_1 \preceq^I R_2$ if $R_1 \preceq^I R_3$ and $R_3 \preceq^I R_2$ for some role family R_3.

Proof. The *I-dominant* relation $\preceq^I$ is transitive from the definition.

Property 2. $R_2 \npreceq^I R_3$ if $R_1 \preceq^I R_2$ but $R_1 \npreceq^I R_3$.

Proof. Assume $R_1 \preceq^I R_2$, $R_1 \npreceq^I R_3$, and $R_2 \preceq^I R_3$. Since $R_1 \preceq^I R_2$ and $R_2 \preceq^I R_3$, $R_1 \preceq^I R_3$ from the property 1. This contradicts the assumption $R_1 \npreceq^I R_3$. Hence, the property holds.

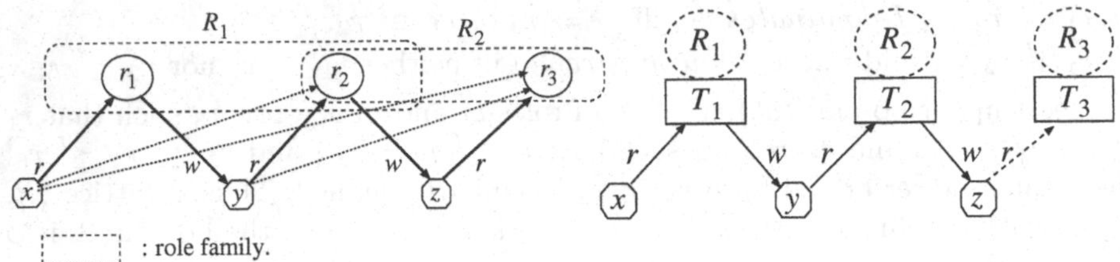

Fig. 8. Information flow

Fig. 9. Information flow

Suppose there are a pair of transactions T_1 and T_2 with purposes R_1 and R_2, respectively, where $R_1 \preceq^I R_2$. Suppose the transaction T_1 reads an object x and writes an object y. Then, T_2 reads the object y and writes an object z as shown in Figure 9. Here, another transaction T_3 with a purpose R_3 would like to read the object z. Suppose $R_1 \not\preceq^I R_3$. From the property 2, $R_2 \preceq^I R_3$ does not hold either. This means, T_3 just compares the purpose $PR(T_3)$ with the purpose of a transaction which has most recently written the object z, i.e. T_2. T_3 can reads the object z if $R_2 \preceq^I R_3$. Otherwise, T_3 cannot read the object z because T_3 might obtain some data of an object from z, which T_3 is not allowed to read.

4 Scheduling and Synchronization of Transactions

4.1 Scheduling of Methods

We discuss how to perform multiple conflicting transactions so as to keep objects consistent and secure. First, suppose a pair of transactions T_t and T_u issue methods op_{ti} and op_{ui} to an object o_i, respectively. First, every method is sent to a scheduler SCH_i of the object o_i, where methods op_{ti} and op_{ui} received from the transactions T_t and T_u are ordered as follows:

Schedule(op_{ti}, op_{ui}) {
  if op_{ti} conflicts with op_{ui},
    if $PR(T_u) \preceq^s PR(T_t)$, /* T_t is more significant than T_u */
      {
        if op_{ti} is *write* and op_{ui} is *read*,
          if $PR(T_t) \not\preceq^I PR(T_u)$, {
            /* illegal information flow might occur */ **abort** T_u; }
        op_{ti} precedes op_{ui} ($op_{ti} \Rightarrow op_{ui}$) in SCH_i;
      }
    else {
      if $PR(T_t) \preceq^s PR(T_u)$, **Schedule**($op_{ui}$, op_{ti});
      else { /* $PR(T_t) \equiv^s PR(T_u)$ or $PR(T_t) \parallel^s PR(T_u)$ */
        if op_{ti} = *write* and op_{ui} = *read*,
          if $PR(T_t) \not\preceq^I PR(T_u)$, {
            /* illegal information flow might occur */ **abort** T_t or T_u; }
          else op_{ti} precedes op_{ui} ($op_{ti} \Rightarrow op_{ui}$);

```
          else opti and opui are arbitrarily ordered (opti || opui);
        }
      }
    else opti and opui are arbitrarily ordered (opti || opui);
}
```

Suppose that a transaction T_t issues a method op_{ti} and T_u issues op_{ui} to a object o_i and op_{ti} conflicts with op_{ui}. In the procedure **Schedule**, the method op_{ti} precedes op_{ui} ($op_{ti} \Rightarrow op_{ui}$) in the schedule SCH_i if T_t is more significant than T_u, i.e. $PR(T_u) \preceq^s PR(T_t)$. Here, suppose that op_{ti} is *write* and op_{ui} is *read*. op_{ti} is performed prior to op_{ui} in SCH_i since $PR(T_u) \preceq^s PR(T_t)$ as shown in Figure 10. Here, if $PR(T_u) \preceq^I PR(T_t)$, no illegal information flow occur. However, illegal information flow might occur unless $PR(T_u) \preceq^I PR(T_t)$. Hence, op_{ti} (*write*) and op_{ui} (*read*) cannot be performed in this order. Either T_t or T_u is aborted since illegal information flow might occur. If $PR(T_u) \preceq^s PR(T_t)$, a less significant transaction T_u is aborted. If $PR(T_u) \equiv^s PR(T_t)$ or $PR(T_u) \parallel^s PR(T_t)$, T_t or T_u is arbitrarily selected and aborted.

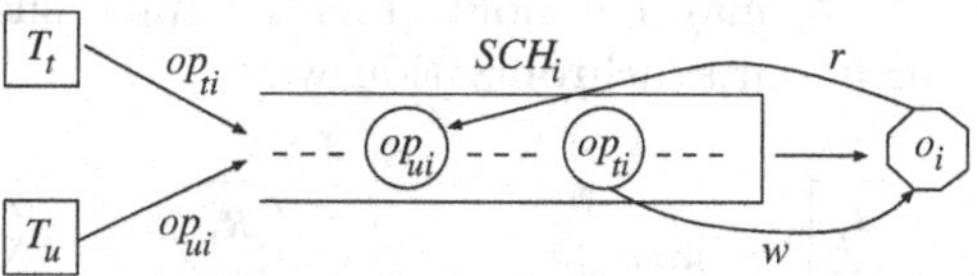

Fig. 10. Scheduler

Since conflicting methods issued by multiple transactions are totally ordered on each object in the significancy of purposes of the transactions, the transactions are serializable in the scheduler SCH_i. In addition, one of transaction T_t and T_u is aborted if illegal information flow would occur.

4.2 Information Flow Check

Methods are performed on an object o_i according to the precedent order $\Rightarrow$ in the schedule SCH_i. A variable $o_i.P$ denoting a role family, i.e. purpose of a transaction which has most recently written the object o_i is manipulated for each object o_i. $o_i.P = \phi$ in the initialization of the system. The scheduler SCH_i outputs a method op_{ti} to the object o_i in the precedent order $\Rightarrow$ obtained in the procedure **Schedule**. op_{ti} is a method issued by a transaction T_t. The top method op_{ti} is performed on the object o_i as follows.

```
Perform(Tt, opti, oi) {
  if opti = write, {
        oi.P = PR(Tt);
        write oi;
  }
  else { /* opti = read */
```

```
        if o_i.P ⪯^I PR(T_t),
            read o_i;  /* no illegal information flow */
        else abort T_t;
    }
}
```

If op_{ti} is *write*, a purpose $PR(T_t)$ of the transaction T_t is stored in a variable $o_i.P$ and op_{ti} is performed on the object o_i [Figure 11]. Next, suppose op_{ti} is *read*. If $o_i.P \preceq^I PR(T_t)$, the transaction T_t reads the object o_i. Otherwise, T_t is aborted since illegal information flow might occur.

Suppose there are four transactions T_1, T_2, T_3, and T_4 with purposes R_1, R_2, R_3, and R_4, respectively, as shown in Figure 12. Suppose $R_1 \preceq^I R_2$. The transaction T_1 reads an object x and then writes another object y. Then, T_2 reads y and then writes an object z. First, suppose T_3 reads the object z. According to the procedure **Perform**(T_3, *read*, z), the purpose R_2 (= $PR(T_2)$) is stored in $z.P$. If $z.P \preceq^I PR(T_3)$, i.e. $R_2 \preceq^I R_3$, T_3 can read z. Here, suppose $R_1 \npreceq^I R_3$. Data in the object x might be brought to the object z through T_1 and T_2. T_3 should not read z since $R_1 \npreceq^I R_3$. According to the properties of the legal information flow relation $\preceq^I$, $R_2 \npreceq^I R_3$ if $R_1 \npreceq^I R_3$ even if $R_1 \preceq^I R_2$. Hence, $R_1 \npreceq^I R_3$ and $R_2 \preceq^I R_3$ may not hold. This example shows that no illegal information flow occur in our synchronization way.

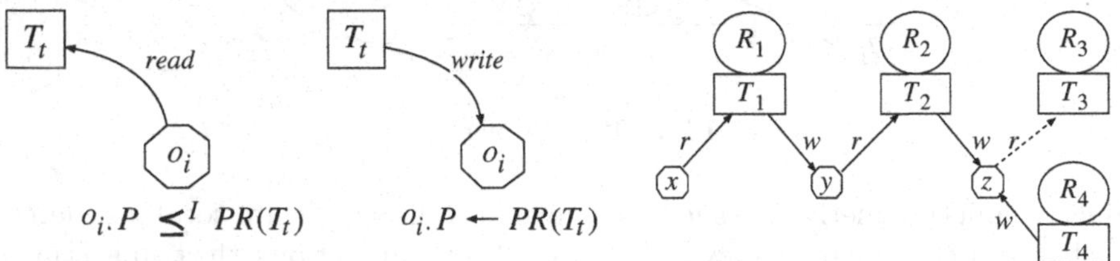

Fig. 11. Information flow check

Fig. 12. Information flow check

5 Concluding Remarks

In information systems, transactions issue conflicting *read* and *write* methods to objects. Conflicting methods are required to be serializable to keep objects mutually consistent. In addition, objects have to be secure. In the access control models, no subject can manipulate an object without access right. However, there is confinement problem, i.e. illegal information flow occur even if only authorized subjects manipulate objects. In this paper, we discuss how to prevent illegal information flow in the role-based access control model. We define a legal information flow relation $\preceq^I$ among role families. If $R_1 \preceq^I R_2$ for role families R_1 and R_2, no illegal information flow occur if a transaction with purpose R_1 is performed prior to a transaction with R_2. We discussed the scheduling and synchronization algorithms to keep objects consistent and secure. Conflicting methods are first ordered in the significancy of roles in the scheduler. Then, a method is performed on an object if no illegal information flow would occur.

In the concurrency control algorithm, discussed here, objects are kept not only consist but also secure in presence of multiple conflicting transactions. We are now evaluating the scheduling and synchronization algorithms.

References

1. Bernstein, P.A., Hadzilacos, V., Goodman, N.: Concurrency Control and Recovery in Database Systems. Addison-Wesley, Reading (1987)
2. Bertino, E., Samarati, P., Jaodia, S.: High Assurance Discretionary Access Control in Object Bases. In: Proc. of the 1st ACM Conf. on Computers and Communication Security, pp. 140–150. ACM Press, New York (1993)
3. Chon, R., Enokido, T., Takizawa, M.: Inter-Role Information Flow in Object-based Systems. In: The Proc. of IEEE 18th International Conf. on Advanced Information Networking and Applications (AINA-2004), pp. 236–343 IEEE Computer Society Press, Los Alamitos (2004)
4. Denning, D.E.: A Lattice Model of Secure Information Flow. Communications of the ACM 19(5), 236–343 (1976)
5. Enokido, T., Takizawa, M.: Concurrency Control Based-on Significancy on Roles. In: Proc. of the IEEE 11th International Conference on Parallel and Distributed Systems (ICPADS2005), pp. 196–202. IEEE Computer Society Press, Los Alamitos (2005)
6. Enokido, T., Takizawa, M.: Role-Based Concurrency Control for Distributed Systems. In: Proc. of the IEEE 20th International Conference on Advanced Information Networking and Applications (AINA-2006), pp. 407–412. IEEE Computer Society Press, Los Alamitos (2006)
7. Enokido, T., Takizawa, M.: Concurrency Control using Subject- and Purpose-Oriented (SPO) View. In: Proc. of the 2nd International Conference on Availability, Reliability and Security (ARES2007), pp. 454–461 (2007)
8. Eswaran, K.P., Gray, J.N., Lorie, R.A., Traiger, I.L.: The Notions of Consistency and Predicate Locks in a Database System. Communications of the ACM 19(19), 624–633 (1976)
9. Ferraiolo, D., Kuhn, R.: Role-Based Access Controls. In: Proc. of 15th NIST-NCSC National Computer Security Conf., pp. 554–563 (1992)
10. Ferraiolo, D.F., Kuhn, D.R., Chandramouli, R.: Role Based Access Control. In: Artech House (2005)
11. Gray, J.: Notes on Database Operating Systems. Lecture Notes in Computer Science 60, 393–481 (1978)
12. Izaki, K., Tanaka, K., Takizawa, M.: Information Flow Control in Role-Based Model for Distributed Objects. In: Proc. of IEEE International Conf. on Parallel and Distributed Systems (ICPADS-2001), pp. 363–370. IEEE Computer Society Press, Los Alamitos (2001)
13. Oracle Corporation: Oracle8i Concepts, vol. 1, Release 8.1.5 (1999)
14. Sandhu, R.S.: Lattice-Based Access Control Models. IEEE Computer 26(11), 9–19 (1993)
15. Sandhu, R.S., Coyne, E.J., Feinstein, H.L., Youman, C.E.: Role-Based Access Control Models. IEEE Computer 29(2), 38–47 (1996)
16. Sybase. Sybase SQL Server, `http://www.sybase.com/`
17. Tari, Z., Chan, S.W.: A Role-Based Access Control for Intranet Security. IEEE Internet Computing 1, 24–34 (1997)
18. Watanabe, K., Sugiyama, Y., Enokido, T., Takizawa, M.: Moderate Concurrency Control in Distributed Object Systems. Journal of Interconnection Networks (JOIN) 5(3), 233–247 (2004)

A Probabilistic Multi-agent Scheduler Implemented in JXTA

André Trudel, Elhadi Shakshuki, and Yiqing Xu

Jodrey School of Computer Science
Acadia University, Wolfville, NS, Canada B4P 2R6
{Andre.Trudel,Elhadi.Shakshuki,072748x}@acadiau.ca

Abstract. Multi-agent technology and constraint satisfaction techniques can be effectively combined and utilized to solve many real-world problems. This paper presents a multi-agent system based on Probabilistic Interval Algebra (PIA) networks to solve distributed scheduling problems. An IA network is a graph where nodes represent intervals and directed edges are labelled with temporal interval relations. A PIA network has probabilities associated with the relations on the edges that are used to capture preferences. The proposed multi-agent system consists of PIA-Agents that are connected via edges to form a network. Each PIA-Agent has ownership and control over a PIA network. A prototype is implemented using JXTA and demonstrated on a university domain to show how the PIA-Agents work together and coordinate their activities to recommend a temporal schedule which is a globally consistent solution which attempts to maximize the desires of each individual PIA-Agent.

Keywords: Allen's temporal relations, CSP, agents, temporal reasoning, JXTA.

1 Introduction

Recently, researchers have combined the intelligent agent and CSP paradigms into single systems. For example, researchers in [2] have analyzed and discussed possible ways of integrating CSP and agent techniques. Other researchers [7] used agents to solve distributed versions of a CSP. Liu and his co-workers [6] presented a multi-agent oriented method for solving CSPs. In their method, distributed agents represent variables and a two-dimensional grid-like environment in which the agents inhabit corresponds to the domains of the variables.

We use Allen's [1] temporal representation approach which is based on intervals and the 13 possible binary relations between them as shown in Table 1. The relations are before (b), meets (m), overlaps (o), during (d), starts (s), finishes (f), and equals (=). Each relation has an inverse. The inverse symbol for b is bi and similarly for the others: mi, oi, di, si, and fi. The inverse of equals is equals. A relation between two intervals is restricted to a disjunction of the basic relations, which is represented as a set. For example, (A m B) V (A o B) is written as A {m,o} B. The relation between two intervals is allowed to be any subset of I = {b, bi, m, mi, o, oi, d, di, s, si, f, fi, =} including I itself.

T. Enokido, L. Barolli, and M. Takizawa (Eds.): NBiS 2007, LNCS 4658, pp. 248–257, 2007.

An IA (Interval Algebra) network is a graph where each node represents an interval. Directed edges in the network are labelled with subsets of I. By convention, edges labelled with I are not shown. An IA network is consistent (or satisfiable) if each interval in the network can be mapped to a real interval such that all the constraints on the edges hold (i.e., one disjunct on each edge is true).

An IA network is a binary constraint satisfaction problem (CSP) with infinite domains. The intervals are the variables. The domain of each variable is the set of pairs of reals of the form (x,y) where x <y. The constraint between two variables i and j is the label on the edge (i,j) in the IA network.

Table 1. Allen's interval relations

Relation	Symbol	Example
X before Y	b	XXX YYY
X meets Y	m	XXXYYY
X overlaps Y	o	XXXX YYYY
X during Y	d	XXX YYYYYYY
X starts Y	s	XXX YYYYYYY
X finishes Y	f	XXX YYYYYYY
X equals Y	=	XXX YYY

A Probabilistic IA network (PIA network) is an IA network with probabilities associated with each interval relation. For example, if we prefer to read the newspaper during breakfast instead of before, we could have: "read newspaper" {d(0.9), b(0.1)} "breakfast".

Directed edges in the network are labelled with subsets of I, and each relation in the subset is assigned a probability. The probabilities on an edge sum to 1. By convention, we list the labels in a set by decreasing order of probability. A PIA network is consistent (or satisfiable) if one disjunct on each edge is true. The probability of a solution is defined to be the product of the probability on each of its edges. Given two solutions, we prefer the one with higher probability. Our proposed system attempts to generate a solution with maximum probability.

A PIA-Agent is an agent which has ownership and control over a PIA network. A node in one PIA-Agent's PIA network can be connected by an edge to a node in another PIA-Agent's network. The individual PIA-Agent networks along with their interconnecting edges, is called a PIA-Agent network. For example, Figure 1 shows a 5 PIA-Agent network that includes a professor, student, secretary, spouse and director. Each node in the network represents a real world event in the PIA-Agent's daily life.

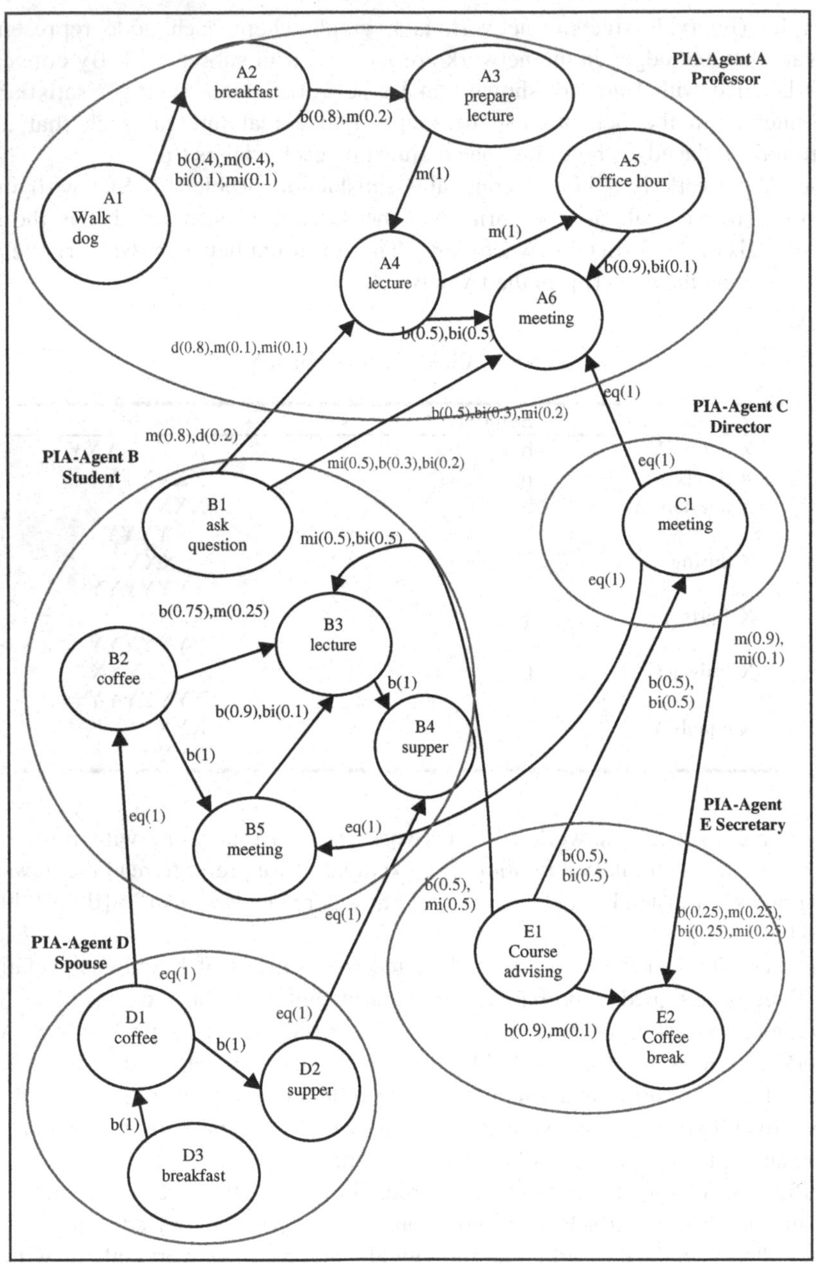

Fig. 1. PIA-Agent Network

The PIA network completely contained within a PIA-Agent is called its internal network. A PIA-Agent's internal network along with the edges that connect the internal network to other networks is called its external network. Note that the external network contains the nodes at both ends of the edges that connect the internal network to other networks. Note that some inter-agent edges have two label sets associated with them. For example, the edge from node B1 to A4 in Figure 1 has the sets {d(0.8),m(0.1),mi(0.1)} and {m(0.8),d(0.2)} (the sets do not necessarily have to contain the same labels). The reason for the dual sets is that the former is associated with the Professor and the latter with the Student (i.e., the Professor prefers that questions be asked after class, while the Student prefers to ask questions during class). When both agents have the same set of labels, we only write it once. Internal network edges will always have one set of labels.

A PIA-Agent has complete control and knowledge of its internal network. For example in Figure 1, only the Professor can make its internal network consistent. Other agents do not know the structure of the Professor's internal network and cannot change any of its labels. An edge between two PIA-Agents is shared by the agents. For example, the edge from node B1 to A4 in Figure 1 is shared by the Student and Professor. They both locally store a personal copy of what they consider to be the label set on the edge. The Professor stores {d(0.8),m(0.1),mi(0.1)} and the Student stores {m(0.8),d(0.2)}. The Professor cannot view or modify the label set stored by the Student, and vice versa. Each PIA-Agent can communicate with every other PIA-Agent.

The problem we consider in this paper has a PIA-Agent network as input. The output is a consistent network where the product of the probabilities on the unique label assigned to each edge is near optimal. Our proposed algorithm makes each PIA-Agent external network locally optimal subject to the constraints imposed by its neighbouring PIA-Agents. Global optimality is desired, but cannot be guaranteed. For example, the solution to Figure 1 is shown in Figure 2. It should be noted that we are not solving a typical IA network as described in [9].

In the next section we describe our algorithm. We then apply the algorithm to the network shown in Figure 1. The following section describes the implementation. Section 5 contains the conclusions and future work.

2 Algorithm

We only provide a high level overview of our algorithm. Full details can be found in [8]. The first step is to assign each PIA-Agent a unique integer ID. ID is used by the algorithm to control the execution order and backtracking. After the IDs are assigned to all PIA-Agents, pairs of agents that share one or more edges need to negotiate to agree on a unique label set for each shared edge. We then run the algorithm in Figure 3 to generate a solution.

3 Example

We use our algorithm to solve the network in Figure 1. Assume the PIA-Agents have finished the pre-processing and negotiation phases of the algorithm. Edge (B1,A4) has the set {d(0.8), m(0.1), mi(0.1)} and initial label d(0.8). Edge (B1,A6) has the set {b(0.5), bi(0.3), mi(0.2)} and initial label b(0.5). Edge (C1,E2) has the set {m(0.9), mi(0.1)} and initial label m(0.9). The last shared edge (E1,B3) has the set {mi(0.5),

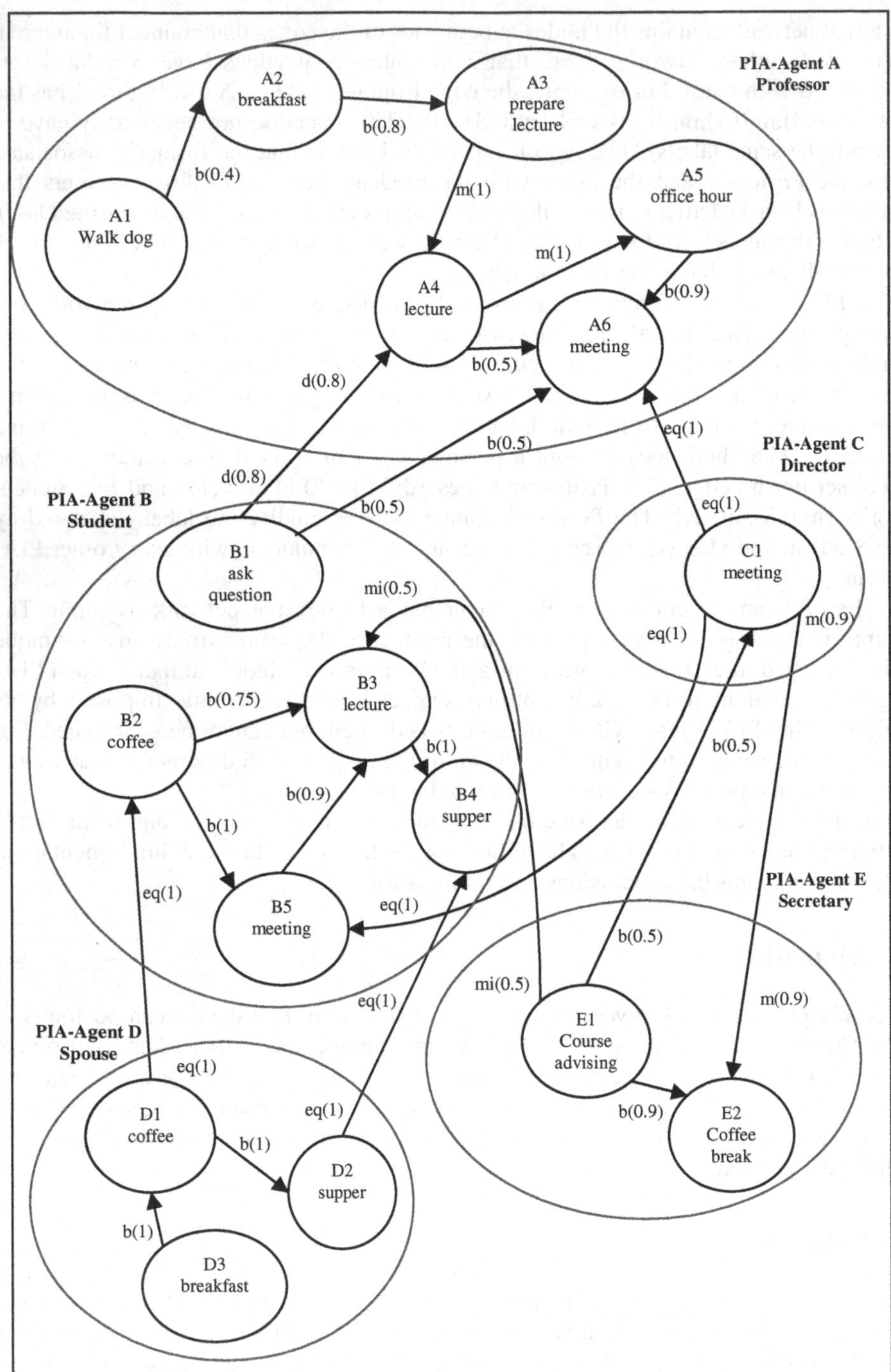

Fig. 2. Global solution

```
1.  current = 1
2.  PIA-Agent ID=current solves its external network.
3.  If a solution is found:
4.    If labels on edges between current and other PIA-Agents
5.    were modified:
6.      Set current to be the minimum of (current+1) and ID's
7.      of the PIA-Agents whose edge labels have been changed
8.      Go to 2.
9.    Else
10.     If current=n then terminate in success
11.        current = current +1
12.        Go to 2.
13. Else terminate in failure
```

Fig. 3. Algorithm to solve PIA-Agents network

bi(0.25), b(0.25)} and initial label mi(0.5). The Professor executes line 2 of the algorithm in Figure 3 and finds a solution to its external network: **{{(B1,A4)=d(0.8), (B1,A6)=b(0.5), (C1,A6)=eq(1), (A1,A2)=b(0.4), (A2,A3)=b(0.8), (A3,A4)=m(1), (A4,A5)=m(1), (A4,A6)=b(0.5), (A5,A6)=b(0.9)}}**. Since the Professor did not change labels on edges to other PIA-Agents, lines 9-11 in Figure 3 sets current=2 (i.e., the Student). The Student then solves its external network: **{{(B1,A4)=d(0.8), (B1,A6)=b(0.5), (C1,B5)=eq(1), (D1,B2)=eq(1), (D2,B2)=eq(1), (E1,B3)=mi(0.5), (B2,B3)=b(0.75), (B2,B5)=b(1), (B3,B4)=b(1), (B5,B3)=b(0.9)}}**. Since the Student also does not change labels on the edges to other PIA-Agents, lines 9-11 in Figure 3 sets current=3 (i.e., the Director). It is then the Director's turn to find a solution (i.e., line 2): **{{(C1,A6)=eq(1), (C1,B5)=eq(1), (E1,C1)=b(0.5), C1,E2)=m(0.9)}}**. Since the Director also finds a solution to its external network without changing labels on Student, Professor and Secretary, lines 9-11 in Figure 3 sets current=4 (i.e., the Spouse). The Spouse then starts to solve its network: **{{(D1,B2)=eq(1), (D2,B4)=eq(1), (D1,D2)=b(1), (D3,D1)=b(1)}}**. Fortunately, the Spouse does not change labels on edges between itself and other PIA-Agents, then lines 9-11 in Figure 3 sets current=5 (i.e., the Secretary). We go to line 2 and the Secretary attempts to find a solution. The Secretary easily finds a solution which does not involve changing labels on edges to other PIA-Agents. The Secretary's solution is: {**{(E1,B3)=mi(0.5), (E1,C1)=b(0.5), (C1,E2)=m(0.9), (E1,E2)=b(0.9)**}}. Since the Secretary is the last agent to execute the algorithm and its current solution is valid and no labels have been modified, the algorithm terminates in success. The final solution is shown in Figure 2.

4 Implementation

This section explains how JXTA is used in our implementation. Other implementation issues are presented in [8].

Our system involves multiple agents which can potentially be residing and executing on different hardware platforms which are geographically isolated. The natural choice of implementation language is Java. We use JXTA [5] to deal with the communication and networking issues. JXTA is an open-source industry leading Peer-to-Peer (P2P) platform, originally developed by Sun Microsystems Inc. JXTA allows users to establish a virtual network with peers on top of the Internet and non-IP networks. It also enables peers to directly communicate, collaborate and share resources independently of their network connectivity.

4.1 Resource Discovery

In a JXTA virtual network, a peer is an application having a unique Peer ID. It has the ability to communicate with other peers over the internet or no-IP networks. In our system, each PIA-Agent is represented by one JXTA peer called a PIA-Peer, which is able to find other JXTA peers on the network and build a pipe to communicate with each other.

All resources in the JXTA network, such as peers, pipes, and services are represented by advertisements. Advertisements are language-neutral metadata structures resource descriptors represented as XML documents.

Usually when a peer logs into a JXTA network, two groups are instantiated: World Peer Group and Net Peer Group. We only use the Net Peer Group as our PIA Peer Group and do not create any other private peer groups. The default services provided by the Net Peer Group fulfills the system's requirements.

In many real world JXTA applications, peers are discovered by searching for their peer advertisements, but we implemented the discovery of peers by searching for the special pipe advertisements instead of the regular peer advertisements. An example of a special pipe advertisement listing is shown in Figure 4.

```
<jxta:PipeAdvertisement xmlns:jxta="http://jxta.org">
	<Id>
		urn:jxta:uuid-
59616261646162614E504720503250337CDA2489269F4E74BB9688AF56FEA1FA04
	</Id>
	<Type>
		JxtaUnicast
	</Type>
	<Name>
		pianetwork:professor-urn:jxta:uuid-
59616261646162614A787461503250326EB11FDACBA4879B2BE85EB276A3DD503
	</Name>
</jxta:PipeAdvertisement>
```

Fig. 4. Pipe advertisement

4.2 Rendezvous Peer Connection

A rendezvous peer is a special peer that can help peers discover other peers on the network by forwarding discovery requests. In our proposed system, there should be at least one rendezvous peer on the PIA network. We set up a regular peer as a rendezvous peer by using the JXTA Configurator, an auto-configuration tool, which is used to configure the JXTA platform for your network environment. The JXTA Configurator is executed only once at the startup of the system.

There are two types of PIA peers: non-rendezvous and rendezvous peers. If a PIA peer is a rendezvous peer, it will send discovery query requests to find other peers as soon as it joins the PIA peer group. If a PIA is not a rendezvous peer, it will start to connect to the rendezvous peers on the JXTA network before sending discovery query requests for other peers in the same peer group.

4.3 Communication Between PIA-Agents

We use JXTA pipes to send data between agents. The pipe service is one of the default core services provided by a JXTA peer group. It is used to create and manage pipe connections between the peers in the same peer group. The pipe service is already implemented and available as a core service within the Net Peer Group. Therefore, any PIA peer is able to load and use this pipe service to interact with other peers once it joins the PIA peer group.

In our proposed system, we implemented a Java Class, Communication, for each PIA-Agent to hold a bi-directional pipe, JxtaBiDiPipe, when it is built. Communication is a wrapper class around most of JxtaBiDiPipe's core functions to handle the bi-directional pipe connection and all the incoming and outgoing messages sent between PIA-Agents. Additionally, Communication provides some new functions to help agents to maintain the corresponding bi-directional pipe, such as checking the connectivity of the pipe.

4.4 KQML Messages

The PIA-Agents exchange their messages using KQML message formats [3]. We implemented a customized KQML parser in the PIA-Agents. When a PIA-Agent receives a message from other PIA-Agents, the parser extracts the desired information such as PIA-Agent ID, name, bad sets, shared edge sets, etc., from the incoming message. Figure 5 shows an example of KQML messages exchanged by PIA-Agents.

```
(ask-one
  :sender Professor
  :senderPeerID: xxx
  :receiver Controller
  :receiverPeerID: yyy
  :language PIA
  :content (TobeFirstAgent))
```

```
(tell
  :sender Controller
  :senderPeerID: yyy
  :receiver Professor
:receiverPeerID:xxx
  :language PIA
:content((firstAgent (firstAgentPeerID xxx))))
```

Fig. 5. Example of messages between PIA-Agents

4.5 GUI

The user interacts with JXTA via a graphical user interface (GUI). A main component of the GUI is a graph visualization tool implemented using JGraph [4]. JGraph provides a powerful API of graph drawing functionalities for java applications.

One of the functionalities of the GUI, is to assist the user to input the nodes, edges and corresponding labels for each PIA-Agent's network. Additionally, our GUI provides flexible graphic features, such as drawing, dragging, re-sizing, redo/undo.

The AWT and Swing classes handle all the interface events, such as menu selections or button clicks. An example of an interaction window is shown in the left hand side of Figure 6. In the top half of this window, the user inputs a particular PIA-Agent's external network. The bottom half of this window displays this particular PIA-Agent's local solution when it is generated.

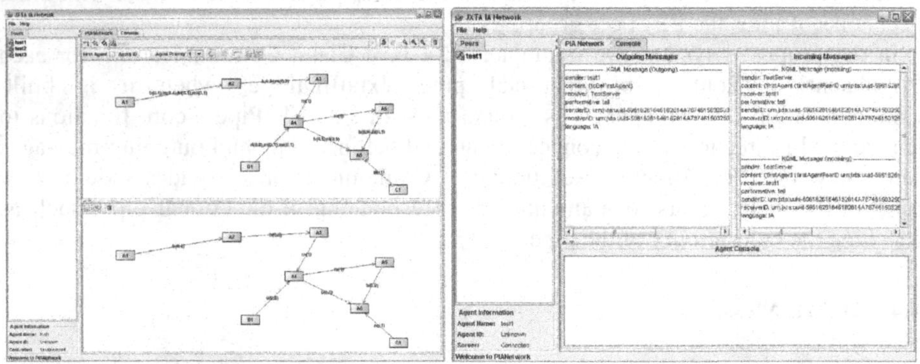

Fig. 6. PIA-Agent Main Pain Panel and Controller Panel

To draw a network, the user must first click the "NODE" button on the tool bar. Each click in the top window of the interface adds a new node. Second, a user selects the button "EDGE" to connect two nodes. Then, he or she is allowed to add labels with or without probability on each edge by double clicking on the corresponding edge. Third, the user can select "ONE SOLUTION" button to generate the possible solution.

The console panel shows all the messages between a particular PIA-Agent and all the other agents. The console is shown the right hand window of Figure 6. There are three information text areas on the console panel. The upper left text area is for outgoing messages and the upper right text area is for incoming messages. The bottom text area displays general system information. The console panels of the various PIA-Agents help the user keep track of the status of the algorithm and overall system by providing real time information.

5 Conclusions and Future Work

PIA-Agents are used to resolve conflicts between sub-graphs to find a global solution to the scheduling problem. We used a university setting example to illustrate how the PIA-Agents find a globally consistent solution which attempts to maximize the desires of each individual involved in the problem domain. A prototype of a distributed time management system is implemented using Java, JXTA and JGraph.

In the future, we are planning to incorporate a learning component in the PIA-Agent architecture, using machine learning techniques and explore and develop different negotiation strategies. We also plan to investigate the possibility of introducing concurrency in our algorithm. For example, while idle an agent can search for and store alternative solutions which may be useful in the future.

Acknowledgments. This project is supported in part by grants from the Natural Sciences and Engineering Research Council of Canada (NSERC) and an internal grant from research and graduate studies of Acadia University.

References

[1] Allen, J.F.: Maintaining Knowledge about Temporal Intervals. Communications of the ACM 26, 832–843 (1983)

[2] Calisti, M., Neagu, N.: Constraint Satisfaction Techniques and Software agents. In: Agents and Constraints Workshop, AIIA'04, Perugia, Italy (2004)

[3] Finin, T., Labrou, Y., Mayfield, J.: KQML as an Agent Communication Language. In: Bradshaw, J.M. (ed.) Software Agents, pp. 291–316. AAA/MIT Press, Cambridge, MA (1997)

[4] JGraph (JGraph, 2006), http://www.jgraph.com/

[5] JXTA (JXTA, 2006), http://www.jxta.org/

[6] Liu, J., Jing, H., Tang, Y.: Multi-agent Oriented Constraint Satisfaction. Artificial Intelligence 136(1), 101–144 (2002)

[7] Makoto Yokoo, M., Durfee, E., Ishida, T., Kuwabara, K.: The Distributed Constraint Satisfaction Problem: Formalization and Algorithms. IEEE Transaction on Knowledge and Data Engineering. 10(5), 673–685 (1998)

[8] Shakshuki, E., Trudel, A., Xu, Y.: A Multi-Agent Temporal Constraint Satisfaction System Based on Allen's Interval Algebra and Probabilities. In: International Journal of Information Technology and Web Engineering (in press, 2007)

[9] van Beek, P., Manchak, D.: The Design and Experimental Analysis of Algorithms for Temporal Reasoning. Journal of Artificial Intelligence Research , 1–18 (1996)

Scheduling Real-Time Requests in On-Demand Broadcast Environments

Kwok-Wa Lam and Sheung-Lun Hung

Department of Computer Science, City University of Hong Kong
83 Tat Chee Avenue, Kowloon, Hong Kong
kwlam@cs.cityu.edu.hk, cshung@cityu.edu.hk

Abstract. On-demand broadcast is an effective approach to disseminating real-time data to mobile clients in mobile environments. Recent studies mostly assume that clients request only a single data item. This assumption may not sufficiently support the increasingly sophisticated real-time applications in mobile environments. In this paper, we present three on-demand broadcast algorithms to cater for multi-item requests with timing constraints. We argue for the case of aggregation of data requests to minimize the broadcast bandwidth and deadline miss rate. The three algorithms try to exploit different properties of system characteristics for aggregation. Our simulation results show that a good aggregation algorithm should consider both data overlapping of client requests and their urgency.

Keywords: On-demand broadcast, real-time systems, data scheduling, mobile computing.

1 Introduction

Mobile computing is becoming important as there is an increasingly need of mobile computing facilities for many people in their jobs and lives. Portable mobile device, such as mobile phones, notebook computers and PDAs are trending to have power computing resources to support more sophisticated applications. As the advance of mobile technology provides the availability of high bandwidth links in the mobile environment, on-demand data broadcast is becoming an effective way to disseminate information dynamically to a large population of mobile clients in many new application areas. Many recent studies [1, 2, 4, 7, 8, 9] on mobile data dissemination have proposed on-demand data broadcast algorithms which try to exploit the characteristics of both broadcasting and on-demand services.

Many real-time applications, such as traffic conditions, stock quotes, airport information services, etc, may have inherent timing constraint requirements. Information must reach the user within a certain deadline for the user to find it useful. Therefore, the system should have real-time design facilities to deliver information to meet clients' data requests with deadline constraints. This real-time requirement is one of our focuses on real-time on-demand broadcast in this paper.

T. Enokido, L. Barolli, and M. Takizawa (Eds.): NBiS 2007, LNCS 4658, pp. 258–267, 2007.

Another design issue is how to schedule data for broadcast according to clients' data requests. This issue has been extensively studied in the past few years [1, 2, 4, 7, 8, 9]. However, most of them considered a restrictive case that mobile clients request for a single data item and the request is satisfied by broadcasting the requested data item. We believe that the algorithms in these studies may not be able to support the increasingly sophisticated business applications.

There are many examples in real-life business applications in which mobile clients may need multiple data items. For example, traders may read a set of stock prices, and try to gain the profit based on the current market status. The query cannot be completely processed until all the requested data items are received. This multi-data-item request requirement makes the request scheduling problem become quite different from that of the single-item case and more challenging.

Obviously, some existing algorithms [1, 2, 7, 8, 9] can be simply extended to handle the new dimension of the scheduling problem by considering the set of requested data items a single aggregated data item. However, mobile clients' requested data items may be overlapped. If a client's data item set is a subset of another client's data item set, broadcasting a larger set of data items can therefore meet both clients' requests and reduces transmission cost. Hence, there is a need to have a well-designed algorithm to exploit the overlapping of mobile clients' data items.

In this paper, we propose three scheduling algorithms which exploit the overlapping of mobile clients' data access patterns by aggregating their requests to efficiently meet mobile clients' requests in order to improve the overall system performance. The rest of this paper is organized as follows. In next section we give a brief discussion of related work. Section 3 describes the system architecture. We discuss the design of different aggregation algorithms in Section 4. The simulation model and experimental results are presented in section 5 and 6 respectively. Finally we conclude the paper with a summary

2 Related Work

Some algorithms [1, 2, 7, 8] have been proposed to determine the broadcast schedule to broadcast data objects to mobile clients. However, these on-demand broadcast algorithms did not consider real-time requirements of client requests.

EDF (Earliest Deadline First) [3] is the most classical scheduling algorithm for real-time systems. Xuan et al [9] showed that on-demand broadcast using EDF achieves better performance. Under the EDF scheme, the server delivers the data objects solely based on the request deadlines. The first data object to be broadcast is the data object requested by the most urgent request (with the earliest request deadline). Note that satisfying the most urgent request may also satisfy other requests for the same data object.

Xu et al. [10] proposed a scheduling algorithm called SIN (Slack time Inverse Number of pending requests), which integrates the access frequency and urgency of data requests to improve scheduling performance. At each broadcast tick, the data object with the minimum sin value is broadcasted. The sin value is defined as the ratio of slack time to the number of pending requests for the data object. Experiments showed that SIN outperforms other existing algorithms over a range of workloads.

Wu et al. in [4, 8] proposed several on-demand broadcast algorithms in real-time systems to investigate the effects of data deadlines and that of preemptive mechanisms on real-time data requests. However, they considered single-item requests as well.

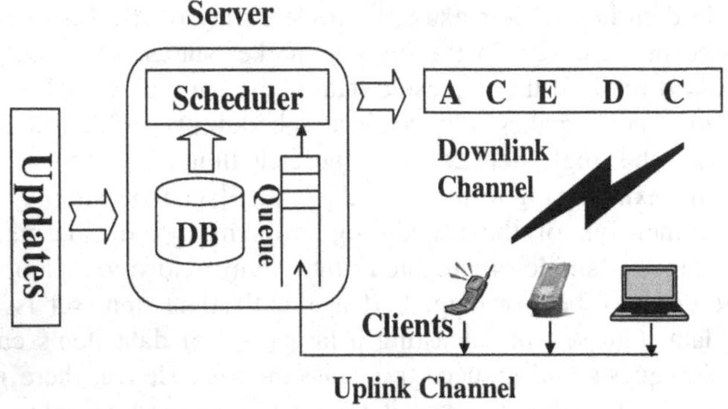

Fig. 1. The system architecture

3 The System Architecture

The system architecture is showed in Figure 1. In this mobile environment, mobile clients maintain their network connection by means of *base stations* equipped with wireless communication capabilities. Each base station serves an area called a *cell.* Clients send requests associated with deadlines to the server through the *uplink* channel. These requests arrived at the server to join the processing queue. According to an adopted scheduling algorithm, the server repeatedly fetches the requested data items in the database and broadcasts them over the *downlink* channel. A client listens to the broadcast channel for the requested data items within its deadline. If the request misses its deadline, there is no value to the client.

A client C_i sends a request Q_i for a set of data items D_i and associated with a timing requirement L_i (an absolute deadline). We call Q the set of all requests received by the server. The server employs an *aggregation* algorithm that processes "similar" requests in the queue. The output of the aggregation algorithm is a collection $M = \{M_\mathrm{i}\}$ where each M_i is a single *aggregated broadcast.* Thus, the server reads $D_{M\mathrm{i}}$ for each M_i in M. For completeness, it is required that $\cup_\mathrm{i}Q_\mathrm{i} = \cup_\mathrm{i}M_\mathrm{i}$. Similarly, $D_\mathrm{q} \subseteq D_{M\mathrm{i}}$ for every $q \in M_\mathrm{i}$. To illustrate these concepts, say client C_1 submits a request Q_1 consisting of a set of data item IDs $D_1 =\{a, b, c\}$, C_2 submits Q_2 with $D_2=\{a, b\}$, C_3 submits Q_3 with $D_3=\{x, y\}$, and C_4 submit Q_4 with $D_4=\{y, z\}$. The server may combine Q_1 and Q_2 into M_1 and Q_3 and Q_4 into M_2 with $D_{M1} =\{a, b, \mathrm{c}\}$ and $D_{M2} =\{x, y, z\}$. Then, the server processes the aggregated requests M_1 and M_2 by reading the requested data items $D_{M1} =\{a, b, \mathrm{c}\}$ and $D_{M2} =\{x, y, z\}$ from the database.

4 Design of Algorithms

The system should consider the data access pattern and the deadline of each request for aggregation in order to maximize data sharing between mobile clients with different timing requirements. Hence, the system performance can be improved in terms of minimizing the broadcast bandwidth and improving the timeliness of the system. In the following, we will present three different aggregation algorithms which exploit different properties of the system characteristics.

4.1 Data-Driven Scheduling

The first algorithm is to exploit the overlapping of the requested data items to aggregate requests, called the Data-Driven Aggregation. First, we may determine the size of M_i using any one of previous algorithms for single-item requests, such as EDF or SIN. For sake of exposition, we choose EDF for selection of the request Q_i to be served and assume a fixed data-item size equal to a *broadcast unit*. After selection, we work out the size of M_i by using its requested data set and deadline.

To illustrate it using an example, we choose a request Q_i with $D_i = \{a, b, c\}$ and relative deadline 10 broadcast units (relative deadline = L_i – current time). Then, the size of M_i is 10 broadcast units with data items a, b, c already packed. Then, we have remaining 7 "data slots" available for aggregation of other requests. One straight-forward way is to use the *next fit* or *best fit* heuristics [5] to aggregate other requests such that M_i is filled with data items of other requests as much as possible and their deadlines will not be missed. These heuristics may be working nicely in the problems of conventional applications of bin packing [5] such as memory allocation. However, these simple heuristics cannot work well in our problem because they do not consider data overlapping in our defined problem and the deadlines of data requests. That is, a data item may serve more than one request combined in M_i.

We define a parameter called, *request data overlap*, *RDO*, for the degree of overlapping between the data item set of a request Q_i and the data item set of M_i by the following formula: $RDO_i = | D_i \cap D_{Mi} | / | D_{Mi} |$. The value of RDO_i can be used to make a decision on how to aggregate the enqueued requests.

```
Function DataDrivenAggregate (pendingRequests Q) {
  select a request Qi from Q based on EDF;
  Put Qi in Mi such that DMi = Di;
  AvailableDataSlots = ⌈(Li – CurrentTime) / B⌉ – |Di|;
    // Li is the deadline of Qi; B is the size of a broadcast unit
  Repeatedly select Qh in Q such that RDOh is the largest and fill Dh in the
        AvailableDataSlots until it is full.
}
```

This algorithm aims to capitalize the overlapping of data items to aggregate requests as much as possible, combining requests which have the similar data requirements with the first request in M_i. Note that the deadlines of all the aggregated requests will also be met as their deadlines must be later than the first request's. Indeed, it will broadcast data items with a higher access frequency. However, it fails to consider deadlines of other requests well except the first one and does not work well in the some situations. We consider the following example.

Example 1: Suppose there are three requests: Q_1, Q_2 and Q_3 request data item sets *{a, b, c}*, *{a, c, d}*, and *{c, e, f}* with relative deadline of 5, 20, 6 respectively. Q_1 will be selected to initialize M_1 because of its earliest deadline. The number of available data slots after initialization is therefore equal to 2. Then, Q_2 will be selected for aggregation since RDO_2 is larger than RDO_3. As a result, M_1 is filled up and $D_{M1} = \{a, b, c, d\}$ will be broadcasted. After this broadcast, the deadline of Q_3 will surely be missed. Obviously, it will be better to aggregate Q_3 in M_1 because of its earlier deadline. Clearly, a variant of the aggregation algorithm is to use deadlines of client requests as a criterion for aggregation.

4.2 Deadline-Driven Aggregation

The second algorithm tries to consider the deadlines of client requests for aggregation, called the Deadline-Driven Aggregation. Like the Data-Driven Aggregation, the size of M_i is also determined by choosing the first request Q_i from Q with the earliest deadline. Available data slots will be worked out after considering the data requests and deadlines of Q_i. The next request with the earliest deadline in Q will be chosen for aggregation. Note that this scheme will only choose the requests with earlier deadlines for aggregation. If the data size of the request Q_n chosen for aggregation due to its earliest deadline is larger than the available data slots, the aggregation will be ended. The scheme will not search for the next request in Q to fill up the available data slots as we found in our simulation experiments that the number of requests missing deadlines is increased. If the scheme continues to search for non-urgent requests in Q for aggregation, the probability of Q_n to miss its deadline will be increased as the broadcast of data items for Q_n will be delayed by the longer broadcast time of the filled-up M_i.

```
Function DeadlineDrivenAggregate (pendingRequests Q) {
  select a request Qi from Q based on EDF;
  Put Qi in Mi such that DM = Di;
  AvailableDataSlots = ⌈(Li – CurrentTime) / B⌉ – |Di|;
    // Li is the deadline of Qi; B is the size of a broadcast unit
  Repeatedly select Qn in Q such that Qn has the earliest deadline to fill Dn in the
    AvailableDataSlots until it is full.
}
```

We revisit Example 1 again, Q_1 will be selected to initialize M_1 because of its earliest deadline and the number of available data slots is therefore equal to 2. Then, Q_3 will be selected for aggregation instead of Q_2 as the deadline of Q_3 is earlier than Q_2. As a result, M_1 has been filled up and $D_{M1} = \{a, b, c, e, f\}$ will be broadcasted and Q_1 and Q_3 will be satisfied. Obviously, Q_2 will also be satisfied in the next broadcast. Hence, all three client requests can be served. Let's consider another example to better understand the characteristics of the Deadline-Driven Aggregation.

Example 2: Suppose there are three requests: Q_1, Q_2 and Q_3 request data item sets *{a, b, c}*, *{ d, e}*, and *{a, c, f}* with relative deadline of 5, 7, 9 respectively. Again, Q_1 will be selected to initialize M_1 because of its earliest deadline and the number of available data slots is therefore equal to 2. Since the requested data items of Q_2 do not have overlapping with M_1, Q_2 will not be aggregated into M_1 and M_1 with data items, $\{a, b, c\}$ is broadcast. Then, Q_2 will be selected to initialize M_2 with two available data slots for aggregation. Note that after M_1 has been broadcast, the relative deadline of Q_2 is changed to 4. Again, since Q_3 does not have overlapping data items with M_2 with data items $\{d, e\}$, no aggregation can be made and M_2 is broadcast. Subsequently, M_3 with data items $\{a, c, f\}$ will be broadcast for Q_3. We can see that it will be better to aggregate Q_1 and Q_3 together and all three requests can be met. With this aggregation, the system can save two broadcast units. Hence, the drawback of the Deadline-Driven Aggregation is that it fails to make full use of data overlapping for aggregation to minimize the broadcast bandwidth.

4.3 Data-Overlapping Versus Aggregated Slack Time

Hence, we will present another algorithm which attempts to integrate both data overlapping and urgency of client requests to solve the problems of both the data-driven and deadline-driven aggregation algorithms. We define another simple measure to select requests for aggregation. We call this algorithm the Data-Overlapping versus Aggregated Slack Time algorithm (OvS).

$OvS_i = (RDO_i + 1)$ / aggregated slack time of Q_i

where the term of $RDO_i + 1$ considers the case that when there is no overlapping of data requests and the slack time of Q_i, i.e., urgency of Q_i, can therefore be incorporated for making aggregation decisions. The aggregated slack time of Q_i is the slack time of Q_i if it was aggregated into a broadcast set. The OvS algorithm is similar to the Data-Driven Algorithm except using OvS_j instead of RDO_j for selection of requests for aggregation. The OvS Aggregation tries to achieve an optimal balance between data overlapping and urgency of client requests.

Let's revisit Example 2 with the OvS Aggregation. The OvS_2 and OvS_3 are 1/2 and 3/5 respectively. Then, Q_3 will be selected first for aggregation with two $M_1 = \{a, b, c, f\}$ and $M_2 = \{d, e\}$ to be broadcast. Two broadcast units of bandwidth can be saved.

5 Simulation Model

We describe the simulation model used for performance evaluation. The simulation model was implemented by using CSIM [6]. The main parameters and settings for the experiments are shown in Tables 1. Except explicit stating, we examine the execution of various scheduling algorithms using the default parameters. This model consists of a single server and NUMCLIENT clients. The bandwidth of downlink is BANDWIDTH and the time unit is 0.01 second. A request's deadline is given by:

Deadline = Arrival_Time + (1 + ε) * D * Service_Time, where ε is a random number selected uniformly from the range (LMIN, LMAX). D is a random number selected uniformly from the range (DMIN, DMAX), and service time is the size of a broadcast unit.

The client access pattern follows a commonly used Zipf distribution [11] with parameter Ω where $0 \leq \Omega \leq 1$. It becomes increasingly skewed as the parameter Ω increases from 0 to 1. When Ω = 0, it is the uniform distribution and data items have similar popularity, while Ω = 1, it is the strict Zipf distribution and is highly skewed. In the Zipf distribution, the first data item is the most frequently accessed data item, while the last data item is the least frequently accessed.

Table 1. System parameter settings and default values

Parameter	Description	Default	Range
NUMCLIENT	The number of clients in a cell	100	50 ~ 300
NUMARRIVAL	The number of requests per client	100	
DBSIZE	The number of data objects in database	100	
BANDWIDTH	Broadcast bandwidth	100 Kbytes/sec	
DMIN	The minimum number of data items	3	1 ~ 5
DMAX	The maximum number of data items	5	3 ~ 7
LMIN	Minimum laxity time	15	10 ~ 20
LMAX	Maximum laxity time	30	20 ~ 30
Ω	Zipf distribution parameter	0.8	0.0 ~ 1.0
THINKTIME	Think time	5 time units	Exponential distribution

The server continually broadcasts data items based on mobile clients' on-demand requests, while the clients continuously monitor the broadcast channel to get the data items. Each client is simulated by a process that runs a continual loop to generate requests. After it receives all the data items that it has requested, the client waits for a period of THINKTIME (Exponential distribution), and then makes the next request. The followings metrics are adopted to evaluate the performance of the algorithms.

Deadline Miss Rate: For real-time systems, deadline miss rate is the primary performance metric, which is the ratio of the number of requests missing their deadlines to the number of total requests.

Saved Broadcast Ratio: This metric is used to measure the effectiveness of the aggregation mechanism in saving the broadcast bandwidth. The ratio is derived by dividing the difference between the total number of data objects received by clients and the number of data objects broadcast by the total number of data objects requested by all clients.

6 Experimental Results

In addition to the three proposed aggregation algorithms, namely Data-Driven Aggregation (DDA), DeadLine-Driven Aggregation (DLDA) and the OvS, we have developed a baseline model (EDF) which does not consider aggregation for performance comparison. We present the performance results of the algorithms based on a detailed simulation study. The results are obtained when the system is in a stable

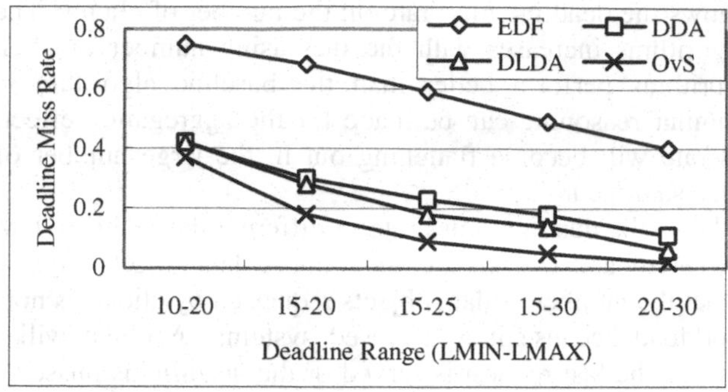

Fig. 2. Deadline miss rate vs deadline range

state and the simulations ended until a confidence interval of 0.95 with half-widths of less than 5% about the mean was achieved.

Figure 2 shows that the deadline miss rates of client requests in different ranges of request deadlines. We would like to examine the effect of deadline range, the LMIN and LMAX range. Recall that ε is a random number selected uniformly from the range (LMIN, LMAX). We specify the range in the form: LMIN – LMAX. The larger the LMIN and LMAX are, the looser the deadline is.

As expected, the deadline miss rate of all algorithms drops when the deadline range increases because the longer the deadline is, the more likely the requests will not miss their deadlines. All our algorithms perform significantly better than the baseline algorithm. We expected that the aggregation algorithms resemble EDF in the worst case in which there is no data overlapping between each consecutive request. But, if data overlapping occurs, the aggregation not only saves the broadcast bandwidth by aggregating data items into a single broadcast set, but also helps other requests in the queue meet their deadlines because these requests will be consequently processed sooner. The ripple effect explains that the performance of the aggregation algorithms is much better than the baseline algorithm.

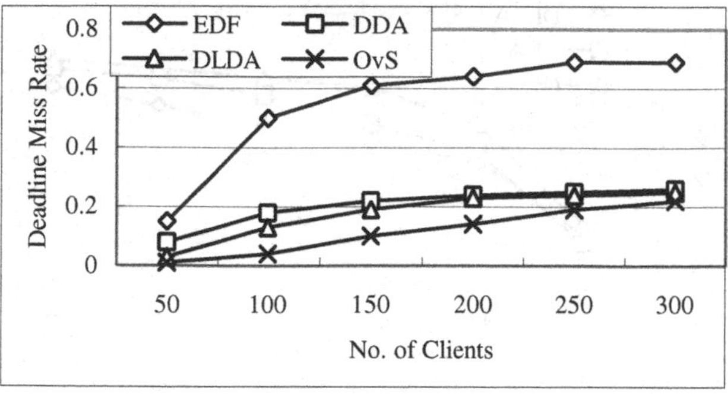

Fig. 3. Deadline miss rate vs no. of clients

Figure 3 shows the deadline miss rate on the number of clients. The deadline miss rate of all algorithms increases with the increasing number of clients. Again, our proposed algorithms perform better than the baseline algorithm in a significant magnitude. Similar reasoning can be made for the aggregation effect. However, the deadline miss rate will become flattening out in the large number of clients as the system has been saturated.

Figure 4 shows the deadline miss rate in different data ranges (DMIN – DMAX). The larger the DMIN and DMAX are, the number data objects requested by clients is bigger. Note that the number of data objects requested by clients is not proportional to the server workload because it is a closed system. A client will submit another request only when the last request is served or the deadline is missed. Also note that the deadline of a request is proportional to the number of data objects requested. So, for EDF, the deadline miss rate rises only slightly when the data range increases. However, for the aggregation algorithms, as the data range increases, there are more opportunities to have data overlapping, leading to a drop of deadline miss rate.

Figure 5 shows the saved broadcast ratio which is the ratio of the broadcast bandwidth with aggregation and without aggregation. The saved broadcast ratio

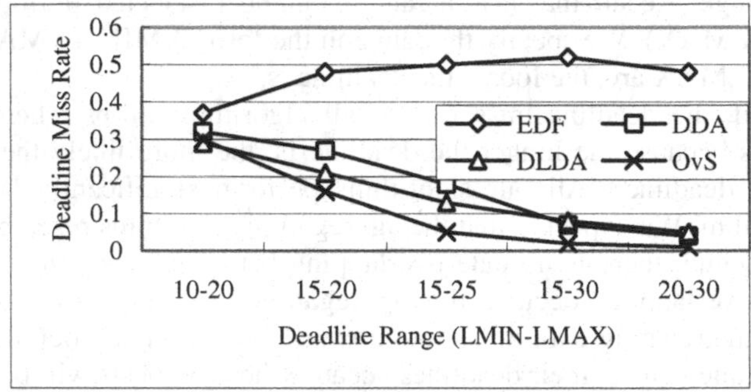

Fig. 4. Deadline miss rate vs data range

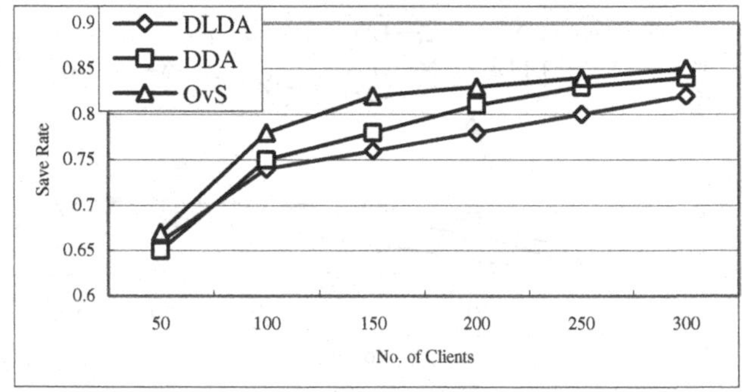

Fig. 5 Saved broadcast ratio

increases with the increasing number of clients. The trend is sensible because with the increasing number of clients, the probability of clients requesting the same data items increases, bringing about the effect of aggregation to minimize the broadcast bandwidth. The OvS has the best performance in saving bandwidth because it strikes a balance between data overlapping and meeting request deadlines. It has the least deadline miss rate, leading to a higher total number of data objects received by all clients. Moreover, it considers data overlapping in selecting requests for aggregation so that number of data objects broadcast can be minimized.

7 Conclusion

On-demand broadcast is an effective data dissemination approach for mobile computing. Most of recent studies consider a restrictive case of single-item requests of mobile clients. We argue that this model does not support many real-life applications well. We extend on-demand broadcast to cater for multi-item requests with timing constraints. We believe that the approach of aggregating data requests is practical and effective to minimize the broadcast bandwidth and deadline miss rate. We have presented three aggregation algorithms and discussed their performance characteristics, strengths and weaknesses. Our simulation results show that the aggregation algorithms perform much better than the algorithms without aggregation.

References

1. Aksoy, D., Franklin, M.: RxW: A Scheduling Approach for Large-Scale On-Demand Data Broadcast. IEEE/ACM Transactions on Networking 7(6) (December 1999)
2. Acharya, S., Muthukrishnan, S.: Scheduling On-demand Broadcasts: New Metrics and Algorithms. ACM MobiCom'98 , 43–54 (October 1998)
3. Liu, C.L., Layland, J.W.: Scheduling Algorithms for Multiprogramming in Hard Real-time Environments. J. of ACM 20(1), 46–61 (1973)
4. Wu, X., Lee, V.C.S.: Wireless real-time on-demand data broadcast scheduling with dual deadlines. Journal of Parallel and Distributed Computing 65(6) (2005)
5. Coffman, E.G., et al.: Approximation algorithms for bin packing: A survey. In: Hochbaum, D. (ed.) Approximation Algorithms for NP-Hard Problems (1996)
6. Schwetman, H.: CSIM user's guide (Version 18). MCC Corporation
7. Vaidya, N.H., Hamed, S.: Scheduling Data Broadcast in Asymmetric Communication Environments. ACM/Baltzer Journal of Wireless Networks 5(3), 171–182 (1999)
8. Wu, X., Lee, V.C.S., Ng, J.: A Preemptive Scheduling Algorithm for Wireless Real-Time On-Demand Data Broadcast. RTCSA 2005 (2005)
9. Xuan, P., Sen, S., Gonzalez, O., Fernandez, J., Ramamritham, K.: Broadcast on Demand: Efficient and Timely Dissemination of Data in Mobile Environments. RTAS'97, 38–48 (June 1997)
10. Xu, J., Tang, X., Lee, W.-C.: Time-Critical On-Demand Broadcast: Algorithms, Analysis, and Performance Evaluation. Technical report (2003)
11. Zipf, G.K.: Human Behavior and the Principle of Least Effort. Addison-Wesley, Massachusetts (1949)

A Fair Replica Placement for Parallel Download on Cluster Grid

Chih-Ming Wang[1], Chu-Sing Yang[2], and Ming-Chao Chiang[1]

[1] Department of Computer Science and Engineering,
National Sun Yat-sen University, Kaohsiung, Taiwan, R.O.C.
{wangcm,mcchiang}@cse.nsysu.edu.tw
[2] Department of Electrical Engineering,
National Cheng Kung University, Tainan, Taiwan, R.O.C.
csyang@mail.ee.ncku.edu.tw

Abstract. Grid technologies congregate numerous computers to provide powerful computing and massive storage. In data-intense applications, Data Grids are developed to cope with the efficiency of data access. Replication is one of the methods to elevate the access performance. When a file is replicated, it can be downloaded from all the nodes with that file in parallel, thus reducing the access latency. Therefore, a fair and adaptive replication strategy for high speed transmission is important. In this paper, we design such a strategy to duplicate popular files to beneficial nodes in the grid networks. All the users deserve the same quality of transmission. The contributions of our mechanism are to average the transmission cost and evenly distribute the workload for download. Simulation results are also given to demonstrate the performance of our replication strategy.

1 Introduction

Grid computing is an emerging technology for scientific, physical, and biological applications, focusing on distributed computing and resource sharing. In recent year, the most widely used software for constructing grid networks is certainly the Globus Toolkit developed by the Globus Alliance [1]. All kinds of resources are congregated via the broadband network to cooperate to get the work done quickly. Nowadays, the exploiting empires include IBM, Sun, SGI, NEC, Entropia, and so on. They almost dominate the development of grid.

Cluster takes advantage of the local resources to cooperate, but grid breaks this restriction. It connects all the resources available on all the networks worldwide by the supporting software. The differences between Grid and cluster are primarily the dynamic and heterogeneous resources, which can be located anywhere for scalability. In a grid system, a job can be divided into many sub-jobs and dispatched to multiple nodes to get it computed in parallel. When the results are reassembled in one node, the job is accomplished. The goals are to reduce the job completion time and balance the workload between all the grid nodes. Moreover, not only the computing power, but also all kinds of resources can be shared, which include both hardware and

T. Enokido, L. Barolli, and M. Takizawa (Eds.): NBiS 2007, LNCS 4658, pp. 268–277, 2007.

software such as CPU, memory, storage, files, databases, and so on. Grid efficiently integrates the various resources via the networks [2]. In a storage system, files are usually replicated to resolve the access latency problem. Identical files may be stored in different storage subsystems for fault tolerance, parallel download, or fast discovery. Grids continue all the characteristics of distributed systems and storage systems. Consequently, research on grids can be divided into that on the computing grid and that on the data grid [3]. The computing grid offers a model for solving massive computational problem. The data grid focuses on three issues: (1) The replica management, which manages the creation or deletion of replica on a massive storage [9][11][12][13]. (2) The replica selection [4], which chooses the best nodes to obtain the resources for download or cooperation [7][10]. (3) The replica catalog, which maps logical file name to physical location address for discovery [8]. In this paper, our focus will be on the replica management.

Bandwidth is certainly one of the most important resources in a data grid [5][6]. A popular file may become a hotspot and thus cause bottleneck at a node because there are a lot of downlinks occurring at the same time. Obviously, the number of user requests is also a crucial factor to affect the bandwidth. Replication is one of the methods to elevate the access performance. When the bottleneck occurs at a node, it means that that node is overloaded and requires to be alleviated. On the other hand, when a file is requested by a lot of users, it indicates that the file is very popular and should be duplicated. But the question is where the replica should be placed? In order to reduce the transmission cost, we must know that a high bandwidth node may not have numerous requests whereas a node with numerous requests may not have sufficient bandwidth. Bandwidth and user requests need to be considered simultaneously as far as downloading is concerned. Therefore, designing an efficient replication strategy to put the replica to an appropriate node is very important. In this paper, we propose a replica placement scheme to overcome the bottleneck problem and to average the access latency for fairness on cluster grid system.

The rest of this paper is organized as follows. Section 2 is the related work about replica placement. In Section 3, we state the problem of replication on cluster grid. Our algorithm is proposed in Section 4. Section 5 shows the simulation results and gives analysis. Section 6 concludes the paper and suggests some possible future research works.

2 Related Works

As previous studies show, replica placement problems are usually handled based on either the centralized or hierarchical network structure. In [11], NoReplication, BestClient, Cascading, PlainCaching, Caching plus Cascading and FastSpread are proposed to estimate the performance. Among these schemes, Cascading and FastSpread perform the best, but with a tradeoff. FastSpread performs better than Cascading in terms of the bandwidth consumption and response time when the access patterns are totally random, but the storage overhead is higher than Cascading. In [13], the authors propose a new placement algorithm for the replicas so that the workload of user requests among these replicas is balanced. In [11] and [13], only the load of user requests is considered. Afterwards, the network load and user requests are estimated together as the parameters of equations for replication.

Four schemes, all of which outperform both Cascading and BestClient, are proposed to place the replica to the best node by calculating an expected utility and risk [12]. Of the four schemes, MinimizeExpectedUtil and MinimizeMaxRisk are two better schemes. MinimizeExpectedUtil computes, for each node to which the file may be duplicated, the sum of products of the number of user requests and the minimum transmission cost for all the nodes as the expected utility, where the minimum transmission cost is defined to be the cost for the transmission of the file from the closest node with that file. Then, the node with the minimum expected utility is chosen to be the target node for replication. MinimizeMaxRisk calculates the risk index for each node by multiplying the number of requests of a file by the minimum transmission cost. Finally, the replica is placed at the node with the maximum risk index.

All of the above discuss the single node download. Nowadays, network communication tends to move to peer to peer. In that case, each node is both a server and a client. Later, parallel download technologies are developed to accelerate the speed of transmission. In a sharing environment, all users deserve the same quality of service whenever they access the resources. Therefore, we prefer to replicate popular file to a node that can provide a fair download performance for every user in parallel. In this paper, we propose a new replica placement mechanism on cluster grid in which all the hosts communicate in peer-to-peer mode. Our strategy averages the transmission cost and alleviates the workload of popular nodes.

3 Problem Description

3.1 Cluster Grid

PCs can be organized to form a large network system using grid technology. Each node communicates across network. In the same subnet, each PC has a high bandwidth for the transmission to each other. For that reason, we group them to form a cluster which may locate at a city, a campus, or a company. Nodes in each cluster elect a head for managing all the cluster members and exchanging information about probed bandwidth. In order to reduce the number of control messages and bandwidth consumption, we adopt the bandwidth result of the head as the result of nodes in a cluster. In addition, the head can be dynamically changed in a cluster according to the workload. We describe the problem that may arise in the following section.

3.2 Problem Statement

Replicas are created for fault tolerance, parallel download, or fast discovery. We state the replication problem for multiple nodes download in this paper. In a single node download, the user just downloads a file from a best node for which the transmission cost is the lowest. When a node in a grid system triggers the replication, a file is copied to a best node according to the evaluation result based on the number of user requests and minimum transmission cost as defined in [12]. In multiple nodes, the file is divided into blocks each of which can be downloaded from many different nodes in parallel [7]. It accelerates the speed of transmission and evenly distributes the workload. If we employ the schemes in [12], it hides a problem about fairness for multiple download. The results would benefit a larger group, but not all the users in a grid system. Note that all nodes deserve the same quality of services. They must provide a fair transmission environment for all the users no matter which node is used by the user to access file.

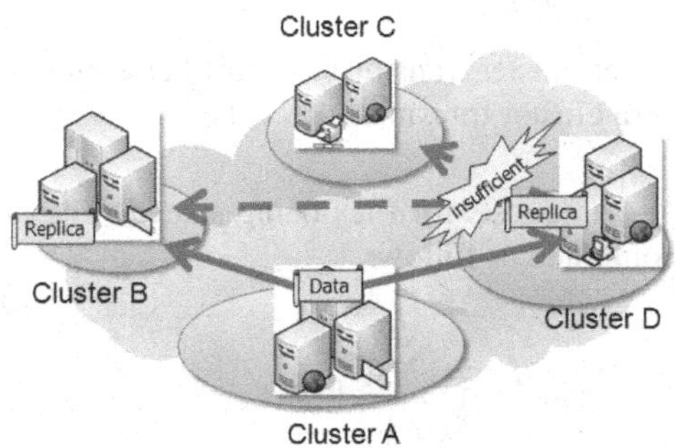

Fig. 1. Parallel Download Environment

For example, if the bandwidth of the replica node with maximum expected utility or risk is insufficient to support all the downloading, it may cause a large number of users still downloading a large portion of the file from the source node. In this case, the parallel download cannot perform well because it tends to fall back to the single node download. Also, the workload of the source node does not cut down obviously, and it may trigger another replication. For the example shown in Fig. 1, one node in Cluster *A* replicates a file to a node in Cluster *D* using the replica placement algorithm, but the bandwidth of Cluster *D* is insufficient for the transmission of that file to Cluster *B* and Cluster *C*, the workload of the source node may not be diminished. It is very likely that, another replication will occur, and the file may be replicated to a node in Cluster *B* or Cluster *C*. Therefore, the replication mechanism in a single node download environment cannot work appropriately for parallel download environment. In order to offer a fair and fast transmission in a grid system, we design a replica placement scheme to distribute the workload and average the transmission cost on cluster grid system.

4 A Fair Replica Placement Mechanism

4.1 Overview

Bandwidth and the number of user requests are two primary factors as far as replication is concerned. In order to conserve the bandwidth, we log the bandwidth between clusters only by head that can decrease the control message flow. In this paper, the transmission cost is defined to be inversely proportional to bandwidth. If there are $n + 1$ clusters in the grid system, we can obtain a symmetric transmission cost matrix T as follow:

$$T = \begin{bmatrix} T_{00} & T_{01} & . & . & T_{0n} \\ T_{10} & . & & & T_{1n} \\ . & & T_{ij} & & . \\ . & & & . & . \\ T_{n0} & T_{n1} & . & . & T_{nn} \end{bmatrix} \qquad (1)$$

where T_{ij} represent the inter cluster transmission cost between cluster C_i and C_j for $i \neq j$; otherwise, T_{ij} is the intra cluster transmission cost.

Each node logs the user requests for files being shared. The number of request for each cluster F_i can be computed as follow:

$$F_i = \sum_{j=1}^{m_i} F_{ij} \qquad (2)$$

where m_i is the number of nodes in cluster i. F_{ij} is the number of files requested of node j in cluster i. we calculate the total requests F_i for each cluster i.

4.2 Time to Activate Replication

The time to activate the replica placement mechanism is the initial step of our algorithm. The average bandwidth that a node provides is defined as follow:

$$avg(B) = \frac{B_{Max}}{L} \leq B_\tau \qquad (3)$$

where B_{Max} is the maximum upload bandwidth that a node S_k in C_i can provide, L is the number of downloading links from S_k, and B_τ is a threshold of the minimum bandwidth that is restricted by each node.

All the nodes in a grid system apply Eq. (3) periodically. If the average bandwidth is lower than $B_\tau$during a period t, the replica placement mechanism will be activated. The period t is set up by each node. The active node chooses a popular file with maximum number of requests as an object for replication.

4.3 Placement Algorithm

In a cluster environment, we use Fig. 2 for the purpose of illustration of various values. T_{ij} is the transmission cost. F_i is the total requests in cluster C_i.

When a node triggers the replica placement mechanism, it calculates an average cost which includes both the intra (IA) and inter (IR) communication costs for nodes with maximum user requests for that file in each cluster. A node with the minimum

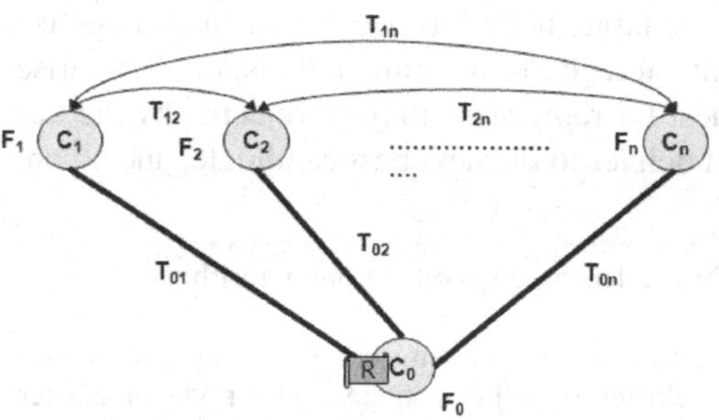

Fig. 2. A Cluster Environment

average transmission cost will be selected as the target for replication. The evaluation function E_i is as given below:

$$IA_i = [F_i - Max(F_{ik})] \times T_{ij} \quad i = j \text{ and } 0 \leq k \leq m_i \tag{4}$$

$$IR_i = \sum_{j=0}^{n} F_j \times T_{ji} \qquad i \neq j \tag{5}$$

$$R_i = \sum_{j=0}^{n} F_j - Max(F_{ik}) \quad 0 \leq k \leq m_i \tag{6}$$

$$E_i = \frac{IA_i + IR_i}{R_i} \tag{7}$$

For multiple download, Eq. (4) and Eq. (5) use MinimumExpectedUtil to calculate the IA_i and IR_i for the node k with $Max(F_{ik})$ in C_i, respectively, that are the sum of all the products of the remainder number of user requests and the transmission cost for one replication case. R_i is the total remainder number of user requests. The purpose of our strategy is to duplicate the file to a node that provides minimum average transmission cost. The replica placement algorithm is shown in Fig. 3.

Fig. 4 is an illustration of our strategy. As Fig. 4 shows, there are 11 nodes and 4 clusters in the grid system. We assume that the local transmission rate is 1. The bottleneck occurs at node S_1 and it is ready to replicate a file. In a single download environment [12], the result of MinimizeExpectedUtil and MinimizeMaxRisk algorithms will require that the file be replicated to S_9 in Cluster D. But this is not fair to other nodes because it cannot offer a minimum average transmission cost as we described in section 5. In our scheme, when S_1 in Cluster A triggers the replica placement mechanism, the values of E_A, E_B, E_C, and E_D can be computed as 10.37, 11.33, 11.77, and 14.25, respectively, using the evaluation function defined in Eq.(7). Obviously, it would perform an intra replication because the value of E_A is minimal. The file is replicated to a node in Cluster A with maximum requests. Note that if there are a lot of nodes with equal requests in one cluster, one can be chosen randomly. Accordingly, the file is replicated to S_2 or S_3. In another case, when the T_{CD} and T_{BD} are varied to 10, then the values of E_A, E_B, E_C, and E_D are 10.37, 6.89, 7.33, and 8, respectively. Thus, the inter replication is performed because $E_A > E_B$. The file is replicated to a node with maximum requests in Cluster B.

Moreover, once the target node for the placement strategy is determined, problems such as insufficient storage or it being a hotspot may arise in the target node. Therefore, the request for replication may be rejected by the target node. In that case, the replication must deliver to the next best candidate, and so on.

Algorithm 1. The pseudo code of our algorithm

```
Input: the transmission cost matrix T, the number of user request F_i
for each cluster C_i with m_i nodes. The node in cluster C_p which
activates the replication mechanism
Output: replicate the file to node S_k in cluster C_f
begin
    MinCost = ∞
        for i ← 0 to |C| do
            for j ← 0 to m_i do
                find node S_j with max request F_ij in C_i
                max_req_node = S_j
            end
            calculate E_i
            if E_i < MinCost then
                MinCost = E_i
                cluster_num = i
                target_node = max_req_node
            end
        end
        replicate the file to target_node in C_cluster_num
end
```

Fig. 3. Algorithm of fair Replica Placement

5 Simulation

5.1 Dynamic Co-Allocation Scheme (DCA)

In [7], the author employed the prediction techniques [5][6] and developed several co-allocation mechanisms to establish connections between servers and a client. The most interesting one is called Dynamic Co-Allocation. The file that a client wants is divided into "*k*" disjoint blocks of equal size. Each available server is assigned to deliver one block in parallel. When a server finishes delivering a block, another block is delivered, and so on, until the entire file is downloaded. Faster servers with high bandwidth can deliver the data quickly, thus serving larger portions of the file requested when compared to slower servers. In our previous work [10], we also proposed two schemes to improve download performance. In this section, we employ DCA as the multiple nodes download scheme to evaluate the performance after replication is applied.

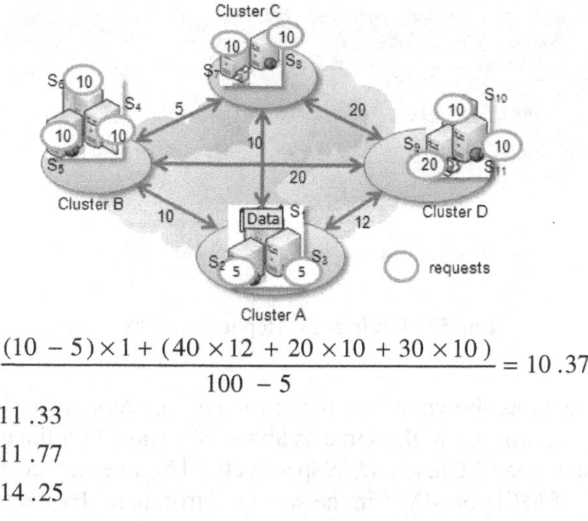

$$E_A = \frac{(10-5)\times 1 + (40\times 12 + 20\times 10 + 30\times 10)}{100-5} = 10.37$$

$$E_B = 11.33$$

$$E_C = 11.77$$

$$E_D = 14.25$$

Fig. 4. An Example of Our Replica Placement Mechanism

5.2 Simulation Result and Analysis

In parallel download environment, we will keep using the example in Fig. 4 for the purpose of illustration. As Fig. 4 shows, there are 2 nodes providing a requested file after replication. Suppose that the file is divided into 5 blocks. Deliver time is the time required to transmit one block. We ádopt the dynamic co-allocation (DCA) scheme to allocate the blocks for download after applying our replication algorithm, MinimizeExpectedUtil (MEU), and MinimizeMaxRisk (MMR), respectively. Finish time means the time sub-job in one node is accomplished. We get the maximum value as the job completion time.

According to the MEU or MMR, the results of replica placement are the same. The file and replica are located at S_1 and S_9 as shown in Fig. 5. All the requested nodes can download the file from them simultaneously. S_2 and S_3 are the members of Cluster *A*; they download the file from S_1 only after DCA. The reason is that the condition gives less blocks, and the intra bandwidth is larger than the inter bandwidth, and thus all blocks are allocated to one node for faster transmission. Furthermore, the requests of nodes in Cluster *B* are equal. The evaluation results will tend to be equal under the same condition. Cluster *C* is the same. Consequently, we show one result to represent the evaluation results of nodes in Cluster *B* and Cluster *C*, respectively. After DCA, nodes with equal number of requests in Cluster *B* get 3 blocks from S_1 and 2 blocks from S_9, nodes with equal number of requests in Cluster *C* get 3 blocks from S_1 and 2 blocks from S_9. The average cost of these two clusters can be computed as 400. In addition, the load of download can be distributed, that is 60% of all the blocks allocated to S_1 and 40% to S_9 for the download.

MEU				MEU			
C_B: S_4, S_5, S_6	Replica	$C_A : S_1$	$C_D : S_9$	C_C: S_7, S_8	Replica	$C_A : S_1$	$C_D : S_9$
	Deliver time	100	200		Deliver time	100	200
	Allocate blocks	3 (60%)	2 (40%)		Allocate blocks	3 (60%)	2 (40%)
	Finish time	300	400		Finish time	300	400
Average cost time		(400+400)/2=400					

Fig. 5. DCA in MEU Replication Environment

In our strategy, as shown in Fig. 6, the file and the replica are located at S_1 and S_4. Assuming the conditions are the same as above, we show that the evaluation results of nodes in Cluster *C* and Cluster *D,* respectively. The average cost is 300 that is less than the result of MEU or MMR in the same environment. Evaluation results are done to show that for multiple nodes download, our strategy outperforms both MEU and MMR.

Ours				Ours			
C_C: S_7, S_8	Replica	$C_A : S_1$	$C_B : S_4$	C_D: S_9, S_{10}, S_{11}	replica	$C_A : S_1$	$C_B : S_4$
	Deliver time	100	50		Deliver time	120	200
	Allocate blocks	2 (40%)	3 (60%)		Allocate blocks	3 (60%)	2 (40%)
	Finish time	200	150		Finish time	360	400
Average cost time		(200+400)/2=300					

Fig. 6. DCA in Our Replication Environment

6 Conclusions

In this paper, we first described the previous work on replica placement and then proposed a new mechanism for parallel download environment. Replica placement affects the download performance. For fairness, we define an evaluation function to decide where to replicate a file. And our strategy not only reduces the average cost but also distributes the workload of providers. In the future, optimal algorithms for placement of replicas need to be studied. Also, we can treat grid systems as a large data storage system. Furthermore, we consider applying it to handle the e-learning system.

Acknowledgements. This work was supported in part by a sub-plan of "National IPv6 Development and Promotion Project for NICI IPv6 Backbone Division" (I-0600) from Ministry of Transportation and Communications and in part by

National Science Council, R.O.C. under contract number 95-2221-E-006-509-MY2. We would like to take this opportunity to thank both organizations for their financial support.

References

1. The Globus Project: http://www.globus.org/
2. Foster, I., Kesselman, C., Tuecke, S., International, J.: The Anatomy of the Grid: Enabling Scalable Virtual Organizations. Supercomputer Applications 15(3) (2001)
3. Allcock, W., Chervenak, A., Foster, I., Kesselman, C., Salisbury, C., Tuecke, S.: The Data Grid: Towards an Architecture for the Distributed Management and Analysis of Large Scientific Datasets. Journal of Network and Computer Applications (2001)
4. Vazhkudai, S., Tuecke, S., Foster, I.: Replica Selection in the Globus Data Grid. In: IEEE/ACM International Symposium on Cluster Computing and the Grid, pp. 106–113 (2001)
5. Vazhkudai, S., Schopf, J.M.: Predicting Sporadic Grid Data Transfers. In: IEEE International Symposium on High Performance Distributed Computing, HPDC-11 2002, pp. 188–196 (July 2002)
6. Vazhkudai, S., Schopf, J.M., Foster, I.: Predicting the Performance of Wide Area Data Transfers. In: Vazhkudai, S., Schopf, J.M., Foster, I. (eds.) International Parallel and Distributed Processing Symposium, IPDPS 2002, pp. 34–43 (April 2002)
7. Vazhkudai, S.: Enabling the Co-Allocation of Grid Data Transfers. In: International Workshop on Grid Computing, vol. 17, pp. 44–51 (2003)
8. Li, D., Xiao, N., Lu, X., Wang, Y., Lu, K.: Dynamic self-adaptive replica location method in data grids. In: IEEE International Conference on Cluster Computing, pp. 442–445 (December2003)
9. Stockinger, H., Samar, A., Allcock, B., Foster, I., Holtman, K., Tierney, B.: File and Object Replication in Data Grids. Journal of Cluster Computing 5(3), 305–314 (2002)
10. Chang, R.S., Wang, C.M., Chen, P.H.: Replica Selection on Co-Allocation Data Grids. In: Second International Symposium on Parallel and Distributed Processing and Applications, Hong Kong (2004)
11. Ranganathan, K., Foster, I.: Identifying Dynamic Replication Strategies for High Performance Data Grids. In: Proceedings of the second International Workshop on Grid Computing, Denver, CO, USA, pp. 75–86 (November 2002)
12. Rahman, R.M., Barker, K., Alhajj, R.: Replica Placement in Data Grid: Considering Utility and Risk. In: ITCC 2005. International Conference on Information Technology: Coding and Computing, 2005, 04-06 April 2005, vol. 1, pp. 354–359 (2005)
13. Lin, Y.-F., Liu, P., Wu, J.-J.: Optimal Placement of Replica in Data Grid Environments with Locality Assurance. In: The 12th International Conference on Parallel and Distributed Systems (ICPAD'06)

Querying Similarity in Metric Social Networks

Jan Sedmidubský, Stanislav Barton, Vlastislav Dohnal, and Pavel Zezula

Masaryk University
Brno, Czech Republic
[xsedmid,xbarton,dohnal,zezula]@fi.muni.cz

Abstract. In this paper we tackle the issues of exploiting the concepts of social networking in processing similarity queries in the environment of a P2P network. The processed similarity queries are laying the base on which the relationships among peers are created. Consequently, the communities encompassing similar data emerge in the network. The architecture of the presented metric social network is formally defined using the acquaintance and friendship relations. Two version of the navigation algorithm are presented and thoroughly experimentally evaluated. Finally, learning ability of the metric social network is presented and discussed.

1 Introduction

The area of similarity searching is a very hot topic for both research and commercial applications. Current data processing applications use data with considerably less structure and much less precise queries than traditional database systems. Examples are multimedia data like images or videos that offer query-by-example search, product catalogs that provide users with preference-based search, scientific data records from observations or experimental analyses such as biochemical and medical data, or XML documents that come from heterogeneous data sources on the Web or in intranets and thus does not exhibit a global schema. Such data can neither be ordered in a canonical manner nor meaningfully searched by precise database queries that would return exact matches.

This novel situation is what has given rise to similarity searching, also referred to as content-based or similarity retrieval. The most general approach to similarity search, still allowing construction of index structures, is modeled in metric space. Many index structures were developed and surveyed recently [12]. However, the current experience with centralized methods [6] reveals a strong correlation between the dataset size and search costs. Thus, the ability of centralized indexes to maintain a reasonable query response time when the dataset multiplies in size, its *scalability*, is limited. The latest efforts in the area of similarity searching focus on the design of distributed access structures which exploit more computational and storage resources [2,7,4,3]. Current trends are optimizing and tuning the well known distributed structures towards better utilization of the available resources.

Another approach to design the access structure suitable for large scale similarity query processing that is introduced in this paper emerges from the notion

T. Enokido, L. Barolli, and M. Takizawa (Eds.): NBiS 2007, LNCS 4658, pp. 278–287, 2007.

of *social network*. A social network is a term that is used in sociology since the 1950s and refers to a social structure of people, related either directly or indirectly to each other through a common relation or interest [10]. Using this notion, our approach places the peers of the distributed access structure in the role of people in the social network and creates relationships among them according to the similarity of the particular peer's data. The query processing then represents searching for a community of people, i.e., searching for peers related by a common interest, for example, maintaining similar data.

Using this data point of view our designed metric social network is a cognitive knowledge network according to the terminology stated in [9] that is described as *who thinks who knows what* where it is not who you know but it is what who you know knows. This means that the network links are created on the basis of the particular peers' knowledge (stored data) rather than on being acquainted with other peers. As for the navigation, social networks exhibit the *small world network topology* [11] where most pairs of peers are reachable by a short chain of intermediates – usually the average pairwise path length is bound by a polynomial in $\log n$. Therefore it is anticipated that a small amount (around six) of transitions will be needed to find the community of peers holding the answer to a query posed at any of the participating peers in the network.

Unlike the usual access structures that retrieve a total answer to each query, the presented approach focuses on retrieving the *substantial part* of the answer yet with *partial costs* compared to the usual query processing. The concepts of social networking towards the approximative query processing in large scale data have already been introduced in related works [1,8].

The paper is structured in following sections. In Section 2, the architecture of the access structure is detailed. In Section 3, the preliminary experimental results are reviewed to present the nature and behavior of the proposed approach. Finally, the conclusions are drawn in Section 4.

2 Architecture

Our social network comprises of nodes (peers) and relationships between them. The relationships identified always relate to a particular query processed by the network and its retrieved answer. In general, we distinguish relationships of two types: the friendship and a relation of acquaintance.

2.1 Nodes of the Social Network

A node (peer) itself, besides the assigned piece of data, remembers also the history of the queries that it has been asked. To each query the recognized set of friends and acquaintances is also remembered for future optimization of a similar query processing. So, a network peer P is $P = (D, H)$ where $D = \{o_1, \dots o_l\}$ represents the assigned piece of data and $H = \{h_1, \dots h_m\}, h_i = (Q, L_P^{Acq}(Q), L_P^{Fri}(Q))$ represents the history of queries with the pair of ordered lists of retrieved acquaintances and friends regarding the particular query Q. For example as a query a usual range query can be considered: $R(q, r)$ where

q is a query object and r is a predefined range. The peer which is asked to answer a query Q in the social network is denoted as P_{start}. Consequently, partial answers $A_{P_i}(Q)$ are passed from the peers P_i of the network to P_{start}. The final answer is $A(Q) = \bigcup_{i=1}^{n} A_{P_i}(Q)$ where n denotes the total number of peers that participated on the answering.

2.2 Measuring Quality of the Query Answer

As we have seen, the total answer can be divided into pieces regarding the peers that participated on the total answer to a query Q. To distinguish which peer answered better, the *quality* is measured by defining a *quality measuring function* $Qual(A_{P_i}(Q))$. It returns a quality object q_i that represents the quality of the peer's answer. Since this object is not necessarily a number, we also define a function to compare two quality objects:

$$compare_{qual}(q_1, q_2) = \begin{cases} -1 & q_1 \text{ is worse than } q_2 \\ 0 & q_1 \text{ is same as } q_2 \\ 1 & q_1 \text{ is better than } q_2 \end{cases}$$

The quality of the total answer is determined by applying the quality measuring function on $A(Q)$. An ordering $\preceq$ which we call the *q-ordering* is defined on the peers' answers $A_{P_1}(Q), \ldots, A_{P_n}(Q)$ in $A(Q)$ according to their qualities. The quality objects are then $q_i = Qual(A_{P_i}(Q))$. The sequence of peers' answers is ordered according to the q-ordering when the following holds:

$$i_1 \ldots i_n : q_{i_a} \preceq q_{i_b} \Leftrightarrow a < b \Leftrightarrow compare_{qual}(q_{i_a}, q_{i_b}) \neq 1$$

Intuitively, when the peers are ordered with respect to the position of their answers in the q-ordered set of partial answers, they are ordered by their ability to answer the particular query Q.

2.3 Acquaintance and Friendship Relations

As we mentioned earlier, we distinguish two relationships in our social network. Firstly, the relationship of friendship represents the similarity of peers – two peers give a similar answer to same query. Secondly, the relationship of acquaintance denotes that the target of the relationship took part in the answer passed to the recipient. In the following, we will use the answer size in objects as the measure of quality, i.e., $Qual(A_P(Q)) = |A_P(Q)|$.

A set of acquaintances for a given query Q is defined as a set of participating peers in the total answer $Acq(Q) = \{P | A_P(Q) \neq \emptyset\}$. Friends are identified in the set of acquaintances as peers that at which the similarity of the data kept could be anticipated: $Fri(Q) = \{P \mid |A_P(Q)| > c \cdot |A(Q)|\}$. The friendship relationship according to the particular query Q is assigned only to those peers that contributed to the answer with a significant partial answer, which is expressed by the positive-value constant c. Then, according to a query Q, a peer P is an acquaintance $P^{Acq}(Q) \Leftrightarrow P \in Acq(Q)$. Similarly, with respect to a query Q, a peer P is a friend $P^{Fri}(Q) \Leftrightarrow P \in Fri(Q)$. Intuitively, the set of acquaintances and friends of each peer that took part in the query processing can be determined using the following functions:

$$Acq_P(Q) = \begin{cases} Acq(Q) & P \in Fri(Q) \vee P = P_{start}(Q) \\ \emptyset & \text{otherwise} \end{cases}$$

$$Fri_P(Q) = \begin{cases} Fri(Q) & P \in Fri(Q) \\ \emptyset & \text{otherwise} \end{cases}$$

For a given query Q, the relationships in the social network are then formed by the mathematical relations defined among the peers:

$$P_1 \sim_Q^{Acq} P_2 \Leftrightarrow P_2 \in Acq_{P_1}(Q)$$

$$P_1 \sim_Q^{Fri} P_2 \Leftrightarrow P_1 \in Fri_{P_2}(Q), \quad P_1 \in Fri_{P_2}(Q) \Leftrightarrow P_2 \in Fri_{P_1}(Q)$$

The relationships are stored in the history as two lists of peers ordered according to the q-ordering of the partial answers in $A(Q)$ with respect to their qualities. The ordering respects the position of the peer's answer in the q-ordered $A(Q)$. Each of the lists comprises of pairs of a peer P_i and a quality object $q_i = Qual(A_{P_i}(Q))$:

- $L_P^{Fri}(Q)$ ... a list of friends of the peer P for a query Q sorted by *q–ordering*;
- $L_P^{Acq}(Q)$ ... a list of acquaintances of P for Q sorted by *q–ordering* .

2.4 Navigation

The query processing using the social network follows the common world concepts for searching. Basically, the best acquaintance regarding the particular subject is located and then his friends are contacted to return their part of the answer to the querist.

The acquaintances are contacted firstly because they represent the entities that have answered before. Initially, the P_{start} goes through its history of processed queries and finds the most similar query Q' to the query Q that is processing now. For query Q', also the lists of acquaintances and friends are retrieved from the history. The query Q is then forwarded to the best acquaintance. This concept is formalized in Algorithm 1. In general, the query can be passed to more then one acquaintance, it depends on the particular navigation algorithm implementation. The process of the query forwarding can be repeated more times to find the peer that is most promising to hold the searched data. At each peer, a different query can be retrieved from the history as the most similar to Q. The stop condition of the query forwarding is when the contacted peer's quality is better than any of his acquaintances to which it could pass the query.

When the best acquaintance regarding the particular query is found, it returns its part of the query answer to the querist. Then it looks up in the history for the most similar query and retrieves the set of friends associated with that query and forwards the query Q to them as described in Algorithm 2. The query is

Algorithm 1. Query forwarding algorithm `forwardQuerySimple`

Input: P_{start}, contacted peer P, query Q, last peer's quality *lastQi*

get entry $E = (Q', L_P^{Acq}(Q'), L_P^{Fri}(Q'))$ from history H with Q' most similar to Q
P' = best acquaintance from $L_P^{Acq}(Q')$
if $compare_{qual}(Qual(A_{P'}(Q')), lastQi) > 0$ **then**
    forwardQuery(P_{start}, P', Q, $Qual(A_{P'}(Q'))$)
else
    for all $F \in L_P^{Fri}(Q')$ **do**
        answerQuery(F, P_{start}, Q)
    end for
    answerQuery(P, P_{start}, Q)
end if

Algorithm 2. Simple query answering procedure `answerQuery`

Input: current peer P, P_{start}, query Q

get all objects that satisfy Q
send retrieved objects to P_{start}

passed also to friends because it is supposed that they hold similar data which will form substantial parts of the query answer $A(Q)$. After contacting, the peers return their partial answers $A_{P_i}(Q)$ to P_{start}.

3 Experimental Results

In this section, we present an experimental evaluation of the proposed distributed access structure for searching in metric data. The experiments have been conducted on two datasets represented by vectors having three and fortyfive dimensions respectively. The 45-D vectors represent extracted color image features compared using a quadratic-form distance. The distribution of the dataset is quite uniform and such a high-dimensional data space is extremely sparse. The 3-D vectors were obtained as the three most-important dimensions of 45-D vectors. The number of vectors in each dataset was 100,000.

3.1 Network Initialization

The peers in the network have been created using the distributed version of the M-tree [5] indexing structure – each peer corresponds to one M-tree leaf node. Besides the data distribution among peers, the M-tree was also used to evaluate the precise total answer to queries.

Firstly, the distributed M-tree is created on the provided dataset. Next, the peers are assigned their pieces of data.[1] The relationships in the network are then acquired by posing queries to the created M-tree and processing its answer retrieved from the peers in the network. This process is called *learning*.

[1] For both datasets, the M-tree consisted of 47 leaf nodes – the data have been distributed among 47 peers.

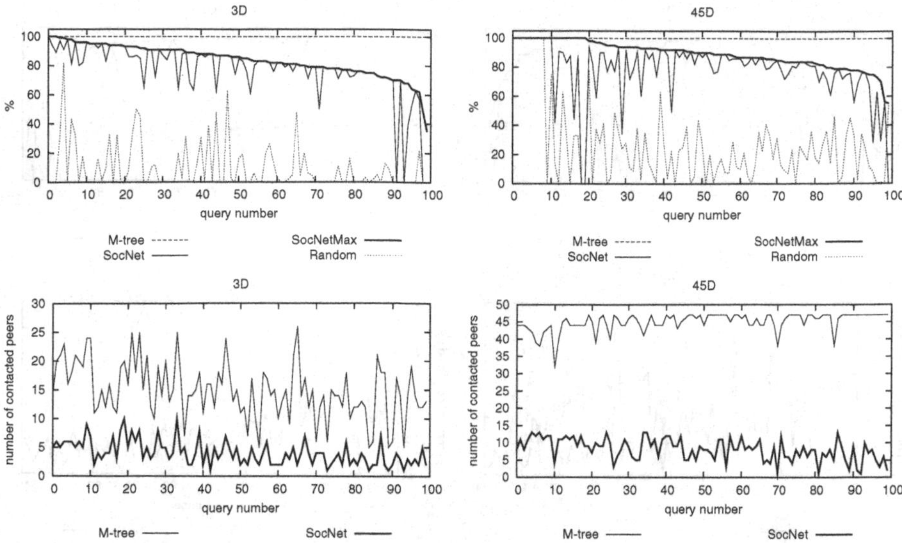

Fig. 1. Results of one hundred queries processed using the social network compared to the total answer of the M-tree: (top row) Recall and (bottom row) Costs

Intuitively, the longer the learning process is the better the social network query processing is afterwards. In the set of experiments regarding the recall and costs of the query processing using the social network, the learning process comprised of 500 queries processed using the M-tree.

3.2 Recall and Costs

To demonstrate the properties of querying process in the social network, we used the basic variant of algorithm described in Section 2.4. A recall of one hundred queries processed using the built social network is presented in Fig. 1. The queries represent range queries with randomly picked objects with a fixed radius of 200 and 2,000 for the 3-D and 45-D data, respectively. These radii have been chosen because they returned on average 3-5% of data.

The queries in Fig. 1 are ordered in a descending manner with respect to the SocNetMax recall values. Both figures demonstrate the percentage of the total answer retrieved using the social network. The recall of SocNetMax value denotes a maximal part of the total answer that could have been retrieved contacting the same amount of peers that the social network (SocNet) did, i.e. if the social network has contacted eight peers, the SocNetMax represents the percentage of objects from the total answer represented by the best eight peers. Finally, Random represents the percentage of the total answer retrieved from the randomly picked peers which amount is the same as the social network has contacted.

The costs of a query processed presented in Fig. 1 are defined as the amount of peers that are contacted in order to answer the query – contacted by the *answerQuery* procedure. We can see that the amount of the peers contacted per

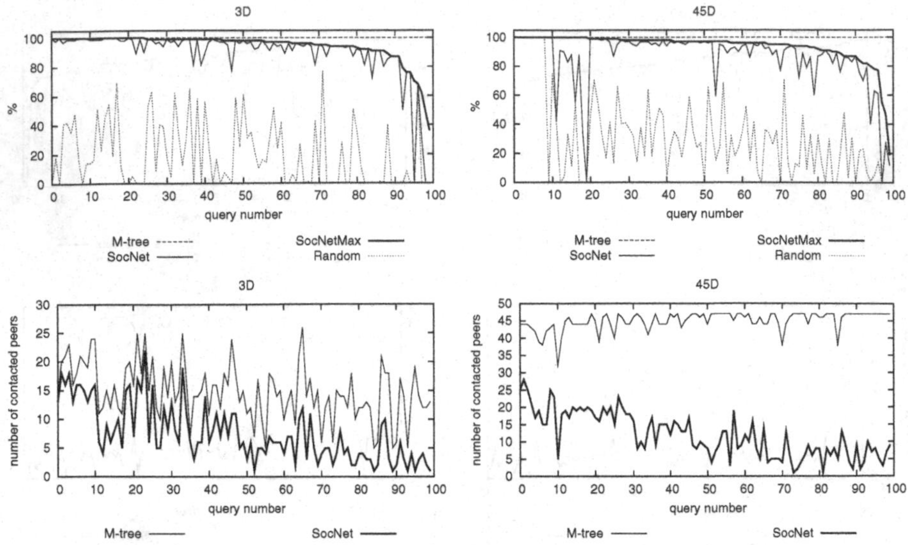

Fig. 2. Results of queries processed by the social network using the *forwardQueryFOAF* navigation algorithm: (top row) Recall and (bottom row) Costs.

query by SocNet is substantially smaller than the numbers of the M-tree in the case of the 3-D data. The gap between those two curves is even greater for the 45-D data. This is caused by the worse clusterability of the latter dataset, since distance between any pair of the objects is more or less the same in this high dimensional data.

The fluctuations in both figures are strictly related, i.e. recall is decreasing with the decreasing number of peers used to answer queries. Such a behavior of SocNet is caused by insufficient social information available to some peers. For the 45-D data, the recall exhibits higher fluctuations than for the 3-D data, which can be attributed to the fact that the complete result is spread over more nodes.This is also proportional to the ratio between the number of contacted peers by the M-tree and by SocNet. An improved query routing strategy tries to eliminate such instability and is presented in the following section.

3.3 Friend-of-a-Friend Query Forwarding

The great differences between SocNet and SocNetMax in Fig. 1 present a fair amount of instability of the SocNet access structure. We have enhanced the navigation algorithm towards the greater stability of the gained results yet with the emphasis on sustaining the low query processing costs. The enhanced query answering procedure is described in Algorithm 3. Despite calling the enhanced answering routine, the query forwarding procedure (Algorithm 1) remains the same. We will refer to this enhanced algorithm as the *forwardQueryFOAF*.

Using the *forwardQueryFOAF* navigation algorithm, the set of peers that participate in the final answer grows because the contacted community of the

Algorithm 3. Enhanced query answering procedure `answerQueryFOAF`

Input: contacted peer P, P_{start}, query Q

$S = \{E = (Q', L_P^{Acq}(Q'), L_P^{Fri}(Q')) \mid$ query object q' satisfies $Q\}$
for all $E \in S$ **do**
  for all $F \in L_P^{Fri}(Q')$ **do**
    answerQueryFOAF(F, P_{start}, Q)
  end for
end for
get all objects that satisfy Q
send retrieved objects to P_{start}

similar peers grows larger. The trends of the results gained in terms of recall and costs can be read from Fig. 2. The queries on which we have measured the properties of the enhanced navigation algorithm are the same as those on which we measured the simple algorithm in the previous subsection.

3.4 Learning Abilities

In the introduction to the architecture of the designed social network, we have mentioned that the qualities of answers to each query are being stored in peers that participated in the query processing, i.e., the social network is being updated. For the structure's evaluation purposes, this feature was disabled during the experiments conducted in the previous section.

In this section, we demonstrate the ability of the designed social network to learn itself towards better query processing. The experimental results are presented using only the 3-D dataset because the results gained on the other dataset were very similar.

To measure the ability to learn, a fixed testing set consisting of twenty randomly picked queries was used. The method is that after processing each 50th query, the self-adaptability of the social network is turned off and the recall and costs on the testing set is examined. Progress of average recall and cost values on the testing queries during time represents the ability of the social network to learn. Two initial states of the network were used. Firstly, the social network is well trained using 250 queries processed by the M-tree. Secondly, this state represents a state of the network that is not trained yet. The relationships in the network were created randomly and assigned to processed queries by the M-tree.

Figure 3 demonstrates the evaluation of the training abilities of the social network using the *forwardQuerySimple* algorithm and *forwardQueryFOAF* algorithm for navigation. In this figure, the curves *recall 1* and *costs 1* represent results initiated in the well-trained social network. On contrary, the *recall 2* and *costs 2* demonstrate the same abilities on the randomly initialized network. Also the costs of the M-tree are presented. The cost values are presented as a proportion of connected peers to the total amount of peers in the network.

The presented results demonstrate the inability of the social network equipped with the *forwardQuerySimple* to refine its social information towards more precise query answering. This is caused by the insufficient overall quality of the

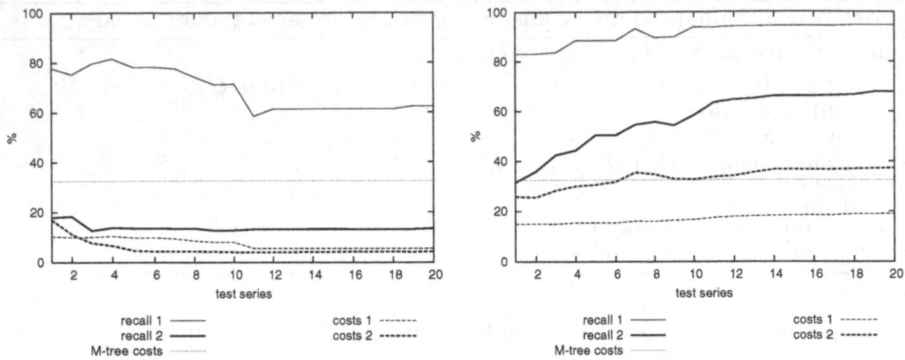

Fig. 3. Learning abilities of the social network access structure: (left) using *forwardQuerySimple* and (right) using *forwardQueryFOAF*

answer retrieved from the network. This inability is underscored by the poor results when deployed on the random initial state social network resulting.

On the other hand, using the *forwardQueryFOAF* algorithm to process the queries in the social network yields better results proved by the rising curve representing improving recall values starting at both well-trained and random initial states of the social network. This fact proves that the algorithm and the training abilities are communicating vessels since the more precise answers the better the learning ability is.

4 Concluding Remarks and Future Work

Distributed processing of similarity queries currently attracts a lot of attention because of its inherent capability of solving the issue of data scalability. We have proposed an approach based on social networking which is able to answer any similarity query modelled using metric space paradigm. The principle exploited in this proposal models social relationships with regards to specific queries. As a result, a multigraph is created in which individual communities sharing similar data can be identified. The presented experiment trails confirm suitability and auspiciousness of such approach. Moreover, the network with the enhanced navigation algorithm is able to evolve autonomously while improving quality of query results.

For future work, various aspects of navigation strategies will be deeply studied in order to design more sophisticated and possibly self-adapting policies. The peers in our social networks were assigned with data objects based on the M-tree clustering principle. Influence of such data partitioning will be verified. Also dynamicity in the sense of peers' joining and leaving the network will be investigated. This is also related to the dynamicity from the data point of view where the data content of individual peer can change, which invalidates relationships established in the network so far.

Acknowledgements

Partially supported by: the EU IST FP6 project 045128 (SAPIR), the national research project 1ET100300419, the Czech Grant Agency project 201/07/P240.

References

1. Akavipat, R., Wu, L.-S., Menczer, F., Maguitman, A.G.: Emerging semantic communities in peer web search. In: P2PIR '06: Proceedings of the international workshop on Information retrieval in peer-to-peer networks, pp. 1–8. ACM Press, New York (2006)
2. Banaei-Kashani, F., Shahabi, C.: SWAM: A family of access methods for similarity-search in peer-to-peer data networks. In: CIKM '04: Proceedings of the Thirteenth ACM conference on Information and knowledge management, pp. 304–313. ACM Press, New York (2004)
3. Batko, M., Novak, D., Falchi, F., Zezula, P.: On scalability of the similarity search in the world of peers. In: Proceedings of First International Conference on Scalable Information Systems (INFOSCALE 2006), Hong Kong, pp. 1–12. ACM Press, New York (May 30 - June 1, 2006) (2006)
4. Bender, M., Michel, S., Triantafillou, P., Weikum, G., Zimmer, C.: MINERVA: Collaborative P2P search. In: VLDB '05. Proceedings of the 31st international conference on Very large data bases, VLDB Endowment, pp. 1263–1266 (2005)
5. Ciaccia, P., Patella, M., Zezula, P.: M-tree: An efficient access method for similarity search in metric spaces. In: Jarke, M., Carey, M.J., Dittrich, K.R., Lochovsky, F.H., Loucopoulos, P., Jeusfeld, M.A. (eds.) Proceedings of the 23rd International Conference on Very Large Data Bases (VLDB 1997), Athens, Greece, August 25-29, 1997, pp. 426–435. Morgan Kaufmann, San Francisco (1997)
6. Dohnal, V., Gennaro, C., Savino, P., Zezula, P.: D-index: Distance searching index for metric data sets. Multimedia Tools and Applications 21(1), 9–33 (2003)
7. Ganesan, P., Yang, B., Garcia-Molina, H.: One torus to rule them all: Multi-dimensional queries in P2P systems. In: WebDB '04: Proceedings of the 7th International Workshop on the Web and Databases, pp. 19–24. ACM Press, New York (2004)
8. Linari, A., Weikum, G.: Efficient peer-to-peer semantic overlay networks based on statistical language models. In: P2PIR '06: Proceedings of the international workshop on Information retrieval in peer-to-peer networks, pp. 9–16. ACM Press, New York (2006)
9. Monge, P.R., Contractor, N.S.: Theories of Communication Networks. Oxford University Press, New York (2003)
10. Wasserman, S., Faust, K., Iacobucci, D.: Social Network Analysis: Methods and Applications (Structural Analysis in the Social Sciences). Cambridge University Press, Cambridge (1994)
11. Watts, D.J., Strogatz, S.H.: Collective dynamics of 'small-world' networks. Nature 393(6684), 440–442 (1998)
12. Zezula, P., Amato, G., Dohnal, V., Batko, M.: Similarity Search: The Metric Space Approach. In: Advances in Database Systems, vol. 32, Springer, Heidelberg (2005)

Performance Evaluation of Dynamic Probabilistic Flooding Using Local Density Information in MANETs

Aamir Siddique, Abdalla M. Hanashi, Irfan Awan, and Mike Woodward

Mobile Computing, Networks and Security Research Group
School of Informatics, University of Bradford,
Bradford, BD7 1DP, U.K.
{asiddiq3,a.m.o.hanashi,i.u.awan,m.e.woodward}@bradford.ac.uk

Abstract. Flooding is an obligatory message dissemination technique for network-wide broadcast within mobile ad hoc networks (MANETs). The conventional blind flooding algorithm causes broadcast storm problem, a high number of unnecessary packet rebroadcasts – thus resulting in high contention and packet collisions. This leads to significant network performance degradation. Because of the highly dynamic and mobile characteristics of MANETs, an appropriate probabilistic broadcast protocol can attain higher throughput, significant reduction in the number of rebroadcast messages without sacrificing the reachability. This paper proposes a new probabilistic approach that dynamically fine-tunes the rebroadcasting probability for routing request packets (RREQs). We assess the performance of the proposed approach by evaluating it against the ad-hoc on demand distance vector (AODV) routing protocol (which follows blind flooding approach), fixed probabilistic approach and the existing dynamic probabilistic approaches. The simulation results reveal that the proposed approach demonstrates better performance than the existing approaches.

1 Introduction

Mobile ad hoc networks (MANETs) are self-organizing mobile wireless networks that do not rely on a preexisting infrastructure to communicate. Network-wide dissemination is used widely in MANETs [1] for the process of route invention, address resolution, and other network layer tasks. For example, on demand routing protocols such as ad-hoc on demand distance vector (AODV) [8] and dynamic source routing (DSR) [12] use the broadcast information in route request packets to construct routing tables at every mobile node [3]. The lively nature of MANETs, however, requires the routing protocols to refresh the routing tables regularly, which could generate a large number of broadcast packets at various nodes. Since not every node in a MANET can communicate directly with the nodes outside its communication range, a broadcast packet may have to be rebroadcast several times at relaying nodes in order to guarantee that the packet can reach all nodes. Consequently, an inefficient broadcast approach may generate many redundant rebroadcast packets [5].

There are many proposed approaches for dissemination in MANETs. The simplest one is the flooding. In this technique, each mobile host rebroadcasts the broadcast

T. Enokido, L. Barolli, and M. Takizawa (Eds.): NBiS 2007, LNCS 4658, pp. 288–297, 2007.

packets when received for the first time. Packets that have already been received are just discarded. Though flooding is simple, it consumes much network resources as it introduces a large number of duplicate messages. It leads to serious redundancy, contention and collision in mobile wireless networks, which is referred to broadcast storm problem [2].

In this paper, we propose a dynamic probabilistic broadcast approach that can efficiently reduce broadcast redundancy in mobile wireless networks. The proposed algorithm dynamically calculates the host rebroadcast probability according to number of neighbor nodes information. The rebroadcast probability would be low when the number of neighbor nodes are high which means host is in dense area and the probability would be high when the number of neighbor nodes are low which means host is in sparse area.

We evaluate our proposed approach against the simple flooding approach and the fixed probabilistic approach, dynamic approach [3] and adjusted probabilistic [4] by implementing them in a modified version of the AODV protocol. The simulation results show that broadcast redundancy can be significantly reduced through the proposed approach.

The rest of this paper is structured as follows. Section 2 includes the background and related work of dissemination in MANETs. Section 3 presents the proposed dynamic probabilistic approach, highlighting its distinctive features from the other similar techniques. The parameters used in the experiments and the performance results and analysis to evaluate the effectiveness and limitation of the proposed technique are presented in Section 4. Section 5 concludes the paper and outlines the future work.

2 Related Work

This section analyses the related work which directly or indirectly aims at reducing the number of broadcast packets generated by the flooding algorithm. The high number of redundant broadcast packets due to flooding in MANETs has been referred to as the Broadcast Storm Problem [2].

There are five proposed flooding schemes [6] in MANETs called probabilistic, counter-based, distance-based, location-based [2] and cluster-based [2, 6]. In the probabilistic scheme, when receiving a broadcast message for the first time, a host rebroadcasts the message with a fixed probability P. The counter-based scheme inhibits the rebroadcast if the message has already been received for more than C times. In the distance-based scheme a node rebroadcasts the message only if the distance between the sender and the receiver is larger than a threshold D.

The location-based scheme rebroadcasts the message if the additional coverage due to the new emission is larger than a bound A. Finally, the cluster-based scheme uses a cluster selection algorithm to create the clusters, and then the rebroadcast is done by head clusters and gateways. The authors conclude by the efficiency of the location-based scheme [2], but these end additional area coverage protocols need a positioning system.

Cartigny and Simplot [1] have described a probabilistic scheme where the probability P of a node for retransmitting a message is computed from the local density n (i.e., the number of neighbors) and a fixed value k for the efficiency parameter to achieve the reachability of the broadcast. This technique has the drawback of being locally uniform. In fact, each node of a given area receives a broadcast and determines the probability according to a constant efficiency parameter (to achieve some reachability) and from the local density [1].

Zhang and Dharma [3] have also described a dynamic probabilistic scheme, which uses a combination of probabilistic and counter-based schemes. The value of a packet counter does not necessarily correspond to the exact number of neighbors from the current host, since some of its neighbors may have suppressed their rebroadcasts according to their local rebroadcast probability. On the other hand, the decision to rebroadcast is made after a random delay, which increases latency.

Bani Yassein et al. [4,7] have proposed fixed pair of probabilistic broadcast scheme where the forwarding probability p is adjusted by the local topology information. Topology information is obtained by proactive exchange of "HELLO" packets between neighbors.

For both approaches presented in [3] and [4] there is an extra overhead i.e., before calculating the probability, average number of neighbor nodes should be known in advance.

3 Dynamic Probabilistic Broadcasting Algorithms

As studied earlier, traditional flooding suffers from the problem of redundant message reception. The same message is received multiple times by every node, which is inefficient, wastes valuable resources and can cause high contention in the transmission medium. In fixed probabilistic flooding the rebroadcast probability P is fixed for every node. This scheme is one of the alternative approaches to flooding that aims to limit the number of redundant transmissions. In this scheme, when receiving a broadcast message for the first time, a node rebroadcasts the message with a predetermined probability P. Thus every node has the same probability to rebroadcast the message, regardless of its number of neighbors.

In dense networks, multiple nodes share similar transmission ranges. Therefore, these probabilities control the number of rebroadcasts and thus might save network resources without affecting delivery ratios. Note that in sparse networks there is much less shared coverage; thus some nodes will not receive all the broadcast packets unless the probability parameter is high. Therefore, setting the rebroadcast probability P to a very small value will result in a poor reachability. On the other hand, if P is set to a very large value, many redundant rebroadcasts will be generated.

A concise sketch of the dynamic probabilistic flooding algorithm is shown below and works as follows. On hearing a broadcast message *msg* at host node N for the first time, the node rebroadcasts a message according to a calculated probability with the help of neigbour nodes of N, Therefore, if node N has a high probability P, retransmission should be likely, Otherwise, if N has a low probability P retransmission may be unlikely.

3.1 Algorithm

This algorithm relays the packet (pkt) for ith node with probability *P*.

Step (1)

Input Parameters:

pkt(i) : Packet to relay by ith node.

P(*i*) : Rebroadcast probability of packet *(pkt)* of ith node.

RN(*i*) : Random No for ith node to compare with the rebroadcast probability *P*.

S_{nbr} (*i*) : Size/No of neighbour nodes of ith node.

Output Parameters:

Discpkt(*i*) : Packet *(pkt)* will be discarded for node(i), if it is in the packet list of ith node.

Rbdpkt (*i*) : Packet *(pkt)* will be rebroadcasted by ith node, if probability *P* is high.

Drpkt(*i*) : Packet *(pkt)* will be dropped by ith node, if probability *P* is low.

DPFlood(msg): Dynamic Probabilistic Flooding

1: Upon reception of message *(msg)* at node (i)
2: if message *(msg)* received for the 1st time then
3: Go to step (2)
4: Relay the packet *(pkt)* with probability *P*
5: else
6: Drop *pkt*
7: endif

Step (2)

This function calculates the Rebroadcast Probability *P* of ith node

Input Parameters:

S_{nbr} (*i*) **:** Size/No of neighbour nodes of ith node.

Output Parameters:

P(*i*) : Rebroadcast probability of packet *(pkt)* of ith node.

Probability (S_{nbr}(i)): Rebroadcast Probability for ith node

1: Set *P* := 1
2: Go to step (3)
3: $P := \prod_{i=0}^{S_{nbr(i)}} P * P_{\max}$
4: if $P < P_{\min}$ then
5: $P = P_{\min}$
6: endif
7: return (*P*)

Step (3)

This function calculates the size/No of neighbour nodes of ith node

Input Parameters:

nbrTable(i) **:** Neighbor table for ith node.

Output Parameters:

$S_{nbr}\ (i)$: Size/No of neighbour nodes of ith node.

NBRsize(nbrTable): Size of the neighbour nodes

1: if nbrTable->size = = 0 then
2:   return (o)
3: else
4:   return (nbrTable->size)
5: endif

The proposed algorithm dynamically adjusts the rebroadcast probability *P* at each mobile host according to the number of neighbor nodes. The value of *P* is different in different areas. In a sparser area, the rebroadcast probability is large whilst in the denser area, the probability is low. Compared with the probabilistic approach where *P* is fixed and comparing with the existing approaches [4,5], the proposed algorithm achieves higher throughput, lower latency, higher reachability and higher saved rebroadcast. The proposal algorithm is scalable algorithm which can be used for any number of nodes in mobile ad hoc network (MANETs) with different number of connections. Algorithm in this paper is tested against only two techniques [3,4], results show better output for our algorithm.

4 Performance Analyses

In this section, we evaluate the performance of the proposed dynamic probabilistic flooding algorithm. We compare the proposed algorithm with a simple flooding algorithm and fixed flooding. We implement all the three algorithms using AODV protocol. The metrics for comparison include the average number of routing rebroadcast requests, reachability, the throughput and end-to-end delay.

A. Simulation Setup

We have used the GloMoSim network simulator (version 2.03) [9] to conduct extensive experiments to evaluate behaviour of the proposed dynamic probabilistic flooding algorithm. We study the performance of the broadcasting approaches in the situation of higher level application, namely, the AODV routing protocol [8,10,11] that is included in the GloMoSim package. The original AODV protocol uses simple blind flooding to broadcast routing requests. We have implemented two AODV variations: one using probabilistic method with fixed probability, called FPAODV (AODV + fixed probability), and the other based on dynamically calculating the rebroadcast probability for each node, called P-AODV (AODV + dynamic probability). In our simulation, we use a 600m × 600m area with random waypoint

Table 1. Summary of the parameters used in the simulation experiments

Parameter	Value
Network range	600m×600m
Transmission range	250m
Number of mobile nodes	80
Number of connections	20, 30, 40
bandwidth	2Mbps
Traffic type	Constant bit rate (CBR)
Packet rate	100 packet per second
Packet size	512 bytes
Simulation time	900s

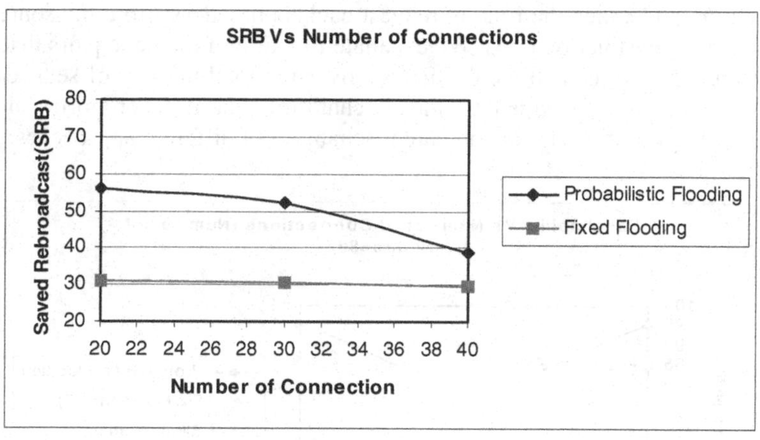

Fig. 1. SRB vs. Connections

model of 80 mobile hosts. The network bandwidth is 2 Mbps and the medium access control (MAC) layer protocol is IEEE 802.11[3]. Other simulation parameters are shown in Table 1.

The main idea behind the proposed approach is to reduce the rebroadcasting number in the route discovery phase, thus reducing the network traffic and decrease the probability of channel contention and packet collision. As a result, end-to-end delay can also be reduced and the throughput can be improved.

Since our algorithm is based on a probabilistic approach, it does not fit every scenario, as there is a small chance that the route requests cannot reach the destination. It is necessary to re-generate the route request if the previous route request failed to reach the destination. We study the performance of the broadcast approaches in these scenarios.

B. Saved Rebroadcasts (SRB)

In our algorithm, the rebroadcast probability is dynamically calculated. In sparser area, the probability is high and in denser area the probability is low. SRB is the ratio of the number of route request (RREQs) packets rebroadcasted over total number of route request (RREQs) packets received, excluding those expired by time to live (TTL).

Fig. 1 shows that our improved algorithm can significantly reduce the saved rebroadcast (SRB) for network with 80 nodes, no mobility, and varying number of connection.

C. Reachability

The metric of reachability measures the ratio of nodes that can receive a broadcast packet. We study the reachability in the context of the AODV routing protocol. We randomly select source–destination node pairs and check if a packet can reach the destination node from the source node. If there exists a route from the source node to the destination node, then the routing request packets broadcast from the source node have reached the destination node. We calculate the ratio of the node pairs that have a route between the source and the destination over the total number of selected pairs. This ratio is not exactly equal to the reachability, but it is proportional to the reachability. We use this ratio to compare reachability of different approaches.

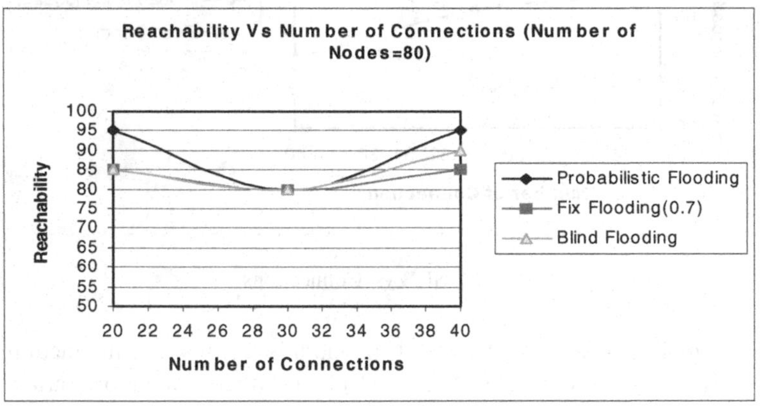

Fig. 2. Reachability Vs. Connections

Fig. 2 shows the reachability for a network with 80 nodes, 20, 30 and 40 connections of source-destination pairs. The figure shows that dynamic probabilistic algorithm has higher reachability than fix probabilistic flooding and simple flooding at 20 and 40 connections. Reachability for all approaches with 30 connections is surprisingly same. This can be attributed to the increasing number of collisions of rebroadcast packets. We have noted that the extra rudandency of route request (RREQ) transmissions result more contentions and collisions. In network with higher number of transmissions i-e higher number of connections dynamic probabilistic algorithm shows 95% reachbility

D. Throughput

Throughput is an important metric that measures the transmission ability of a network.The average throughput is calculated as the mean volume of data that is actually delivered to the destination within each time unit. We compare the throughput in this section.

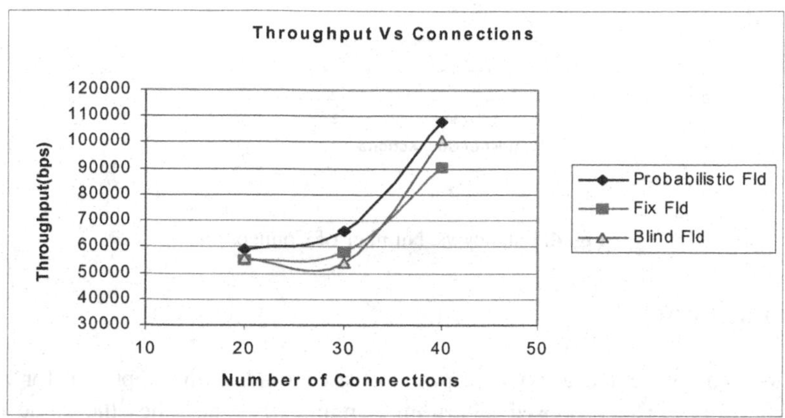

Fig.3. Throughput vs. Number of Connections

Fig. 3 shows that our algorithm achieves better throughput values than from other algorithms with no mobility. It is clearly predicted that the throughput increases when traffic load increases.

E. Latency

We measure the broadcast latency for the three approaches. We record the start time of a broadcast as well as the time when the broadcast packet reaches the last node.

The difference between these two values is used as the broadcast latency. Since rebroadcasts can cause collision and possible contention for the shared channels, the improved probabilistic approach incurs the lowest number of rebroadcasts and consequently generating the lowest latency.

Fig. 4 shows the latency for different levels of traffic load. Our algorithm has better results for less number of connections i-e 20 and 30 but as we increase the number of connections it shows that results are better than fix flooding but surprisingly blind flooding has good results than other two approaches which might be because of higher number of retransmission. As expected, the proposed improved probabilistic algorithm displays lower latency than blind flooding and fixed probabilistic approach.

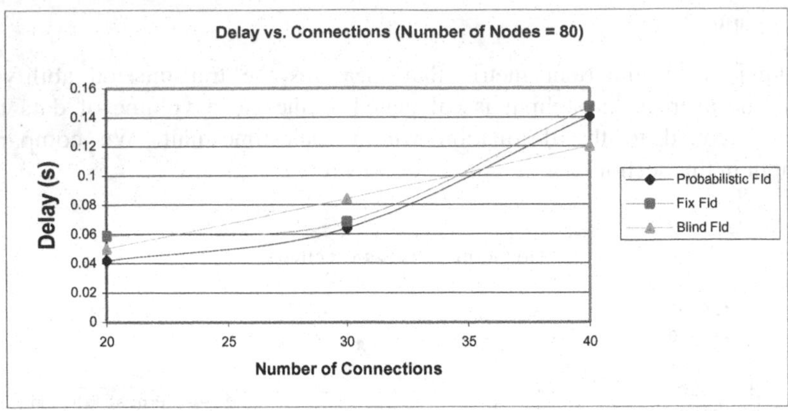

Fig. 4. Latency vs. Number of Connections

5 Conculsion

This paper has presented a dynamic probabilistic broadcasting approach for mobile ad-hoc networks. The proposed algorithm dynamically fine tunes the value of the rebroadcast probability for every host node according to the neighbors information. Our simulation results prove this approach can generate less rebroadcasts than that of the fixed-value probabilistic approach, dynamic [3] and adjusted probabilistic [4], while keeping the reachability high. It also demonstrates lower broadcast latency than all the existing approaches.

For future work it would be interesting to explore the algorithm for mobility in mobile ad-hoc network using neighbors information. We also plan to evaluate the Performance of dynamic probabilistic flooding on the Dynamic Source Routing (DSR) algorithm.

References

1. Cartigny, J., Simplot, D.: Border node retransmission based probabilistic broadcast protocols in ad-hoc networks. Telecommunication Systems 22(1-4), 189–204 (2003)
2. Tseng, Y.-C., Ni, S.-Y., Chen, Y.-S., Sheu, J.-P.: The broadcast storm problem in a mobile ad hoc network. Wireless Networks 8(2/3), 153–167 (2002)
3. Zhang, Q., Agrawal, D.: Dynamic probabilistic broadcasting in manets. Journal of ParallelDistributed Computing 65, 220–233 (2005)
4. Yassein, M.B., Khaoua, M.O., et al.: Improving route discovery in on-demand routing protocols using local topology information in MANETs. In: Proceedings of the ACM international workshop on Performance monitoring, measurement, and evaluation of heterogeneous wireless and wired networks, Terromolinos, Spain, pp. 95–99. ACM Press, New York (2006)

5. Stefan, P., Mahesh, B., et al.: MISTRAL: efficient flooding in mobile ad-hoc networks. In: Proceedings of the seventh ACM international symposium on Mobile ad hoc networking and computing, Florence, Italy, pp. 1–12. ACM Press, New York (2006)
6. Williams, B., Camp, T.: Comparison of broadcasting techniques for mobile ad hoc networks. In: Proc. ACM Symposium on Mobile Ad Hoc Networking & Computing (MOBIHOC 2002), pp.194—205 (2002)
7. Bani-Yassein, L.M.M.M., Ould-Khaoua, M., Papanastasiou, S.: Performance analysis of adjusted probabilistic broadcasting in mobile ad hoc networks. International Journal of Wireless Information Networks, 1–14 (March 2006)
8. Perkins, C.E., Royer, E.M.: Ad-hoc on-demand distance vector routing. In: Proceedings of the 1999 Second IEEE Workshop on Mobile Computing Systems and Applications, New York, pp. 90–100. IEEE Computer Society press, Los Alamitos (1999)
9. Zeng, X., Bagrodia, R., Gerla, M.: GloMoSim: a library for parallel simulation of large-scale wireless networks. In: PADS '98. Proceedings of the 1998 12th Workshop on Parallel and Distributed Simulations, Banff, Alb., Canada, May 26-29,1998, pp. 154–161 (1998)
10. Sasson, Y., Cavin, D., Schiper, A.: Probabilistic broadcast for flooding in wireless mobile ad hoc networks. In: Proc. IEEE Wireless Communications & Networking Conference (WCNC 2003), pp. 1124—1130 (March 2003)
11. Sasson, Y., Cavin, D., Schiper, A.: Probabilistic broadcast for flooding in wireless mobile ad hoc networks, EPFL Technical Report IC/2002/54, Swiss Federal Institute of Technology(EPFL) (2002)
12. Johnson, D.B., Maltz, D.A.: Dynamic source routing in ad hoc wireless networks. In: Imielinski, T., Korth, H. (eds.) Mobile Computing, New York, pp. 153–181. Academic Publishers, San Diego (1996)

A Token Bucket Model with Assured Forwarding for Web Traffic

Salvador Alcaraz[1], Katja Gilly[1], Carlos Juiz[2], and Ramon Puigjaner[2]

[1] Miguel Hernández University,
Departamento de Física y Arquitectura de Computadores,
Avda. del Ferrocarril, 03202 Elche (Spain)
{salcaraz,katya}@umh.es
[2] University of Balearic Islands,
Departament de Ciències Matemàtiques i Informàtica,
Carretera de Valldemossa, km 7.5, 07071 Palma de Mallorca (Spain)
{cjuiz,putxi}@uib.es

Abstract. In this paper we present PLF (Promotion of Long Flows). PLF tries to promote web traffic using the Token Bucket Model in a DiffServ framework. This algorithm preserves the high priority for short flows but tries to allocate some long flows in the high priority class level, in order to improve some performance parameters of the long ones. Finally, we present PLFwp (Promotion of Long Flows with Penalization) in order to detect (and cancel) the effect of these extremely long flows over the global performance. We analyze the results for packet loss and web transmission latency.

Keywords: Web traffic, DiffServ, Token bucket, QoS, Short and long flows.

1 Introduction

The best effort service model of the Internet, where all packets and flows have equal status is not being able to provide packet delivery guarantees. This model is unsuitable for applications with Quality of Service (QoS) constraints. The early 1990s saw a large number of frameworks being proposed for supporting QoS over the Internet.

The Integrated Services Model (IntServ) [1] was one of the IETF first proposal to achieve QoS over the Internet traffic. In this model, routing devices are required to hold the status information of each flow going through that device. One single reason why IntServ has not been accepted in the Internet is its absence of per-flow QoS scalability beyond the Intranet environment. Typically more than 250,000 simultaneous flows pass through Internet Core routers. Maintaining a state for such a large number of flows requires computing resources.

IETF proposed another framework, the Differentiated Services Model (DiffServ) [2] that could support a scalable form of QoS. DiffServ operates at class level, where a class is an aggregate of many such flows. For example, packets

T. Enokido, L. Barolli, and M. Takizawa (Eds.): NBiS 2007, LNCS 4658, pp. 298–307, 2007.

coming from a set of source addresses or packets of a certain size, may fall into one class. DiffServ architecture adheres to the basic Internet philosophy, where the complexity is relegated to the Edge device while preserving simplicity of the Core device. Per-hop behaviors (PHBs) have been standardized into two classes by the IETF: *Expedited Forwarding (EF)* [3] and *Assured Forwarding (AF)*[4]. The main goal of the PHB-AF is to deliver the packets reliably. The PHB-AF is suitable for non-real time services such as TCP applications.

Several strategies have been proposed to achieve some kind of treatment for web traffic. Due to the web traffic's nature and the fact that the most of web traffic flows are short, in [5] the authors define a preferential treatment for short over long flows. In [6], QoS using control theory and predictability are applied both over DiffServ framework. In [7] uses RED Active Queue Management for provides better network performance for short-lived web traffic. In [8,9] the authors propose solutions based on load balancing and admission control.

In this paper, we propose a new algorithm (PLF, *Promotion of Long Flows*). It is in a DiffServ framework and PHB-AF, based on flow size, with a special handle of short flows in order to improve its performance for QoS. It also tries to achieve a certain QoS over the rest of long flows. We use the Token Bucket Model to assess the amount of priority available bandwidth to allocate long flows in the high level priority class.

The remainder of this paper is organized as follows: section 2 includes a short description of our architecture with DiffServ framework, Edge and Core devices and priority queueing scheduling. Section 3 describes the traffic and workload model. PLF algorithm is described in section 4. Afterwards, we present different performance metrics that we have analyzed. In section 6 we present another variant and the performance results. Finally, some concluding are presented.

2 System Architecture

Our experiments are based on a dummbell architecture (Fig. 1 (a)), where we can distinguish: *(i) Client area*, where the HTTP traffic is generated by HTTP client with HTTP request to HTTP servers, at the other side of the system; *(ii) Servers area*, where HTTP servers attend the incoming request from client; and *(iii) DiffServ area*, with the Edge router and Core router. The Edge router classifies packets by marking them and the Core router forwards/drops packets.

PHB-AF introduces two components in the operation of the DiffServ area: a packet marking mechanism administered by profile meters or traffic conditioners at Edge devices and a queue active management at Core devices. The packet marking mechanism monitors and marks packets according to the service profile at the Edge of a network. If the incoming traffic conforms the service profile, the packets are marked with a high priority and receive better service. Otherwise, the packets belonging to the non-conform part of a flow are marked with a low priority and receive low priority at the Core device. The Edge router classifies packets in function of the algorithm implemented, i.e. the action to perform with incoming packets: to drop them, to queue them in the queue-IN or in the

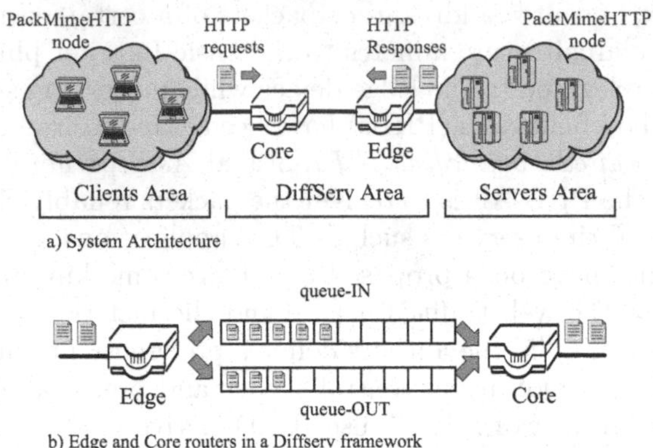

Fig. 1. System architecture

queue-OUT. The virtual queues (Fig. 1 (b)), queue-IN and queue-OUT, both are managed under RED discipline: queue-IN ($max_{th} = 30$, $min_{th} = 10$, $max_p = 0.02$, $w_p = 0.002$) and queue-OUT ($max_{th} = 24$, $min_{th} = 8$, $max_p = 0.10$, $w_p = 0.002$).

We have deployed the Token Bucket Model [10] in the Edge device (Fig. 2 (a)). This model has two main components: CIR (*Committed Information Rate*) in bps, and CBS (*Committed Burst Size*) in Bytes. The bucket is filled with tokens at a CIR rate, and with CBS of maximum of capacity. The incoming packet that according with the service profile is marked with high-priority and it is also sent to queue-IN. On the other hand, the incoming packet not according with the service profile is marked with low-priority and it is sent to queue-OUT. Therefore packets sent to queue-IN spend tokens, and packets sent to queue-OUT not spend tokens. In our case, the service profile holds the rules to distinguish between short and long flows.

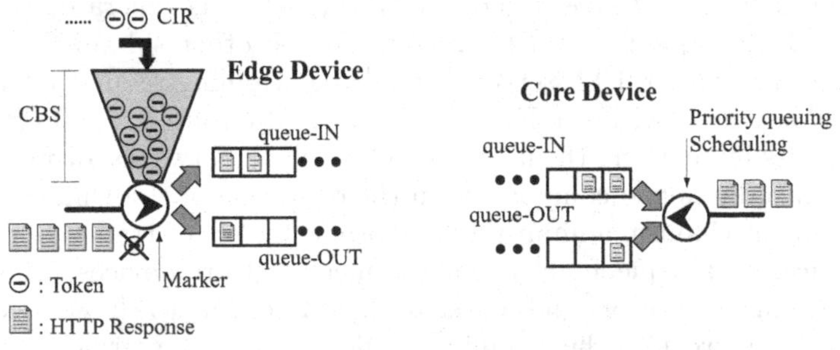

Fig. 2. Edge and Core devices

The Core device (Fig. 2 (b)) performs the scheduling of the packets by selecting which packet should be removed from which queue. In our research, we have worked with Priority Queuing (PQ) scheduling, alleviating the Core device of the computational load and assigning priority to queue-IN over queue-OUT. With PQ we have set the queue-IN like the high priority queue with QoS, and the queue-OUT without QoS (best-effort service).

3 Traffic and Workload Model

We have used NS-2 simulator [11] with PackMime Traffic Model [12] to generate the traffic and workload model. The PackMime includes a model of HTTP traffic, called PackMime-HTTP. The traffic intensity generated by PackMime-HTTP is controlled by the *rate* parameter, which is the average number of new connections started each second.

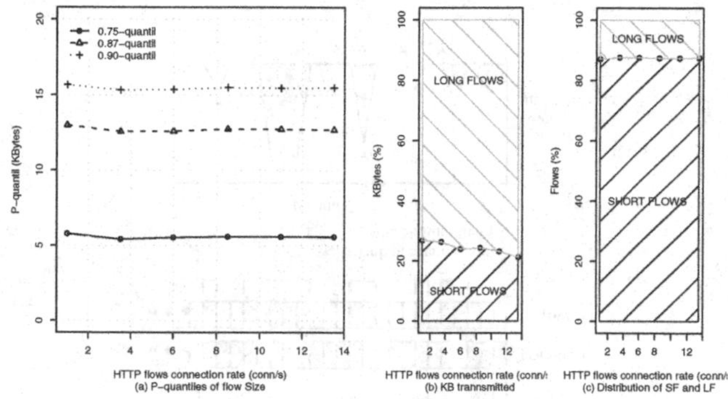

Fig. 3. (a) 0.75-quantile, 0.87-quantile and 0.90-quantile of the flow size; (b) Total of KB transmitted by SF and LF; (c) Total distribution of SF and LF

Some studies show us the distribution and classification of the web flows in Internet [13]: *short flows (SF)* and *long flows (LF)*. The division criteria is the flow size. Depending on the partial size of the flow, the incoming packets will be classified like *SF* or *LF*. So, according to [13]:

> *"...most (e.g. 80%) of the traffic is actually carried by only a small number of connections (elephants), while the remaining large amount of connections are very small in size or lifetime (mice). In a fair network environment, short connections expect relatively fast service than long connections..."*

With the traffic model used, PackMime-HTTP, we have fixed the flow size threshold in 13 KB for the simulation batches and after the simulation, we get the next results (Fig. 3 (a)): (i) the 0.87-quantile of the flow size is around 13 KB; (ii) between 20-30% of traffic (KB) is carried by a small number of flows (SF); (iii) between 80-90% of live connections are SF.

4 PLF: Promotion of Long Flows

Our proposed algorithm is based on the Token Bucket traffic specification with the parameters: CIR and CBS. The main idea is to continue with a high priority for SF, forwarding its packets to queue-IN, and PLF also tries to exploit the gaps in the available bandwidth by queueing packets of LF into queue-IN.

Let $T = T_{SF} + T_{LF}$ the incoming traffic to the DiffServ area, consists of traffic from SF (T_{SF}) and traffic from LF flows (T_{LF}). Let *Bucket* the bandwidth available for QoS. Then $Gap = Bucket - T_{SF}$ will be the available bandwidth for promotion of LF (Fig. 4).

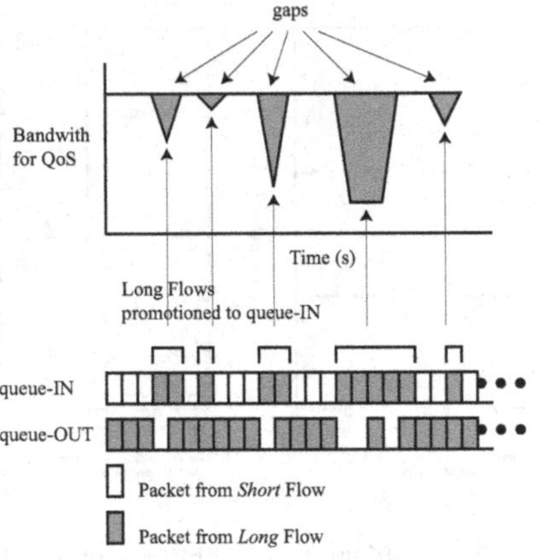

Fig. 4. Distribution of gaps in the bandwidth

To avoid the synchronizing flows and to get a progressive promotion of long flows, we will make a stochastic function (δ). This function will be based on *Gap* and *Bucket*. Then, for all incoming packets P from a LF (denoted P^{LF}), we can define $Prob(P^{LF})_{queue-IN}$ like the probability of P is sent to queue-IN; and $Prob(P^{LF})_{queue-OUT}$ like the probability of P is sent to queue-OUT (1):

$$\begin{aligned} \delta &= \frac{Gap}{Bucket} \\ Prob(P^{LF})_{queue-IN} &= \delta \\ Prob(P^{LF})_{queue-OUT} &= \overline{\delta} \end{aligned} \quad (1)$$

and PLF algorithm will be:

Let F_i flow i
Let P_j^i packet $j/P_j^i \in F_i$
Let S_i size of F_i
Let Th threshold
Let $Type_f$ of (SHORT,LONG)
Let $Bucket$ size of bucket
Let Gap available gap of bandwidth
then
$\forall$ incoming P_j^i
  $S_i = \sum_{i=1}^{j} Size(P_j^i)$
  $Type_f = (S_i \leq Th?SHORT : LONG)$
  Case $Type_f$ of
    $SHORT$:
      $P_j^i \longmapsto queue_{IN}$
      break
    $LONG$:
      $Gap = Bucket - Size(P_j^i)$
      $\delta = \frac{Gap}{Bucket}$
      with probability δ : $P_j^i \longmapsto queue_{IN}$
      with probability $\overline{\delta}$: $P_j^i \longmapsto queue_{OUT}$
      break
  $endCase$
  $Bucket = Bucket - Size(P_j^i)$

5 Performance Parameters

Several experimental studies [13,14] have shown that Internet traffic exhibits a really high variability, where HTTP traffic is carried, mainly, by SF, and it has an important temporal constraints depending on customer satisfaction. So, in this paper, we have analyzed the interactions between SF and LF, and we have compared the results with other well-known proposal, like DropTail and RED. We have isolated the analysis of HTTP flows, analyzing the next performance parameters for SF and LF: packet loss and latency.

5.1 Packet Loss

Packet loss has an important effect over web systems performance. The most significant cause of packet loss in networks is packet discard within routers in the presence of congestion, and the outcomes is the overload and a low performance of the system.

In Fig. 5 we have represented the evolution of packet loss with the HTTP Traffic Load (conn/s). Due to the special handle of short flows, with high-priority in the DiffServ framework, PLF gets lower packet loss rate than DropTail and RED, for all values of Traffic Load. The packet loss is near 0, practically. Due to early dropping of RED, it presents a high values of packet loss. In the second graphics (Long Flows), we can see that the packet loss for PLF is always under the DropTail and RED.

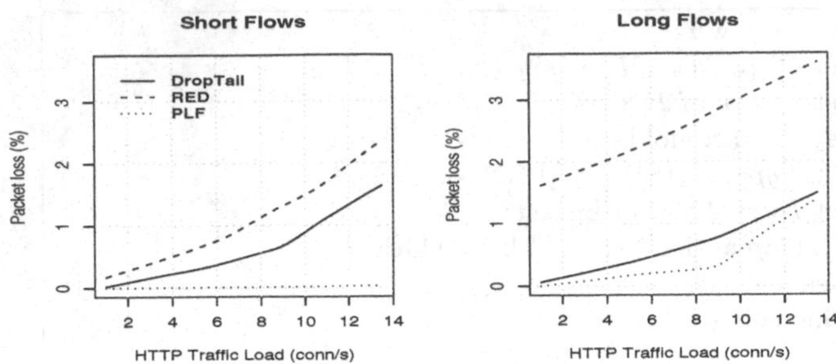

Fig. 5. Packet loss

5.2 Transmission Latency

Packet delay has been the main metric of network performance since the earliest days of the Internet, and, in particular, web Transmission latency (latency for short), could be one of the most important performance parameters for web traffic. We will analyze the latency from the point of view of client. So, the latency measures the time interval starting when a HTTP client launch the request HTTP, and ending when the last packet of the HTTP response arrives at client node.

We use 3D-graphics (Fig. 6) to visualize the evolution of the Latency (Z-axis) with the HTTP Traffic Load (X-axis) and Flow size (Y-axis), and with the numerical values of the table.

6 PLFwp: Promotion of Long Flows with Penalization

The main problem of the PLF is the *extremely* long flows. Suddenly, some flows have a lot of packets, hundreds of them. The result is these packets take up the available gap impeding other flows can use the bandwidth for QoS. So, we are going to penalized these extremely long flows, with the function γ. For this purpose, γ must be another stochastic function (2) of the minimum (Min_{flow}), maximum (Max_{flow}) sizes of live flows and the flow size (S_i). So, now we can redesign $Prob^{LF}_{queue-IN}$ and $Prob^{LF}_{queue-OUT}$ with δ and γ in (2).

$$\begin{aligned} \gamma = 1 - \frac{Max_{flow} - S_i}{Max_{flow} - Min_{flow}} \\ Prob^{LF}_{queue-IN} = \delta * \overline{\gamma} \\ Prob^{LF}_{queue-OUT} = (\delta * \gamma) + \overline{\delta} \end{aligned} \tag{2}$$

In Fig. 7 we have depicted the mean of transmission latency and 95% confidence interval. We observe a light improvement of the latency and very similar confidence intervals for SF. About LF, the confidence intervals are more different, and also, with PLFwp we get a ligth improvement for latency.

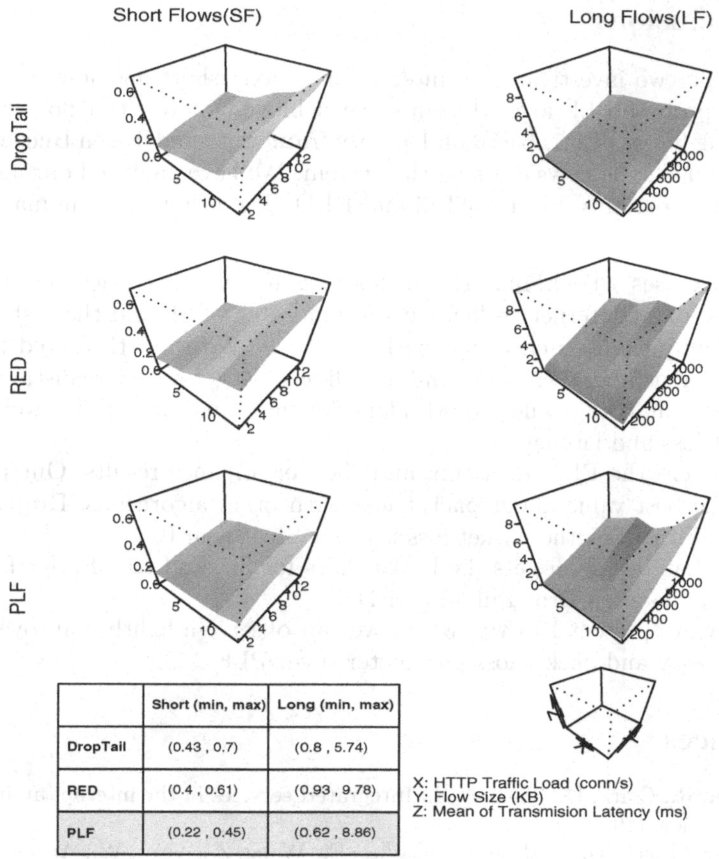

	Short (min, max)	Long (min, max)
DropTail	(0.43 , 0.7)	(0.8 , 5.74)
RED	(0.4 , 0.61)	(0.93 , 9.78)
PLF	(0.22 , 0.45)	(0.62 , 8.86)

Fig. 6. 3D graphics for Mean of transmission latency. The table shows the minimum/maximum values for this parameter.

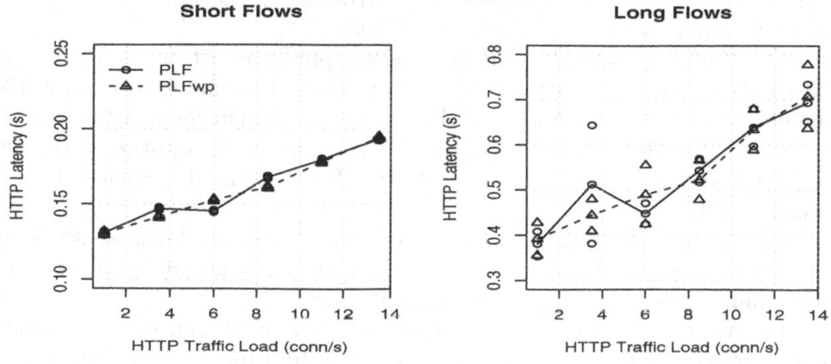

Fig. 7. Mean of transmission Latency with 95% confidence interval

7 Conclusions

In this paper we investigate the interaction among short and long web traffic flows. We propose PLF algorithm in order achieve QoS to short flows but promoting long flows. PLF is based on DiffServ framework and Token Bucket Model for management the flows crossing the system. We have analyzed our algorithm with other algorithms, like DropTail and RED. The results are summarized below:

1. We have uses a PackMime-HTTP traffic generator. It carries out the latest studies about Internet traffic, with around 80% of SF and the rest LF, but the mainly traffic is carry out with a few LF. With our threshold (13 KB) to distinguish between short and long flows, we get a very realistic results
2. We have analyzed some important performance parameters for web traffic: packet loss and latency.
3. We present the PLF algorithm and the performance results. Our proposal gets the best value about packet loss with other algorithms, DropTail and RED. With PLF, the packet loss rate for SF is near 0.
4. About Latency, PLF gets the best results for SF, and for LF, our PLF gets a results between DropTail and RED.
5. Finally, we present PLFwp, where we can observe a lightly improvement of the latency and packet loss parameters over PLF.

References

1. Braden, R., Clark, D., Shenker, S.: Integrated services in the internet architecture: An overview (1998)
2. Blake, S., Black, D., Carlson, M., Davies, E., Wang, Z., Weiss, W.: An architecture for differentiated service (1998)
3. Jacobson, V., Nichols, K., Poduri, K.: Rfc 2598, an expedited forwarding phb (1999)
4. Heinanen, J., Baker, F., Weiss, W., Wroclawski, J.: Assured forwarding phb group (1999)
5. Chen, X., Heidemann, J.: Preferential treatment for short flows to reduce web latency. Comput. Networks 41, 779–794 (2003)
6. Zhou, X., Cai, Y., Chow, E.: An integrated approach with feedback control for robust web qos design. Computer Communications Journal 29, 3158–3169 (2006)
7. Claypool, M., Kinick, R., Hartling, M.: Active queue management for web traffic. In: Proc. of the 23rd IEEE International Performance, Computing and Communications Conference (IPCCC), pp. 531–538. IEEE Computer Society Press, Los Alamitos (2004)
8. Gilly, K., Alcaraz, S., Juiz, C., Puigjaner, R.: Resource allocation study based on burstiness for a web switch. In: Proc. of 4th International Information and Telecommunication Technologies Symposium (2005)
9. Gilly, K., Alcaraz, S., Juiz, C., Puigjaner, R.: Service differentiation and qos in a scalable content-aware load balancing algorithm. In: Proc. of 40th Annual Simulation Symposium (2007)
10. Ahmed, N.U., Wang, Q., Barbosa, L.O.: Systems approach to modeling the token bucket algorithm in computer networks. Mathematical Problems in Engineering 8, 265–279 (2002)

11. The Network Simulator NS-2: http://www.isi.edu/nsnam/ns/
12. Cao, J., Cleveland, W.S., Gao, Y., Jeffay, K., Smith, E D., Weigle, M.: Stochastic models for generating synthetic http source traffic. In: Proc. IEEE INFOCOM, Hong Kong, Mar 2004, pp. 1547–1558. IEEE Computer Society Press, Los Alamitos (2004)
13. Guo, L., Matta, I.: The war between mice and elephants. In: ICNP '01: Proceedings of the Ninth International Conference on Network Protocols, Washington, DC, USA, p. 180. IEEE Computer Society Press, Los Alamitos (2001)
14. Paxson, V., Floyd, S.: Wide area traffic: the failure of poisson modeling networking. IEEE/ACM Transactions on 3, 226–244 (1995)

An Analytical Approach to the Efficient Real-Time Events/Services Handling in Converged Network Environment

Natalia Kryvinska[1], Peter Zinterhof[1], and Do van Thanh[2]

[1] Department of Scientific Computing, University of Salzburg,
Jakob-Haringer-Str. 2, 5020 Salzburg, Austria
n-v-kryvinska@gmx.net, peter.zinterhof@sbg.ac.at
[2] Department of Telematics, Norwegian University of Science and Technology,
O.S. Bragstads plass 2B, N-7491 Trondheim, Norway
thanh-van.do@telenor.com

Abstract. Converged network seamlessly integrates different communications media such as data, voice and multimedia on a single platform. It refers to convergence both types of network and technologies as well as convergence between the different layers of network architecture. In this paper, we examine a priority-based queuing model and perform the mathematical analysis of different media calls processing in converged network environment. We use for this purpose a queuing system model M3/G3/1/NPRP in order to process effectively input jobs/requests (or packets). Tasks within this queuing system get a higher priority if they are handling a real-time event. We present in our paper mathematical results of the expected response and waiting time, and build hypothetical diagrams for the further practical usage in real-time system. A modeling method developed in this paper will be used for the fast configuration and testing of new converged network applications and services.

Keywords: Converged Network, M3/G3/1 priority-based queuing model, Non-PRe-emptive Priority (NPRP), Real-time Event, VoIP, Integrated Services.

1 Introduction

Networks of today and tomorrow are built on the convergence of voice, multimedia, and data. In this environment, data networks carry voice, video, and data traffic along a managed, secure, and transparent backbone. A converged network affords interoperability among differing communication platforms and allows to have the full range of possibilities that bandwidth allows. This network moves toward a single protocol that can handle the convergence of multiple data types. The marketplace trend is undoubtedly on the way to tighter and better integration of networks because of increased technical performance and lower total IT costs. But, a converged network must be standardized and robust enough in order to handle audio, video, and e-business transactions with the higher requirement degree of security. It has to

T. Enokido, L. Barolli, and M. Takizawa (Eds.): NBiS 2007, LNCS 4658, pp. 308–316, 2007.

integrate seamlessly different communication types: for the delivering of e-mails and faxes that can be read over the PC or the phone, to allow for the live videoconferencing, and to let users initiate and receive phone calls at the PC [1, 2, 4].

Mainly, information exchanged over the public telecommunication networks has been voice. Present voice communication networks (e.g., Intelligent Networks) utilize digital technology via circuit-switching. The circuit-switching establishes a dedicated path (circuit) between the source and destination. This environment provides fixed bandwidth, short and controlled delay. It provides satisfactory quality of services and does not require a complicated encoding algorithm. Also, in circuit switching, capacity and resources cannot be shared by other users, thereby hindering the system's overall efficiency. In packet-switched network, data is split into packets containing destination identification that are sent and routed independently. It implements store-and-forward switching of discrete data units (packets), and implies statistical multiplexing. This is an ideal environment for non real-time data, where the performance of a best-effort delivery model in terms of throughput is more desirable than delivery of packets within bounded delay and jitter. Crudely sending voice or video data over such a network will lead to poor and even unacceptable quality [3, 5].

To transport voice (e.g., real-time media) over a packet-switched network, it is required a mechanism (e.g., Voice over Internet Protocol - VoIP). The goal of VoIP is to provide the efficiency of a packet-switched network while rivaling the quality of a circuit-switched network. The quality of VoIP does not yet match the quality of a circuit-switched telephone network, but there is an abundance of activity in developing protocols and speech encoders for the implementation of the high quality voice service. The redoubtable problem is that the Internet was designed for data communications; consequently, packets suffer a long and variable delay that decreases voice quality. To overcome this problem, protocols are being developed to provide a certain share of network resources for each voice call through the network. On the whole, many proprietary technologies for VoIP are available, and it is expected that these applications expand as the technologies mature into certified standards - forming a single standard that is an amalgamation of current schemes [4].

In order to overcome mentioned above problems while transporting real-time media in packet-switched networks, we examine in this paper a priority-based queuing system model for the performance of the mathematical analysis of different media calls processing in converged network environment. We assign prioritization rules for different categories of requests (e.g., packets), taking into consideration their importance. Tasks within a queuing system get a higher priority if they are handling a real-time event [4, 6, 14].

We present in our paper theoretical results of the expected response and waiting time in order to build hypothetical diagrams for the further practical usage. To be precise, we give normalized values of main parameters (e.g., arrival rate, service time, time in system). And, when applying real values of λ and μ, we have possibility to compare theoretical and practical results (for example, comparison of the theoretical values of time in system T, with practical ones), which gives great opportunity to modify and/or adjust real parameters for the better performance of the whole system.

2 Priority Queuing Models for the Real-Time Events Handling

In practical queuing systems (e.g., telecommunication and computer networks), demand consists of jobs of different types. These job types may or may not have different arrival and service characteristics. Rather than treat them all equally and serve them in a first-in first-out (FIFO) order or according to some symmetric scheduling policy, it is often desirable to discriminate among the different job types, giving a better quality of service to some, at the expense of others. The usual mechanism for doing that is to operate some sort of priority policy [7, 9].

Lets us assume that there are K job types, numbered 1, 2, ..., K. Type i jobs arrive in an independent Poisson process with rate λ_i; their service requirements have some general distributions, with mean $s_{1i}(1/\mu_i)$ and second moment s_{2i} $(1/\mu_i^2)$, where $i = 1, 2, \ldots, K$. For each type, we establish a separate unbounded queue, where jobs wait in order of arrival. The service is provided by a single server (Figure 1).

The different queues are served according to a priority assignment, which is assumed to be in inverse order of type indices. Thus, type 1 has the highest priority, type 2 the second highest, ..., type K the lowest. Whenever a scheduling decision has to be made as to which job to serve next, the job selected is the one at the head of the highest priority (lowest index) non-empty queue. This means, of course, that a type i job may start service only if queues 1, 2, ..., i-1, are empty (i=2, 3, ..., K) [8, 10, 11].

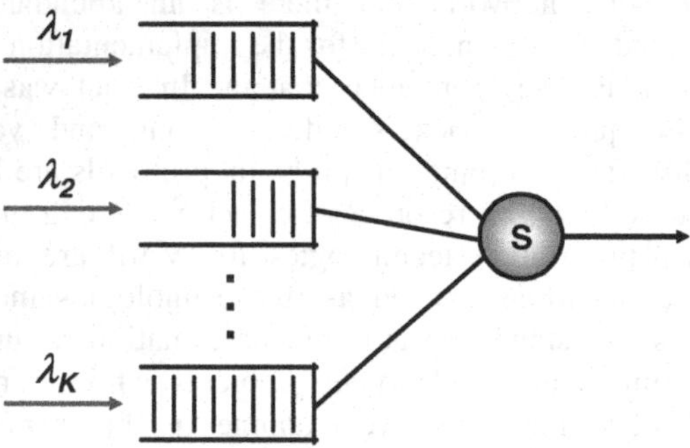

Fig. 1. Queuing system with single server

In computer communication networks users or jobs are assigned as a priority-based on their importance. Tasks within an operating system get a higher priority if they need to handle a real-time event. On communication links short messages are often given priority over long messages, and status or control messages are given priority over data messages.

There are two types of priority scheme. With head-of-line systems, also known as non-preemptive systems, once a customer has commenced service, he or she will not be interrupted by a higher priority customer who arrives after service has started. The higher priority customer will join the waiting-line ahead of any lower priority customers present, and within the same priority class customers are served first-come-first-served.

The other type of priority scheme is called pre-emptive, where a higher priority customer will pre-empt the server if the server is dealing with a lower priority customer. Once the higher priority customer has been served, service of the lower priority customer will resume where it left off. Complex sequences of the server switching between customers of several different priorities may occur, where an arriving customer pre-empts the server, only to be pre-empted in turn by a later-arriving yet-higher priority customer [11, 13].

It is important to note that both of these priority schemes require priority to be assigned to classes of customers independent of individual service-times. It may be that classes of customers do in fact have different service-times, either constant per class or different distribution per class. If customers are assigned a priority-based on their individual service-time requirements, then a different analysis is needed [12, 16].

In our article, for the implementation of the real-time services in packet-based infrastructure, we select non-preemptive scheme, which allows data packets not to be thrown from serving system, when a packet with higher priority comes. What does it give to the users that send data information (e.g., faxes, documentation, different text files, and so on) through the network? One of the main parameters of QoS in non real-time systems is the delivery of complete, not destroyed, not lost, and so on, information. With non-preemptive scheme in converged network, we support these requirements.

But, what does it give for the users of real-time services. For them, the main parameter of QoS is delivery time (e.g., minimum delivery delay). Giving them higher priority, we also can support them with good QoS.

And, finally, what does prioritization bring for converged network at all? It allows to support both types of services (e.g., non real-time and real-time) with tolerable QoS.

In the next section, we present and motivate $M_3/G_3/1/NPRP$ queuing system (based on non-preemptive priority scheme) usage in our network model.

3 An Analysis of Main Network Parameters by M3/G3/1/NPRP System

In this section, we perform a mathematical analysis of the main network/system parameters (e.g., waiting time, time in system) in converged network using non-preemptive scheme. For this purpose, we use well-known M/G/1 queuing system.

The arrival process is assumed to be Poisson distribution, which means the incoming packet's process is Markovian (**M**/G/1). The pattern of the service time distribution in the queuing system is general distribution (M/**G**/1) in order to have more precise formulas for waiting time and average time in system. The packets arrive into the serving system have difference in length and service time, which will widely vary (eg., this is not modeled by exponential distribution, but more *general distribution*). There three levels of priority will be considered (e.g., for multimedia packets – the highest, first class; for voice packets – the second, and for the data – the lowest, third class) according to their importance. The serving system is based on a single server (M/G/**1**), which means only one-server treats the packets from all input queues. The packets are served according to the **N**on-**PR**e-emptive **P**riority discipline. So, the proposed model is called as $M_3/G_3/1/NPRP$ (Figure 2) [9, 11].

The definition of the scheduling policy is to specify what happens if a higher priority job arrives and finds a lower priority one in service. One possibility is to take no action other than place the new arrival in its queue and await the scheduling decision that will be made on completing the current service. The priorities are then said to be non-preemptive, or head-of-the-line. The condition for stability is that the total load should be less than 1: $\rho_1+\rho_2+\ldots+\rho_k < 1$.

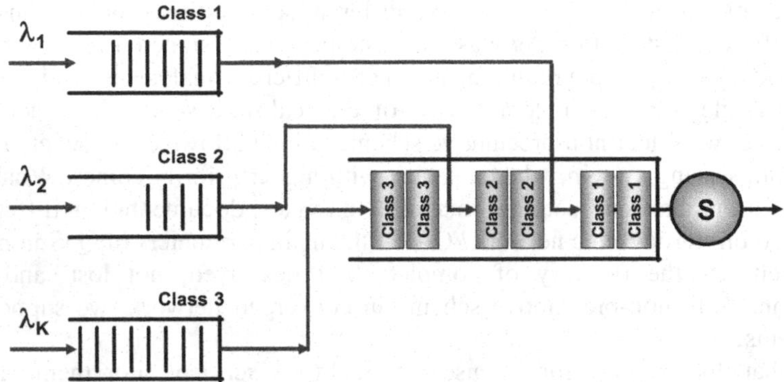

Fig. 2. $M_3/G_3/1$ NPRP system

We use the following characteristics. There are *n* classes of customers. A class-1 has priority over class-2, which in turn has priority over class-3, and so on. For each class of customer we specify the parameters [11, 12, 17]:

λ_j - arrival rate, $j=1\ldots n$;
T_{Sj} - average service-time, $j=1\ldots n$;
C^2_{Sj} – coefficient of variation squared for the service time, $j=1\ldots n$.

The total arrival rate is

$$\lambda=\lambda_1+\lambda_2+\ldots+\lambda_n=\sum_{j=1}^{n}\lambda_j \tag{1}$$

The *j*-th partial traffic intensity is the traffic intensity up to and including the *j*-th customer class is

$$u_j=\sum_{i=1}^{j}\lambda_i T_{Si} \qquad j=1,\ldots,n. \tag{2}$$

We define that $u_0=0$, and the total server utilization is $\rho=u_n$.
The second moment of service-time for each customer class is

$$s_{2j}=T_{Sj}^2\left(1+C_{Sj}^2\right) \tag{3}$$

The second moment of overall service time is

$$s_2 = \sum_{i=1}^{n} \frac{\lambda_i}{\lambda} s_{2i} \tag{4}$$

For non-preemptive priority system, with a head-of-line scheme, once a customer has commenced service that customer will not be interrupted by a customer of higher priority who arrives later. It is necessary to have $\rho < 1$, for the system to be stable.

The average waiting time for each class is

$$T_{W_j} = \frac{\lambda_{S2}}{2(1-u_{j-1})(1-u_j)} \qquad j = 1,\ldots,n. \tag{5}$$

The average waiting time over all classes is

$$T_W = \sum_{j=1}^{n} \frac{\lambda_i}{\lambda} T_{Wj} \tag{6}$$

The average time in system we obtain using the basic relationship that time in system is service time plus waiting time. This we apply to each class, and then the weighted average is taken to get the overall average time in system. The average time in system for each class is

$$T = T_W + T_S \tag{7}$$

And, the average time [4, 6] in system overall is

$$T = \sum_{j=1}^{n} \frac{\lambda_i}{\lambda} T_j \tag{8}$$

In Figure 3, we show the average waiting time for each class and over all classes. We use normalized values of main parameters (e.g., arrival rate - λ, and service rate - μ). According to the most important teletraffic theory balance equation (e.g., system stability), where λ/μ must always be less than <1, in this study, we set $\mu = 1$, and change λ on interval from 0.001 (e.g., about zero) till 0.999 (e.g., it is not allowed to reach "1" because of system balance/stability). Different variants of λ and μ distributions are needed to be studied. But, it is out of scope of this paper. The y-axis presents the normalized values of waiting time in the queue (Figure 3) and the time in the system (Figure 4) [12, 18].

From the diagram presented in Figure 3, we can make the following conclusions. According to calculations done using formulas (1) ÷ (6), the longest waiting time is T_{W3}, obtained for the lowest, 3rd priority class (e.g., for the data packets). The shortest waiting time - T_{W1}, is for packets from multimedia users. For the 2nd priority class packets (e.g., from voice users), the waiting time does not differ so much from the 1st class. It shows that voice packets will have to wait in the queue only little bit longer than multimedia packets. So, we can say that QoS requirements (e.g., minimal waiting delay) are met for the first and the second priority classes. For the third class packets this parameter is not important. The average waiting time - T_W over all classes has pattern similar to the 3rd class waiting time - T_{W3}, but values are lower than T_{W3}. It can be easily predictable from the equation (6). In priority-based network, average waiting time or average time in system over all classes is not an important parameter, since it is more abstract feature. It is used to check whether the results of calculations of waiting time for every class are correct.

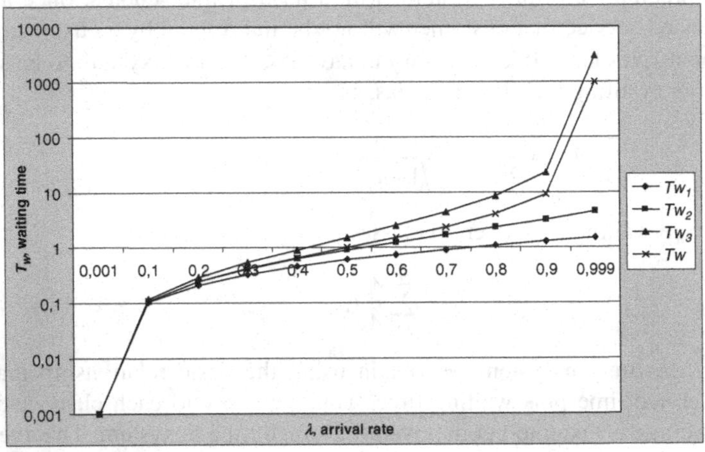

Fig. 3. Average waiting time for each class and over all classes

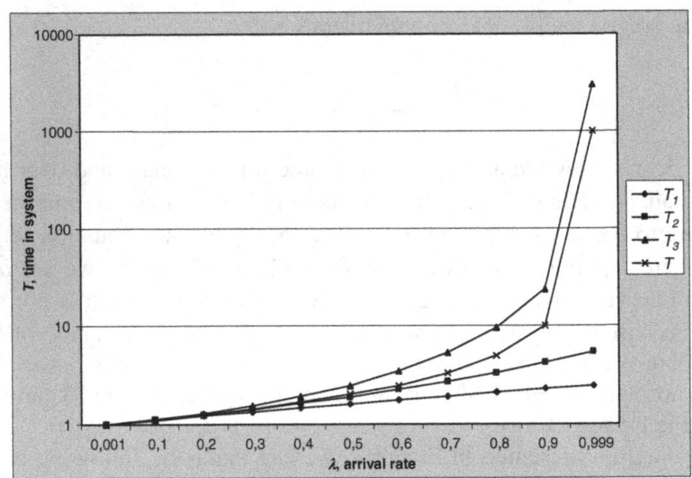

Fig. 4. Average time in system for each class and over all classes

The calculations of the average time in system are done using formulas (1) ÷ (8). The numerical results for the expected time, that a packet spends in system, which is the sum of waiting time in the queue and service time, are given in Figure 4. From the Figure 4 we can see that the time which a packet with the highest priority (e.g., multimedia) spends in system does not make big influence on the traffic from the 2nd priority (e.g., voice), what is very important for the real-time event handling, e.g., QoS support. And, the time in system, as well as the waiting time for the third priority class packets will be very high with high rates of the server utilization (e.g., when the packets with higher than 3rd priority class are coming with high rate λ).

But, we can see also the difference in shapes in Figures 3 and 4 when the λ gets values from 0÷0.1. The waiting time growing dramatically in logarithmic scale (Figure 3), while the time in system - smoothly (Figure 4). This happens because of no packets arrive at the beginning of this interval, so every packet arrives (e.g., from any class) will not have to wait in queue or wait very short time. And, from this point packets from the 3rd priority start to wait because higher priority packets are coming [11, 19].

4 Conclusions

Converged networks deliver a new generation of integrated data, voice, and multimedia applications on a single platform. This allows reducing of maintenance costs by eliminating redundant hardware, communications facilities and supporting staff. But, real-time applications have different characteristics and requirements from those of traditional data applications. Because of their real-time nature, voice and multimedia applications tolerate minimal variation of delay affecting delivery of their packets. These kinds of traffic are also intolerant of packet loss, out-of-order packets, and jitter, all of which gravely degrade the quality of the voice and multimedia transmission delivered to the recipient end user. To effectively transport voice/multimedia traffic over IP, the special mechanisms are required that ensure reliable delivery of packets with low and controlled delay [4, 6, 13].

In order to meet mentioned above requirements while transporting real-time media in packet-switched networks, we examined in this paper a priority-based queuing system model for the performance of the mathematical analysis of different media calls processing in converged network environment. We assigned prioritization rules for different categories of requests (e.g., packets), taking into consideration their importance. Tasks within a queuing system get a higher priority if they are handling a real-time event.

We built here a theoretical model that will be used for the calibration of working system/network performance parameters. For instance, it is possible using the model to determine what the processing rate should be for a certain arrival rate to obtain a certain waiting time.

Exactly in the "calibration" feature is laying a high value of this mathematical model since a certain processing rate can be obtained by adding more processors, more memory, etc.

References

1. Hall, P.: The evolution of managed network services in an application-centric world, Extracted from an Ovum report, Ovum (May 2006)
2. White paper: Unified Communications in a Converged Network, Electronic Data Systems Corporation (February 2002)

3. White paper: Operational Excellence in Triple Play Service Delivery: The Role of Policy-Enabled Subscriber Service Management, Alcatel, Bridgwater Systems, 08 (2005)
4. Doshi, B.T., Eggenschwiler, D., Rao, A., Samadi, B., Wang, Y.T., Wolfson, J.: VoIP Network Architectures and QoS Strategy. Bell Labs Technical Journal 7(4), 41–59 (2003)
5. White paper: Route Analysis for Converged Networks: Filling the Layer 3Gap in VoIP Management, Packet Design (2005)
6. Technical Report MS-CIS-01-31: Overview of Voice over IP, University of Pennsylvania (February 2001)
7. Dziong, Z., Liao, K.-Q., Mason, L.G.: Flow control models for multi-service networks with delayed call set up. In: Dziong, Z., Liao, K.-Q., Mason, L.G. (eds.) Proceedings of IEEE INFOCOM'90, pp. 39–46. IEEE Computer Society Press, Los Alamitos (1990)
8. Tijms, H.: Stochastic Modeling and Analysis - A Computational Approach. John Wiley & Sons, Chichester (1986)
9. Mitrani, I.: Probabilistic modelling. Cambridge University Press, Cambridge (1998)
10. Koole, G., Nain, P.: On the value function of a priority queue with an application to a controlled polling model. Springer Queueing Systems 34, 199–214 (2000)
11. Tanner, M.: Practical Queueing Analysis, IBM McGraw-Hill Series (1995)
12. Kleinrock, L., Gail, R.: Solution Manual for Queueing Systems. Computer Applications, Technology Transfer Institute, vol. II (1986)
13. Position Paper: Centralized vs. distributed IP Telephony systems - Convergence options for the customer-driven enterprise, Nortel Networks (2005)
14. Special Report by NetworkWorld. In: Denoia, L., Randall, T., Bennett, S., Taylor, S., Hettick, L., Greene, T. (eds.) Planning and Migration Strategies for IP Telephony, NetworkWorld (2005)
15. Howard, R.A.: Dynamic Programming and Markov Process. The MIT Press, Cambridge, Massachusetts (1960)
16. Tcha, D., Jin, C., Lutz, S.: Link-by-link bandwidth allocation in an integrated voice/data network using the fuzzy set approach. Computer Networks and ISDN Systems 1988/89 16, 217–227 (1988/1989)
17. Ash, G.: Dynamic Routing in Telecommunications Networks. McGraw-Hill, New York (1998)
18. Field, A.J., Harrison, P.G., Bradley, J.T., Harder, U.: Modelling Techniques and Tools for Computer Performance Evaluation. Elsevier Journal Special Issue Performance Evaluation 54(2), 77–206 (2003)
19. Harrison, P.G., Patel, N.M.: Performance modelling of communication systems and computer architectures. Addison-Wesley, Reading (1993)

Command Transition Probability Analysis on Mobile Internet Command Sequences

Toshihiko Yamakami

[1] ACCESS, 2-8-16 Sarugaku-cho, Chiyoda-ku, Tokyo, 101-0064 Japan
Toshihiko.Yamakami@access-company.com
[2] Graduate School of Engineering, Kagawa University, 2217-20 Hayashi-cho, Takamatsu-city, Kagawa, 761-0396 Japan

Abstract. We have witnessed rapid growth of mobile Internet capabilities in the mobile handsets. The penetration of the user life increases the need to establish a methodology to capture the user behavior patterns in order to improve satisfaction of the mobile web users. In order to cope with the design evaluation needs, the author proposes a long-term command transition probability analysis on mobile clickstreams. The observation showed that the first command ratio did not depend on the menu order, but that the ratio to terminate the command sequence depended on the order. This gives a positive outcome from the command transition analysis in the mobile clickstream.

1 Introduction

We have witnessed explosive growth of mobile handsets capable of Internet access. The Internet access from mobile handsets exceeded that from PC in Japan. The number of wireless IP-connected users reached 85.2 million users in Japan in May 2007, which was 89.1 % of total wireless subscribers. This high penetration demands content providers to improve their capability to design and evaluate mobile web. The mobile Internet users are characterized as *easy-come and easy-go*. With the user interface limitation, it is difficult to ask users why they came and why they are leaving. This prompts the need to develop some methodologies to complement the lack of the direct user feedbacks. The author assumes the long-term mobile clickstream can be a source to obtain implications of the mobile web menu structure to improve the user interface design. The user identifiers provided by wireless carriers enables the long-term observation. In order to facilitate user feedbacks to the mobile web menu structures, the author proposes a command transition analysis using long-term mobile clickstream logs. The paper describes the method to identify the command transition patterns and implications from the exploratory analysis.

T. Enokido, L. Barolli, and M. Takizawa (Eds.): NBiS 2007, LNCS 4658, pp. 317–324, 2007.

2 Purpose of the Research and Related Works

2.1 Purpose of the Research

The aim of this study is to identify a methodology to extract the feedbacks for user interface design using real mobile clickstream logs to facilitate efficient design-implement-feedback cycle in the mobile Internet.

2.2 Related Works

The mobile clickstream catches researchers' attention with the advance of the wireless Internet. Yamakami performed the regularity analysis in the mobile Internet with time slot count [1]. Halvey presented the significance of time of day in mobile clickstreams [2] to indicate the weekday/weekend user behavior differences. Halvey showed that the day-of-week-based Markov models explain WAP logs better than the models without day-of-week considerations [3]. The mobile web design evaluation using user trackable long-term logs was unexplored in the past literature. It should be noted that the mobile clickstream analysis is obscured due to widespread WML 1.x use with multiple cards per page. The widespread use of Compact HTML enabled detailed user interaction analysis in Japan.

3 Method

In order to improve the mobile web design, it is critical to get the user feedbacks for the web design. The mobile clickstream is a resource that is available in most of the web services. The unique characteristics of the mobile Internet include the user identifiers provided by the wireless carriers to enable content charging. The author considers this long-term user-trackable clickstream log can be used to identify the implicit user feedbacks to the mobile web design.

The author proposes a transition probability comparison method to identify long-term transitions of user navigation to obtain user behavior characteristics to a specific mobile web. The processing flow for monthly transition probability analysis is depicted in Fig. 1.

The detailed flow in the preprocessing part is outlined in Fig. 2. The preprocessing program can support two levels of threshold values to identify sessions: 500 seconds and 14400 seconds (4 hours). In this research, the author uses only the short-term sessions with 500-second timeout values. In the drawing part, the command groups are split into news article groups with labels (c_n : where n is 1, 2, ...) and other groups with label *misc*. Each label denotes a separate news category. The *misc* groups include subscribing, unsubscribing and other services. Other services include quiz, keyword alert registration, and weekly keyword ranking news. In this article, the author uses the P notation: $P(c_i \rightarrow c_k)$ denotes the probability from the c_i command groups to the c_k command groups when a user performs one of the c_i command groups. The transitions within the same command groups are illustrated with circles with arrows.

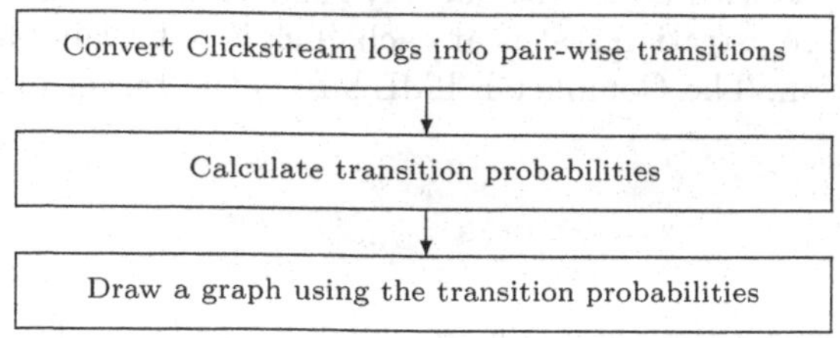

Fig. 1. Outline of Processing Flow

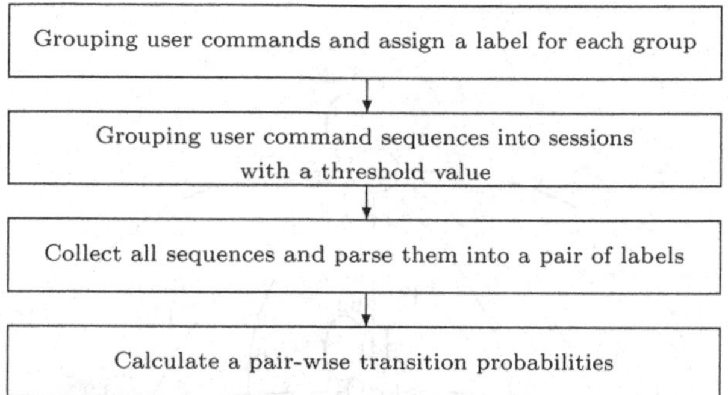

Fig. 2. Outline of Preprocessing Flow

The author implemented an analysis system for the mobile clickstreams. The data sources are monthly mobile clickstream logs with user identifiers (UIDs). The preprocessing part was implemented by PHP ver 4.12 [4]. The calculation and graph drawing parts were implemented by R ver 2.1.1 [5].

4 A Case Study

4.1 Data Set

The observation target is a commercial news service in the mobile Internet. The service is available on the three different mobile carriers. The service is charged for monthly subscription fee. The log stores the unique user identifier, time stamped, command name and content shorthand name. The services were launched from 2000 to 2001, and continue up to today. The target service provides 40 to 50 news articles per week on weekdays. the commercial mobile service charges the monthly subscription fee to the users, approximately 3 US dollars per month. UID is usually 16 or more unique alphanumeric character long, e.g. "310SzyZjaaerYlb2". The service uses Compact HTML [6], HDML, and MML that is a dialect of HTML. The site can be accessible from registered and non-registered users. Many non-registered users have only short sessions. In order to exclude this non-registered users, the author performed the preprocessing to exclude clickstreams with users without any registration records from Aug 2000 to July 2002. The registration status at each click is not available, but this gives some approximation. The Compact HTML site is the target of research in this paper.

4.2 Result

The author performed the command sequence transitions. For each node, the sum of the probabilities on the outgoing arcs is 100 %, including the self-destination arc. A Compact HTML based service's command transition probabilities during January 2001 to March 2001 depicted in Fig. 3.

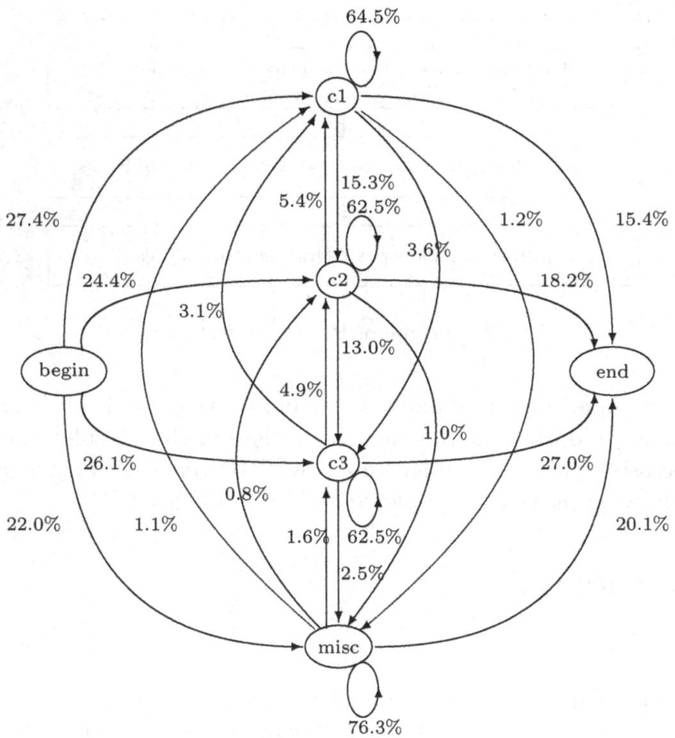

Fig. 3. Transition Probability among Command Groups (A Compact HTML site, Jan 2001 - March 2001)

The transition probabilities in Aug 2000, Nov 2000, Feb 2001, and May 2001 are shown in Figs. 4, 5, 6, and 7, respectively. The transition probabilities are approximately same with small differences in each month. The notable difference for each arc probability comparison are $P(begin \rightarrow c2)$ pattern with 17.4 % and 29.1 % and $P(begin \rightarrow misc)$ with 32.7 % and 19.3 %, in Aug 2000 and May 2001.

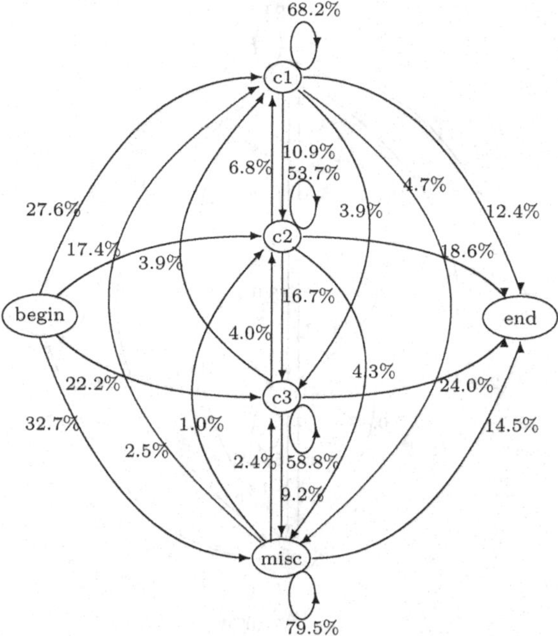

Fig. 4. Transition Probability among Command Groups (Aug 2000)

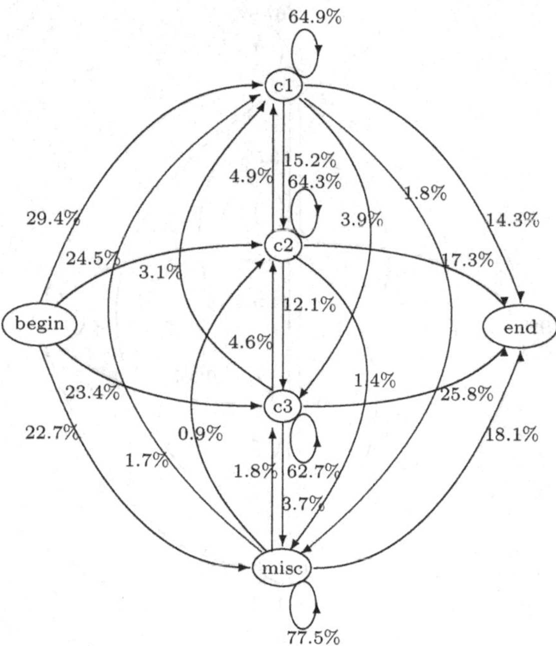

Fig. 5. Transition Probability among Command Groups (Nov 2000)

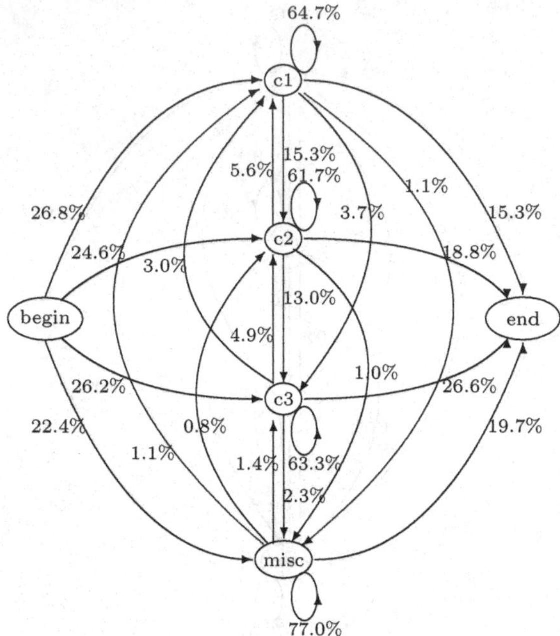

Fig. 6. Transition Probability among Command Groups (Feb 2001)

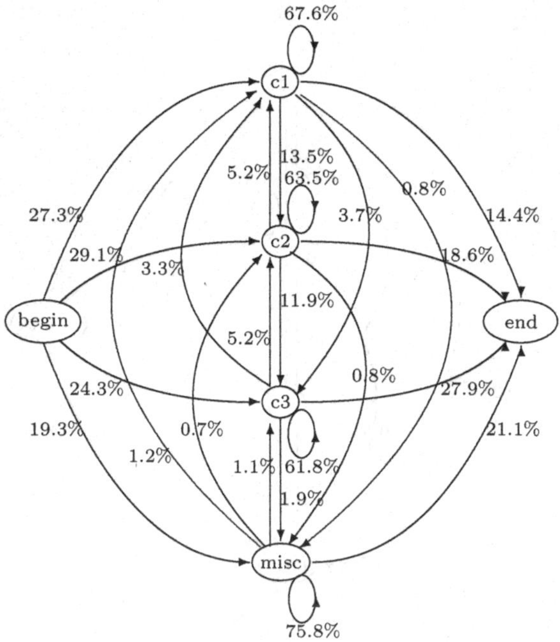

Fig. 7. Transition Probability among Command Groups (May 2001)

4.3 Discussion

The author examined the transition probability graphs and identifies the following three patterns:

- The first command ratio in a session,
- The last command ratio in a session, and
- The stay ratio within a command group

These three factors are considered to be the user preference to the group.

From observation, the first command ratio is generally divided into three different groups. This indicates that the user preference is reflected to the first command choice. The last command ratio is biased to the last category (c_3). This indicates that the user has the tendency to move from top to down and ends at the final category. In this sense, the menu reordering may impact the order of reading. The last command ratio, the ratio to the end state, may relate to the user satisfaction. However, the highest ratio in the last category is likely attributed to the menu order. The stay ratio within a command group seems stable from 53 % to 79 %. The stay ratio for the first group (c_1) is slightly higher than the other groups except misc groups. It is highest in all the four observations. This may relate to the easiness of access from the menu order.

This observation shows the importance of the menu order. The order may not impact the ratio of access, but the reading order is impacted by the menu order from the author's observation. The transition ratio $P(c_1 \rightarrow c_2)$ or $P(c_2 \rightarrow c_3)$ is always higher (double or triple) compared to the reverse directions. On the contrary, $P(c_1 \rightarrow c_3)$ and $P(c_3 \rightarrow c_1)$ are similar in all four cases.

From the graph, the author considered the effect of the menu order to the first command is not significant despite of the author's expectation. The first command ratio is slightly biased to the first menu (c_1), but it did not match the author's expectation in advance. The reordering of the menu is not needed from this observation. The personalized reordering may be useful, but it needs further investigation.

The challenges in the mobile web design include a) simplicity of the menu structure and b) frequently updated volatile content. Both factors come from the user interface constraints, The result shows that the long-term observation enables identification of service-specific user navigation patterns under these challenges.

4.4 Limitations

This method can be applicable to a wide range of mobile applications with clickstream logs. The limitations of this study include cross-service comparisons and verifications with user assessment to follow-up the implications.

The author used ad hoc time out values to identify sessions. The proper value to identify the sessions is for further studies.

The target web sites have the free headline news at the top of the menu choice. The logs to the free part were not logged for this analysis.

The data set was obtained from the 2001 data. The basic interaction patterns to access periodically updated news articles in the mobile Internet are supposed to be similar. Also, the major content language for mobile Internet shifts from WML 1.x to XHTML Mobile Profile, or even full HTML in some cases. This trend is aligned to the study based on Compact HTML. However, it is better to verify in the recent data.

5 Conclusions

As the mobile Internet penetrates into every-day life, it increases importance to coin a methodology to capture user feedbacks. In order to capture implicit user feedbacks, the author used long-term user-trackable mobile clickstream logs. The author proposed a command-transition probability analysis to identify the user interface design guidelines and long-term transitions on user navigation patterns. The author identified the menu order impacts on the command-transition probability patterns. The author showed the fact that the menus order does not impact the first command choice for users, but impacts the cross-category transitions. This gives positive evaluation for the command transition probability analysis to obtain feedbacks from mobile clickstreams for the mobile Internet user design. The method is based on clickstream logs, therefore, it is applicable to a wide range of mobile web applications.

References

1. Yamakami, T.: Regularity analysis using time slot counting in the mobile clickstream. In: Proceedings of DEXA2006 workshops, pp. 55–59. IEEE Computer Society Press, Los Alamitos (2006)
2. Halvey, M., Keane, M., Smyth, B.: Predicting navigation patterns on the mobile-internet using time of the week. In: WWW2005, pp. 958–959. ACM Press, New York (2005)
3. Halvey, M., Keane, M., Smyth, B.: Time based patterns in mobile-internet surfing. In: CHI'06, pp. 31–34. Springer, Heidelberg (2006)
4. The PHP Group: Php hypertext processor (2003), available at `http://www.php.net/`
5. R Development Core Team: R: A language and environment for statistical computing. R Foundation for Statistical Computing, Vienna, Austria (2005) ISBN 3-900051-07-0
6. Kamada, T.: Compact HTML for small information appliances. W3C Note (Febraury 9, 1998) (1998), available at: `http://www.w3.org/TR/1998/NOTE-compactHTML-19980209`

A Solution for Congestion and Performance Enhancement by Dynamic Packet Bursting in Mobile Ad Hoc Networks

Young-Duk Kim, Yeon-Mo Yang, and Dong-Ha Lee

Daegu Gyeongbuk Institute of Science and Technology (DGIST)
Deoksan-Dong 110, Jung-Gu, Daegu, 700-742, Korea
{ydkim,yangym,dhlee}@dgist.org

Abstract. In mobile ad hoc networks, most of on demand routing protocols such as DSR and AODV do not deal with traffic load during the route discovery procedure. To solve the congestion and achieve load balancing, many protocols have been proposed. However, existing load balancing schemes just avoid the congested route in the route discovery procedure or find an alternative route during a communication session. To solve this problem, we propose a new scheme which uses the packet bursting mechanism in congested nodes. The packet bursting, which is originally introduced in IEEE 802.11e QoS specification, is to transmit multiple packets after channel acquisition. Thus, congested node can forward buffered packets quickly and prevent bottleneck. Each node begins to transmit packets in normal mode whenever its congested status is dissolved. We also propose two threshold values to define exact overloaded status adaptively; one is interface queue length and the other is buffer occupancy time. Through a experimental simulation study, we compare our protocol with normal on demand routing protocols and show that the proposed scheme is more efficient and effective especially when network traffic is heavily loaded.

Keywords: Ad hoc networks, Medium Access Control (MAC), Packet bursting, Load balancing.

1 Introduction

A mobile ad hoc network (MANET) is a self-configuring network of mobile hosts connected by wireless links without fixed infrastructure like a base station. In MANETs hosts are free to move randomly, and thus network topologies may change rapidly and unpredictably. Devising an efficient routing protocols for MANETs has been a challenging issue and DSDV (Destination Sequence Distance Vector) [1], DSR (Dynamic Source Routing) [2], AODV (Ad-hoc On-demand Distance Vector) [3] are such protocols for tackling the issue. One of the most popular MAC protocols for MANETs is the IEEE 802.11 [4, 5] which defines the distributed coordinated function (DCF) as a fundamental channel access mechanism to support asynchronous data transfer.

T. Enokido, L. Barolli, and M. Takizawa (Eds.): NBiS 2007, LNCS 4658, pp. 325–334, 2007.

Recently, the requirements for real time and multimedia data traffic have been requested more seriously. In this situation, the occurrence of congestion is inevitable in MANETs due to their limited bandwidth constraints. Furthermore, by the route cache mechanism in the existing protocols, the route reply from intermediate node during the route discovery procedure leads to traffic concentration on a certain node. When a node is congested, several problems can occur such as packet loss by buffer overflows, long end-to-end delay of data packets, poor packet delivery ratio, and much control packet overhead related to reinitiating the route discovery procedure. In addition, the congested node consumes more energy to route lots of packets, resulting in much more network partitions.

In this paper, we propose a new effective scheme called Dynamic Packet Bursting Algorithm (DPBA), which is intended to dissolve traffic congestion and can be easily implemented with current on demanding routing protocols such as AODV and DSR. This scheme is motivated from the IEEE 802.11e [6] QoS operation, which uses packet bursting mechanism. When a certain node is believed to be congested, it begins to make burst packets until overloaded status is dissolved. To decide whether congestion occurs or not, each node monitors number of packets in its interface queue and defines dynamical threshold values, which is the length of buffer and the period of packet buffered time. By using the packet bursting scheme in the congested node, we can achieve traffic alleviation, and improve performance in terms of packet delivery ratio and end-to-end delay, etc.

The rest of this paper is organized as the follows. In Section II, we review standard IEEE 802.11 MAC protocol including its enhanced version, IEEE 802.11e and other related works with load balancing. In Section III, we illustrate the detail operation of our proposed protocol. Performance evaluation by simulations is presented in Section IV. Finally, concluding remarks are given in Section V.

2 Related Works

2.1 IEEE 802.11 DCF Protocol

The overall operation of IEEE 802.11 DCF is described in Figure 1. The basic operation is a Carrier-Sense Multiple Access with Collision Avoidance (CSMA/CA) mechanism with a random back-off time. Before a station starts transmission, it should contend for shared medium. To avoid packet collision in transmission, the DCF also defines an optional mechanism for unicast frames, which are Request-To-Send (RTS) and Clear-To-Send (CTS) control frame. When the wireless medium is detected as idle for fixed interval, which is Distributed Inter-Frame Space (DIFS), the sender and receiver start to exchange RTS and CTS, respectively, prior to the actual data frame transmission to reserve the channel. Between control frames are transmitted, the Short Inter-Frame Space (SIFS), which is smaller than DIFS, is used. The other stations which overhear the RTS or CTS frame defer their transmission by maintaining Network Allocation Vector (NAV) which is a timer for the remaining time of any ongoing packet transmission. Another mechanism of the IEEE 802.11 is that an acknowledgment (Ack) frame which is sent by the receiver on successful reception of a data frame. The Short Inter-Frame Space (SIFS), which is smaller than

DIFS, is the time interval between reception of a data frame and transmission of its Ack frame. By using this small interval between transmissions, stations can prevent collision among others.

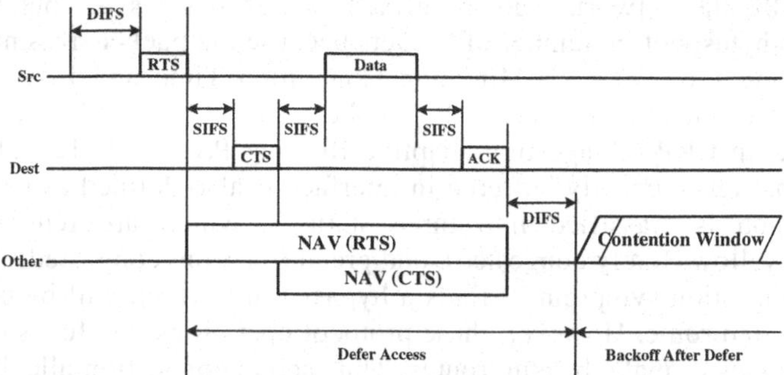

Fig. 1. IEEE 802.11 DCF

2.2 IEEE 802.11e QoS Specification

To support enhanced QoS, IEEE 802.11e is proposed to support QoS in WLANs, and it is aimed to support the transport of real time multimedia applications and defines a Transmission Opportunity (TXOP) in Hybrid Coordination Function (HCF) mode. The TXOP is the basic unit of allocation of the right to initiate transmission on the stations without any contention. When the station receives a QoS poll which contains the entire of TXOP during PCF mode called a polled TXOP. Transmission of two QoS data frames during a single TXOP is shown in Figure 2, where the entire of TXOP should be protected by the NAV set and whole transmission time for two data and Ack frames is less than the TXOP limit announced by the AP. Within a TXOP, all sequences nominally also separated by a SIFS.

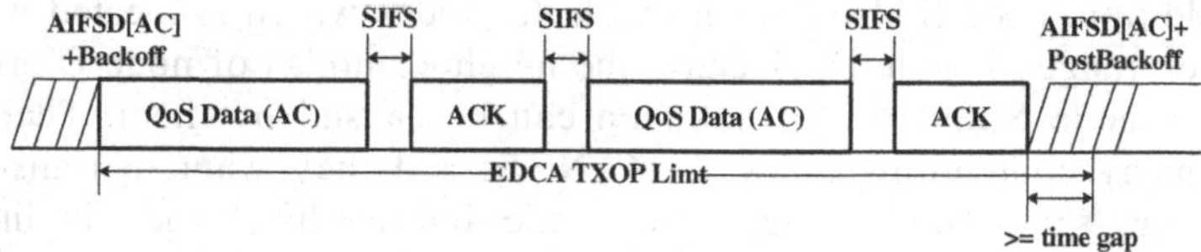

Fig. 2. IEEE 802.11e TXOP Bursting

2.3 Other Protocols with Load Balancing

There is OAR (Opportunistic Auto-rate) [7] which allows to transmit multiple packets at high quality channel. However OAR is based on multi rate environment and executes packet bursting for only a single flow, which congests next hop nodes, instead. Thus, it is not the solution for congestion. In network layer, there are many routing protocols that consider load balancing as the primary route selection criterion, which are as followed. In DLAR (Dynamic Load Aware Routing Protocol) [8], the network load is defined as total number of buffered packets. And in LBAR

(Load-Balanced Ad hoc Routing) [9], the network load is defined as total number of active routes passing through the node and its neighbors. During the route discovery procedure, load information on all paths from the source to a destination is forwarded to the destination node. In TSA (Traffic-Size Aware Routing) [10], the network load is defined as traffic sizes of routes, which is presented in bytes, not in number of packets because the packet sizes may vary. In MCL (Routing Protocol with Minimum Contention Time and Load Balancing) [10], the network load is defined as the number of neighbors which content with a source node. In CRP (Congestion-adaptive Routing Protocol) [12], although the number of packets currently buffered in interface is also defined as network load, the congestion is classified into three statuses, which are red (very likely congested), yellow (likely congested), and green (far from congested). If a node is aware of congestion symptom, it finds a bypass route which will be used instead of the congested route. However, these protocol operations just focus on avoiding congested routes or make backup routes. Thus actual congestion alleviation is not shown.

3 Basic Operation of DPBA

In this section, we present the proposed protocol DPBA to improve the performance by making burst packets when congestion occurs in mobile ad hoc networks.

3.1 Basic Operation

Most MAC protocol for MANETs use IEEE 802.11 described in the previous section. When a node S transmits a data frame to node D, it transmits a RTS frame to D and node D replies with a CTS frame. The other nodes that hear a control frame that is not destined to themselves defer their transmission. Thus, node S have to contend with neighbor nodes located within the transmission range of it. In addition, node S also contend with the nodes which is located within the transmission range of node D. Because the neighbor nodes of node D are hidden terminals to node S and packet collision can be caused by them. Therefore, if there are many contending nodes in MANETs and they want to transmit their frames at the same time, congestion at the intermediate node is inevitable. Moreover due to the contention with other nodes, total throughput is also degraded, which is described in figure 3.

Figure 3 shows a topology example of DPBA. There are three active routes which are (S3-N1-I-N5-D3), (S2-I-N4-D2), (S1-N2-I-N3-D1). When three sources transmit their packets to destinations, the intermediate node I can be easily congested. In addition, node I need three channel accesses in order to relay packets, which requires large overhead and increases end-to-end packet delay. To solve this problem, when the intermediate node detects congestion symptom, it transmits multiple packet by a packet bursting scheme.

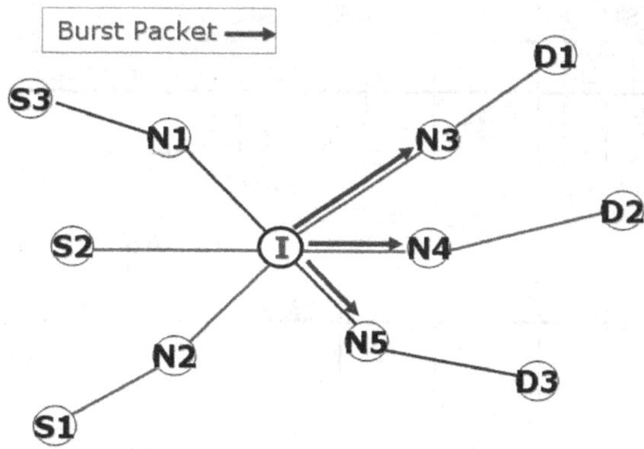

Fig. 3. Topology example for proposed scheme

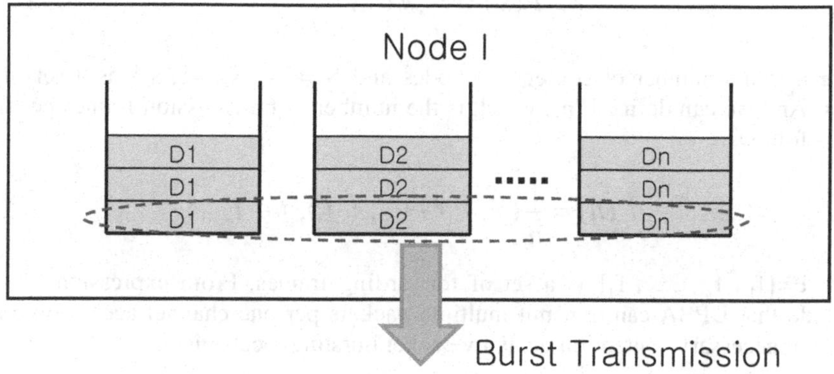

Fig. 4. Overal operation of DPBA

Figure 4 describes the basic operation of DPBA. In the MAC layer of each intermediate node, it maintains independent multiple queues for several data traffic. When the data packet is arrived at MAC layer from the network layer, DPBA module classifies them and stores in the appropriate queue by destination MAC address from frame header. If the intermediate node acquires the wireless channel access right, it can transmit multiple packets which are stored at the head of each separate queue by packet bursting.

The detail mechanism of DPBA for channel access is illustrated in figure 5. DPBA assumes that all nodes use IEEE 802.11 with RTS/CTS extension for channel access, which is explained in the previous section. When node I wins the channel contention, three data frames are transmitted in a burst packet. During the packet bursting period, there are no additional contention delay such as RTS/CTS exchange and DIFS. Node I exchanges only data and ack frames.

As shown in figure 5, when it is assumed that all nodes compete with each other for shared wireless channel, we can define $P(s_i)$, which is channel access probability of each node in the contention range.

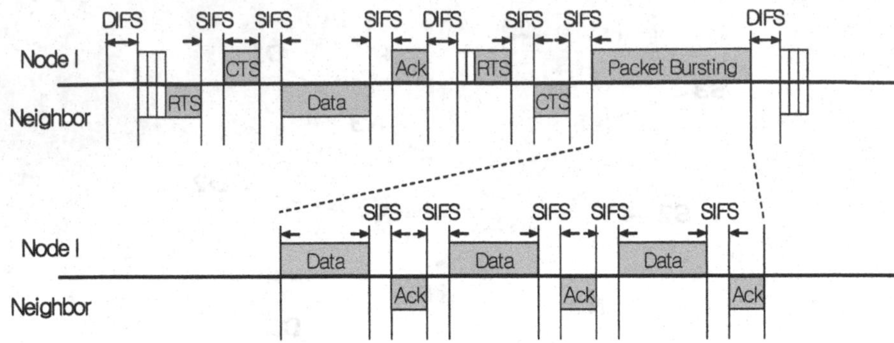

Fig. 5. Channel access mechanism of DPBA

$$P(s_i) = \frac{1}{n}, s_i \in S \tag{1}$$

where n is the number of contending nodes and S = $\{s_1, s_2, \ldots, s_n\}$ as a set of all nodes. And we can define F(n), which is the number of transmission frames per time unit as follows.

$$F(n) = \frac{1}{n}(f_1 + f_2 + \ldots + f_n), f_i \in F \tag{2}$$

where F=$\{f_1, f_2, \ldots, f_n\}$ is a set of forwarding frames. From expression (2), we conclude that DPBA can transmit multiple packets per one channel access time and reduce unnecessary contention delay by packet bursting mechanism.

3.2 Algorithm for Congestion Detection

When a node use DPBA scheme, it have to find out whether it is congested or not. Thus DPBA needs an adaptive algorithm for congestion detection.

Although DPBA is an efficient scheme for multiple packet transmission, unnecessary packet bursting may prevent channel acquisition opportunity of other nodes. So we define two threshold values which can detect the actual congestion status of the node. The first threshold is Queue-Threshold (Q_{max}) which is the number of buffered packets of interface queue. For example, when Q_{max} is 30 and a node buffered more than 30 packets, we believe that it is congestion environment.. The second threshold is Time-Threshold (T_{max}) which is the packet residence time in the interface queue when Q_{max} condition is satisfied. Q_{max} information alone is not enough to evaluate the actual load status of a node because the queue length can be high for a short period in a temporal situation even though the node is not overloaded. In addition, due to the various data rate of each node, packet process capacity is also different from each other. When time the packet residence time greater than T_{max}, we believe that it is real congested situation. Thus the node use DPBA to reduce traffic load.

4 Performance Evaluation

4.1 Simulation Environment

To evaluate the performance of the proposed protocol, we used the ns-2 simulator (version 2.28) [13] with AODV routing protocol. It is assumed that 50 mobile nodes are randomly placed in a 1500m x 300m rectangle network area. All mobile nodes moved freely at the given maximum speed of 10m/s with the pause time of 50 during the simulation time of 300 seconds. The radio propagation range for a node is set to 250m. The number of data connections are 20 and all source nodes generate constant bit rate (CBR) traffic. Each pair of source and destination nodes of a connection is randomly selected without duplicate sources. In order to represent different network traffic load, we used five different packet rates of 5, 10, 15, 20, and 25 with two different packet sizes of 512 bytes and 128bytes. The maximum buffer size of each node's interface is set to 50 and three different buffer Queue-Threshold values of 45, 20, 10 and three different Time-Threshold values of 5, 3, and 2 are used for the simulation study.

4.2 Simulation Result

Figure 6 shows the averaged number of dropped packets in a node's interface queue by buffer overflows. As shown in the figure, DPBA provides less buffer overflows because during the route discovery procedure DPBA can transmit multiple packets and can solve traffic congestion in the network while the other protocols have frequent packet drops by buffer overflows, which eventually leads to route breakdowns.

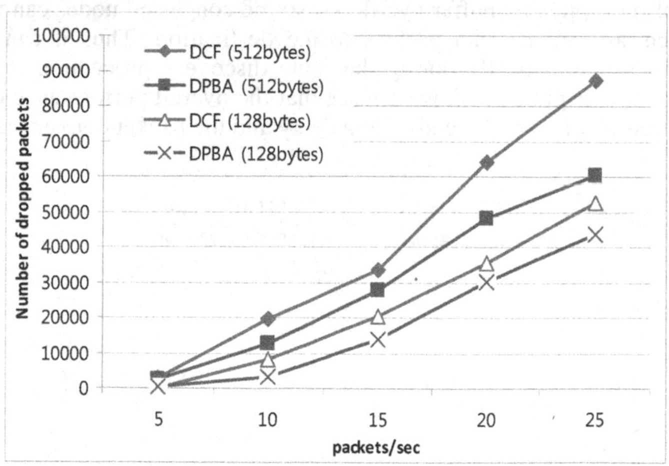

Fig. 6. Number of dropped packets

Figure 7 shows the packet delivery ratios of DPBA and DCF as a function of traffic load. The delivery ratio of DPBA is better than that of DCF due to less frequent buffer overflows. However, when the packet rate is over 25, delivery ratios of all the protocols are saturated because the entire network is congested.

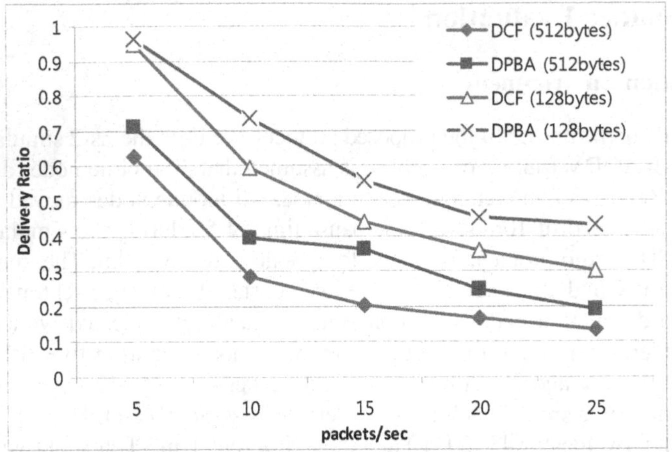

Fig. 7. Packet delivery ratio

Figure 8 shows the packet end-to-end delay as a function of traffic load. When the network traffic load increases, the end-to-end delay also increases. However, the delay of DPBA does not increase rapidly because this protocol can alleviate traffic of bottleneck nodes and congested routes. Moreover, when we used 512 bytes packet, DPBA can reduce transmission delay by eliminating unnecessary contention overhead. In DCF mode, the end-to-end delay decreases when the packet rate is above 15. When the traffic load is high and the intermediate nodes are congested, the RREQ packets are also dropped by buffer overflows, so the congested nodes can not forward RREQ packets as well as data packets to the destination. Thus it can detour the congested nodes automatically during the route discovery procedure. In the figure, when compared to original DCF, we can see that the overall performance of DPBA is highly improved in terms of the end-to-end delay and the packet delivery ratio.

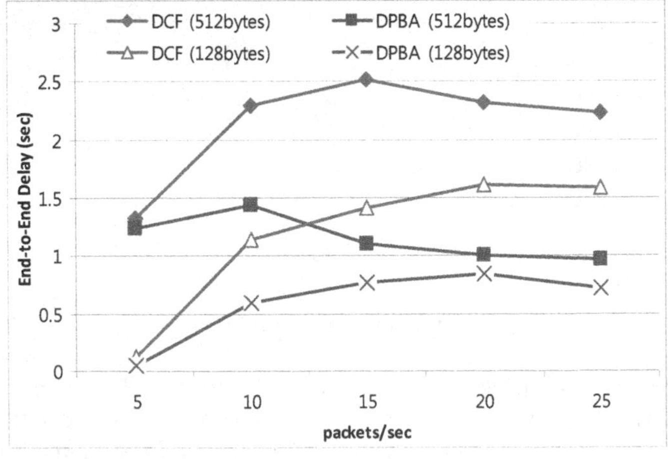

Fig. 8. End-to-end delay

Finally, Table 1 and Table 2 show the comparison of the performance with different buffer threshold values (Queue-threshold and Time-threshold) of DPBA in order to confirm the actual congestion situation when a packet size is 512 bytes. Although it is not easy to select the optimal values, we can see that the buffer threshold value affects the protocol's performance by setting differently. In both scenarios of different packet rates, we can find that DPBA shows the best performance when Q_{max} is 25 and T_{max} is 1.0 sec.

Table 1. Various threshold values of DPBA with 5 packets/sec

Threshold		5 packets/sec		
Q_{max}	T_{max}	Delivery Ratio	End-to-End Delay	Overflow Dropped
45	2	0.69	1.45	2736
20	1	0.71	1.32	2250
10	0.5	0.71	1.34	2312

Table 2. Various threshold values of DPBA with 20 packets/sec

Threshold		20 packets/sec		
Q_{max}	T_{max}	Delivery Ratio	End-to-End Delay	Overflow Dropped
45	2	0.22	1.38	52137
20	1	0.24	1.01	48180
10	0.5	0.24	1.16	49375

5 Conclusion

In mobile ad hoc networks, congestion can lead to performance degradation such as many packet losses by buffer overflows and long end-to-end delay. However, existing load balancing protocols only consider routing with an alternative route. That is, they do not solve actual congestion status of a node. In this paper, we have proposed DPBA (Dynamic Packet Bursting Algorithm) which can monitor the congested node in route and can transmit multiple packets by packet bursting during the communication session. By using burst packet, the congested node does not need to defer to send another packet. We also defined two buffer thresholds to confirm the actual congestion environment. Simulation study shows that DPBA shows a good performance in terms of packet delivery ratio, end-to-end delay, when a network is heavily loaded.

References

1. Perkins, C.E., Bhagwat, P.: Highly Dynamic Destination Sequenced Distance-vector Routing (DSDV) for Mobile Computers. Comp. Commun. Rev., 234–244 (October 1994)
2. Johnson, D.B., Maltz, D.A., Hu, Y.-C.: The Dynamic Source Routing Protocol for Mobile Ad Hoc Networks (DSR). Internet Draft, IETF Mobile Ad hoc Networks (MANET) Working Group

3. Perkins, C.E., Royer, E.: Ad-hoc on-demand Distance Vector Routing. In: Proc. 2nd IEEE Wksp. Mobile Comp. Sys. App. (February 1999)
4. IEEE 802.11, Part 11: Wireless LAN Medium Access Control (MAC) and Physical Layer (PHY) Specifications, Standard, IEEE (June 1997)
5. Cro, B.P., Kim, J.G.: IEEE 802.11 Wireless Local Area Networks. IEEE Communications magazine (December 1999)
6. IEEE 802.11e/D3.0, Draft Supplement to Part 11: Wireless Medium Access Control (MAC) and physical layer (PHY) specifications: Medium Access Control (MAC) Enhancements for Quality of Service (QoS) (May 2002)
7. Sadeghi, B., Kanodia, V., Sabharwal, A., Knightly, E.: OAR: An Opportunistic Auto-Rate Media Access Protocol For Ad Hoc Networks. In: ACM Mobicom 2002 (2002)
8. Lee, S.-J., Gerla, M.: Dynamic Load-Aware Routing in Ad hoc networks. In: Proceedings of IEEE ICC 2001 (2001)
9. Hassanein, H., Zhou, A.: Routing with Load Balancing in Wireless Ad hoc Networks. In: ACM MSWiM (July 2001)
10. Altalhi, A.H., Richard III, G.G.: Load-Balanced Routing through Virtual Paths. In: IPCCC 2004 (2004)
11. Kim, B.C., Lee, J.Y., Lee, H.S., Ma, J.S.: An Ad-hoc Routing Protocol with Minimum Contention Time and Load Balancing. In: IEEE Global Telecommunications Conference (2003)
12. Tran, D.A., Raghavendra, H.: Routing with congestion awareness and adaptivity in mobile ad hoc networks. In: Wireless Communications and Networking Conference (2005)
13. McCanne, S., Floyd, S.: NS network simulator. URL: http://www.isi.edu/nsnam/ns

Empirical Study of Design Pattern Usage in Peer-to-Peer Systems

Markus Aleksy[1], Martin Schader[1], Christian Seifried[1], and Makoto Takizawa[2]

[1] University of Mannheim
Department of Information Systems
[2] Tokyo Denki University
Department of Computers and System Engineering

Abstract. In this paper, we present the results of our analysis in which we investigated the different existing peer-to-peer systems with regard to design pattern usage. In the course of our analysis, we mainly concentrated on patterns concerned with the classification of distributed systems. In the following, the design patterns investigated are examined in more detail in their usage context and possible alternative solutions are discussed.

1 Introduction

The peer-to-peer (P2P) concept has experienced a revival over the last few years. The approach does not describe the exchange of data or how the communication between two participants takes place; rather, it is much more an architectural form that can be applied to all levels of a system. Put simply, a peer-to-peer system makes it possible for two or more equal participants to spontaneously form a network and to collaborate over it. In this way, it is not dependant on any central coordination entity.

During the development of a complex system, such as a peer-to-peer system, there are many different problems that appear again and again. At this point, the application of design patterns may be called for. Design patterns are simple and concise solutions for frequently occurring programmer tasks. A design pattern documents a comprehensive and viable solution, won through experience, to frequently recurring problems during program design.

The primary benefit of a design pattern lies in the delineation of a solution for a particular class of problems. Additional advantages are derived from the fact that each pattern has a name. This simplifies discussion amongst software developers by allowing for abstract dialog about software structure. Design patterns are, in this way, basically language independent. In the development of object-oriented software, they serve as an accepted tool for design structuring. The usage of tested and proven design patterns can lead to shorter development times, minimization of mistakes, and a higher application quality.

The design patterns found to be particularly useful for the development of P2P systems according to our analysis can be grouped as follows:

T. Enokido, L. Barolli, and M. Takizawa (Eds.): NBiS 2007, LNCS 4658, pp. 335–344, 2007.

- Communication
  One of the most crucial aspects for the proper functioning of a P2P system is communication between peers. If the developer fails to install a well-designed communication infrastructure that can be used to exchange all the required information such as routing messages, lookup/location queries and results etc., the backbone of the P2P system will be missing. For the design and implementation of such a foundational system layer it is therefore essential to apply reliable and well-suited procedures. In this context, design patterns such as *Acceptor-Connector*, *Forwarder-Receiver*, *Non-blocking Buffered I/O*, *Fire and Forget*, and *Asynchronous Completion Token* should be considered.
- Location of data, peers and services
  In order for a P2P system to operate successfully it must be possible to locate other peers participating in the network and the data and services they offer. Design patterns such as *Lookup*, *Location*, and *Service Locator* put forward valuable approaches to the solution of this problem.
- Resource Management
  In this category, we subsume design patterns that describe solutions to the problem of controlling and managing access to and availability of peers and the resources they own. Typical representatives are, for example, the *Leasing* pattern and the *Heartbeat* pattern.
- Caching
  Caching and *Evictor* are to be mentioned as examples of design patterns that specify mechanisms to care for an optimized placement of data within the P2P network.
- Security
  This category comprises design patterns like *Security Policy* or *XML Firewall*, which are concerned with security aspects and are applicable to P2P systems.

2 Empirical Study

Among the goals of our study was the examination of the following questions:

- Which design patterns appear to be especially well suited for designing a P2P system?
- Are design patterns typically used to the same extent in all of the different categories introduced above?

We defined a set of design patterns to be looked for in our analysis. This set was mainly drawn from standard literature in the field, such as [4], [9] and [13]. [13], for example, served as a source for selecting existing design patterns for the area of "Communication", and [9] provided design patterns for the categories "Location", "Resource Management", and "Caching". This selection was extended with several other design patterns drawn from papers published at specific technical conferences such as "Pattern Languages of Programs (PLoP)" conferences or the "European Conference on Pattern Languages of Programs (EuroPLoP)".

Our study is based on the analysis of seven different peer-to-peer systems; with the architectures LimeWire and Gridella being discussed in detail here and the remaining architectures only schematically depicted due to existing space restrictions.

2.1 LimeWire-One Client for the Gnutella Network

The application LimeWire is available as either a free (opensource) version or a pro-version that is subject to charges. The following analysis is based exclusively on the opensource version of the client in version 4.8.1.

Introduction and Classification of the System

LimeWire is a client primarily designed for file sharing [11]. Through an additional feature, it can also be used as a simple chat-client. Thus, it can be classified as a file sharing application as well as, to a smaller degree, as a messaging application. LimeWire was developed for use in the Gnutella network.

Gnutella is a pure, unstructured and loosely coupled peer-to-peer system: it functions without central components; the peers do not save additional information about other peers that could allow for a structuring of the network; and peers can participate in the system at any time without having to login to a group. The protocol itself specifies with only five message types how the communication among clients and the routing is to take place. However, the transfer of data following a successful search is not conducted over the Gnutella network any longer but through a direct HTTP transfer.

Used Design Patterns

The central component of the client is the class `RouterService`, which builds a part of the interface between the backend, responsible for the entire network functionality, and the GUI. Through the design pattern *Façade*, a uniform access by the GUI is made possible. The class `ActivityCallback` allows the backend to communicate with the GUI via *Callbacks*. In this way, the *Observer* pattern is applied. In Table 1, this pattern as well as other generally used design patterns are presented as an overview.

LimeWire primarily uses TCP connections to send and receive routing messages as well as for data transfer. The configuration of the responsible subsystem and the procedure for accepting and connecting a connection follows the design pattern *Acceptor-Connector*. In this context the pattern *Active Object* is also applied.

The routing functionality of LimeWire is implemented in the class `MessageRouter`. Here the design pattern *Non-Blocking Buffered I/O* is applied through a multi-threading strategy. Two threads are assigned to each connection. One thread waits for incoming messages as long as the connection is open and handles these in accordance with their types. In doing so, user administrators are determined through different routing table objects. A suitable reply or a message

Table 1. Overview of the design patterns used by LimeWire

Design Pattern	Affected Class(es)
Active Object	ConnectionManager
Composite	Spamfilter
Decorator	PaneItemMainLabel
Evictor	ConnectionWatchdog
Façade	RouterService
Factory Method	ConnectionManager
Iterator	ConnectionManager, DownloadManager
Mediator	GUIMediator
Monitor Object	ManagedConnection
Observer	ActivityCallback
Proxy	NotifyUserProxy, OptionsTreeNode
State	HTTPUploader
Strategy	SpamFilter
Singleton	Cookies
Template Method	MessageRouter, StandardMessageRouter
Wrapper Façade	WindowsLauncher

itself is passed along to the user administrators. During the handover, a message is put into a queue that is controlled by the second thread of the connection. In this independent control flow of the user administrator, the message is sent over the associated connection, ensuring that neither the quality of receiving nor dispatching messages impairs the other.

In using the design pattern *Asynchronous Completion Token*, a connection does not need to link threads or to save the current status in order to be successfully carried out, which would have been necessary in part for the processing of the replies to the sent messages. The ACTs are implemented through the different message types such as `PingRequest` or `PingReply`. In addition to the identification of the originating peer and additional information about it, they include the TTL and Hopcounter, which are adapted corresponding to the versions of the *Chain of Service* and *Non-Opaque ACTs*, and that can be passed on to more peers.

In handling `PingRequests` and their subsequent replies (`PingReplies`, or `Pongs`), the design patterns *Caching* and *Heartbeat* are brought into action. Unknown `Pongs` from other peers received over all connections are saved in a cache (`PongCacher`) before they are forwarded to the originating peer using the `PingRequest`. In this way, later `Pings` can be answered with the `Pongs` from the cache and will not be distributed further in a broadcast method. In order to ensure that the `Pongs` are still valid, Heartbeat messages reporting all current connections are sent regularly by the class `Pinger`. The connected peers can also use their cache in this way to reply with `Pongs`.

LimeWire designates peers that accept incoming connections and that have a good connection to the network as ultra-peers. The differentiation is carried out by the class `SupernodeAssigner`. Ultra-peers save, according to the idea of pattern *Location*, the addresses and the release of data from leaf-peers (in the role Location Service) and the addresses of other ultra-peers (Locator) in the class `HostCatcher`. Leaves mostly do not accept incoming connections and communicate with the Gnutella network only over an ultra-peer. In this way, ultra-peers take on the role of a go-between.

To solve the bootstrapping problem, during the first connection to the network, LimeWire uses a list of preconfigured ultra-peers. This list consists of such ultra-peers that are identified as being reliable during running operation. Additionally, LimeWire makes use of the GwebCaches inserted in the Gnutella network. These are small programs that can be executed on conventional web servers, prepare lists of Gnutella peers, and allow peers to register themselves in the lists. GwebCaches correspond extensively to the concept of the design pattern *Lookup*. Because of this, Gnuttella should be classified as a hybrid form. Since GwebCaches are however not critical for the functioning of the network and are not a main component of it, the classification as a "fragmented form" is justified.

In LimeWire, as with most file sharing programs, there are almost no integrated security mechanisms. Users can only exclude certain data from search results or refuse connection to certain IP addresses through the definition of filters. A secure transfer of content or coded communication with other peers is not possible. Only updates of the programs themselves are tested for authenticity with the help of public code from LimeWire. The data that a peer obtains from other peers are merely tested through a hash value to see whether or not they were transferred correctly.

Assigning self-organizing rights to specific peers or users is also not possible. It can only be stipulated as to when a peer is to be regarded as a freeloader and whether or not it should be offered data. This approach is comparable to a simple and incomplete application of the pattern *Role-Based Access Control*; it is not applied, however, in the source code.

2.2 Gridella-Implementation of the P-Grid-Approach

The peer-to-peer system P-Grid, as opposed to the Gnutella protocol, was developed according to a scientific approach ([1], [2]). Like Gnutella, P-Grid is a pure peer-to-peer system; however, regarding certain aspects, it is expanded as covered in more detail in the following. The P-Grid-based client Gridella is also implemented in Java and available in the Version 1.

Introduction and Classification of the System

P-Grid was developed at the École Polytechnique Fédérale de Lausanne (EPFL) and is not a finished applicable implementation that can be assigned to a specific application domain. Rather, it is a scientific approach to a peer-to-peer search system that is to be implemented in a concrete application. P-Grid is based on a virtual binary search tree (cf. DHT) that is distributed throughout peers in a network and that allows for efficient and quick searches for data filed in the network. For the data, P-Grid builds keys that are to serve as the basis for the search and that, as opposed to many other DHT-based search systems, are built in such a way that parts of the complete reference chain can be searched for.

Furthermore, peer replicas exist-several peers are responsible for the same path in the tree, meaning for the same data. The addresses of these replicas are also saved by the peers in order to compensate in the case that individual peers are offline, so that the inquiries can be distributed over several peers, and in order to keep the depth of the tree small.

P-Grid also provides an algorithm that allows system updates to be carried out that also take into consideration the replication of data. This is not possible in most other peer-to-peer systems or is only insufficiently implemented. With the help of this update mechanism, a decentralized Reputation or Trust Management System, is also possible with P-Grid.

Due to previously detailed characteristics, the P-Grid is a structured, decentralized approach. Since a search tree can be built through local interaction of peers without the peers having knowledge of the structure of the entire tree and since peers can enter the network at any point in time, a loosely coupled system is realized.

Used Design Patterns

Gridella is a file sharing application that was also developed at the EPFL [14]. Its client can communicate both through a Gridella protocol and the Gnutella protocol. Gridella as well uses an HTTP channel for the data transfer after successful searches. Table 2 summarizes the general patterns. In case of repeated use of individual patterns, only one reference is given.

Table 2. Overview of the design patterns used by Gridella

Design Pattern	Affected Class(es)
Active Object	`ConnectionManager, SearcherManager`
Façade	`PGrid`
Factory Method	`PGridReader`
Iterator	`MessageManager`
Monitor Object	`PGridReader`
Observer	`MessageManager`
Singleton	`PGrid`
Template	`Host, PGridHost`
Wrapper	`Host, PGridHost`

Gridella uses the TCP protocol for the communication amongst the peers. In order to allow incoming connection requests, a listener is created in the application's main method directly after starting, which creates a server socket on a specific port. As suggested in the design pattern *Acceptor-Connector*, an acceptor takes over those tasks in its class that are necessary for initializing incoming connections. The acceptor decides whether a connection is an HTTP GET query for transferring data, or a connection for setting up the P-Grid used for sending search messages. If the latter is the case, the acceptor exchanges the necessary information at the beginning of the connection and registers these with the `ConnectionManager`, which logs connections with other hosts.

For forwarding search queries and the resulting responses (Routing), also in Gridella the design pattern *Non-Blocking Buffered I/O* is used. However, differing from the process in LimeWire, there is no automatic assignment to every connection of two threads that are responsible for processing inputs and outputs. Instead, initially only one thread is assigned, which is responsible for the connection's incoming messages. For sending through an already existing connection, depending on the kind of message to be sent, an existing, already waiting thread is reactivated.

When creating new threads in the method `startSearch`, the design pattern *Active Object* is used in order to process the search in an individual control flow. The creating of the threads remains transparent to the method that calls them up. When processing search queries that are started locally by the application's user through an object of the class `SearchTab`, the design pattern *Asynchronous Completion Token* is utilized.

Design patterns such as *Caching* or *Location* are not used. In addition, no further security mechanisms are incorporated. Therefore, the available Gridella application is more suitable for Intranet applications, e.g., for file sharing systems for shared documents and files that are based on a central search system and realized through P-Grids.

2.3 Further References for the Usage of Design Patterns in Peer-to-Peer Systems

In the last two sections, two existing opensource peer-to-peer systems were analyzed with regard to their design pattern usage. This included thorough source code analysis and system documentation of both systems. In this section, we provide brief overviews of further peer-to-peer systems, in which the use of various design patterns is proven.

One of these systems is the JXTA project [18]. JXTA is a peer-to-peer platform based on six basic protocols that allow any device to communicate with each other. In 2002, the JXTA protocols were submitted to the Internet Engineering Task Force for standardization. JXTA is a specification of protocols for peer-to-peer applications and is not a complete solution. For developers wanting to implement a peer-to-peer application using JXTA, a reference implementation of the JXTA project exists in Java. JXTA itself is independent of programming languages, application domains, and the concrete peer-to-peer architecture. Therefore, it can be used for any peer-to-peer system. Its multi-purpose usability is due to the fact that the developer still has to implement many services and functions such as the concrete search methods or bootstrap mechanisms. The analysis regarding the usage of design patterns, therefore, focuses on the design of the protocols as well as on the reference implementation within the JXTA project. The JXTA protocols are XML-based and set up in such a way that good use of this works design patterns, mainly in the area of security, is allowed.

Table 3 summarizes all references of the analyzed systems. In addition to name and version of the analyzed peer-to-peer systems, the table lists characteristic features of their architecture and the kind of application the system can be classified as. The last column lists all design patterns and pattern languages that are explicitly referred to or can be identified in the source code. Most of the listed references result from comments and references of the developer or designer in technical reports or the respective systems documentation. For applications that are not available as an opensource application, this is the only possibility to learn about the use of design patterns. However, wherever a validation of the use of design patterns is possible through analyzing the source code, this analysis is conducted.

Table 3. Further references for the usage of design patterns in the framework of peer-to-peer systems

P2P System	Application Domain / Architecture	Used Design Patterns and Pattern Languages
Frost [16], Version 03-02-2005	Distributed content storage (anonymous), based on Freenet; pure, unstructured	Abstract Factory, Caching, Observer, Singleton
FSS [12], Version 1.0	File sharing; pure, coupled, unstructured	Blackboard, Caching, Key Management, Location, Observer, Proxy, Role-based Access Control
JXTA Protocols [17], Version 2.0	P2P platform; will be first determined through concrete implementation	Caching, Leasing, Location, Publisher-Subscriber, Wrapper Façade
Phex [10], Version 2.1.4.80	File sharing; pure, unstructured	Acceptor-Connector, Active Object, ACT, Caching, Coordinator-Worker, Fire and Forget, Monitor Object, Non-blocking Buffered I/O, Wrapper Façade
ProActive [7], Version 2.2	Distributed computation; pure, structured, coupled	Active Object, Adapter, Chain of Responsibility, Composite, Decorator, Façade, Factory, Heartbeat, Key Management, Location, Observer, Consumer-Producer, Proxy, Security Policy, Singleton, Strategy

3 Summary and Conclusions

In the previous sections, a total of seven existing peer-to-peer systems were analyzed based on the usage of design patterns. The implementations of the systems came from a scientific environment (P-Grid, ProActive, FSS) as well as from the commercial side (LimeWire, JXTA). Moreover, the examined systems can be assigned to different application domains. The systems differentiate themselves from each other also with regard to the occurrence of characteristic architectural attributes. Despite these different pre-conditions, the usage of design patterns could be recognized for all examined systems. Often, an explicit reference to the use of a concrete design pattern in the source code, technical reports or the documentation is present.

Regarding the implementations for which we did not have access to the source code, this was actually the only possibility to collect information about the potential use of design patterns for the architectural designs of those systems. However, in those cases that allowed the assessment of the application of design patterns by analyzing the source code, we used this opportunity. Very often, the class names used in the implementations already indicated realizations of design patterns. Other useful criteria for the detection of design patterns were drawn from [15]. Further, [3], [6], and [8] provided useful concepts for the search for design patterns.

In the two systems presented in detail, P-Grid or Gridella respectively and LimeWire, it is clear that mainly the design patterns for the communication within a peer-to-peer network are already used in order to realize the basic functionality of a system. However, in both systems as well as in the additional systems analyzed, also patterns such as *Caching* and *Leasing* were used in order to optimize or to expand the existing implementation.

Most of the analyzed systems show a deficit in the area of security. Only JXTA, ProActive, and FSS offer sufficient security mechanisms (respectively, the possibility of using them in the case of JXTA), as suggested in the respective patterns pointed out in this work. Therefore, mainly the file sharing applications still have a need for expanding their systems.

The technical literature provides several design patterns or pattern languages, e.g. the *Pattern Language for Key Management*, the *Pattern Language for Security Models* or the *Security Policy* pattern, that could be very useful here. They address security issues relevant to P2P systems, such as authorization, role-based access control or more specific topics like encrypted and partially anonymous message exchange as described by patterns like *Sealed Envelope* or *Sealed and Signed Envelope*.

Further, it is evident that the systems with the most extensive functionality, ProActive and LimeWire, also show the most extensive use of design patterns. This indicates that design patterns are suitable for use during the development of complex systems such as peer-to-peer systems. It also becomes clear that many patterns are already known to software developers and are not only used in reference implementations.

This shows that design patterns are deliberately used during the development and design of peer-to-peer applications. Certainly, it occurs that a given solution is similar to a design pattern without the developer even knowing this. However, such a case indirectly proves the suitability of the pattern in this context.

References

1. Aberer, K.: P-Grid: A self-organizing access structure for P2P information systems. In: Proc. of the 6th Int. Conf. on Cooperative Information Systems, Trento, Italy (2000)
2. Aberer, K., Hauswirth, M.: Peer-to-peer information systems: concepts and models, state-of-the-art, and future systems. In: Proc. of the 18th Int. Conf. on Data Engineering, San Jose, USA (2001)
3. Antoniol, G., Fiutem, R., Cristoforetti, L.: Design pattern recovery in object-oriented software. In: Proc. of the 6th Int. Workshop on Program Comprehension, Ischia, Italy (1998)
4. Buschmann, F., Meunier, R., Rohnert, H., Sommerlad, P., Stal, M.: Pattern-Oriented Software Architecture: A System of Patterns. John Wiley & Sons, Chichester (1996)
5. Gamma, E., Helm, R., Johnson, R., Vlissides, J.: Design Patterns: Elements of Reusable Object-Oriented Software. Addison-Wesley Longman, Redwood City, CA, USA (1996)
6. Heuzeroth, D., Holl, T., Högström, G., Löwe, W.: Automatic Design Pattern Detection. In: Proc. of the 11th IEEE Int. Workshop on Program Comprehension, Portland, USA (2003)
7. Institut National de Recherche en Inoformatique et en Automatique: ProActive Manual (2005), `http://www-sop.inria.fr/oasis/ProActive/doc/ProActiveManual.pdf`
8. Kim, H., Boldyreff, C.: A method to recover design patterns using software product metrics. In: Proc. of the 6th Int. Conf. on Software Reuse, Vienna, Austria (2000)
9. Kircher, M., Jain, P.: Pattern-Oriented Software Architecture: Patterns for Resource Management. John Wiley & Sons, Chichester (2004)
10. Koukkoullis, G.: Phex-The Gnutella P2P Filesharing Client (2005), `http://phex.kouk.de/`
11. Lime Wire LLC: LimeWire.org-Open Source P2P Filesharing (2005), `http://www.limewire.org`
12. Sanmarti, M.: P2P File Sharing Service (2002), `http://www.bath.ac.uk/comp-sci/hci/mobile/p2p.html`
13. Schmidt, D.C., Rohnert, H., Stal, M., Schultz, D.: Pattern-Oriented Software Architecture: Patterns for Concurrent and Networked Objects. John Wiley & Sons, Chichester (2000)
14. Schmidt, R.: Gridella: an open and efficient Gnutella-compatible Peer-to-Peer System based on the P-Grid approach (2002), `http://www.p-grid.org/Papers/TR-IC-2002-71.pdf`
15. Streitferdt, D., Philippow, I., Riebisch, M.: Design Pattern Recovery in Architectures for Supporting Product Line Development and Application (2003), `http://www.theoinf.tu-ilmenau.de/riebisch/publ/04-phil.pdf`
16. The Frost Project Website (2005), `http://jtcfrost.source-forge.net/`
17. The Internet Society JXTA v2.0 Protocols Specification (2004), `http://spec.jxta.org/nonav/v1.0/docbook/JXTAProtocols.html`
18. Traversat, et al.: Project JXTA 2.0 Super-Peer Virtual Network (2004), `http://www.jxta.org/project/www/docs/JXTA2.0protocols1.pdf`

Improvement of JXTA Protocols for Supporting Reliable Distributed Applications in P2P Systems

Fatos Xhafa[1], Raul Fernandez[2], Thanasis Daradoumis[2], Leonard Barolli[3], and Santi Caballé[2]

[1] Polytechnic University of Catalonia
Department of Languages and
Informatics Systems Barcelona, Spain
fatos@lsi.upc.edu
[2] Open University of Catalonia,
Department of Information Sciences Barcelona, Spain
adaradoumis@uoc.edu
[3] Department of Information and Communication Engineering
Fukuoka Institute of Technology (FIT) Fukuoka, Japan
barolli@fit.ac.jp

Abstract. In any distributed application, the communication between the distributed processes/nodes of the distributed systems is essential for both reliability and efficiency matters. In this work we address this issue for distributed applications based on JXTA protocols. After a careful examination of the current version of JXTA protocols, we observed the need for improving the original JXTA protocols, such as pipe services, to ensure reliable communication between peer nodes and the discovery and presence service to increase the performance of the applications. The re-implemented protocols have been validated in practice by deploying a P2P network using nodes of PlanetLab platform and testing each of the extended protocols using this real P2P network.

1 Introduction and Motivation

The reliability of distributed applications has been largely investigated by researchers of the distributed computing community. While reliability issues are generally well understood for operating systems and classical distributed systems and LANs (see e.g. [3]), there is still few work in addressing these issues for the emergent computational systems. With the development of Internet and other new technologies, distributed systems and applications are becoming the indispensable approach for solving complex problems. Therefore, the reliability issue is nowadays being investigated for Web-based distributed systems / applications (e.g. [6,13,11]) and Grid-based computing (e.g. [2,7]). Moreover, P2P systems are evolving towards an important paradigm for distributed computing. Each time more, P2P systems are used beyond file/data sharing applications, for developing large scale distributed applications that benefit from the immense

T. Enokido, L. Barolli, and M. Takizawa (Eds.): NBiS 2007, LNCS 4658, pp. 345–354, 2007.

computing power contributed by millions of peers worldwide. Projects such as "Folding@Home on the PS3" by seti@home for studying the protein folding by utilizing the new Cell processor in Sony's Playstation 3 are allowing to achieve performance previously only possible on supercomputers. The main challenge in developing large-scale P2P applications is how to develop efficient, scalable and reliable distributed systems from inexpensive unreliable computers contributed to P2P network by millions of individuals. One of the today's technologies used in developing P2P systems is JXTA [1,9,10]. This is a recent technology, which has been used in several P2P projects [5] and is currently drawing the attention of many researchers and developers of the P2P and Grid computing. In particular the reliability and efficiency issue is being studied for JXTA-based applications (e.g. [4,12]).

This work is motivated by the need to support the development of efficient and reliable P2P applications using JXTA protocols. To this end, we have carefully analyzed the current JXTA protocols and report here several limitations of most important protocols of JXTA. After examining and pointing out such limitations, we further propose a solution to them through re-implementation/extensions without damaging the genericity of JXTA protocols. More precisely, in this work we have considered the following protocols and services: *Peer Discovery Protocol*, *Discovery Service*, *Peer Information Protocol*, *Peer Information Service*, *Peer Resolver Protocol*, *Resolver Service*, *Pipe Binding Protocol* and *Pipe Service*, *Endpoint Routing Protocol* and *Endpoint Service*. Our approach is validated in practice by deploying a real P2P network using the nodes of the PlanetLab platform [8], a planetary scale distributed infrastructure, and have experimentally evaluated the performance and reliability of the re-implemented protocols.

The rest of the paper is organized as follows. We give in Section 2 the evaluation of the JXTA protocols and their limitations. In Section 3 we present the re-implementation of the JXTA protocols; their experimental evaluation is given in Section 4. Finally, we conclude in Section 5 with some remarks and indicate directions for future work.

2 The JXTA Protocols and Their Limitations

2.1 The JXTA Protocol and Services

The services offered by JXTA library are based on its own protocols and serve as the starting point in the development of a P2P network using JXTA. Certainly, it is upon the developer to extend/implement these services according to his needs. JXTA offers essentially six protocols, each one with its corresponding services. In fact, in developing JXTA-based P2P applications, not all these protocols and services are necessarily used. These protocols and services are the following:

- *Peer Discovery Protocol* and *Discovery Service*, which serve to advertise the proper resources and to discover the resources of other peers.
- *Peer Information Protocol* and *Peer Information Service*, which are in charge of obtaining state information of local or remote peers.

– *Peer Resolver Protocol* and *Resolver Service*, which are used for sending a general query to one or more peers and receiving one or more responses in order to interchange desired information.
– *Pipe Binding Protocol* and *Pipe Service*, which serve for establishing a virtual communication channel, that is a *pipe*, to enable sending and receiving data from other peers.
– *Endpoint Routing Protocol* and *Endpoint Service* for routing to other peers. The route information contains an ordered sequence of relay peers that must be used to send a message to the specified destination peer.
– *Rendezvous Protocol* and *Rendezvous Service*, which constitute the mechanisms through which peers can be subscribed to a propagated service or a source peer can propagate a message to all peers subscribed to the service.

2.2 Limitations of JXTA Protocols

In any P2P network, independently of its specific purposes, there are several key issues to tackle: (a) publishing and receiving services; (b) the network connection; and (c) message sending/receiving. JXTA offers protocols and services to support these needs, however, as shown in this work, they have several limitations that we overcame by adding new functionalities to the original services. We present next these limitations of JXTA protocols.

Managing the presence mechanism. The presence of a peer node in a peerGroup of the JXTA network is provided by the document of presence notification. This document is published by each peer and reaches the local cache of all peers, where it will "stay" for a certain time. The presence mechanism is very important for the JXTA network in order for a peer's advertisement and therefore its services, to reach all peers that are present. Most importantly, the rendezvous must know all peers connected to the peergroup because the rendezvous is in charge of synchronizing the local caches of peers and compute the routes to be used by any peer to reach all the connected peers of the group. The advertisement document is of the type *PeerAdvertisement* and must periodically be published in order for other peers of the group to know the updated presence information of the peer that publishes the advertisement document. However, this publishing is not done automatically in JXTA; hence any application using JXTA must manage it by its own! Essentially, any JXTA-based application has to manage the information of the updated presence (a sort of presence refreshment) of any peer node in any peerGroup it belongs to.

Managing the connection to groups. In any mixed P2P network, that is, a P2P network in which we have *broker peers* and *client peers* [12], any client peer can be connected only to one peerGroup by discovering and establishing communication with a rendezvous. Therefore it is necessary to have a broker peer in any peerGroup, which must act as a rendezvous in order to achieve that client peers get connected and the broker could notify the presence of the peer to the rest of the nodes of the peerGroup. It should be noted that the connection to a peerGroup is done differently depending on whether the peerGroup is specific or is a general group. The general group is the *NetPeerGroup*, the peerGroup to which must get connected any peer to join the JXTA network and to collaborate/work with other peers. On the other hand, the connection to other peerGroups is not indispensable for the peer to start working in the JXTA network, but rather it serves to make much more specific the peer's characteristics and functionalities. Moreover, using broker peers and brokerage services, the number of peers that could be used for a certain purpose can be reduced. In JXTA, there are no such mechanisms for broker peers.

Managing the communication mechanism. In JXTA, pipes are used as a basic direct communication mechanism between two peers belonging to the same peer-Group. Pipes are of two types: InputPipe and OutputPipe. Clearly, if a peer A wants to send a message to a destination peer B, it is necessary that an instance of A's outputPipe must be connected to an instance of B's inputPipe. In order to establish this connection, the peer A must know the B's inputPipe and the peer B must accept messages from the A's outputPipe. This is achieved in JXTA by using descriptions of pipes in a way that they are unique, that is an inputPipe can only receive messages from an outputPipe having the same description. The description is done in XML documents, called PipeAdverstisement, which is of type advertisement and has defined, besides its unique identifier, several parameters such as name, type and description. Therefore in order for the peer A to send a message to the peer B, both inputPipe and outputPipe must be defined in the same PipeAdvertisement and both peers must agree which one to use. Thus, we have to find the appropriate protocol to assure the communication among all peers of the same peerGroup. Again, this is not assured by JXTA pipes. Moreover, JXTA pipes do not assure nor notify the failure that might occur in message delivery and once a message is sent out, it is not attempted again in case of failure.

3 Improvements of JXTA Protocols

In order to overcome the limitations of the JXTA protocols shown in the previous section, we re-implemented the JXTA protocols/services by adding new functionalities and control to the original services offered by JXTA.

Managing the presence and service mechanisms. Recall that the presence is done through the presence notification document. This document must be periodically published in order for other peers of a peerGroup to know the presence of the peer. This is one of the limitations of JXTA that we have solved by adding to peer's functionalities, the publishing of its own PeerAdvertisement periodically. In this way, the peers of the peerGroup will know the presence of the peer and hence they will send to the peer their future advertisements. Moreover, in order for the peer to know all services of the P2P network, it has to discover such services, which are found in different advertisements and are stored in local cache.

Again, the peer's cache must be frequently updated. One way to do this, is to look up local caches of peers in the peerGroup by sending queries. A query is a request sent to all peers of the peerGroup which, upon reaching a peer, examines its local cache, and recollects all the advertisements of the specified type. When such query reaches a rendezvous, it recollects all advertisements of all peers of the peerGroup.

Finally, the results of the query are stored in the local cache of the peer, which can use them later on for its purposes. The main issue here is thus the synchronization of the local cache of a peer with local caches of other peers of the peerGroup. To this end, in our implementation, a query is sent periodically to all peers of the peerGroup. More precisely this is done in a new module[1], called DiscoveryOverlay, as shown in Fig. 1.

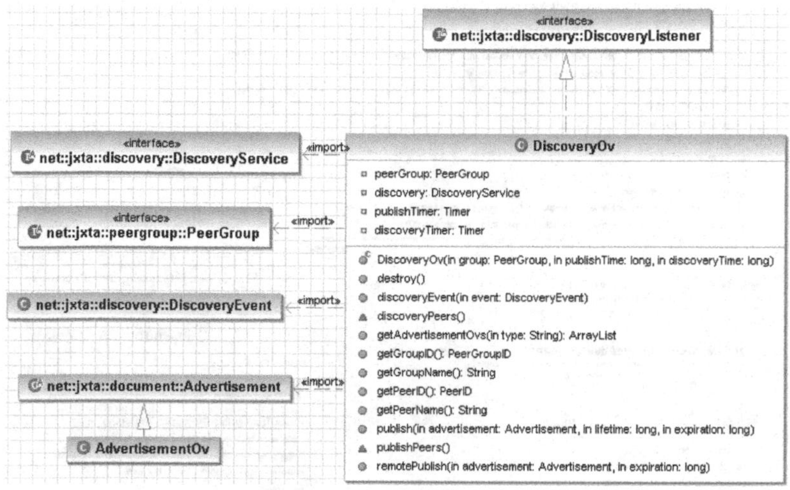

Fig. 1. UML diagram of the overlay module

Managing the connection to groups. Recall that any peerGroup needs a rendezvous peer. The principal peerGroup is that of NetPeerGroup, the connection to which is done according to the peer's configuration: (a) connection to the default rendezvous of JXTA. This is certainly inefficient since we cannot control the rendezvous; (b) connection to rendezvous pre-specified by the concrete JXTA application; (c) connection to rendezvous specified in a rendezvous list. In this later case, the JXTA application just needs to know the address where to find the rendezvous list. Note that the rendezvous list can be changed independently of the application, which is desirable in P2P applications. Moreover, once a peer is connected to the P2P network through the principal peerGroup, it can join any peerGroup by knowing the GroupAdvertisement of such groups. However, for this to be done, the peerGroups must exist, there must be at least one rendezvous and the GroupAdvertisements must be propagated. In our P2P network of broker peers and client peers, the brokers are the governors of the network and the organization of the groups. Thus broker peers are in charge of creating the groups and propagate the GroupAdvertisement accordingly.

[1] The abbreviation ***Ov*** stands for *Overaly*, which refers to the new implementation.

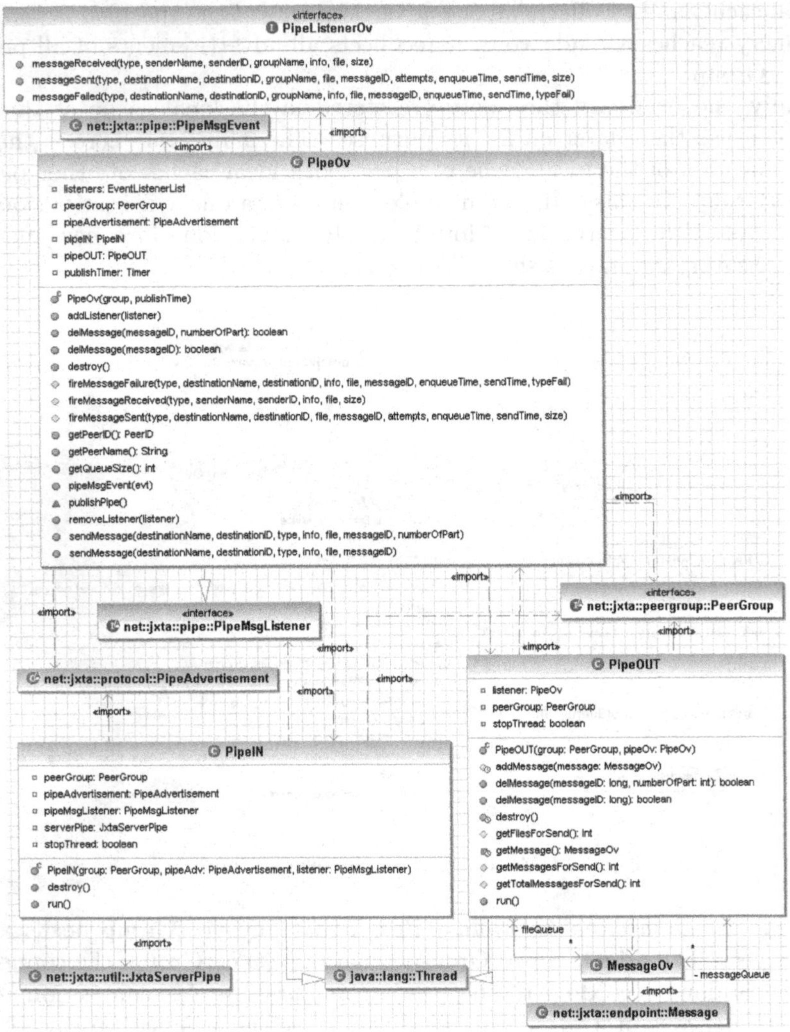

Fig. 2. UML diagram of the Pipe Service re-implementation

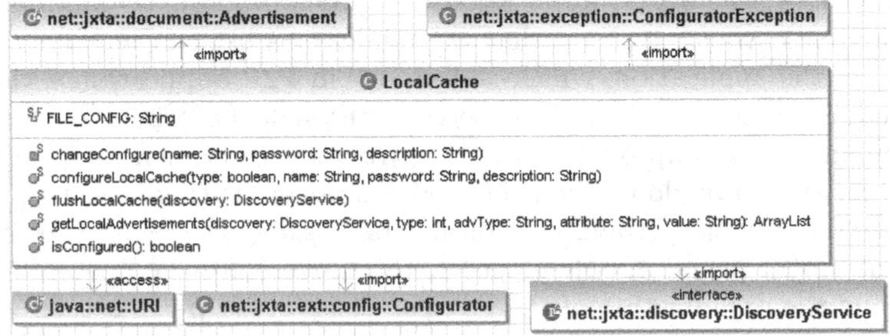

Fig. 3. UML diagram of information management re-implementation

Managing the communication mechanism. Recall that in order for a peer to send a message to another peer, there must exist a connection between an outputPipe and inputPipe defined in the same PipeAdvertisement and therefore both peers have to agree on which PipeAdvertisement to use. One possible solution would be to create a PipeAdvertisement for any possible connection between any two peers of a peerGroup according to a predefined protocol. This is not efficient given the large number of different PipeAdvertisements needed to manage the connections.

We decided then to create a unique PipeAdvertisement by a concrete peer in a peerGroup, having thus operative only one inputPipe through which to receive messages from all the rest of peers of the peerGroup. It is necessary to find a way to create such a unique PipeAdvertisement per peer and how other peers can know the peer's PipeAdvertisement. Since in JXTA, each peer has its unique PeerID, we associate a PipeAdvertisement with a peer by including the PeerID in PipeAdvertisement variables. Once the PipeAdvertisement is created, the source peer has to create an outputPipe and the destination peer has to create an inputPipe, both of them defined with the same PipeAdvertisement.

We have thus implemented this approach for the case of receiving and sending messages and pipe services (details are omitted). We show in Fig. 2 the UML diagram of the re-design of the JXTA pipe services mechanisms.

Managing the peer's state information. As already mentioned, keeping updated information of the network is crucial in P2P applications. To this end, we have implemented functionalities that allow to recollect information on the nodes of the network and publish it periodically through advertisements. More precisely, each time a node changes its state, due to any network event or application event, the node's state information is updated. This information is defined at three levels: for the last k hours, for the current session and for all sessions (historical data). The peer node publishes this information using advertisements, which are periodically published. Moreover, the peer node computes several statistics, which are sent together with the peer's state information; thus, any peer can use statistical information of other peers for efficient decision-taking. To this end, we have implemented a module LocalCache, which has functionalities to control the local cache of the peer (see Fig. 3).

4 Testing the Re-implementations of the JXTA Protocols

4.1 Deployment of the P2P Network Using PlanetLab Nodes

In order to evaluate the performance of the re-implemented protocols, first we deployed the P2P network using nodes of the PlanetLab [8], a planetary-scale platform[2]. The sample set of PlanetLab's machines forming our slice was about 25 nodes. Moreover we used the cluster nozomi.lsi.upc.edu (a main control node + five computing nodes).

[2] At present, composed up of 784 nodes at 382 sites.

4.2 Reliability Tests and Computational Results

We conducted several experiments to test the reliability and efficiency of the re-implemented protocols. The experimenting was done twice (for the original and re-implemented version) under the same P2P network of PlanetLab nodes.

Testing the presence and service management. When a peer client joins the network for the first time, its local cache is created empty. Next, the local cache must get synchronized, at first place, with the local cache of the rendezvous and then with those of other peers of the same peerGroup. On the other hand, if the peer has already joined the P2P network in previous sessions, the advertisement are stored in its local cache. We observed and experimentally measured that the synchronization for the first connection takes, as expected, much more time than when the peer has already done some prior sessions in the P2P network.

Once the peer has its local cache synchronized, we experimentally studied the peer's services. Peer's services are implemented in a way that each service can have its lifetime and its publishing frequency. We briefly mention here three scenarios that we considered: (a) Statistics services: these services distinguish for their long lifetime (e.g. order of minutes) and a high publishing frequency (e.g. order of seconds, say, 30 seconds). By monitoring the statistics of the P2P nodes, we observed that these services correctly kept the information on all peers. (b) Rendezvous services: these services include criteria for choosing a peer for efficient computation or efficient data transmission, which require that the rendezvous' advertisements must be synchronized because through it are synchronized the local caches of other peers. (c) Peer common services (e.g. information on peer node): these services have usually a short lifetime, otherwise in case the peer is disconnected from the P2P network its services would be *alive* even the node is not present in the network. Experimental values showed that 60 seconds was a good value for the lifetime of such services, meaning that an invalid service could be alive during that time but because the publishing time is inferior to that, a new publishing could take place.

The time connection to a peerGroup. Recall that at least one rendezvous of the general group must be permanently operative so that different peers will try to join the network by trying to connect to the rendezvous. In order to increase the possibilities that a peer will always establish connection to a rendezvous we used a rendezvous list implementation. The experimental data showed that, although it could take more time to establish the connection (now a peer has to examine the list of rendezvous), it considerably increases the possibility of a peer to establish connection with a rendezvous. In fact with our real P2P network, we did not observe failure to establish connection.

The communication test. One important parameter to measure is the pipe connection times, which depending in the type of peer and the network could vary considerably. Essentially, in order to establish a pipe, JXTA has to previously do some communications based in a communication protocol and each of these connections has its ping time. Due to this variability, considering a fixed timeout (say

2 secs) turned out to not be a good choice; it worked very well for cluster-based P2P network but it was not reliable for a geographically distributed P2P network. This motivated precisely one of the improvements presented in this work, namely, the progressive augmentation of the window timeout, which in our experiments was upper bounded by 40 seconds. Recall that in our re-implementation of pipes, if a message is not delivered to destination peer, it is attempted again to send it. Thus, the number of attempts depends on the time window used. The experiments showed that by progressively increasing the time window to at most 40 seconds, almost all messages were sent to destination. By using this approach less than 2% of messages that could not be delivered (e.g. because the peer is already disconnected) were reported as errors as opposed to 32% of undelivered messages that were reported as errors with a fixed timeout (see Fig. 4).

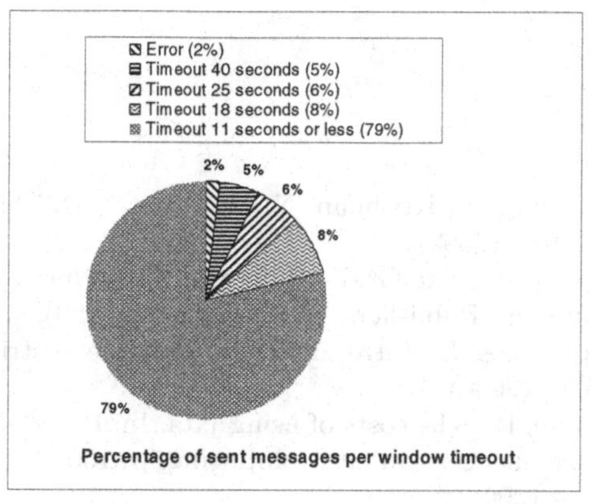

Fig. 4. Time out values and the corresponding percentage of sent messages

Information management test. In our approach, each node publishes a large quantity of information and therefore peer nodes of the P2P network have better knowledge of the peerGroup / the network and can use the information of other peers in decision-taking process. In this context, we considered as a test finding the best peer for efficiently running a task from many candidate peers. In absence of information about the other peer nodes, the task assignment would essentially reduce to a random assignment, which is not efficient. By using the information published by the peer nodes brokers are able to find the best peer among different candidates. Thus, we implemented a data-evaluator model as part of brokerage services to identify the best peer for executing a task.

5 Conclusions and Future Work

In this work we have analyzed the JXTA protocols/services and have shown several limitations of these protocols regarding the efficiency and reliability of P2P JXTA-based applications. The analyzed protocols include discovery, peer information, peer resolver, and pipe binding protocols/services, among others. We then proposed and re-implemented these protocols in order to overcome the identified limitations. The proposed improvements of the JXTA protocols have been validated in practice using a real P2P network deployed in nodes of PlanetLab platform. The experimental results showed the improvement of both efficiency and reliability of JXTA protocols and services.

In our future work we plan to use the re-implemented protocols in large-scale JXTA-based applications for data intensive computing in highly dynamic environment using a large number of unreliable peer nodes.

Acknowledgements

This work has been partially supported by the Spanish MCYT project TSI2005-08225-C07-05.

References

1. Brookshier, D., Govoni, D., Krishnan, N., Soto, J.C.: JXTA: Java P2P Programming. Sams Publishing (2002)
2. Foster, I., Kesselman, C.: The Grid - Blueprint for a New Computing Infrastructure. Morgan Kaufmann Publishers, San Francisco (1998)
3. Guerraoui, R., Rodrigues, L.: Introduction to Reliable Distributed Programming. Springer, Heidelberg (2006)
4. Halepovic, E., Deters, R.: The costs of using jxta. In: Proceedings of the 3rd International Conference on Peer-to-Peer Computing, p. 160. IEEE Computer Society Press, Los Alamitos (2003)
5. JXTA Projects: `https://communications.dev.java.net/`
6. Keidl, M., Seltzsam, S., Kemper, A.: Technologies for E-Services. In: Benatallah, B., Shan, M.-C. (eds.) TES 2003. LNCS, vol. 2819. Springer, Heidelberg (2003)
7. Krepska, E., Kielmann, Th., Sirvent, R., Badia, R.M.: A service for reliable execution of grid applications. In: 2nd CoreGRID Integration Workshop, Krakow, Poland, October 2006, pp. 232–242 (2006)
8. Planet Lab: `http://planet-lab.org/`
9. Li, S.: Early Adopter JXTA. Wrox Press Information Inc. (2003)
10. Oaks, S., Traversat, B., Gong, L.: JXTA in a Nutshell. O'Reilly (2003)
11. Ostrowski, K., Birman, K.: Extensible web services architecture for notification in large-scale systems. In: International Conference on Web Services. IEEE Computer Society Press, Los Alamitos (2006)
12. Riasol, J.E., Xhafa, F.: Juxta-cat: a jxta-based platform for distributed computing. In: Proceedings of the 4th International Symposium on Principles and Practice of Programming in Java, pp. 72–81. ACM Press, New York (2006)
13. Peterson, R., Ramasubramanian, V., Sirer, E.G.: Corona: A high performance publish-subscribe system for the world wide web. In: Proceedings of Networked System Design and Implementation, California (2006)

A Ring Infrastructure for Neighbor-Centric Peer-to-Peer Applications

Oliver Haase, Alfred Toth, and Jürgen Wäsch

HTWG Konstanz - University of Applied Sciences, Constance, Germany

Abstract. We propose a peer-to-peer system that supports distributed virtual world applications. For these applications, the connections between directly neighboring peers are of the utmost importance. To minimize wide area network traffic and average latency, peers that belong to the same subnet, are grouped together, and these groups are interconnected via wide area connections. To build up and maintain this optimized peer-to-peer structure, we developed a set of protocols that efficiently handle the joining and leaving of peers as well as failure situations. Peers are aranged in the logical ring structure using a two-step discovery and join procedure. The first step uses broadcast messages to discover peers in a local subnet, followed by a local join. If no peer answers in the local subnet, a remote join is performed. With the implemented recovery procedures, our peer-to-peer system can survive multi-node failures in a local subnet as well as the failure of an entire subnet.

1 Introduction

Peer-to-peer networks support a variety of different applications, including file sharing, telecommunication, multimedia streaming, web caching, distributed collaboration, and shared virtual world implementations. Evidently, a good peer-to-peer infrastructure has to efficiently support the needs of its applications [1]. For file sharing applications, e.g., the pre-dominant operation is the retrieval of a (key, value) pair for a given key. Many peer-to-peer infrastructures, such as distributed hash tables [2,3,4,5,6], are optimized for exactly this retrieval operation.

For distributed shared virtual world applications, however, the situation is different. Typically, the virtual world is divided into separate, neighboring areas that are distributed among the participating peers. Data exchange mainly takes place between neighboring areas, because the beings that inhabit the virtual world can move from one area to a neighboring one.

One example of a shared virtual world is Aqualife, a peer-to-peer application that simulates a distributed ecosystem. In Aqualife, each participating peer runs a part of the virtual global aquarium, and hosts fish that interact with each other, and that can swim from one peer to another. A peer has a preceeding and a succeeding neighbor that its fish can swim to and from, so that as a result all peers together form a logical ring. When a new peer joins the community, it needs to connect to a succeeding and to a preceeding neighbor, but its actual

T. Enokido, L. Barolli, and M. Takizawa (Eds.): NBiS 2007, LNCS 4658, pp. 355–364, 2007.

position in the ring is irrelevant from the application point of view. Thus, to minimize network traffic and latency, it is advisable to build the peer ring upon the topological proximity of the peers.

Topological proximity takes into account not only the geographical distance between two peers, but also the characteristics of the interconnecting network including bandwidth, throughput, and latency. Evidently, determining the topological distance between any two peers is a complex and costly task; what is even more, it is a metric that varies over time, as the network load and other parameters change. Also, it is generally not possible to map the surface of the earth onto a ring while at the same time preserving topological distances.

On the other hand, the single one type of proximity that has the greatest impact on both network load and latency, is whether or not two peers belong to the same subnet. Taking that differentiation into account is very beneficial and, at the same time, feasible with comparably simple and robust procedures.

Our peer-to-peer infrastructure groups peers that belong to the same subnet together in a chain, and interconnects these local chains to a global ring, see Figure 1. This approach minimizes the amount of wide area network traffic and the average latency. In addition, it reduces the number of connections that have to traverse firewalls and NAT boxes, and that need to be taken special care of.

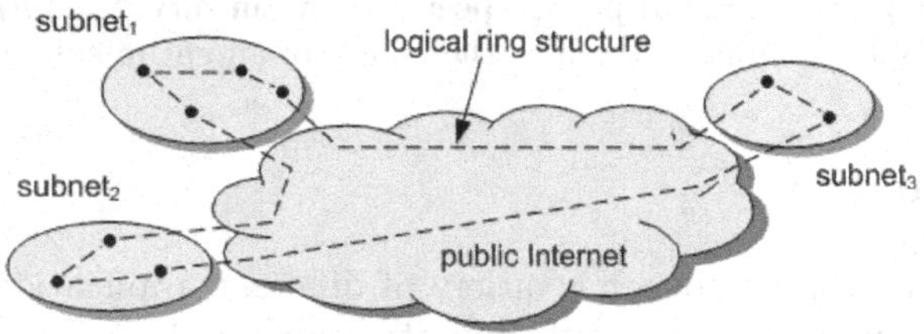

Fig. 1. Global ring structure interconnecting local peer chains

We achieve this optimized peer-to-peer structure by a two-step discovery and join procedure. In the first step, the new peer broadcasts a discovery request into its subnet. If at least one local peer replies, the new peer initiates a *local join* procedure to have itself inserted into the local peer chain.

If no local peer responds to the discovery broadcast, the new peer performs the second step of the discovery procedure and uses a bootstrap server to be put in contact with any one peer in the community. The new peer uses the contact to request a *remote join* procedure. During this procedure, care is taken not to place the new peer between two peers that belong to the same subset, so as not to corrupt the optimal structure shown in Figure 1.

The bootstrap server is the only central entity in an otherwise serverless peer-to-peer infrastructure. It helps new peers to contact the existing community by maintaining a partial list of known peers in its peer cache. To ensure scalability, the bootstrap server caches the addresses of a constant number of peers only and operates completely statelessly on a simple request-response protocol. Its cache replacement technique continuously updates the peer cache with new, alive contact points. This technique quickly detects inactive peers and discards them; it optimizes load balancing with respect to the join procedure; it includes even peers that have joined the community without interrogating the bootstrap server; and it diversifies the content of the peer cache across the entire peer-to-peer community [7].

2 Network Topology

Each peer a in our peer-to-peer network is identified by a globally unique identifier ID_a. We define connections between two peers a and b as follows: if a peer a knows the IP adress of peer b, there exists a (directed) connection from a to b. If both a connection from a to b and from b to a exist, we say that a connection exists *between* a and b.

From an application point of view, the peer-to-peer overlay network constitutes a logical *ring* (cf. Figure 1). This means that each peer maintains dedicated connections to its *succeeding* and *preceeding* peer in the ring. We call this type of connections *primary connections* (cf. Figure 2).

Each subnet A in the global ring has assigned a unique subnet identifier SID_A, which is known by all peers within A. The peers in a subnet that are connected to a peer in another subnet are called *edge peers*, otherwise the peers are called *inner peers* (cf. Figure 2). Subnets that are connected via their edge peers are called *neighboring subnets*.

Peers within a subnet can be totally ordered by their unique IDs. In our topology, we assume that the peers within a subnet form an ordered chain from the edge peer with the smaller ID (*lower* edge peer) to the edge peer with the greater ID (*upper* edge peer) in the subnet. Successor connections of peers point to peers with the next greater ID within the same subnet, predecessor connections point to the peers with the next smaller ID, respectively. Exception are the two edge peers in a subnet: the predecessor connection of the lower edge peer point to the upper edge peer in the preceeding network, the successor connection of the upper edge peer point to the lower edge peer in the suceeding subnet (cf. Figure 2). In case the ring is fully contained in a subnet, i.e., it is constituted solely by peers of the same network, both edge peers of the subnet are connected with each other.

To enable efficient recovery in case of failures, e.g., when a local or remote peer becomes unavailable, peers maintain so called *secondary* connections, in addition to the primary connections that constitute the application layer ring (cf. Figure 2). Each inner peer maintains 6 secondary connections: It knows both edge peers of the preceeding and the succeeding subnets, as well as the upper edge peer of the next-to-preceeding subnet and the lower edge peer of the next-to-succeeding subnet. Edge peers maintain only 4 secondary connections, since their successor (predecessor) primary connection already points to the lower (upper) edge peer of the succeeding (preceeding) subnet.

Since a peer in a subnet can efficiently determine the edge peers of its local subnet by broadcast, we do not maintain secondary connections from inner

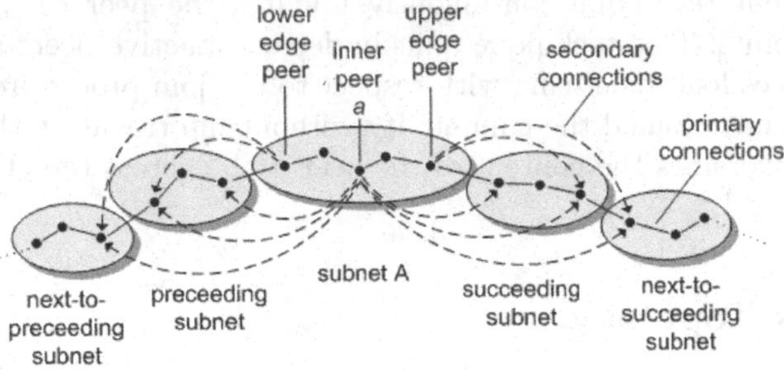

Fig. 2. Peer-to-peer network topology and terminology

peers to the local edge peers. This decision is based upon the observation that broadcasting delivers accurate information about the local edge peers and is comparatively cheap, whereas stored information about edge peers can become out of date. This approach is not applicable to determine edge peers of neighboring subnets, since broadcasts are confined to subnet boundaries.

Please note, that, in our ring topology, it is possible for a peer to maintain connections to itself. In case the ring consists only of a single peer a, all primary and secondary connections point to a itself. Moreover, some secondary connections might be redundant, in case the ring spans less than four subnets. We allow this redundancy for the sake of a uniform treatment of the join and leave procedures and recovery.

3 Joining and Leaving

When a peer joins or leaves the peer-to-peer community, certain primary and secondary connections need to be updated. In this section we present the procedures to perform these structural updates.

3.1 Local Join

When a new peer, a, wants to join the network, it first broadcasts a `discovery request` into its local subnet. Whether or not at least one peer replies within a certain time frame, determines if a local or a remote join is performed. In this section, we assume peer a to receive at least one reply to its `discovery request`.

After the `discovery request` has been sent out, peer a waits for a time period that is long enough for a preexisting local peer to reply. Within subnet boundaries where communication is extremly fast, this period can be comparably short. In most cases, all local peers will reply within the time limit; however, for the local join procedure to succeed, the reply of only one peer suffices, as we will see in the following.

In the reply, each responding peer sends its ID to a. Peer a selects the peer, b, with the ID closest to its own and sends a `local join request` to it. For the following considerations, let us assume ID_a to be greater than ID_b; the opposite case is treated symmetrically.

As a measure to ensure correctness even if some peers failed to respond in time to *a*'s `discovery request`, peer *b* checks whether *a* indeed belongs between *b* and its current successor, *c*. If ID_c is less than ID_a, *b* rejects the `local join request` and refers *a* to peer *c* instead. Otherwise, *b* prepares the join procedure by sending a `lock request` to its current successor, *c*. If *c* were not locked, a concurrent join request to peer *c* of another new peer that also belongs between *b* and *c* could corrupt the ring structure.

Once the join lock is set in both *b* and *c*, peers *a*, *b*, and *c* update their primary, i.e., predecessor and successor, connections in the usual way so as to effectively insert *a* in between *b* and *c*. In addition, peer *b* transmits the subnet ID and its secondary connections to *a*. As a result, *a* knows the edge peers of the preceeding and succeeding subnets, as well as the near edge peers of the next-to-preceeding and the next-to-succeeding subnets.

If *a* has become a new edge peer, the secondary connections of all peers in the four neighboring (preceeding, succeeding, next-to-preceeding, next-to-succeeding) subnets need to be updated. To this end, *a* uses its newly aquired secondary connections to inform the near edge peers in the four neighboring subnets of the change. These edge peers use local broadcast messages to spread the information to all their local peers that update their secondary connections accordingly.

3.2 Remote Join

If the new peer, *a*, gets no response to its `discovery request`, it represents a new subnet, *A*. At this point, *a*'s ID is made the subnet ID of *A*, SID_A, and will be propagated to any future peers in *A*, as described in section 3.1.

Peer *a* now contacts the bootstrap server, whose address is known through out-of-band means. The bootstrap server puts peer *a* into contact with a randomly selected peer, *b*, of another subnet, to which *a* sends a `remote join request`. If *b*, however, is an inner peer, it cannot perform the remote join itself because that would disrupt the local structure in *b*'s subnet. Instead, *b* determines its local edge peers (see section 2), randomly choses one, say *c*, and refers peer *a* to *c*. After *a* has sent the `remote join request` to *c*, *c* initiates the update of the primary connections of all involved peers, i.e., *a*, *c*, and *c*'s current remote neighbor, *d*. As a result, *a*'s subnet has been inserted between two other subnets.

In the next steps, all secondary connections have to be established and updated, respectively. This is done by information propagation through the four neighboring subnets of peer *a*, as sketched in Figure 3. The direct neigbors of *a* broadcast the existence of *a* into their local subnets (1). As a result, all peers in the directly neighboring subnets can update their secondary connections accordingly. In step (2), the far edge peers in these subnets send a notification back to *a* enabling it to set its preceeding and succeeding far edge peer connections. Also, these far edge peers propagate the update to their direct neighbor in the next-to-preceeding and next-to-succeeding subnets (3). The edge peers in these subnets broadcast the update to their local peers (4a), and send a notification back to a (4b) which sets its final two secondary connections. Please note that steps (4a) and (4b) can be performed concurrently.

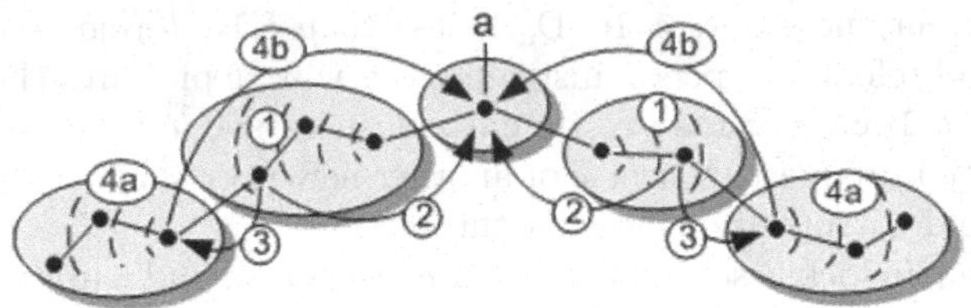

Fig. 3. Propagation of secondary connection information after remote join

3.3 Leave

When a peer, a, wants to leave the peer-to-peer community, it first sends lock messages to its predecessor, b, and its successor, c. As a result, b and c cannot perform any other join or leave operation before a's leave has been completed, thus avoiding inconsistencies stemming from concurrent operations affecting the connections of the same peers. In the next step, a sends references to each other to b and c, which update their primary connections accordingly. Finally, a unlocks b and c, enabling them to accept future join and leave requests.

If a was an edge peer, the secondary connections of the peers in the four neighboring subnets need to be updated as well. The updated information is propagated by means of local broadcast messages and handed-off from the direct neighboring subnets to the next-to-direct neighboring subnets by point-to-point message exchange between the respective edge peers. This process is very similar to the secondary connection update in the case of a remote join operation as explained in section 3.2.

4 Recovery

In case one or more peers fail (due to hardware or software failures) or become disconnected from the network (due to network failures), recovery procedures must take place to rebuild the ring structure.

When a peer detects a failure, it initates the appropriate recovery procedure. Considering our ring topology, we can distinguish three different kinds of failures. First, one or more inner peer fail within a subnet. Second, an edge peer fails within a subnet. Third, a subnet as a whole becomes unavailable.

4.1 Inner Peer Failure

If an inner peer fails, recovery can be handled locally within the subnet the failed peer belongs to. The peer a that detected that its preceeding (succeeding) peer failed, simply sends a broadcast message in the subnet stating that peer a

looks for a new predecessor (successor). All alive peers that miss a successor (or predecessor) answer upon this broadcast with their unique peer ID and their IP address. Peer a re-connects with peer b, where $|ID_a - ID_b|$ is minimal. Since the peers within a subnet are totally ordered by their unique peer IDs, a re-connects with the the correct peer to close the ordered chain in the subnet and, thus, close the ring. Simultanous failures of neighboring inner peers are handled with this approach like the failure of a single peer.

4.2 Edge Peer Failure

If an edge peer e fails, the peer a that detects the failure determines if the failed edge peer belongs to the same subnet as a or to a neighboring subnet. In the former case, a uses its secondary connection to the upper (lower) edge peer of the preceeding (succeeding) subnet to re-connect to this peer and to close the ring. At the same time, peer a becomes a new edge peer of its subnet.

In the latter case, i.e., if the failed edge peer e belongs to a different subnet, peer a is itself an edge peer. Peer a uses its secondary connection to the lower (upper) edge peer b of the preceeding (succeeding) subnet to get a "handle" to the subnet S where e belongs to. The edge peer b initiates a local search for the new upper (lower) edge peer in S and returns this information to a. Peer a re-connects to this peer to close the ring. In both cases, recovery results in updates of secondary connections which is done analogously to join and leave (cf. section 3).

4.3 Subnet Failure

The case that a complete subnet gets unavailable, can not directly be recognized. The situation that both edge peers of a subnet can not be reached does not imply that all peers in the subnet became unavailable. We have to wait for a specific period of time in which we allow the subnet to recover from local edge peer failures to close the ring again. If this does not happen, the edge peer that detected the failure of the subnet uses its secondary connection to the upper (lower) edge peer of the next-to-preceeding (next-to-succeeding) subnet (cf. Figure 2) to reconnect to this edge peer and, hence, to close the ring again.

Summarizing, using the described recovery procedures, our peer-to-peer ring infrastructure can survive failures of one or more inner peers, one or both edge peers of a subnet and an entire subnet. Of course, there exist situations where the peer-to-peer ring system can not recover from a failure: if two or more neighboring subnets fail, our system can not recover from this situation.

In this case, there exist several possibilities to react and to bring the remainder of the peer-to-peer system again into a consistent state. For example, all peers can simply terminate. If configured, they can restart afterwards and build up a new, differently structured, ring. An alternative is to enable a global ring search for the "open ends" of the ring followed by re-connecting the "open ends" and, hence, closing the ring. In the current implementation, the system terminates and restarts again.

More details on recovery in our peer-to-peer ring system and its implementation can be found in [7].

5 Implementation

The presented protocols and mechanisms have been fully implemented in Java [7]. All broadcast messages use datagram sockets for UDP/IP broadcast within subnet boundaries. All point-to-point communication uses the Java Remote Method Invocation (RMI) mechanism which exchanges request/response message pairs over TCP/IP; this comprises all messages for joins (both local and remote), leaves, heart-beating, propagation of secondary connection information, and last not least the exchange of application level payloads.

Due to Java's platform independence, the software should run on any machine that provides a Java 5 runtime environment, or higher. However, the otherwise fully portable system uses one platform specific system call to access the MAC (media access control) address of a peer machine. This system call has been tested on Windows, Linux, Solaris, and MacOS, and should also work on any other UNIX based operating system.

For deployment, we use Java Web Start technology. A Web Start enabled Java application can be dynamically downloaded from a web page, similar to an Java applet except that a Web Start application runs outside the protected applet sandbox and, thus, is allowed to communicate with other peers in the network. Also, using Web Start ensures that each client always runs the latest version of the software, which dramatically simplifies deployment and versioning.

6 Related Work

The topologies of most distributed hash table approaches seem, at first glance, similar to our approach. They use logical ring structures to divide the address space up amongst the peers, and they use some notion of routing tables, finger tables, or neighbor lists to keep connections to a number of other peers in the overlay network, which resembles some similarity with the secondary connections in our approach [2,4,5,6]. In the case of Chord [2], e.g., each peer maintains a so called finger table that consists of references to the peer opposite to itself in the ring, to the peer a quarter rotation ahead, to the peer an eighth rotation ahead, and so on. As a result, with the need to store (and keep up-to-date) $O(\log n)$ connections, an arbitrary peer can be reached in $O(\log n)$ steps in a Chord ring of n peers, performing a distributed binary search. Other distributed hash table approaches vary in the technical details, but follow the same principle.

A peer being able to efficiently reach any other peer in the network is essential for a distributed hash table, because the storage and retrieval of (key, value) pairs are the primary operations. From the application point of view, the peer-to-peer community is an interconnected set of data stores that cooperate to jointly provide a uniform address space. When a peer is asked for a specific key, it is mandatory that it may help to efficiently retrieve the (key, value) pair independent of where it is hosted in the overlay network. In a distributed hash table, the connections with the adjacent neighbors are of no greater relevance than the connections with any other peers. Putting physically close peers into topological proximity in the peer-to-peer overlay network, is not helpful and, thus, not a design goal.

This is in sharp contrast to our approach that is tailored for virtual world applications that pose significantly different requirements upon the underlying peer-to-peer infrastructure [8,9]. Here, what the application sees is exactly the ring topology, and thus the connections with the adjacent neighbors are of the utmost importance. All application level data exchange goes through these connections only. Consequently, grouping physically close peers together is a highly desirable design goal for an infrastructure of this type.

Finally, the routing structures in a distributed hash table, such as the Chord finger tables, contain suitable subsets of *primary* connections, as they are used during regular operations. Our secondary connections between non-adjacent peers, in contrast, are required to ensure robustness and reliability and are only used to restore operability in case of a system or network failure.

7 Conclusion and Future Work

We have presented operations and protocols that establish and maintain a ring infrastructure for neighbor-centric peer-to-peer applications. Even though the primary topology is simple, the need for robustness and failure tolerance in a volatile and vulnerable environment such as the public Internet, makes the structures and procedures rather complex. In particular, we use different categories of secondary connections to protect the peer-to-peer overlay network against various degrees of failures.

A next step is to extent the ring to a grid structure that spans a virtual globe, with each peer having four neighbor, rather than two. Clearly, the challenge with this extension is to find a good trade-off between complexity stemming from the secondary connections and protection against multiple simultaneous node and network failures.

Other interesting conclusions relate to the Java RMI implementation rather than the protocols themselves. For one, the RMI built-in detection of a failure in the remote node is far too slow in a mixed Linux/Windows environment. We had to implement an application layer time-out mechanism to overcome this issue. An even more serious problem is communication between two peers with a firewall in the middle. The standard Java RMI solution to this problem is to tunnel RMI requests over HTTP. This, however, requires a peer that sits behind a firewall either to run an HTTP server, or the external HTTP server in the subnet to forward incoming RMI-over-HTTP requests via a specific CGI script to the target peer. Both options are rather heavy-weight and are likely to conflict with the security policies in the subnet.

Therefore, many peer-to-peer networks employ an approach where a peer behind a firewall actively contacts a rendez-vous peer outside the firewall to establish contact with its outside neighbors. Then, TCP connections are kept open to the direct neighbors over which data can then be exchanged as desired. However, because Java RMI uses a simple request response protocol, the lifespan of a TCP connection is left to the operating system and cannot be controlled by the peer-to-peer infrastructure. In a follow-up project we plan to extend Java RMI in a way that better suits the need of a peer-to-peer infrastructure.

References

1. Hauswirth, M., Dustdar, S.: Peer-to-Peer: Foundations and Architecture (in German). Datenbank Spektrum 5, 5–13 (2005)
2. Morris, R., Karger, D., Kaashoek, F., Balakrishnan, H.: Chord: A Scalable Peer-to-Peer Lookup Service for Internet Applications. In: Proceedings of ACM SIGCOMM 2001, San Diego, CA, pp. 149–160. ACM Press, New York (2001)
3. Ratnasamy, S., Francis, P., Handley, M., Karp, R., Schenker, S.: A scalable content-addressable network. In: Proceedings of ACM SIGCOMM 2001, San Diego, CA, pp. 161–172. ACM Press, New York (2001)
4. Zhao, B., Huang, L., Stribling, J., Rhea, S., Joseph, A., Kubiatowicz, J.: Tapestry: A resilient global-scale overlay for service deployment. IEEE Journal on Selected Areas in Communications 22, 41–53 (2003) Special Issue on Service Overlay Networks.
5. Rowstron, A., Druschel, P.: Pastry: Scalable, decentralized object location, and routing for large-scale peer-to-peer systems. In: Guerraoui, R. (ed.) Middleware 2001. LNCS, vol. 2218, pp. 329–350. Springer, Heidelberg (2001)
6. Aberer, K.: P-Grid: A Self-Organizing Access Structure for P2P Information Systems. In: Batini, C., Giunchiglia, F., Giorgini, P., Mecella, M. (eds.) CoopIS 2001. LNCS, vol. 2172, pp. 179–194. Springer, Heidelberg (2001)
7. Toth, A.: Ein ringbasiertes Peer-to-Peer-System auf Basis Java RMI. HTWG Konstanz - University of Applied Sciences, Diplomarbeit (2007)
8. O'Connell, K., Dinneen, T., Collins, S., Tangney, B., Harris, N., Cahill, V.: Techniques for handling scale and distribution in virtual worlds. In: Proceedings of the 7th ACM SIGOPS European Workshop, ACM SIGOPS, pp. 17–24. ACM Press, New York (1996)
9. Walch, J., Steggles, P.: User intent as a bandwidth conservation heuristic in shared virtual environments. In: IMSA, pp. 5–10 (2002)

Semantic Query Routing in SenPeer, a P2P Data Management System

David Faye[1], Gilles Nachouki[2], and Patrick Valduriez[2]

[1] LANI, Université Gaston Berger de Saint-Louis, Sénégal
David.Faye@univ-nantes.fr
[2] LINA, Université de Nantes, France
Gilles.Nachouki@univ-nantes.fr,
Patrick.Valduriez@inria.fr

Abstract. A challenging problem in a schema-based peer-to-peer (P2P) system is how to locate peers that are relevant with respect to a given query. In this paper, we propose a new semantic routing mechanism in the context of the SenPeer *P2P Data Management System* (PDMS). SenPeer is an unstructured P2P system based on an organization of peers around super-peers according to their semantic domains. Our proposal is based on the use of a distributed data structure, called expertise table, maintained by the super-peers and describing data at the neighboring peers. This table, combined with matching techniques, is the basis of a semantic overlay network. Semantic links are exploited for efficient query propagation towards peers that may have relevant data. We give a performance evaluation of our semantic query routing with respect to important criteria such as precision, recall and number of messages. The results show that our algorithm significantly outperforms a baseline algorithm without semantics.

1 Introduction

PDMS aim at overcoming the scalability problems of data integration systems by combining P2P and distributed database techniques. Peers join the system by providing their own schemas and matching their respective schemas to discover their acquaintances for effective data sharing. In such a setting, a major problem is efficient query routing across peer data sources, i.e. deciding to which peers the query must be sent for efficiency and effectiveness. To motivate our discussion, let us consider a PDMS[6] where experts and scientists share data about the development of the Senegal river. The data are covered by topics such as hydraulics, agronomic research, health, etc. For these multidisciplinary applications, schema sharing and efficient query routing are crucial in order to enable users discovering remote data sources.

Unstructured P2P systems typically employ flooding and random walk approaches to locate files, which result in much network traffic and low recall/precision. To improve performance, peer clustering and indexing allow peers to select from an index the relevant peers to send a query to. In some PDMS with

T. Enokido, L. Barolli, and M. Takizawa (Eds.): NBiS 2007, LNCS 4658, pp. 365–374, 2007.

complex queries facilities, peer selection relies on the use of semantic descriptions of peers. We observe that they are essentially based on statistical observations and exploit, in some cases, a shared ontology, or a taxonomy. In some cases, flooding is unavoidable.

In this paper, we propose a new semantic routing mechanism in the context of SenPeer, a PDMS with various data models and ontologies. We assume an unstructured P2P system where peers are connected to super-peers according to their semantic domains. In SenPeer, the knowledge of a peer is represented through a semantic network (called *sGraph*) which can represent data conforming to various data models. To interact, super-peers maintain expertise tables describing data at the semantically linked (super)-peers and define semantic mappings between their content descriptions. These mappings are the basis of semantic overlay network where peers having similar schemas form a semantic neighborhood. This semantic overlay is exploited further to address query propagation. Our routing technique is applied in the presence of several data models provided that there are wrappers which undertake the transformation of the query to a suitable query language for each data source. We make the following contributions :

(i) We introduce the SQUEL language, for exchanging queries between peers.
(ii) We propose a distributed data structure called *expertise table* that is used for advertising content shared by a peer.
(iii) we propose a semantic routing algorithm of queries toward relevant peers.
(iv) We provide an experimental validation. The results show that our routing algorithm significantly outperforms a baseline algorithm without semantics.

The remainder of this paper is organized as follows. Section 2, introduces our semantic overlay. Section 3 presents our semantic query routing algorithm. Section 4 gives an experimental validation. Section 5 discusses relevant work. Finally, Section 6 concludes and discuss our future work .

2 Semantic Overlay

In this section, we present the techniques for the semantic overlay formation.

2.1 Basic Context

Assume a PDMS in which each peer hosts a data source. Our main goal is the efficient search across the PDMS by routing queries only to relevant peers. To support peer autonomy, network self-organization, we choose an unstructured super-peer network. We adopt a super-peer network topology that combines the efficiency of centralized search with the autonomy, load balancing and robustness of distributed search. Peers are attached to super-peers according to their topic of interest or semantic domain. Each super-peer SP_j responsible of a semantic domain D_j suggests a schema SS_j for that domain. However, each peer describes its data with its own schema S_i. Moreover, each peer P_i submits queries with its own query language. For these reasons, we use : (1) a schema exchange format called *sGraph* that allows to exchange semantically associated schemas across the network without making any assumptions about the peers data models; (2) a query exchange format called SQUEL that allows to exchange queries between peers. These considerations are taken into account in our query routing strategy.

2.2 Semantic Reconciliation in SenPeer

In SenPeer, each peer exports its schema in a data model-independent representation called *sGraph*. An *sGraph* is an edge-labeled directed graph whose nodes correspond to the elements in the source schemas (such as tables, columns, XML attributes, etc.) and whose edges are taken in the set of possible semantic relations between elements in those schemas. Additionally, every node n_i is associated with a set $syn(n_i)$ of keywords (essentially synonyms added by the owners of the schemas at design-time) which provides more linguistic information about the node to guide mapping discovery. Figure 1 depicts a portion of the *sGraph* representing a schema (here a relational schema) about the cultures practised on the grounds of the Senegal river basin. For simplification, some keywords have been omitted. The schema elements are not filled and the nodes filled correspond to type nodes. To discover mapping between two nodes

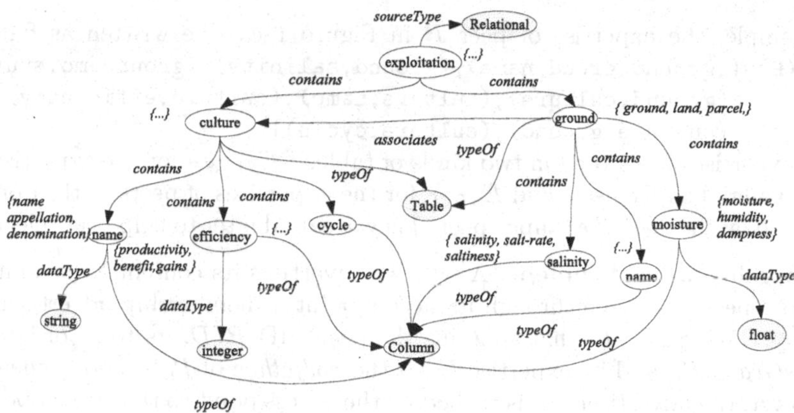

Fig. 1. Partial *sGraph* about the cultures practised on the grounds of the river basin

n_p and n_k, we use a semantic matchmaker which performs dynamic *sGraph* matching. Based on a similarity measure $Sim(n_p, n_k)$, this matchmaker takes into account both linguistic and structural features of the nodes to be compared. The linguistic similarity $S_l(n_p, n_k)$ computes the level of matching based on the meaning of their synonym sets $syn(n_p)$ and $syn(n_k)$. The neighborhood similarity $S_v(n_p, n_k)$ captures their similarity based on their context of appearance in the two *sGraph*. It is proportional to the number of matching neighbors the nodes have in their neighborhood and their level of matching. The similarity

$Sim(n_p, n_k)$ is evaluated as follow :

$$Sim(n_p, n_k) = \lambda_l.S_l(n_p, n_k)+\lambda_v.S_v(n_p, n_k) \text{ where } \lambda_l, \lambda_v \geq 0 \text{and} \lambda_l+\lambda_v = 1. \quad (1)$$

A detailed description of the matching process and the similarity measures can be found in [2]. These mappings are stored in two kinds of matrices : $M_{\mathcal{SP}/\mathcal{SP}}$ for the mappings between the schemas of super-peers and $M_{\mathcal{SP}/\mathcal{P}}$ for the mappings between the schema of a super-peer and the schemas of its peers. These mappings are the basis of a semantic overlay on top of the underlying physical network.

2.3 Semantic Overlay Formation

A semantic domain appears when a new super-peer SP_j, called *domain godfather*, joins the PDMS with a suggested schema SS_j. First, the super-peer defines its expertise and publishes a domain advertisement. Then, it can process requests from linked super-peers or membership requests from peers.

Expertise Description. Upon joining a super-peer, a peer registers a semantic description (automatically inferred from its *sGraph*) of the elements it wants to share. The expertise of a peer P of *sGraph* SG is defined as follows :

$$Exp(P) = \{(n_p, m_p) \in SG \mid contains(n_p, m_p)\}. \quad (2)$$

For example, the expertise of peer P in Figure 1 can be written as follows:

```
Exp(P)={(ground,groud_name),(ground,salinity),(ground,moisture),
        (ground,culture),(culture,name),(culture,efficiency),
        (culture,ground),(culture,cycle)}.
```

These expertises are stored in two kinds of tables : $E_{\mathcal{SP}/\mathcal{SP}}$ for the expertises of the acquainted super-peers and $E_{\mathcal{SP}/\mathcal{P}}$ for the expertises of peers in the domain sponsored by the *godfather* super-peer. They are used later to help peer selection.

Membership advertisement. A peer P_i advertises its content by sending to the super-peer backbone through its access point a membership advertisement $MA_i = (PID, S_i, E_i, T)$ that contains the peer's ID PID, its topic of interest T, its *sGraph* S_i, and its expertise E_i. If the *godfather* of P_i has not joined the PDMS yet, the advertisement is cached by the access point so that it will be able to advertise the *orphan* peer when its *godfather* joins the network. If the *godfather* of its semantic domain has been found, the matching process is done by the *godfather* to find mappings between the peer's *sGraph* and the suggested schema of the semantic domain. If the super-peer accepts the membership request, it stores the peer's expertise in its expertise table $E_{\mathcal{SP}/\mathcal{P}}$, the mappings in its mapping matrix $M_{\mathcal{SP}/\mathcal{P}}$ and sends a membership approval to the peer P_i.

Domain advertisement. A new super-peer SP_j advertises its domain by sending to its neighbors a domain advertisement $SDA_j = (DID, SS_j, E_j, T_j, \epsilon_{acc}, TTL)$ containing the domain ID DID, the suggested schema SS_j, the corresponding expertise E_j, the topic area of interest T_j, the minimum semantic similarity value required to establish semantic mapping between the suggested schema SS_j and the schemas of others (super-)peers. To carry out efficient communication and message forwarding among super-peers during domain foundation we combine a constrained flooding algorithm[7] that decreases duplicate queries with a TTL mechanism that helps reducing the radius of the discovery query coverage. When receiving a domain advertisement, a super-peer SP_r invokes the semantic matching process to find mappings between its suggested schema SS_r and the received suggested schema SS_j. The semantic mappings found are stored in $SP_r^{\prime}s$ mapping matrix $M_{\mathcal{SP}/\mathcal{SP}}$ and sent also to SP_j which can approve or reject them. If the collaboration has been accepted, each one stores the other's expertise in its expertise table $E_{\mathcal{SP}/\mathcal{SP}}$. SP_r forwards also the advertisement SDA_j to the peers it has early cached their advertisements to be interest by topic T_j.

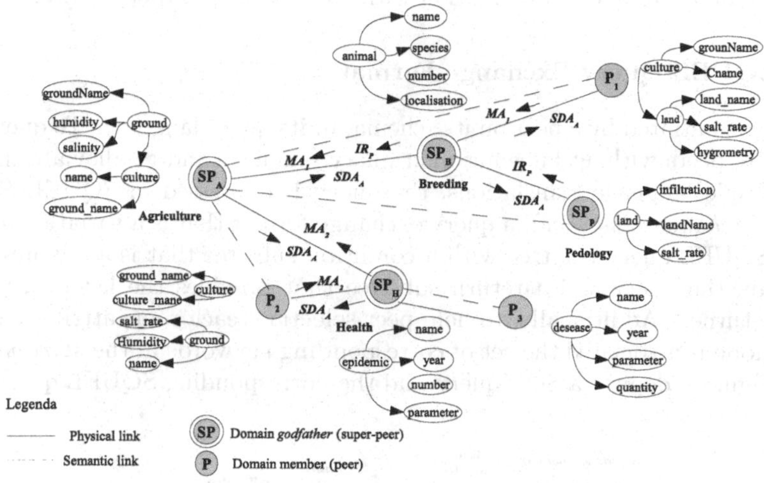

Fig. 2. Semantic communities formation during matching process

2.4 Example

Figure 2 depicts the role of semantic reconciliation in the domain formation process in a PDMS dealing with *Agriculture*, *Pedology*, *Breeding* and *Health* semantic communities. For simplicity, we give a minimal representation of each *sGraph*. Assume that SP_A joins the PDMS to define the *Agriculture* domain. It sends a domain advertisement SDA_A to its physical neighbors (i.e., SP_B and SP_H). According to the constrained flooding algorithm and the TTL, the advertisement is propagated to SP_P and the other peers for which SP_B and SP_H have early cached their advertisements for being interested by this domain. Here these other peers are P_1 and P_2. Super-Peer SP_P replies to SP_A (because *Agriculture* and *Pedology* topics are linked) by sending an interest request IR_P containing the matching elements found during the matching process, before waiting for approval. Thus, the resulting mappings are added in the mapping matrix $M_{\mathcal{SP}/\mathcal{SP}}$ of the corresponding super-peers. SP_B and SP_H are not interested and thus do not reply to SP_A. P_1 and P_2 interested by the *Agriculture* domain send their membership advertisement MA_1 and MA_2 to SP_A which can apply the matching process between the peer schemas and the schema it suggests. SP_A sends an accept notification to P_1 and P_2 if the matching has been successful and stores the mapping found in its mapping matrix $M_{\mathcal{SP}/\mathcal{P}}$.

3 Semantic Query Routing Mechanism

In this section, we introduce the SQUEL language for exchanging queries between peers and a semantic-based routing algorithm. This algorithm, shows how to select the set of relevant remote peers to forward a query by combining domain-aware query propagation with the notion of expertise table.

3.1 SQUEL Query Exchange Format

A query is initiated by a peer on its schema, in its query language. To query data of remote peers without knowing their query language and to alleviate the need for multiple language translations, the query is expressed in SQUEL(*SenPeer Query Exchange Language*), a query exchange format that is a variation of QEM [5]. A SQUEL query is a tree with a condition sub-tree that is an expression to constrain the query and a return sub-tree that provides the list of attributes to be returned. Additionally, to help peer selection, each root, attribute or sub-query node is associated the set of corresponding keywords in the *sGraph* of the peer. Figure 3 depicts a SQL query and the corresponding SQUEL query.

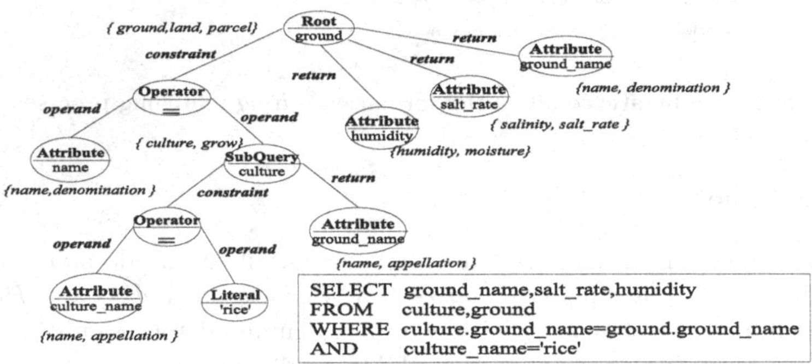

Fig. 3. A SQL query and its corresponding SQUEL query

3.2 Semantic Query Routing Algorithm

The semantic routing algorithm exploits the semantic overlay and the expertise tables of the local super-peer for both intra and inter-domain query propagation. Assume that peer P_i of *godfather* super-peer SP_j, issues a query Q on its schema with its query language, we distinguish the following main steps:

***Step 1.* Query subject extraction.** The query is first expressed in the SQUEL format. Then, the resulting query Q_s is routed to the *godfather* super-peer which extracts the query subject. The subject of a query Q_s is an abstraction of the query in terms of nodes of the query tree as follows:

$$Sub(Q_s) = \{(n_q, m_q) \in Q_s \mid return(n_q, m_q)\} \cup \{(n_q, m_q) \in Q_s \mid \exists\, o_q \in Q_s \wedge constraint(n_q, o_q) \wedge operand(o_q, m_q)\}. \quad (3)$$

For example, the subject of query Q_s in Figure 3 can be written as follows :

```
Sub(Q)={(ground,name),(ground, salt_rate),(ground,humidity),
    (culture,culture_name), (culture, ground_name)}.
```

***Step 2.* Peer selection.** The *godfather* super-peer selects the most knowledgeable peers for the query or their *godfathers* super-peers, by matching the query subject to the set of expertises that are stored in its expertise tables $E_{\mathcal{SP}/\mathcal{SP}}$ and $E_{\mathcal{SP}/\mathcal{P}}$. The selection is based on a function *Cap* that measures the capacity of a peer of expertise $Exp(P)$ on answering a given query of subject $Sub(Q)$.

$$Cap(P, Q) = \frac{1}{|Sub(Q)|}\Big(\sum_{s \in Sub(Q)} \max_{e \in Exp(P)} S_s(s, e)\Big). \quad (4)$$

The function *Cap* is based on the similarity S_s(defined in our previous works [2]) of the synonym sets associated to the elements of $Sub(Q)$ and $Exp(P)$. Each selected super-peer applies *Step 2* in its own domain for finding promising peers for the incoming query Q. Note that these descriptions are only used to facilitate peer selection and they do not hamper query processing. Indeed, it is easier to match these two structures rather than doing a complete graph matching process between *sGraph* and SQUEL query graph. After peer selection, we use the original query with its structure and rewrite it towards the selected peers.

***Step 3.* Query routing.** Once the set of relevant (super-)peers has been identified, the *godfather* super-peer SP_j of P_i sends the query to those promising peers or to their godfathers super-peers by using their ID, IP addresses and the underlying physical network.

***Example** (Semantic routing).* Consider that peer P_2 in Figure 2 submits to its godfather super-peer SP_A the query Q described in Figure 3. SP_A uses the semantic overlay to forward the query. To this end SP_A evaluates the capacity of each of its semantic neighbors P_1 and SP_P . As result, the following capacity values are returned $cap(Sub(Q), Exp(P_1)) = 0.8$ and $cap(Sub(Q), Exp(SP_P)) = 0.65$. On the basis of this result, SP_A sends the query Q to the selected semantic neighbors before waiting for reply.

4 Validation

In this section, we describe the performance evaluation of our routing algorithm with a SimJava-based simulator. We use recall and precision metrics borrowed from Information Retrieval, number of messages per query trace and response time, for different network sizes. We apply them at the peer selection level with number of peers ranging from 50 to 3000 and 10 super-peers with two settings :

- ***Setting A :*** peers are randomly clustered to super-peers. The super-peer selects randomly a set of peers to forward the query. This is our baseline.
- ***Setting B :*** peers are bounded to super-peers according to their interest. We apply our expertise-based selection algorithm to find relevant nodes.

The variation between the response times and the numbers of messages for the two settings is very low for network size less than 500 peers and 10 super-peers. This is due to the fact that in *Setting A*, the peers are also clustered and query broadcast is done between super-peers. By increasing the network size by a factor of 10, the response time increases for a factor of 3% and 5% for *Setting B* and *Setting A* respectively. The variation becomes very significant because when the network size increases for a factor of 60, response time increases by a factor of 40 for *Setting A* and 16 for *Setting B*. We observe the same phenomena for the number of messages. Figures 6 indicates that in *Setting A*, the recall shows

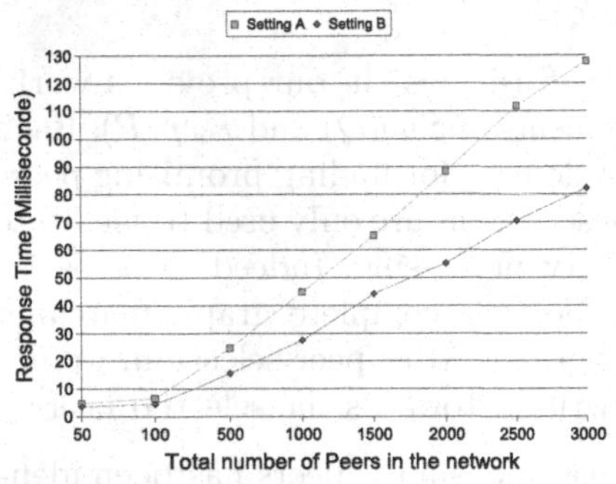

Fig. 4. Response Time

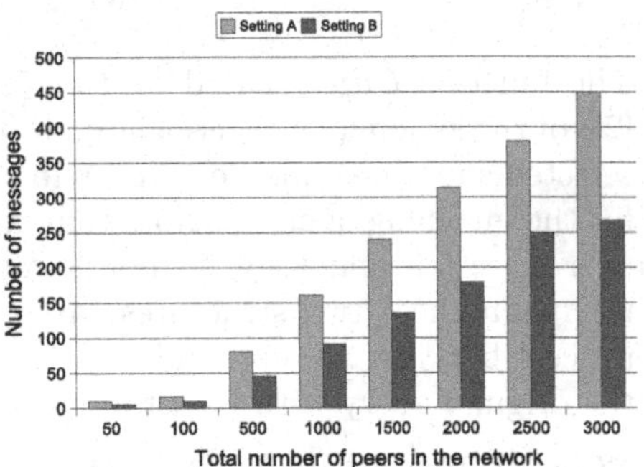

Fig. 5. Number of Messages

constant behavior regardless of the network size, approximately 25%. The recall of *Setting B* increases with the size of the network and reaches a percentage of almost 60% for a network of 3000 peers. Considering the number of messages per query, we observe that in *Setting B*, to reach a recall of 60%, we need less than 250 messages compared to *Setting A* which needs more than 450 messages to reach a recall of only 25%. Figure 7 shows that the peer selection in *Setting A* results in low precision of 1.5% that decreases when the number of peers increases, despite a high number of messages. In contrast, in *Setting B*, the precision is improved by the selectivity of the peer selection algorithm. At the same time, the number of messages is reduced because queries are sent only to promising peers. It can be inferred from these results that our semantic routing mechanism provides better results in term of recall and precision, reduces query distribution effort significantly compared to the baseline.

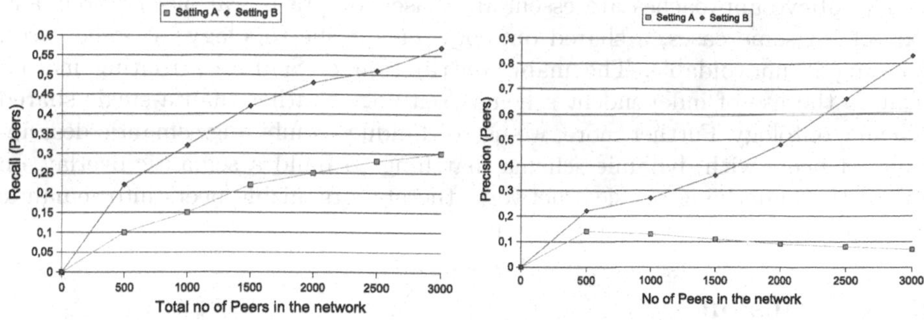

Fig. 6. Recall Rate

Fig. 7. Precision Rate

5 Related Work

This section gives an overview of routing algorithms in P2P systems. Efficient query routing in P2P systems has already been discussed in the literature [7][9]. Semantic query routing techniques are required to improve effectiveness and scalability of search processes for resource sharing in P2P systems. The unstructured P2P systems typically employ flooding and random walk to locate data, which results in much network traffic. To improve their performances, peer clustering and indexing allow peers to select from an index the right peers to send a query to. Structured overlays such as CAN and Chord use distributed hash table (DHT) for providing good scalability and efficient query routing performance. The use of semantics has been introduced to improve query routing techniques. In the INGA[8] algorithm, to find relevant peers, each peer maintains in a lazy manner a semantic shortcut index by analyzing the queries that are initiated remote peers and that transit via the peer. The main limitation of this routing approach is the unavoidable flooding of the network with messages, when a new peer that has not yet replicated any remote knowledge joins the network or when peers contain limited information about previous queries. Recently, schema and ontology frameworks have been used to support complex queries and address the lack of semantics in P2P routing algorithms. For instance, in Edutella[1], a RDF-based semantic routing architecture, nodes are clustered according to their interests and intra-(inter-)cluster routing algorithms are defined for providing efficient query routing. However, the routing protocol requires a specific topology between super-peers. The SQPeer[3] routing strategy uses intentional schemas (RVL Views) for determining relevant peer bases through the fragmentation of query patterns. However, since each view corresponds to a peer advertisement, it should be broadcast to the P2P network. In Bibster[4], data are structured and queries formulated according to a shared common ontology and routed in the network according to the expertise descriptions known by the peer. Based on the semantic similarity between a query and the expertises of the others nodes, a peer can select appropriate peers for query forwarding.

The above approaches are essentially based on statistical observations and exploit, in some cases, a shared ontology, or specific topology. In some cases, flooding is unavoidable. The main contribution of SenPeer's routing mechanism is the use of independent schemas/ontologies rather than a single shared schema/ontology. Further more, we use techniques combining semantic descriptions of peers with dynamic schema matching to build a semantic overlay, on top of the underlying physical network, thereby organizing peers into semantic communities for efficient query routing.

6 Conclusion

In this paper, we proposed a new routing algorithm in a PDMS in the context of multiple data models and query languages. The peers advertise the content they want to share by their expertise and discover acquainted peers by schema matching techniques. The peers' expertises and the semantic mappings are the basis of a semantic overlay organizing the network into semantic domains. The introduction of super-peers in combination with expertise tables and domain-aware query routing reduces the workload of peers by distributing queries to the appropriate subset of peers. From experiments with different parameters we obtain results that show that the community-based routing combined with the concept of expertise table outperforms significantly a baseline algorithm without semantic. Future work related to our proposal includes query planning, query optimization and answer fusion.

References

1. Nejdl, W., Wolf, B., Qu, C.: Edutella: A P2P networking infrastructure based on RDF. In: 11th International World Wide Web Conference, Hawaii, USA, May 2002 (2002)
2. Faye, D., Nachouki, G., Valduriez, P.: SenPeer: un système pair-à-pair de médiation de données. Revue ARIMA, vol. 4 (2006)
3. Sidirourgos, E., Kokkinidis, G.: Efficient Query Routing in RDF/S schema-based P2P System. In: 4th Hellenic Data Management Symposium (HDMS'05), Athens (2005)
4. Haase, P., Broekstra, J., Ehrig, M.: Bibster-A Semantics-Based Bibliographic P2P System. In: International Semantic Web Conference, Hiroshima (November 2004)
5. Panchapagesan, B., Hui, J., Wiederhold, G., Erickson, S.: The INEEL Data Integration Mediation System. In: International ICSC Symposium on Advances in Intelligent Data Analysis (AIDA'99), Rochester, NY (June 1999)
6. Rousset, M.C., Adjiman, P., Chatalic, P., Goasdoué, F., Simon, L.: SomeWhere in the Semantic Web. In: International Conference on Current Trends in Theory and Practice of Computer Science, Prague (January 2006)
7. Vuong, S., Li, J.: An Efficient Content Routing Algorithm in Large P2P Overlay Networks. In: 3rd International Conference on P2P Computing, Sweden (2003)
8. Tempich, C., Staab, S.: A lazy learning approach to effective query routing in peer-to-peer based networks for rdf data. In: WWW conference, USA (2004)
9. Zhuge, H., Liu, J., Feng, L.: Query Routing in a Peer-to-Peer Semantic Link Network. Computational Intelligence 21(2), 197–216 (2005)

Jamjuree Cluster: A Peer-to-Peer Cluster Computing System

Kasame Tritrakan, Pakit Kanchana, and Veera Muangsin

Dept. of Computer Engineering, Chulalongkorn University,
Pratumwan, Phrayathai, Bangkok, Thailand
{kasame.tr,pakit.k}@student.chula.ac.th, veera.m@chula.ac.th

Abstract. Peer-to-Peer computing, which aggregates idle computing cycles and storage space from PCs on the Internet, is a new approach to establish a high performance computing system. In this paper, we introduce Jamjuree Cluster, a cluster middleware suite that is an integration of cluster computing and peer-to-peer computing concepts. Jamjuree Cluster creates a single system image from PCs on a peer-to-peer network, and provides a parallel programming environment, file system, and batch scheduling like in a typical cluster system.

Keywords: cluster computing, peer-to-peer computing, JXTA.

1 Introduction

Cluster computing [1] and peer-to-peer computing [2] are two different approaches with the same goal to create scalable computing systems. The cluster computing approach is to build a computer system from commodity-of-the-shelf (COTS) hardware components connected with a local area network. The main objectives are high-performance, high-availability, scalability and cost-effectiveness. The cluster is controlled by cluster middleware to make all computers' resources (CPU, memory, and storage) work together as a single computer, or in other words, to create a single system image. Parallel programming environment and batch scheduling are available to support parallel and high-throughput computation, respectively. A computer cluster has centralized management and works in a client-server fashion.

Peer-to-peer (p2p) computing is an approach to gather computing resources and enable network collaboration. A p2p system typically consists of personal computers that connect to the Internet and arbitrarily participate in p2p activities. Due to fast growing processing power, storage capacity and network capability of personal computers, a global p2p network is potentially the largest pool of computing power. Nowadays, millions of people are using p2p file sharing applications or participating in distributed computing projects like Seti@home [3]. In its ideal concept, there is no centralized control in a p2p network. Every computer is equal and can act as a client and a server at the same time. However, in practical p2p systems, some mechanisms such as indexing can be performed more efficiently in a centralized manner.

Unlike computer clusters, most p2p networks at present are application-specific and based on different p2p architectures. In other words, there does not exist a general

T. Enokido, L. Barolli, and M. Takizawa (Eds.): NBiS 2007, LNCS 4658, pp. 375–384, 2007.

purpose p2p system in use today. Also, most of them are built on different software frameworks. Although there is a mature programming framework such as JXTA [4], it only provides primitive components and protocols for building more complicated services and applications. These reasons make it difficult for a user to use many different applications at the same time and for a developer to create a new application that works with others.

We propose that there must be a higher-level framework than that is provided by an existing framework such as JXTA. This can be done by applying some concepts of cluster computing onto p2p computing. The target is a general-purpose p2p architecture that provides a single system image. We also introduce Jamjuree Cluster, a middleware suite that is a proof-of-concept.

2 Jamjuree Cluster Architecture

We decided from the very beginning to build our p2p-cluster system on JXTA, a widely-accepted p2p software framework, rather than implementing a new one. However, many extensions are necessary. First, we need a library and services on top of JXTA so that the middleware and applications can be developed more easily than using JXTA library alone. After that, some essential components are required to create a cluster-like behavior. These include a shared file system and a job scheduler.

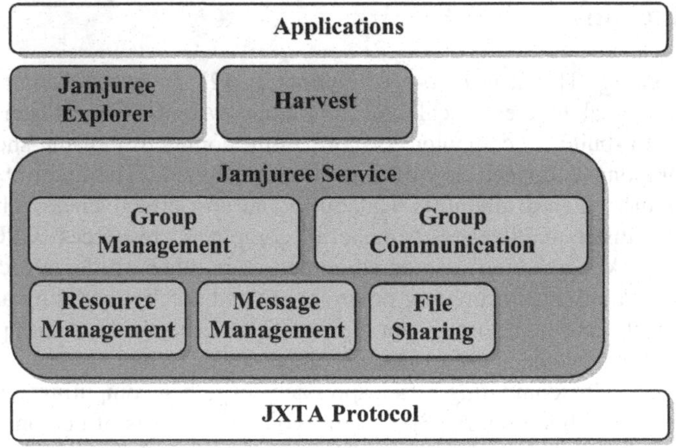

Fig. 1. Jamjuree Cluster Architecture

Fig. 1 shows the organization of Jamjuree p2p cluster architecture. On top of JXTA Protocol layer is Jamjuree Service layer that provides group-wise functionalities. On top of that is the clustering layer that consists of Jamjuree Explorer, a shared file system, and Harvest, a job scheduler.

3 Jamjuree Service

The objectives of Jamjuree Service are to be an easy-to-use library for p2p programming and to provide basic functions for a p2p system. It employs JXTA protocol and services in the background. The API of Jamjuree Service is simpler than JXTA, so that programmers can develop their applications faster and with fewer failures. The commonly used functions in p2p applications include as creating, publishing, and discovering advertisements, sending messages among peers, working in peergroup, file sharing, etc. Jamjuree Service also simplifies multistage operations found in JXTA and therefore reduces programming errors.

3.1 Jamjuree Service Architecture

The JXTA framework is divided into two layers, platform layer and service layer [4]. The Jamjuree Service layer lies on top of JXTA and more particularly connects to the JXTA service layer. Note that it is only a higher level API that simplifies programming and working with JXTA, not a service that improves the performance of JXTA. The application layer lies upon Jamjuree Service layer.

3.2 Components and Mechanism

Jamjuree Service can be divided into 4 groups of classes classified by functionality.

- *Group Service*

The group service acts as an operation center that can command and monitor every other module. Its main service is to set up a p2p environment of JXTA and manage the information when the environment changes. Almost every single command in our library must be invoked through it.

- *Resource Management*

Resource Management discovers resources by sending discovery messages to search for peers, peergroups, and other advertisements. The corresponding responses from other peers are returned to the requester and then stored in its local cache. It periodically explores the local cache for updates and check if each known peer is reachable and report to the API listener if a cache-updated event occurs, e.g. new peer, new group, or new pipe is found, a pipe is unreachable.

- *Message Management*

This module manages incoming and outgoing messages which relate to JXTA's input pipe and output pipe, respectively. In general, an input pipe is automatically created when Jamjuree Service starts and rebuilt every time the peer moves to another peergroup. If a new input pipe is created, the current pipe will be disabled.

An output pipe, which is used to send a message to any peer's input pipe, is created every time an application calls `sendMsg()`. A message that is sent to a destination peer is also attached with a sender's input pipe name and pipe ID as well.

- *File Sharing*

Jamjuree Service provide an API for file sharing, which allow peers to share, unshare, search, and download file contents across the peergroup. Jamjuree Service provide two implementations of file sharing with a common interface based on two JXTA services, namely CMS (Content Management System) [5] and GISP (Global Information Sharing Protocol) [6].

Jamjuree Service supports most general functions of p2p applications. With using JXTA's well constructed protocols, Jamjuree Service can be a basement for p2p applications which serves availability, reliability, and scalability. These properties consolidate Jamjuree Service to be used for developing a highly reliable distributed cluster system.

4 Jamjuree Explorer

Jamjuree Explorer is developed with Jamjuree Service API. It allows each peer to browse other peers' files and directories in the network as like they are local. Files and directories are organized in hierarchy like directory structure. Each peer has its own root directory and each file in this directory is shared in the peergroup and presented as hierarchy under the root directory which named as the same as owner's name.

Fig. 2 illustrates how this application works. Peer1 and Peer2 are peer names and represented as root directories of Peer1 and Peer2, respectively. Each peer traverses into its root directory and publishes its directory structures to the network. Each peer discovers directory structure in the network and is returned those published Structure messages which are used to rebuild the directory structure locally. Consequently, Peer1 and Peer2 share the same view of virtual directory structure as depicted in Fig 2(c). Note that each peer does not own real content of one another's files but stores only structure information.

Jamjuree Explorer uses file sharing function, more particularly GISP, of Jamjuree Service to implement. GISP file sharing approach in Jamjuree Service not only

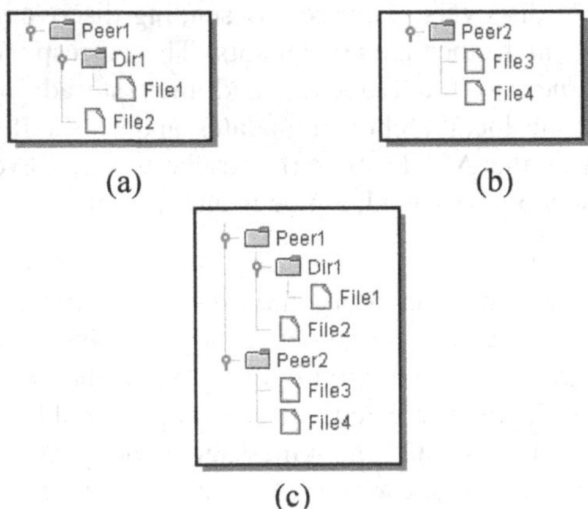

Fig. 2. Directory Structure of Peer1 (a), Peer2 (b) and virtual directory structure combining Peer1 and Peer2 (c)

provides file content sharing across the peergroup, but also enables DHT technique for some specific applications. Jamjuree Explorer uses this feature to do indexing.

Key and value are the main keywords in DHT. Key and value pairs are uniformly distributed among the peergroup. This is done by using hash function of the key and the peer ID. In Jamjuree Explorer, key and value pair concept are applied to the messages. The messages related to the mechanism are classified into two groups.

1. Structure message is a message that is used to organize hierarchy of a file or a directory. It sets parent full path as a key and sets file or directory name as a value. Examples of structure messages related to Peer1 in Fig2 are :
   - ("/", "<Dir>Peer1/</Dir>")
   - ("/Peer1/", "<Dir>Dir1/</Dir>")
   - ("/Peer1/", "<File>File2</File>")
   - ("/Peer1/Dir/", "<File>File1</File>")
2. File Metadata message is a message that keeps information of a file, including Content Advertisement which is used in transferring process. It sets full path name as a key and file information as a value.

Structure and File Metadata messages are distributed among peers in the peergroup. Each peer periodically traverses into its own root directory and distributes Structure and File Metadata messages among the peergroup.

In order to discover directory structure, each peer starts from sending a query message by setting a keyword as "/". The first group of messages that will be returned are Structure messages the represents each peer names in the peergroup. This happens because the only messages that use "/" as a key are directories which names as the peer name. Next step, the first key and directories are concatenated, e.g. "/" + "Peer1/" = "/Peer1/" and "/" + "Peer2/" = "/Peer2/", and used as next keywords to be queried. Each query which uses a directory name as a keyword might return file names or directory names or both. If a directory name is returned, it will be used to query into its subdirectory. Otherwise, if a file name is returned, it stops querying in this branch. A File Metadata message is used if a peer wants to download the relevant file. With the directory structure, a peer can get full path name of a file and use this path to query for the Content Advertisement which is needed for downloading that file.

Every key-value pair messages are put into the network by calling GISP `insert()` method instead of sending a message via Jamjuree Service `sendMsg()` method because we aim to apply DHT mechanism for management.

4.1 P2P File System

Jamjuree Explorer presents a view of directory structure which is like a traditional file system on a single machine. This could be possible to apply its mechanism to be a virtual file system. We have modified Jamjuree Explorer to be a p2p file system which can support our distributed computation. The primary requirements of the proposed file system are listed as follows.

1. Each peer must share the same view of file structure, i.e. peers have the same reference to each relevant file.

2. Each peer must share its storage space to store others' file in order to create replicas of each file.
3. If peers' shared files or directories are updated, other peers who share the same resources must be update for consistency.

Originally designed Jamjuree Explorer distributes indexing of file system structure and file information. GISP module responds for key-value pairs of messages, as described above, but not responds for file contents. The solution is to let peers have responsible for the file content. A tricky way is that let each peer explore its own stored File Metadata messages and downloads that relevant file into its local cache. GISP mechanism always replicates each message to multiple peers, so this trick would help create some copies of the file content and distribute them in the network. These replicas not only stored in the local cache in the same hierarchy as overall structure, but also be continually shared to network. Now querying for a file using a keyword would return more than only one Content Advertisement but all correspondences of it occur. If a peer who shares this file go offline unexpectedly, others could have responsible to share the relevant file to fill up the required amount of replicas. This serves the second requirement.

In order to check for update of a file, a file version is required. We add an attribute to the File Metadata message, <timestamp></timestamp>. This attribute is a long integer number that represent the last modified time in millisecond. Root directory and every subdirectory periodically check for file modification by comparing last modified time of each file. If modification occurs with a file, it immediately publishes a new advertisement to the network, attaching with the new modified time. The old Content Advertisements will not be completely replaced but a peer downloading the file can inspect for the newest file. Also if the peers that are responsible for the modified files have found the changes from the new File Metadata, they download the new files overwriting the old ones. This completes the third requirement.

4.2 File Replication

To improve availability and fault-tolerant, the file replication mechanism is adopted. After file is put into the root directory, the specific number of replicas will be propagated to local cache of other neighbor peers. This also can reduce the time to access file because its may be able to download from its local cache. Users also can disable this feature to achieve personal policy.

5 Harvest

In this section, we introduce Harvest, a job manager on a p2p network. Harvest harnesses the processing power from idle participants' PCs in Jamjuree Cluster to execute jobs. Harvest operates on the Jamjuree Service and uses Jamjuree Explorer as file system for storing input and output files. In Harvest, superpeer model [7], p2p communication fashion and advertisement mechanism [8] have been applied to improve scalability and reduce server's network load [9]. Furthermore, using a superpeer model, the system also achieves fault-tolerant.

5.1 Harvest Architecture

Peers in Harvest are organized into many peergroups. Each peergroup is a collection of peers that have agreed upon a common set of services and defines its own joining policy. It represents as a cluster system. A peer may belong to more than one peergroup simultaneously. Each peergroup advertises its activities and other information associated with the group in order to be discovered and joined by an interested peer. Peers in Harvest are divided into 2 categories – clients and superpeers.

A *client* is a peer that joins and participates to a peergroup. A client can take roles of a *job submitter* by submitting jobs, and a *volunteer* by offering to execute jobs. A client has a monitoring daemon, which working like a typical screensaver program, for determining the idle status. A client can join and leave the system freely at any time.

A *superpeer* works as a server for a group of clients. A peergroup may contain more than one superpeer. It is responsible for answering the queries for its clients. Its primary functions are matching job with volunteer, and jobs and peers monitoring. This may also requires among the superpeers in the peergroup. Communication between peergroups is only required for group discovery.

In sending queries, a client sends all queries (group discovery, resource discovery and offering, etc.) to and gets answers from its connected superpeer only. If the query cannot be answered by the superpeer, it propagates the query to its neighbor superpeers. When the answer is found, the response is sent back to the original superpeer, and then to the client.

5.2 Advertisement Mechanism

In distributed and heterogeneous resources environments, it is hard to determine the characteristics of a peer and define the usage policy. We adopt the advertisement model introduced by Condor to handle the matching between job and volunteer.

Advertisement mechanism uses the advertisements to represent the characteristics and policies or requirements of the computers and jobs. In Harvest, there are two types of advertisement – job advertisement, and resource advertisement.

A *job advertisement* holds necessary information about that job such as jobID, fileID of input, JXTA network information, minimum requirements to run the job, and the command to run the job.

A *resource advertisement* describes the specifications of the client machine including hardware, software, and usage policies.

Computer owners and users who submit jobs define the specifications and policies of their machines and jobs in form of description file, which will be used to generate the job advertisement and resource advertisement. These advertisements are sent to their connected superpeer for resources and jobs registration and are used for matching. For compatibility with JXTA, our advertisement is represented in the XML format.

5.3 Job Characteristics

Jobs that can be submitted to Harvest are batch job, which can be run from command line. A job must have certainly input and output file names, which specified in job description file. We suggest that jobs should be computing-intensive job because the network bandwidth in p2p network is unpredictable and typically much less than cluster system.

5.4 Job Submission Protocol

Job submission protocol (Fig. 3.) is designed for the dynamic computing model where job submitters and volunteers can leave the system at any time.

The processes start with a job owner puts the input files (compressed into a zip file to reduce file size) in the root directory of Jamjuree Explorer and edits a job description file. Harvest then automatically establishes the job advertisement and register with the connected superpeer. The superpeer also maintains a database of resource advertisements that have been registered by clients when they enter the system. The superpeer finds a suitable match between volunteer and that job. The superpeer then notifies the volunteer for assigning the job. The volunteer uses fileID of input file specified in received job advertisement to download the file from Jamjuree Explorer and starts executing job. When job is finished, the output file is sent into Jamjuree Explorer (by putting in the root directory) and notifies the superpeer with fileID of output file. The superpeer then forwards the notification to the job submitter. Job submitter invokes Jamjuree Explorer to retrieve the result back. The result files contains output, error message, and log file. All of them are compressed into a zip file in order to reduce transferred file size.

With usage of Jamjuree Explorer, the input and output file will be replicated to prevent the lost of job. Consider the case that the job submitter leaves the system before the job is dispatched, the superpeer can submit it using a replica of the input file. And the case when processing node leaves before the submitter online and retrieve the output file, the submitter also can instead download other replicas.

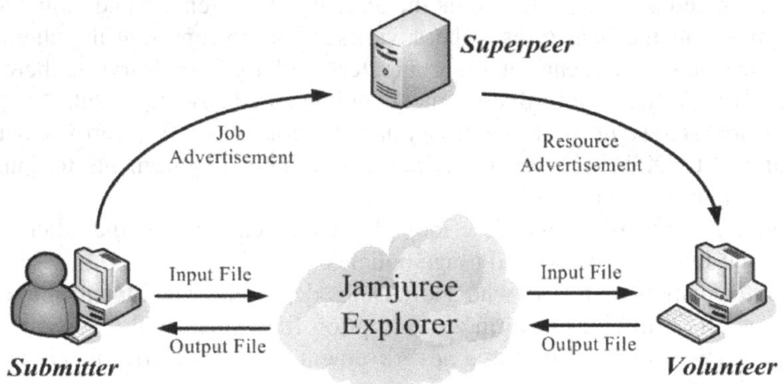

Fig. 3. Job Submission Protocol

5.5 Job Monitoring and Resubmission

In some circumstances, the job owner may not be able to monitor its jobs. For example, it may have to disconnect from the network for a long period. Since superpeers are more available than other peers in the group, it should provide a job monitoring or resubmission service. However, this puts extra work on the superpeer.

The superpeer maintains the status of its client peers and their jobs. Once the job is initiated, the superpeer periodically monitors the status of the volunteer peer and the progress of the jobs. If the volunteer peer is not responding or the job is not in progress, the superpeer finds a new volunteer for the job on behalf of the job owner.

5.6 Superpeer Redundancy

A superpeer has a tendency to become overloaded with too many clients or become a single point of failure. The problems can be partially solved by connecting a client to redundant superpeers. Another solution for overloaded superpeers is selecting another superpeer from the clients and transforming a client to a new superpeer. This process is also needed if a superpeer leaves the system. Changing connecting superpeer does not much affect the working processes because the finished job can be transferred to the original submitter by using information in attached job advertisement instead of information stored in superpeer. However, job being in queue will be lost. If a job submitter is notified changing of connected superpeer, it has to resubmit the jobs that have not been matched yet.

6 Implementation Status and Future Work

The first version of Jamjuree Cluster has been completed and it is now being tested. Many applications have been written with Jamjuree Service API, including instant messaging and games. The distributed computing feature has been tested with many applications including prime number searching and POV-Ray, a 3D animation rendering application. Currently, we are also trying to enable the capability to connect a p2p network with a Grid computing system.

7 Conclusions

In this paper, we have proposed a cluster computing system operating on a peer-to-peer network called Jamjuree Cluster. It is composed of 3 main services, Jamjuree Service which is a programming model and environment, Jamjuree Explorer which is a file system, and Harvest which is a job manager. In Jamjuree Service, we provide a library for peer-to-peer programming on JXTA protocol that make it easier to develop a peer-to-peer applications. Jamjuree Explorer provides a high availability virtual file system. Finally, a job management system using processing power from participant peers, called Harvest, which employs a advertisement mechanism and peer-to-peer communication to utilized clients' bandwidth for transferring file instead of superpeers' bandwidth. This benefits when number of clients increase, system overall bandwidth also increases.

References

1. Buyya, R.: High Performance Cluster Computing: Architectures and Systems, 1st edn. Prentice-Hall PTR, Englewood Cliffs (1999)
2. Alto, P., Milojicic, D.S., Kalogeraki, V., Lukose, R., Nagaraja, K., Pruyne, J., Richard, B., Rollins, S., Xu, Z.: Peer-to-Peer Computing. Technical Report HP Laboratories (2002)
3. Anderson, D.P., Cobb, J., Korpela, E., Lebofsky, M., Werthimer, D.: SETI@home: An experiment in public-resource computing. Communications of the ACM 45, 56–61 (2002)
4. Traversat, B., Abdelaziz, M., Duigou, M., Hugly, J.-C., Pouyoul, E., Yeager, B., Arora, A., Haywood, C.: Project JXTA 2.0 Super-Peer Virtual Network. White Paper. Sun Microsystems, Inc. (2003)
5. http://cms.jxta.org/
6. Kato, D.: GISP: Global Information Sharing Protocol - a Distributed Index for Peer-to-Peer Systems. In: Proceedings of the Second International Conference on Peer-to-Peer Computing, pp. 65–72 (2002)
7. Carlo, M., Domenico, T., Oreste, V.: A super-peer model for resource discovery services in large-scale grids, Future Generation Computer Systems, pp. 1235–1248 (2005)
8. Raman, R., Livny, M., Solomon, M.: Matchmaking: Distributed Resource Management for High Throughput Computing. In: 7th IEEE International Symposium on High Performance Distributed Computing (HPDC7), pp. 140–147. IEEE Computer Society Press, Los Alamitos (1998)
9. Tritrakan, K., Muangsin, V.: Using peer-to-peer communication to improve the performance of distributed computing on the Internet. In: Proceedings of the 19th International Conference on Advanced Information Networking and Applications, vol. 2, pp. 295–298 (2005)

Evaluations on Classified Selection of Dense Vectors for Vegetable Geographical Origin Identification System Using Trace Elements

Nobuyoshi Sato[1], Minoru Uehara[2], Koichiro Shimomura[3], Hirobumi Yamamoto[3], and Kenichi Kamijo[3]

[1] Faculty of Software and Information Science, Iwate Prefectural University
152-52, Sugo, Takizawa, Iwate 020-0193 Japan
nobu-s@iwate-pu.ac.jp
[2] Depertment of Information and Computer Sciences, Toyo University
2100, Kujirai, Kawagoe, Saitama 350-8585 Japan
uehara@cs.toyo.ac.jp
[3] Plant Regulation Research Center, Toyo University
1-1-1, Izumino, Itakura, Gunma 374-0193 Japan
{shimomur,yamamoto,kamijo}@itakura.toyo.ac.jp

Abstract. Recently, in Japan, some farming districts established their locality as brands, and prices of agricultural products differs from their grown places. This induced some agricultural food origin forgery cases. Food traceability systems are introduced and some are now in operation to solve this problem. However, food traceability systems have vulnerabilities in their nature because they traces only artificially attached IDs. So there are possibility to forge ID and packages, and switching the vegetables in packages. So, we developed a geographical origin identification system for vegetables by using their trace element compositions. Trace element means very small quantities of elements. This system gathers trace element data of vegetables when shipping from farms, and stores them into databases located in farming districts. In case of a vegetable which has doubtful geographical origin is found in markets, their trace element compositions are measured and compared with data in databases to find its actual geographical origin. Our system judges geographical origin by whether correlation coefficient. This requires calculating correlation coefficients for identifying one and all stored data. However, this is not scalable for the number of data. In this paper, we describe a method to limit the number of data to be used to calculate correlation coefficients before calculating them, and realize scalability.

Keywords: Geographical origin identification by trace element compositions, efficient retrieval of dense vector.

1 Introduction

Recent years in Japan, some farming districts established their districts as brands; their products are traded in expensive values. This gave rise to forging geographical

T. Enokido, L. Barolli, and M. Takizawa (Eds.): NBiS 2007, LNCS 4658, pp. 385–396, 2007.

origin of agricultural products and problems to guaranty food safety. To solve these two problems, food traceability systems are now on the way to be used universally. However, since food traceability systems employ artificial materials such as barcode, RFID tags as ID attached into cardboard box and containers, it is possible to forge IDs, packages, and switching packages or contained foods.

In these situation, we developed a vegetable geographical origin identification system which distinguishes differences of trace element compositions of vegetables depend on cultivated places [1]. Here, trace element means that very small quantities of elements; and it is a technical term in chemists. Normally, vegetables are cultivated on the soil. Since trace element compositions of the soil differ from districts, even farms, absorbed trace element compositions in vegetables also differ. In our system, trace element compositions are measured at farms when shipping, they are registered in databases located in each farming district. In case of a vegetable of which cultivated place is cheated was found, its trace element composition is measured and it is compared to all registered trace element data. Correlation coefficient between doubtful one and one of stored data is calculated for comparison. If the correlation coefficient overcomes a certain threshold, it is considered that two vegetables may be cultivated the same farm. In case of a vegetable of which geographical origin seem to be cheated is found, its trace element composition is measured and compared to all registered data in databases. If geographical origin of doubtful vegetable by food traceability system is included in a set of geographical origin by our system, it is considered that geographical origin of doubtful vegetable is not cheated, otherwise, it is considered that it is cheated and its real geographical origin is a certain farm which has the highest correlation coefficient.

In our system, trace element compositions are expressed as high dimensional vectors. Our system compares query vector and stored vectors in databases by calculating correlation coefficient. This is one-to-one comparison, and this is a obstruction to make system scalable. To realize scalability, there are two possible strategies; the one is to narrow target of one-to-one comparison, the other is to develop yet another techniques rather than one-to-one comparison. However, the latter is not realistic way. Therefore, we have realized a certain extent of success to realize efficiency by using Similarity Preserve Hash (SPH)[2], presented by Moses Charikar. This method succeeded to reduce the number of one-to-one comparison and time to identify. SPH itself is jock job method and it is not enough efficient. However, we invented employment of SPH and we reduced time to retrieve data from database to about few seconds [3]. Although SPH can be used for practical generic method to narrow high dimensional dense vector, reducing retrieval time by SPH seem to reach the limit. Therefore, in this paper, we discuss on a method to reduce retrieval time to extract trace element data from database by encoding trace element compositions into some classes. This method aims at distribution of values of trace element compositions.

Organization of this paper is as following; in Section 2, we describe some related works on geographical origin identification. In Section 3, we explain our vegetable geographical identification system. In section 4, we discuss on requirements to classify trace element compositions, and describe a method to encode the classes. In section 5, we will show evaluation. Finally, we will conclude.

2 Related Works

There are some experimental works by agricultural chemists to identify geographical origin of agricultural products using trace element compositions. These works initially done for products those producing place and year are important such as wine [4], coffee [5], tea [6] and rice [7] and so on.

In these works, firstly agricultural chemists establish methods to experiment and measure, and they analyze result data mainly using cluster analysis, and they show that trace element compositions differ from geographical origin of agricultural products. Generally, papers on agricultural chemistry focused on only method to experiment and measurement and statistically processed data, the does not have interest on statistical analysis method and information system for geographical origin identification. Furthermore, relatively obscurity method such as cluster analysis is chosen to prevent criticize against data.

3 Geographical Origin Identification System

At first, we describe our proposed method to identify geographical origins of vegetables using their trace element compositions. In our method, trace element composition of both shipped vegetables from and gathered vegetables on food distribution channel are compared as vector forms, and if angle of two vector is almost 0, corresponding farm is judged as a geographical origin. Trace element compositions are standardized. And, angle of vectors are calculated as correlation coefficient.

At first, we describe how to standardize trace element compositions. Let $\boldsymbol{X}_i = (x_{i,1}\ x_{i,2}\ \dots\ x_{i,m})$ be a vector which expresses trace element composition of a sampled vegetable i. Here, m means the number of elements which employed to identification, e represents element. Each of element y_{ie} of standardized vector $\boldsymbol{Y}_i=(y_{i,1}\ y_{i,2}\ \dots\ y_{i,m})$ for i are calculated as following

$$y_{i,e} = \frac{x_{i,e} - \overline{x_e}}{s_e} \tag{1}$$

Here, $\overline{x_e}$ is an average trace element compositions for e whole of all samples, s_e is standard deviation for e whole of samples.

Next, we calculate a correlation coefficient between an identifying sample which gathered from distribution channel and $\boldsymbol{X}_i$. Let trace element composition vector of identifying sample be $\boldsymbol{U} = (u_1\ u_2\ \dots\ u_m)$. Firstly, U is standardized by following

$$v_e = \frac{u_e - \overline{x_e}}{s_e} \tag{2}$$

Here, $\boldsymbol{V}=(v_1\ v_2\ \dots\ v_m)$ expresses standardized vector of $\boldsymbol{U}$. Next, the correlation coefficient of them is calculated as follows

$$r_{Y_i,V} = \frac{\sum (y_{i,m} - \overline{y}_i)(v_m - \overline{v})}{\sqrt{\sum (y_{i,m} - \overline{y}_i)^2}\sqrt{\sum (v_m - \overline{v})^2}} \tag{3}$$

When $r_{Y_i,Y}$ overcomes a suitable threshold near 1, $\boldsymbol{X}_i$ and $\boldsymbol{U}$ are considered that they are grown in the same field of a farm. Note that there may exists some $\boldsymbol{X}_i$s that overcomes the threshold, and not always $\boldsymbol{X}_i$ which have the maximum $r_{Y_i,V}$ is the real geographical origin. Therefore, the result of this geographical origin identification process should be treated carefully. The realistic usage of our proposing method is to use verify geographical origin information by food traceability system. In this case, if the geographical origin by food traceability system is included in a set of geographical origins of which correlation coefficient overcomes a certain threshold, geographical origin information is verified as valid Otherwise, it is considered as cheated information.

To prevent possibility of iniquity, it is desirable that trace element compositions of vegetables are measured, stored at agricultural organizations on faming districts. So we decided to locate distributed databases which accumulate trace element compositions onto farming districts. Fig.1 shows the overview of proposing system. Databases which accumulate trace element compositions are located onto agricultural organizations in each district as DataSite. Furthermore, to cope to iniquity by agricultural organization on each district, a ControleSite is installed in an agricultural authority organization. In addition to Fig.1, there are some retrieval clients which only throws query trace element composition data and catches the result of geographical origin identification.

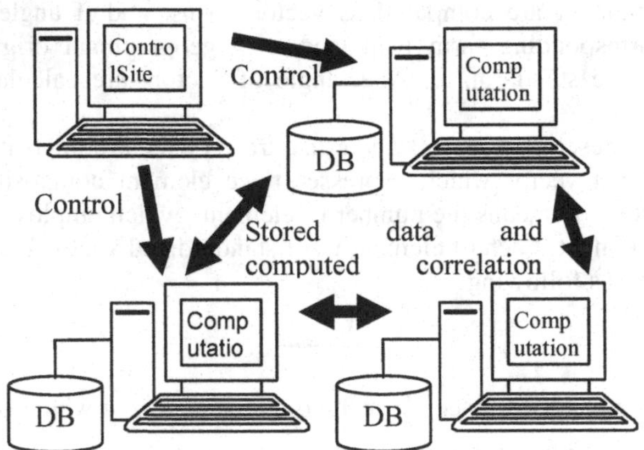

Fig. 1. The System Overview

Next, data stored in databases are standardized as following:

1. Computation of averages of each data

As average of a data of element e in site i, $\overline{x}_{i*_e}$ is calculated as follows:

$$\overline{x}_{i*_e} = \frac{1}{m_i}\sum_{j=1}^{m_i} x_{ije} \tag{4}$$

As average data of e of all samples in all sites, $\overline{x}_{**_e}$ is as follows:

$$\bar{x}_{**e} = \frac{1}{\sum_{i=1}^{n} m_i} \sum_{i=1}^{n} m_i \bar{x}_{i*e} \tag{5}$$

Here, $\bar{x}_{i*e}$ can be calculated from only local data of each site i. The $\bar{x}_{i*e}$ and m_i are gathered by the Control Site, and the Control Site calculates $\bar{x}_{**e}$.

2. Calculation of standard deviation of all data.

A standard deviation s_e of e in the all site is as follows:

$$\begin{aligned} S_e &= \sqrt{\frac{1}{\sum_{i=1}^{n} m_i - 1} \sum_{i=1}^{n} \sum_{j=1}^{m_i} (x_{ije} - \bar{x}_{**e})^2} \\ &= \sqrt{\frac{1}{\sum_{i=1}^{n} m_i - 1} \sum_{i=1}^{n} d_{ie}} \end{aligned} \tag{6}$$

Here, $d_{ie} = \sum_{j=1}^{m_i} (x_{ije} - \bar{x}_{**e})^2$ is a sum of squares of residuals of the element e in the site i. After computing d_{ie} in each site, the Control Site gathers them, and calculates s_e.

3. Standardization of each data.

Let a standardized vector of j-th sample in the sitte i be $\boldsymbol{Y}_{ij} = (y_{ij1}\ y_{ij2}\ \ldots\ y_{ijl})$. Each element of the vector can be calculated as follows:

$$y_{ije} = \frac{x_{ije} - \bar{x}_{**e}}{s_e} \tag{7}$$

Therefore, $\boldsymbol{Y}_{ij}$ can be calculated in the site i.

In case of our proposing classification method described in section 4 is employed, each Data Site calculates classified code of stored trace element data. Classified code is used to select target to calculate correlation coefficients when identifying, In case of SPH is employed, each site calculates SPH of all data, and stores them to their own database. Also, each site sends SPH values to Control Site to use select Data Site which have similar trace element composition data to given query.

Here, we describe behavior to identify geographical origin.

1. A client for identification c requests identification by sending a vector of identifying vegetable's trace element composition $\boldsymbol{U} = (u_1\ u_2\ \ldots\ u_l)$, name of crop, breed and shipped date to Control Site. If classify code or SPH is employed, c calculates it and send it together.
2. In case of classified code or SPH is employed, Control Site enumerates a set S of Data Site i having data which are similar to given data, and sends S to c. Otherwise S will be all Data Sites.
3. In case of classified code or SPH is employed, c obtains standardized trace element compositions Y_{ij} which matched SPH or classify code. Otherwise, skip this step.

4. c calculates correlation coefficients between identifying sample and obtained data from each site as follows:

$$r_{(Y_{ij}U)} = \frac{\sum_{e=1}^{l}(u_e - \overline{u})(y_{ije} - \overline{y}_{ij*})}{\sqrt{\sum_{e=1}^{l}(u_e - \overline{u})^2}\sqrt{\sum_{e=1}^{l}(y_{ije} - \overline{y}_{ij*})^2}} \quad (8)$$

5. c treats combination of i and j those $\boldsymbol{r}_{(Y_{ij}U)}$ overcomes a threshold t as result of identification. If there are some combinations of i and j, c treats combinations of i and j those shipping date, breed and geographical origin is the same to identifying sample as proper. Otherwise, all combinations are shown to user.

4 Class Coding of Trace Element Compositions

Calculation of correlation coefficients between trace element compositions of identifying vegetables and trace element compositions data in databases is needed to realize geographical origin identification using trace element compositions by proposing method. Here, we should pay attention to that proposing method have interests to only data which have high correlation coefficient between identifying vegetable. Although values of correlation coefficients are not known before calculation, however, if the subject data for calculation can be limited, necessary time to calculate correlation coefficients can be reduced because the number of one-to-one comparison using floating point instructions can be limited.

Calculation target selection by Similarity Preserve Hash (SPH) which we employed before needs bit width times of floating point computation. So SPH have limitation to select calculation targets fast. To accelerate target selection, a method which uses only integer operations, can only a time of operation is desired.

Generally, in loose vectors, there are well known efficient methods when registering, retrieving data and in space usage. However, no efficient method known that satisfies these three requirements at the same time. Here, we describe a method to reduce necessary time when registering and retrieving data, at the sacrifice of space usage.

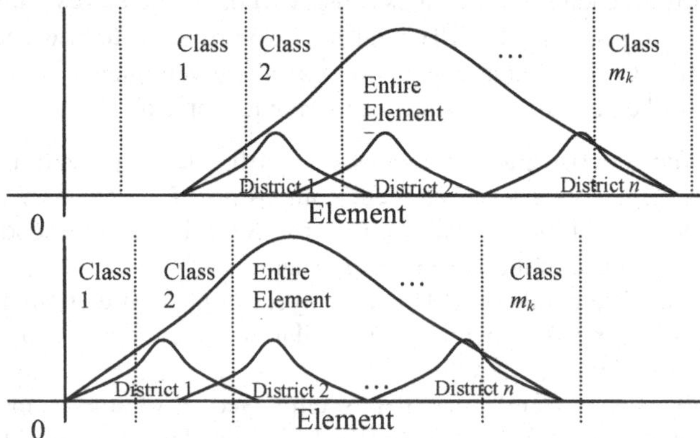

Fig. 2. Distribution of trace element compositions on all districts and their classification

At first, we discuss on trace element compositions themselves. Trace element compositions entire of all districts have normal distribution or its variant, it is thought. Because there is no negative quantity in trace element compositions, left bottom may sharply falls. In addition, it is thought that trace element compositions of each farm and farming district have normal distribution or its variants. Also, these distributions in each farm have similar value. This is shown in Fig. 2.

Based on these characteristics, we thought of a method to classify a trace element composition value x_{Adh}, element A of h-th sampled vegetables in district d. Let $\overline{x}_A$ be average of all x_{Adh}, s_A be standard deviation of it. x_{Adh} is standardized by following, and standardized trace element composition y_{Adh} has standard Gaussian distribution.

$$y_{adh} = \frac{x_{Adh} - \overline{x}_A}{s_A} \tag{9}$$

Divide range of y_{Adh}, $-\infty \le y_{Adh} \le \infty$ to b sections, and name each of sections as g (g = 1, 2, 3, …, b) from lower. A section for y_{Adh} can be determined by finding minimum g which satisfies following:

$$F(z_{Adh}) = \int_{-\infty}^{z_{Adh}} \frac{1}{\sqrt{2\pi}} e^{-y_{Adh}^2} \le \frac{g}{b} \tag{10}$$

Here, possibility that one of y_{Adh} is classified to each one of section g is equal. As actual implementation, only to do is to calculate percentiles that divide the normal distribution into g sections, and just compare given y_{Adh} and these percentiles. Therefore, it is expected that calculation to classify given y_{Adh} is enough fast.

Here, we must pay attention to that trace element compositions in the same farm field have possibility which are classified into two or more sections. Although contrivance to device to divide sections may decrease the possibility, however, it cannot make it zero. That is, when a trace element composition Q_A for element A of query Q, there is possibility that trace element composition data in database which have high correlation coefficient between Q_A may exists in near section $g_{QA}\pm$l. If these trace element composition data in database is not included in target to calculate correlation coefficients, the result of geographical origin identification will be incorrect. This means that in case of the number of dividing sections is too lot, neighbor sections must be searched to find data correctly. On the other hand, the number of dividing sections is too few, classifying and dividing into sections have no effect. In addition, This will require a coding method to express these divided sections and check all neighbor sections in few computation cost as possible as.

Next, we describe an effective coding method of divided sections. This method determines that whether a trace element compositions data in the database matches to calculate correlation coefficient between given query by using only integer operations. At first, allocate b bit with of space for code of element A. A bit string $b^b \ldots b^2 b^1$ expresses a section which trace element composition of A belongs. Then, bit strings for all elements are concatenated and the entire of bit string expresses approximate trace element composition of an actual vegetable. In case of a trace element composition data of A classified into section g, g-th bit of bit string for A is set to 1 and other bits are set to 0. In retrieving data, all corresponding bit for desired retrieval target sections is set to 1. That is, in case of all sections of g^{QA}±l should be searched, just all bits corresponding to g^{QA}±l are set to 1. Let each of trace element data for A in database be d_A. Target data to calculate correlation coefficient satisfies following:

$$d_A \,\&\, b_{QA} \neq 0 \tag{11}$$

The entire of trace element compositions of an actual vegetable can be expressed using $e{\times}b$ width of bit string when e sorts of elements are employed and each of them occupies b bit width of classification code. If $e{\times}b$ is less than or equal to bit width of integer register, only one time of integer operation is needed to judge a trace element data in database meets to target to calculate correlation coefficient. In 32 bit width of integer register, 8 sorts of elements can be employed when each trace element composition divided into 4 classes for an integer operation. If the bit string exceeds integer register bit width, integer operation can be repeated in only few costs.

Here, we discuss on necessary time to select target data to calculate correlation coefficients. Necessary time to select target using SPH is $O(n)$ when n expresses the number of target trace element data in database[3]. Although proposing method using classification needs $O(n)$. However, to compared with SPH requires at least bit width times of floating point operations, proposing method only requires $\lfloor e \times b / x \rfloor + 1$ times of integer operations when x expresses bit width of integer register. Here, $\lfloor y \rfloor$ means a floor function that gives the maximum integer which does not exceeds y.

Geographical origin identification by our system finally requires one-to-one comparison which needs floating point operations Therefore, target of one-to-one comparison must be restricted to enough few. At now, there is two million farms are in Japan. We estimate 5% of them may ship the same crop and breed at the same time. So our system must handle hundred thousand of trace element data effectively. We have evaluated geographical origin identification method itself by simulation before, there was 100 to 1000 data which are similar to given vegetable's trace element composition. These similar trace element data in database are candidate of real geographical origin of identifying vegetable. So it is most effective in case of the number of target to calculate correlation coefficient is reduced to 100 to 1000 by proposing classification and coding method. The number of sections to be divided b can be settled as following expression:

$$d' = \frac{t}{b^e} \approx d \tag{12}$$

Here, let the number of trace element data to be selected be d, and let the number of trace element composition data in database which are the same crop and breed be t, and e sorts of elements are used to identification.

5 Evaluations

We evaluated proposing classification and coding method using simulated trace element composition database which is the same we used to evaluate SPH. Table 1 shows that necessary time to classification and coding of trace element compositions and store the result to database. We employed a dual Xeon 3.0GHz, 1GB of memory

PC. FreeBSD 6.2-RELEASE is installed in this PC, and PostgreSQL 8.1.4 is used as database. Necessary times are almost the same and it takes so short for hundred thousands of data. Calculation of classification and coding is needed when registering new trace element data. However, necessary time to this calculation for each one of trace element data is ignorable short time.

Table 1. Necessary time to classify coding

The number of classes	Execution Time [m:s]
3	1:29.18
4	1:19.31
5	1:19.63

Table 2 shows that necessary time to select target to calculate correlation coefficients. All takes less than 1 second, and all of differences of necessary time seem to be error range. Since SPH, we employed before took about 3 seconds, proposing method is enough faster.

Table 2. Necessary time to select target to calculate correlation coefficients

#classes	Execution Time [s]	Execution time in when neighbors are searched [s]	
		One neighbor for each side	Two neighbors for each side
3	0:00.55	0:00.68	-
4	0:00.62	0:00.53	0:00.33
5	0:00.28	0:00.51	0:00.33

Table 3 shows that the number of selected data in database by proposing classifies coding method. Our geographical origin identification system calculates correlation coefficients between identifying vegetable and these selected data. In most cases data are selected into 1/10 or fewer. In case of two neighbors for each side is searched for 4 classes, it seem to fail to select enough. In other cases, short necessary time to calculate correlation coefficients is expected.

Fig. 3 shows correlation coefficients vs. recall ratio for whether neighbors are searched and the number of classes. Here, recall ratio 1.0 means that all targets to

Table 3. The number of selected trace element data by classify coding in case of neighbor are searched

The number of classes	Maximum	Minimum	Average
3, 1 neighbor	62510	5807	13708
4, 1 neighbor	11408	1504	3639
4, 2 neighbors	100001	11158	28967
5, 1 neighbor	3405	558	1308
5, 2 neighbors	55303	3478	11169

calculate correlation coefficients are selected and there were no leakage. So we counted the number of selected items for recall ratio 1.0 by searching entire of database without proposing method and/or SPH. In explanatory notes in Fig. 3, "no neighbor" means that target trace element data are picked up from only query's classified sections. "1 neighbor" means that both sides of classified sections are searched. "2 neighbors" means two neighbor sections for each side are searched. In lower correlation coefficients, recall ratios in all cases change to worse. However, our geographical origin identification system has no interests to data which have lesser correlation coefficients between identifying vegetable. So degeneration of recall ratio in less than 0.9 will be acceptable. In every cases of no neighbors of classified section is searched, recall ratios are extremely worth and they are not acceptable. So At least, searching from both side neighbors is needed.

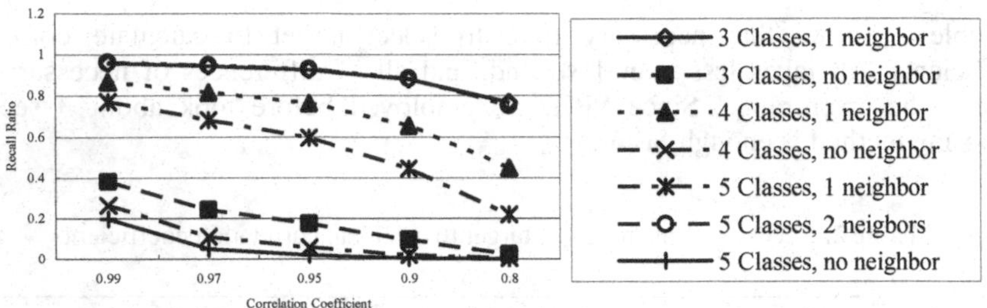

Fig. 3. The number of classification and recall ratio

Here, we discuss on why recall ratio degenerates in lower correlation coefficients and in cases of no neighbor is searched. Correlation coefficient is equivalent to angle of two vectors. Note that lengths of two vectors are not considered. Therefore, it is possible case that two vectors have correlation coefficient 1.0 but they are not equal. That is, only direction from the origin is the same and their lengths differ. This situation is the same in cases of correlation coefficient is 0.9, interested by our geographical origin identification system. Infinite numbers of vectors exist which accords $\cos^{-1}\theta=0.9$. Here, θ expresses angle to an identifying vegetable's vector. Let ***B*** as a set of vectors of which length is equal to identifying vegetable's query vector q and angles between q are θ. Shape of B will be a cone, of which apex is the origin. Also all vectors which are form the origin and passes the surface of the cone satisfies $\cos^{-1}\theta=0.9$, even if the lengths of them differ. Our proposing method does not considered length of vector and it assumes that vectors which have almost the same length to identifying vegetable's query' vector.

The next problem is the same as above problem in its nature. First, we assume a query Q made from trace element composition, and trace element composition data in database A and B. The, we consider in cases of correlation coefficients between Q and A, B are $r_{QA}=r_{QB}$ or $r_{QA}\approx r_{QB}$. Here, we assume an extreme condition that each element of A is roughly the same to each element of Q. In case of each element of B is almost the same to Q except an element and an element differs so, $r_{QA}=r_{QB}$ or $r_{QA}\approx r_{QB}$ will be satisfied too. However, in proposing classification and coding method, an element so differs is classified to class which is not targeted to search. As this result, recall ratio degenerates.

Geographical origin identification method we described in section 3 employs 6 elements and it is relatively robust method[1]. That is, if trace element compositions of vegetables grown in the same farm varied, thanks to the number of employed elements, this make only few influence to the result of geographical origin identification. Our geographical origin identification method allows nearly 50% variation in case of only an element varies and others almost the same, 10% variation in case of all elements vary. Target selection by proposing classification and coding method can cope with later case, but cannot be applied to former case. However, in real world, former case is rare it is thought.

6 Conclusion

In this paper, we described a method to accelerate computation time to identify geographical origin of vegetables by using their trace element compositions. Also we showed evaluation of it including recall ratio. Our geographical origin identification method requires calculation of correlation coefficients between trace element composition of an identifying vegetable and trace element composition data stored in database. However, it is inefficient that to calculate correlation coefficients between identifying one and all stored data. Our method described in this paper classifies trace element compositions into some sections, and by devising code expression of classes. This enables to judge a data in database is suitable for target to calculate correlation coefficient by only a integer operation. Although we are dissatisfied to recall ratio, proposing method realized quite faster target selection than SPH we employed before.

Acknowledgements. This work was supported by "University-Industry Joint Research" Project for Private Universities; subsidy by MEXT (Ministry of Education, Culture, Sports, Science and Technology), 2003-2007.

References

[1] Sato, N., Uehara, M., Tamaoka, J., Shimomura, K., Yamamoto, H., Kamijo, K.: A Distributed Geographical Origin Identification System for Agricultural Products by Trace Element Compositions. International Journal of Computer Science and Network Security 5(10), 55–63 (2005)

[2] Charikar, M.S.: Similarity Estimation Techniques from Rounding Algorithms. In: Proc. of 4th Annual ACM Symposium on Theory of Computing, pp. 380–388. ACM, New York (2002)

[3] Sato, N., Uehara, M., Tamaoka, J., Shimomura, K., Yamamoto, H., Kamijo, K.: Efficient Target Selection in Similarity Preserve Hash for Distributed Geographical Origin Identification System of Vegetables. In: Proc of The 9th International Workshop on Network-Based Information Systems, pp. 40–44 (2006)

[4] Baxter, M.J., Crews, H.M., Dennis, M.J., Goodall, I., Anderson, D.: The determination of the authenticity of wine from its trace element composition. Food Chemistry 60(3), 443–450 (1997)

[5] Anderson, K.A., Smith, B.W.: Chemical Profiling to Differentiate Geographic Growing Origins of Coffee. J. Agric. Food Chem. 50(7), 2068–2075 (2002)
[6] Fernádez-Cáceres, P.L., Martín, M.J., Pablos, F., González, A.G.: Differentiation of Tea (Camellia sinensis) Varieties and Their Geographical Origin According to their Metal Content. J. Agric. Food Chem. 49(10), 4775–4779 (2001)
[7] Yasui, A., Shinodh, K.: Determination of the geographic origin of brown-rice with trace-element composition (in Japanese). Bunseki Kakagu 49(6), 406–410 (2000)

Integrated Biomedical System for Ubiquitous Health Monitoring

Arjan Durresi[1], Arben Merkoci[2], Mimoza Durresi[3], and Leonard Barolli[4]

[1] Louisiana State University, Baton Rouge LA 70803, USA
durresi@csc.lsu.edu
http://www.csc.lsu.edu/~durresi
[2] Universitat Autònoma de Barcelona, Barcelona, Spain
[3] Franklin University, Columbus OH, USA
[4] Fukuoka Institute of Technology, Fukuoka, Japan

Abstract. We propose a distributed system that enables global and ubiquitous health monitoring of patients. The biomedical data will be collected by wearable health diagnostic devices, which will include various types of sensors and will be transmitted towards the corresponding Health Monitoring Centers. The permanent medical data of patients will be kept in the corresponding Home Data Bases, while the measured biomedical data will be sent to the Visitor Health Monitor Center and Visitor Data Base that serves the area of present location of the patient. By combining the measured biomedical data and the permanent medical data, Health Medical Centers will be able to coordinate the needed actions and help the local medical teams to make quickly the best decisions that could be crucial for the patient health, and that can reduce the cost of health service.

1 Introduction

The aging of populations is becoming a social and economical challenge worldwide. For example, according to [1] "In the United States alone, the number of people over age 65 is expected to hit 70 million by 2030, doubling from 35 million in 2000, and similar increases are expected worldwide." On the other hand, many elderly people suffer from chronic diseases that require medication and clinic visits on a regular basis. Therefore, for this growing category of people, it is crucial to monitor the health condition all the time. Health monitoring can save lives, improve the quality of life for many, and last but not least, it can reduce the const of health care, by enabling early interventions. The cost of the health care is a growing problem too, for example, expenditures in the United States for healthcare will grow to 15.9% of the GDP ($2.6 trillion) by 2010 (Digital 4Sight's Healthcare Industry Study) as a result of the accumulative impact of chronic degenerative diseases in the elderly and their increasing dependence on the health care system.

Next generation networked medical devices and health management systems are envisioned to be ubiquitous systems of networked systems for secure, reliable,

T. Enokido, L. Barolli, and M. Takizawa (Eds.): NBiS 2007, LNCS 4658, pp. 397–405, 2007.

privacy-preserving, cost-effective and personalized quality health care, leading not only to better health-care delivery, but also to improving peoples quality of life in general. Unfortunately, current medical devices are still mostly standalone subsystems with proprietary designs. Medical workers often need to manually transfer data among several machines.

There are various research projects going on in the direction of using sensor and network technologies for health services. The closest work to our solution is *I-Living* [2,3], an assisted-living supportive system, beng developed by researchers at the University of Illinois at Urbana-Champaign. The major goal of *I-Living* is to assist elderly people to get the needed health services, while staying at home.

At the *Center for Future Health (CFH)* at University of Rochester [4] the smart medical home prototype consists of infrared sensors, computers, bio-sensors, and video cameras. The key services to be provided are medical advisory, which provides a natural conversational interface between the patient and health care expert, motion and activity monitoring, pathogen detection and skin care, and personal health care recording for consumer-provider decision support.

The *Aware Home* project at Georgia Tech [5] targets to create a home environment that is aware of its occupants' whereabouts and activities. The services provided by *Aware Home* range from enhancing social communications such as providing digital portrait of elderly people to their family members, to memory aids that assist users in resuming interrupted activities based on playbacks of past events recorded by video camera.

The smart in-home monitoring system at University of Virginia [6] focuses on data collection with the use of a suite of low-cost, non-intrusive sensors. The information collected is logged and analyzed in an integrated data management system (that is linked to the Internet). The system essentially collects information in a passive manner and does not directly interact with elderly people.

The major industry research effort is perhaps led by the age-in-place advanced smart-home system at Intel [7]. It aims to help elderly people with Alzheimer's diseases, by integrating four major technologies: sensors, home networks, activity tracking, and ambient displays. The sensors located in the home environment sense the locations of the people and the objects in the home.

Differently from the above mentioned strategies, our goal is to provide ubiquitous health monitoring, at home, and outside it, all the time. People need to have their health conditions under control not only when they are at home, but everywhere. In our technological society, we are proud of our ubiquitous communication or computing capabilities, but we think, it would be a point of even higher proud, if we could have ubiquitous health monitoring, which would improve the life quality for many. If our technology is not used to improve people's life, what is it good for?

We define the following requirements for our architecture:

1. **Reliability:** Due to the sensitive nature of our system, it should work even when various components might fail. For example, to guarantee the connectivity of the patients to the system, we propose to use complementary multiple wireless technologies.

2. **Quality of Service:** The system should provide high Quality of Service. For this reason, our communication protocols and our information management systems have to be designed and dimensioned with this requirement in mind.
3. **Security and Privacy:** Are a must for the whole system. The system will guarantee confidentiality, integrity, authentication, and privacy of data.

The rest of the paper is organized as follows. Section 2 provides an overview of our system architecture. In Section 3 we discuss the communication architecture. Section 4 presents our information management and security architecture. We conclude in Section 5.

2 Architecture Overview

In Fig. 1 we show an overview of the architecture that we are proposing for the Ubiquitous Health Monitoring System.

The biomedical data will be generated by multiple sensors that can be integrated in devices wearable by patients, such as necklaces, bracelets, etc. Sensors could include Carotid Dopplers, ECG Nanotrodes, biochip based on tissue/fluids Quantum Dots, etc. The measured biomedical data could include vital signs, such as the glucose level, blood pressure, heart bit rate, arterial oxyhemoglobin saturation level, etc.

The measured biomedical data will be transmitted via multiple complementary wireless networks, through the Internet, towards the appropriate Health Monitoring Center (HMC), where this data will be integrated with the permanent medical data of the given patient. Therefore, the medical personnel at HMC will be able to monitor various vital signs at desirable time granularity. Should

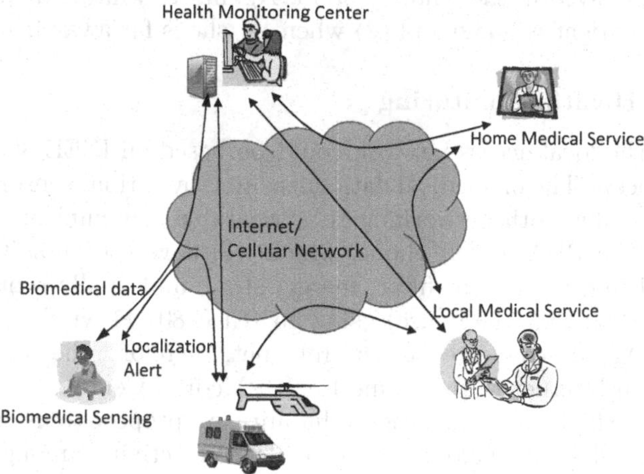

Fig. 1. System Architecture. Patient's biomedical data will be sent via multiple wireless networks to the appropriate Health Monitor Center, which will coordinate the activities among the Home and Local Medical Services and various emergency services.

the readings suggest any abnormal health situations, medical instructions can be given and actions can be taken before the situations deteriorate.

If needed, the personnel at HMC can consult with the patient's personal doctor, whose information is kept at Home Medical Center. Depending on the situation, HMC can coordinate the immediate medical service in the closest or more appropriate local medical facility using the best transportation service available. HMC can also coordinate a quick location discovery of the patient, in order to minimize the delays in providing the medical help, delays that in many cases make the difference between life and death.

Our goal is to monitor the patient's health everywhere, in their homes and outside. Therefore, we will distinguish two typical scenarios: (1) When the patient is at home or in the surrounding area; and (2) When the patient is far away from his home, for example in another city. To cover both cases, we propose a distributed health monitoring system. Therefore, the Health Monitoring Center functionalities will be distributed over the territory. In case (1), when the patient is at home, his/her measured biomedical data will be sent to the Home Health Monitoring Center. On the other hand, in case (2), when the patient is in another location, far away from his/her home, the measured biomedical data will be sent to the corresponding Visitor Health Monitoring Center.

In Section IV, we will discuss in more details the level of distribution of HMC and capacity planning issues of the system.

3 Communication Architecture

While there are various communication components in our architecture, as shown in Fig. 1, we will focus in this paper on the access communication architecture, which is between the patient and the Internet, as the most critical part of communications involved in the whole system. Again, we will distinguish two cases (1) when the patient is home and (2) when he/she is far away from home.

3.1 Home Health Monitoring

In this case, the local access network could be based on IEEE 802.11 family of wireless protocols. The biomedical data, measured by various sensors, will be sent using wireless Bluetooth networking to a wearable communication/computing device, such as a PDA or cell phone, which will have special software to treat the measured information, to filter, merge, store, and finally sent it to an Access Point (AP) (inside the house) using an IEEE 802.11 wireless interface. We assume that AP are connected to the Internet, therefore, the biomedical data, will go through Internet to the Home Health Medical Center.

To guarantee high communication reliability, we propose to use multiple complementary wireless technologies to provide connectivity among the patients and the system. Therefore, while IEEE 802.11 could be, as explained above, one way of network access, other solutions should be investigated and possibly be used as alternative interface. For example, the patient wearable communication/computing device could be equipped, beside the IEEE 802.11 interface,

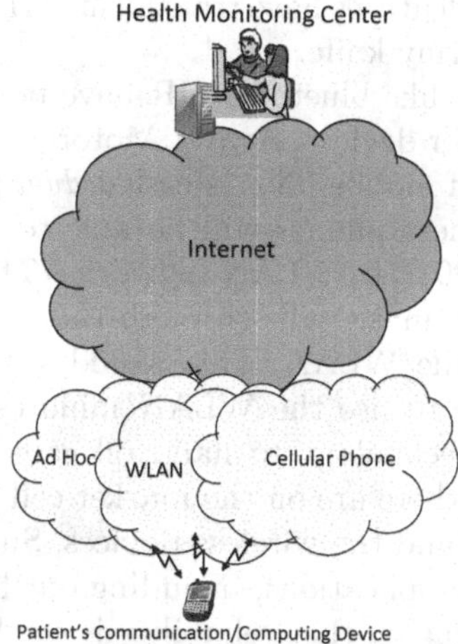

Fig. 2. The patient communication device, after collecting the measured biomedical data from various sensors, will communicate using multiple wireless networks with the Health Monitoring Center via Internet

with cellular phone, IEEE 802.16, and other wireless interfaces, as shown in Fig. 2. So when the patient is out of the reach of his/her IEEE 802.11 network, the data will be sent via cellular network, IEEE 802.16 or other interfaces. In case all such interfaces fail, which most likely will happen when the patient is not close to his home, we propose an ad hoc wireless network, which will be explained in more detail in Section 3.2.

3.2 Mobile Health Monitoring

When patients are away from their homes, again we propose multiple complementary wireless networks to be used as access network between the patient and the Internet.

In the case of mobile conditions, we propose cellular phone to be used as the first choice for the access network. The reason is that cellular phones are becoming ubiquitous telecommunication devices. Beside the low cost, their multitude of features, make cellular phones our most used personal communication devices. It is estimated that there are over 2 billion cell phones worldwide [8]. These phones typically have low power transceivers which typically transmit data and voice up to a few miles where the mobile tower (base station) is located. This base station connects the cellular phone to the backbone telephone network. The mobile phones cannot communicate when they are unable to connect to the base station.

The capabilities of these phones have also increased dramatically over the last few years. In addition to the standard telephone features, the phones also Instant Messaging, MMS, Internet access etc. More advanced features like music and video streaming, digital camera, and document scanner are being bundled with the cell phone. These features have transformed the cell phone from a simple phone to a digital Swiss army knife.

More advanced features like bluetooth, IR have been added to allow the cell phone to connect with other devices. Avaya, Motorola, and Proxim are planning to introduce a new class of mobile phones called *dual phones* [9,?], also referred to as the dual phones. These phones will be able to make voice calls over the cellular network and the 802.11a WLAN networks. The advantage of using this phone is that the user can make calls through the WLAN infrastructure when he is able to connect to the WLAN. This would save money because the cell phone user would be able to use the WLAN minutes for free. The companies have also developed the technology to hand off calls between the WLAN and cellular network. Already there are on the market cell phones able to connect to both the cellular network and the wireless devices. Such an ability could allows them to be used in many applications, including our health monitoring system.

We would like to stress again that reliability is the key distinguishing characteristic of our proposed architecture. Therefore, one important case is that when neither cellular phone system nor various WLAN technologies are available to patients in specific locations. For such cases we propose to use cell phones as ad hoc devices. As a consequence, existing cell phones in the area will create an ad hoc network (using similar interfaces such as IEEE 802.11) and will forward messages (containing biomedical data) even when the cellular infrastructure is not working.

We have developed routing [11,12] and broadcast protocols [13,14,15] to be used over ad hoc networks of cell phones. For example, our Adaptive Geometric Broadcast Protocol (AGB) for Heterogeneous Wireless Ad Hoc Networks [13],[16],[14] starts with a geometric approach and adapts itself to real conditions to use at best the available resources. Consequently, AGB is simple, robust and very scalable. On the other hand, our Adaptive Routing and Energy Management (AREM)[17],[18],[11,12], an adaptive cosslayer communication protocol, dynamically adapts the transmission ranges to minimize the delay and the energy consumption, and to prolong both node and network lifetimes. For the particular case when patients are traveling on highways, we have proposed another intervehicle communication protocol [19] that can be used to connect patients to the health monitoring system.

4 Information Management and Security Architecture

The information management architecture is shown in Fig. 3. The territory is covered by distributed Health Monitoring Centers. Each patient will be affiliated with a Home Health Monitoring Center (HHMC), which has a Home Data Base (HDB), where the permanent medical data of the given patient are stored. The permanent medical data are periodically updated from the corresponding Home Medical Service (personal doctor).

When the patient is located inside the coverage area of his/her HHMC, the measured biomedical data will be sent to this center, to be merged there with his/her

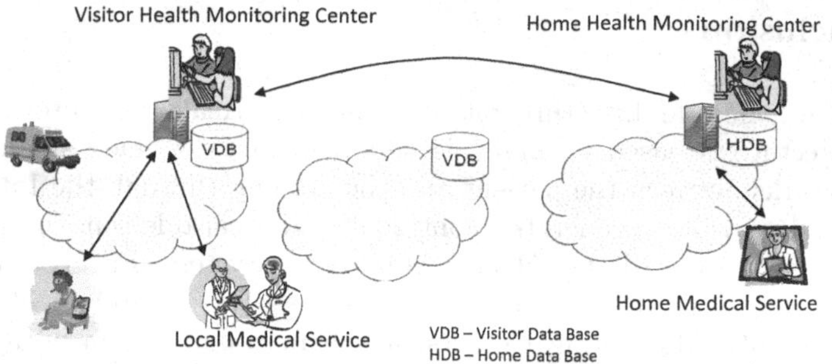

Fig. 3. The Health Monitoring Centers are distributed over the territory. Each patient is affiliated with a Home Health Monitoring Center, which keeps his/her permanent medical data. The patient will be served by the corresponding Visitor Health Monitoring Center (if he/she is not in his area), which in collaboration the his/her Home Health Monitoring Center will coordinate the activities among the Local and Home Medical service.

permanent medical data. Then, the personnel of HHMC, in collaboration with that of the patient's Home Medical Service, will coordinate the needed actions.

When the patient is located far away from his home, he/she will be covered by a given Visitor Health Monitor Center (VHMC), and the measured biomedical data will be stored in the Visitor Data Base (VDB) of this center. When needed, the VHMC will contact the HHMC to retrieve the permanent medical data of the patient from the HDB, update the VDB, and merge them with the measured biomedical data. Then, the personnel of VHMC will coordinate the activities among the Home Medical Service and the Local Medical Service, to provide the best medical help to the patient.

One important aspect of the Information management System is its capacity dimensioning. When Visitor Health Monitoring Centers cover large areas, the load work for each one of them could be high too. On the other hand, small coverage areas of Visitor Health Monitoring Centers, would distribute the load among them, but would increase the coordination load among them. Therefore, a careful tradeoff dimensioning of the system is needed, to provide the best and quickest service to the user.

All information flows in the system should be secure. We propose that before each exchange of information between two parts, cryptography authentication should take place first. So, the patient and the given HHMC or VHMC should authenticate each other. The same should happen between HHMC and VHMC, HMC and (Local of Home) Medical Service. Therefore, we assume that all parties share the needed keys among them. Using session keys, all exchanges of data will be end-to-end encrypted to guarantee the required confidentiality. Also, all exchanges of information will be protected from integrity point of view, with the appropriate digital signatures. Due to its delicate nature, the system will guarantee the privacy of biomedical data. Only authorized medical personnel will have access on the data and when it is needed. Solutions such as we have proposed in [20,21] could be used for such purpose.

5 Conclusions

We propose a new architecture for a Ubiquitous Health Monitoring System. Our architecture is based on multiple complementary wireless communication access networks between the patient and the system, through the Internet. The biomedical data will be generated continually by wearable sensing devices. We propose to have a distributed Health Monitoring System. Each patient will be affiliated with e Home Health Monitoring Center. The territory will be covered by Visitor Health Monitoring Centers, which in collaboration with the Home Centers will provide the needed coordination among the Home and Local Medical Services, to quickly respond to any medical situation in the best and secure way.

References

1. Huang, G.T.: Monitoring Mom: As population matures, so do assisted-living technologies. Technical Review 20 (July 2003)
2. Assited Living Project Web page at University of Illinois at Urbana-Champaign. [Online]. Available: `http://lion.cs.uiuc.edu/assistedliving/index.html`
3. Wang, Q., Shin, W., Liu, X., Zeng, Z., Oh, C., Li, B.A., Caccamo, M., Gunter, C., Gunter, E., Hou, J., Karahalios, K., Sha, L.: I-Living: An Open System Architecture for Assisted Living. In: Proceedings of IEEE SMC, [Online] Available (2006), `http://lion.cs.uiuc.edu/assistedliving/publications/I-Living.pdf`
4. University of Rochester, Center of Future Health. [Online]. Available: `http://www.futurehealth.rochester.edu/news/`
5. Georgia Institute of Technology, Aware Home. [Online]. Available: `http://www.cc.gatech.edu/fce/ahri/`
6. University of Virginia, Smart In-Home Monitoring System. [Online]. Available: `http://marc.med.virginia.edu/projectssmarthomemonitor.html`
7. Intel Corporation, Age-in-Place. [Online]. Available: `http://www.intel.com/research/prohealth/cs-aginginplace.htm`
8. Cellularonline, `http://www.cellular.co.za`
9. `http://www.networkworld.com/news/2004/072604avaya.html`
10. `http://www.pcworld.com/news/article/0,aid,116334,00.asp`
11. Durresi, A., Paruchuri, V., Barolli, L.: Delay-Energy Aware Routing Protocol for Sensor and Actor Networks. In: Proceedings of the 11th IEEE International Conference on Parallel and Distributed Systems ICPADS'2005, Fukuoka, Japan, July 20–22, pp. 292–298. IEEE Computer Society Press, Los Alamitos (2005)
12. Durresi, A., Paruchuri, V., Barolli, L.: Delay-Energy aware Routing Protocol for Heterogeneous Ad Hoc Networks. Journal of Interconnection Networks (JOIN) 7(1), 37–49 (2006)
13. Durresi, A., Parachuri, V., Iyegar, S., Kannan, R.: Optimized Broadcast Protocol for Sensor Networks. IEEE Transaction on Computing 54(8), 1013–1024 (2005)
14. Durresi, A., Parachuri, V., Jain, R.: Geometric Broadcast Protocol for Heterogeneous Wireless Sensor Networks. Journal of Interconnection Networks (JOIN) 6(3), 193–208 (2005)
15. Durresi, A., Parachuri, V.: Broadcast Protocol for Energy-Constrained Networks. IEEE Transaction on Broadcasting 53, 112–119 (2007)

16. Durresi, A., Parachuri, V.: Geometric Broadcast Protocol for Sensor and Actor Networks. In: Proceedings of IEEE AINA 2005, Taipei, Taiwan, March 27-29, pp. 343–348. IEEE Computer Society Press, Los Alamitos (2005)
17. Paruchuri, V., Basavaraju, S., Durresi, A., Kannan, R., Iyengar, S.: Random Asynchronous Wakeup Protocol for Sensor Networks. In: Proceedings of BroadNets'04 San Jose, CA, pp. 710–717 (October 2004)
18. Durresi, A.: Architectures for Heterogeneous Wireless Sensor Networks. In: Proceedings of the 16th Annual IEEE International Symposium on Personal Indoor and Mobile Radio Communications - PIMRC'2005, Berlin, Germany, September 11 - 14, IEEE Computer Society Press, Los Alamitos (2005)
19. Durresi, M., Durresi, A., Barolli, L.: Adaptive Intervehicle Communications. International Journal of Wireless Information Networks, Springer Science 13(2), 151–160 (2006)
20. Durresi, A., Paruchuri, V., Iyengar, S.: A lightweight protocol for data integrity in sensor networks. In: Proc. of The International Conference on Intelligent Sensors, Sensor Networks and Information Processing ISSNIP 2004, Melbourne, Australia (December 2004)
21. Durresi, A., Paruchuri, V., Barolli, L., Kannan, R.: Anonymous communication protocol for sensor networks. International Journal of Wireless and Mobile Computing (IJWMC) (2007) (in press)

Tree Graph Views for a Distributed Pervasive Environment

Tuyêt Trâm Dang Ngoc[1] and Nicolas Travers[2]

[1] ETIS Laboratory - University of Cergy-Pontoise, France
Tuyet-Tram.Dang-Ngoc@u-cergy.fr
[2] PRiSM Laboratory - University of Versailles, France
Nicolas.Travers@prism.uvsq.fr

Abstract. The pervasive Internet and the massive deployment of sensor devices have lead to a huge heterogeneous distributed system connecting millions of data sources and customers together [Fra01]. On the one hand, mediation systems [BGL+99, DNJT05] using XML as an exchange language have been proposed to federate data accross distributed heterogeneous data sources. On the other hand, work [MSFC02, AML05, BGS01, NDK+03] have been done to integrate data from sensors. The challenge is now to integrate data coming from both "classical" data (DBMS, Web sites, XML files) and "dynamic" data (sensors) in the context of an ad-hoc network, and finally, to adapt queries and result to match the client profile.

We propose to use the TGV model [TDNL06, TDNL07a] as a mobile agent to query sources across devices (sources and terminal) in the context of a rescue coordination system. This work is integrated in the PADAWAN project.

Keywords: XQuery evaluation, Tree Graph View (TGV), Pervasive environment, Rescue Coordination.

1 Introduction

The pervasive Internet and the massive deployment of sensor devices have lead to a huge heterogeneous distributed system connecting millions of data sources and customers together.

On one side, data sources are heterogeneous as they can be of different types (relational, text, XML, streaming value, etc.) and can have different update frequencies (from "never" for some text document to "always" for sensors value) and their autonomy (from non-manageable obfuscated black box that just provide values to a full access management on a DBMS). On the other side, there can be different profiles of clients: access permission, terminal capabilities, user preferences, etc.

To deal with distributed heterogeneous and autonomous data sources, mediation systems have been widely studied [Wie92, MFK01, NGT98, BGL+99, DNJT05]. Such mediation systems [Wie92] provide a uniform interface to a multitude data sources using mediators and wrappers to handle respectively distributivity and heterogeneity.

T. Enokido, L. Barolli, and M. Takizawa (Eds.): NBiS 2007, LNCS 4658, pp. 406–415, 2007.

XML [BPSM98], has become the preferred format to represent semi-structured data [Abi97] and an effective way to define any type of data that can be represented as a tree.

Moreover, XQuery [W3C05] has proved to be an expressive and powerful query language to query XML data both on structure and content, and to make transformation on the data. In addition, its query functionalities come from both the database community (filtering, join, selection, aggregation), and the text community (supporting and defining function as text search).

TGV (Tree Graph View) [Tra06, TDNL06, TDNL07a] is a Tree Pattern-based model (such as TPQ [CJLP03] and GTP [AYCLS01]) to model XQuery queries. This model is suitable to our needs since :

- it supports the complexity of the full untyped-XQuery specification: relational and set operator, aggregation, ordering, nested reconstruction, conditional predicate, etc.
- it is designed for a mediation context accessing to distributed autonomous and heterogeneous data sources: its structure identifies data collections and dependencies between them. An annotation model in layers allows to annotate any piece of information (location of the source(s), cost model, etc) that can be useful a evaluation time. Finaly, transformation rules have been defined to optimize and evaluate the TGV to produce the result.

The rest of this paper is organized as follows. To start off with, we motivate the need for a mobile semi-structured model in a pervasive environment in Section 2 and we express issues and related works in Section 3. Further, we recall the TGV model and functionalities in Section 4 and show how it is suitable to our context. We then present some extensions to the TGV model that would make it more suitable to a pervasive environment (Section 5). In the end, we conclude in Section 6 and present future directions of our work.

2 Context

In the global context of our work, different types of data sources and terminal client are dissiminated all over a network consisted of traditional IP routing and addressing (e.g. the Internet), and ad-hoc routing scheme.

2.1 Motivational Scenario

The application scenario is the deployment of a Rescue Coordination Center after or during a disaster (fire, earthquake, flood, etc.) A truck (Figure 1) carries the PADAWAN proxy, some access points (wire, wireless WI-FI, SINK, etc.) and an Internet Access.

Using these gateway access points, the PADAWAN proxy can reach three types of networks:

- *Wireless ad-hoc Sensor Network [Toh01] (ad-hoc WSN)*: Sensors are deployed (eg. from helicopter or embedded in the rescue team equipment) in

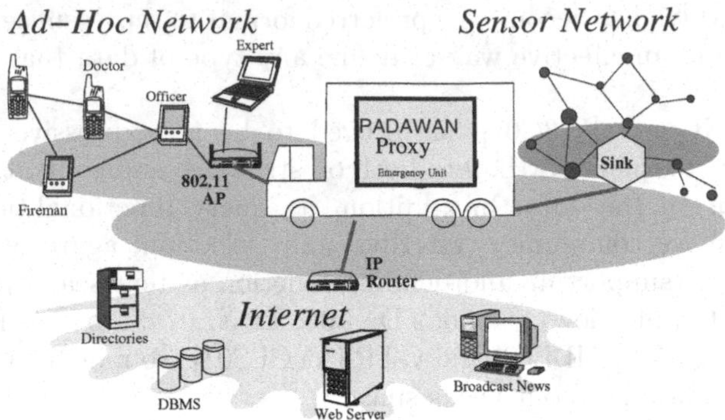

Fig. 1. Deployment of a Rescue Coordination Center

the monitoring area to form a WSN. The entry point is a *sink* (a node with large resources that collects statistics from nodes in its coverage and generally remains in a static location).
- *private network and/or ad-hoc network*: used by the rescue team (firemen, officers, doctors, emergency unit)
- *the Internet*: to access databases, web site, directories, etc.

Using such a system, depending of their profile and access rights, not only the members of the rescue team, but the experts and the press can access to an integrated view on all sources related to the disaster and query it.

2.2 PADAWAN

The rescue scenario relies on the PADAWAN (a Proxy for All Devices Accessing the World And Neighborhood) infrastructure. The PADAWAN infrastructure is seen as a graph where links are networks links (radio or wire), and nodes are either data sources, client terminals or the PADAWAN proxy itself.

Data Sources. We define by **source**, any device that provides data: DBMS, sensors, web sites, RSS feeds, legacy applications, directories, files, etc. We consider different kinds of (non-exclusive) heterogeneity:

- *data type*: sources can have a relational, text-based, semi-structured, unstructured model. The query language can differ : SQL, XQuery, OQL, contains function, http request, etc. and so the result format : tuple, XML, objects, text lines, text documents, etc.
- *autonomy*: except for some databases managed by the PADAWAN administrators themselves, the major number of sources are autonomous and just communicate what their owner want them to communicate. They mainly just provide data to reply to requests more or less supported, and rarely give their internal information (cost model, data statistics, schema, etc.)
- *update frequency*: some data sources can be considered as static or semi-static sources where data do not change frequently, eg. Web pages, LDAP

directories, some databases. Other data sources are considered as dynamic, as their information update very frequently or on each request (RSS feed, sensors measure).

Clients. All kind of clients can access to PADAWAN to query the sources: from a simple pager to a complex application manipulating huge volume of sources. Available data and results are processed using specific views based on client profile. These views are computed depending on:

- *user preference*: eg. the firemen officer want to know about the temperature measured by each sensors, the press just needs to access the average temperature of the site.
- *user access rights*: eg. the rescue team has access to the personal medical information of injuried people, others don't.
- *client terminal capabilities*: eg. the cell-phone used by the firefighter does not have the same display capabilities as the laptop computer of the rescue cooordination officer, so large volume of information, images and video is not applyable in every case.

The PADAWAN Proxy. The core of the system is the PADAWAN proxy (that is located in the rescue truck). This proxy is a mediator system collecting and requesting all available data coming from deployed sensors, and embedded systems used by the rescuers received via the access points, and also from databases and RSS feeds from the Internet.

The Figure 2 shows a query Q and its XQuery representation. We suppose that, for example, information on building occupation is stored in a relational DBMS located on an Internet site, and that sensors are deployed over an ad-hoc sensor network reachable by a sink access point.

Let **Q** be the query that *"list every buildings occupied by more than 100 inhabitants, and for each, get the district and the list of maximum temperature measured by the sensors located in the same district."*

XQuery Request	XML Result
for *$a* **in** /buildings/building	<districtMonitoring>
where *$a*/description/inhabitant > 100	<location> *Yellow Lake* </location>
return	<temperatures>
<districtMonitoring>	<temperature> *14* </temperature>
<location> {*$a*/district} </location>	</temperatures>
<temperatures>	</districtMonitoring>
{ **for** *$b* **in** //sensor	<districtMonitoring>
where	<location> *Green Valley* </location>
$b/deploymentArea/district = $a/district	<temperatures>
return	<temperature> *163* </temperature>
<temperature> {*$b*/max_temp} </temperature>}	<temperature> *25* </temperature>
</temperatures>	<temperature> *43* </temperature>
</districtMonitoring>	</temperatures>
	</districtMonitoring>

Fig. 2. Query, XQuery request for Query Q and XML result

3 Issues and Related Works

Mediation systems [BGL+99, DNJT05] based on mediator/wrappers architecture [Wie92] using XML as an exchange language have been proposed to federate data accross distributed heterogeneous data sources. The heterogeneity of the data type is handled by *wrappers* that act as "translators" from the source native query language and result to the common query language and model used by the mediator. The mediator decomposes the user into subqueries sent to wrappers, and recomposes the final result, and thus, manages the distributed aspect of the system.

Many work [MSFC02, AML05, BGS01, NDK+03] have been done to integrate data from sensors. The first type of approach considers the sensor network as a virtual [MSFC02] or materialized [BGS01] relational table. The second type of approach as in the IrisNet [NDK+03], considers the web as a "huge" XML document, using DNS extension to locate nodes of the XML document. However, these works are not designed to be integrated with other DBMS in a heterogeneous environment, using queries with complex functionalities.

The challenge is how to evaluate XQuery across the graph composed of heterogeneous sources, heterogeneous clients and heterogeneous infrastructure.

We propose to use the TGV model to deal with this problem. We recall the TGV basis in the next section, and show how it is suitable to our needs.

4 Tree Graph View (TGV)

TGV (Tree Graph View). [Tra06, TDNL06, TDNL07a] is a Tree Pattern-based model (such as TPQ [CJLP03] and GTP [AYCLS01]) designed to represent XQuery request and its evaluation. The TGV supports all the functionnalities of untyped-XQuery, uses an intuitive representation compliant with mediation issues, and provides a support for optimization and information.

4.1 TGV Example

This TGV representation of the XQuery Q (Figure 2) is shown on Figure 3 (a). The tree patterns of the two data collections of the query are shown in circles. The intermediate and final result construction are represented within boxes. Dependencies are shown by hyperlink lines binding the patterns or the pattern nodes: join on the two source tree patterns and projection from one node or tree pattern to another. The nested `temperature` in `temperatures` is also supported (the $t box).

This type of representation is suitable to a mediation system as subpart of the requests can be identified and also dependencies between them.
The TGV model has been fully formalized using Abstract Data Types in [Tra06].

4.2 Annotation

Set of elements of the TGV can be annotated for (a) any *granularity* of information and (b) any *type* of information (cost models and statistics, location, constraint, accuracy, security, rule tracability).

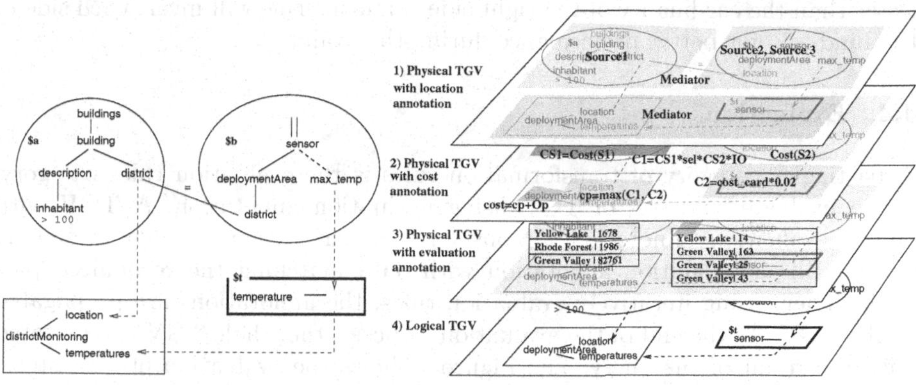

Fig. 3. (a) TGV of the Query **Q** - (b) TGV Annotation Layers View

Using annotation, a TGV can be viewed on any type of annotation that has been defined on it. On Figure 3 (b), the original logical TGV ④ has three annotated views:

① *location annotation*: each location of the execution of subparts of the TGV is reported on the associate set of TGV elements on the TGV. *In our example, the information on* `buildings` *can be retrieved from a source* `Source1` *that is a DBMS accessible from the Internet. The information on* `sensors` *are retrieved from* `Source2` *and* `Source3` *that are located on two SINKS respectively located on the* `Yellow Lake` *and on the* `Green Valley`*. The other parts of the TGV are evaluated by the mediator, located on the PADAWAN proxy.*

② *time cost annotation [LDNL07]*: the time cost execution are annotated on subparts of the TGV. The time costs are evaluated using cost models.

③ *evaluation annotation*: This annotation layer is used to evaluate the TGV. The evaluation annotations are intermediate or final results that have been evaluated on subparts of the TGV. The evaluation process is described in the subsection 4.4 ("evaluation").

The annotation specification [TDNL06, LDNL07] are generic enough to annotate any subpart of the TGV, including money cost, energy cost (battery for sensors), accuracy, etc.

4.3 Transformations

In [TDN07], a pattern-based language for extensible rules has been defined for TGV. The subpart of the TGV that match the rule condition pattern is transformed into another pattern by applying transformation rules. Annotations can also be considered in the rule condition. For instance, during the optimization phase, cost annotation can be used to generate better plan: the rule condition can express that if the estimated cardinality of left side of an bind-join is much lesser than the cardinality of the right side, than the rule will invert each side of the bind-join for better performance during the evaluation.

4.4 Evaluation

A particular category of transformation rules is the evaluation rules category, which evaluate subparts of TGV using evaluation annotation. A TGV with empty evaluation annotation is considered as an execution plan. Matching sources fill the evalution annotation with data matching the recognized patterns. Then, using iteratively evaluation rules, the annotations are propagated in the TGV. At the end of the evaluation, process, the whole TGV is annotated with the result of the query. The Figure 4 shows the evaluation process steps. Starting from the TGV Query on Figure 3 with empty evaluation annotations, the Source Tree Patterns are annotated (7a) with matching information retrieved from the appropriate sources (using location annotation). Then the transformation rule matching the join hyperlink apply (7b), then the aggregation rule (7c) and finally, the projection rule annotates the whole TGV with the evaluation annotation containing the final result (7d) that can be returned as an XML document (Figure 2 (left column)).

A similar evaluation approach has been developped in Mutant Query Plan [PMT03].

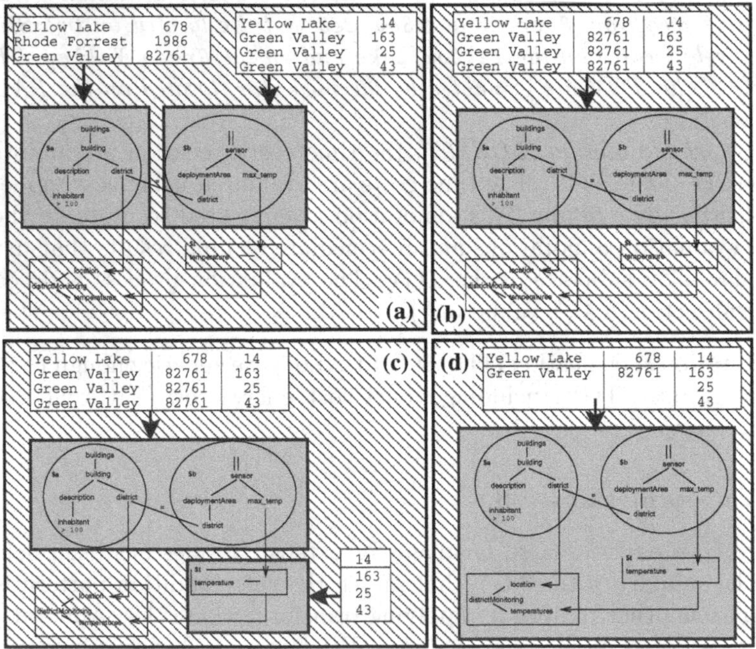

Fig. 4. Evaluation of a TGV

5 TGV in a Pervasive Environment

5.1 TGV Mobile Agent

The TGV evaluation by transformation rules on annotations is very well adapted to a mobile agent platform. The TGV Mobile Agent move between nodes across the graph. Each node of the graph:

– applies evaluation rules on the matched TGV, to fill evaluation annotations
– reads location annotations to route the TGV to the next concerned node

Query processing using Mobile Agent -but in relational context- has been developped in the work of [MHMM05]. Using the TGV model, mobile agent would be able to query on semi-structured distributed data, and thus be used in a heterogeneous environment.

5.2 Views on TGV

A client profile is represented by a view. A view is a request, and so can be represented by a TGV. Each client has a view constructed from the user preference, the user access permission and the client terminal capabilities. The profile is modeled as a view (a TGV request) that is applied to the client request (another TGV request). Such TGV merging has been developed in [DNGT04] via mapping.

5.3 TGV* (TGV Star)

When a source connects to the PADAWAN proxy, the associated wrapper send the source description to the proxy. The source description is also a TGV with as many annotation views as different types of information provided. As this TGV is a TGV where all paths of supported tree patterns (as in dataguide [GW97]) are annotated, this TGV is called TGV* (TGV star). All TGV* are sent by wrappers to the PADAWAN proxy and merged to make a big TGV* on the proxy. This TGV* is then used by the proxy to annotate TGV user request with information about location, cost, etc.

6 Conclusion

In this article, we have presented the TGV as a model suitable for distributed evaluation of an XQuery request over a pervasive environment, using a rescue coordination scenario.

– as a representation [TDNL07b] of the full-untyped XQuery specification, the TGV inherits of all the power of the XQuery language (relational and set operator, aggregation, ordering, nested reconstruction, conditional predicate, etc.)
– its tree pattern based structure and dependencies, make it suitable to a multi-sources context

- its annotation layers view is designed for a distributed environment
- merging rules make views on request easy to evaluate, and thus, client profile easy to consider
- its evaluation rules by using annotation and transformation make the distribuated TGV evaluation feasable on autonomous nodes. Thus, with routing consideration, moving TGV to mobile agent can be done.
- its extensible optimisation rules, allows us to process TGV efficiently.

Future Works. In this paper, we consider that sources description (metadata) are centralized on the PADAWAN proxy as a kind of a Yellow Page service. The scenario context of the coordination of rescue teams legitimates this approach.

In a more general context, it would be interesting to distribute the metadata all over the network. This raise the problem of maintaining such a distributed index of metadata. We are currently studying whether a P2P DHT approach is suitable to our needs, and how to distribute the TGV* in this way.

If we choose to distribute the data sources description, there won't be a central PADAWAN proxy anymore, and any node could then be considered as a PADAWAN proxy for other nodes, with more or less capabilities. This approach will transform the whole PADAWAN architecture into a P2P network that will be applied in the context where no critical coordination is needed.

Reflexion about routing TGV as a mobile agent would then have to be done. To optimize queries execution, nodes can also cache data and source description from TGV they forward to other nodes.

Acknowledgement

This work is done as part a of the PADAWAN project supported by the ANR.

References

[Abi97] Abiteboul, S.: Querying Semistructured Data. In: Proceeding of the 6th International Conference on Database Theory, Delphi, Greece (1997)

[AML05] Abadi, D.J., Madden, S., Lindner, W.: Reed: Robust, efficient filtering and event detection in sensor networks. In: VLDB, pp. 769–780 (2005)

[AYCLS01] Amer-Yahia, S., Cho, S., Lakshmanan, L.V.S., Srivastava, D.: Minimization of Tree Pattern Queries. In: SIGMOD Conference (2001)

[BGL+99] Baru, C., Gupta, A., Ludascher, B., Marciano, R., Papakonstantinou, Y., Velikhov, P.: XML-Based Information Mediation with MIX. In: ACM-SIGMOD, Philadelphia, USA, ACM Press, New York (1999)

[BGS01] Bonnet, P., Gehrke, J., Seshardi, P.: Toward sensor database systems. In: Conference on Mobile Data Management (2001)

[BPSM98] Bray, T., Paoli, J., Sperberg-MacQueen, C.: Extensible Markup Language (XML) 1.0 (W3C Recommendation) (1998)

[CJLP03] Chen, Z., Jagadish, H.V., Laksmanan, L.V.S., Paparizos, S.: From Tree Patterns to Generalized Tree Patterns: On efficient Evaluation of XQuery. In: Very Large Data Bases, Germany, pp. 237–248 (2003)

[DNGT04] Dang-Ngoc, T.-T., Gardarin, G., Travers, N.: Tree graph view: On efficient evaluation of xquery in an xml mediator. In: Proc. of BDA (2004)

[DNJT05] Dang-Ngoc, T.-T., Jamard, C., Travers, N.: XLive: An XML Light Integration Virtual Engine. In: Proc. of BDA (2005)

[Fra01] Franklin, M.J.: Challenges in ubiquitous data management. Informatics , 24–33 (2001)

[GW97] Goldman, R., Widom, J.: Dataguides: Enabling query formulation and optimization in semistructured databases. In: VLDB (1997)

[LDNL07] Liu, T., Dang-Ngoc, T.-T., Laurent, D.: Cost framework for a distributed semi-structured environment. In: Database Management and Application over Networks (DBMAN) 2007 (to appear)

[MFK01] Manolescu, I., Florescu, D., Kossmann, D.: Answering XML Queries over Heterogeneous Data Sources. In: 27th Intl. Conf. VLDB, Roma, Italy, pp. 241–250 (2001)

[MHMM05] Marsit, N., Hameurlain, A., Mammeri, Z., Morvan, F.: Query processing in mobile environments: A survey and open problems. In: Distributed Frameworks for Multimedia Applications (DFMA) (2005)

[MSFC02] Madden, S., Szewczyk, R., Franklin, M.J., Culler, D.E.: Supporting aggregate queries over ad-hoc wireless sensor networks. In: WMCSA (2002)

[NDK+03] Nath, S., Deshpande, A., Ke, Y., Gibbons, P.B., Karp, B., Seshan, S.: Irisnet: An architecture for internet-scale sensing services. In: VLDB (2003)

[NGT98] Naacke, H., Gardarin, G., Tomasic, A.: Leveraging Mediator Cost Models with Heterogeneous Data Sources. In: ICDE, pp. 351–360 (1998)

[PMT03] Papadimos, V., Maier, D., Tufte, K.: Distributed query processing and catalogs for peer-to-peer systems. In: CIDR (2003)

[TDN07] Travers, N., Dang-Ngoc, T.-T.: An extensible rule transformation model for xquery optimization. In: International Conference on Enterprise Information Systems (ICEIS) 2007

[TDNL06] Travers, N., Dang-Ngoc, T.-T., Liu, T.: Tgv: an efficient model for xquery evaluation within an interoperable system. International Journal of Interoperability in Business Information Systems (IBIS) 2 (2006)

[TDNL07a] Travers, N., Dang-Ngoc, T.-T., Liu, T.: Tgv: a tree graph view for modelling untyped xquery. In: Database Systems for Advanced Applications (DASFAA) (April 2007)

[TDNL07b] Travers, N., Dang-Ngoc, T.-T., Liu, T.: Untyped xquery canonization. In: Workshop on Emerging Trends of Web Technologies and Applications (WebETrends) 2007

[Toh01] Toh, C.K.: Ad Hoc Wireless Networks: Protocols and Systems. Prentice Hall, Englewood Cliffs (2001)

[Tra06] Travers, N.: Optimization Extensible dans un Médiateur de Données XML. PhD thesis, University of Versailles (2006)

[W3C05] W3C. An XML Query Language (XQuery 1.0) (2005)

[Wie92] Wiederhold, G.: Mediators in the Architecture of Future Information Systems. Computer 25(3), 38–49 (1992)

A Distributed Resource Furnishing to Offload Resource-Constrained Devices in Cyber Foraging Toward Pervasive Computing

MinHwan Ok, Ja-Won Seo, and Myong-soon Park*

Dept. of Computer Science and Engineering / Korea University
Seoul, 136-701, Korea
mhok@ieee.org, jawon@ilab.korea.ac.kr, myongsp@ilab.korea.ac.kr

Abstract. Mobile devices are pursuing the succession of desktop PCs these days. Cyber Foraging is the project that investigated overcoming scarce computing resources and reducing the power consumptions of mobile devices. In this paper, we propose a framework for remote execution of mobile devices in the way of delivering user data and invoking and manipulating the software of a surrogate with VNC-style interface. This resource furnishing system has the merits of remote application execution, and automatic file transfer. Remote execution is provided via VNC-style interface that is user-friendly. Performance evaluation shows the feasibility of the resource furnishing system, for both data transfers over wired and wireless network.

Keywords: Mobile Device, Storage Server, Remote Execution, Virtual Network Computing, Cyber Foraging.

1 Introduction

The Internet is a resource pool of powerful hardware and various software sharable. Some software, specific for use in desktop PCs or requiring high processing capability are increasingly engaging faster processing speed, larger memory area and more storage space. Most of these software require powerful hardware, which has superior processing unit, huge main memory and vast auxiliary storage. These characteristics make those software unmovable, and any user who needs those software may use them through Internet.

Mobile devices are pursuing the succession of desktop PCs these days. However, mobile devices should be small and light to support mobility, so they use a small flash memory instead of a hard-disk of large data space. In the case of PDAs, these are usually equipped with RAM in size of 256~512MB. Cell-phones or smart phones permit smaller memory space. It is hard to deal with multimedia data such as mpg, and installing large software such as database engines or using database in mobile devices. Furthermore, mobile devices have low processing capability and it has been a barrier

* Corresponding author.

T. Enokido, L. Barolli, and M. Takizawa (Eds.): NBiS 2007, LNCS 4658, pp. 416–425, 2007.

in applying various services of the wired environment. Cyber Foraging[1] is the project to research about the pervasive computing. It proposed a mechanism to augment the computational and storage capabilities of mobile devices. Cyber foraging realized that mobile devices forages the resources of nearby public computing facilities connected to the wired Internet through high bandwidth networks. These public computing facilities, named a *surrogate*, play the role of computing and data staging server. Actual processing and substantial data transfer is carried out by the surrogates, what is similar to the concept network computing. Cyber foraging illustrated two kinds of service. One is the data staging that mobile devices can store the data on surrogates and the other is the remote execution. The remote execution is a service that an application of mobile devices' user can utilize resources of the nearby surrogates.

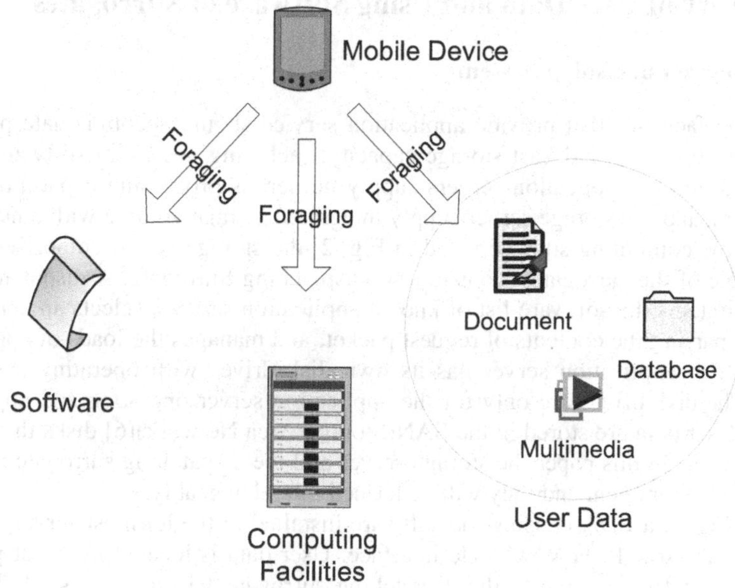

Fig. 1. Resources in Cyber Foraging for a Mobile Device

In the previous works related to cyber foraging, the software codes should be re-written to run in distributed computing environment. However, this consumes very much effort, but even not practical for some specific software. To use those software at mobile devices, a concept of Virtual Network Computing[2] is a good candidate. The mobile device would be a thin client only receiving the screen of the software running at a computing facility over wireless network by VNC. The difficulty in adapting the concept VNC is its frequent screen refresh. For instance, PDA users can access and download packet data from networks at the maximum speed of 2.4Mbps in CDMA 2000 1x EV-DO. In maximal download speed, the application screen in size of 640x480 can be delivered as a whole once per about 1 second. This screen refresh rate seems to be too low. However a changed part of the screen is only transferred in practice, thus the actual refresh rate would be near 10 times per second.

Another important component for cyber foraging is surrogate discovery. Versatile Surrogate Discovery, VERSUDS[1], is an on-going project for this objective and this work conforms to the mechanism of VERSUDS. In this paper, we propose a framework for remote execution of mobile devices in the way of delivering user data and invoking and manipulating the software of a surrogate with VNC-style interface that is user-friendly. In the next section, delivery of user data and using the software with the concept of VNC is introduced. The system architecture and managing user data are described in Section 3. In Section 4, the file transfer module implementation for unstable wireless bandwidth is described and experimentation results are presented. Section 5 deals with related works. The last section summarizes this work.

2 Delivery of User Data and Using Software of Surrogates

2.1 Resource Furnishing System

Computing facilities that provide application service should accommodate plenty of processing resources and vast storage capacity, including necessary software set for users. A dozen of application servers supply numerous processing capabilities from server farm, and the storage server supply integrated storage volume with a number of disks. In the computing sites depicted in Fig. 2, the storage server comprises an important role of the surrogates, constituting Dispatching Surrogate. A dispatching surrogate maintains the software list of known application servers, selects an application server by parsing the contents of request packet, and manages the loads of application servers. Each application server has its own disk drives with operating system installed. The disk drives are only for the application server operation and application running. User data are stored in the SAN(Storage Area Network)[6] disks through the storage server. In this paper the storage server and the dispatching surrogate indicates an identical component and they will be termed interchangeably.

In the Fig. 2, a PDA is using the software installed in the leftmost server of application server farm 1 via VNC-style interface. User data is located in the dispatching surrogate 2 and transferred to the dispatching surrogate 1 to be processed. The next subsection describes the procedure in detail.

2.2 Interrelations Among a Mobile Device, Surrogates, and Application Servers

A mobile device, dispatching surrogates, application servers, and VERSUDS are four major components in this work. The procedure of Fig. 3 implies the roles of the major components.

In this resource furnishing system, user data is transferred from other storage server to one application server of the installed software. Once the user uploads the data to one of storage servers, the data is automatically transferred to be processed. For this purpose a *Sharable Storage* is devised and it is the home space of data collected by the user. The user login to the sharable storage and use the software of each application server, and data are automatically transferred between each computing site and the sharable storage, each time the user commits the transfer. System architecture is described in the next section including automatic data transfer[5].

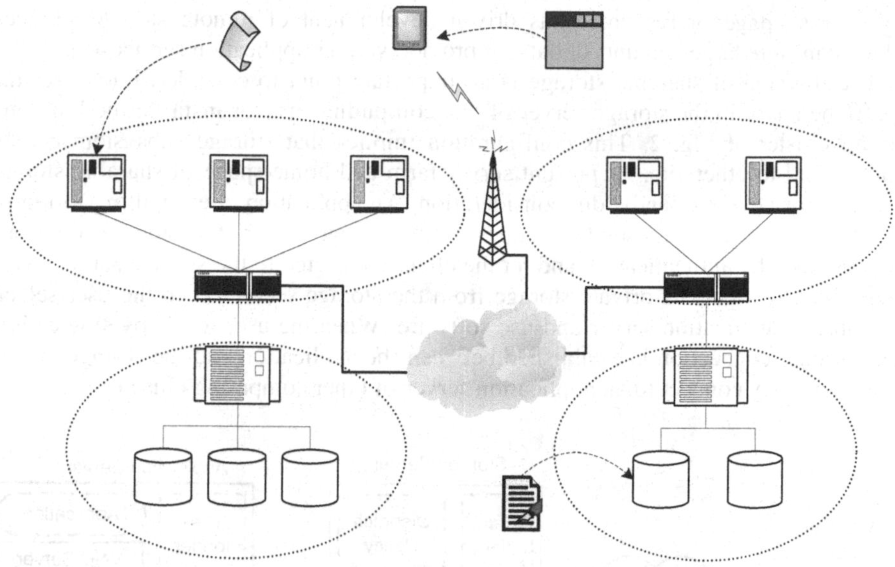

Fig. 2. Two computing sites constitute a part of resource furnishing system with server farms and their storage subsystems

(1) Mobile Device	Discovery a nearby surrogate by VERSUDS
(2) Mobile Device	Request to the selected surrogate
(3) Dispatching Surrogate	Parse the request and Determine the type of application
(4) Dispatching Surrogate	Relay the request to the application server in which the software installed
(5) Application Server	Establish a direct connection to the Mobile Device with VNC-style interface
(6) Application Server	Invoke the software and Get user data transferred to its dispatching surrogate
(7) Mobile Device	Manipulate the invoked software

Fig. 3. Operation Sequence of Resource Furnishing System

3 System Architecture

For the software runs its application server in conventional manner and manipulated via VNC-style interface, the majority of the system is composed of modules for data transfer. Therefore the performance of data transfer is of primary concern in this work, since the user manipulate the software directly. We have adopted a storage subsystem for mobile devices of our previous works[4,5], and the subsystems shows good performance in their characteristics of block-level I/O. Similar to this work, the mobile device's shortage of resources has driven development of remote storage services, which can store large amounts of data, or provide various application services[5].

The location of sharable storage is an important point to consider. Each user has the home space in the storage server of one computing site, for instance the left computing cluster of Fig. 2. This configuration implies that storage subsystem can be immigrated to other site. At present server farm and home space of sharable storage coexists for network bandwidth consideration. An application client willing to log on the storage server should send its request to the storage server. The storage server admits the user by authentication and let the client connected to the storage server. After login the client gets its private storage from the storage server. Then the user selects appropriate application server and use software. When the user logon by single sign-on, a secure connection is established between the application and the storage server. The client may connect to an application server of other computing cluster.

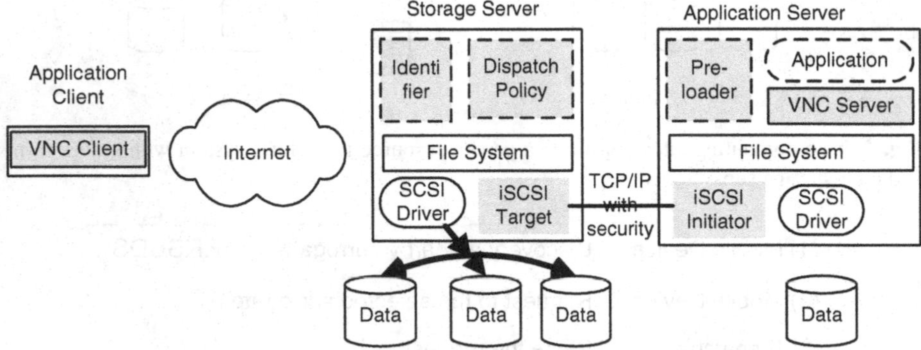

Fig. 4. System architecture to supply processing resources and secure storage

User data is transferred to storage server manually, and transferred to the application server automatically. Fig. 4 depicts system architecture with sharable storage. Since the iSCSI protocol can make clients access the SCSI I/O devices of a storage server over IP network, a client can use the remote storage at other computing site transparently without the need to pass through the remote storage server's file system[7]. The user's home space is recognized as the application server's a local storage by a particular network device driver[4]. Once the application requests a data file to the device driver, *iSCSI Initiator* in the figure, it relays the request to the other network device driver, *iSCSI Target*, of the storage server. The storage server starts to transfer user data to application server by the network device drivers. When the application server transfers data to the storage server, data blocks are delivered via *iSCSI Initiator* and *iSCSI Target*. For performance reason, they I/O in block-level[8] that provides requested blocks of an opened file to the remote server and updates corresponding blocks when modification occur. Block I/O outperforms file I/O and moreover it does not adhere to a certain file system. *Dispatch Policy* module parses the request and selects an application server to relay the request. The user may select more than one application server concurrently. *Identifier* module monitors connections with application servers and maintains each connection, i.e. connection re-establishment and transfer recovery.

Pre-loader module caches the user data in home space for computing clusters not equipped with dedicated broadband network lines. This module is described further in the next section. The application server and the storage server can exchange data through Internet for the data are transferred in iSCSI protocol.

4 File Transfer over Wireless Network

Before preloaded into the storage server, user data need be transferred to the user's home space at its (remote) storage server. The mobile device uploads/downloads the data files via nearby storage server to its storage server. As the bandwidth of wireless network is very low than that of wired network, the primary concern in performance issues is the delivery of the data files from/to the storage server to/from the mobile device. Frequently the bandwidth of wireless network isn't stable; the resource furnishing system is equipped with a communication module for unstable bandwidth. In this section transfer performance is measured between the mobile device and a nearby storage server over wireless network through an experiment with the effects of potential parameters in order to adjust transfer throughput to unstable wireless bandwidth.

4.1 Experiment Setup

Our experiment consists of a PDA and a storage server connected to Internet with CDMA 2000 1x EV-DO network, as shown in Fig. 5. The Initiator module embedded in PDA based on Windows CE can transmit iSCSI command and data to the target of storage server for I/O. We set the experimentation environment as shown in Table 1.

Table 1. Summary of Experimentation Environment

	Storage Server	PDA
OS	Linux 8.0	Windows CE 4.0
CPU	PIII 800 Mhz	Intel Strong ARM SA-1110
Memory	256MB	32MB
NIC	1 Gbps LAN	CDMA 1x EV-DO

PDA users can access and download packet data from networks at the maximum speed of 2.4Mbps in CDMA 2000 1x EV-DO. The maximum speed of uploading is 307.2Kbps.

We consider throughput as performance metrics, which is the total number of application-level bytes carried over an iSCSI connection divided by the total elapsed time taken by the application, as expressed in Bytes per millisecond (B/ms). We used the system timer of PDA which is based on WinCE in order to measure throughput. Total elapsed time was measured as the time interval from the initial time when the experiment program started generating the first byte of data to the time when the last byte of data was confirmed to have been sent (received).

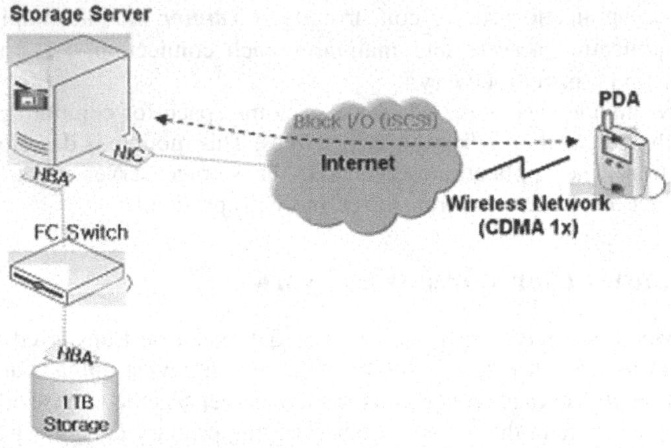

Fig. 5. Experiment of File Transfer over Wireless Network

We conducted two kinds of experiments with an I/O stream of 5 megabytes. In the first experiment, commands of the PDA for 5 megabytes read operation are passed through wireless link. Then the target of the storage server sends data to the initiator of the PDA. In the second experiment, commands of the PDA for 5 megabytes write operation are passed through wireless link. The initiator of the PDA sends the commands then data to the target of the storage server.

4.2 Experiment Results

Fig. 6 shows the result from the first experiment for 5 megabytes read operation in CDMA network. We first examined the effect of the Number of sectors per command with the parameter MaxRecvDataSegmentLength(MRDSL) from 512bytes to 8Kbytes respectively. The Number of sectors per command is increased from 16 to 2048, which increases the expected command size from 8Kbytes to 1024Kbytes due to a 512 bytes sector size for our system. In the wireless network, the results related to the values of MRDSL from our experiment are different from those in a stable wired network. The throughputs are better at the MRDSL values of 1Kbytes, 2Kbytes and 4Kbytes than the values of 512bytes and 8Kbytes. At the Number of sectors per command value of 2048, the throughput of 2Kbytes MRDSL is increased by 48% and 52% respectively compared with those of 512bytes and 8Kbytes MRDSL.

In write operation, the Number of sectors per command is kept constant at 1024 (512Kbytes) and the MaxBurstLength (MBL) varies from 512Bytes to 256Kbytes. We use the fixed Number of sectors per command. Fig. 7 shows that the throughput is increased as MBL increases from 512Bytes to 128Kbtyes in a wireless network, after that there is a slight decrease in throughput when MBL is around 256Kbytes. The same kinds of decreases in throughput happen in read operations too, which are caused by the narrow bandwidth of CDMA network. In a write operation, the result is

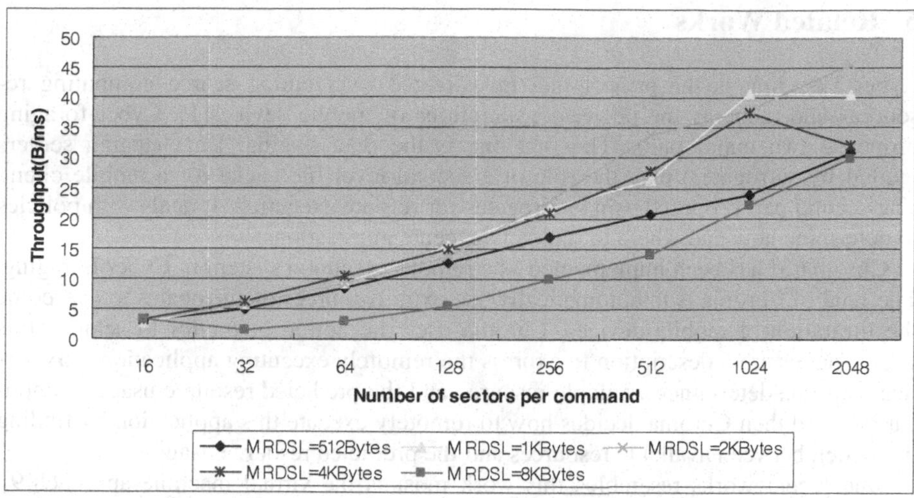

Fig. 6. Effect of Number of sectors per command on throughput for 5 Mbytes Read operation in CDMA

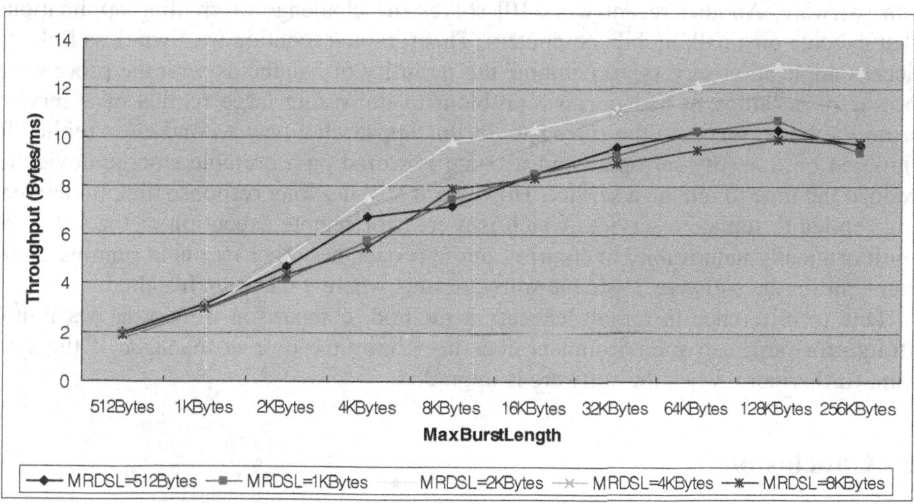

Fig. 7. Effect of MaxBurstLength on throughput for 5Mbytes Write operation in CDMA network

more obvious because the CDMA 2000 1x EV-DO network has the narrower bandwidth for upload than that for download.

Throughout the experiments, the storage server is able to adjust transfer rates by respective parameters according to the network delays of unstable wireless network.

5 Related Works

Cyber Foraging is the project that investigated overcoming scarce computing resources and reducing the power consumptions of mobile devices[1]. Cyber foraging proposed two major parts. The first one is the data staging. Data staging servers (called by surrogates) play the role of a second-level file cache for a mobile client. The second part proposed using surrogates for remote execution. It deals with policies to determine how and where to remotely execute applications.

Chroma[3] has been implemented as a remote execution system in Cyber Foraging. The goal of Chroma is to automatically use extra resources of surrogates to overcome the limitation of mobile devices. Chroma uses the notion of *tactics* to achieve this goal. Tactics are a description to express the remotely executing applications. By tactics, Chroma determines available resource and the predicted resource usage of application. And then Chroma decides how to remotely execute this application by finding the match between available resources and the predicted resource usage.

One recent works resembles this work most is the virtual machine approach[9]. Linux VServer is adopted for remotely execution the application. The VServer enables a single hardware platform to run a number of virtual machines with complete isolation, flexibility, resource control, and ease of cleanup. It is a practical approach for unmovable software however, has the potential limitation of virtual machine to run software. Another recent work[10] solves the challenge of creating applications that execute on small, mobile computers. This remote execution uses wireless links to access application servers, to combine the mobility of handhelds with the processing power of desktops. It had intrinsic problem in delivering large replica of a service from the home server to the surrogate. In this approach a new second-class replica is initiated on a nearby surrogate and its state is stored on a portable storage device to reduce the time to initiate a service. However it still has long response time in delivering replica to initiate a service, which is a cost for remote execution of the software built originally unmovable. In contrast, our approach has other merits in running environment for the software, since the software runs where it has been installed.

Due to difference in remote execution method, comparison in approaches is not straightforward, native environment does not annoy the user or manager of the system, furthermore, when the software is upgraded.

6 Conclusion

For mobile devices lack sufficient resource to run a software or handle large files, we proposed a framework to furnish resources for remote execution together with data delivery. This work is different from other work by using VNC-style interface in running software.

While the software runs at an application server, user data are to be transferred to the storage server of the application server. Preliminary functionalities for data transfers are proposed in our previous works[4,5] and we implemented and tested the communication module for wireless network in this work. In the experiments a way is derived to adjust transfer throughput to unstable wireless bandwidth with the potential parameters.

The application client necessitates only the VNC-style interface. Required resources are all foraged from the resource furnishing system. The model behind this system is very similar to the Web service system and it is planed the system would incorporated in the form of a pervasive computing infrastructure on Internet.

References

1. Balan, B., Flinn, J., Satyanarayanan, M., Sinnamohideen, S., Yang, H.: The Case for Cyber Foraging. In: Proc. ACM SIGOPS European Workshop. ACM Press, New York (2002)
2. Richardson, T., Stanfford-Fraser, Q., Wood, K.R., Hopper, A.: Virtual Network Computing. IEEE Internet Computing 2(1), 33–38 (1998)
3. Balan, R.K., Satyanarayanan, M., Park, S.Y., Okoshi, T.: Tactics-Based Remote Execution for Mobile Computing. In: Proceedings of MobiSys 2003: The First International Conference on Mobile Systems, Applications, and Services, San Francisco, CA, USA (May 2003)
4. Kim, D., Ok, M., Park, M.-s.: An Intermediate Target for Quick-Relay of Remote Storage to Mobile Devices. In: Gervasi, O., Gavrilova, M., Kumar, V., Laganà, A., Lee, H.P., Mun, Y., Taniar, D., Tan, C.J.K. (eds.) Computational Science and Its Applications – ICCSA 2005. LNCS, vol. 3481, pp. 1035–1044. Springer, Heidelberg (2005)
5. Ok, M., Kim, D., Park, M.-s.: UbiqStor: Server and Proxy for Remote Storage of Mobile Devices. In: Zhou, X., Sokolsky, O., Yan, L., Jung, E.-S., Shao, Z., Mu, Y., Lee, D.C., Kim, D., Jeong, Y.-S., Xu, C.-Z. (eds.) Emerging Directions in Embedded and Ubiquitous Computing. LNCS, vol. 4097, pp. 22–31. Springer, Heidelberg (2006)
6. Clark, T.: IP SANs: A Guide to iSCSI, iFCP, and FCIP Protocols for Storage Area Networks. Addison-Wesley, Reading (2002)
7. Lu, Y., Du, D.H.C.: Performance study of iSCSI-based storage subsystems. IEEE Communication Magazine 41, 76–82 (2003)
8. Block Device Driver Architecture: http://msdn.microsoft.com/library/en-us/wceddk40/html/_wceddk_system_architecture_for_block_devices.asp
9. Goyal, S., Carter, J.: A Lightweight Secure Cyber Forging Infrastructure for Resource-constrained Devices. In: The Sixth IEEE Workshop on Mobile Computing Systems and Applications, pp. 186–195 (2004)
10. Suu, Y.Y., Flinn, J.: Slingshot: Deploying Stateful Services in Wireless Hotspots. In: Annual Conference on Mobile Systems, Applications and Services, pp. 79–92 (2005)

Trust Model for Mobile Devices in Ubiquitous Environment

Zhefan Jiang and Sangwook Kim

Department of Computer Science, Kyungpook National University,
Sankyuk-dong 1370, Bukgu, Daegu, Korea
{zfjiang,swkim}@cs.knu.ac.kr

Abstract. In ubiquitous computing environment, people carrying their mobile devices (eg., mobile phone, PDA, embedded devices) expect to access locally hosted services or resources anytime, anywhere. These mobile devices have restricted capabilities and security supports. Traditional security management systems used definite access control policies for each role or user in each domain server or agent. But in ubiquitous environment, it is hard to specify authorization policies for mobile users and it is inflexible and unavailable for security management of users or mobile devices. To solve these problems, we need trust-based management mechanism as a reference to security management systems. Trust model contains trust relationship and calculation of trust value. Experiences and recommendations are the factors to calculate trust value. In this paper, we design a trust model to calculate trust value and a trust management architecture which can be running in various domain servers and mobile devices.

1 Introduction

In ubiquitous computing environment, people carrying their mobile devices (eg., mobile phone, PDA, embedded devices) expect to access services or resources anytime, anywhere. But they don't know these services are trustworthy or not. At the same time, service domains don't know how to trust mobile users. Traditional security management systems used definite access control policies for each mobile user or device. But in ubiquitous environment, it is hard to specify authorization policies and it is inflexible and unavailable for security management. Trust-based security management defines a trust model to allow entities to compare the trustworthiness of other entities for security decisions[12]. It captures the dynamic aspects and human intuitions about trust for using in security management. It enhances the existed security management and makes more easier to do collaboration works.

In this paper, we propose a trust model for mobile users. This model is used experience and recommendation as factors to compute trust value. We present new computation method to compute trust value according to transaction history and enhance the recommendation protocol to propagate recommendation requests. We also designed a trust-based management system which can be used in mobile devices or domain servers.

T. Enokido, L. Barolli, and M. Takizawa (Eds.): NBiS 2007, LNCS 4658, pp. 426–434, 2007.

The remainder of this paper is structured as follows. In section 2, we describe some related work. Section 3 shows our trust model which includes the trust relationship and calculation algorithms of trust value. We present our trust management architecture in section 4. Finally, we draw some conclusions and outlines directions for future work.

2 Related Work

In this section, we briefly highlight several existing trust management systems. The basic part in trust management system is the trust model which defines trust relationships and the computation mechanisms for trust value.

The mains trust factors calculating trust value are experiences and recommendations. For instance, in [2,3] mainly used experience between a trust and a trustee. [4,5,7,9] used both experience and recommendation to calculate trust value. VTrust used both experience and recommendation as trust factors, it calculated experience value which given weight for each action[6]. These researches considered that each negative or positive action gave the same effect to evaluate trust value. [8] designed a trust evolution model, they used mathematical and probabilistic model to calculate trust value. In [11], they set more weight to negative actions when they calculated experience value. In [13], the authors distinguished transaction amounts and computes different impact factors when computing trust values. In [13], the authors distinguished transaction amounts and computes different impact factors when computing trust values. These works considered different impact factors to compute trust value with different views and implemented their trust management systems.

In this paper, we propose a dynamic trust model for mobile devices. We consider security level of a target service and give more weight to continuous negative actions to calculate experience value. And we enhanced our recommendation protocol to propagate recommendation re-quests. We also consider security capabilities of mobile devices to reduce risks.

3 Proposed Trust Model

A Trust model defines trust relationship and the computational mechanism for trust value.

3.1 Trust Relationship

Truster(Tr) trusts Trustee(Te) to perform actions to the specific Services(Se) when Contexts(Cs) are satisfied during a TimePeriod(TP). Tr and Te can be users or intelligent devices. As are performed actions to the Tr's resources. TV is a trust value. Trust value is the number in the range [-1, 1]. The value in the positive region is used to express trust and in the negative region is used to express distrust. 1 means complete trust and -1 means complete distrust. 0 indicates trust neutral value.

{ Tr, Te, TV, Se, Cs, TP }

3.2 Experience

Experience is the most important and direct factor to evaluate a trust value. It is calculated by the past interactions between a truster and a trustee. The calculations of the trust value are different from the domain management applications and administrators disposition. This disposition also determines how trust value is updated after interactions[11].

As an interaction result, an action can be a positive action(a+ = 1)or a negative action(a- =1). For calculation of experience value, we consider following several matters. First is the security level of a target service. For instance, one negative action performed on a target service which the security level set to high and one negative action performed on a target service which security level set to low. These two actions have different effects on the trust evaluation. Security level(SL) is a integer number in the range [1, n] according to the service domain or applications. N is the highest security level.

$$Va_j = \max\{ \frac{a_j * 2^{cn}}{Total_a} * \frac{SL_j}{SL_n}, -1 \} \tag{1}$$

Intuitively, trust is hard to gain, easy to lose[8]. The continuous negative actions give more effect than non-continuous negative actions. And second continuous negative action has given more disappointment than the first negative action to a truster. So we give more weight to continuous negative actions. We use equation(1) to calculate each action value Va_j, which is rewarded or penalized according to past interaction.

a_j is a jth action, it can be positive action or negative action. $Total_a$ is the total action number of 1 period. SL_n is the highest security level in an applying domain and SL_j is a security level of target service which jth action performed. cn is a counter number of continuous negative actions, cn is established by default to 0, cn is increased to 1 when continuous negative actions performed. For instance, if there are two continuous negative actions, cn is increased to 1, if there are three continuous negative actions, cn is increased to 2. After that, a positive action performed, it set to 0 again.

The current trust value according to experience(EV_i) is recalculated according to previous trust value(EV_{i-1}) and the current action value. User can configure weight ß to current action Va, ß is in the range[0,1]. We configure 0.5 as a default weight. The new trust value is calculated according to equation(2):

$$EV_i = EV_{i-1} * (1 - |ß * Va_j|) + ß * Va_j \tag{2}$$

Figure 1 shows the experiments of experience evaluation using 30 actions performed in 1 period. We assume the initial trust value is 0 and the target services are classified into four security levels(unclassified=1, classified=2, secret=3, top secret=4). We can see the trust value was drop faster when the continuous negative actions performed. And trust values are changed according to weight ß.

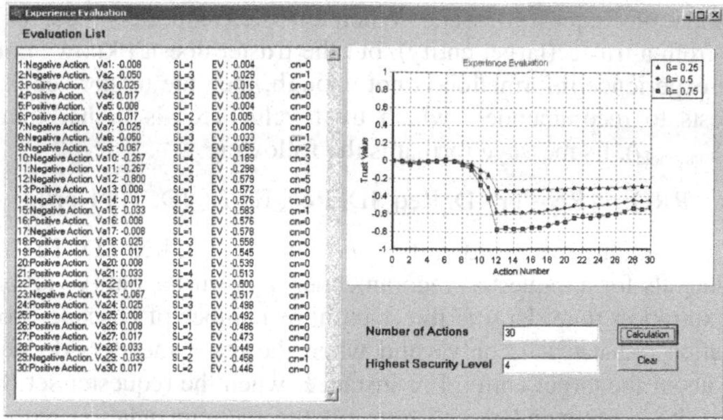

Fig. 1. Experience Evaluation according to Continuous Negative Actions and ß

3.3 Recommendation Protocol

Recommendation is used when there in no experience or insufficient information between a truster(requester) and a target entity(trustee). A truster sends recommendation request messages to recommenders who have a trust value higher than a certain threshold. Recommendation protocol is used to exchange recommendation messages as shown in Figure 2. In our recommendation protocol, a truster can set Hop which the maximum number of cascade propagation of recommendation request. It is only valid when the recommenders do not have trust information about the target entity. For instance, when the requester(Truster) set the Hop as 1, it means that the recommenders can transmit the recommendation requests as a requester to another trust entity and set the Hop as 0 and set the new TP as a TP/2.

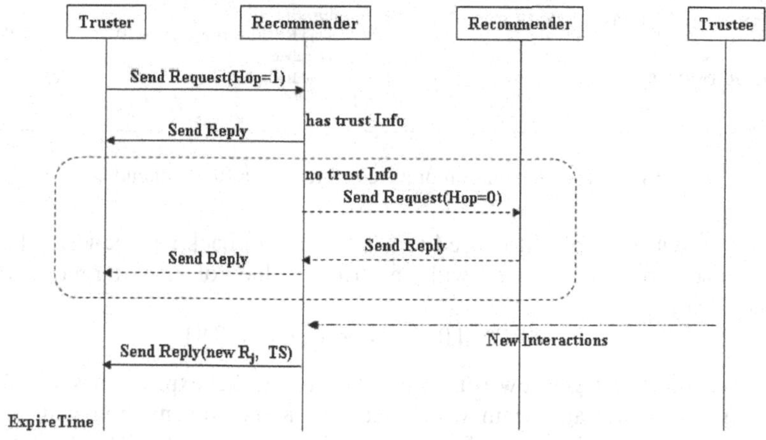

Fig. 2. Recommendation Protocol

Recommendation Request Message: When a truster(requester) receives the interaction request from a trustee(target entity), but the truster doesn't know about trustee or consider the experience information is not enough, then the truster sends recommendation requests to recommenders which trust value(TR_j) is higher than a specific threshold($TV_{threshold}$). Its message format is the following:

RRQ::={Reqster_ID, Req_ID, Rec_ID Te_ID, TP, Hop}

Req_ID is the unique request identifier and Reqster_ID, Rec_ID, Te_ID are identifiers or credentials for a requester, recommender, and trustee entity. TP is the request message's expiration time. Hop is the maximum number of cascade propagation of recommendation request. It is only valid when the recommenders do not have trust information about the target entity. For instance, when the requester set the Hop as 1, it means that the recommenders can transmit the recommendation requests as a requester to another trust entity and set the Hop as 0 and set the new TP as a TP/2. 0 means that the recommenders don't send requests to others any more. RV is a recommendation value for a trustee. R_j is jth recommender's recommendation value. m is the total number of recommenders. Figure 3 shows the algorithm and implementation of a truster and recommender.

Requester implementation	Recommender implementation

{
RV = 0; Hop = h;
search Recommenders which $TR_j > TV_{threshold}$
send RRQ(Reqster_ID, Req_ID, Rec_ID Te_ID, TP, h);
 	
calculate RV{
while(Timeout(send_time + time_period) == true)
{
listen(RRP(Rec_ID, Req_ID, R_j, TS);
if receive two RRP from one Rec_ID
compare(TS1, TS2) refresh Rj;
}
$RV = \sum_{j=1}^{m}(R_j \cdot TR_j) / (\sum_{j=1}^{m} TR_j)$
}
if(no RRP) RV = 0;
}
	{
	listen(RRQ(Tr_ID, Req_ID, Rec_ID, Te_ID, TP, h));
	search Te;
	if known (Te)
	$R = TV_{Te}$
	send(RRP(Rec_ID, Req_ID, R, TS));
	if refresh (TV_{Te})
	send RRP(RecID, ReqID, R, TS));
	else
	if(Hop == 0)
	R= null;
	send RRP(Rec_ID, Req_ID, R, TS);
	else
	send RRQ(Reqster_ID, Req_ID, Te_ID, TP/2, (h-1));
	calculate RV;
	send RRP(Rec_ID, Req_ID, R, TS);
	}

Fig. 3. Implementation of a Requester and a Recommender

Recommendation Reply: It is used to send response back per request. The recommender sends reply message with a trust value of the target entity and TS(Timestamp).

RRP::={Rec_ID, Req_ID, R, TS}

If the recommender get new trust value before the TP expired, it sends a recommendation replay message again which set new R(recommendation value) and TS. The final recommendation value(RV) is used in computing final trust value for the trustee.

3.4 Trust Evaluation

For evaluating the trust value(TV), a truster may assign different weights to the experience factor and recommendation factor according to equation(3). EV is the trust value according to experience with weight = a. RV is the recommendation value according to recommendation. The weights will specify in trust evaluation policy.

$$TV = EV * a + RV * (1-a) \qquad (0 <= a <= 1) \tag{3}$$

3.5 Risk Management

In this paper, we propose two schemes to reduce risks. First scheme is comparing the minimum security requirements of target services for interaction and security capabilities of mobile devices.

The security capabilities for mobile devices include secure communication protocol, cryptographic algorithms, authentication schemes. But they are still restricted. Although a truster and trustee has a trust relationship and the trust value is high, if the security capabilities for mobile devices can't be satisfied with the security requirements for the target objects, the access request could be denied. For instance, the domain server specifies that accessing a file transfer service must use SSL protocol, but if the mobile device has not support this secure protocol. So domain server can deny this request.

Second is implicit in trust evaluation to reduce risks. It is a scheme that if a truster has a low trust value for a trustee, this trustee only can access the service which has a low security level. For instance, a truster can configure risk rules as shown in Figure 4.

security level 1 -1 <= TV < -0.5
security level 2 -0.5 <= TV < 0
security level 3 0 <= TV < 0.5
security level 4 0.5 <= TV <= 1

Fig. 4. Risk Rules

If the truster has a trust value which equals -0.6 for a trustee, the trustee only can access the target service which security level is 1.

4 Trust Management System

We design our trust management architecture as shown in Figure 5. It includes a security manager and a trust agent. A trust agent is an assembly of software components for the trust management.

Security manager: It consists of a request analyzer, monitor, access control manager and policy repository. When a trustee sends a service request for interaction, the request analyzer analyzes the request information. The access control manager is responsible for searching the policy repository about the target service's security level(SL) and security requirements and the minimum trust value. Then it sends these information to the trust agent to evaluate trust value. It makes a decision the request would be granted or denied. The policy repository stores the security policies which specify service name, security level, trust value. The monitor is monitoring the status of domain resources and events.

Trust Agent: It consists of experience, recommendation protocol, trust inference engine, risk manager and a trust policy repository. Experience collects interaction history for each trustee and calculates the experience value. Recommendation protocol sends recommendation requests and receives recommendation reply from recommenders. Trust policy repository stores trust policies and trust values for each trustee.

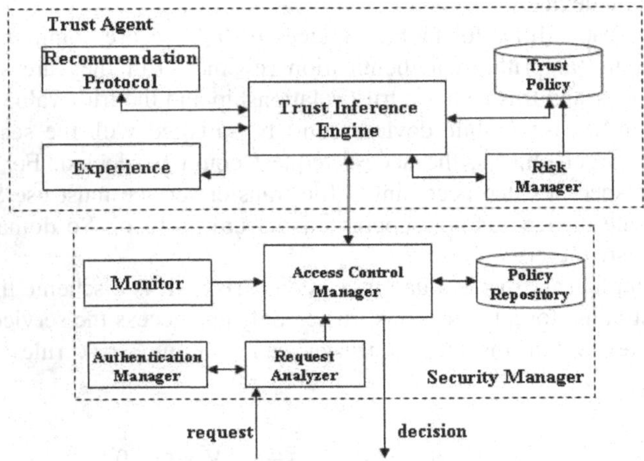

Fig. 5. Trust Management Architecture

Trust policy specifies as following 7 fields like the trust relationship. a is the weight of experience value and ß is the weight of last action value of interaction.

[Trustee, Services, TrustValue, Contexts, ValidTime, a, ß]

The risk manager is responsible for analyzing the risks. The trust inference engine refers to trust policies and computes new trust value. Then it sends the new trust value and risk information to security manager to make a decision for requests.

We have implemented the trust management system. Figure 6 shows the experiment of our trust management system and recommendation process. We used two domain servers which has our trust management system. Domain Server 1 has the trust information for PDA and it calculated the mobile user's trust value according to interaction history. When this mobile user move to another service domain and want to access services, but domain server 2 doesn't have trust information about this mobile user. If domain server 2 trusts domain server 1, domain server 2 sent recommendation request to domains server 1 and made a decision according to recommendation value.

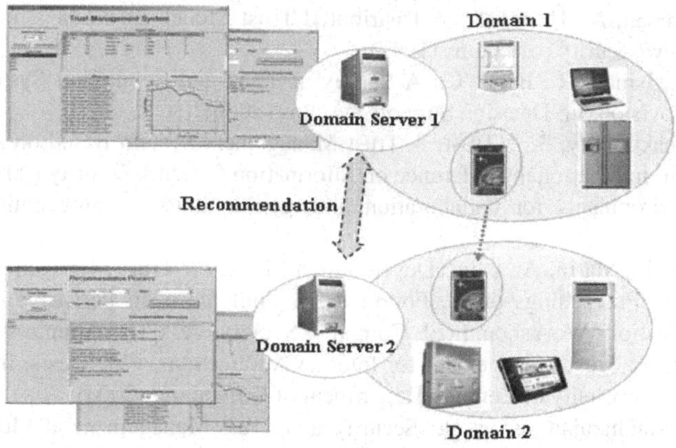

Fig. 6. Trust Management System and Recommendation Process

5 Conclusion and Future Work

We have designed a trust model for mobile users and devices. It enhances the existed security management and makes more easier to do collaboration works. This model is used experience and recommendation as factors to compute trust value. It can express that each action's effects are different according the security level of target service and continuous negative action counters. We also enhance the recommendation protocol to propagate recommendation requests.

We also implemented a trust management system to be used in mobile devices or domain servers. Our model minimizes the risks from the restricted security capabilities of mobile devices. Now we are analyzing the performance of our trust model. Furthermore, we will develop more efficient trust management system for using a various domains.

Acknowledgement

This research was supported by the MIC of Korea, under the ITRC support program supervised by the IITA(IITA-2006-C1090-0603-0026).

References

1. Gambetta, D.: Can we trust trust? In: Gambetta, D. (ed.) Trust, Making and Breaking Cooperative Relations, pp. 213–237. Basil Blackwell, Oxford (1988)
2. Virendra, M., Upadhyaya, S.: Securing Information through Trust Management in Wireless Networks. In: Workshop on Secure Knowledge Management (2004)
3. Shi, J., von Bochmann, G., Adams, C.M.: A Trust Model with Statistical Foundation. In: 18th International Federation for Information Processing (IFIP) World Computer Congress TC1 WG1.7 Workshop on Formal Aspects in Security and Trust (2004)

4. Abdul-Rahman, A., Hailes, S.: A Distributed Trust Model. In: Proceedings of the workshop on New security paradigms (1997)
5. Josang, A., Ismail, R., Boyd, C.: A Survey of Trust and Reputation Systems for Online Service Provision. In: Decision Support Systems (2006)
6. Ray, I., Chakraborty, S.: VTrust: A Trust Management System Based on a Vector Model of Trust. In: International Conference on Information Systems Security (2005)
7. Secure environments for collaboration among ubiquitous roaming entities (SECURE) (2001)
8. Almenarez, F., Marin, A., et al.: Developing a Model for Trust Management in Pervasive Devices. In: Proceedings of the Fourth IEEE Conference on Pervasive Computing and Com-munications Workshop. IEEE Computer Society Press, Los Alamitos (2006)
9. Grandison, T.: Trust Management for Internet Applications. PhD thesis, Imperial College of Science, University of London, Department of Computing (2003)
10. Lin, C., Varadharajan, V., et al.: Security and Trust Management in Mobile Agents: A New Perspective. In: Proceedings of The Second International Conference on Mobile Technology, Application and Systems (November 15-17, 2005)
11. Jameel, H., Hung, L., et al.: A Trust Model for Ubiquitous Systems based on Vectors of Trust Values. In: Proceedings of the Seventh IEEE International Symposium on Multimedia. IEEE Computer Society Press, Los Alamitos (2005)
12. McKnight, D., Chevany, N.: The Meanings of Trust. Working paper, Carlson School of Management, University of Minnesota (1996)
13. Wang, Y., Lin, F.: Trust and Risk Evaluation of Transactions with Different Amounts in Peer-to-Peer E-Commerce Environments. In: The IEEE International Conference on e-Business Engineering. IEEE Computer Society Press, Los Alamitos (2006)

PoQBA: A New Path Admission Control for Diffserv Networks

Enrique Pena, Miguel Rios, Christian Oberli, and Vladimir Marianov

Department of Electrical Engineering
Pontificia Universidad Catolica de Chile
Casilla 306, Correo 22, Santiago-Chile

Abstract. In most DiffServ networks there is a bandwidth broker (BB) that manages the network resources. One of the many tasks of this broker is to perform admission control on the flows entering the network. When there are many frequent calls, the network is large, or the admission control scheme is very complex, the bandwidth broker can become part of the problem instead of the solution. In those cases the broker might act as a bottleneck, limiting the number of flows entering the network and rejecting some of them even if there are still enough resources available. This is why distributed and hierarchical architectures of bandwidth brokers are needed. We introduce PoQBA: an algorithm that adapts book-ahead optimization to path oriented hierarchical broker architecture. The results show that the performance of this algorithm has several advantages compared to normal hierarchical systems and the Hose model.

Keywords: QoS Broker, Admission Control.

1 Introduction

The DiffServ architecture is capable of providing well defined end-to-end service not only inside, but between different network domains. It is based on two types of agents: edge and core routers. Core routers are kept as simple as possible in order to achieve scalable results. To do so, the edge routers aggregate traffic into flow classes based on previously negotiated service level agreements (SLA). These SLAs are complex business related contracts that cover a wide range of issues, including network availability guarantees, payment models and other legal and business necessities. Among these parameters, SLA also contains Service Level Specifications (SLS) that characterize the QoS requirements and the Per Hop Behavior (PHB) a flow class must receive. Core routers schedule the different packets based on these PHB. They only have to deal with a few flow classes instead of every single flow that arrives to the network. This makes them simple and independent of the amount of flows in the system.

The Bandwidth Broker (BB) is the management entity of the system. It has full knowledge of the topology and resources of the network. In general terms, BB's main function is to control and administrate the network resources, allowing

T. Enokido, L. Barolli, and M. Takizawa (Eds.): NBiS 2007, LNCS 4658, pp. 435–445, 2007.

new flows to enter the net, negotiating and monitoring the QoS constrains for every client, and configuring the resources to accomplish these tasks [1]. This paper will focus on one of the main functionalities of the BB: admission control. The BB must decide which flows to accept and which one to reject based on the actual resources available and the requirements of each flow. it is of great interest for network administrators to configure the BB, so it performs this admission control while trying to maximize their profit [11].

Centralized architectures are very efficient in resource allocation but might introduce some scalability problems. In particular, the ability of a single BB to handle large volumes of flows is debatable. The simplest solution is to use several BBs, in order to share the processing load between them. Distributed systems are a reasonable solution but require a very strict coordination [3].

Another way to achieve scalability is using hierarchical models, where a central agent coordinates several edge agents. Such idea is used in [4], where a central BB assigns bandwidth quotas dynamically to several edge BBs. These edge agents perform the admission control based on the amount of quota assigned to them. In [5] it is proposed some modifications to this quota-based scheme in order to reduce the complexity of the admission control process. A hybrid scheme is proposed in [6] where edge BBs start to work when the load on the central BB becomes large.

In this paper we use optimization techniques proposed for centralized architectures in order to reduce the overhead and increase the profit of a hierarchical architecture. Scalability and resource optimization are issues that have been studied separately, but there is no previous work that analyzes them together. The paper main contribution is proposing a scalable BB architecture, capable of performing resource allocation optimization. This new model achieves better results than common hierarchical architectures, and can be easily implemented in large networks, solving the traditional scalability problems of other optimization models.

The paper is organized as follows: Section 2 explains in detail the admission control module of a BB and the different approaches to perform this task, discussing their advantages and disadvantages. Section 3 shows the profit optimization model. Section 4 explores the potentiality of using path instead of link constrains and introduces PoQBA as a new approach to perform admission control. Section 5 presents simulation results of the proposed algorithm and some discussion based on them. Finally, there are some general conclusions.

2 Admission Control in Bandwidth Brokers

The admission control module is a fundamental part of a BB. Its main purpose is to evaluate if there are enough resources to satisfy the QoS requirements before allocating a new flow in the network [7]. It is possible to express all QoS constrains in terms of only a bandwidth requirement. Parameters like loss ratio can be assured if sufficient bandwidth is reserved. Other constraints such as delay and jitter can be pre-evaluated using PHB or PDB [1]. For monitoring the network resources, there are two major approaches: link and path based admission control. The first one uses link state information to see if there is enough capacity available for a flow. When a request arrives the BB searches the available bandwidth in every link between the source and its destination. Link based methods are very efficient in terms of resource utilization. They assure that all flows are accepted if there is enough bandwidth along its path. There is no sub-utilization of the network, but this approach has scalability problems. The other method to perform admission control is using path states instead of link state information. The path between node A and node B is defined as the set of links a flow uses to go from A to B. A path can consist of one or more links and usually the number of paths is less than the number of links. The allocation of bandwidth to paths can be done by static or dynamic methods [4]. One of the advantages of the path approach is that it can easily be adapted to distributed or hierarchical structures of BBs.

Scalability issues. The best way to perform admission control, is using all the available information and a single agent making the decisions. This might become unpractical in networks with large topologies or high demands. Issues to be considered are i) Frequency and number of the requests and ii) Memory and time requirement for processing the requests. We propose a solution that uses a distributed architecture of BBs and simplifies the memory requirements by adapting a path approach, solving the scalability problem.

Book-ahead and resource optimization. It is very difficult to design systems able to admit every request generated without the over-provision of resources. This is why efforts are centered in designing systems that maximize the network utilization. Two types of requests are considered: Instant requests, which have to be answered in a very short time, and book-ahead requests, which arrive with some anticipation. Book-ahead requests make possible for networks administrators to make optimization and admit those flows that maximize their profit. Instant and book-ahead requests co-exist in many of today's networks and they must share the same resources.

3 Proposed Solution: Path Model

This paper proposes the path model as a simple way to perform optimization in distributed BB architectures. It uses paths instead of links in the bandwidth constraints. It also uses discrete time windows and can be defined as the following integer optimization problem:

$$MAX \sum_{i=1}^{N} b_i \cdot x_i \cdot (stop_i - start_i) \tag{1}$$

subject to

$$\sum_{i \in Pr(j,t)} b_i \cdot x_i \leq Bp(j,t) \; j \in P \; t = 1 \ldots d \tag{2}$$

$$0 \leq x_i \leq 1 \; \forall i \tag{3}$$

$$x_i \qquad integer \tag{4}$$

where N: number of requests arriving to the system, b_i: bandwidth for request i, x_i: 1 if request i is accepted and 0 if not, $stop_i$: stop time of request i, $start_i$: start time of request i, $Bp(j,t)$: available bandwidth of path j at time t, P: set of paths, r: number of requests, l: number of links, p: number of paths, d duration time of the problem defined as the time between the earliest start and the latest stop time of the requests.

There are a few things to consider about the path methods. The number of constraints are $d.p + 2.r$. Considering that usually the number of paths p is less than the number of links l this is an improvement.

It is also very important to notice that each request uses only one path. This implies that the $Pr(j)$ sets are independent, therefore, the problem can be separated into p small problems, considerably reducing the complexity. In other words, each path can be solved independently without any loss in the full problem, making this path approach very interesting for big networks. This characteristic also makes very easy to distribute the work in several BBs and adapt a scalable architecture.

4 PoQBA

Most of previous works solve the optimization problem using one central broker that manages all the information of the network. The scalability of such solutions can be a serious problem. Trying to apply distributed or hierarchical bandwidth brokers architectures directly to link admission control isn't as straight as it seems. Many coordination issues should be addressed, and each resulting broker would still have to deal with great memory requirements.

One way to solve the scalability problem is using paths tables instead of links tables. This approach is easy to implement but it has the problem of sub-utilization of the resources. In this section we propose PoQBA: an algorithm that adapts book-ahead optimization to a path oriented hierarchical broker architecture. The results show that the performance of PoQBA has several advantages compared to normal hierarchical systems and the Hose model [9].

PoQBA uses a two level hierarchical broker structure. On the top level there is a central broker (CBB) with full knowledge of the network states and topology. On the lower level there are many edge brokers (EBB) that manage independent set of paths and are coordinated by the central broker. These edge agents perform path based admission control optimization. They ask for path quota to the CBB every time they run out of bandwidth on certain path. The CBB uses link states tables to assign the quotas. The advantage over the simple link based algorithm is that the number of times this table is used is very low, because of the traffic aggregation the quota makes. In simple link admission the states tables are accessed for every request, while in PoQBA this table is accessed only when quota is requested.

The states tables can be timeless or time aware. The timeless approach simplifies the CBB. It only have to manage a table with a size equal to the number of links of the network. The problem is that it needs from the EBBs to send a message when they release a quota and that leads to profit decrease because of bandwidth waste. On the other hand, the time aware approach needs of large tables and special structures to handle the bandwidth of links over time.

The EBB is the key structure. When requests arrive, they are put on a list with a maximum capacity. The EBB gathers requests until one of two things happens: a) the list is full, or b) one of the requests is about to expire.

These events trigger the optimization problem and a solution is found using the path algorithm described above. Before rejecting a request, the broker puts it on a waiting list and asks for more quotas. If the quota is granted, then the optimization problem is solved again using the requests on the waiting list. Only when the CBB says there is no quota for the path the request can be rejected. There are many parameters that should be specified. Their effect can affect significantly the performance of the algorithm.

- Quota size: It should be chosen carefully. A small quota size means a great amount of packets for quota assignment, therefore too many overhead in the network and potential bottleneck on the CBB. Large quota sizes leads to waste of bandwidth and lower profits.
- List size: The list size affects the optimality of the solution. Short lists will probably find less optimal solutions since they gather few requests. They will also lead to frequent solving of the optimization problems. Big list would seem to be a better solution. This is not necessary true. With more requests on the list each problem size increases and takes more to be solved. It is also important to notice that the list size should consider the nature of the requests. It is better not to include requests too far in the future, because they will have little competition and, therefore, would be accepted immediately. Another problem is that, with big lists, the answer time of the requests increases. It is clear that clients will like their request to be answered as soon as possible, therefore network administrators face a new challenge. To avoid this kind of problems in [6] it was proposed an adaptive algorithm that dynamically changes the list size in order to obtain low response time and high profit.
- Time window length:This parameter affects the potential size of the states tables. For optimality purposes this window size should be as small as possible. But small windows mean a great number of them to cover a determinate amount of time. Therefore the window size should be chosen with some relation to the average length of the transmissions.

5 Performance Evaluation

The performance evaluation of PoQBA was made using the NS-2 simulation tool. Although NS-2 provides some DiffServ and QoS extensions, it was necessary to implement new agents like the EBB and the CBB in order to perform the simulations. It was also necessary to create a source agent, able to send bandwidth requests and wait for its answer, before generating any traffic. The optimization problems were solved using glpk (gnu linear programming kit), which is an external solver software that can be easily used by the agents in the NS-2 code.

Simulated Algorithms. For comparison purposes there were 4 different BB schemes implemented: Three of them are already known architectures used as a reference for PoQBA. All of them were tested under the same traffic conditions to ensure a fair comparison.

- SLAC (simple link admission control): This is a link based algorithm where every request is processed as soon as it arrives. There is no optimization capability. One CBB manages the entire network and performs admission control for every link in the request's path. There is a link table with the available bandwidth for each time slot. There is no necessity to have a request list. This is the simplest way to make admission control.
- HM (book-ahead link optimization): This scheme uses the hose model. The amount of bandwidth each edge router can admit was pre-calculated using the traffic characteristics. In this scheme there is a single BB that manages the entire network. It gathers some requests on a list and then solves an optimization problem trying to maximize the network utilization.
- PoQ (path-oriented-quota based): This structure follows the algorithm proposed in [4]. This path based approach has a CBB that give path quotas to EBBs. Each EBB performs admission control based on the quota assigned to it. Quota is asked or released depending on the remaining bandwidth for each path. There is no optimization done here. The CBB is kept simple and manages a timeless link table, while the EBBs manage time-aware path tables. This means that quota de-allocation must be triggered by a message from the EBB to the CBB. This hierarchical structure allows to deal with scalability issues at the cost of reducing the network utilization and of some overhead.
- PoQBA (path oriented with book-ahead optimization): Our proposed structure takes a part of the PoQ scheme and adapts it to make book-ahead optimization. It has two BB levels. The CBB is exactly the same as the one of the PoQ scheme. The EBB gathers a list of requests and performs optimization along paths. When the available bandwidth is over, the EBB asks for more quota from the CBB and puts the remaining requests on a waiting list. Requests are rejected only if a negative response for more quotas is received or it is about to expire and no quota is available at the moment, otherwise it waits on a list until quota is allocated for its path.

Simulations Scenarios. The proposed BB architectures were tested two different scenarios. Each one of them was defined by a specific topology and requests pattern. Two different topologies were used. The first one is a very simple bottleneck network as shown in figure 1 b). On one end of the network, there are N sources connected to an edge router. On the other end, there is a single sink. All links have 100Mbs capacity and 5 ms delay. This topology permits an easy control over the actual load of the network and is the simplest scenario for comparison. The second topology is a star network with a central node connected to N edge nodes as shown in figure 1 a). All links have the same capacity (100Mbs) and delay (5ms) parameters. Each edge receives flows form a couple of clients and clients act as sink and sources of traffic. This is a more realistic scenario to prove the true performance of the algorithms.

Every request consists of three random parameters: star and stop time and bandwidth. The arrival time is also a random number. The time between its arrival and the actual start of the transmission is defined as the anticipation time (10 time slots). The traffic characteristics proved to be very important in the performance, therefore, two different types of requests were defined based on the size of the corresponding traffic. The first one has a large bandwidth requirement respect to the link's capacity and its duration is rather long (1 Mbps, 50 timeslots); meanwhile, the second is smaller in bandwidth and has a shorter duration (0.5 Mbps, 25 time slots). Every simulation has an average load

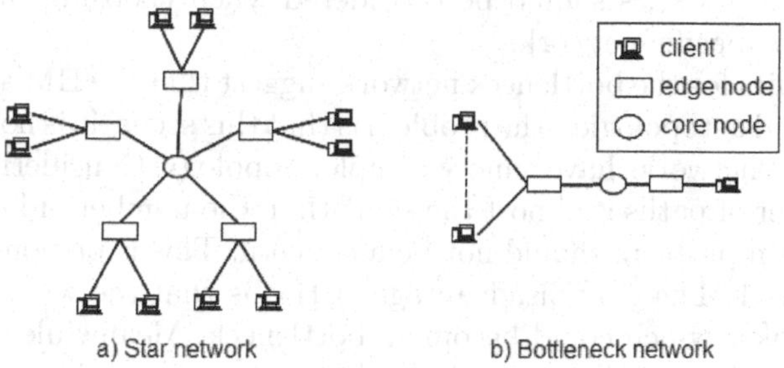

Fig. 1. Networks topologies

which is obtained by carefully choosing the number of requests generated. The simulation duration is 200 seconds, long enough to avoid transient's interferences in the results, the time slot duration is 1 second, the quota size 7.5 Mb and the request list size 10 requests. Each scenario was simulated several times to obtain a proper confidence interval at 95%.

Simulation Results. One of the key performance variables is the total profit of the network. As mentioned before, this profit was measured as the total bandwidth utilization expressed as Mb*seconds. Figure 2a shows the profit obtained in a bottleneck network for different loads. It is clear that, for low loads, all the algorithms get to the same result. This can be explained by the fact that there is plenty of bandwidth available at every time so all incoming requests should be accepted, no matter the admission control scheme. As the load increases, the differences between algorithms become more evident. As expected, the most profitable approach is the HM. In this case the hose model has great results since the "virtual link" is exactly the same as the bottleneck link, therefore there is no information lost in the relaxation. On the other hand the PoQ approach gives the lowest profits. The SLAC and PoQBA approaches show almost the same behavior. In the PoQBA algorithm the profit loss produced by the use of quotas is compensated by choosing the most profitable requests.

Using large requests on the bottleneck network shows some impressive results. In figure 2b the PoQBA scheme is better than the SLAC one. This shows that

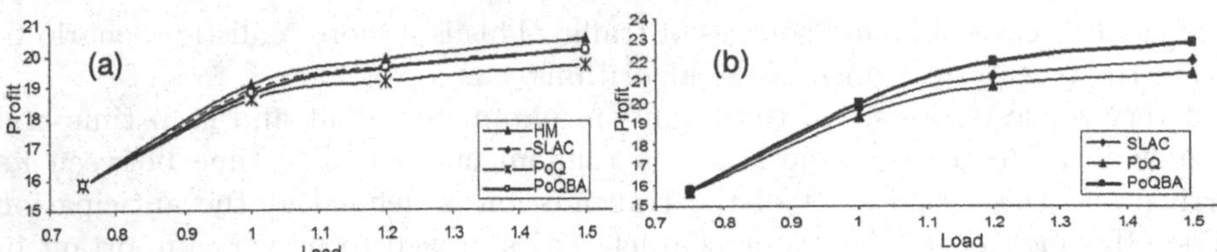

Fig. 2. (a) Profit for small requests on a bottleneck network. (b) Profit for large requests on a bottleneck network.

the optimization algorithms work better when the bandwidth of the requests is considerable larger in proportion to the links' capacities. This suggests that the traffic characteristics should be considered when choosing the appropriate algorithm for a specific network.

While graphics for the bottleneck network suggest that the HM approach is the best for this kind of topologies, the problem is that this scenario is not very realistic and most of the networks have a more complex topology. Considering that in this case the number of paths is almost the same than the number of links, the size of the optimization problem should not be a concern. This is demonstrated by the results of Table 1. The only disadvantage of HM is that the whole work is done by a single broker which could become a bottleneck. Meanwhile in the PoQBA approach the work is distributed in the 4 edge routers decreasing the memory and processing requirements of the brokers.

Table 1. Optimization problems for HM and PoQBA in a bottleneck network

Load	**No of problems solved (HM)**	**Average problem size (HM)**	**No of problems solved (PoQBA)**	**Problems per broker (PoQBA)**	**Average problem size (PoQBA)**
0.75	120	780	136	34	703
1	160	759	173	43	718
1.2	192	757	205	51	722
1.5	240	741	253	63	713

A more realistic comparison is achieved using the star topology. Under this more complex scenario the results are different. Figure 3a shows the profit obtained for different values of requests per second. The more requests the higher the profit in all cases due to a higher load over the network. The first think to notice is that under this scenario the HM is no longer very effective. It achieves worst results than the path oriented methods when there are many requests. This is because the hose model can give erroneous results, admitting flows when there is no bandwidth left in some links of the path and rejecting others when there is still bandwidth. Such errors happen due to the use of a single "virtual link" instead of all the real links. The error percentage increases with the number of requests per second (9% for 60 requests per second). These type of errors could be reduced with a better way to control the virtual link capacity.

Clearly in the star network the simple link admission control (SLAC) gives higher profit than the path based algorithm. But, as shown in Table 2, both path approaches reduce significantly the number of times the link table is accessesd (a high time consuming process). This reduces the processing load of the central broker between 40 to 100 times. In networks where the BB is a potential bottleneck this is a huge advantage since the SLAC approach could be unpractical.

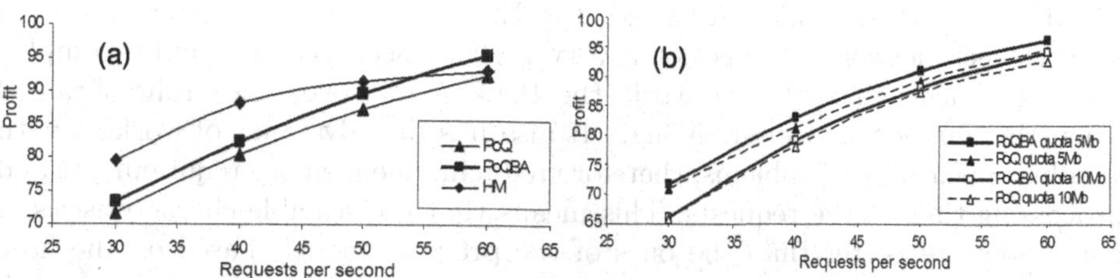

Fig. 3. (a) Profit for a star network. (b) Profit for different quota sizes on a star network.

Figure 3a also shows that PoQBA get better profits than the simple PoQ, since there is a significant reduction (up to a 60%) in the number of quota related control packets.

As seen in figure 3b the size of the quota is an important parameter too. The PoQBA is always better than the PoQ, but for small quota sizes the profit is higher and gets closer to the SLAC values. It is also important to see that for high rates of requests the profit difference between the quota sizes become smaller. The list size effect shows that the profit increases with the number of requests in the list. It also shows that the there is certain list value at which the profit stop increasing. This happens because in large list values there is always a request that expires before the list is full. This implies that there is an optimum value for the list size that depends on the nature of the requests and the anticipation of them to the actual traffic transmission.

Table 2. Link table accesses

Requests per second	SLAC	PoQ	PoQBA
30	6000	153	131
40	8000	120	102
50	10000	102	94
60	12000	110	108

5.1 Results Discussion

The first thing to notice from the simulations is that the simple link admission control (SLAC) has very good results. Then, for small network where a single central broker can manage all the domain's requirements or networks with low utilizations, the SLAC is the right choice. Naturally, the problem is the scalability of this method. The solution is to use other algorithms that give scalability at the cost of lower profits. The simulations also showed that the PoQBA has some very interesting results. First of all, compared to the traditional PoQ, it gets to higher resources utilizations and considerably reduces the amount of control packets (up to 60%). This means that the PoQBA is more profitable and reduces the overhead of the network. PoQBA also proved to be better than the algorithms based on the Hose model. Although the HM seems to have better results in a bottleneck network, this is not a very realistic scenario. In a more complex topology, such as the star network, the PoQBA improved the profit obtained when the number of requests is high. It also has the advantage of working with smaller optimization problems, therefore reducing the memory requirements and processing time of the requests. This means that the scalable characteristics of our model are better than the ones of the previous models based on the hose model. Finally, it is important to notice that by adapting some parameters such as the quota and the list size, this algorithm can adapt to overhead requirements and response times.

6 Conclusions

This paper shows that by using path instead of links tables, the optimization problem reduces it size considerably (becoming a scalable solution) and can be distributed in several brokers easily. The main contribution of this work was to introduce a new algorithm that combines the scalability of path approaches with the profitability of using an optimization model. This new algorithm proved not only to increase the networks utilization, but also to reduce the amount of overhead of traditional path based methods. It also revealed to be a better alternative than the price-based approach, since it has better scalable characteristics. This makes PoQBA the best choice for hierarchical architectures maximizing the profits with a low overhead.

Acknowledgments. This work was partially funded by Fondecyt (1060695) and Conicyt (ACT-32).

References

1. Sohail, S., Jha, S.: The survey of bandwidth broker. Tech. Rep. UNSW CSE TR 0206, University of New South Wales, Sydney, Australia (2002)
2. Bouras, C., Stamos, K.: Examining the Benefits of a Hybrid Distributed Architecture for Bandwidth Brokers. In: 24th IEEE International Performance, Computing and Communications Conference, pp. 491–498. IEEE Computer Society Press, Los Alamitos (2005)
3. Bhatnagar, S., Nath, B.: Distributed Admission Control to Support Guaranteed Services in Core-Stateless Networks. In: 22th Annual Joint Conference on the IEE Computer and Communications Societes, vol. 3, pp. 1659–1669 (2003)

4. Zhang, Z., Duan, Z., Hou, Y.T.: On Scalable Design of Bandwidth brokers. IEIC Trans. Commun. 84(8), 2011–2025 (2001)
5. Rhee, W., Lee, J., Yu, J., Kim, S.: Scalable Quasi-Dynamic-Provisioning-Based Admission Control Mechanism in Differentiated Service Networks. ETRI Journals 26(1), 27–37 (2004)
6. Bouras, C., Stamos, K.: An adaptive Admission Control Algorithm for Bandwidth Brokers. In: Third IEEE International Symposium in Network Computing and Applications, pp. 243–250. IEEE Computer Society Press, Los Alamitos (2004)
7. Menth, M., Kopf, S., Mibrandt, J.: A Performance Evaluation Framework for Network Admission Control Methods. Network Operations and Management Symposium. 1, 307–320 (2004)
8. Greenberg, A., Srikant, R., Whitt, W.: Resource Sharing for Book-Ahead and Instantaneous-Requests Calls. IEE/ACM Transactions on Networking (1999)
9. Duffield, N., Goyal, P., Greenberg, A., Mishra, P., Ramakrishnan, K., Van Der Merwe, J.: A Flexible Model for Resource Management in Virtual Private Networks. ACM SIGCOMM Computer Communication Review. 29(4), 95–108 (1999)
10. Chabra, C., Erlebach, T., Stiller, B., Vulkadinovic, D.: Price-based Call Admission Control in a Single DiffServ Domain. TIK-Report 135 (2002)
11. Bouras, C., Stamos, K.: Evaluating Admission Control Modules for Bandwidth Brokers in DiffServ Networks Using ns-2. In: 13th International Conference on Telecommunications (2006)

An Adaptive Call Admission Control Approach for Multimedia 3G Network

Waqas Ahmad[1], Irfan Awan[1], and Makoto Takizawa[2]

[1] Mobile Computing, Networks and Security Research Group
School of Informatics, University of Bradford, UK.
mr_waqasahmad@hotmail.com, i.u.awan@bradford.ac.uk
[2] Department of Computers and Systems Engineering,
Tokyo Denki University, Japan
Makototaki@aol.com

Abstract. The rapidly growing mobile demands have reinforced the network providers to emphasize on the basic customer needs and the resource management. The two main areas such as capacity management and data service provisions have engulfed the research field. This research paper attempts to cover both these issues in terms of Call Admission Control (CAC). Paper presents an adaptive technique built upon our previous static CAC research. The scheme provides differentiated admission to various delay sensitive (DS) and delay tolerant (DT) traffic streams for both Handover Request (HOR) and New call Request (NCR) according to current load intensity. It is based on an effective pre-emption priority in order to reduce the forced handover failure probability. Service nature and customer behaviour have been considered to lay down the different levels of priorities that were assigned at different stages of CAC Scheme in order to achieve optimal quality of service (QoS) for urban area (metropolitan) cell.

1 Introduction

The ever growing mobile market and introduction of variant services in the wireless networks has enlightened the need for optimized connection admission control (CAC) Schemes and has fuelled an extensive research work in this area. The main objective of this paper is to recognize multi-service type traffic and their prioritization depending upon service type and customer behavior. A hybrid of queuing and channel allocation priorities is presented in the proposed models.

The Quality of Service (QoS) standards are derived from the customer demands. It has been witnessed that majority of the technological advancements in late 20th century are influenced by the customer requirements. So is the case of mobile cellular industry, the introduction of modern day data services are an out come of customer demands. It is very vital to enlighten the concept of QoS because QoS provisioning is the center of all research done in CAC mainly due to the scarcity of resources in radio networks. The acceptance and rejection of a call is dependent upon QoS deterioration, as whenever the call is accepted there is some level of QoS deterioration. There are

T. Enokido, L. Barolli, and M. Takizawa (Eds.): NBiS 2007, LNCS 4658, pp. 446–455, 2007.

three levels of QoS; Bit Level parameters such as energy to noise ratio [1]; Packet Level parameter such as packet loss but majority of the research work is done in at Call Level. In Call Level QoS, the dropping and blocking probabilities are the QoS parameters [1].

Stochastic Prioritized Call Admission Control Algorithms can be divided into two major types [1,2,3]; such as Static and Adaptive CACA. In cellular systems the geographical distribution of coverage area is of great importance and can be used to organize CAC approaches. Local CAC Schemes consider only one cell and the Global CAC Schemes span over cluster or even entire network [4]. The major aims of CAC Schemes are [5] to maximize channel utilization in a fair manner to all flows, minimize the Dropping Probability of handover calls, minimize the reduction of service of connected calls and minimize the Blocking Probability of new calls.

In this paper we emphasis on a single cell CAC and Call Level QoS parameters are taken into consideration. The two QoS parameters taken into account are Blocking Probability (loss of new call) and Dropping Probability (loss of handover request) [21].

The rest of this paper is organized as follows: Section 2 includes the related work in the field of CAC Schemes and the traffic prioritizing. Section 3 presents two proposed models and a Basic priority model for comparison. Performance evaluation through simulation results are presented in Section 4. Paper is summarized in Section 5.

2 Related Work

The modern day cellular mobile networks aim to provide multimedia services including voice, data and video being the predominant ones. It creates more importance for clever designing of CAC algorithms as they ought to manage capacity distribution. In order to understand the behavior of each traffic type, the traffic is characterized on its time dependency [6]. The traditional voice call is considered as real time or delay sensitive traffic type, where as the data and video streaming are more tolerant to time; so named as non-real time or delay tolerant. It has become imperative to understand the behavior of each service type in order to derive optimized CAC Scheme.

Also the growing strength of mobile customers has forced the cell size to decrease in order to maximize the frequency reuse; this has resulted in an evident increase of number of handover calls; the calls that are carried through one cell to another. It is a universal understanding that call dropped during the talk time is more annoying than the initial rejection of connection. This has been the major driving force behind early CAC Schemes e.g., [2,7], but since we have a significant increase in number of types of traffic therefore the priority distribution has to be more specific.

Many queuing priority techniques for new call and handover traffic have been reported in the literature, e.g., [2,7-10]. These papers generally discuss various ways to assign priorities via queuing techniques. A basic categorization of queuing priority is also presented in [11] as pre-emptive and non pre-emptive. Although pre-emptive technique to prioritize a service type over another has been encouraging [6,12], yet majority of existing work handles the non pre-emptive queuing priority in CAC Schemes.

CAC Scheme is useless without an effective channel allocation technique. There is an ample amount of literature available to analyze the channel assignment and its effect on prioritizing service types e.g. [2,12,13,14]. Most of the channel allocation schemes lay the stress upon forced termination probability of handover traffic. The concept is to provide an extra cushion to the most sensitive traffic with respect to the QoS deterioration, through channel prioritizing.

Traditionally Poisson Process was the sole provider for the depiction of traffic behavior, discussed in [15,16]. But since the introduction of IP data traffic, the bursts caused due to file downloading or congested SMS traffic, can no more be effectively modeled through Poisson Process. Therefore the implementation of 2-state Markov Modulated Poisson Process (MMPP) to model the IP traffic was considered more relevant and efficient [15].

In [6], authors have divided the traffic in two categories of real time and non real time, each handover and new call has both of the above categories. The distribution of the input traffic is according to Poisson Process. It is concluded in [6], that the pre-emptive technique has improved the QoS for real time handover traffic; also the queuing priority for non-real time traffic has decreased the blocking probability. The proposed models discussed in next section of the paper are mainly inspired by the work in [6]. The aim was to use the pre-emption not only a priority between real time and non real time, but also assigning higher priority to one of the real time traffic through higher degree of pre-emption.

3 Proposed Scheme

This section explains the Adaptive CAC approach in detail which was built upon the static techniques [22]. As mentioned above the traffic is segregated upon the factor of time dependency, the traffic that is sensitive to latency is taken as Delay Sensitive (DS) such as voice and video, where as the traffic that is relatively time independent is labeled as Delay Tolerant (DT) general data and video streaming. Mentioned in [6], [15], [16], it was considered effective to model the data IP traffic as 2-state MMPP; where as the DS calls for both handovers and new calls were depicted by Poisson Process. The proof that IP traffic modeling is more realistic through MMPP than traditional Poisson Process can be seen in [18] and [19]. The input model has four traffic types handover DS (HDS), new call DS (NDS), handover DT (HDT) and new call DT (NDT). Following are few equations of input model, influenced from the work of [20]:-

Let λ_{ds} be the mean arrival rate for delay sensitive traffic and λ_{dt} is the mean arrival rate for delay tolerant data traffic. As they share the over all traffic of new call or handover, therefore:-

$$\lambda_{ds} = \gamma\lambda \tag{1}$$

$$\lambda_{dt} = (1 - \gamma)\,\lambda \tag{2}$$

As we know that λ_{dt} is modeled by 2-state MMPP, so the aggregate or average arrival rate would as:

$$\lambda_{dt} = P(B_{dt})\lambda_{dtB} + P(NB_{dt})\lambda_{dtNB} \tag{3}$$

$$P(B_{dt}) = \gamma_{dtNB} / \gamma_{dtB} + \gamma_{dtNB} \quad (4)$$

$$P(NB_{dt}) = \gamma_{dtB} / \gamma_{dtB} + \gamma_{dtNB} \quad (5)$$

$P(B_{dt})$ is the Probability of being in a state where the bursty arrivals are generated (λ_{dtB}). Similarly the $P(NB_{dt})$ is the Probability of being in a state where the arrivals are modeled through a non bursty arrival rate such as (λ_{dtNB}). Both of these probabilities are calculated as shown above through the switching probabilities of the two states.

This paper is a sequel to a previous attempt by us (*) [22], where it was established that Pre-emptive static scheme provides the best QoS standard. The static scheme (c.f., Fig 1) had basic queuing priority for both HDT and NDT, where as the high priority HDS and NDS were facilitated by the introduction of pre-emption in shared capacity area. Also the capacity was segregated into section for new call, handover and shared channels.

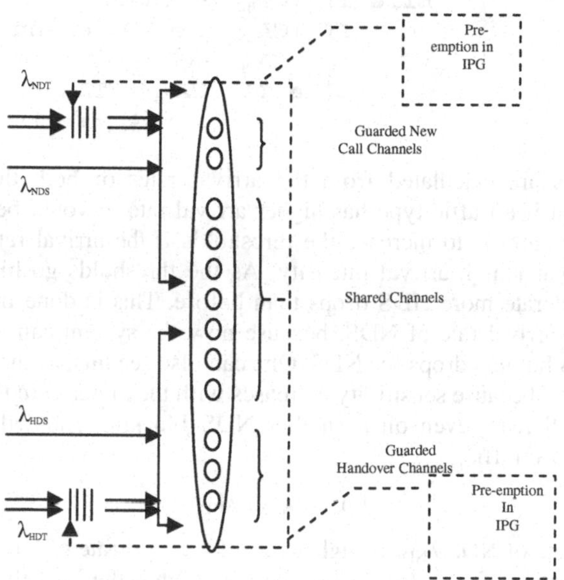

Fig. 1. Pre-emptive Static Model, pictorial layout

The proposed algorithm only focuses on NDS and HDS adaptability (c.f., Fig 2). This keeps the computation simple and as there is no queue for HDS and NDS, it proves to be effective approach to improve QoS. The idea is to change the channel priority on run time. As the traffic behaviour is changed, accordingly the channel priority is also updated. The algorithm on run time keeps a record of over all Delay Sensitive traffic loss.

The logic is to maintain thresholds for HDS and NDS traffic. If the drops from the previous update till now are more than the threshold of HDS then a channel from shared (pre-emptive) channels are allocated purely for HDS arrivals. This makes sure that by next update there are lesser drops of HDS, eventually it will bring the drops of

HDS down to the required threshold. Same adaptive technique is used to bring the NDS blocks back to the threshold. The ultimate aim is to bring the drops within the two thresholds.

$\mathbf{Cd_{HDS}}$	Current HDS drop proportionality (HDS Drop / Total DS Drop).
$\mathbf{TH_{HDS}}$	Threshold for maximum HDS drop
$\mathbf{TH_{NDS}}$	Threshold for maximum NDS drop
$\mathbf{CA_{CH}}$	Currently Adapted Channels
$\mathbf{TA_{CH}}$	Maximum number of adaptive channels

```
If (Cd_HDS > TH_HDS)
    If (CA_CH are NDS channels)
        CA_CH –
     Else If (CA_CH < TA_CH)
              CA_CH ++
Else If (Cd_HDS < TH_NDS)
     If (CA_CH are HDS channels)
        CA_CH –
     Else If (CA_CH < TA_CH)
              CA_CH ++
```

The thresholds are calculated from the arrival rates of both the Delay Sensitive traffics. So that if a traffic type has higher arrival rate it would be allocated realistic thresholds. The aim is to increase the thresholds if the arrival rate of NDS is more than HDS to cater high arrival intensity. As the thresholds go high this means that system will tolerate more HDS drops than before. This is done in order to facilitate the increasing arrival rate of NDS, because now the system can accommodate more drops for HDS but less drops for NDS. One can also see this, as the sensitivity to react for NDS blocks, because sensitivity increases with the increase in the thresholds. Now the system will react even on a smaller NDS blocking and will allocate adaptive channels to NDS traffic.

$$Pn_{\lambda} = \lambda_{NDS} / \lambda_{HDS} \tag{6}$$

If the arrival rate of NDS λ_{NDS} is higher than the arrival rate of HDS λ_{HDS}, then λ_{NDS} is taken as proportion of λ_{HDS} (6), just to see how high is the λ_{NDS} than λ_{HDS}. To increase the thresholds in the favour of increased λ_{NDS}, the shift to thresholds is calculated (7). As mentioned above that the algorithm can accommodate 9 times higher λ_{NDS} than λ_{HDS}. Therefore in (7) the proportionality is divided and multiplied by 0.3. As 0.3 is the maximum rise in thresholds, this is done for the sake of translation of arrival rate increase into threshold increase. The concept is that 0.3 is the maximum increase in thresholds and up till 0.3 there are maximum 9 levels of increase. Therefore translation of level in terms of 0.3 is calculated which gives you the shift.

$$Th_{shift} = (Pn_{\lambda} / 9) * 0.3 \tag{7}$$

Once the shift is calculated it is simple added to the existing thresholds, resulting in higher tolerance for HDS drops. (8, 9)

$$TH_{HDS} = TH_{HDS} + Th_{shift} \tag{8}$$

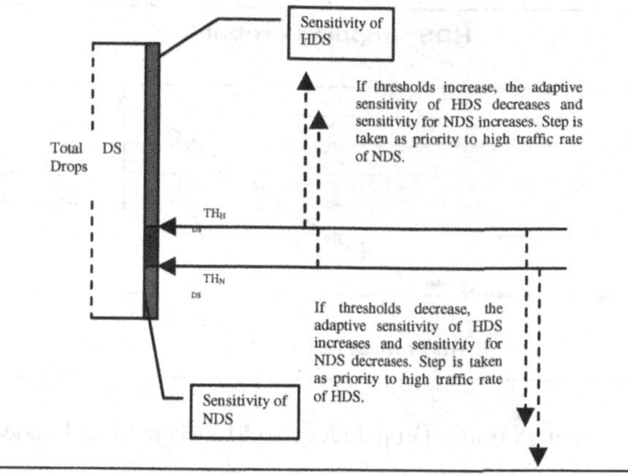

Fig. 2. Adaptive Sensitivity Technique

$$TH_{NDS} = TH_{NDS} + Th_{shift} \tag{9}$$

Similarly if λ_{HDS} is higher than λ_{NDS}, the thresholds should be brought down. Therefore the same procedure is conducted so that the shift is subtracted from the existing thresholds. Also to remind this time its other way around, so the proportionality (Ph_{λ}) of λ_{HDS} is calculated in terms of λ_{NDS}.

4 Result Discussion

This section deals with the discussion of simulation results. The discussion illustrates the improvement in the Adaptive technique over Static Model. An overloading traffic scenario is described as following, keeping all the switching rates constant:-

$\lambda_{Ndtb} = 0.3$; $\lambda_{Ndtnb} = 0.1$;$\lambda_{Hdtb} = 0.3$; $\lambda_{Hdtnb} = 0.1$; $\lambda_{Nds} = 0.2$;
$\mu_{Ndt} = 0.1$, $\mu_{Hdt} = 0.1$, $\mu_{Nds} = 0.1$, $\mu_{Hds} = 0.1$,
$\mathbf{N}_{HGC} = 4$; $\mathbf{N}_{NGC} = 2$; $\mathbf{S}_{CH} = 10$
Handover Delay Tolerant Queue = 10
New Call Delay Tolerant Queue = 10

4.1 Pre-emptive Static Model Vs Pre-emptive Adaptable Model

The first result discussion is about the improvement of QoS in existing pre-emptive model [22]. As the HDS traffic increases, the adaptive model should assign the adaptive priority of dedicated channels to HDS traffic. This results in a better QoS as compared with the previous model.

The adaptive scheme was aimed at cutting the resources of HDS traffic and allocating adaptive priority to NDS in order to eliminate the injustice. There was an intuitive hope that adaptive algorithm will also improve QoS regarding HDS traffic. In Fig. 3 one can witness the fact that adaptive algorithm has improved the QoS. The improvement at arrival rate 1.5 is 1.18%, though it is small yet it is significant as we are dealing with the highest priority service call of pre-emptive model.

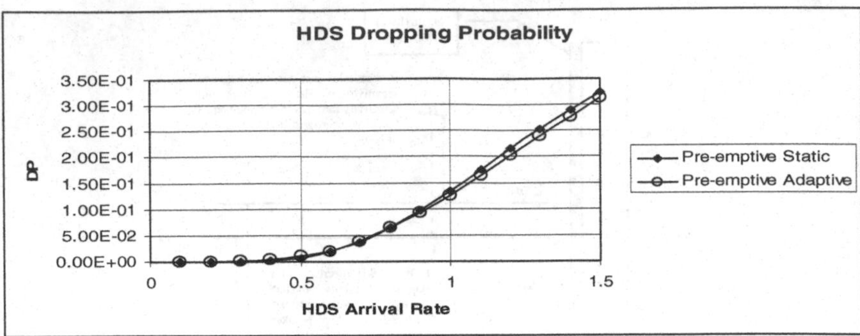

Fig. 3. Comparison of HDS traffic Drop under two Models in Over Loaded Traffic Scenario

To decrease the blocking probability of NDS traffic was the vital aim for adaptability. In order to create some flexibility in prioritization, the expectation from the adaptive model is to realise the arrival intensity and adjust according to that.

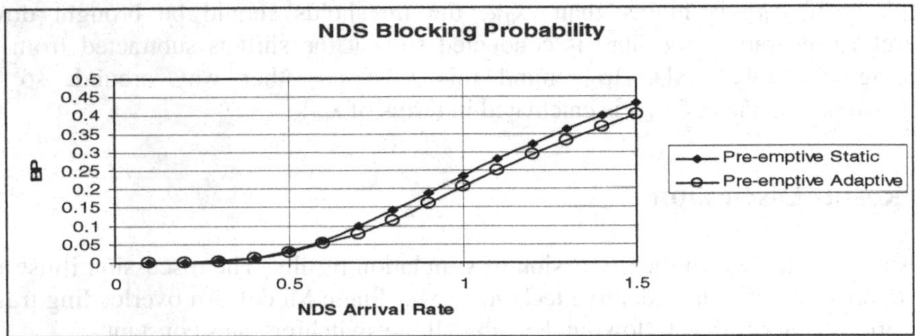

Fig. 4. Comparison of NDS traffic Block under two Models in Over Loaded Traffic Scenario

Fig. 4 presents the proof to the logic behind the adaptive scheme, as NDS has a higher arrival rate so it is justified with the allocation of adaptive channels. In the above graph one can see the struggle to adapt between 0.6 and 0.8. Between that region the adaptive scheme is finally allocating complete 10 channels for adaptation. Mainly because the arrival rate of NDS has reached to appoint where there is no scope of further adaptation and only complete channel allocation can result in satisfactory results.

In order to see the maximum effect on NDS traffic we introduce another traffic scenario which has high handover traffic.

$\lambda_{Ncdt} = 0.2$; $\lambda_{Hodt} = 0.6$; $\lambda_{Hods} = 0.6$;
$\mu_{Ncdt} = 0.3$, $\mu_{Hodt} = 0.3$, $\mu_{Ncds} = 0.2$, $\mu_{Hods} = 0.2$,
$\mathbf{N}_{HGC} = 4$; $\mathbf{N}_{NGC} = 2$; $\mathbf{S}_{CH} = 10$ (Adaptive Channels)
Handover Delay Tolerant Queue = 10
New Call Delay Tolerant Queue = 10

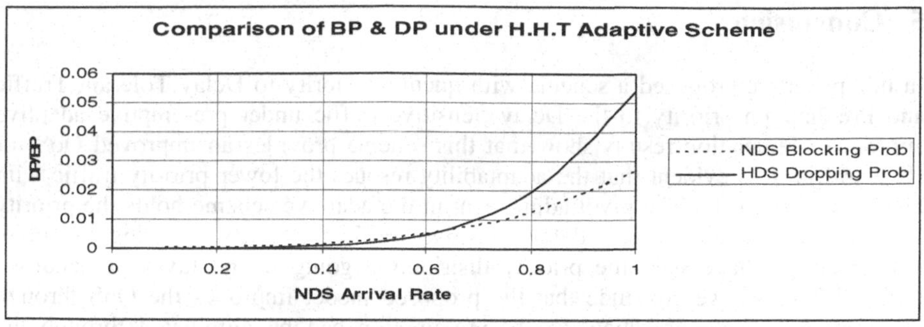

Fig. 5. Comparison of NDS & HDS traffic under High Handover Traffic Scenario

The graph in Fig. 5 illustrates the struggle between the two traffics (HDS & NDS). Close observation of the graph reveals that up till 0.6 at x-axis the HDS traffic has a lower loss, as it has a higher arrival rate than the NDS traffic. But when the NDS arrival rate increases the shift of adaptability goes in the favour of NDS traffic resulting in a drop of packet loss as compared with the HDS traffic.

This fact is more evident if the pivot of thresholds which was adjusted at ThHD = 0.55 and ThND = 0.45, is moved lower. By moving the initial pivot low we effectively shift the priority to HDS traffic. This will clearly show the struggle of two traffic types.

4.2 Pivot Effect

Pivot is the focal point of the two thresholds from where they adapt upwards and downwards in the favour of NDS and HDS traffic respectively. Fig. 6 shows the significance of pivot, as in this graph the pivot is lower down as compared with fig. 6. Therefore it is evident that HDS traffic struggles for long to stay low in packet loss but eventually the NDS traffic is allocated with maximum adaptive channels to show a lower packet drop. The increasing NDS traffic should be allocated with adaptive channels once the arrival rate is more than the arrival rate of HDS traffic.

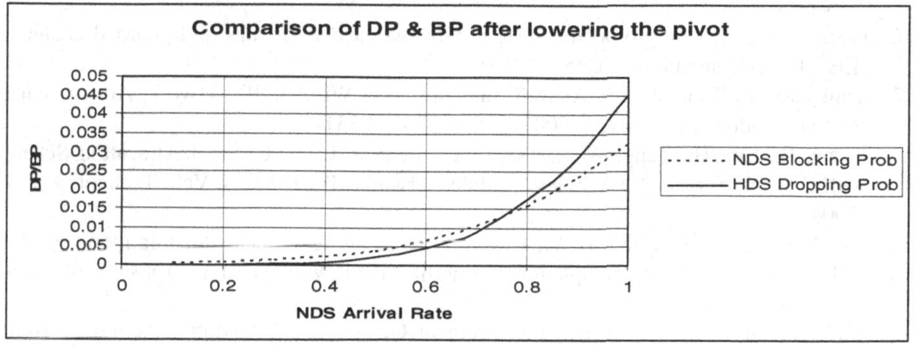

Fig. 6. Comparison of NDS & HDS traffic under High Handover Traffic Scenario

5 Conclusion

In this paper we proposed a scheme with queuing priority to Delay Tolerant Traffic and Pre-emption priority to the Delay Sensitive traffic under pre-emptive adaptive approach. Simulation results show that this scheme provides an improved QoS for HDS traffic. It is evident that the adaptability rescues the lower priority traffic with high arrival intensity. The pivot adjustment in the adaptive scheme holds the priority distribution between the two delay sensitive traffic types. By lowering the pivot adjustment we have seen the priority distribution going in the favor of handover traffic. Therefore we conclude that the proposed model improves the QoS through pre-emption and the injustice due to pre-emption can be eliminated through the adaptive scheme.

References

1. Ghaderi, M., Boutaba, R.: Call Admission Control in Mobile Cellular Networks. A Comprehensive Survey. ACM Digital Library (February 2006), ISSN 1530-8669
2. Fang, W.Y., Zhang, Y.: Call Admission Control Schemes and Performance Analysis in Wireless Mobile Networks. IEEE Trans. Veh. Technol. 51(2), 371 (2002)
3. Lodi, C.Q., Marca, J.R.B.: Performance of a Dynamic Multiple Class Admission Control Strategy For Wireless Systems. IEEE trans. Veh. Technol. 3, 1083 (2004)
4. AKL, R., Parvez, A.: Global versus Local Admission Control in CDMA Cellular Networks. In: CITSA (2004)
5. Moorman, J.R., Lockwood, J.W., Kang, S.: Real-Time Prioritized Call Admission Control in Base Station Scheduler. In: WOWMOM, Boston, MA, USA (2000)
6. Wang, J., Zeng, Q., Agarwal, D.P.: Performance analysis of pre-emptive and priority reservation handoff schemes for integrated service based wireless mobile networks. IEEE Transa. Mobile Compu. 2(1), 66–75 (2003)
7. Yoon, C.H., Un, C.K.: Performance of personal portable radio telephone systems with and without guard channels. IEEE J. Select Areas Comm. 11(6), 911 (1993)
8. Aboelaze, M., Elnaggar, A., Musleh, M.: A Priority Based Call Admission Control Protocol with Call Degradation of Cellular Networks. IEEE Wireless Comm. Sys. Sympo. 71–75 (2004)
9. Awan, I., AlBegain, K.: Performance Modelling of Differentiated services in 3G mobile Networks
10. Guerin, R.A.: Queuing-blocking system with two arrival streams and guarded channels. IEEE Trans. Commun 36(2), 153 (1988)
11. Toni Janevski Book: Traffic Analysis and Design of Wireless IP Network. Artech House, Boston, London, pp. 118–124 (2003) ISBN 1-58053-331-0
12. Ferng, H., Lin, H., Teng, W.C., Tsai, Y.C., Peng, C.C.: A Channel Allocation Scheme with Dynamic Priority for Wireless Mobile Networks. IEEE Trans. Veh. Technol. 3, 1143 (2004)
13. Lai, W.K., Jin, Y.J., Chen, H.W., Pan, C.Y.: Channel assignment for initial and handoff calls to improve the call completion probability. IEEE Vech. Techno. Tansc. 52(4), 876–890 (2003)
14. Chen, J., Cao, D.: Performance Improvement Of Prioritized handoff Schemes In Multi-Service Mobile Cellular Systems. In: Proc. IEEE Canadian Conf. Electrical & Comp. Engineering 02, vol. 3, pp. 1347–1351 (2002)

15. Muscariello, L., Meillia, M., Meo, M., Marsan, M.A.: An MMPP-based hierarchical model of Internet traffic. In: Communications, 2004. IEEE International Conference, vol. 4, pp. 2143–2147 (2004)
16. Nogueira, A., Valadas, R.: Analysing the versatility of the 2-MMPP traffic model. In: CSNDSP'2000. Proc. of the Second International Symposium on Communication Systems Networks and Digital Signal Processing, Bournemouth, UK, July 18-20, 2001, pp. 261–266 (2001)
17. Das, S.K., Jayaram, R., Kakni, N.K., Sen, S.K.: A call Admission & control scheme for quality of service (QoS) provisioning in the nest generation wireless networks, vol. 6, pp. 17–30. Kluwer Academic Publisher, Dordrecht (2000)
18. Nogueira, A., Valadas, R.: Analysing the versatility of the 2-MMPP traffic mode. In: CSNDSP'2000. Proc. of the Second International Symposium on Communication Systems Networks and Digital Signal Processing, Bournemouth, UK, July 18-20, 2001, pp. 261–266 (2001)
19. Muscariello, L., Meillia, M., Meo, M., Marsan, M.A.: An MMPP-based hierarchical model of Internet traffic. In: Communications, 2004. IEEE International Conference, vol. 4, pp. 2143–2147 (2004)
20. Onvural, R.O.: Book: Asycnronous Transfer Mode Networks Performance Issue. Artech House, Boston, London, pp. 461 - 463 (1995)
21. Stallings, W.: Book: Wireless Communications & Networks, 2nd edn. Prentice-Hall, Englewood Cliffs (2005)
22. Ahmad, W., Awan, I.: Performance Evaluation of CAC Schemes for Multi-Service Traffic Environment in 3G Networks. SCS Simulation: Transactions of the Society for Modelling and Simulation International (to appear, 2007)

Spatial Correlation Code Based Data Aggregation Scheme for Maximizing Network Lifetime

Sangbin Lee, Younghwan Jung, Woojin Park, and Sunshin An

Department of Electronics and Computer Engineering,
Korea University, Seoul, Korea
{kulsbin,youngh,wjpark,sunshin}@dsys.korea.ac.kr

Abstract. A wireless sensor network consists of many micro-sensor nodes distributed throughout an area of interest. Each node has a limited energy supply and generates information that needs to be communicated to a sink node. The basic operation in such a network is the systematic gathering and transmission of sensed data to a base station for further processing. During data gathering, sensors have the ability to perform in-network aggregation (fusion) of data packet routes to the base station. The lifetime of such a sensor system can be defined as the time during which the sensor information is gathered from all of the sensors and combined at the base station. Given the location of the sensors, the base station and the available energy at each sensor, the main interest is to find an efficient manner in which data can be collected from the sensors and transmitted to the base station at a given rate, so as to maximize the system lifetime. A zone based data aggregation scheduling scheme is presented to accomplish this. The experimental results demonstrate that the proposed protocol significantly outperforms other methods in terms of the energy saving and system lifetime.[1]

Keywords: Data Aggregation, Maximum Network Lifetime, Scheduing Spatial Correlation, Wireless Sensor Networks, Zone.

1 Introduction

Recent advances in micro sensor technology and low power analog/digital electronics have led to the development of distributed, wireless sensor device networks [1]. In the future, it is envisioned that sensor networks will consist of hundreds of inexpensive nodes that can be readily deployed in physical environments to collect useful information (e.g. seismic, acoustic, medical and surveillance data) in a robust and autonomous manner. However, there are several obstacles that need to be overcome before this vision becomes a reality [2]. These obstacles arise from the limited energy, computing capabilities, and communication resources available to sensors. Therefore, reducing the energy consumption of such networks is the most important design consideration.

[1] This research was Supported by a Korea University Grant.

T. Enokido, L. Barolli, and M. Takizawa (Eds.): NBiS 2007, LNCS 4658, pp. 456–465, 2007.

Data aggregation has been put forward as an essential paradigm for wireless routing in sensor networks [3]. Most previous related works [4], [2] aimed to reduce the energy consumed by sensors during the process of data gathering. Directed diffusion [4] is based on a network of nodes that can coordinate their operation, in order to perform distributed sensing of an environmental phenomenon. This approach allows significant energy savings to be achieved, when intermediate nodes are employed to aggregate responses to queries. LEACH analyzes the performance of the cluster-based routing mechanism with in-network data compression [2]. In PEGASIS [10], sensors form chains so that each node transmits and receives information from a close neighbor. Gathered data moves from node to node, becomes aggregated and is eventually transmitted to the base station.

Wireless Sensor Networks (WSNs) are characterized by the dense deployment of sensor nodes that continuously observe a physical phenomenon. Due to the high density in the network topology, sensor observations are highly correlated in the space domain. These spatial correlations, along with the collaborative nature of the WSN, bring significant potential advantages for the development of efficient communication protocols well-suited for the WSN paradigm. Typical WSN applications require spatially dense sensor deployment in order to achieve satisfactory coverage [2]. As a result, multiple sensors record information about a single event in the sensor field. Due to the high density in the network topology [5], spatially proximal sensor observations are highly correlated, with the degree of correlation increasing with decreasing inter-node separation. Therefore, it may not be necessary for every sensor node to transmit its data to the sink; instead, a smaller number of sensor measurements might be adequate to communicate the event features to the sink within a certain reliability/fidelity level. There has been some research effort to study the correlation in WSN [5]. However, most of these existing studies investigated the theoretical aspects of the correlation, and they do not provide efficient networking protocols which exploit the correlation in the WSN. In a recent effort, joint routing and source coding was introduced in [6] to reduce the amount of traffic generated in dense sensor networks with spatially correlated records. While this technique reduces the number of bits transmitted; from the network point of view, the number of transmitted packets remains unchanged, whereas it could be further minimized by regulating the network access based on the spatial correlation between the sensor nodes. In this paper, the Spatial Correlation Code based data Aggregation (SCCA) scheme is proposed to maximize the network lifetime. SCCA is operated in a framework that models the spatial correlations in wireless sensor networks. The proposed protocols can significantly outperform the previous methods in terms of the energy saving and network lifetime.

The remainder of this paper is organized as follows. In Section 2, we state the problem and, in Section 3, we present the SCCA algorithm whose primary purpose is to prolong the network lifetime. In Section 4, we show the numerical results obtained using the above analytical framework. Finally, concluding remarks are discussed in Section 5.

2 Model and Problem Formulation

2.1 Network Model

We consider a multi-hop wireless network with n nodes. The nodes communicate with each other via wireless links. The nodes in the network and possible communications between the nodes are represented by a directed graph When $G=(V,E)$. Here, $V = \{ v_1, v_2, \ldots, v_n\}$ represents the set of nodes in the network and E represents the set of directed edges in the network. Given a link $e \in E, t(e)$ is used to represent the transmission end of the link e and $r(e)$ to represent the receiving end of the link e. A link e is considered to be active if there is a transmission from $t(e)$ to $r(e)$. Given a node $v \in V, l_{in}(v)$ denotes the set of links terminating at node . In other words, $l_{in}(v) = \{ e \in E : r(e) = v\}$. Similarly, for a given node $v \in V$, $l_{out}(v)$ denotes the set of edges emanating from $l_{out}(v) = \{ e \in E : t(e) = v\}$. As in a previous work [2], [4], [10], we make the simplistic assumption that an intermediate sensor can aggregate multiple incoming packets into a single outgoing packet. Therefore, the value of can only be one. Note that the model includes the special case where the underlying graph is a complete graph (every pair of nodes can directly communicate with each other), in which the path loss for those nodes not in range is set to zero. We assume that each sensor generates one data packet per time unit to be transmitted to the base station. For simplicity, we refer to each time unit as a round. The information from the assigned sensors needs to be aggregated at each round and be sent to the base station. Further, each node has a battery with a finite, non-replacement energy, Whenever a sensor transmits or receives a data packet, it consumes some energy from its battery. The base station has an unlimited amount of energy available to it.

2.2 Formatting of Zones by Exchanging Control Packets

SCCA groups the sensor nodes into zones. The prevalence of spatial correlation in environmental phenomena makes it possible to schedule the process of aggregation of the nodes. SCCA uses three types of short, fixed-size signaling packets $(Query, SCC, U)$ for grouping. The formatting of the zones operates in three phases: query, broadcasting and update. In the query phase, when user in base station wants to gather the data (e.g. temperature, light), Base station transmits the query packet to the sensor network. This query packet contains the application type (e.g. temperature, light), and the location of base station, and the user-specified error threshold, τ, interchangeable with a user-provided error-tolerance threshold. In the broadcasting phase, all sensor nodes in sensor network broadcast the spatial correlation code (SCC) packets and are grouped into zones when a TAG-like [8] forwarding tree is built using a user-specified error threshold, τ. The SCC-packet contains the addresses (sID, zID), geographical information of the node, the user-specified error threshold, τ, and the sensing value (e.g. temperature). where sID is a identification of the sensor node and zID is a identification of the zone. A user-provided error threshold, τ, is used while building the zones. Each node decides to join a zone based on the values of Neighbor sensing Value (NV) and My local sensor Value (MV) , if $MV < NV \pm NV \times \tau$, then the sensor node registers the zID of the node that broadcasts SCC and is included in the same zone. In the update phase, those sensor nodes that receive the SCC packet transmit the update packet, called the U-packet. This packet contains the geographical position of the node and the sensing value. We assume that the base station can gather all data about sensor $(sID, zID, Location)$ through exchanging control packets as Fig. 1.

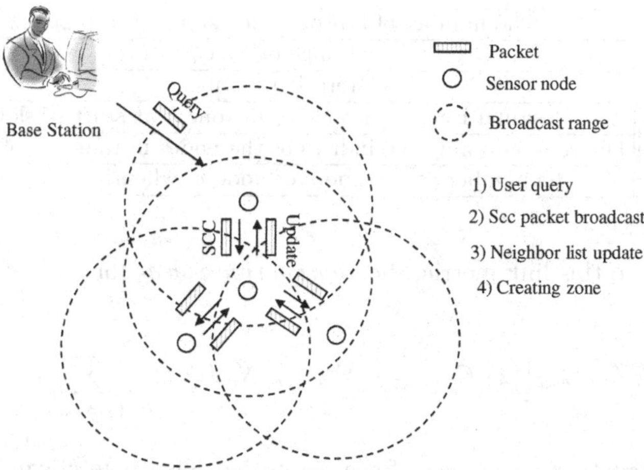

Fig. 1. Formatting zone by Exchanging control packets

2.3 Energy Model

where E_{ctrans} is the energy utilized by the transmitter circuits (PLLs, bias currents, etc.) and digital processing. This energy is independent of distance; E_{crec} is the energy consumed by the receiver circuits, E_{caggre} is the energy consumed by data aggregation, and β_{ij}^{α} accounts for the radiated power necessary to transmit over a distance d_{ij} between node v_i and node v_j. As in [7], we assume that

$$E_{ctrans} = E_{crec} + E_{circuit} \tag{1}$$

Thus, the overall expression for E in Eq.3, which we refer to as the link metric hereafter, simplifies to

$$E = 2 \cdot E_{circuit} + E_{caggre} + \beta d_{ij}^{\alpha} \tag{2}$$

With the notation in Table 1., a model for the energy consumption per bit at the physical layer is

$$E = E_{ctrans} + E_{crec} + E_{aggre} + \beta d_{ij}^{\alpha} \tag{3}$$

Table 1. Notation

Notation	Description
α	Path loss $(2 \leq \alpha \leq 5)$
β	Constant $[Joule/(bits \cdot m^{\alpha})]$
L_{SCC}	Size of SCC packets $[bits]$
L_U	Size of location update packets $[bits]$
L_G	Size of generated packets $[bits]$
$L_{in}(i)$	The number of $l_{in}(i)$
$M(z_k)$	The number of sensor nodes grouped into $zonek$
r_i	Range of SCC_i
f	Iteration number
$\varepsilon_i^k(f)$	Residual Energy of node v_i in zone k at start of slot f
$\zeta_i(r_i)$	The set containing the indices of the nodes in range r_i of node v_i
$N_i(r_i)$	The number of neighbors of node v_i when its range is r_i

According to this link metric, the *aggregation power* for node v_i is expressed as Eq.4

$$P_i^{Aggre} = L_G\Big[(2 \cdot E_{circuit} + E_{caggre})N_{in}(i) + \sum_{l_{in}(j)=l_{out}(i)} \beta d_{ij}^{\alpha}\Big] \quad (4)$$

The *constructing zone power* for node v_i that has range r_i can be computed from Eq.5

$$P_i^{Inf}(r_i) = L_{SCC}\left[\beta r_i^{\alpha} + N_i(r_i) \cdot E_{circuit}\right] + L_U\left[2N_i(r_i) \cdot E_{circuit} + \sum_{m \in \zeta_i(r_i)} \beta d_{mi}^{\alpha}\right] \quad (5)$$

Therefore, the expected residual energy for node v_i is expressed as

$$\varepsilon_i^k(f+1) = \varepsilon_i^k(f) - \frac{P_i^{Aggre}}{M(z_k)}, \qquad (\varepsilon_i^k(1) = \varepsilon_i^k(0) - P_i^{Inf}(r_i)) \quad (6)$$

The expression βr_i^{α} represents the energy needed to transmit one bit over a distance r_i ; thus $L_{SCC} \cdot \beta r_i^{\alpha} + L_{SCC} \cdot E_{circuit}$ is the energy needed for node v_i to transmit the SCC-packet in its range, whereas each of the neighbor nodes in its range expends only $L_{SCC} \cdot E_{circuit}$ to receive the SCC-packet. By adding these two components, we obtain the first line of Eq.5. Then, each of the neighbor nodes transmits an U-packet. The energy expenditure has again a constant factor, $L_U \cdot E_{circuit}$, plus a factor, $L_U \cdot \beta d_{mi}^{\alpha}$, which depends on the distance between the transmitting node v_m and node v_i. Moreover, v_i expends $L_U \cdot E_{circuit}$ to receive the each of the U-packets of the neighbors. By summing all of these components, which depend on the mobility rate of the nodes in the network, we obtain the final expression for P_i^{Inf}. In other words, P_i^{Inf} is the average energy which is needed to allow node v_i to obtain topology information within the range r_i.

3 Data Aggregation

In this section, we describe the development of the data aggregation scheduling scheme based on the zone & energy model proposed in the previous section. Because sensor nodes in the same zone have high spatial correlation, there is no need for all of them to transmit their data packets. Therefore, using scheduling, we elect only one sensor node to aggregate and transmit its data packets for the sake of minimizing the network energy consumption.

3.1 Scheduling Based Data Aggregation

TDMA schemes have been proposed wherein the slot length is optimally assigned according to the routing requirements, while minimizing the total energy consumption across the network. In particular, during the time slot assigned by the TDMA scheme, the corresponding node works in active mode. After finishing its data transmission, it turns off all of its circuits and enters sleep mode. In this way, the energy consumption can be minimized. In the previous section, we refer to each time slot as a round. We define the lifetime T_{net} of the network as the number of rounds until first zone is drained of its energy. A data aggregation schedule specifies, for each round, how the data packets from all of the sensors are collected and transmitted to the base station. A data aggregation schedule has one aggregation tree for each round. The lifetime of a schedule is equal to the lifetime of the network under that schedule. The objective is to find a schedule that maximizes the network lifetime T_{net} by balancing the energy consumption of each zone.

3.2 SCCA Algorithm

In this section, we discuss how to obtain a schedule from an admissible flow network. Recall that a schedule is a collection of directed trees, rooted at the base station, that span all of the zones, with one such tree for each round. Each such tree specifies how the data packets are aggregated and transmitted to the base station. We call these trees aggregation trees. An aggregation tree may be used for one or more rounds.

- **Step 1.** Constructing an Aggregation Tree

In this protocol, the sensor nodes are grouped into zones based on their spatial correlation. In Fig.2, the aggregation is formed among the zones at different levels of the hierarchy. The level is defined by the node which is the farthest from the base station in each zone. The hop counts of these nodes are the level of the zones. In Fig.2, the zones are used to construct the Aggregation Tree using the level of each zone. Each admissible aggregation tree is assigned to a round by the scheduling algorithm. After step 1 is processed, step 2 is processed at each admissible aggregation tree.

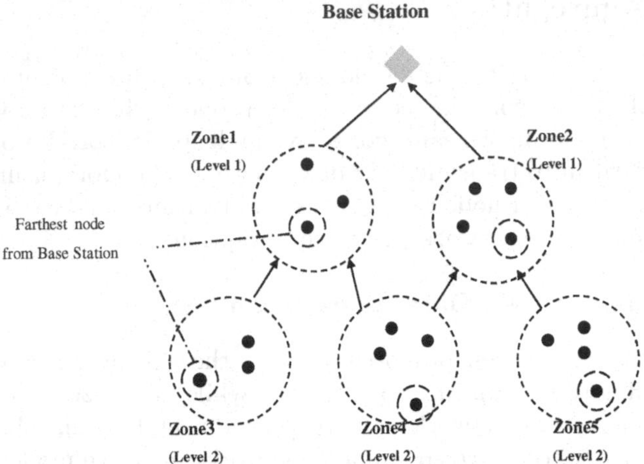

Fig. 2. Construction of Aggregation Tree

- **Step 2** Hierarchical election of representative node

In step 2, a schedule is constructed based on the residual energy of the sensor nodes in each zone. In order to maximize the network lifetime, the average energy consumption per zone must be minimized. Therefore, the representative node (r_{level}-node) that has the most residual energy, in the case where the data is transmitted to the next level zone, is selected among the sensor nodes in the same zone. Only the r_{level}-node aggregates and transmits the data packet to the next level zone. In this case, the most important considerations are the residual energy of the sensor node, the distance of the link, and the number of sensor nodes grouped into each zone. The greater the number of sensor nodes grouped into the zone, the lower the average energy consumption per zone. For each zone, the algorithm first computes Eq.6 and then Eq.7. As a result, in each zone, it elects the r_{level}-node to be assigned to the TDMA slot.

$$\varepsilon_j^k(f+1) = \max\{\varepsilon_i^k(f+1)\}, \qquad \forall k \tag{7}$$

First, the algorithm elects the r_1-node by computing Eq.6 and Eq.7 among the sensor nodes in the highest level zones (1-level) that have links to the BS. Then, the algorithm elects the r_2-node by computing Eq.6 and Eq.7 among the sensor nodes in those zones of the 2-level that have links to the r_1-node. This procedure is repeated until it elects the r_{level}-nodes for all zones. Also, step 2 is repeated for all admissible aggregation trees. In this case, all other nodes that are not elected switch to sleep mode. Therefore, these nodes consume only sleep power (P_{sleep}). Eq.8 shows the expected residual energy of each sleep node.

$$\varepsilon_i^k(f+1) = \varepsilon_i^k(f) - \frac{P_{sleep}}{M_k}, \qquad j \neq i \tag{8}$$

- **Step 3.** Selection of Aggregation Tree

Based on the elected r_{level}-nodes obtained through step 2, the algorithm computes Eq.9 for all admissible aggregation trees. Eq.9 shows the residual energy of the aggregation tree after round (T) has elapsed. E_{AT} is the sum of the residual energy of all r_{level}-nodes and sleep nodes.

$$E_{AT}(f+1) = \sum_k \Big(\sum_i \varepsilon_i^k(f+1) + \sum_j \varepsilon_j^k(f+1) \Big). \quad (9)$$

- **Step 4.** Iterative Execution

The process of steps 2 $\sim$ 3 is iterated until the first zone is drained of its energy. (i.e. $\sum_i \varepsilon_i^k(f+1) + \sum_j \varepsilon_j^k(f+1) = 0$).
Through steps 2 $\sim$ 4, the appropriate aggregation tree is assigned at each round. As a result, the lifetime of the sensor network is $T_{net} = T \times f$.

4 Performance Evaluation

4.1 Experimental Setup

We evaluate the performance of the proposed algorithm via simulation in this section. The simulation settings are as follows. In our experiment, we set $\alpha = 2, \beta = 100pJ/bit/m^\alpha$, $E_{circuit} = 50pJ/bit$ and $E_{caggre} = 100pJ/bit$ for the power consumption model. The initial energy reserve ε_v on each sensor is $1J$. We set the data packet sizes, $L_{SCC} = 128bits, L_U = 128bits, L_G = 1000bits$. The maximum transmission range of each sensor is $25m$ and the base station is located at (25,150).

Table 2. Parameters of the model used for the simulations

	Scenario 1	Scenario 2	Scenario 3	Scenario 4
Field	$50m \times 50m$	$100m \times 100m$	$50m \times 50m$	$50m \times 50m$
n	*variables*	*variables*	*variables*	*variables*
r_i	$10m$	$20m$	*variables*	$10m$
τ	5 %	5 %	5 %	*variables*

We are particularly interested in the typical scenarios encountered in sensor networks applications. The model depends on several input parameters, and on the appropriate choice of these parameters which are highly dependent on the technology and on the target applications. We vary these parameters in order to study their relevant effects on the network performance. Moreover, we believe that the realistic tuning of these parameters must be aided by the real hardware implementation of the considered protocols. We present the simulation results for the scenarios illustrated in Table.2. We compare the performance of our protocol with that of other data aggregation protocols (PEGASIS [10], CMLDA [9]).

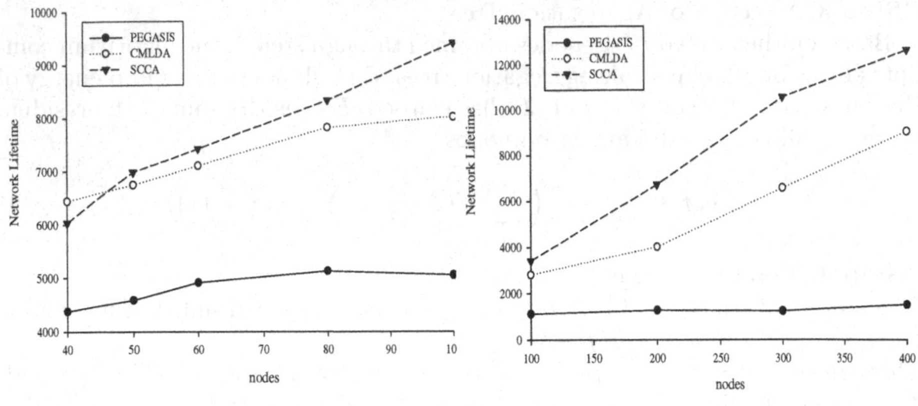

Fig. 3. Scenario 1

Fig. 4. Scenario 2

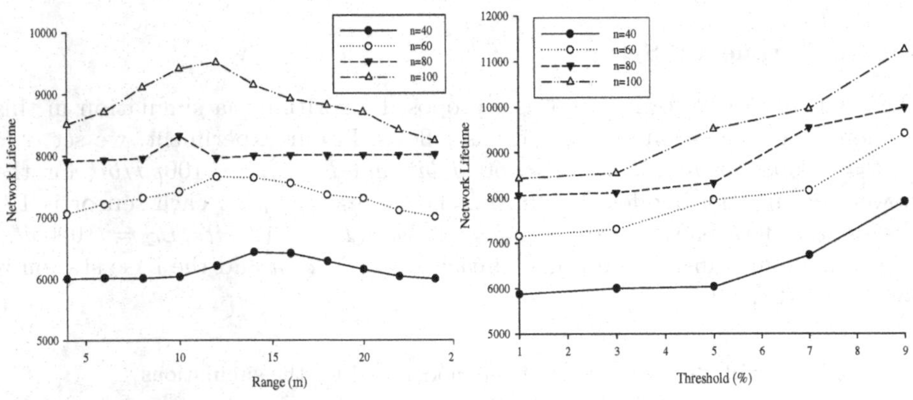

Fig. 5. Scenario 3

Fig. 6. Scenario 4

4.2 Experimental Results

In the case of Scenario 1, the network lifetime given by the SCCA is longer than that given by the other protocols. In Fig.3, the SCCA performs 1.07 to 1.7 times better than the LRS protocol and 0.98 to 1.2 times better than the CMLDA protocol. In the case of Scenario 2, the network lifetime given by the SCCA is always significantly longer than that given by the other protocols. Fig.4, the SCCA performs 2.7 to 7.7 times better than the LRS protocol and 1.2 to 1.4 times better than the CMLDA protocol. We observe that as the network size grows, SCCA is able to at least double the lifetime returned by the LRS protocol. In the case of Scenario 3, Fig.5 shows the tradeoff between the energy required to construct the zone and the size of the zone. As the SCC range increases, the energy required to construct the zone increases, but the number of transmissions decreases. In the case of Scenario 4, we show the impact of τ on the network performance. From Fig.6, we observe that a large value of τ will slightly increase the network lifetime, because as τ increases, the size of the zone increases.

5 Conclusion

The paper investigates the zone based data aggregation scheduling scheme in wireless sensor networks. By jointly designing the routing and link layer to minimize the sum of the transmission energy and circuit processing energy, the aggregation energy and some interesting results are obtained. The benefit of spatial correlation is also studied in a sensor network, with a protocol for maximizing the network lifetime. The results show that significant energy savings can be made by taking advantage of the spatial correlation, which increase the network lifetimes compared with the other data aggregation protocols. It is also shown that the energy savings vary according to the number of nodes, range, and threshold. As a result, the network lifetimes change adaptively. In order to improve this algorithm, we will study the impact of mobile data sinks on the lifetime of sensor networks, and present our observations.

References

1. Kahn, J.M., Katz, R.H., Pister, K.S.J.: Mobile Networking for Smart Dus. In: Proceedings of 5th ACM/IEEE Mobicom Conference (1999)
2. Heinzelman, W., Kulik, J., Balakrishnan, H.: Adaptive Protocols for Information Dissemination in Wireless Sensor Networks. In: Proceedings of 5th ACM/IEEE Mobicom Conference (1999)
3. Heidemann, J., et al.: Building Efficient Wireless Sensor Networks with Low-Level Naming. In: Proceedings of 18th ACM Symposium on Operating Systems Principles, October 21-24, 2001. ACM, New York (2001)
4. Intanagonwiwat, C., Govindan, R., Estrin, D.: Directed diffusion: A scalable and robust communication paradigm for sensor networks. In: Proceedings of 6th ACM/IEEE Mobicom Conference, Boston, Massachusetts, United States (2000)
5. Vuran*, M.C., Akan, O.B., Akyildiz, I.F.: Spatio-temporal correlation: theory and applications for wireless sensor networks. Proceedings of Computer Networks, 45 (2004)
6. Scaglione, A., Servetto, S.D.: On the interdependence of routing and data compression in multi-hop sensor networks. In: Proceedings of the ACM MOBICOM 2002, Atlanta, GA, USA. ACM, New York (2002)
7. Heinzelman, W.B., Chandrakasan, A.P., Balakrishnan, H.: An Application-Specific Protocol Architecture for Wireless Microsensor Networks. IEEE Transactions on Wireless Communications 1(4) (2002)
8. Madden, S.R., Franklin, M.J., Hellerstein, J.M., Hong, W.: TAG: Tiny AGgregation service for ad-hoc sensor networks. In: Proceedings of OSDI (December 2002)
9. Dasgupta, K., Kalpakis, K., Namjoshi, P.: An Efficient Clustering-based Heuristic for Data Gathering and Aggregation in Sensor Networks. In: Proceedings of WCNC(2003)
10. Lindsey, S., Raghavendra, C.S.: PEGASIS: Power Efficient Gathering in Sensor Information Systems. In: Proceedings of IEEE Aerospace Conference (March 9-16, 2002)

A Mesh-Based QoS Aware Multicast Routing Protocol

Dayin Promkotwong and Ohm Sornil

Department of Computer Science, National Institute of Development Administration
118, Serithai Road, Bangkapi, Bangkok 10240, Thailand
{dayin,osornil}@as.nida.ac.th

Abstract. Due to the rising popularity of multimedia applications and potential commercial usages of mobile ad hoc networks (MANETs), quality of service (QoS) in MANET has become necessary to support those needs. In this paper, we propose a QoS aware multicast routing protocol (QMRP) based on mesh architecture which offers bandwidth guarantees for applications in MANETs. Experimental evaluations are carried out in a simulated environment. The results show that the proposed protocol outperforms ODMRP, a mesh-based multicast routing protocol in a variety of environments.

Keywords: quality of service, mesh architecture, multicast routing protocol.

1 Introduction

Wireless mobile networks and devices are becoming increasingly popular as they provide supports for applications anywhere and anytime. Traditional wireless mobile communications are usually supported by wired, fixed infrastructure; a mobile node is only one hop away from a base station. In contrast, the class of Mobile Ad Hoc Network has no fixed infrastructure or central administration. Each mobile node acts either as a host generating flows, being the destination of flows from other mobile nodes, or as a router forwarding flows directed to other mobile nodes. Due to the unpredictable locations and mobility of mobile nodes in MANETs, classical routing protocols used on wired networks are not suitable for MANETs. Protocols defined for ad hoc networks are classified as reactive protocols and proactive protocols.

Reactive protocols are characterized by mobile nodes acquiring and maintaining routes on demand while proactive protocols are characterized by all mobile nodes maintaining routes all the time. Examples of reactive protocols are DSR (Dynamic Source Routing) [2] and AODV (Ad Hoc On-demand Distance Vector) [10]. Examples of proactive protocols are OLSR (Optimized Link State Routing) [5] and TBRPF (Topology Dissemination Based on Reverse-Path Forwarding) [9]. These protocols have been analyzed and compared in a number of papers. The main conclusion of these comparisons is that none of them is the best for all environments. Depending on several aspects such as mobility, load of the network, diameter of the network, a protocol may give better performance than others.

Nowadays in MANETs, network hosts work in group to carry out a given task, therefore, multicasting plays an important role in MANETs. Multicast routing

T. Enokido, L. Barolli, and M. Takizawa (Eds.): NBiS 2007, LNCS 4658, pp. 466–475, 2007.

protocols in MANETs include CAMP [6], AMRoute [1], AMRIS [13], and ODMRP [8]. Among these, ODMRP is considered a superior one. It is a mesh-based protocol instead of a tree-based. To establish a mesh for each multicast group, ODMRP employs the concept of forwarding groups [4]. However it does not support quality of service.

QoS is usually defined as a set of service requirements that need to be met by a network while transporting packets from a source application to their destinations. The network needs are governed by the service requirements of end user applications. A network is expected to guarantee a set of measurable prespecified service attributes to applications in terms of end-to-end performance, such as delay, bandwidth and jitter.

A few protocols have been developed for supporting QoS in MANETs. QoS-AODV [11] enables AODV routing decision based on QoS by adding an extension to messages during route discovery. QoS-Aware Routing protocol [3] considers bandwidth constraints for supporting real-time video or audio transmissions; focuses on exploring different ways to estimate available bandwidth; incorporating QoS into the route discovery procedure; and providing feedback to the application through a cross-layer design.

2 A Mesh-Based QoS Aware Multicast Routing Protocol (QMRP)

2.1 Multicast Mesh Creation

A multicast mesh is created when a source node needs to send data to receiver nodes. The source node broadcasts a RouteRequest packet as shown in Fig. 1. A combination of source address, sequence number and multicast address uniquely identifies the RouteRequest packet. An intermediate node will not rebroadcast the RouteRequest packet if the RouteRequest packet has the same source address, sequence number and multicast address as what it has received before by consulting its RouteRequest cache. When an intermediate node receives a RouteRequest packet, it updates its local RouteRequest cache and increases the HopNumber field in the RouteRequest packet before rebroadcasting the packet.

Once a receiver node receives a RouteRequest packet, it updates its RouteRequest cache and broadcasts a RouteReply packet. If the upstream node receives a RouteReply packet, it will set the Forwarding Flag and Forwarding Timeout fields in Forwarding table, and rebroadcasts the RouteReply packet. An upstream node of a receiver node is a node that sends the RouteRequest packet to the receiver. Thus, when an upstream node of a receiver receives a RouteReply packet, its node address must be similar to the upstream node's address in the RouteReply packet that the receiver sends (i.e., a reverse path). However, if a receiving node is not an upstream node, it will set the Neighbor Flag and Neighbor Timeout fields, but it will not rebroadcast the RouteReply packet. When the source node receives a RouteReply packet, a route has been established and is ready to deliver data.

A multicast mesh consists of source nodes, receiver nodes, forwarding nodes and links connecting them [7]. Two proposed alternatives for the processing at a receiver when it receives a RouteRequest packet are:

1. QMRP_nw: The receiver node sends a RouteReply packet once it receives the first non-duplicate RouteRequest packet (regarded as the shortest path), updates its RouteRequest cache, and rebroadcasts the RouteRequest packet because the receiver node itself may also be a forwarding node for other receiver nodes.
2. QMRP_w: When the receiver node receives the first non-duplicate RouteReply packet, it wait for a period of time for other RouteRequest packets. After the waiting time is over, it compares the quality of routes and updates its RouteRequest cache with the information of the best route determined so far. QMRP selects the best route based on Forwarding Count and Non-Forwarding Count and gives preference to the route with the highest value of Forwarding Count. And it rebroadcasts the RouteRequest packet because the receiver node itself may also be a forwarding node for other receivers.

Type	Source Address	Sequence Number	Multicast Address	Up-Stream	Hop-Number	Forwarding Count	Non-Forwarding Count

Fig. 1. Packet header

Fig. 1 shows the packet header relevant parts of header are adjusted during mesh creation and maintenance, for example, QMRP_nw model is used, Forwarding Count and Non-Forwarding Count fields are not used. The Type field is used separate type of packets from one another. Values of the Type field are shown in Fig.2.

Type	
RouteRequest	RouteRequest packet initiated by a source node for multicast mesh creation
RouteReply	RouteReply packet initiated by a receiver node to set up a route
Data	Data packet
OnDemand-Maintenance	OnDemandMaintenance packet initiated by a node that detects a link failure to discover a new route
OnDemand-MaintenanceReply	OnDemandMaintenanceReply packet initiated by a receiver node to set up a new route
Periodic-Maintenance	PeriodicMaintenance packet initiated by a source node in period time
Periodic-MaintenanceReply	PeriodicMaintenanceReply packet initiated by a receiver node to set up a new route

Fig. 2. Values of the Type field

Source Address	Sequence Number	Multicast Address	Upstream
...	...	...	...

Fig. 3. RouteRequest cache

Fig. 3 shows the structure of the RouteRequest cache. A cache is maintained at each node to check for RouteRequest duplicates. It is used to check upstream for setting the Forwarding Flag field of the Forwarding table and resending RouteReply packet when it receives a RouteReply packet. When a node receives a RouteRequest packet, it checks for duplicates, and if the RouteRequest packet is not duplicated, a record is inserted into the cache.

During the multicast mesh creation, a node broadcasts a RouteRequest packet only when the residual bandwidth is greater than the required bandwidth.

Forwarding Flag	Time Stamp	Neighbor Flag	Time Stamp
...	...	...	...

Fig. 4. Forwarding table

Once a node receives a RouteReply packet, it checks whether it is a forwarding node and/or a neighbor node then sets corresponding fields in its Forwarding table (shown in Fig 4), accordingly.

The purpose of a forwarding node is to rebroadcast Data, OndemandMaintenance, or PeriodicMaintenance packets that it receives, and the purpose of a neighbor node is to rebroadcast OndemandMaintenance or PeriodicMaintenance packets in a similar fashion to the forwarding node, however, it will not rebroadcast Data packets that it receives.

2.2 Bandwidth Estimation

Because bandwidth is shared among nodes, and each node has no knowledge about each other, QMRP is designed for each node to periodically broadcast hello message (Table 1 illustrates the structure of a hello message). When a node receives a hello message, it knows its first and second neighbors and their bandwidth usages. The node consolidates information from hello messages in its Bandwidth cache. Then it estimates the residual bandwidth as follows:

$$\text{Residual bandwidth} = \left(\frac{Raw\ Channel\ Bandwidth - Total\ BandwidthConsumed}{Weight\ Factor} \right)$$

QMRP needs to know the bandwidth consumed by the first and the second neighbors to avoid the hidden problem. Even though the hidden problem may also occur in the third neighbor, this situation is not happen frequently. The receiver also calculates the maximum bandwidth:

```
if (HopNumber = 1)
        MinBandwidth = MinBandwidth
Else if (HopNumber = 2)
        MinBandwidth = MinBandwidth/2
Else if (HopNumber = 3)
        MinBandwidth = MinBandwidth/3
Else MinBandwidth = MinBandwidth/4
```

The maximum bandwidth is added to the RouteReply packet's header. When an upstream node receives the RouteReply packet, it updates the maximum bandwidth in its memory, to be used for maintaining bandwidth estimation.

During the mesh maintenance process, a node that receives an OnDemandMaintenance (or a PeriodicMaintenance) packet compares its residual bandwidth to the maximum bandwidth in its memory. If the residual bandwidth is less than the maximum bandwidth; the maximum bandwidth must be updated to the residual bandwidth.

Table 1. Hello message structure

Node Address	Consumed bandwidth	Time Stamp
Sender	Sender's consumed bandwidth	Sending time
Neighbor node 1	Node 1's consumed bandwidth	Sending time
Neighbor node 2	Node 2's consumed bandwidth	Sending time
…	…	…
Neighbor node n	Node n's consumed bandwidth	Sending time

2.3 Multicast Mesh Maintenance

We propose two alternatives for route maintenance: on demand maintenance and periodic maintenance.

On demand maintenance

QMRP starts the maintenance process only when a forwarding node cannot send data to any forwarding node on the route, that is, it does not receive hello message from any forwarding node which is not the one sending Data packets to it. The node broadcasts an OnDemandMaintenance packet to find a new route from this node to a receiver node if the maximum bandwidth is greater than the bandwidth the application required.

When a node receives an OnDemandMaintenance packet, it updates its Maintenance cache, increases HopNumber field of packet header and rebroadcasts the OnDemandMaintenance packet if it is a neighbor node, and its maximum bandwidth is greater than the required bandwidth. Once a receiver node receives an OnDemandMaintenance packet, it broadcasts an OnDemandMaintenanceReply packet to set up a new route. QMRP uses this maintenance method to avoid maintenance of unnecessary routes by starting the maintenance from a node that link failure occurs to reduce the control overhead.

Fig. 5 (b) when node10 receives a Data packet, it knows that it has no forwarding node to send data to (i.e., it does not receive a hello message from any forwarding node to which it needs to send the data). Node10 starts maintaining the multicast mesh by broadcasting an OnDemandMaintenance packet. When node9 (or node11) receives the OnDemandMaintenance packet, it updates its Maintenance cache and rebroadcasts the OnDemandMaintenance packet if it is a neighbor node. When a receiver node receives the OnDemandMaintenance packet, it updates the Maintenance cache and broadcasts an OnDemandMaintenanceReply packet to set up a reverse path.

Periodic route maintenance

A source starts the mesh maintenance periodically. Periodic maintenance proceeds in the similar fashion to the multicast mesh creation, involving only nodes in the mesh and neighbor nodes. Source broadcasts a PeriodicMaintenance packet periodically. When a node receives a PeriodicMaintenance packet, it rebroadcasts the PeriodicMaintenance packet. When a receiver node receives the PeriodicMaintenance packet, it sends a PeriodicMaintenanceReply packet to its upstream node. During this process, before a node sends the PeriodicMaintenance packet, it compares the maximum bandwidth to the required bandwidth and rebroadcasts the PeriodicMaintenance packet.

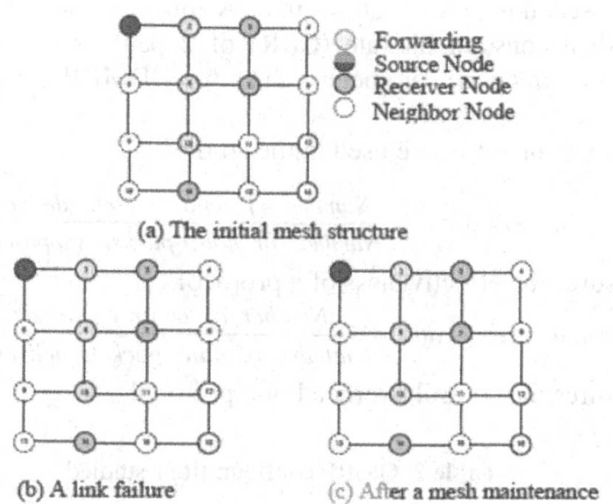

Fig. 5. On demand maintenance

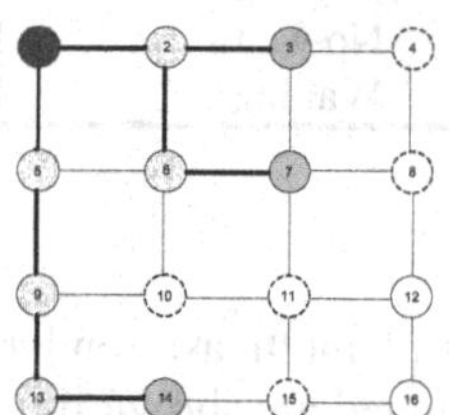

Fig. 6. After periodic maintenance

Source Address	Sequence Number	Multicast Address	Upstream
...	...	...	...

Fig. 7. Maintenance cache

Fig. 6 illustrates a mesh after a session of periodic maintenance. The result mesh is difference from that in Fig. 5 because periodic maintenance starts maintenance at a source node while on demand maintenance starts at an intermediate node.

Fig. 7 shows Maintenance cache. This cache is similar to the RouteRequest cache but it is used for the maintenance purpose.

3 Experimental Evaluation

3.1 Simulation Environment

In this research, we use GloMoSim [12] to create a simulation environment. The environment models a network of 50 mobile nodes placed randomly within a 1000m 1000m area. Twenty receiver nodes are selected randomly. Radio propagation range for each node is 250m, and the channel capacity is 2Mbps. Each simulation run is executed for 600 seconds of simulation time. A multicast source generates 512-byte data packets with a constant bit rate (CBR) of 2 packets per second. Every node moves in a random direction. Parameter values for ODMRP are set according to that described in [8].

Two performance measures are used in the studies:

- $$Packet\ delivery\ ratio = \frac{Number\ of\ data\ packets\ delivered\ to\ receivers}{Number\ of\ data\ packet\ supposed\ to\ be\ received}$$ measures the effectiveness of a protocol.
- $$Control\ overhead\ ratio = \frac{Number\ of\ control\ packets\ transmitte\ d}{number\ of\ data\ packets\ delivered\ to\ receivers}$$ measures the control overhead of a protocol.

Table 2. QMRP configurations studied

	Receiver Process	Maintenance Approch
QMRP_nw_ondemand	No waiting	On demand
QMRP_w_ondemand	Waiting	On demand
QMRP_nw_periodic	No waiting	Periodic
QMRP_w_periodic	Waiting	Periodic

3.2 Results

Mobility speed and the number of multicast senders are varied in the experiments. Four configurations of QMRP studied are shown in Table 2.

3.2.1 Mobility Speed

First, we study effects of mobility speeds and waiting periods to the performance of QMRP_w_ondemand and QMRP_w_periodic. Each node moves in a random direction, using a random speed between 10 to 70 km/hr. We randomly select 5 multicast sources and 20 receivers from 50 mobile nodes.

The results of QMRP_w_ondemand are shown in Fig. 9. We can observe that QMRP_w_ondemand with the waiting period of 0.2 seconds (w_0.2s) has higher packet delivery ratio than do other configurations. This method, a receiver does not wait long before sending a RouteReply packet back to the source node. When nodes move at higher speeds, QMRP with the waiting periods of 0.2 seconds (w_0.2s) and 0.5 seconds (w_0.5s) experience performance drops. On the contrary, control overhead ratios are higher when nodes move at higher speeds.

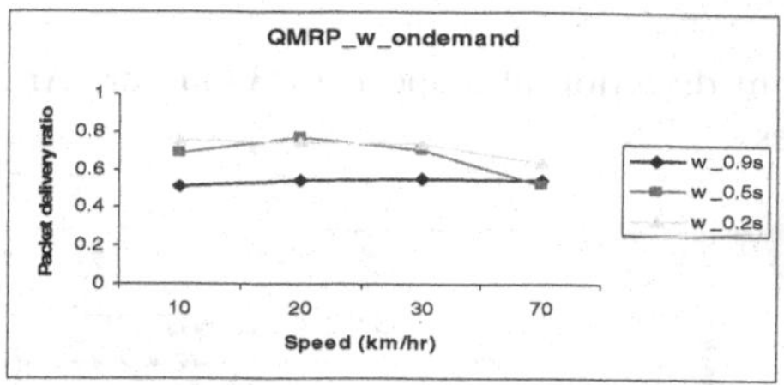

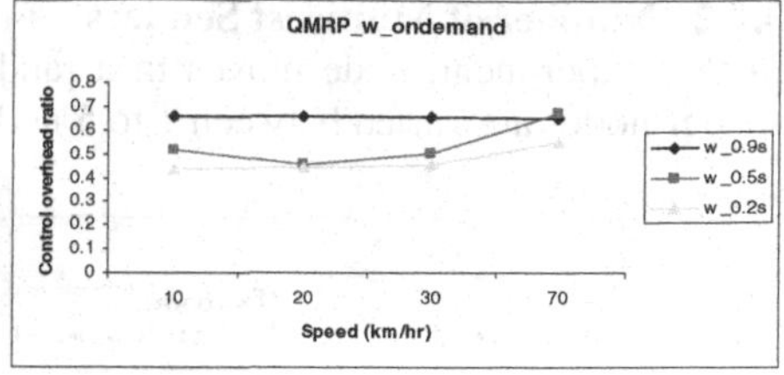

Fig. 9. Packet delivery ratios and control overhead ratios of QMRP_w_ondemand at different mobility speeds

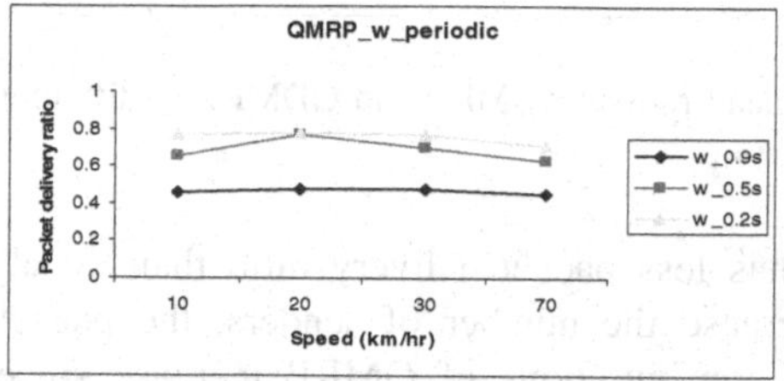

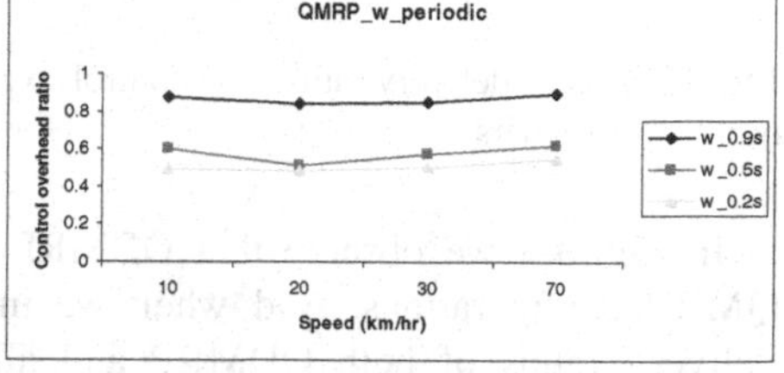

Fig. 10. Packet delivery ratios and control overhead ratios of QMRP_w_periodic at different mobility speeds

Fig. 10 shows the results of QMRP_w_periodic. We can see that QMRP_w_periodic has higher packet delivery ratio than does QMRP_w_ondemand. This is because QMRP_w_ondemand performs maintenance more frequently than does QMRP_w_periodic, especially at higher mobility speeds.

Next, we compare the performance of different configurations of QMRP and that of ODMRP. In Fig. 11, we observe that ODMRP has less packet delivery ratio than do all QMRP configurations. This is because QMRP performs bandwidth reservation and accepts only routes that satisfy bandwidth requirements. QMRP_nw has a higher packet delivery ratio than QMRP_w. QMRP_nw_ondemand has higher packet delivery ratio at higher mobility speeds. This is because at high mobility speeds QMRP prefers route to be established quickly. QMRP_nw_periodic has the best packet delivery ratio, and even at high mobility speeds the packet delivery ratio does not drop. ODMRP has higher control overhead ratio than all QMRP configurations since during its maintenance process, QMRP induces only multicast mesh and neighbor nodes.

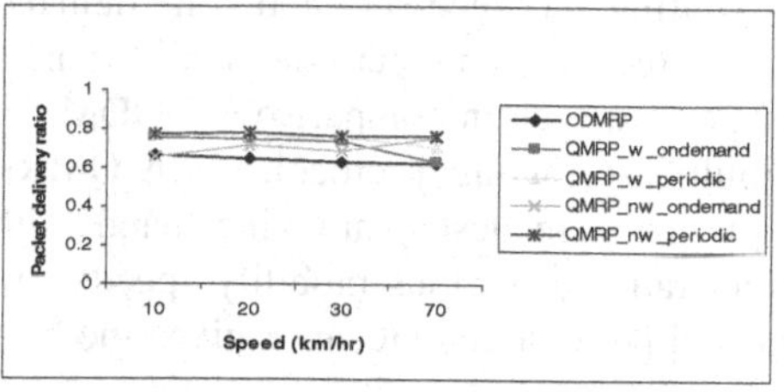

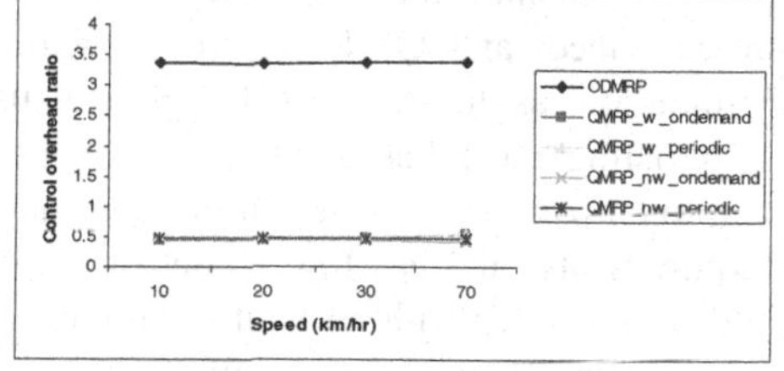

Fig. 11. Packet delivery ratios and control overhead ratios of QMRP and ODMRP at different mobility speeds

3.2.2 Number of Multicast Senders

In this experiment, node moves in a random direction at a speed of 3.6km/hr. And sender nodes are varied between 1 to 5 nodes.

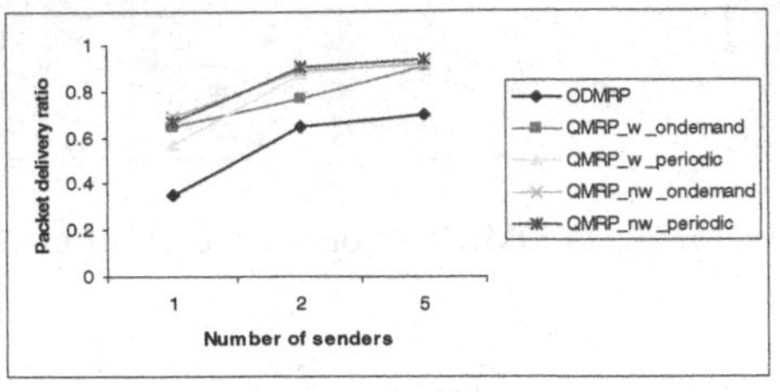

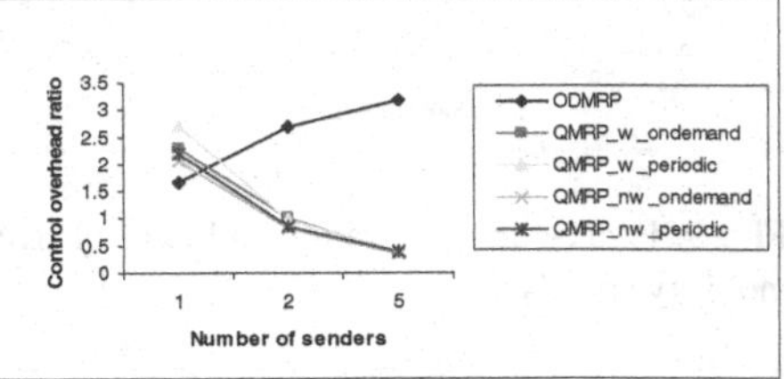

Fig. 12. Packet delivery ratios and control overhead ratios of QMRP and ODMRP at different number of senders

In Fig. 12, we observe that ODMRP has less packet delivery ratio than do all QMRP configurations. And when we increase the number of senders, the packet delivery ratios of both ODMRP and all configurations of QMRP increase since ODMRP and QMRP use the forwarding group concept. The more senders are selected, the more forwarding nodes are set and the more paths are redundant. QMRP_nw with ondemand and periodic maintenance have better performance than do QMRP_w with similar configurations. When the number of senders increases, the control overhead ratio of ODMRP increases as well. On the contrary, when the number of senders increases, the control overhead ratio of ODMRP decreases. This is due to the fact that when the number of senders increases, the number of control packets of QMRP also increases, however the number of packets delivered increases at a faster rate, therefore the control overhead ratio is low. In ODMRP, when the number of senders increases, the number of delivered packets slowly increases in comparison to QMRP, causing the control overhead to rise higher.

4 Conclusion

In this paper, we propose a mesh-based QoS aware multicast routing protocol for MANETs. Four different configurations are proposed and studied: QMRP with waiting at receiver and on demand maintenance, QMRP with waiting at receiver and periodic maintenance, QMRP with no waiting at receiver and on demand maintenance, and QMRP with no waiting at receiver and periodic maintenance. Simulation results show QMRP gives better performance in comparison to ODMRP, an existing mesh-based ad hoc network multicast routing protocol, since QMRP employs bandwidth reservation and accepts only requests satisfying bandwidth requirements; and has lower control overhead ratios at various mobility speeds. In addition, QMRP with no waiting at receiver and periodic maintenance gives the best performance than other configurations.

References

1. Bommaiah, E., Liu, M., McAuley, A., Talpade, R.: AMRoute: Ad Hoc Multicast Routing Protocol. IETF (1998)
2. Broch, J., Maltz, D.A., Johnson, D.B.: The Dynamic Source Routing Protocol for Multihop Wireless Ad Hoc Networks, pp. 139–172. Addison-Wesley Longman Publishing, Redwood City,CA, USA (2001)
3. Chen, L., Heinzelman, W.: QoS-aware Routing Based on Bandwidth Estimation for Mobile Ad Hoc Networks. IEEE Journal on selected areas in communications (2005)
4. Chiang, C.C., Gerla, M., Zhang, L.: Forwarding Group Multicast Protocol (FGMP) for Multihop. Mobile wireless network(Cluster computing), pp. 187–189 (1998)
5. Clausen, T., Jacquet, P.: Optimized Link State Routing Protocol (OLSR). IETF (2003)
6. Garcia-Luna-Aceves, J.J., Madruga, E.L.: The Core-Assisted Mesh Protocol. IEEE Journal on selected areas in communications, 1380–1394 (1999)
7. Lee, S., Kim, C. (eds.): A New Wireless Ad Hoc Multicast Routing Protocol, pp. 121–135. Elsevier North-Holland publisher, Amsterdam (2002)
8. Lee, S., Su, W., Gerla, M.: On Demand Multicast Routing Protocol (ODMRP) for Ad Hoc Networks. IETF (2000)
9. Ogier, R., Templin, F., Lewis, M.: Topology Dissemination Based on Reverse-Path Forwarding (TBREF). IETF (2004)
10. Perkin, C., Royer, D.M., Das, S.R.: Ad Hoc On Demand Distance Vector (AODV) Routing. IETF (1993)
11. Renesse, R., Ghassemian, M., Aghyami, A.H.: QoS Enabled Routing in Mobile Ad Hoc Networks. 3G Mobile Communication Technologies (2004)
12. UCLA Parallel Computing Laboratory and wireless Adaptive Mobility Laboratory: GloMoSim
13. Wu, C.W., Tay, Y.C., Toh, C.K.: Ad Hoc Multicast Routing Protocol utilizing Increasing id-numbers (AMRIS) functional specification. IETF (1998)

Virtual Large-Scale Disk System for PC-Room

Erianto Chai[1], Minoru Uehara[1], Hideki Mori[1], and Nobuyoshi Sato[2]

[1] Dept. of Information and Computer Sciences, Toyo University, 2100 Kujirai, Kawagoe, Saitama, 350-8585, Japan
[2] Faculty of Software and Information Science, Iwate Prefectural University, 152-52, Sugo, Takizawa, Iwate, 020-0193 Japan
eriaji@gmail.com, uehara@toyonet.toyo.ac.jp, mori@toyonet.toyo.ac.jp, nobu-s@iwate-pu.ac.jp

Abstract. There are many PCs in a PC room. For example, there are 500 PCs in our University. Each PC has a HDD, which is typically not full. If the disk utilization is 50% and each PC has a 240GB HDD, there is 60TB (500x120GB) free disk space. The total size of the unused capacity of these HDDs is nearly equal to the capacity of a file server. Institutions, however, tend to buy expensive appliance file servers. In this paper, we propose an efficient large-scale storage system that combines client free disk space. We have developed a java-based toolkit to construct a virtual large-scale storage system, which we call VLSD (Virtual Large-scale Disk). This toolkit is implemented in Java and consists of RAID (Redundant Arrays of Inexpensive/Independent Disks) and NBDs (Network Block Device). Using VLSD, we show how to construct a large disk that consists of multiple free spaces distributed over networks. VLSD supports typical RAID and other utility classes. These can be combined freely with one another.

Keywords: RAID, Network Block Device, Storage System.

1 Introduction

The requirements of higher education are growing. Companies expect graduates to maintain Linux servers and to administer networks, something which only privileged users are allowed to do. However, it is difficult for a beginner to become a privileged user. Consequently, we have developed a plan to use a virtual machine, such as VMware, Microsoft Virtual PC 2004, and so on, to allow students to learn how to maintain Linux servers in a safe environment. In this way, virtual machines are very useful in advanced education. These virtual machines, however, require much disk space. VMware recommends 8GB as the HDD capacity for Linux and 16GB for Windows. In our experience, Windows actually requires 24GB HDD capacity. This means that 40-120TB disk capacity is required for 5000 students.

An appliance file server with a 60TB capacity, was considered for this purpose. A commercial company quoted 250 million yen (about 2 million dollars) for such a file server. However, we already have 500 PCs. If we add 120GB HDDs to all our PCs at

T. Enokido, L. Barolli, and M. Takizawa (Eds.): NBiS 2007, LNCS 4658, pp. 476–485, 2007.

a cost of 150 dollars per HDD, a 60TB distributed file server can be realized at a cost of just 75 thousand dollars. The ratio of cost saving is 1:33, making this more important than any other factor, such as performance, dependability or maintainability. We therefore propose a distributed storage system and develop a toolkit to aid in the construction of such a system. We call this toolkit VLSD (Virtual Large-scale Disk).

We assume that a VLSD is used in the following educational environment. There are 512 client PCs, each running both Windows and Linux. Linux runs on VMware in Windows as a guest OS. Each client has at least 170GB free disk space. Therefore, the total available space is 70TB. We construct the distributed storage system using this free space. We can use the file system via a Linux file server, which supports NFS for Linux clients and SMB/CIFS for Windows. The Linux file server can be either real or virtual.

VLSD is a toolkit for developing virtual large scale disks, and can run on any platform that supports Java, since VLSD is 100% pure Java. Using VLSD, both Linux and Windows can be either a client or a server. A VLSD disk server creates a disk file on its own file system, and then publishes it as a remote disk for VLSD clients to share. VLSD is independent of the file system, and can combine Linux disk files with Windows disk files. In addition, VLSD can construct a virtual 64 bit file system on a 32 bit system.

VLSD can concatenate multiple virtual disks, thereby increasing the storage capacity. VLSD supports typical RAID classes, such as RAID0, 1, 4, 5, and 6, and can construct multiple hierarchies of RAID combining any RAID class with any other RAID class.

The remainder of this paper is organized as follows. In Section 2, we introduce several related works and give details of the problem. In Section 3, we introduce our VLSD toolkit. We then evaluate the VLSD and discuss the results. Finally, we offer our conclusions.

2 Related Works

2.1 64 Bit File Systems

We need more than a 64 bit file system to construct a large-scale storage system. Here, a 64 bit file system means that the seek pointer of a file is represented as a 64 bit integer. Initially we wish to construct a 70TB storage system, but in the future, we intend constructing 4EB storage systems. A 64 bit file system theoretically allows us to construct a 16EB storage system. However, this is not really feasible because Java's long is a 64 bit signed integer. In practice, the maximum disk capacity is less than 8GB if Java is used.

SGI's XFS is a popular 64 bit file system running on Linux. UFS2 is also popular in FreeBSD. Sun's ZFS is provided for Solaris. In a sense, ZFS is the greatest file system because it uses 128 bits. In this paper, we use XFS because the file server runs on Linux.

2.2 Distributed File Systems

When we set about constructing a large-scale storage system, we tried mounting several isolated disks using a distributed file system, such as SMB/CIFS, NFS [1], NRFS [2], Gfarm [3], GPFS [8], Lustre [9], JDFS [4] and CaFS [5].

In Windows, SMB/CIFS is the de facto standard protocol for implementing network drives. Linux can also be a SMB/CIFS server using Samba, which enables it to maintain Windows accounts easily.

In UNIX, including Linux, FreeBSD and so on, NFS is the de facto standard protocol for implementing distributed file systems. Windows can also be an NFS server using Microsoft Service for UNIX (SFU). However, it is not so easy for Windows to maintain Linux accounts in SFU. We therefore, have to choose another protocol suited to a different client.

NRFS realizes RAID1 on NFS. However, it is best suited to small-scale storage, because NRFS is based on RAID1 (mirroring), which does not increase storage capacity. Therefore, NRFS is not suitable for increasing storage capacity.

Gfarm is a wide area virtual file system that realizes large-scale storage on Grids. In this sense, a virtual file system is a service that provides a virtual view of a uniform, logical file system to applications running on different physical file systems. In Gfarm, replication is used to improve fault tolerance and to allow parallel distributed processes. The replication is based on the principle of RAID0 and as such, Gfarm is also not suitable for increasing storage capacity. This does not however, mean that it is impossible for Gfarm to increase storage capacity. Furthermore, Gfarm is based on Linux and both Linux and Windows clients can use it. However, Gfarm cannot use Windows HDDs. Since we need a multi-platform solution, Gfarm is not suited to our purpose.

IBM's GPFS (General Parallel File System) is a high performance cluster file system based on NFS. Therefore, GPFS has the same problems as NFS and Gfarm.

Lustre is also a high performance cluster file system like GPFS. Unlike GPFS, it has been developed as open source software. Lustre however, also has the same problems as GPFS.

JDFS is a 100% pure Java distributed file system for Java applets and applications. JDFS provides Java applets and applications to a network transparent distributed file system. However, it cannot be used in applications compiled in native code. CaFS is an extended version of JDFS. It is suited to desktop searching. JDFS can mount several disks; however, it cannot concatenate the disks. Therefore, the maximum file size is limited to the minimum disk size.

We have identified two essential problems in the file system based approach. The first problem is not being able to utilize the full capacity of the storage. For example, when we try to construct 60TB of storage using 120GB HDDs, the maximum size of a file must be less than 120GB. The total size of all files in a directory must also be less than 120GB. In addition, it is impossible for this kind of physical file system to create a file greater than 2GB. The second problem is dependent on a particular platform such as Linux. Almost all distributed file systems are based on the NFS protocol, yet NFS is not suited to Windows. Windows clients have a larger capacity of HDDs than a Linux server.

In this way, a file system based on a distributed storage system such as NFS can neither stripe physical storage devices nor concatenate them. Therefore, we employ a disk based approach, in which a virtual disk is created in a physical file system.

2.3 NBD

An NBD (Network Block Device) [6] is a virtual disk that is popular with Linux users and consists of a server and client. The server is a user process that allows the sharing of any physical file as a virtual block device on the network. An NBD client is a device driver that transfers read/write accesses to the NBD server. When an application uses NBD, v-node transfers read/write access to an NBD device. An NBD's major device number is reserved as 43.

NBDs are included in many Linux distributions. However, if not, it is easy to install an NBD. The NBD server is ported to Windows and other UNIX systems. Linux can easily realize dependable storage using both NBD and the software RAID (Redundant Array of Independent Disk) of the Linux kernel.

There are several variations in NBD. ENBD (Enhanced NBD) employs block-journaled multi-channel communication and may be working now. GNBD (Global NBD) [12] is an extended NBD for clustering. A GNBD server allows simultaneous access for its clients and is included in RedHat, Fedora Core, etc.

NBD is the simplest solution for our requirements. Of course, NBD is based on a disk based approach. It is easy to modify because it is open source and is supported in several OS including Linux and Windows. We employ the NBD protocol as a disk level storage protocol. We allow connecting a NBD device locally because NBD is not secure.

FreeBSD's GEOM may be better than NBD. However, it is dependent on FreeBSD and so we did not choose it.

2.4 RAID

The most important problem for large-scale storage is dependability. Generally, the MTTF of a system that consists of N disks is 1/N of the MTTF of each disk. RAID is a solution to this problem [7].

There are 7 levels in RAID. RAID0 stripes without redundancy but increases the capacity. RAID1 mirrors but does not increase capacity. In RAID2, data is striped at a bit level. RAID2 can correct erroneous data using ECC (Error Correcting Code) such as Humming code, but it is not used because ECC has no advantage over parity. In RAID3, data is striped at a bit or byte level. RAID3 employs parity instead of ECC. Parity is easier to compute than ECC, and is stored on a particular disk. RAID4 is similar to RAID3, but in RAID4, data is striped at a block level instead of at a bit or byte level. The parity disk becomes a bottle neck in both RAID3 and RAID4. In RAID5, parities are distributed on the data disk. RAID6 can mask 2 faults using 2 parities.

RAID can be implemented in either hardware (HW) or software (SW). Currently, HW RAID is popular because it is faster than SW RAID. However, in HW RAID, special hardware, called a RAID controller, is required. The CPU of a RAID controller is slower than the CPU of the host computer. Thus, SW RAID is available for file servers. Furthermore, SW RAID is the only solution for networking RAID.

Single level RAID is not suited to our requirements. RAID hierarchy is a typical multiple level RAID. Much research has been done on hierarchical RAID. AutoRAID [10] combines RAID1 with any other RAID. HiRAID [11] combines any RAID with any other RAID. In this sense, VLSD is similar to HiRAID. However, VLSD is not only SW RAID, but also a network disk.

3 VLSD

We now describe the VLSD (Virtual Large Scale Disk) toolkit for large-scale storage.

3.1 System Overview

In this section, we design a 70TB distributed storage system in the environment as described in Section 1. In our system, there are 512 client PCs which each provide 170GB free disk space. The total free space is 87TB. However, a client PC may be shut down by an inexperienced user. The distributed storage system is no more reliable than a conservative file server. So, we overcome this problem by using hierarchical RAID such as HiRAID. We employ RAID66, which is two layered RAID6.

Figure 1 shows a typical organization of RAID66 which consists of 512 PCs. The number of disks in the upper layer is 512/N where N is the number of disks in the lower layer. When N is small, the MTTF of RAID6 in the lower layer is large. So, the MTTF of the entire system is also large. However, whether N is small or large, the efficiency of the HDD capacity is low. The efficiency is at its maximum when N = $512^{1/2}$=22. As a result, the number of disks in both layers should be the same, providing, in this case, a total of 484 disks (=22x22). This is less than the number of clients available, namely 512. The total storage capacity is 68TB and the disks of 28 (512 minus 484) clients are reserved as spares.

The VLSD is a toolkit for constructing large-scale storage systems. It is written in pure Java, and is thus independent of any platform on which Java runs, such as Windows, Linux, and so on. Even if there is no native NBD server in an OS, VLSD can be used on it. VLSD includes software RAID and NBD and consists of typical RAID classes and an NBD client/server. Using VLSD, we can combine any RAID and NBD device with one another.

In Linux, the maximum number of devices with the same major number is 256. Therefore, it is impossible to implement our storage system using only NBD. VLSD uses ports instead of devices. The number of ports is also limited in the NBD server of VLSD. The NBD server keeps a port while using the virtual disk. Although the number of ports is greater than the number of devices, it is still not sufficient. It is possible to construct a single layer even when the number of clients is several thousand. However, it is difficult to construct the system in such a way when the number of clients increases. In this case, the system must be constructed hierarchically. Hence, we provide an RMI based remote disk server (DiskServer) to overcome this problem.

Both the command "nbd-server" of Linux and the command "nbdsrvr" of Windows can share a single file as a virtual disk. Thus, they are not suited to FAT32 because its maximum file size is limited to 2GB. For example, when a PC has 120GB of free space, 60 (120GB/2GB) NBD servers are required. On the other hand, VLSD can concatenate multiple files as a single JBOD (Just a Bunch Of Disks). In this sense, VLSD is better than native NBD.

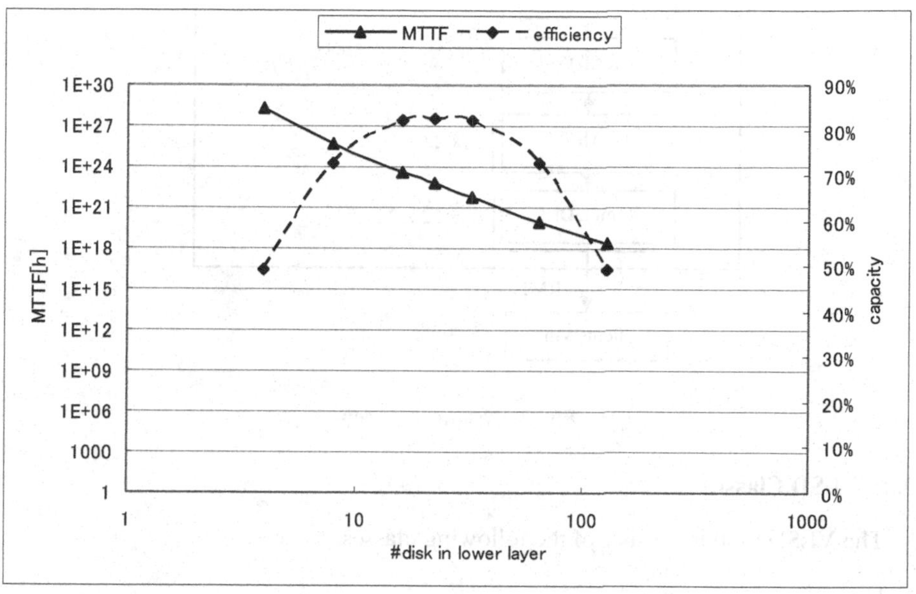

Fig. 1. MTTF and efficiency in RAID66

Figure 2 shows an example of distributed storage using VLSD. There are 500 Windows or Linux clients, which connect to the file server using NFS or CIFS. A client also serves as a DiskServer collecting its free space as a JBOD. Each DiskServer provides 170GB and there are at least 484 DiskServers in the system. The file server is also a Linux machine running Samba. Using Samba, the file server supports Windows clients via SMB/CIFS, and also supports Linux clients directly via NFS. The file server has an nbd-client (i.e. NBD device), which connects locally to an NBDServer. The NBD protocol is not secure, but in this case, this is not a problem. The NBDServer consists of a top-level RAID6. The RAID6 consists of 22 RAID6s in the upper layer. Each RAID6 in the upper layer consists of 22 RemoteDisks in the lower layer. There are thus 484 RemoteDisks in the file server. We have implemented the file server using Debian GNU/Linux.

This system has advantages over and above those of a conventional file system. It does not need any sub-servers, and it allows the addition of many more clients.

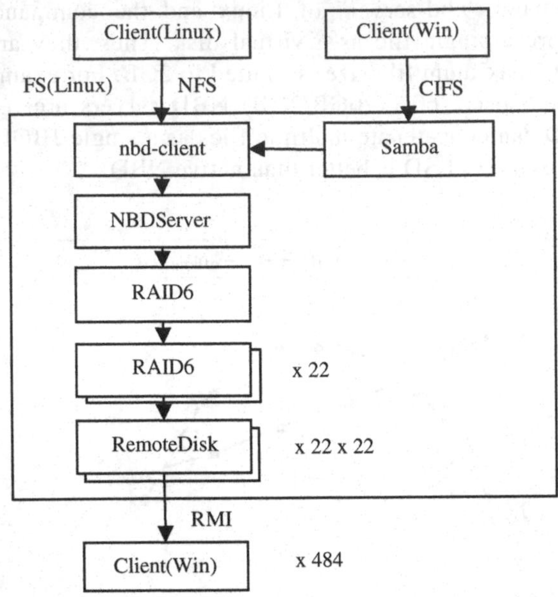

Fig. 2. System Overview

3.2 VLSD Classes

The VLSD toolkit consists of the following classes.

- Disk
  This is the interface that defines the specification of all disks.
- SingleDisk
  This is a wrapper which creates a single disk from another single disk.
- PagedDisk
  This is a wrapper which converts byte-boundary access to page-boundary access.
- VariableDisk
  This is a wrapper which creates a variable capacity disk from another single disk. A variable disk has a k-tree structure. The size of each node is 8KB. A leaf node has 8KB data. An intermediate node has 1024 pointers to nodes. Each node is dynamically allocated on demand. The maximum depth of the tree is 6. The maximum capacity of the whole disk is 4EB. However, the overhead is 0.1% of the capacity.
- FileDisk
  This is a fixed capacity disk created from a single file. The physical capacity is equivalent to the logical capacity.
- MemoryDisk
  This is a fixed capacity disk created from a byte array in memory.

- NBDServer

This is an NBD server, providing free space to the storage system in the form of a virtual disk. In this research, an NBDServer runs on each client PC in order to provide access to the free space on the local disk. The client OS is either Windows or Linux. The NBDServer can run on either OS because it is implemented in Java. A client has several disks and/or a client uses a FAT32 disk. In FAT32, the maximum file size is 2GB. In this case, the NBDServer is combined with JBOD which concatenates the separate free spaces.

- NBDDisk

This is an NBD client.

- DiskServer

An NBD device is based on a connection oriented protocol. It occupies a port per connection and so there may be a bottleneck for port resources. Thus, we provide a DiskServer which does not depend on the number of ports because it uses Java RMI.

- RemoteDisk

This is the client class of a DiskServer. It can access the virtual disk provided by the DiskServer via RMI.

- DiskCache

This is a cache based on LRU.

- JBOD

This can concatenate multiple disks into a single disk without redundancy. It is usually used to increase the capacity. The capacity of each sub-disk need not be the same. The total capacity is the sum of all parts because JBOD does not stripe.

- RAID0

The class of RAID0. RAID0 is used to increase capacity. In contrast to JBOD, as described later, RAID0 stripes and so has slightly better performance than JBOD. However, it truncates the size to the minimum size of the files. For example, when we begin to construct RAID0 using a 100GB HDD, a 120GB HDD and a 160GB HDD, the capacity of RAID0 is limited to 100GB. In this case, we should use JBOD to increase capacity. However, RAID0 is expected to increase performance. A file system gathers super nodes that manage other i-nodes. In such a system, the system load of the file system will increase as the scale of the system grows. RAID0 may distribute the system load because of striping. RAID0 stripes in byte units.

- RAID1

The class of RAID1. RAID1 copies the operations to mirror the contents. It works well if at least one disk works well. So, it is resilient to t-faults if n>t, where n is the number of disks. It is highly reliable but does not increase capacity.

- VotedRAID1

This is similar to RAID0, but differs in that it votes to mask bit errors. Thus, it requires more than 3 disks. It is the most reliable in the RAID family.

- RAID4

The class of RAID4. It is not used because RAID5 is better than RAID4.

- RAID5

The class of RAID5. It is similar to a RAID4 but differs in that parities are distributed to data disks. It has the same reliability as RAID4 but may have better performance than RAID4.

- RAID6
The class of RAID6. It needs two parity disks because it is based on P+Q. It is more reliable than RAID5.

4 Evaluation

In this section, we evaluate the performance of VLSD. Figure 3 shows the performance comparison of VariableDisk with FileDisk. Here, the X-axis is the total disk capacity and the Y-axis is the response time when the disk is formatted to XFS. As shown in this figure, VariableDisk performs better than FileDisk. The physical size of VariableDisk is smaller than that of FileDisk. This is the reason why the format time of VariableDisk is less than that of FileDisk.

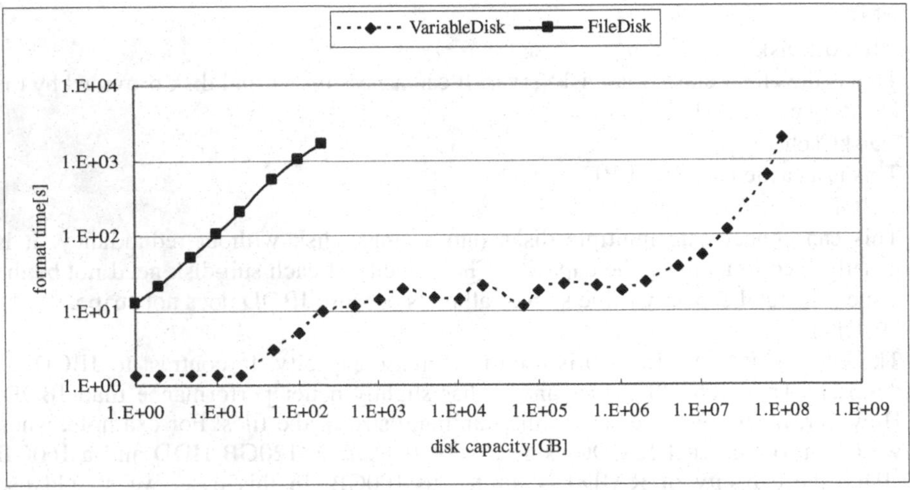

Fig. 3. The performance comparison of VariableDisk with FileDisk

We built the prototype file server on a virtual machine. It runs on a PC (CPU: AMD Athlone 64 X2 Dual Core Processor 3800+; Memory: 2GB; LAN: 100 base). The guest OS is Debian GNU/Linux (Memory 1GB) and the host OS is Windows 2003. The throughput between VM and VM is 480Mbps, the throughput between VM and the host is 192Mbps, and the throughput between VM and the remote host (CPU: Intel Pentium 4 3GHz; Memory: 1GB; OS: Windows XP) is 64Mbps. In our experience, the bottlenecks are Samba and the network but not VLSD.

5 Conclusions

This paper describes VLSD, a toolkit for constructing large-scale storage systems. It is available to construct a large disk in an environment such as PC-rooms where there are many PCs that have free disk space. VLSD has enough functionality to construct such a system without special hardware, and can decrease the cost of storage systems.

Our future work includes the need to improve the performance of the VLSD. We intend to employ multiple path access to improve both performance and reliability. In addition, we will try to improve the maintainability, as it is difficult to maintain many disks in the current system.

References

1. Shepler, S., et al.: NFS version 4 Protocol, http://www.ietf.org/rfc/rfc3010.txt
2. NRFS Project Team: NRFS, http://www.ssscore.org/nrfs/
3. Grid Datafarm: Gfarm file system, http://datafarm.apgrid.org/index.en.html
4. Uehara, M.: A Distributed File System for Java Applet based Distance Learning. In: Proc. of 2004 Symposium on Applications and the Internet(SAINT 2004), pp. 145–151 (2004) (2004.1.29)
5. Uehara, M.: Change Aware Distributed File System for A Distributed Search Engine. In: Proc. of 2004 IEEE International Conference on Multimedia and Expo(ICME2004), PD5(4-4), pp. 1–4. IEEE, Los Alamitos (2004) (2004.6.29)
6. Wouter Verhelst: Network Block Device, http://nbd.sourceforge.net/
7. Chen, P.M., Lee, E.K., Gibson, G.A., Katz, R.H., Patterson, D.A.: RAID: High-Performance, Reliable Secondary Storage. ACM Computing Surveys 26(2), 145–185 (1994)
8. Barkes, J., Barrios, M.R., Cougard, F., Crumley, P.G., Marin, D., Reddy, H.: Theeraphong Thitayanun: GPFS: A Parallel File System, IBM, http://publib-b.boulder.ibm.com/Redbooks.nsf/RedbookAbstracts/sg,24515.html?Open
9. Cluster File Systems, Inc.: Lustre: scalable, secure, robust, highly-available cluster file system, http://www.lustre.org/
10. Wilkes, J., Golding, R., Stealin, C., Sullivan, T.: The HP AutoRAID hierarchical storage system. ACM Trans. Computer Systems 14(1), 108–136 (1996)
11. Baek, S.H., Kim, B.W., Joung, E.J., Park, C.W.: Reliability and performance of hierarchical RAID with multiple controllers. In: Proc. of 12 th annual ACM sumposium on Principles of Distributed Computing, pp. 246–254. ACM, New York (2001)
12. GNBD Project Page http://sourceware.org/cluster/gnbd/

Application of Default Logic in an Intelligent Tutoring System

Sylvia Encheva[1] and Sharil Tumin[2]

[1] Stord/Haugesund University College, Bjørnsonsg. 45, 5528 Haugesund, Norway
sbe@hsh.no
[2] University of Bergen, IT-Dept., P. O. Box 7800, 5020 Bergen, Norway
edpst@it.uib.no

Abstract. Default logic is often used for solving knowledge representation problems in a compact, robust and flexible way. One of goals of intelligent systems is to provide efficient evaluation students' responces. Often they operate only with the answers to a single question addressing learning a new term, understanding a new concept or mastering a new skill. However, experimental practice shows that asking several questions about the same item results in inconsistent and/or incomplete feedback, i.e. some of the answers are correct while others are partially correct or even incorrect. In this paper we propose use of default logic in an intelligent tutoring system as a way of resolving the problem with inconsistent and/or incomplete input.

Keywords: Knowledge assessment, learning, logic.

1 Introduction

The issue of rewarding partially correct answers has been addressed by many authors. Intelligent systems have been designed to assign scores related to the importance of missing or incorrect part of an answer. Such systems are meant to facilitate the process of knowledge assessment. While trying to be efficient in evaluating students' responces these systems operate with the answers to a single question addressing learning a new term, understanding a new concept or mastering a new skill. However, experimental practice shows that asking several questions about the same item results in inconsistent and/or incomplete feedback, i.e. some of the answers are correct while others are partially correct or even incorrect. In this paper we propose use of default logic in an intelligent tutoring system as a way of resolving the problem with inconsistent and/or incomplete input.

The rest of the paper is organized as follows. Related work and statements from default logic may be found in Section 2. The main results of the paper are placed in Section 3. The system architecture is described in Section 4. The paper ends with a conclusion in Section 5.

T. Enokido, L. Barolli, and M. Takizawa (Eds.): NBiS 2007, LNCS 4658, pp. 486–494, 2007.

2 Background

Default theory was first introduced in [10]. Distinction between definite consequences and default consequences was first discussed in [1]. Ten-valued logic was used in [12] and [13] to order default theories and distinguish different sorts of information. Ten-valued logic composed of four basic and six composed values was applied in [16] for performing implication, justification, and propagation in combinatorial circuits.

A level-based instruction model is proposed in [7]. A model for student knowledge diagnosis through adaptive testing is presented in [3]. An approach for integrating intelligent agents, user models, and automatic content categorization in a virtual environment is presented in [14]. Previous research indicates that interactive-engagement classes can achieve at higher levels than more didactic classes, and that students in active-engagement computer-based physics classes outperform students who receive traditional instruction [4].

The Questionmark system [5] applies multiple response questions where a set of options are presented following a question stem and the student can select any number and combination of those options. They are significantly more complex than multiple choice questions where the student can select only one among the suggested options. If a student marks some of the correct options (but not all) and or some of incorrect options his/her responce can be correct, incorrect, partly correct or partly incorrect. The final outcome is correct or incorrect because the system is based on Boolean logic [2], [19].

A default theory is a pair $\Delta = (D, W)$ where D is a set of default rules and W is a set of quantifier-free formulas [10]. A set S of formulas is deductively closed if $S = Th(S)$, where Th is the usual deductive closure operator. A set E of formulas is an extension of Δ if it coinsides with the smallest deductively closed set E' of formulas satisfying the conditions:

- $W \subseteq E'$,
- $\forall \alpha : \beta_1, \beta_2, ..., \beta_n / \gamma \in D, \alpha \in E', \neg\beta_i \notin E, i = 1, .., n$ implies $\gamma \in E'$.

A formula derived from a theory is either a definite consequence by W or a default consequence by D. A formula is

- a credulous conclusion of Δ if it belongs to some (but not all) extensions, and
- a skeptical conclusion of Δ if it belongs to all extensions.

Default consequences are results of two modes of inferences - skeptical or credulous reasoning. The logic used here for default reasoning has the following truth values:

- t - true
- f - false
- $\perp$ - undefined
- $\top$ - contradictory
- $d\top$ - contradictory by default

- dts - skeptically true by default
- dfs - skeptically false by default
- dtc - credulously true by default
- dfc - credulously false by default
- $*$ - undetermined by default

A bilattice is a set equipped with two partial orderings - truth ordering $\leq_t$ and knowledge ordering $\leq_k$. The t partial ordering $\leq_t$ means that if two truth values a, b are related as $a \leq_t b$ then b is at least as true a. The k partial ordering $\leq_k$ means that if two truth values a, b are related as $a \leq_k b$ then b labels a sentence about which we have more knowledge than a sentence labeled with a.

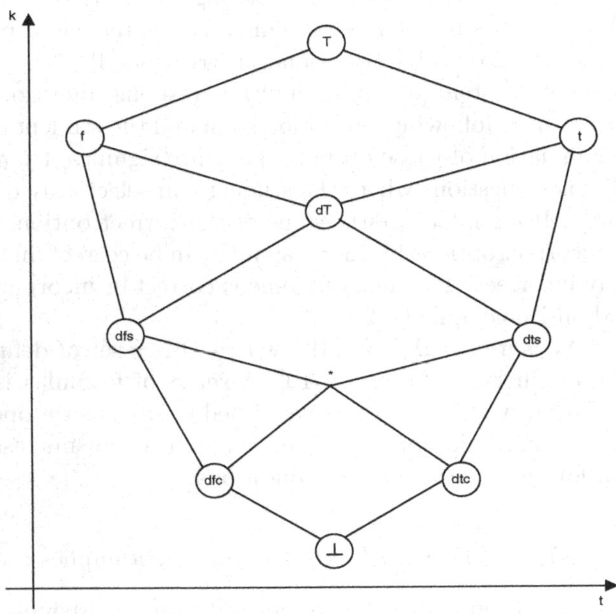

Fig. 1. Bilattice

The ten truth-values form a bilattice (Fig. 1) under $\leq_t$ and $\leq_k$ [13]. These values are related as follows

- $\bot \leq_k dtc, dfc \leq_k * \leq_k dts, dfs \leq_k d\top \leq_k t, f \leq_k \top$,
- $f \leq_t \top, d\top \leq_t t;\quad dfs \leq_t d\top \leq_t dtc$, and
- $f \leq_t dfs \leq_t dfc \leq_t *, \bot \leq_t dtc \leq_t dts \leq_t t$.

The values $t, f, \top$ denote definite consequences by W and the values $dts, dfs, d\top, dtc, dfc, *$ denote default consequences by D, $\bot$ denotes that no information is available. Knowledge ordering concerns the certainty of information - first order logical consequences are more certain than skeptical default consequences, which are more certain than credulous default consequences. The truth ordering shows degree of truth, f. ex. 'true' has a higher degree of truth than 'skeptically true by default', which has a higher degree of truth than 'credulously true by default'.

3 The Default Logic

Questions in a test should provide information about

- the student's knowledge,
- the subtler qualities of discrimination, judgment, and reasoning necessary in scientific reasoning,
- evaluate the student's judgment as to whether cause and effect relationships exist, and
- student's comprehension of a described situation.

Based on the relations among the truth values from Section 2 we propose the following:

- Two correct answers imply understanding of the concept. The assigned truth-value is t. The process of questioning is terminated.
- One correct answer and one partially correct answer imply doubt about the student's understanding of the concept. The assigned truth-value is dts. The system first provides additional explanations and then suggests to the student to answer to the same question that has received a partially correct answer.
- One correct answer and one unanswered question imply doubt about the student's understanding of the concept. The assigned truth-value is dtc. The system first provides additional explanations and then suggests to the student to answer one new question taken from the database.
- One correct answer and one wrong answer imply some doubt about the student's understanding of the concept. The assigned truth-value is $\top$. The system first provides additional explanations, selected theory and examples, and then suggests to the student to answer again to the question that has previously received a wrong answer and one new question taken from the database.
- Two partially correct answers imply doubt about the student's understanding of the concept. The assigned truth-value is $d\top$. The system first provides additional explanations selected theory and examples, and then suggests to the student to answer to the same questions.
- One partially correct answer and one one unanswered question imply doubt about the student's understanding of the concept. The assigned truth-value is $*$. The system first provides additional explanations and then suggests to the student to answer two new questions taken from the database.
- One partially correct answer and one wrong answer imply doubt about the student's understanding of the concept. The assigned truth-value is dfs. The system first provides additional explanations selected theory and examples, and then suggests to the student to answer three new questions taken from the database.

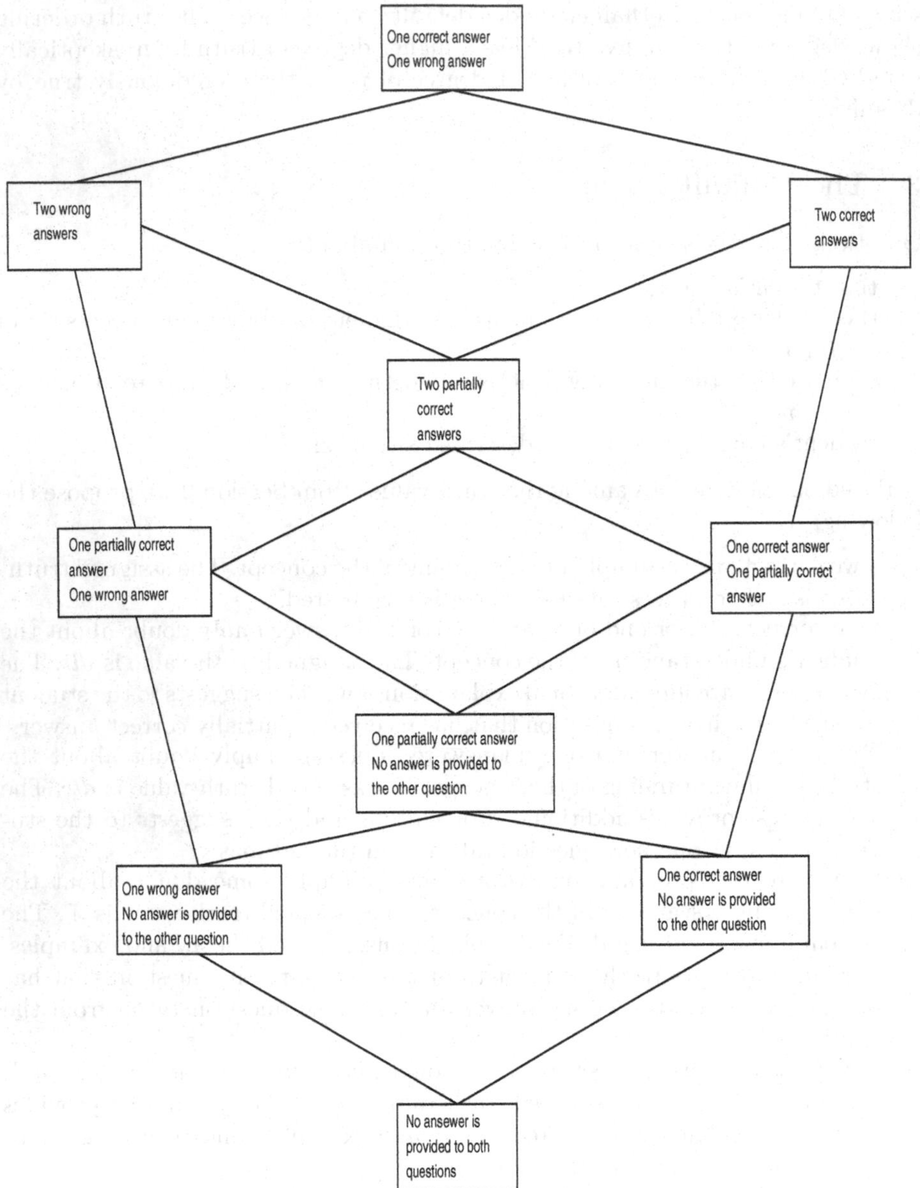

Fig. 2. A bilattice for different answer combinations

– One wrong answer and one unanswered question imply doubt about the student's understanding of the concept. The assigned truth-value is dfc. The system first provides additional explanations selected theory and examples, and then suggests to the student to answer to the question that has previously received a wrong answer and two new questions taken from the database.

- Two wrong answers imply lack of understanding of the concept. The assigned truth-value is *f*. The system first provides additional explanations and then suggests to the student to answer the same questions plus two new questions taken from the database.
- Two unanswered questions imply doubt about the student's understanding of the concept. The assigned truth-value is $\perp$. The system first provides additional explanations and then suggests to the student to answer the same questions plus one new question taken from the database.

A bilattice relating the response combinations is presented on Fig. 2.

4 System Architecture

4.1 System Framework

An intelligent tutoring system based on default logic is useful to students who do their study in a mixed mode learning environment. Such a system must support the traditional the three layered system architecture of presentation, application and data as well as the following sub-systems:

1. Presentation: a Web server that will provide students and teachers with Web user interface to Web based applications for example user registration, user login and MCT and Web pages for example learning objects, test results and user status;
2. Application: users related applications, learning related applications and integration with multi-agents sub-system that provide personal intelligent tutoring of a particular subject;
3. Data: a database that stores user information and status, meta data to learning objects, logical and inference rules related to tests.

Initially the system is provided with all relevant learning objects for a particulars line of study. The teachers responsible for the subjects are also responsible for providing the system with contents and meta-data of learning objects. These learning objects are to be used as a knowledge base for teaching concepts. For each concept thought in a particular unit, some test applications are made to assess students understanding. A test is made of two questions. Each test will result in one of the possible logical consequences as shown on Fig. 2. Following the guide line from Section 3 each consequence will lead a student to a particular learning path depending on the result of a particular test and his/her learning history. Using feedback from students experiences, the teachers can incorporate new tests and learning objects at any time to improve the quality of the tutoring system.

4.2 System Implementation

A typical Web server infrastructure using open sources and free software tools can be used to implement the system. It is a combination of free software tools which include a Web server from apache.org, a database server from sqlite.org and a scripting programming language from python.org on a Linux operating environment.

The Apache server is complemented with security module mod_ssl using OpenSSL toolkit and Python language interpreter module using mod_python. The OpenSSL toolkit implements security libraries for Secure Sockets Layer (SSL v2/v3) and Transport Layer Security (TLS v1) protocols as well as a full-strength general purpose cryptography library. The mod_ssl makes it possible to support secure HTTPS communications between client and server. The mod_python makes it possible to program applications in Python language. Since the interpreter is compiled into the Web sever, mod_python handler is hundreds time faster the using Common Gateway Interface (CGI) method of invoking application softwares. Python provides powerful set of standard libraries like for example networking and database connectivity modules. Using sqlite3 module, a Python program can be directly connected to a SQLite database.

SQLite is a library that provides a lightweight disk-based database. We connect to a database directly from within an application. It does not require a separate database server process to be up and running and allows accessing the database using a nonstandard variant of the Structured Query Language also known as SQL query language. Some applications can use SQLite for internal data storage since SQLite supports database directly in RAM (random access memory).

The deployed Web application server is made of:

1. an Apache front end Web server,
2. a Python based Web application middle-ware for dynamic content, data integration and user interface to software agents,
3. a number of back end databases provided by SQLite for data store of both static and dynamic data.

Together with the Web application server implementation is a service support multi-agents sub-systems. The communication among sub-systems and Web application server is based on remote procedure call using XML (Extensible Markup Language) also known as XML-RPC. The Web application middle-ware and the rules-based intelligent tutoring sub-systems exchange request/response messages in XML using HTTP (Hyper Text Transfer Protocol). The separation of these two software service units makes it possible to modularly design and implement the system as loosely couple independent sub-systems. This is complemented by using multiple databases for different purposes.

The Web application middle-ware and the software agents run independently of each other. As such, they can be situated on different servers. Each of these sub-systems has its own disk-based database. The Web application server implements the Web side of the system while the software agents implement the logical side of the intelligent tutoring side of users, learning a particular subject.

All students using the system must first be registered to the system thus obtaining users identity in the form of identification and password data pair to be used during authentication process. Each registered user will have a user database assign to her. The binding between a user and her database is done at login time. An authenticated user will be given session data that is saved in the user Web browser cookie and is used to identify user for that particular session. The session data is an encrypted piece of information containing user identification, user database name and other operational data. All interaction data for a particular user is stored in her user database. Data stored in users and system databases is used to provide information to sub-systems in decision making processes.

Given a certain result of a test, at a particular student learning state, the intelligent tutoring agent sub-systems will provide the student with the best action to be taken to increase the probability that she will assimilate a piece of knowledge. This optimal learning path is calculated by the system in response to the student interactions and previous learning history.

The users stack profiler module keeps track of user activities history in a stack like data structure in the user database. Each event, like for example response/result of a test or a change of learning flow after following a hint given by the system, is stored in this particular user database. This module provides the percepts to the intelligent modules of the software agents sub-system. The users stack profiler communicates directly with the agents by sending massages over the XML-RPC communication channel. By using some common data stored in the database, the users stack profiler indirectly affects the behavior of the user's agents and vise verse.

The publisher module, in the Web application middle-ware, compiles a page to be presented to a particular user dynamically depending on the user current state and recommendation provided by the intelligent tutoring agent sub-systems. The presentation styles are controlled by declarations in templates files. The publisher module uses a particular template file and together with dynamic variables determined by the user test results, current state and activities history produces an HTML document to be sent back to user Web browser. This module also acts as a handler when a user requests a page or sends a form back to the Web server.

Each learning unit is atomic, self-contained and reusable. The dynamic page publisher makes use of these learning units to provide students with a dynamic and personalized learning material as a direct reaction to students' interaction to the system.

5 Conclusion

Default logic is often used for solving knowledge representation problems in a compact, robust and flexible way. The application of default logic allows more sophisticated feedback and development of better marking schemes. An intelligent tutoring system based on the logical model discussed in this paper is useful to students who do their study in a mixed mode learning environment.

References

1. Ginsberg, M.L.: Multi-valued logics: a uniform approach to inference in artificial intelligence. Computational Intelligence 4, 265–316 (1988)
2. Goodstein, R.L.: Boolean Algebra. Dover Publications, Mineola, NY (2007)
3. Guzmàn, E., Conejo, R.: A model for student knowledge diagnosis through adaptive testing. In: Lester, J.C., Vicari, R.M., Paraguaçu, F. (eds.) ITS 2004. LNCS, vol. 3220, pp. 12–21. Springer, Heidelberg (2004)

4. Huffman, D., Goldberg, F., Michlin, M.: Using computers to create constructivist environments: impact on pedagogy and achievement. Journal of Computers in mathematics and science teaching 22(2), 151–168 (2003)
5. http://www.leeds.ac.uk/perception/v4_mrq.html
6. Johnstone, A.: Effective Practice in Objective Assessment, www.physsci.heacademy.ac.uk/Publications/PracticeGuide/
7. Park, C., Kim, M.: Development of a Level-Based Instruction Model in Web-Based Education. In: Luo, Y. (ed.) CDVE 2004. LNCS, vol. 3190, pp. 215–221. Springer, Heidelberg (2004)
8. Priest, G.: An Introduction to Non-Classical Logic, Cambridge (2001)
9. Prior, A.N.: A Statement of Temporal Realism. In: Copeland, B.J. (ed.) Logic and Reality: Essays on the Legacy of Arthur Prior. Clarendon Press, Oxford (1996)
10. Reiter, R.: A logic for default reasoning. Artificial Intelligence 13, 81–132 (1980)
11. Sabetzadeh, M., Easterbrook, S.: Analysis of Inconsistency in Graph-Based Viewpoints: A Category-Theoretic Approach. In: Proceedings of the 18th IEEE International Conference on Automated Software Engineering (ASE'03), Canada, October 6-10, 2003, pp. 12–22. IEEE Computer Society Press, Los Alamitos (2003)
12. Sakama, C.: Ordering default theories. In: Proceedings of the 18th International Joint Conferance on Artificial Intelligence, pp. 839–844. Morgan Kaufmann, San Francisco (2003)
13. Sakama, C.: Ordering default theories and nonmonotonic logic programs. Theoretical Computer Science 338(1-3), 127–152 (2005)
14. Santos, C.T., Osòrio, F.S.: Integrating intelligent agents, user models, and automatic content categorization in virtual environment. In: Lester, J.C., Vicari, R.M., Paraguaçu, F. (eds.) ITS 2004. LNCS, vol. 3220, pp. 128–139. Springer, Heidelberg (2004)
15. Sim, K.M.: Bilattices and Reasoning in Artificial Intelligence: Concepts and Foundations. Artificial Intelligence Review 15(3), 219–240 (2001)
16. Tafertshofer, P., Granz, A., Antreich, K.J.: Igraine-an implication GRaph-bAsed engINE for fast implication, justification and propagation. IEEE Transaction on Computer-Aided Design of Integrated Circuits and Systems 19(8), 907–927 (2000)
17. Tamir, P.: Justifying the selection of answers in multiple-choice items. International Journal of Science Education 12, 563–573 (1990)
18. Tsovaltzi, D., Fiedler, A., Horacek, H.: A Multi-Dimensional Taxonomy for Automating Hinting. In: Lester, J.C., Vicari, R.M., Paraguaçu, F. (eds.) ITS 2004. LNCS, vol. 3220, pp. 722–781. Springer, Heidelberg (2004)
19. Whitesitt, J.E.: Boolean Algebra and Its Applications, Dover Publications (1995)

Consolidating with Media Streaming Server and Network Storage Card

YongJu Lee[1], SongWoo Sok[1], HagYoung Kim[1], MyungJoon Kim[1], and CheolHoon Lee[2]

[1] Dept. of Internet Server Group, Digital Home Research Division, Electronics and Telecommunications Research Institute, 161 Gajeong-Dong, Yuseong-Gu, Daejeon, Korea
{yongju,swsok,h0kim,joonkim}@etri.re.kr
[2] System Software Lab., Dept. of Computer Engineering, Chungnam National University, Daejeon 305-764, Korea
chlee@ce.cnu.ac.kr

Abstract. Recently there have been a large number of multimedia demands of IP-based applications in tremendous Internet world. However, Internet-based multimedia services typically do not offer any quality of service because of its own characteristics such as network bandwidth. In case of Korea, assumption that dense residential communities sharing their livings and information have their infrastructures like high speed communication network is able to achieve quality of service at a close range. This trend creates new market by creating new type of service in Korean-style Internet server. In this paper, we design and implement the high performance media streaming server focusing on local communities which obtain high speed network bandwidth, using streaming-accelerated network storage card which is enable to offer "zero-copy" interfaces and raw-disk I/O.

1 Introduction

Multimedia content on websites can be accessed in one of two ways: either by downloading the entire content, or by using a streaming server. The streaming server enables a client to start viewing the content much faster, and is the preferred method for long streaming or for watching real-time events on a network. Anyone who has played multimedia streams over the Internet has encountered its quality's degradation severely. However, multimedia services in Korean-style residential district with dense complexity are more adaptable to deploy high-density playback because of abundant Internet infrastructure and closer network nodes. In order to provide a high quality service for multimedia demands, powerful network bandwidth is needed. In this purpose, network storage add-on card (NSCard) for streaming-acceleration is made recently. This NS card can transfer stream data from disks to end users directly in a zero-copy technique via the network without any intervention of host processor in the server[1, 2]. The streaming server with this powerful NS card allows support for varying

T. Enokido, L. Barolli, and M. Takizawa (Eds.): NBiS 2007, LNCS 4658, pp. 495–504, 2007.

quality of service streaming and for providing more plenty of concurrent users. Therefore, we design and implement the high performance streaming server on network-storage card. The main contribution of this paper is the deployment of an NS card and the development of high performance streaming server using it. Through alleviating CPU's burden and gaining zero-copy based I/O bandwidth, we have proved to reach the limits of a system significantly if it is well-configured and apparently used. The remainder of this paper is structured as follows. In section 2, we analyze the present problems and introduce an NS card's practical strength and weakness. In section 3, we discuss our high performance streaming server's architecture and implementation in detail. And then, we show the efficacy of our system through extensive experiment in Section 4. Finally, we conclude the paper in Section 5.

2 System Requirements

In this section, we present preliminary requirements for deploying an NS card and obtaining better performance in Linux. An NS card has its own software device drivers: Stream Disk Array(SDA), PCI Memory(PMEM), TCP Offloading Engine(TOE). Streaming data copied to the PMEM is directly transmitted to network without additional memory copy operations(so-called zero-copy)[3]. Zero-copy technique using above drivers gives better performance if a system is well-configured and used appropriately. SDA is a special purpose disk array optimized for large sequential disk accesses in a way of pipelined I/O.(e.g. a SDA device driver support 1M/512K/256K/128K block sizes). These large block sizes make easier way to alleviate numbers of read() operations, but streaming server designer must consider units of buffering/caching and also be aware of the fact that a fixed block size is not changed dynamically because of applying to modify a unit size in a system widely, is not used in common with separate files because of interval's differentiation among files. Peripheral memory is equipped with DRAM memory modules and is dedicated to temporary buffer on disk-to-network data path without user's context switching. In general, PMEM is not adaptable to calculating like a main memory.(e.g. PMEM's memcpy/memset call is approximately four or five times slower than main memory's). This limitation also is considered for designing non-arithmetic streaming operations. Lastly, TOE provides protocol-based offload network interfaces without modification in the light of an application developer. In general, a streaming server makes use of threads for each connection to clients because of the independency among connections. Demands of large scale performance lead to the difficulty of this approach because of many threads. However, the Native POSIX Thread Library(NPTL) is encouraged to us for using independent thread handling without system degradation[4]. Together with this effort, we choose an N:M model to improve CPU's time-slice ticks and to avoid silly waiting. In conventional operation, we allocate a main memory and opens a suitable file and a socket. Thereafter, we read a file and send its data until end-of-file. In our fast-path I/O operation, we prepare a PMEM device and allocate a SDA_SIZE's memory using new interface like *'pmem_alloc(device_id)'*. Next, we read a file without additional API's modification. The reason is that we also implements zero-copy supported file system(EXT3NS)[5]. One of fast-path I/O and legacy I/O is determined by an argument to the system call in a user buffer address. If read()'s buffer is a general main memory as shown Fig. 1(a), there is no additional work in file system(e.g. *generic_file_read*()). However, if a PMEM address space is in use, SDA's software interface, for example *ext3ns_sda_file_read*() in our file system, is called, as shown in Fig. 1(b).

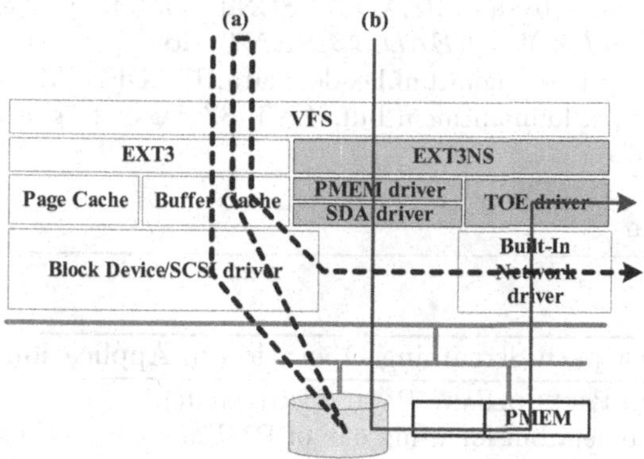

Fig. 1. Basic Streaming Operation in User/Kernel Space

Table 1. Fast-path I/O in Kernel Space

```
// This function is located in kernel space.
ssize_t  ext3ns_file_read(struct file *filp, char *buf, size_t count, loff_t *ppos)
{
   pmem_addr_t pmem_paddr = (*__ns_virt_to_phys)((const void*)buf);
// If a user requests a pmem buffer, read() calls
// ext3ns_sda_file_read() using zero-copy. If not,
// generic_file_read() is called as though a general file system
   if( pmem_paddr && (*pmem_check)((unsigned)pmem_paddr) >=0)
         ext3ns_sda_file_read(filp, buf, count, ppos);
   else
         generic_file_read(filep, buf, count, ppos);
}
```

Table 1 shows fath-path I/O operation in kernel space. We check a memory address in read() system call, and it braches off legacy buffered-I/O and raw-disk I/O. Algorithm 1 and 2 show comparison between conventional- and our fast-path I/O- streaming operations

Algorithm 1. General Streaming Operation in Application Space

```
procedure VOID PSEUDO_GENERAL_STREAMER()
  ▷ We can allocate a send_buffer using malloc() for payload and header of streaming data. HEADER means a streaming protocol's header such as RTP(Realtime Transport Protocol).
    char main_mem_buf[PAYLOAD_SZ+HEADER_SZ];
    while !eof do
        read_sz = read(file_fd,main_mem_buf+HEADER_SZ,PAYLOAD_SZ);
  ▷ mayIgo() is a trivial function name for rate's controlling during interval. SENT_SZ is a unit of sending bytes and READ_SZ_SENT is a total packet size.
        while mayIgo()! = READ_SZ_SENT do
            memcpy(main_mem_buf,header_data,HEADER_SZ);
            send(sock_fd,main_mem_buf,SENT_SZ,flags);   ▷ general send() function
        end while                                        ▷ do until mayIgo()
    end while                                            ▷ do until eof
end procedure
```

Algorithm 2. Fast-path Streaming Operation in Application Space

```
procedure VOID PSEUDO_FAST-PATH_STREAMER()
  ▷ We declare a pmem_buf for using one of PMEM's address space.
    char *pmem_buf=NULL;
    char main_mem[HEADER_SZ];
    pd = pmem_init("/dev/ns0");                          ▷ first NSCard
    pmem_buf = pmem_alloc(pd);                           ▷ pmem allocates
    while !eof do
        read_sz = read(data_file_fd,pmem_buf,SDA_SIZE);
        while mayIgo()! = READ_SZ_SENT do
            memcpy(main_mem,header_data,HEADER_SZ);
            struct iovec datavec[2];
            datavec[0].iov_base = main_mem;              ▷ a pointer of main memory
            datavec[0].iov_len = HEADER_SZ;
            datavec[1].iov_base = pmem_buf;              ▷ a pointer of PMEM
            datavec[1].iov_len = PAYLOAD_SZ;
  ▷ Assign message header using datavec array.
            struct msghdr msg.msg_iov = (struct iovec*)&datavec;
            sendmsg(sock_fd,msg,SENT_SZ,flags);          ▷ sendmsg() function
            pmem_buf += PAYLOAD_SZ;
  ▷ pmem_buf's location must be rearranged for next pumping. This means that we hold a pmem unit until SENT_SZ reaches fragmentation numbers (e.g. is equal to division PAYLOAD_SZ into SDA_SIZE )
        end while                                        ▷ do until mayIgo()
    end while                                            ▷ do until eof
    pmem_free(pmem_buf);                                 ▷ pmem deallocates.
    pmem_fin(pd);                                        ▷ release a pmem block.
end procedure
```

3 Media Streaming Server Architecture

As shown in Fig. 2, our media streaming server can be implemented in a network in the form of several transcoding proxy streaming severs(TPSSs) and a content streaming server(CSS) to perform streaming and transcoding on-the-fly. There are same nature that TPSS and CSS can deliver the streaming data to the client, but especially, TPSS has the additional functionality that it transcodes streaming data to adaptive stream rate via hardware Digital Signal Processing units(DSPs) or software transcoders. Hence, it consists of a main process (hereafter "MP") and an ns process (hereafter "NP") which number is the same as number of network storage card, for example 4 , in given figure. An RtspDaemon thread of the media streaming server,which basically controls streaming data using RTSP/RTP[6, 7, 8], creates an RtspThreadController thread which controls the creation and assignment of an RtspStackThread and has a FIFO which keeps a great number of RTSP connections. The RtspThreadController thread also passes an RTSP connection to the RtspStackThread through PIPE. The RtspStackthread manages maximum number of RTSP connections, manipulates RTSP messages and stores them to the specific shared memory area. If a recvIPCNSSharedMemory thread in specific NP receives an RTSP request, it is added by a session manager to the session manager's map table.

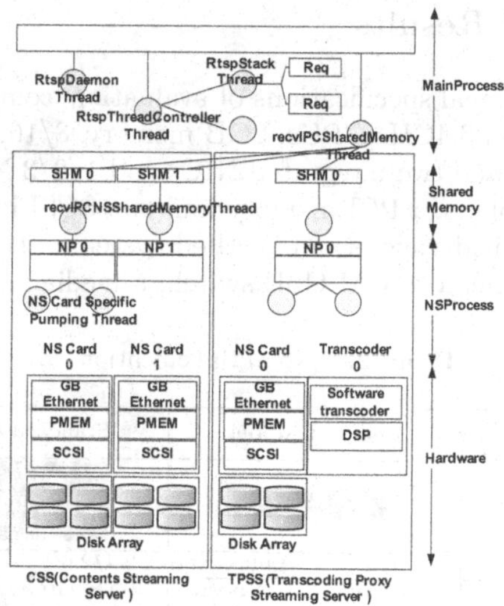

Fig. 2. MainProcess(MP)/NSProcess(NP) Architecture

Fig. 3 shows a streaming engine class diagram which consists of a lot of subclasses for manipulating streaming requests. Each filled-box represents a representative class name including a member class in a lined-box. First of all, the MainProcess class acts on controlling RTSP protocol, communicating with

NSProcess, monitoring system health, providing a short structured textual description(SDP: Session Description Protocol[9]), and manipulating clients' connections. Secondly, the NSProcess class consists of IPCSubController, Configurator and SessionManager. The IPCSubController communicates with MP from reserved area. Thirdly, the StreamingService class loaded by the SessionManager dynamically contains a variety of MPEG-1/2/4 services that have their own TCP/UDP/RTP sender instance which determines when and how much data should be sent to the client in a way like unicast/multicast types.

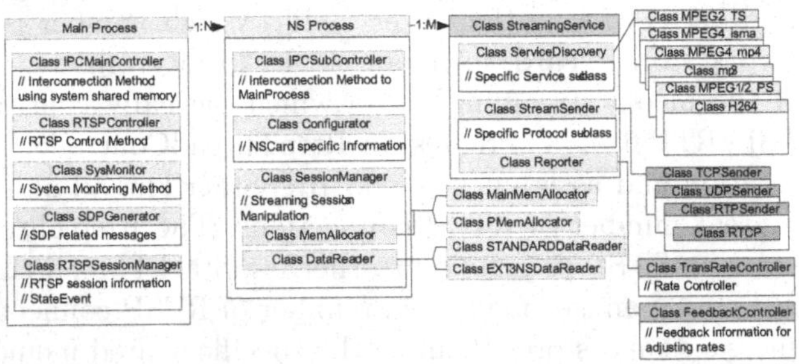

Fig. 3. Streaming Engine Class Diagram

4 Experimental Results

Table 2 shows the principal specifications of evaluation/commercial platform. A node contains two Xeon 3.4GHz CPUs, 2GB memory, 8/16/24 disks(configured as StripingOverSDA), and two integrated NICs and 1/2/3 NSCards which integrates two GbE controllers, a PCI memory and two SCSI interfaces.

Fig. 4 shows a detailed view of out testbed system. The testbed consists of a shooter Linux machine, a 3COM GbE switch, a media streaming server node

Table 2. System Specification

Model / *Feature*	Compact Model	Standard Model
System Feature		
OS/FS	Linux Kernel 2.4/2.6	
NS/HDD	1 NS with 2Gbps ports Max. 6 Hot-swap 876GB	3 NS with 6Gbps port Max. 24 Hot-swap 3.5TB
Interface	IPSTB/IPTV/OpenCable,OCAP,DOCSIS v2.0	
NSCard image	SCSI Connector, Disk Controller, SCSI Connector, Intel 80321 IOP, SDRAM 512MB, Dual Ethernet Connector, Network Controller, PCI-to-PCI Bridge	

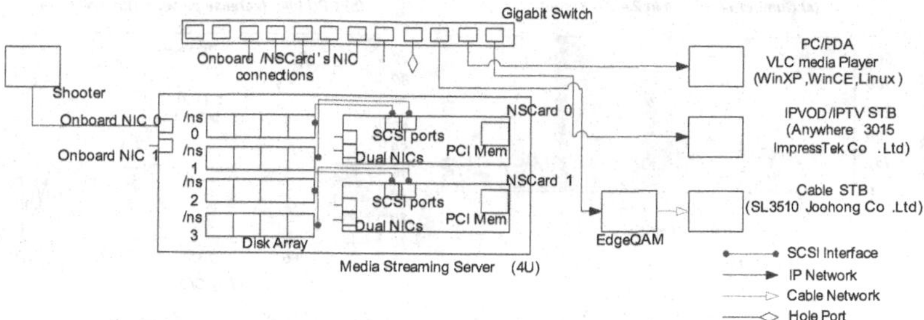

Fig. 4. Testbed Environment

with two NSCard and 16 disk arrays, an EdgeQAM for converting IP packets to RF signals and client terminals, e.g. PC/PDA player as open source VideoLan Player, IPVOD/IPTV STB and CableSTB,respectively[10, 11, 12, 13]. An NS card is interconnected by a disk array for serving large volumes and a Gigabit interface for controlling and transmitting streaming data in a form of zero-copy by help of a PCI Memory. Moreover, a port of Gigabit switch must be configured by a dummy port, namely a black hole, in a way that merely flows into the port whether physically connected or not[14]. We can also set up an ARP table in Linux system to add an address mapping entry for flowing the selected port[15]. To simulate to determine how well the media streaming server can transmit data to clients, the shooter Linux machine generates virtual client requests via RTSP messages using in-house utility, so-called "PseudoPlayer", which is implemented to deal with virtual user connections. The PseudoPlayer utility has several parameters: the content name, virtual client's address, streaming server address. Using input parameters, the PseudoPlayer is possible to execute a various way of protocols such as UDP, TCP and RTP. Through the PseudoPlayer's request, A media streaming server can receive virtual RTSP messages and interacts with individual clients, select a NS card (e.g. selection is also another part of research as Contents Distribution framework, we can fix a simple round-robin approach for testing) and streams data to the clients. To evaluate the throughput of concurrent sessions, the majority of streams ,as has been noted above, must be discarded at the switch hardware level besides browsing several streams and measuring for packet loss.

In Fig. 5(a), we measure the maximum number of streams on four different types. "Ideal NIC Limitation" is computed by division of NS card's NIC capacity by a bitrate (e.g., 200 streams are equal to the division of 2 GbE NICs by 10Mbps at 1 NS card). Its parameters are two hundred video objects,a 10Mbps bitrate, 1/2/3 various NS cards. Streaming requests are partitioned among a node's mount points (e.g, "/ns0" has 50 video objects) according to a Zipf distribution(e.g., of 0.47) and arrived at the node according to a fixed rate poisson process[16, 17]. Fig. 5(b),(c) and (d) show CPU idle/non-idle utilization under two NS cards. We measure streaming throughput on three different type of operating kernels: (i) standard Linux kernel without NS cards, (ii) Linux 2.4 kernel with the zero-copy patch and NS cards,

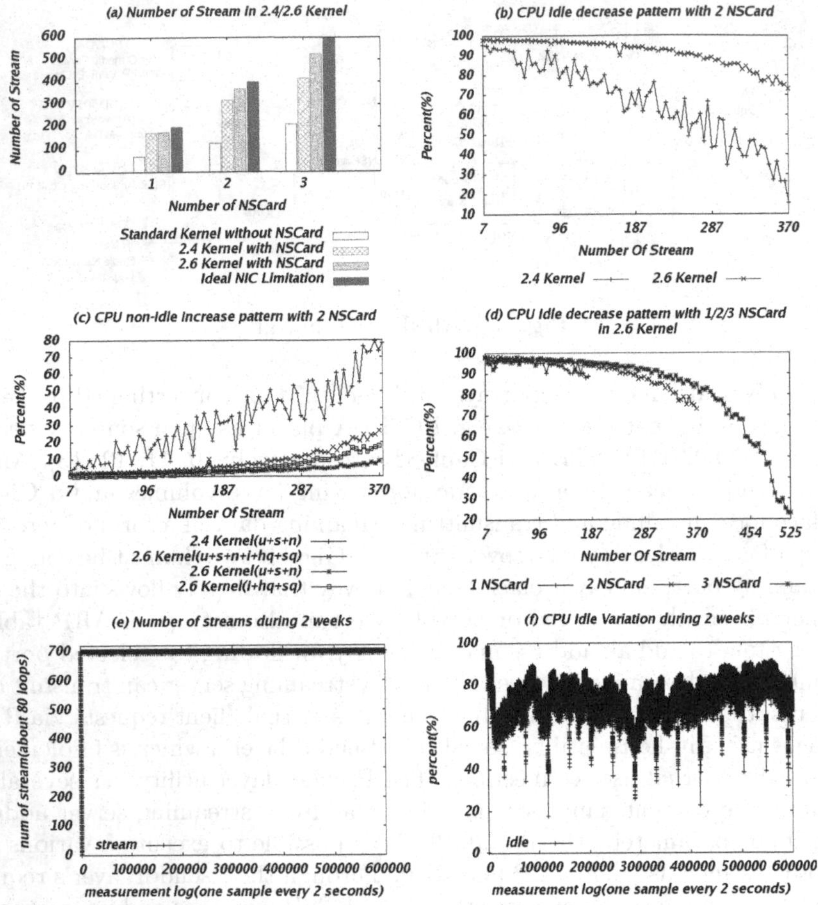

Fig. 5. Number of Stream/CPU Usage Patterns

(iii) Linux 2.6 kernel with the zero-copy patch and NS cards. X axis denotes the number of NS cards(up to 3 cards) and Y axis is the maximum number of streams without jitter. Linux 2.6 kernel equipped with NS cards gives better performance than standard Linux kernel and Linux 2.4 kernel. Linux 2.4 kernel's CPU idle pattern lead to more diverse and unstable values than 2.6 kernel's. Especially, its value is about 5 times lower than that of 2.6 kernel at the case of 370 streams, as shown in Fig. 5(b). Fig. 5(d) also demonstrates example of no interference even if a node equips up to three NS cards within the limits of the maximum PCI slots. Fig. 5(e)(f) depict,respectively, number of streams and CPU idle variation curve in the event of seamless 700 streams during two weeks. Fig. 6 shows the number of zero-loss streams in various content types. "Standard 2/4 NIC" means standard Linux 2.4 kernel with legacy NICs and "1/2 NS cards" also means Linux 2.4 kernel with the zero-copy patch and NS cards. This test report is offered by Telecommunications

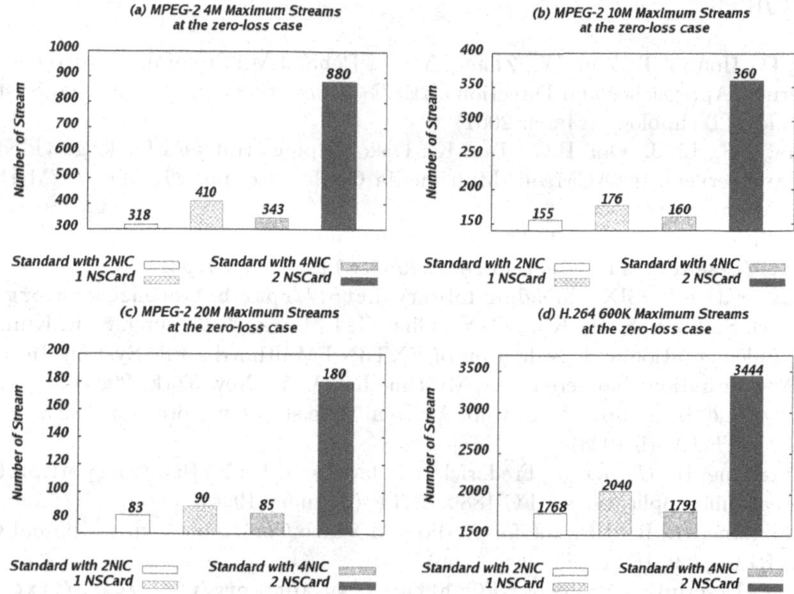

Fig. 6. MPEG-2 4/10/20M,H.264 600K's Server Stream Capacity between standard and 1/2 NSCard-enabled system in Linux 2.4 Kernel(source: TTA test reports)

Technology Association(TTA) which provides an organization for national telecom standardization and certificated test[18].

5 Conclusion

In this paper, we have presented a media streaming server with streaming-accelerated hardware and deployed Korean-style Internet server specialized on HD-level services. Especially, we have demonstrated collaboration streaming operations and fast-path I/O functionality via NS cards. Performance evaluation shows the improvement in streaming throughput without CPU's burden. Future works include supporting Fibre channel interface and integrating Content Delivery Network(CDN).

Acknowledgement

This research is based on a part of Next-Generation Internet Server, so-called NGIS, project for the purpose of development of a Korean-style server to provide HDTV-level streaming service up to one thousand client in the high speed communication network of 2-20 Mbps.

References

1. Wu, D., Hou, Y.T., Zhu, W., Zhang, Y.-Q., Peha, J.M.: Streaming Video over the Internet: Approaches and Directions. IEEE Transactions on Circuits and Systems for Video Technology (March 2001)
2. Chua, T.S., Li, J., Ooi, B.C., Tan, K.: Disk striping strategies for large video-on-demand servers. In: ACM Int. Multimedia Conference, pp. 297–306. ACM Press, New York (1996)
3. An Efficient Zero-Copy I/O Framework for Unix: `http://research.sun.com/techrep/1995/smli_tr-95-39.pdf`
4. Linux: Native POSIX Threading Library, `http://nptl.bullopensource.org/`
5. Ahn, B.-S., Sohn, S.-H., Kim, C.-Y., Cha, G.-I., Baek, Y.-C, Jung, S.-I., Kim, M.-J.: Implementation and Evaluation of EXT3NS Multimedia File System. In: Proc. ACM international conference on Multimedia. ACM, New York (2004)
6. Schulzrinne, H., Lanphier, R., Rao, A.: Real time streaming protocol (RTSP) RFC 2326. IETF (April 1998)
7. Schulzrinne, H., Casner, S., Frederick, R., Jacobson, V.: RTP: a transport protocol for real-time applications RFC 1889. IETF (January 1996)
8. Schulzrinne, H.: RTP Profile for Audio and Video Conferences with Minimal Control. RFC 1809, IETF (January 1996)
9. Session Description Protocol RFC: `http://www.ietf.org/rfc/rfc2327.txt`
10. EdgeQAM vendor: `http://www.harmonicinc.com`
11. Opensource VideoLanClient Player Project: `http://www.videolan.org`
12. IP based solution vendor: `http://www.impresstek.co.kr/en/`
13. Cable STB vendor: `http://www.joohong.co.kr`
14. L2 Switching Basics - MAC learning: `http://www.ciscopress.com/articles/article.asp?p=101367\&rl=1`
15. Lee, Y.-J., Min, O.-G., Kim, H.-Y.: Performance Evaluation Technique of the RTSP based Streaming Server. In: ACIS Intl. Conf. on Computer and Information Science, vol. 4(1) (July 2005)
16. Zipf's Law: `http://en.wikipedia.org/wiki/Zipf's_law`
17. Poisson Distribution: `http://mathworld.wolfram.com/PoissonDistribution.html`
18. TTA: `http://www.tta.or.kr/English/new/main/index.htm`

Design of the Tile-Based Embedded Multimedia Processor –TEMP–

Shinya Toji, Minoru Uehara, and Hideki Mori

Department of Open Information Systems Graduate School of Engineering
Toyo University, Saitama, Japan
{gz0600171,mori,uehara}@toyonet.toyo.ac.jp

Abstract. An advanced multimedia processing unit is needed for the DVD player, the music player, and the video game machine, etc., we propose a sub-processor for advanced multimedia processing for built-in usage. We achieve the necessary arithmetic capacity equal with the processing, only for the multimedia by proposing multimedia processing is done by extended instruction. The tile processor is adopted as architecture of the processor. The tile processor can reduce the wiring delay that happens because of tile positioning, and is suitable for the miniaturization required for built-in processors. Moreover, the high parallel processing ability of the tile architecture is the best for media operations involving same operation and repetitions of data volume. With the aim of time efficiency, SIMD style operation was installed. However with device miniaturization a high level of integrations necessary

Keywords: Embedded System, Tile-Based Processor.

1 Introduction

The rapid evolution of multimedia due to the spread of the Internet in the latter half of the 20th century has created demand for devices such as cellular phones and DVD players, with high-speed voice image data processing. For this, the ability to execute the image data processing and the voice processing, etc. in real time is necessary. As a result, the multimedia processor appeared in general-purpose CPUs which depended on a multimedia extension instruction with special MMX instructions. Given the nature of the miniaturization (embedding multimedia capable processors etc) it follows that a high level of integration is necessary. It fallows too that RSP and reliability are also demanded. So, we propose tile architecture and SIMD type multimedia extension instruction for the multimedia processing which is appropriate for built-in processors using reduced time interval.

The wiring delay often found in processors with a high level of integration built in is significantly reduced with tile architecture. This design reduces the wiring delay between tiles by limiting communication proximity only to/and between tiles in close physical.

T. Enokido, L. Barolli, and M. Takizawa (Eds.): NBiS 2007, LNCS 4658, pp. 505–512, 2007.

The SIMD (Single Instruction Multiple Data) instruction is an instruction, via which two or more pieces of data can be processed by one instruction. As SIMD allows high speed operations, such as simultaneous processing and repetition processing, image processing and filtering processing for voice processing is possible. Moreover, it becomes easy to change and debug the algorithm because it is program based rather than hard-wired. It follows then that Rapid System Prottyping (RSP) can be assured. In this paper, the enhanced instruction set for multimedia, in accordance with INTEL MMX, is defined and implemented on tile architecture.

2 Related Works

2.1 TRIPS

The tile processor named TRIPS presently under research at Texas University utilizes a concept of data flow architecture [1]. TRIPS consists of 16 processing elements in 4×4 arrays, which consist of integer units, floating point arithmetic units, input ports, output ports, operand buffers, and routers. The 16 (4 x 4) processing arrays are the main core, and the instruction cache, the data cache, and the registers are located in the immediate surroundings of the core. Each tile communicates with adjacent tiles. Each tile executes the instruction as soon as data arrives. This part looks like the architecture of the data flow machine. In the case of instruction fetch, delay occurs. To eliminate this delay, two or more instructions are fetched at the same time.

Figure 1 shows the block diagram of 4×4 TRIPS processors.

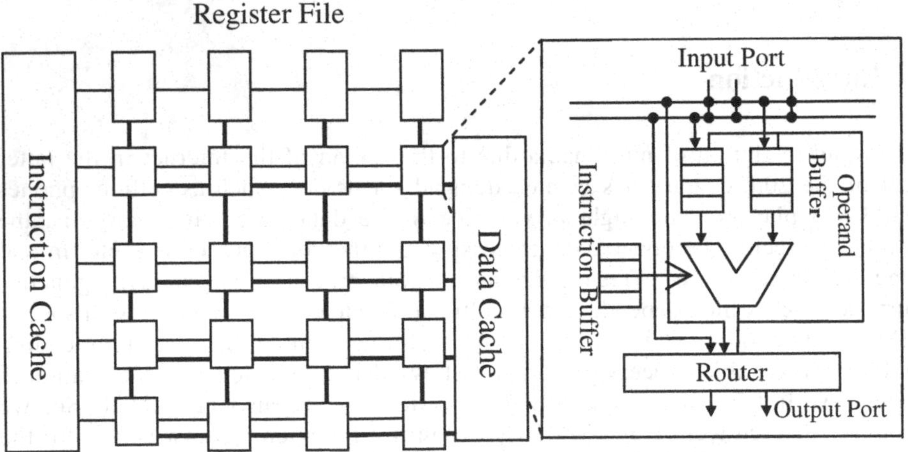

Fig. 1. Block diagram of 4×4 TRIPS processor

Please punctuate a displayed equation in the same way as ordinary text but with a small space before the end punctuation.

2.2 Data Flow Machine

The data flow method is based on the computing model described Dennis in 1974 [2].

The operation of the data flow method is shown in Figure 2. The nodes in the data flow graph show the input-output line of the data known as arc links and shows operations such as addition, and subtraction, etc. It starts by putting the data token in the input link of the data flow graph. Afterwards, the calculation is executed according to the following rules [3].

A node fires when all tokens in the input link become available.

When the node fires, the token is removed from the input link, and the node sends the token corresponding to the operation to the output link.

Figure 2 shows the actual operation example.

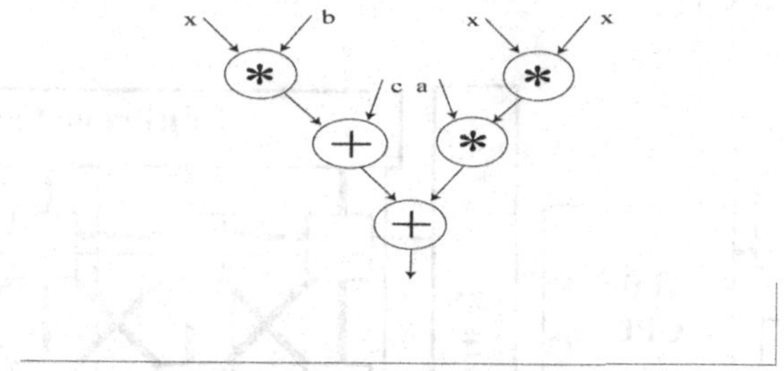

Fig. 2. Dataflow Graph of $ax^2 + bx + c$

In TRIPS, each node in the graph corresponds to a tile. There is another rule in the data flow model. It is that "Only one token can exist in the one link at one time". This rule however does not apply, when the data flow graph is used repeatedly, in which case, redundancy must be inserted. So, a dynamic computing model that applies tags to the token is expedient. Accordingly, one token or more is allowed to be put in each link in a dynamic computing model because tags are applied to the token.

And, the rule of the ignition changes as follows.

The node fires when the token with the same tag becomes available in the input link. The input token is removed after it has fired, and a new tag is applied to the output token, and the node sends it to the output link.

The operation begins when a complete data set is stored in the operand buffer, TRIPS doesn't actually operate dynamically. TRIPS are however based on the idea of data flow architecture.

3 Tile-Based Embedded Multimedia Processor (TEMP)

The Tile-Based Embedded Multimedia Processor (TEMP) operates as follows;

- TEMP executes only multimedia processing as an assistant processor. When an Instruction is executed, it gets data from the main processor through a common register. The instruction is stored by an instruction register of TEMP. TEMP executes a similar instruction as an MMX instruction with the applicable and data. The operation result is sent from the data cache to main CPU□

- Operation tiles are arranged in a 4-by-4 grid. Data flows multi-directionally along the grid with significant wiring delay reductions, while the addition of the diagonal data flow option seems to have a negative effect on wiring delay evasion, the increased flexibility more than compensates.
- To execute TEMP first breakdowns a complex multimedia instruction into simple instruction sets. TEMP hands a sets to each tile. In addition, it stores the data which is necessary to begin a calculation to a register. A tile upon operation completion sends the result to the next tile. TEMP executes an SIMD instruction by repeating this process.
- As most multimedia data consists of 256 gradations, a data set size of 8bit was instituted. TEMP executes an SIMD instruction to process eight 8bit data at a time. Accordingly, SIMD operation sets of TEMP results in a doubling of available processing.

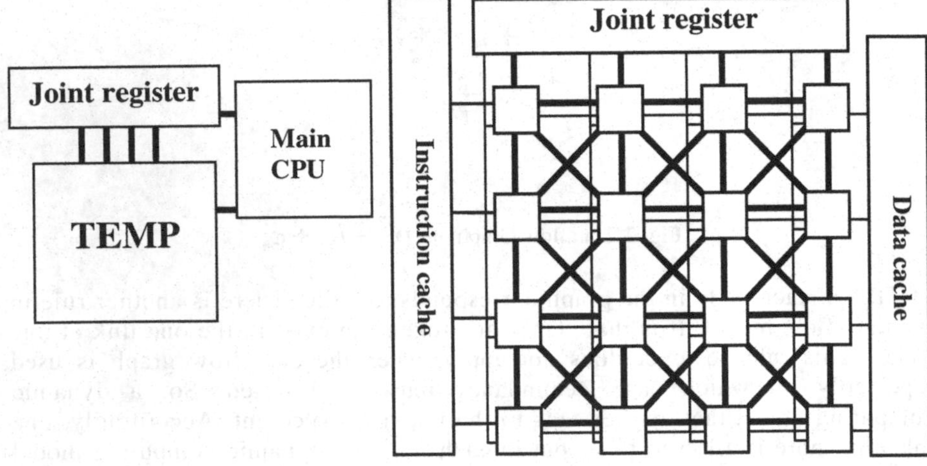

Fig. 3. Design of TEMP

32bit			
Data A(8bit)	Data B(8bit)	Data C(8bit)	Data D(8bit)

Fig. 4. Packed data type

4 Decision of Instruction

Temp utilizes MMX instructions to execute operations. (See Table1 for full instruction list) List is simple. As a store instruction has been added to same tiles operation can be automatically results send to the data cache.

Each instruction packet consists of 4bit as an operation cord to distinguish an order, and 4bit to decide a destination of an operation result and 8bit for immediate data. It is 16bit in total. Figure 5 is form of an instruction packet. Conventional loading of instruction is non-existent.

OP(4bit)	DEST(4bit)	IMME(8bit)

Fig. 5. Form of an instruction packet

Table 1. An instruction of an operation tile

operation code	instruction name	action
0000	THR	Through A
0001	AND	A and B
0010	OR	A or B
0011	EOR	A eor B
0100	NOT	Not A
0101	ADD	A + B
0110	SUB	A - B
0111	MUL	A * B
1000	ADDI	A + immediate data
1001	SUBI	A - immediate data
1010	MULI	A * immediate data
1011	NOP	No Operation
1100	ST	Store A
1101	SL	Shift left A
1110	SRL	Shift right logical A
1111	SRA	Shift right arithmetic A

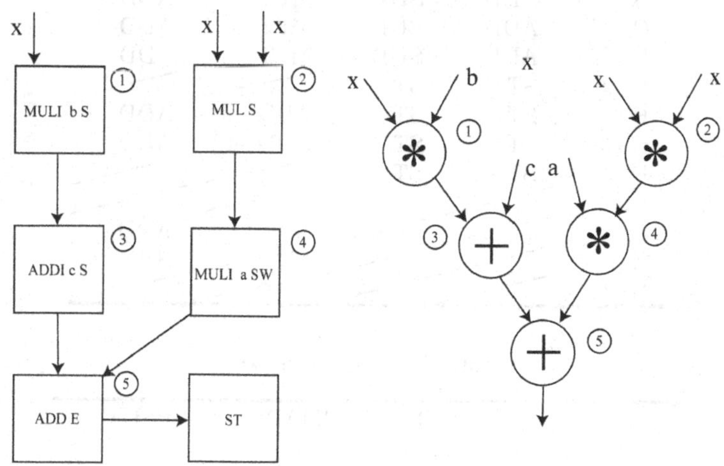

Fig. 6. Operation example with TEMP

When it uses an instruction from table 1, TEMP can execute a calculation as shown in figure 6. In addition, TEMP executes a similar instruction in an MMX instruction such as PADD, PSUB, PMULL, and PMADD. In addition, it can easily execute processing -We named PSUM- to calculate sum of the eight data in addition to an MMX instruction.

5 Allocation of Tile Algorithm

The TEMP made was able to four SIMD instructions -PADD and PSUB and PMADD and PSUM-.Table 3 shows allocation option

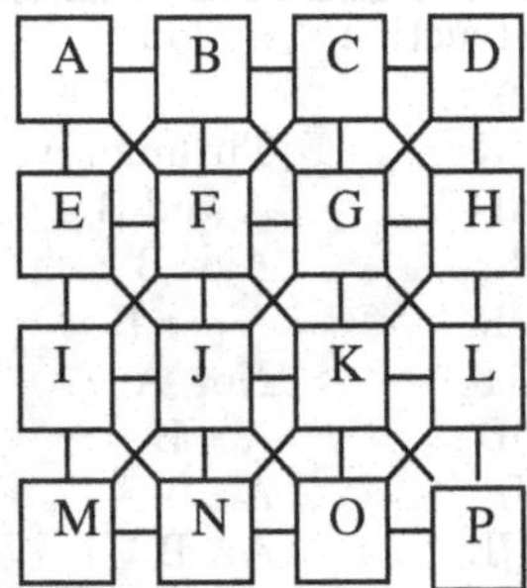

Fig. 7. Tile Allocation

Table 2. Example of an instruction allocation

	PADD	PSUB	PMADD	PSUM
A	ADD	SUB	MUL	ADD
B	ADD	SUB	MUL	ADD
C	ADD	SUB	MUL	ADD
D	ADD	SUB	MUL	ADD
E	ST	ST		
F	ST	ST	ADD	ADD
G	ST	ST	ADD	ADD
H	ST	ST		
I				
J			ST	ADD
K				ST
L~P				

Table 3. Number of clocks

	PADD、 PSUB	PMADD	PSUM
SISD	4clocks	6clocks	7clocks
TEMP(SIMD)	2clocks	3clocks	4clocks

Table 3 shows that clocks of TEMP decrease than SISD, The slanted lines show the tiles which TEMP did not use when it executed a SIMD instruction in table 2. In other words this implementation of SIMD instruction does not make full utilization of the available tiles. Efficiency increases with more complex calculation.

6 Simulation of Tiles

Tiles follow the specifications of the preceding sections. Using a VerilogHDL, design simulation a tile gate level check was conducted. Table 4 shows results of logic synthesis.

Table 4. Performance results of TEMP

	number of the gates	power consumption
Operation tile	1650	12mW

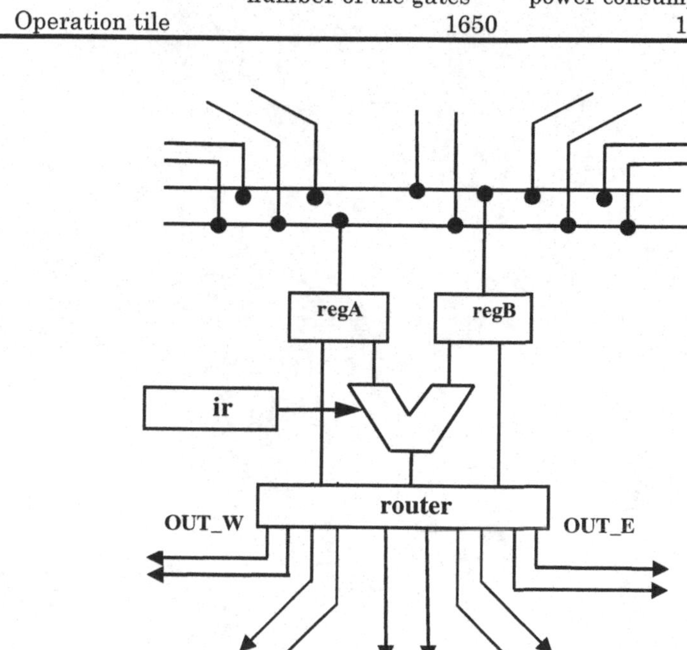

Fig. 8. Operation tile

7 Conclusion

SIMD instruction improves data processing speed but does not fully utilize tile capacity. The simulated performance of tile architecture showed that the proposed architecture is appropriate for multimedia applications. Howevcr in the applications the algorithm allocation presents a challenge and requires further study, perhaps involving more complex calculations.

References

1. Sankaralingam, K., Nagarajan, R., Liu, H., Huh, J., Kim, C.K., Burger, D., Keckler, S.W., Moore, C.R.: Exploiting ILP, TLP, and DLP Using Polymorphism in the TRIPS Architecture. In: 30th Annual International Symposium on Computer Architecture (ISCA), pp. 422–433 (June 2003)
2. Dennis, J.B.: First version of a data flow procedure language. In: Robinet, B. (ed.) Programming Symposium. LNCS, vol. 19, pp. 362–376. Springer, Heidelberg (1974)
3. Sharp, J.A.: Data Flow Computing. Ellis Horwood Limited, Chichester, England (1985)

A Fuzzy-Based Speed-Aware Handoff System for Wireless Cellular Networks

Leonard Barolli[1], Arjan Durresi[2], Fatos Xhafa[3], and Akio Koyama[4]

[1] Department of Information and Communication Engineering
Fukuoka Institute of Technology (FIT)
3-30-1 Wajiro-Higashi, Higashi-ku, Fukuoka 811-0295, Japan
barolli@fit.ac.jp

[2] Department of Computer Science, Louisiana State University
Baton Rouge, LA 70803, USA
durresi@csc.lsu.edu

[3] Department of Languages and Informatics Systems
Polytechnic University of Catalonia
Jordi Girona 1-3, 08034 Barcelona, Spain
fatos@lsi.upc.edu

[4] Department of Informatics, Yamagata University
4-3-16 Jonan, Yonezawa 992-8510, Yamagata, Japan
akoyama@eie.yz.yamagata-u.ac.jp

Abstract. Presently, the wireless mobile networks and devices are becoming increasingly popular to provide users the access anytime and anywhere. The mobile systems are based on cellular approach and the area is covered by cells that overlap each other. In mobile cellular systems the handover is a very important process, which refers to a mechanism that transfers an ongoing call from one Base Station (BS) to another. The performance of the handover mechanism is very important to maintain the desired Quality of Service (QoS). Many handover algorithms are proposed in the literature. However, to make a better handover and keep the QoS in wireless networks is very difficult. In this paper, we propose a fuzzy-based speed-aware handover system. The performance evaluation via simulations shows that proposed system has a good handover decision.

1 Introduction

As the demand for multimedia services over the air has been steadily increasing over the last few years, wireless multimedia networks have been a very active research area [1,2]. The QoS support for future wireless networks is a very important problem. To guarantee the QoS, a good handover strategy is needed in order to balance the call blocking and call dropping for providing the required QoS [3,4].

In the future, the wireless networks will adopt a micro/pico cellular architecture. However, smaller cell size naturally increases the number of handoffs a Mobile Terminal (MT) is expected to make. As the new call arrival rate or load increases, the probability of handoff failure increases. This phenomenon combined with the large number of handoffs before completion of a call increases the forced termination probability of calls [5,6].

T. Enokido, L. Barolli, and M. Takizawa (Eds.): NBiS 2007, LNCS 4658, pp. 513–522, 2007.

Many metrics have been used to support handover decisions, including Received Signal Strength (RSS), Signal to Interference Ratio (SIR), distance between the mobile and BS, traffic load, and mobile velocity, where RSS is the most commonly used one. The conventional handover decision compares the RSS from the serving BS with that from one of the target BSs, using a constant handover threshold value (handover margin). The selection of this margin is crucial to handover performance. If the margin is too small, numerous unnecessary handovers may be processed. Conversely, the QoS could be low and calls could be dropped if the margin is too large. The fluctuations of signal strength associated with shadow fading cause a call sometimes to be repeatedly handed over back and forth between neighboring BSs, in what is called the ping-pong effect [7].

Recently, many investigations have addressed handover algorithms for cellular communication systems. However, its essentially complex to make handover decision considering multiple criteria. Sometimes, the trade-off of some criteria should be considered. Therefore, heuristic approaches based on Neural Networks (NN), Genetic Algorithms (GA) and Fuzzy Logic (FL) can prove to be efficient for wireless networks [8,9,10,11]. In [10], a multi-criteria handover algorithm for next generation tactical communication systems is introduced. The handover metrics are: RSS from current and candidate base transceivers, ratio of used soft capacity to the total soft capacity of base transceivers, the relative directions and speeds of the base transceivers and the mobile node. In [11], a handover algorithm is proposed to support vertical handover between heterogeneous networks. This is achieved by incorporating the mobile IP principles in combination with FL concepts utilizing different handover parameters. However, these algorithms seem to be complex, because the number of fuzzy rules is high.

Rapid progress in the research and development of wireless networking and communication technologies has created different types of wireless communication systems, such as Bluetooth for personal area, IEEE 802.11-based WLANs for local area, Universal Mobile Telecommunications System (UMTS) for wide area, and satellite networks for global networking. These networks are complementary to each other and, hence, their integration can realize unified Next Generation Wireless Systems (NGWS) that have the best features of the individual networks to provide ubiquitous communication for mobile users [12,13,14].

In this paper, in different from other works by considering a mixed cell architecture, we propose a FL-based speed-aware handover system that consist of three FLC. The FLC1 determines the speed of MT. Then, the FLC2 makes the handover decision for slow-speed users and FLC3 for high-speed users. In this paper, we consider a 2-layer structure, where micro cells are in the low layer and macro cells on the upper layer which serve as umbrella. However, the work can be extended considering the universal wireless networks coverage [14].

The structure of this paper is as follows. In Section 2, we present the handover decision problem. In Section 3, we introduce the proposed system. In Section 4, we discuss the simulation results. Finally, some conclusions are given in Section 5.

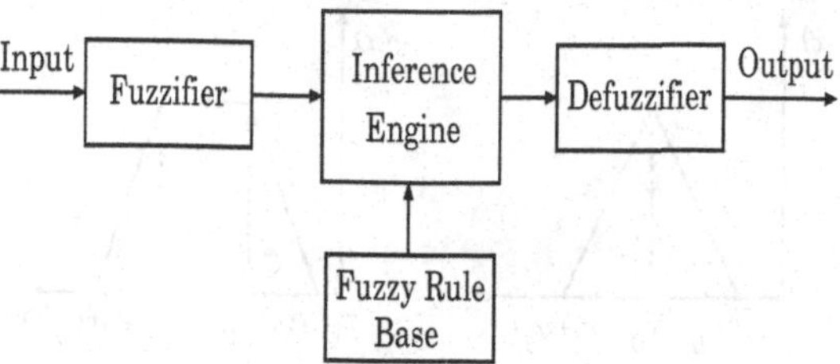

Fig. 1. FLC structure

2 Handover Decision Problem

Handoffs which are consistently both accurate and timely can result in higher capacity and better overall link quality than what is available with today systems. Now with increasing demands for more system capacity, there is a trend toward smaller cells, also known as microcells. Handoffs are more critical in systems with smaller cells, because for a given average user speed, handoff rates tend to be inversely proportional to cell size [5].

The main objectives of handover are link quality maintenance, interference reduction and keeping the number of handoffs low. Also, a handover algorithm should initiate a handoff if and only if the handoff is necessary. The accuracy of a handover algorithm is based on how the algorithm initiates the handover process. The timing of the handoff initiation is also important. There can be deleterious effects on link quality and interference is the initiation is too early or too late. A timely handover algorithm is one which initiates handoffs neither too early nor too late.

Because of large-scale and small-scale fades are frequently encountered in mobile environment, it is very difficult for handover algorithm to make an accurate and timely decision. Handover algorithms operating in real time have to make decisions without the luxury of repeated uncorrelated measurements, or of future signal strength information. It should be noted that some of handover criteria information can be inherently imprecise, or the precise information is difficult to obtain. For this reason, we propose a FL-based approach, which can operate with imprecision data and can model nonlinear functions with arbitrary complexity.

3 Proposed System Model

The Fuzzy Logic Controller (FLC) is the main part of the proposed Fuzzy Handover Decision System (FHDS) and its basic elements are shown in Fig. 1. They are the fuzzifier, inference engine, Fuzzy Rule Base (FRB) and defuzzifier. As shown in Fig. 2, as membership functions we use triangular and trapezoidal membership functions because they are suitable for real-time operation [15].

In Fig. 2, x_0 in $f(.)$ is the center of triangular function; $x_0(x_1)$ in $g(.)$ is the left (right) edge of trapezoidal function; and $a_0(a_1)$ is the left (right) width of the triangular or trapezoidal function.

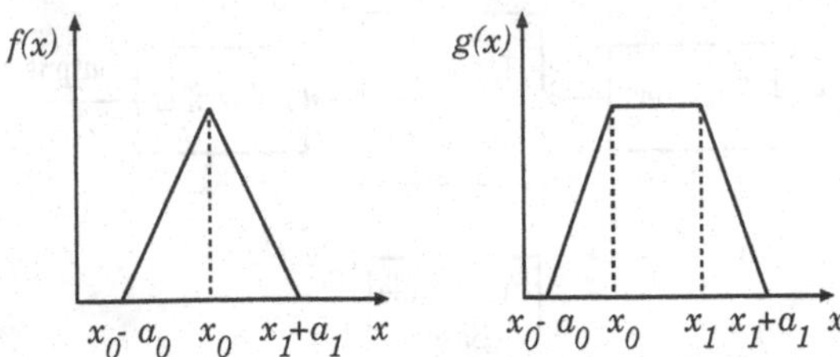

Fig. 2. Triangular and trapezoidal membership functions

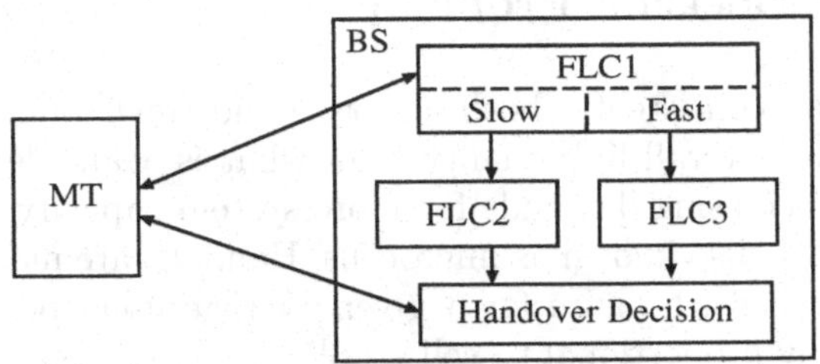

Fig. 3. Proposed system model

The proposed FHDS shown in Fig. 3 has three FLCs. The FLC1 determines the speed of MTs, FLC2 makes the handover decision for slow-speed users, and FLC3 for high-speed users.

3.1 Design of FLC1

The input parameters for FLC1 are: Distance (*D*) and Error ratio (*Er*), while the output linguistic parameter is Prediction factor (*Pf*). The term sets of *D* and *Er* are defined respectively as:

$$T(D) = \{Small, Middle, Far\} = \{Sm, Mi, Fa\};$$
$$T(Er) = \{Small, Normal, Big\} = \{Sl, No, Bi\}.$$

The output linguistic parameter $T(Pf)$ is defined as $\{Slow, Middle, Fast\} = \{So, Ml, Fs\}$.

The membership functions of FLC1 are shown in Fig.4. The FRB forms a fuzzy set of dimensions $|T(D)| \times |T(Er)|$, where $|T(x)|$ is the number of terms on $T(x)$. The FRB1 shown in Table 1 has 9 rules. The control rules have the following form: IF "conditions" THEN "control action".

In order to calculated the distance *D* parameter of moving MT, the BS uses a control message to ask the MT for its position. By considering the transmission time of the control message and the delay time of the received control message, the BS calculates the *D* parameter. If the *D* is small then the speed of MT is slow, on the other hand, when the *D* is large the speed is high. For the *Er* parameter, when the speed of MT is high, the *Er* tends to be high, while when the speed of MT is slow, the *Er* is low.

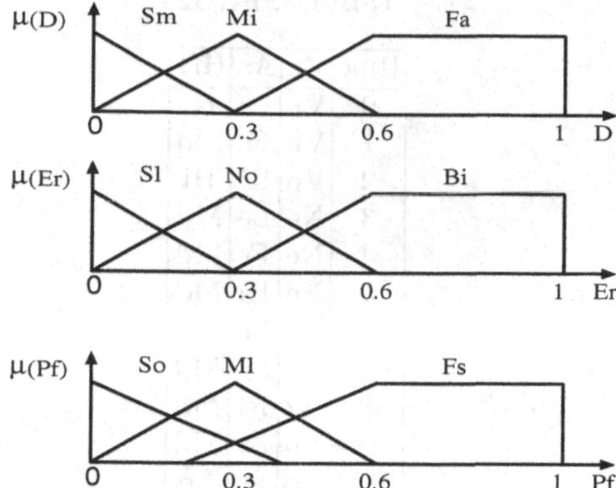

Fig. 4. FLC1 membership functions

Table 1. FRB1

Rule	D	Er	Pf
0	Sm	Sl	So
1	Sm	No	So
2	Sm	Bi	Ml
3	Mi	Sl	So
4	Mi	No	So
5	Mi	Bi	Mi
6	Fa	Sl	Mi
7	Fa	No	Fs
8	Fa	Bi	Fs

By considering D and Er input parameters FLC1 decides the speed of MT. If the speed is slow, then the FLC2 is activated, otherwise the FLC3 makes the handover decision for high speed MT.

3.2 Design of FLC2

When the MT moves with a low speed the probability to change the direction is very high. For this reason, we selected as an input parameter the angle which the MT is approaching the BS (Aa) and the change of the intensity of the Electric Field (Ec). Based on these 2 input parameters, the FCL2 makes the handover decision for low speed MTs.

The term sets of Ec and Aa are defined respectively as:

$$\begin{aligned} T(Ec) &= \{Very\ Negative, Negative, Around\ Zero, Pozitive, VeryPozitive\} \\ &= \{Vn, Ne, Az, Po, Vp\}; \\ T(Aa) &= \{Left, Front, Right\} = \{Le, Fr, Ri\}. \end{aligned}$$

Table 2. FRB2

Rule	Ec	Aa	Hf1
0	Vn	Le	Hi
1	Vn	Fr	Md
2	Vn	Ri	Hi
3	Ne	Le	Md
4	Ne	Fr	Md
5	Ne	Ri	Md
6	Az	Le	Md
7	Az	Fr	Md
8	Az	Ri	Md
9	Po	Le	Md
10	Po	Fr	Lo
11	Po	Ri	Md
12	Vp	Le	Lo
13	Vp	Fr	Lo
14	Vp	Ri	Lo

The term set of the output linguistic parameter $T(Hf1)$ is defined as $\{Slow, Middle, Fast\} = \{Sw, Me, Fs\}$.

The membership functions of FLC2 are shown in Fig. 5. The FRB2 shown in Table 2 has 15 rules.

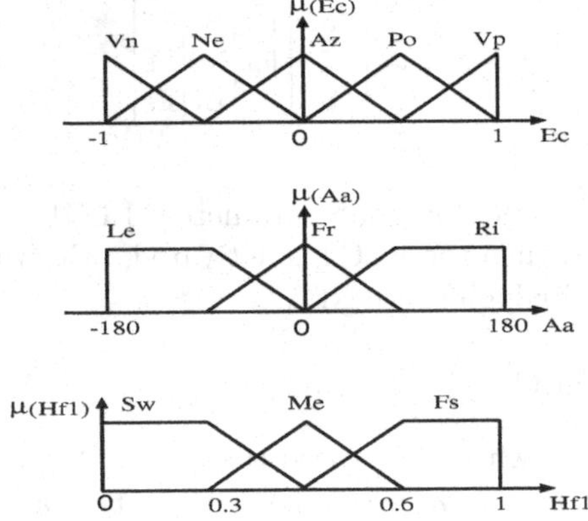

Fig. 5. FLC2 membership functions

3.3 Design of FLC3

In the case when MT moves with a high speed the probability to change the direction is very low. For this reason, we selected as an input parameters for FLC3 the change of the RSS or the electric field intensity for neighbor BSs. The input linguistic parameters are the change of electric field intensity of BS1 ($E1c$) and the change of electric field intensity of BS2 ($E2c$). Based on these 2 input parameters, the FCL3 makes the handover decision for high speed MT.

The term sets of $E1c$ and $E2c$ are defined respectively as:

$$T(E1c) = \{Negative, Around\ Zero, Pozitive\} = \{Ng, Az1, Pi\};$$
$$T(E2c) = \{Negative, Around\ Zero, Pozitive\} = \{Na, Az2, Pz\}.$$

The term set of the output linguistic parameter $T(Hf2)$ is defined as $\{Low, Middle, High\} = \{Lw, Mid, Hg\}$.

The membership functions of FLC3 are shown in Fig. 6. The FRB3 shown in Table 3 has 9 rules.

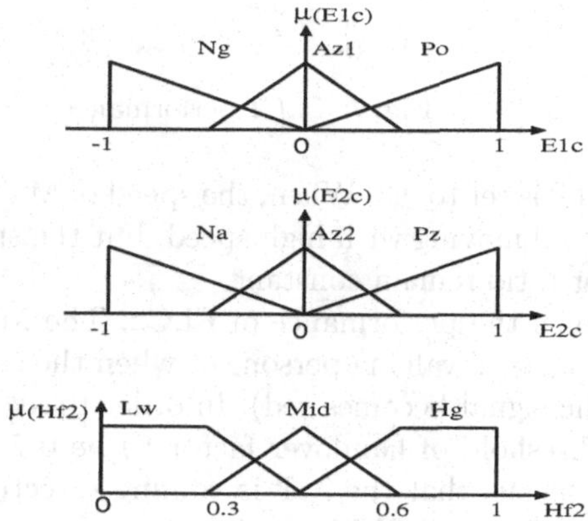

Fig. 6. FLC3 membership functions

Table 3. FRB3

Rule	E1c	E2c	Hf2
0	Ng	Na	Hg
1	Ng	Az2	Hg
2	Ng	Pz	Mid
3	Az1	Na	Hg
4	Az1	Az2	Mid
5	Az1	Pz	Mid
6	Pi	Na	Mid
7	Pi	Az2	Mid
8	Pi	Pz	Lw

4 Simulation Results

The simulation were carried out in Linux Fedora Core5 computer by using FuzzyC software developed in our Laboratory. The performance evaluation for FLC1, FLC2 and FLC3 drawing by MATLAB are shown in Fig. 7, Fig. 8, and Fig. 9, respectively.

In Fig. 7 is shown the performance of FLC1. With the increase of the distance and the error ratio, the prediction factor is increased. The threshold for deciding

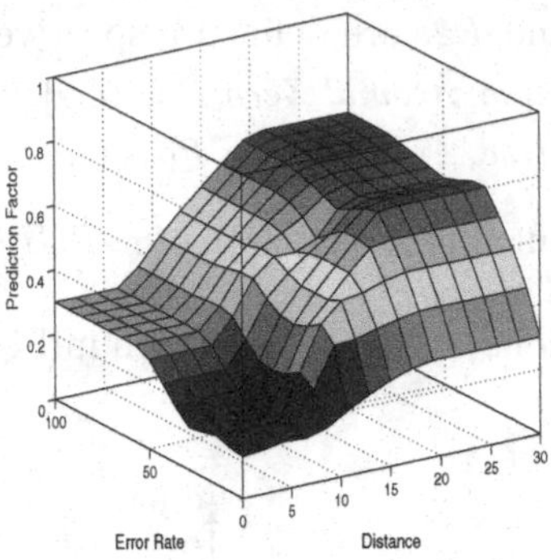

Fig. 7. FLC1 performance

the speed of the MT is set to 0.3. When, the speed of MT is approaching 40km/h, the MT is considered moving with high speed, but the speed is not changing too much, so the error ratio remain constant.

In Fig. 8 is shown the performance of FLC2. The MT is moving with a low speed. This is the case of walking persons or when the cars are slowing down the speed (when traffic signal becomes red). In order to avoid the ping-pong effect, we selected the threshold of handover factor to be 0.7. When the approaching angle is small, it means that the MT is coming directly to the BS. Therefore, the handover factor is small. With the increase of the approaching angle value and the change of the RSS, the handover factor is increased.

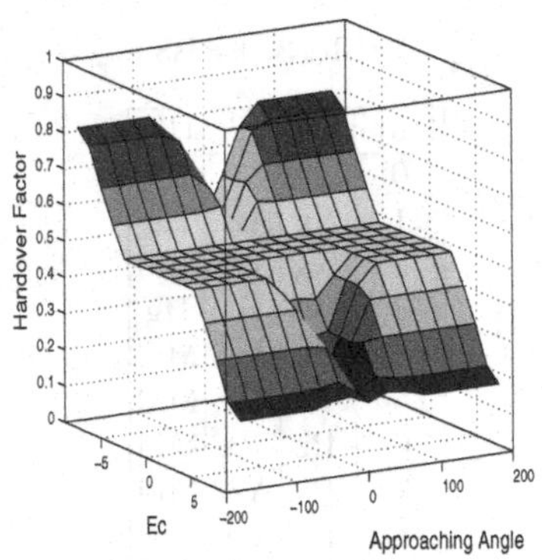

Fig. 8. FLC2 performance

In Fig. 9 is shown the performance of FLC3. This is the case for moving cars, so the probability of changing direction is very small. The threshold for handover factor was set 0.5. The figure shows that with the decrease of the RSS the handover factor is increased. However, when the RSS is high, the handover factor is very small. So, it is not necessary to make handover.

In Table 4, we show the comparison of the proposed FHDS with other fuzzy-based handover systems. Our FHDS needs only 33 rules for making the handover

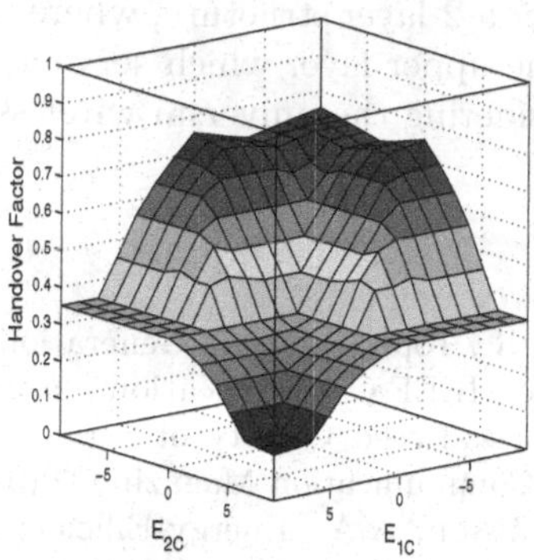

Fig. 9. FLC3 performance

Table 4. Comparison of fuzzy-based systems

Systems	Fuzzy Handover (Ref.[11])	Fuzzy Handover (Ref.[12])	Proposed FHDS
Number of FLC	1	1	3
Number of Input Parameters	4	4	2;2;2
Number of Membership Functions	(3,3,3,3)	(3,3,3,3)	(3,3);(5,3);(3,3)
Number of Fuzzy Rules	81	81	33

decision. However, the algorithms proposed in [11,12] seem to be complex and the number of fuzzy rules is high.

5 Conclusions

In this paper, we proposed a FHDS for wireless cellular networks. In different from other works by considering a mixed cell architecture, we propose a FL-based speed-aware handover system that consist of three FLCs. The FLC1 determines the speed of MTs, FLC2 makes the handover decision for slow-speed users, and FLC3 for high-speed users.

From the simulation results we conclude as follows.

- When the approaching angle is small, it means that the MT is coming directly to the BS, so the handover factor is small.
- With the increase of the approaching angle value and the change of the RSS, the handover factor is increased.
- With the decrease of the RSS the handover factor is increased.
- When the RSS is high, the handover factor is very small. So, it is not needed to make handover.

In this paper, we consider a 2-layer structure, where micro cells are in the low layer and macro cells on the upper layer which serve as umbrella. However, the work can be extended considering the universal wireless networks coverage.

References

1. Berezdivin, R., Breining, R., Topp, R.: Next-Generation Wireless Communication Concepts and Technologies. IEEE Communication Magazine 40(3), 108–116 (2002)
2. Guo, Y., Chaskar, H.: Class-Based Quality of Service over Air Interfaces in 4G Mobile Networks. IEEE Communication Magazine 40(3), 132–137 (2002)
3. Wang, W., Wang, X., Nilsson, A.A.: Energy-Efficient Bandwidth Allocation in Wireless Networks: Algorithms, Analysis, and Simulations. IEEE Transactions on Wireless Communications 5(5), 1103–1114 (2006)
4. Fang, Y., Zhang, Y.: Call Admission Control Schemes and Performance Analysis in Wireless Mobile Networks. IEEE Transactions on Vehicular Technology 51(2), 371–382 (2002)
5. Wong, K.D., Cox, D.C.: A Pattern Recognition System for Handoff Algorithms. IEEE J-SAC 18(7), 1301–1312 (2000)
6. Kovvuri, S., Pandey, V., Ghosal, D., Mukherjee, B., Sarkar, D.: A Call-Admission Control (CAC) Algorithm for Providing Guaranteed QoS in Cellular Networks. International Journal of Wireless Information Networks 10(2), 73–85 (2003)
7. Lin, H.P., Juang, R.T., Lin, D.B.: Validation of an Improved Location-Based Handover Algorithm Using GSM Measurement Data. IEEE Transactions on Mobile Computing 4(5), 530–536 (2005)
8. Fiengo, P., Giambene, G., Trentin, E.: Neural-based Downlink Scheduling Algorithm for Broadband Wireless Networks. Computer Communication 30(2), 207–218 (2007)
9. Barolli, L., Koyama, A., Suganuma, T., Shiratori, N.: GAMAN: A GA Based QoS Routing Method for Mobile Ad-hoc Networks. Journal of Interconnection Networks (JOIN) 4(3), 251–270 (2003)
10. Chan, P.M.L., Sheriff, R.E., Hu, Y.F., Conforto, P., Tocci, C.: Mobility Management Incorporating Fuzzy Logic for a Heterogeneous IP Environment. IEEE Communications Magazine 39(12), 42–51 (2001)
11. Onel, T., Ersoy, C., Cayirci, E.: A Fuzzy Inference System for the Handoff Decision Algorithms in the Virtual Cell Layout Base Tactical Communications System. In: IEEE Military Communications Conference (MILCOM-2002), vol. 1, pp. 436–441 (2002)
12. Mohanty, S., Akyildiz, I.F.: A Cross-Layer (Layer 2+3) Handoff Management Protocol for Next-Generation Wireless Systems. IEEE Transactions on Mobile Computing 5(10), 1347–1360 (2006)
13. Yu, F., Krishamurthy, V.: Optimal Joint Session Admission Control in Integrated WLAN and CDMA Cellular Networks with Vertical Handoff. IEEE Transactions on Mobile Computing 6(1), 126–139 (2007)
14. Hannikainen, M., Hamalainen, T.D., Niemi, M., Saarinen, J.: Trends in Personal wireless Data Communication. Computer Communication 25(1), 84–99 (2002)
15. Dubois, D., Prade, H., Yager, R. (eds.): Fuzzy Sets for Intelligent Systems. Morgan Kaufman Publishers, San Francisco (1993)

WPS and Voice-XML-Based Multi-Modal Fusion Agent Using SNNR and Fuzzy Value

Jung-Hyun Kim and Kwang-Seok Hong

School of Information and Communication Engineering, Sungkyunkwan University, 300, Chunchun-dong, Jangan-gu, Suwon, KyungKi-do, 440-746, Korea
kjh0328@skku.edu and kshong@skku.ac.kr
http://hci.skku.ac.kr

Abstract. The traditional fusion methods of multiple sensing modalities are summarized with 1) data-level fusion, 2) feature-level fusion and 3) decision-level fusion. This paper suggests the decision-level fusion-oriented novel fusion and fission framework, and it implements WPS (Wearable Personal Station) and Voice-XML-Based Multi-Modal Fusion Agent (hereinafter, MMFA) using audio-gesture modalities. Because the MMFA provides different weight and a feed-back function in individual recognizer, according to SNNR(Signal Plus Noise to Noise Ratio) and fuzzy value, it may select an optimal instruction processing interface under a given situation or noisy environment, and can allow more interactive communication functions in noisy environment. In addition, the MMFA provides a wider range of personalized information more effectively as well as it not need complicated mathematical algorithm and computation costs that are concerned with multidimensional features and patterns (data) size, according as it use a WPS and distributed computing-based database and SQL-logic, for synchronization and fusion between modalities.

1 Introduction

A recent study on multimodal interaction describes the potential of multimodality in terms of increased adaptability, robustness and efficiency. There are some well-known approaches towards modeling and prototyping multimodal systems such as RDPM [1, 2], theoretical frameworks (e.g., modality theory [3, 4], TYCOON [5], CARE [6]) and others, which constitute a solid basis for multimodal system design, focusing on task specification, rapid prototyping and Wizard-of-Oz-testing.

However, the next generation HCI for more advanced and personalized PC system such as wearable computer and PDA based on wireless network and wearable computing, may require and allow new interfaces and interaction techniques such as tactile interfaces with haptic feedback methods, and gesture interfaces based on hand gestures, or mouse gestures sketched with a computer mouse or a stylus, to serve different kinds of users. In other words, for perceptual experience and behavior to benefit from the simultaneous stimulation of multiple sensory modalities that are concerned with human's (five) senses, fusion and fission technologies of the information from these modalities are very important and positively necessary.

T. Enokido, L. Barolli, and M. Takizawa (Eds.): NBiS 2007, LNCS 4658, pp. 523–532, 2007.

Consequently, we implement MMFA including synchronization between audio-gesture modalities by coupling the WPS-based embedded KSSL recognizer with a remote Voice-XML user, for improved multi-modal HCI in noisy environments, and suggest improved fusion and fission rules depending on SNNR (Signal Plus Noise to Noise Ratio) and fuzzy value, for simultaneous multi-modality.

This paper is organized as follows. In section 2, we describe an implementation of the WPS-based embedded KSSL recognizer for ubiquitous computing. Web-based speech recognition and synthesis system using Voice-XML is described briefly, in section 3. In section 4, we introduce SNNR and fuzzy value-based the MMFA architecture depending on improved fusion and fission rules, including a synchronization between audio-gesture modalities. In section 5, we evaluate and verify suggested the MMFA with experimental results, and finally, this study is summarized in section 6, together with an outline of challenges and future directions.

2 Embedded KSSL Recognizer

2.1 RDBMS-Based Feature Extraction and Instruction Recognition Models

We constructed 65 sentential and 165 word instruction models by coupling KSSL hand gestures with motion gestures that are referred to "Korean Standard Sign Language Tutor (KSSLT) [7]". In addition, for a clustering method to achieve efficient feature extraction and construction of recognition models based on distributed computing, we utilize and introduce an improved RDBMS(Relational DataBase Management System) clustering module [8], because statistical classification algorithms including K-means clustering, QT(Quality Threshold) clustering, and the Self-Organizing Map(SOM), have certain restrictions and problems, such as the necessity of complicated mathematical algorithm by multidimensional features, relativity of computation costs by pattern size, and minimization of memory swapping and assignment.

2.2 Pattern Recognition Using Fuzzy Max-Min Composition

As the fuzzy logic for KSSL recognition, we applied trapezoidal shaped membership functions for representation of fuzzy numbers-sets, and utilized the fuzzy max-min composition.

$$\begin{gathered} \textbf{For } (x, y) \in A \times B,\ (y, z) \in B \times C, \\ \mu_{S \bullet R}(x, z) = \max_{y} \left[\min \left(\mu_R(x, y), \mu_S(y, z) \right) \right] \end{gathered} \tag{1}$$

Two fuzzy relations R and S are defined in sets A, B and C (we prescribed the accuracy of hand gestures and motion gestures, object KSSL recognition models as the sets of events that occur in KSSL recognition with the sets A, B and C). That is, $R \subseteq A \times B$, $S \subseteq B \times C$. The composition $S{\cdot}R = SR$ of two relations R and S is expressed by the relation from A to C, and this composition is defined in Eq. (1) [9], [10]. $S{\cdot}R$ from this elaboration is a subset of $A \times C$. That is, $S{\cdot}R \subseteq A \times C$. If the relations R and S are represented by matrices M_R and M_S, the matrix $M_{S \bullet R}$ corresponding to $S{\cdot}R$ is obtained from the product of M_R and M_S; $M_{S \bullet R} = M_R{\cdot}M_S$. The matrix $M_{S \bullet R}$ represents

Table 1. The matrix $M_{S \bullet R}$ corresponding to the relations $S \bullet R$

S • R	KSSL recognition model : "YOU"				
Accuracy of motion gestures	**Insignificance**	**Bad_YOU**	**Normal_YOU**	**Good_YOU**	**Best_YOU**
Very_bad	0.9	0.6	0.3	0.2	0.1
Bad	0.6	0.7	0.4	0.2	0.2
Normal	0.3	0.4	0.4	0.3	0.3
Good	0.3	0.3	0.5	0.8	0.7
Best	0.2	0.3	0.4	0.6	0.9

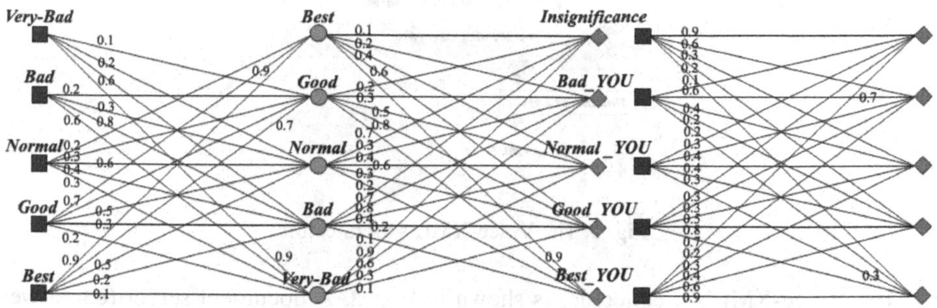

Fig. 1. Composition of fuzzy relation

max-min composition that reason and analyze the possibility of C when A occurs, and it is also given in Table 1 and Fig. 1.

In addition, WPS-based embedded KSSL recognizer calculates and finds a fuzzy value that indicates the posterior probability of a gesture being correctly matched to a KSSL recognition model, via a fuzzy reasoning and composition process, and it recognizes user's various KSSL according to produced fuzzy value. The flowchart of KSSL recognizer is shown in Fig. 4 (in sub-section 4.1) together with an outline and flow-chart of the MMFA.

3 Speech Recognition and Synthesis Using Voice-XML

Voice-XML is a language for creating voice-user interfaces, particularly for the telephone. It uses speech recognition and touch-tone (DTMF keypad) for input, and prerecorded audio and text-to-speech synthesis (TTS) for output. It is based on the Worldwide Web Consortium's (W3C's) Extensible Markup Language (XML), and leverages the web paradigm for application development and deployment. For ASR-engine in architecture of W3C's VXML 2.0 [11], we used the HUVOIS solution that is Voice-XML-based voice software developed by KT Corp. in Korea for those with impaired sight that converts online text into voice and reads out the letters and words punched in through the computer keyboard, thus enabling them to use computers and the internet. The HUVOIS solution consist of HUVOIS-ARS based on HMM, TTS using tri-phone unit and HUVOIS Voice-XML, and supports client-sever network, LSS(Load Share Server) and modular structure.

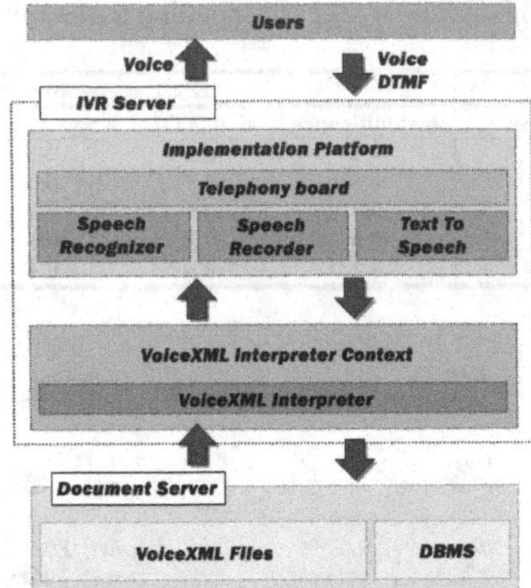

Fig. 2. The Voice-XML's architecture

The Voice-XML's architecture is shown in Fig. 2. A document server (e.g. a web server) processes requests from a client application, the Voice-XML interpreter, through the VXML interpreter context. The server produces Voice-XML documents in reply, which are processed by the Voice-XML interpreter. The Voice-XML interpreter context may monitor user inputs in parallel with the Voice-XML interpreter. For example, one Voice-XML interpreter context may always listen for a special escape phrase that takes the user to a high-level personal assistant, and another may listen for escape phrases that alter user preferences like volume or text-to-speech characteristics. The implementation platform is controlled by the Voice-XML interpreter context and by the Voice-XML interpreter.

4 MMFA Architecture Using SNNR and Fuzzy Value

4.1 Audio-Gesture Fusion Architecture

The fusion scheme consists of seven major steps: 1) the user connects to Voice-XML server via PSTN and internet using telephone terminal and WPS based on wireless networks (including middleware), and then inputs prescribed speech and KSSL, 2) the user's speech data, which are inputted into telephone terminal, is transmitted to ASR-engine in Voice-XML, then ASR results are saved to the MMDS (Multi-Modal Database Server; The MMDS is the database responsible for synchronizing data between speech and KSSL gesture), 3) user's KSSL data, which are inputted into WPS, are recognized by embedded KSSL recognizer, then the WPS transmits and saves recognition results to the MMDS, using middleware over TCP/IP protocol and wireless networks(blue-tooth module), 4) at this point, the user's KSSL and speech data run the synchronization session using internal SQL logic of the MMDS, 5) while suggested the MMFA runs comparison arithmetic (validity check) on ASR and KSSL recognition results with prescribed instruction models by internal SQL logic, the NAT(Noise

Analysis Tool) analyzes noise for user's speech data (wave file) which is recorded by Voice-XML, 6) According to analyzed noise and arithmetic result, the MMFA gives weight into an individual (gesture or speech) recognizer, 7) finally, user's intention is provided to the user through TTS and visualization. The suggested fusion architecture and flowchart of MMFA are shown in Fig. 3 and Fig. 4.

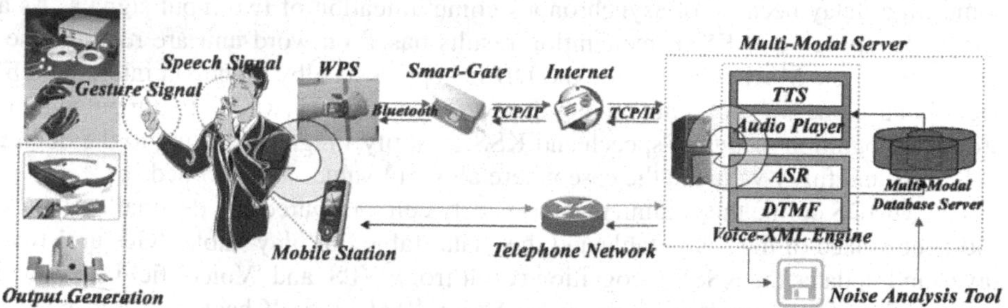

Fig. 3. The components and fusion architecture

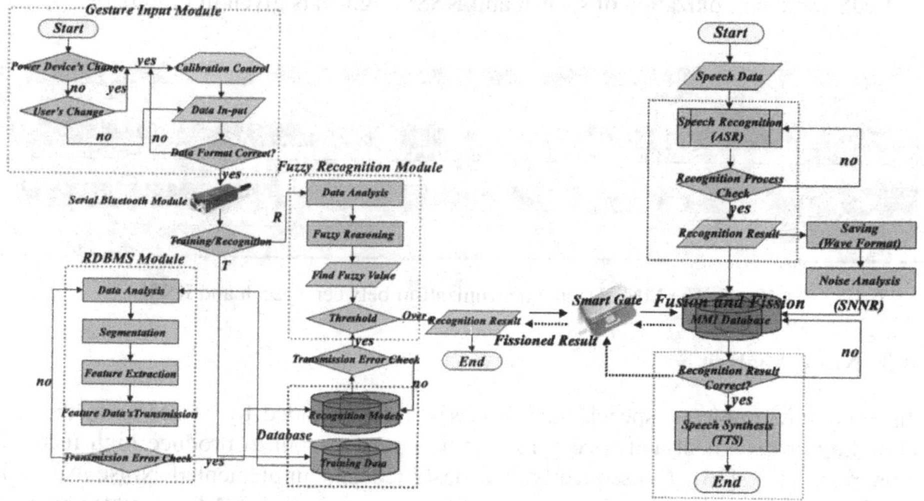

Fig. 4. The flowchart of the MMFA integrating 2 sensory channels with speech and gesture

4.2 Synchronization Between Audio-Gesture Modalities

Human's utterance and gesture representation usually have some time difference and such asynchronous control should occur necessarily in speech synthesis processing of recognition results. All multi-modal inputs are synchronized, because while speech recognizer generates absolute times for words, gesture movements generate *{x, y, t}* triples, and initial work identifies an object or a location from gesture inputs accordingly, as speech understanding constrains gesture interpretation.

This paper solves the asynchronous control problems between speech and gesture signals using a web-logic and word-unit input method based on the database (the MMDS in section 4.1). In other words, for synchronization between speech and gesture signals, after individual speech and KSSL recognizer recognizes inputted speech and the KSSL recognition models, they transmit recognition results into the MMDS for weight application. However, the transmission time of recognition results has some time delay because of asynchronous communication of two input signals. As a result, the speech and KSSL recognition results based on word-unit are recorded sequentially to the MMDS, and while the DB is kept in standby mode via internal web-logic in case one was not input among the two input signals (where, two input signals are the recognition results of speech and KSSL), apply weight according to the degree of SNNR and fuzzy value, in the case where all input values are recorded.

The MMDS define the column mappings between the source and destination tables, and is consisted of the 'play' table and the 'data' table. In 'play' table, 'Gesture' field saves and updates the KSSL recognition result from WPS, and 'Voice' field saves and updates the speech recognition result by Voice-XML, then 'Checking' field checks that all data were inputted in both fields ('Gesture' and 'Voice' field). In addition, in 'data' table, the prescribed instruction models are saved with 'Contents' field. The MMDS for synchronization of speech and KSSL signals is given in Fig. 5.

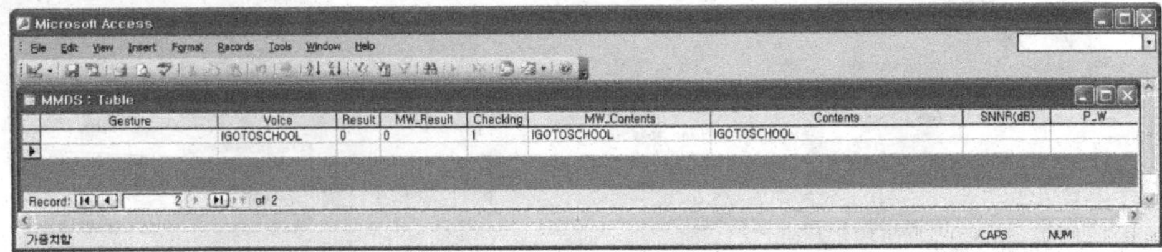

Fig. 5. The MMDS for synchronization between speech and KSSL

4.3 Noise Analysis

In noisy environments, speech quality is severely degraded by noises from the surrounding environment and speech recognition systems fail to produce high recognition rates [12], [13]. Consequently, we designed and implemented Noise Analysis Tool (NAT) for weight decision in individual recognizer. The NAT calculates average energy (mean power; [dB]) for a speech signal that recorded by wave-format in the Voice-XML; and then computes SNNR by Eq. (2), where, P is mean power.

$$SNNR(dB) = 10\log_{10} \frac{P_{signal+noise}}{P_{noise}} \tag{2}$$

4.4 Weight Decision Rules

Speech recognition rate does not usually change to a SNNR of 25 dB, but if the rate lowers, the speech recognition rate falls rapidly. Therefore, the MMFA provides feedback function according to SNNR critical value. In case SNNR critical value for weight decision is ambiguous, according as a feed-back function requests re-input (speech and KSSL) to user for clear a declaration of intention, more improved instruction processing is available. In addition, we utilized an average speech recognition rate as speech probability value for weight decision, and to define speech probability value depending on SNNR, we repeatedly achieved speech recognition experiments 10 times with the 20 test speech recognition models in noisy and clean environments, for every 5 reagents. The average speech recognition rates are given in Table 2.

Table 2. Weight value according to the SNNR and critical value for the feed-back function

SNNR Critical value	Weight value (%)		Average speech recognition rates for the 20 test recognition models (%)						
	Speech (W_S)	KSSL(W_G)	Reagent 1	Reagent 2	Reagent 3	Reagent 4	Reagent 5	Average(S)	Difference
more than 40 [dB]	99.0	1.0	98.2	98.4	97.9	98.5	98.2	98.2	0.9
35 [dB] ≤ SNNR < 40 [dB]	98.0	2.0	97.8	97.3	96.6	97.1	97.5	97.3	0.3
30 [dB] ≤ SNNR < 35 [dB]	96.0	4.0	97.5	96.5	96.6	97.0	97.4	97.0	0.2
25 [dB] ≤ SNNR < 30 [dB]	94.0	6.0	97.2	96.5	96.5	96.9	96.9	96.8	0.2
20 [dB] ≤ SNNR < 25 [dB]	92.0	8.0	96.9	95.9	96.4	96.8	96.8	96.6	2.2
15 [dB] ≤ SNNR < 20 [dB]	*Feed-Back*		*92.4*	*96.2*	*93.8*	*95.2*	*94.1*	*94.3*	*11.1*
10 [dB] ≤ SNNR < 15 [dB]	6.0	94.0	83.6	83.4	83.5	82.6	83.2	83.3	8.8
5 [dB] ≤ SNNR < 10 [dB]	4.0	96.0	71.9.	72.5	70.2	79.5	75.6	74.5	22.4
0 [dB] ≤ SNNR < 5 [dB]	2.0	98.0	53.4	51.3	52.6	51.6	51.3	52.0	14.0
less than 0 [dB]	1.0	99.0	38.5	37.6	37.5	38.2	38.5	38.1	-

$$P\_W = W_S \times S + W_G \times G \tag{3}$$

- *P_W : Expected value after weight application*
- W_S*: Defined Weight for Speech recognition mode in Table 2.*
- W_G*: Defined Weight for KSSL recognition mode in Table 2.*
- *S : speech probability (an average speech recognition rate)*
- *G : KSSL probability (the critical value depending on normalized fuzzy value)*

$$G = \frac{\text{Fuzzy Value\_Current}}{\text{Fuzzy Value\_Max}} = \frac{\text{Fuzzy Value\_Current}}{3.5} \tag{4}$$

- *Fuzzy Value_Current : Fuzzy value to recognize current gesture(KSSL)*
- *Fuzzy Value_Max = 3.5 : The maximum fuzzy value for KSSL recognition*

SNNR and fuzzy value-based weight decision processing for fusion and fission between modalities consists of three major steps: 1) as speech and KSSL probability value, it calls an average speech recognition rate *(S)* depending on the defined SNNR, and fuzzy value *(G)* for KSSL recognition from the MMDS, then apply weights (W_S and W_G) in called-individual probability value, 2) and then calculate a expected value *(P_W)* after weight application via by Eq. (3), 3) return the fission result (speech or KSSL recognition result) by calculated the expected value *(P_W)* to user. Where, the maximum fuzzy value for KSSL recognition is 3.5, and the minimum critical value is 3.2 (in programming). Accordingly, the normalized fuzzy value (*G*) of the embedded KSSL recognizer is defined Eq. (4).

For example, 1) in case SNNR is more than 40 [dB], average speech recognition rate *(S)* using Voice-XML is 98.2%, and then apply weights of $W_S = 99\%$ and $W_G = 1\%$ in Table 2, 2) if *Fuzzy Value_Current* in Eq. (4) is *3.2*, *P_W* that is expected value after weight application is calculated with Table3, 3) by the same principal, individual *P_W* values depending on SNNR and fuzzy value are shown in Table 4. (Because *KSSL probability (G)* is changed according to *Fuzzy Value_Current*, *P_W* is changed justly.) As a result, if *P_W* value is over than 0.917, the MMFA fissions and returns recognition result of speech recognizer based on Voice-XML, while the MMFA fissions the embedded KSSL recognizer in case *P_W* value is less than 0.909. In case *Fuzzy Value_Current* is 3.2, *P_W* values using the Eq. (3) and (4) are given in Table 4.

Table 3. For example; A system of measuring of *P_W* value

Speech		KSSL		A System of Measuring	P_W
W_S	S	W_G	G		
0.99	0.982	0.01	0.914	0.98*0.982 + 0.02*0.914	0.981

Table 4. In case *Fuzzy Value_Current* is 3.2, *P_W* values using the Eq. (3) and (4)

SNNR	Speech		KSSL		P_W
	W_S	S	W_G	G	
more than 40 [dB]	0.99	0.982	0.01	0.914	0.981
35 [dB] ≤ SNNR < 40 [dB]	0.98	0.973	0.02	0.914	0.972
30 [dB] ≤ SNNR < 35 [dB]	0.96	0.970	0.04	0.914	0.968
25 [dB] ≤ SNNR < 30 [dB]	0.94	0.968	0.06	0.914	0.965
20 [dB] ≤ SNNR < 25 [dB]	0.92	0.966	0.08	0.914	0.917
15 [dB] ≤ SNNR < 20 [dB]			*Feed-Back*		
10 [dB] ≤ SNNR < 15 [dB]	0.06	0.833	0.94	0.914	0.909
5 [dB] ≤ SNNR < 10 [dB]	0.04	0.745	0.96	0.914	0.907
0 [dB] ≤ SNNR < 5 [dB]	0.02	0.520	0.98	0.914	0.906
less than 0 [dB]	0.01	0.381	0.99	0.914	0.909

5 Experiments and Results

The experiment environment consisted of a blue-tooth module, wireless haptic devices, WPS based on embedded LINUX operating system, and blue-tooth headset for embedded-ubiquitous computing. That is, data gloves transmit 14 kinds of hand's structural motion data (10 fingers gesture data, 4 pitch & roll data) and the motion tracker transmits 12 kinds of hand's spatial motion data with both hands connected to a WPS via a blue-tooth module. The suggested embedded KSSL recognizer is 283 Kbytes (including images and composite sounds for visual and additive representation) and it can process and calculate 200 samples per seconds on the WPS. For the WPS-based embedded KSSL recognizer, we used 5DT company's wireless data gloves and Fastrak® which are popular input devices in the haptic application field, and utilized blue-tooth module for the wireless sensor network [14]. And the i.MX21 test board was selected, which is developed as the WPS (a wearable platform for the next-generation PC in the Rep. of Korea). The i.MX21 test board consists of an ARM926EJ-S (16KB I-Cache, 16KB D-Cache) CPU, and includes ARM Jazelle technology for Java acceleration and MPEG-4 and H.263 encode/decode acceleration. The i.MX21 provides flexibility for software implementation, for other video encoders, such as packet-video, real-networks and windows media [15].

The experimental set-up is as follows. The distance between the KSSL input module and the WPS with a built-in KSSL recognizer approximates radius 10M's ellipse

Table 5. Average recognition rates for prescribed sentence and word-based instruction models

Evaluation (R:Recognition) / Reagent	Uni-modal Instruction Processing Interface						The MMFA			
	KSSL (%)		Speech (%)				KSSL + Speech (%)			
	Noise or Clean		Noise		Clean		Noise		Clean	
	sentence	word	sentence	word	sentence	word	sentence	word	sentence	word
Reagent 1	**92.8**	**92.7**	**79.5**	**80.4**	**94.5**	**98.7**	**92.7**	**92.6**	**94.5**	**98.7**
Reagent 2	**91.6**	**93.5**	**75.2**	**75.6**	**95.1**	**96.5**	**91.6**	**93.5**	**95.1**	**96.5**
Reagent 3	**92.1**	**93.9**	**78.8**	**78.9**	**95.3**	**96.7**	**92**	**93.9**	**95.3**	**96.7**
Reagent 4	**93.3**	**93.1**	**75.8**	**77.8**	**93.6**	**95.9**	**93.3**	**93.1**	**93.5**	**95.9**
Reagent 5	**93.2**	**93.0**	**77.3**	**78.6**	**94.1**	**95.7**	**93.2**	**93.0**	**94.1**	**95.7**
Reagent 6	**92.3**	**91.7**	**78.7**	**78.9**	**95.4**	**96.6**	**92.2**	**91.7**	**95.4**	**96.6**
Reagent 7	**91.6**	**92.8**	**77.3**	**80.1**	**94.6**	**97.3**	**91.6**	**92.8**	**94.6**	**97.3**
Reagent 8	**91.4**	**93.9**	**72.4**	**74.7**	**97.3**	**97.7**	**91.4**	**93.8**	**97.3**	**97.7**
Reagent 9	**93.0**	**93.2**	**75.8**	**76.2**	**94.7**	**96.8**	**92.9**	**93.2**	**94.7**	**96.7**
Reagent10	**93.1**	**93.4**	**79.5**	**80.6**	**94.6**	**96.9**	**93.1**	**93.4**	**94.6**	**96.9**
Reagent11	**92.3**	**93.5**	**77.2**	**77.9**	**93.7**	**94.2**	**92.3**	**93.5**	**93.7**	**94.2**
Reagent12	**93.7**	**94.1**	**78.2**	**78.9**	**93.8**	**96.3**	**93.7**	**94.1**	**93.8**	**96.3**
Reagent13	**92.1**	**92.4**	**75.2**	**79.3**	**94.8**	**95.9**	**92.1**	**92.4**	**94.8**	**95.9**
Reagent14	**92.6**	**93.1**	**73.9**	**75.6**	**93.9**	**96.8**	**92.6**	**93.1**	**93.9**	**96.8**
Reagent15	**93.9**	**93.5**	**77.7**	**80.1**	**97.8**	**98.1**	**93.9**	**93.5**	**97.8**	**98.0**
Average	**92.60**	**93.20**	**76.83**	**78.24**	**94.88**	**96.67**	**92.57**	**93.17**	**94.87**	**96.66**

form. In KSSL gesture and speech, we move the wireless data gloves and the motion tracker to the prescribed position. For every 15 reagents, we repeat this action 15 times in noisy and clean environments. While the user inputs KSSL using data gloves and a motion tracker, and speak using the blue-tooth headset in a telephone terminal.

Experimental results, the MMFA's average recognition rates for 65 sentential and 165 word instruction models were 94.87% and 96.66% in clean environments (e.g. office space), while 92.57% and 93.17% were shown in noisy environments. The uni-modal and the MMFA's average recognition rates in noisy and clean environment are shown in Table 5.

6 Conclusions

The approaches to Multi-Agent Systems (MAS) varies considerably in many areas, such as computer science, philosophy, mathematics, linguistics, social science, and so on, but even if one limits the analysis to logical systems, one finds that different languages are applied to very similar problems.

This study fuses natural language and artificial intelligence techniques to allow human computer interaction with an intuitive mix of speech, gesture and sign language based on the WPS and Voice-XML. In contrast to other proposed multi-modal interaction approaches, our approach is unique in three aspects: ***First,*** because the MMFA provides different weight and a feed-back function in individual embedded recognizer, according to SNNR and fuzzy value, it may select an optimal instruction processing interface under a given situation or noisy environment, and can allow more interactive communication functions in noisy environment. ***Second***, according as the MMFA fuses and recognizes the sentence and word-based instruction models that are represented by speech and KSSL, and then translates recognition result, which is fissioned according to a weight decision rule into synthetic speech and graphical display by HMD-Head Mounted Display in real-time, it provides a wider range of personalized information more effectively. ***Finally***, the MMFA not need complicated mathematical algorithm and computation costs that are concerned with multidimensional features and patterns (data) size, according as it use a WPS and distributed computing-based database and SQL-logic, for synchronization and fusion between modalities.

Acknowledgement

This research was supported by MIC, Korea under ITRC IITA-2006-(C1090-0603-0046)

References

1. Cenek, P., Melichar, M., Rajman, M.: A Framework for Rapid Multimodal Application Design. In: Matoušek, V., Mautner, P., Pavelka, T. (eds.) TSD 2005. LNCS (LNAI), vol. 3658, pp. 393–403. Springer, Heidelberg (2005)
2. Rajman, M., et al.: Assessing the usability of a dialogue management system designed in the framework of a rapid dialogue prototyping methodology. EAA 90, 1096–1111 (2004)
3. Bernsen, N.O.: Modality Theory: Supporting Multi-modal Interface Design. In: Proc. ERCIM (1993)
4. Bernsen, N.O.: A toolbox of output modalities. In: Representing output information in multimodal interfaces, Roskilde University (1995)
5. Martin, J.-C.: Towards intelligent cooperation between modalities. In: Proc. IJCAI-97, Nagoya, Japan (1997)
6. Coutaz, J., Nigay, L., Salber, D., Blandford, A., May, J., Young, R.M.: Four Easy Pieces for Assessing the Usability of Multimodal Interaction: The CARE Properties. In: Proc.Interact'95, pp. 115–120. Chapman & Hall, Sydney, Australia (1995)
7. Kim, S.-G.: Korean Standard Sign Language Tutor, 1st edn. Osung Publishing Company, Seoul (2000)
8. Kim, J.-H., et al.: An Implementation of KSSL Recognizer for HCI Based on Post Wearable PC and Wireless Networks KES 2006. In: Gabrys, B., Howlett, R.J., Jain, L.C. (eds.) KES 2006. LNCS (LNAI), vol. 4251, pp. 788–797. Springer, Heidelberg (2006)
9. Chen, C.H.: Fuzzy Logic and Neural Network Handbook. McGraw-Hill, New York (1992)
10. kandasamy, W.B.V.: Smaranda Fuzzy Algebra. American Research Press, Seattle (2003)
11. McGlashan, S., et al.: Voice Extensible Markup Language (VoiceXML) Version 2.0. W3C Recommendation (1992), http://www.w3.org
12. Martin, W.H.: DeciBel -The New Name for the Transmission Unit. Bell System Technical Journal (January 1929)
13. NIOSH working group.: STRESS..AT WORK NIOSH, Publication No. 99-101,U.S. National Institutes of Occupational Health (2006)
14. Kim, J.-H., et al.: Hand Gesture Recognition System using Fuzzy Algorithm and RDBMS for Post PC. In: Wang, L., Jin, Y. (eds.) FSKD 2005. LNCS (LNAI), vol. 3614, pp. 170–175. Springer, Heidelberg (2005)
15. i.MX21 Processor Data-sheet: http://www.freescale.com

A Fuzzy Neural Network Based Scheduling Algorithm for Job Assignment on Computational Grids

Kun-Ming Yu[1], Zhi-Jie Luo[1], Chih-Hsun Chou[1], Cheng-Kwan Chen[1], and Jiayi Zhou[2]

[1] Department of Computer Sciences and Information Engineering, Chung Hua University
[2] Institute of Engineering Science Chung Hua University
Hsin-chu, Taiwan 300, ROC
yu@chu.edu.tw

Abstract. Grid computing is an emerging computing architecture that can solve massive computational problems by making use of large numbers of heterogeneous computers. Job scheduling is an important issue in the high performance Grid computing environment. An appropriate scheduling algorithm can efficiently reduce the response time, turnaround time and further increase the throughput. However, finding an optimal grid scheduling algorithm is intractable. In this paper, we propose a high performance scheduling algorithm based on Fuzzy Neural Networks to resolve this problem. In the proposed algorithm, we apply the Fuzzy Logic technique to evaluate the grid system load status, and adopt the Neural Networks to automatically tune the membership functions. Since there are many factors that influence the system's load circumstances; as the number of factors increase, it becomes very difficult to set up the system using general experience. We implemented a Fuzzy Neural Network scheduler based on Globus Toolkit 4 to verify the proposed scheduling algorithm performance. NAS Grid Benchmarks (NGB) was utilized to validate the performance of our scheduling approach. The experimental results show that our proposed algorithm can reduce the turnaround time and has better speed-up ratio than previous methods.

Keywords: grid, fuzzy logic, neural network, fuzzy neural network, grid benchmark.

1 Introduction

Grid computing is a loosely couple distributed system. It uses computing resources that are connected through networks to solve large-scale computational problems [3]. Unlike the traditional cluster system, it can share heterogeneous computing and storage resources. So extending the grid environment is easier than the traditional cluster system. To integrate the resources of the grid system, grid middleware plays a significance role [1, 4, 5], and provides many unique components to enable these resources to communicate with each other.

T. Enokido, L. Barolli, and M. Takizawa (Eds.): NBiS 2007, LNCS 4658, pp. 533–542, 2007.

The open source Globus Toolkit is a popular middleware for constructing a grid computing environment [7]. Globus Toolkit allows users to share securely geographically distributed computing power, databases, and other resources by network connection. This includes many components that users can integrate them conveniently into their applications. Although GT is very convenient for users to construct a grid computing environment, however, there are still some drawbacks when submitting a job with GT. Firstly, many complicated procedures and lots of command-line operations are needed when users submit a job to a grid system using GT. Secondly, submitting jobs to an appropriate computing node with the most available computing resource is an important scheduling problem; however, GT does not provided any information to help users to select the most appropriate node.

Most of the scheduling algorithms determine the system workload by using a threshold. But this approach does not belong in a heterogeneous grid environment, because of the dynamic workload. In our previous work, we proposed a Fuzzy Logic based scheduling algorithm [16] to determine the system workload and performed better than the traditional approaches. However the fuzzy membership functions of the fuzzy variables must be tuned manually and tested many times. With the growth of the number of fuzzy variables, it is too difficult to tune an ideal membership function manually.

In this paper, we proposed a Fuzzy Neural Network which based on the back-propagation network model to train the fuzzy membership functions. The proposed method combines the Neural Network Training Component with the Fuzzy Logic Workload Measurement into a load balancing module. With our approach, the membership functions can be tuned automatically instead of artificial fine-tuning to enhance the system performance conspicuously.

The rest of this paper is organized as follows. Section 2 describes the related work. Section 3 presents the proposed Three-Tier grid architecture. Section 4 describes our load balancing module in detail. Section 5 presents the experimental results. Our conclusions are presented in Section 6.

2 Related Work

In a heterogeneous grid system, the capability of each computing node is different. Therefore, scheduling of a grid system is important, because it allows resources to be used more effectively and enhances the performance of the entire grid system. Many researchers studied the scheduling issues thoroughly [2, 6, 8-11, 14, 16]. Most of the scheduling algorithms determined the system workload by using some fixed thresholds [12, 14-15]. But it is not a good way to determine the system workload. In the heterogeneous grid environment, the system workload is dynamic so precise load information cannot be determined for allocating jobs to the applicable computing nodes.

In our previous work [16], we proposed a Fuzzy Logic Workload Measurement system to measure the system workload of each computing node. With this approach, the workload of each computing node can be forecasted more precisely than using only a threshold. This method allows high performance scheduling to be achieved.

Although using Fuzzy Logic Workload Measurement to measure the system workload of each computing nodes can schedule jobs effectively, it needs manual trial and error to tune the membership function value many times to get a better results. In this paper, we apply the Neural Network to our Fuzzy Logic Workload Measurement to improve this problem. In our proposed Fuzzy Neural Network, it can train the membership function of fuzzy variables automatically and obtain an ideal load balancing result.

3 The Proposed Three-Tier Grid Architecture

In most of the previous approaches, the researchers determined the workload by using a threshold. However, this approach is not suitable for a dynamic environment. Instead of the traditional approaches, we propose a Fuzzy Neural Network based dynamic scheduling scheme that can correctly evaluate the current workload status of each computing node in a grid system. With our scheme, the workload of each computing node in a grid system can be balanced; thereby producing a high performance computing environment. The fuzzy variable membership function does not need to be tuned manually. The proposed three-tier grid architecture consists of a Resource Broker Tier, Grid Head Tier, and Computing Tier, as shown in Fig. 1.

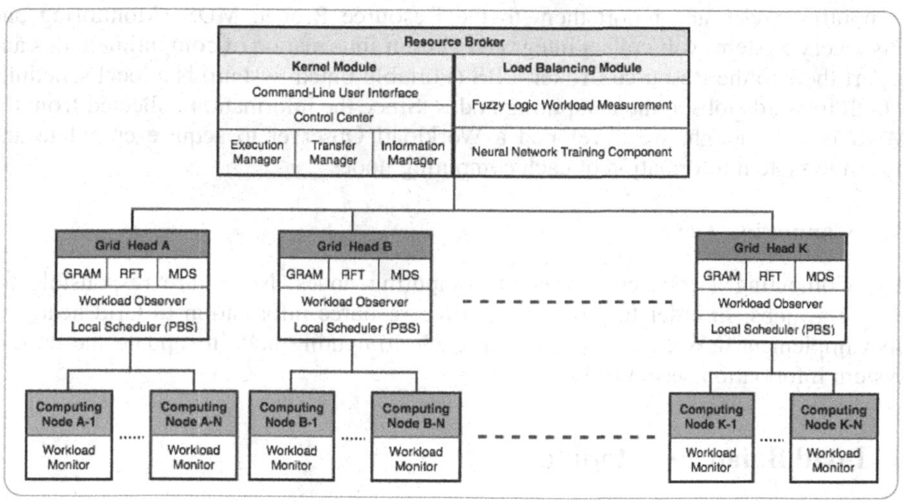

Fig. 1. Three-Tier grid architecture

3.1 Resource Broker Tier

The Resource Broker Tier is comprised of many components and acts as the coordinator between users and resource providers. According to the functionality of components, we grouped the components into two modules in this tier: (1) Kernel Module and (2) Load Balancing Module.

The kernel module includes three layers. The first layer is a Command-Line User Interface. It provides a user friendly interface for job submission. The second layer is the Control Center, it receives user command requirements from the first layer and selects a suitable manager from the third layer to execute them. The third layer is comprised of three managers: (1) Execution Manager: it is used to execute jobs generated from users' requirements; (2) Transfer Manager: it is used to transfer files and related data; (3) Information Manager: it is used to collect information from computing resources.

In the Load Balancing Module, it is composed of Fuzzy Logic Workload Measurement and Neural Network Training Component. The functionality of Fuzzy Logic Workload Measurement is to estimate the workload degree of each computing nodes. And Neural Network Training Component can train the membership functions of fuzzy variables automatically. We will describe the detail of Fuzzy Logic Workload Measurement and Neural Network Training Component in Section 4.

3.2 Grid Head Tier

Grid Head Tier is responsible for submitting jobs to the corresponding computing nodes and communicating with the Resource Broker. Each head is comprised of GRAM, RFT, MDS, PBS and Workload Observer. The first three are GT components. GRAM (Grid Resource Allocation Management) is used to receive commands from the Resource Broker. RFT (Reliable File Transfer) will gather executive results from computing nodes and report them to the Resource Broker. MDS (Monitoring and Discovery System) will collect integrated system information of computing nodes and report them to the Resource Broker. PBS (Portable Batch System) is a local scheduler which forwards jobs to the computing nodes. Since the information collected from the MDS is not enough, we developed a Workload Observer to acquire complete and dynamic system information of each computing nodes.

3.3 Computing Tier

The Computing Tier is composed of computing nodes. Nodes are responsible for executing jobs. In order to provide real time resource information to Grid head, we also implement a Workload Monitor in each computing node to update the current system information periodically.

4 Load Balancing Module

Correctly measure the workload of each computing node in a grid system is an important and difficult issue. By applying the proposed Load Balancing Module, we can accurately evaluate the workload status of each computing node. The Load Balancing Module is comprised of Fuzzy Logic Workload Measurement and Neural Network Training Component. In this section, we will describe them in detail.

4.1 Fuzzy Logic Workload Measurement

In our previous work [16], we presented a workload measurement technique by using Fuzzy Logic. In that work, we apply CPU Utilization and Memory Utilization as the input fuzzy variables. The CPU Utilization includes CPU speed, CPU usage and CPU run queue length. The Memory Utilization consists of the total memory, memory usage and swapped memory. Both fuzzy variables were normalized and characterized by the membership functions defined in (1) to (3).

$$Light\ (x) = \begin{cases} 1, & if\ x<0 \\ 1-2x, & if\ 0 \le x \le 0.5 \end{cases} \tag{1}$$

$$Medium\ (x) = \begin{cases} 2x, & if\ 0 \le x < 0.5 \\ 2-2x & if\ 0.5 \le x < 1 \end{cases} \tag{2}$$

$$Heavy\ (x) = \begin{cases} 2x-1, & if\ 0.5 \le x < 1 \\ 1, & if\ x > 1 \end{cases} \tag{3}$$

The inference rules are used to compute the workload of each node as shown in Table 1. Using the Max-Min inference method and the center-of-gravity defuzzification process, the load degree of each computing node can be obtained.

Table 1. Fuzzy inference rules

Memory \ CPU	**Light**	**Medium**	**Heavy**
Light	Very Light	Medium	Heavy
Medium	Light	Medium	Heavy
Heavy	Medium	Heavy	Very Heavy

Our previous work is described in [16]. The membership function parameters must be tuned to get a better result. In this study, a Fuzzy Neural Network system comprised of a Fuzzy Logic Workload Measurement and a Neural Network Training Component is proposed. The proposed method not only balances the workload of each node well, but also self-organizes the membership functions. The proposed Fuzzy Neural Network architecture is shown in Fig. 2. In the next section, we will describe the Neural Network Training Component in detail.

4.2 Neural Network Training Component

As shown in Fig. 2, the proposed system includes five layers: Input Layer, Hidden Layer X, Hidden Layer Y, Hidden Layer Z and Output Layer. The operations of Neural Network Training Component include feed-forward phase and back-propagation phase, which will be described in the following.

4.2.1 Feed-Forward Phase

In feed-forward phase, the workload information includes CPU Utilization and Memory Utilization as the input to the Input Layer. The input values are then

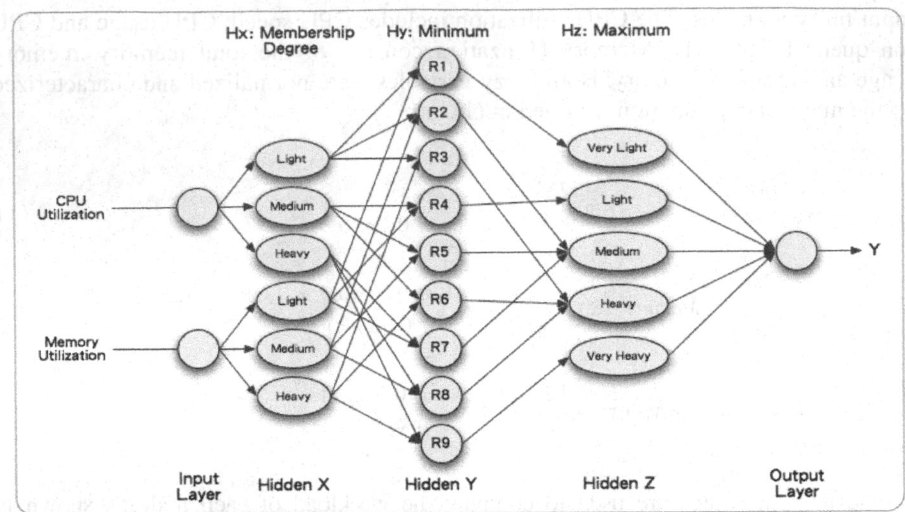

Fig. 2. The Architecture of the Proposed Fuzzy Neural Network

individually fuzzified using three fuzzy sets in the Hidden X layer. The Hidden Y layer displays the nine fuzzy rules applied in this system. For example, rule R_1 indicates that if CPU Utilization is Light and Memory Utilization is Light then the workload is Very Light. In this layer, the neuron computes the minimum value of the fuzzified degrees received from the Hidden X layer, which indicates the degree of match for the condition part of the rule. These minimum values is then send to the linked neuron in Hidden Z layer, and computed by the maximum operator to accomplished the Max-Min rule inference process. The output layer will calculate the workload degree by the center-of-gravity defuzzification.

4.2.2 Back-Propagation Phase

In back-propagation phase, in order to reduce the training overhead, we do the back-propagation training following five times of feed-forward training set. In the training process, it is very important to set the value of tolerance value. The object function is defined as follows:

Avg_{node}: The average grade of each node after five times of feed-forward Process.

Avg_{total} : The average grade of each nodes Avg_{node}.

E_{node}: The object function.

$$Avg_{node} = \sum_{i=1}^{5} y_i / 5 \tag{4}$$

$$Avg_{total} = \sum_{j=1}^{n} Avg_{node_j} / n \tag{5}$$

$$E_{node} = | Avg_{total} - Avg_{node} | + | 0.85 - Avg_{node} | \tag{6}$$

5 Performance Evaluation

To evaluate the performance of our proposed Fuzzy Neural Network scheme, we have constructed a grid computing environment which consist four grid systems by using Globus Toolkit 4, the hardware and software configuration are stated in table 2. We implemented our proposed algorithm along with the Fuzzy Logic, Round-Robin and Random schedulers for performance evaluation.

Table 2. Experimental environment

	Grid A	Grid B	Grid C	Grid D
Grid Head	AMD 1.2GHz 1 GB RAM	P4 2.8GHz 768 MB memory	P4 3.2GHz 1GB RAM	P4 3.2 GHz 1GB RAM
Computing Nodes	AMD XP 1.6GHz 768 MB RAM	AMD XP 1.6GHz 768 MB RAM	P4 3GHz 1GB RAM	P4 3.2 GHz 512 MB RAM
Number of Nodes	7	5	4	8
Software	Debian 3.1r2 ; Globus Toolkit 4.0.2 ; DRBL 1.7.1 ; GCC 3.3.5			

5.1 Experimental Environment

To determine the grid computing performance, many researchers proposed different kinds of benchmark tools and NAS Grid Benchmarks [13] is the most popular. In our experiment we adopted the NAS Grid Benchmarks (NGB) to determine the performance of our proposed scheduling approach. NGB was originally used in NASA (National Aeronautics and Space Administration) to compute the Computational Fluid Dynamics.

In our experiment, we used Embarrassingly Distributed (ED) and Visualization Pipe (VP) testing modules, as shown in Fig. 3 to evaluate the performance of our Fuzzy Neural Network approach and compared with Fuzzy Logic, Round-Robin and

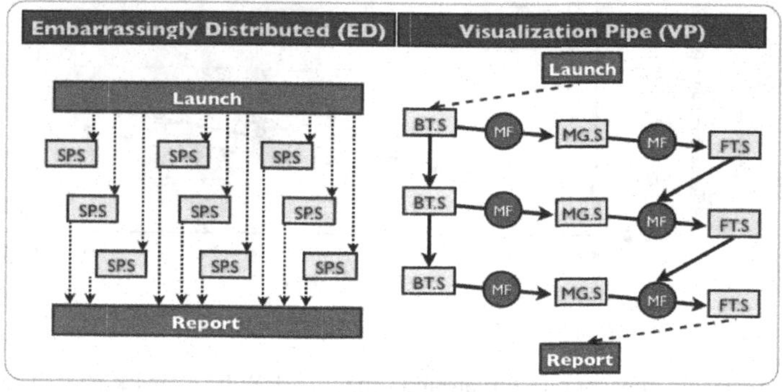

Fig. 3. NGB testing module

Random approaches. The testing module Embarrassingly Distributed (ED) is independent and the module Visualization Pipe (VP) is dependent. These two testing modules are comprised of two different NGB problems: Scalar Pentadiagonal (SP) and Block Tridiagonal (BT). With the difference in the problem sizes, the NGB classes S, W, A, and B were sized from small to large. We used ED.W and VP.W testing modules to evaluate the performance in the following experiments.

5.2 Experimental Results

The turnaround time for executing the ED.W testing module using these four scheduling methods with different number of jobs are shown in Fig. 4. Our proposed scheme had the shortest turnaround time and performed better than the other two

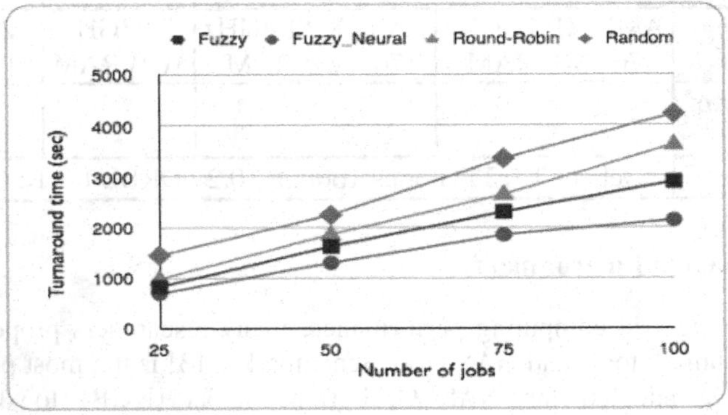

Fig. 4. Performance comparison of turnaround time by ED.W benchmark with different number of jobs

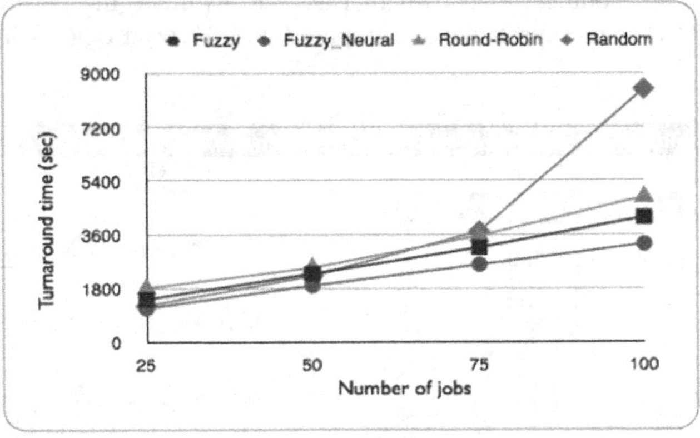

Fig. 5. Performance comparison of turnaround time by VP.W benchmark with different number of jobs

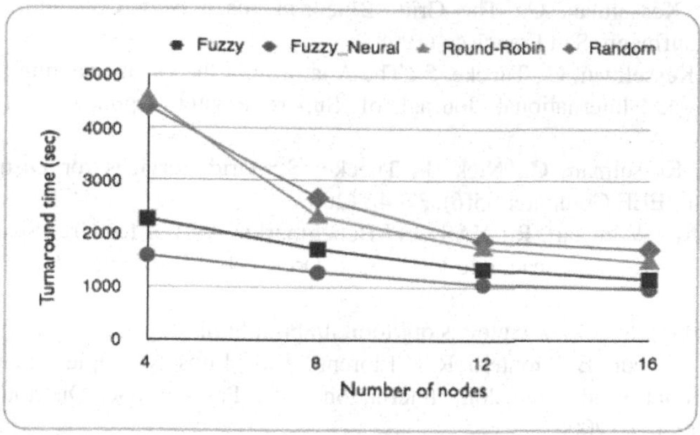

Fig. 6. Performance comparison of turnaround time by ED.W benchmark with different number of computing nodes

approaches when the number of jobs increased. Fig. 5 depicts the turnaround time for executing the VP.W testing module. As shown in the figures, with the growth in the number of jobs, our approach performed better than the other two approaches. The turnaround time with different numbers of nodes is shown in Fig. 6. It illustrates that the Fuzzy Neural approach can reduce the turnaround time when the number of nodes increases. In the experimental results, our Fuzzy Neural approach always produced better performance than the Fuzzy Logic, Round-Robin and Random scheduling methods.

6 Conclusions

We designed and implemented a Resource Broker Module in a grid environment. This module can collect precise workload information from each computing node and automatically process the job submission procedure which originally needs a complicated procedure. In the proposed module, we applied the Fuzzy Logic technique with many fuzzy variables to determine the workload information for each computing node in the grid system. We adopted a Neural Network Training Component to automatically train the membership function defined by the Fuzzy Logic Workload Measurement. We constructed a real grid system using Globus Toolkit 4 and used a well-known benchmark tool to evaluate the system performance. The experimental results show that our approach can reduce the turnaround time efficiently and produce better performance compared with the Fuzzy Logic, Round-Robin and Random scheduling schemes.

References

1. Berman, F., Fox, G., Hey, T.: Grid Computing: Making the Global Infrastructure a Reality. John Wiley & Sons, Chichester (2003)
2. Elmroth, E., Tordsson, J.: An Interoperable, Standards-based Grid Resource Broker and Job Submission Service. In: First International Conference on e-Science and Grid Computing, p. 9 (2005)

3. Foster, I., Kesselman, C.: The Grid: Blueprint for a New Computing Infrastructure. Morgan Kaufmann, San Francisco (1998)
4. Foster, I., Kesselman, C., Tuecke, S.: The Anatomy of the Grid: Enabling Scalable Virtual Organizations. International Journal of Supercomputer Applications 15(3), 200–222 (2001)
5. Foster, I., Kesselman, C., Nick, J., Tuecke, S.: Grid Services for Distributed System Integration. IEEE Computer 35(6), 37–46 (2002)
6. Frumkin, M., Wijngaart, R.: NAS Grid Benchmarks: A Tool for Grid Space Exploration, pp. 247–255. Kluwer Academic Publishers, Dordrecht Manufactured in The Netherlands (2002)
7. Globus (2006), http://www.globus.org/toolkit/about.html
8. Herrera, J., Huedo, E., Montero, R.S., Llorente, I.M.: Loosely-coupled Loop Scheduling in Computational Grids. In: 20th International on Parallel and Distributed Processing Symposium, p. 6 (2006)
9. Montero, R.S., Huedo, E., Llorente, I.M.: Benchmarking of high throughput computing applications on Grids. Instituto Nacional de Te'cnica Aeroespacial Esteban Terradas (INTA) 32(4), 267–279 (2006)
10. Phatanapherom, S., Uthayopas, P., Kachitvichyanukul, V.: Dynamic scheduling II: fast simulation model for grid scheduling using HyperSim. In: Proceedings of the 35th conference on Winter simulation, pp. 1494–1500 (2003)
11. Sabin, G., Sahasrabudhe, V., Sadayappan, P.: On fairness in distributed job scheduling across multiple sites. In: IEEE International Conference on Cluster Computing, pp. 35–44. IEEE, Los Alamitos (2004)
12. Shin, P.-C.: Design and Implementation of a Resource Broker with Network Performance Model on Grid Computing Environments. Master Thesis (2004)
13. Snavely, A., Chun, G., Casanova, H., Wijngaart, R., Michael, A.: Benchmarks for Grid Computing: A Review of Ongoing Efforts and Future Directions. ACM Sigmetrics Performance Evaluation Review 30(4), 27–32 (2003)
14. Song, E., Jeon, Y., Han, S., Jeong, Y.: Hierarchical and Dynamic Information Management Framework on Grid Computing. In: Sha, E., Han, S.-K., Xu, C.-Z., Kim, M.H., Yang, L.T., Xiao, B. (eds.) EUC 2006. LNCS, vol. 4096, pp. 151–161. Springer, Heidelberg (2006)
15. Yagoubi, B., Slimani, Y.: Dynamic Load Balancing Strategy for Grid Computing. Transactions on Engineering, Computing and Technology 13, 260–265 (2006)
16. Zhou, J., Yu, K.-M., Chou, C.-H., Yang, L.-A., Luo, Z.-J.: A Dynamic Resource Broker and Fuzzy Logic Based Scheduling Algorithm in Grid Environment. In: accepted by the International Conference on Adaptive and Natural Computing Algorithms. LNCS, Springer, Heidelberg (2007)

Author Index

Lecture Notes in Computer Science

For information about Vols. 1–4577

please contact your bookseller or Springer

Vol. 4720: B. Konev, F. Wolter (Eds.), Frontiers of Combining Systems. X, 2283 pages. 2007. (Sublibrary LNAI).

Vol. 4708: L. Kučera, A. Kučera (Eds.), Mathematical Foundations of Computer Science 2007. XVIII, 764 pages. 2007.

Vol. 4707: O. Gervasi, M.L. Gavrilova (Eds.), Computational Science and Its Applications – ICCSA 2007, Part III. XXIV, 1205 pages. 2007.

Vol. 4706: O. Gervasi, M.L. Gavrilova (Eds.), Computational Science and Its Applications – ICCSA 2007, Part II. XXIII, 1129 pages. 2007.

Vol. 4705: O. Gervasi, M.L. Gavrilova (Eds.), Computational Science and Its Applications – ICCSA 2007, Part I. XLIV, 1169 pages. 2007.

Vol. 4703: L. Caires, V.T. Vasconcelos (Eds.), CONCUR 2007 – Concurrency Theory. XIII, 507 pages. 2007.

Vol. 4697: L. Choi, Y. Paek, S. Cho (Eds.), Advances in Computer Systems Architecture. XIII, 400 pages. 2007.

Vol. 4685: D.J. Veit, J. Altmann (Eds.), Grid Economics and Business Models. XII, 201 pages. 2007.

Vol. 4683: L. Kang, Y. Liu, S. Zeng (Eds.), Intelligence Computation and Applications. XVII, 663 pages. 2007.

Vol. 4682: D.-S. Huang, L. Heutte, M. Loog (Eds.), Advanced Intelligent Computing Theories and Applications. XXVII, 1373 pages. 2007. (Sublibrary LNAI).

Vol. 4681: D.-S. Huang, L. Heutte, M. Loog (Eds.), Advanced Intelligent Computing Theories and Applications. XXVI, 1379 pages. 2007.

Vol. 4679: A.L. Yuille, S.-C. Zhu, D. Cremers, Y. Wang (Eds.), Energy Minimization Methods in Computer Vision and Pattern Recognition. XII, 494 pages. 2007.

Vol. 4678: J. Blanc-Talon, W. Philips, D. Popescu, P. Scheunders (Eds.), Advanced Concepts for Intelligent Vision Systems. XXIII, 1100 pages. 2007.

Vol. 4673: W.G. Kropatsch, M. Kampel, A. Hanbury (Eds.), Computer Analysis of Images and Patterns. XX, 1006 pages. 2007.

Vol. 4671: V. Malyshkin (Ed.), Parallel Computing Technologies. XIV, 635 pages. 2007.

Vol. 4660: S. Džeroski, J. Todorovski (Eds.), Computational Discovery of Scientific Knowledge. X, 327 pages. 2007. (Sublibrary LNAI).

Vol. 4659: V. Mařík, V. Vyatkin, A.W. Colombo (Eds.), Holonic and Multi-Agent Systems for Manufacturing. VIII, 456 pages. 2007. (Sublibrary LNAI).

Vol. 4658: T. Enokido, L. Barolli, M. Takizawa (Eds.), Network-Based Information Systems. XIII, 544 pages. 2007.

Vol. 4657: C. Lambrinoudakis, G. Pernul, A M. Tjoa (Eds.), Trust and Privacy in Digital Business. XIII, 291 pages. 2007.

Vol. 4656: M.A. Wimmer, J. Scholl, Å. Grönlund (Eds.), Electronic Government. XIV, 450 pages. 2007.

Vol. 4655: G. Psaila, R. Wagner (Eds.), E-Commerce and Web Technologies. VII, 229 pages. 2007.

Vol. 4654: I.Y. Song, J. Eder, T.M. Nguyen (Eds.), Data Warehousing and Knowledge Discovery. XVI, 482 pages. 2007.

Vol. 4651: F. Azevedo, P. Barahona, F. Fages, F. Rossi (Eds.), Recent Advances in Constraints. VIII, 185 pages. 2007. (Sublibrary LNAI).

Vol. 4649: V. Diekert, M.V. Volkov, A. Voronkov (Eds.), Computer Science – Theory and Applications. XIII, 420 pages. 2007.

Vol. 4647: R. Martin, M. Sabin, J. Winkler (Eds.), Mathematics of Surfaces XII. IX, 509 pages. 2007.

Vol. 4645: R. Giancarlo, S. Hannenhalli (Eds.), Algorithms in Bioinformatics. XIII, 432 pages. 2007. (Sublibrary LNBI).

Vol. 4644: N. Azemard, L. Svensson (Eds.), Integrated Circuit and System Design. XIV, 583 pages. 2007.

Vol. 4643: M.-F. Sagot, M.E.M.T. Walter (Eds.), Advances in Bioinformatics and Computational Biology. XII, 177 pages. 2007. (Sublibrary LNBI).

Vol. 4642: S.-W. Lee, S.Z. Li (Eds.), Advances in Biometrics. XX, 1216 pages. 2007.

Vol. 4641: A.-M. Kermarrec, L. Bougé, T. Priol (Eds.), Euro-Par 2007 Parallel Processing. XXVII, 974 pages. 2007.

Vol. 4639: E. Csuhaj-Varjú, Z. Ésik (Eds.), Fundamentals of Computation Theory. XIV, 508 pages. 2007.

Vol. 4638: T. Stützle, M. Birattari, H.H. Hoos (Eds.), Engineering Stochastic Local Search Algorithms. X, 223 pages. 2007.

Vol. 4637: C. Kruegel, R. Lippmann, A. Clark (Eds.), Recent Advances in Intrusion Detection. XII, 337 pages. 2007.

Vol. 4635: B. Kokinov, D.C. Richardson, T.R. Roth-Berghofer, L. Vieu (Eds.), Modeling and Using Context. XIV, 574 pages. 2007. (Sublibrary LNAI).

Vol. 4634: H.R. Nielson, G. Filé (Eds.), Static Analysis. XI, 469 pages. 2007.

Vol. 4633: M. Kamel, A. Campilho (Eds.), Image Analysis and Recognition. XII, 1312 pages. 2007.

Vol. 4632: R. Alhajj, H. Gao, X. Li, J. Li, O.R. Zaïane (Eds.), Advanced Data Mining and Applications. XV, 634 pages. 2007. (Sublibrary LNAI).

Vol. 4628: L.N. de Castro, F.J. Von Zuben, H. Knidel (Eds.), Artificial Immune Systems. XII, 438 pages. 2007.

Vol. 4627: M. Charikar, K. Jansen, O. Reingold, J.D.P. Rolim (Eds.), Approximation, Randomization, and Combinatorial Optimization. XII, 626 pages. 2007.

Vol. 4626: R.O. Weber, M.M. Richter (Eds.), Case-Based Reasoning Research and Development. XIII, 534 pages. 2007. (Sublibrary LNAI).

Vol. 4624: T. Mossakowski, U. Montanari, M. Haveraaen (Eds.), Algebra and Coalgebra in Computer Science. XI, 463 pages. 2007.

Vol. 4622: A. Menezes (Ed.), Advances in Cryptology - CRYPTO 2007. XIV, 631 pages. 2007.

Vol. 4619: F. Dehne, J.-R. Sack, N. Zeh (Eds.), Algorithms and Data Structures. XVI, 662 pages. 2007.

Vol. 4618: S.G. Akl, C.S. Calude, M.J. Dinneen, G. Rozenberg, H.T. Wareham (Eds.), Unconventional Computation. X, 243 pages. 2007.

Vol. 4617: V. Torra, Y. Narukawa, Y. Yoshida (Eds.), Modeling Decisions for Artificial Intelligence. XII, 502 pages. 2007. (Sublibrary LNAI).

Vol. 4616: A. Dress, Y. Xu, B. Zhu (Eds.), Combinatorial Optimization and Applications. XI, 390 pages. 2007.

Vol. 4615: R. de Lemos, C. Gacek, A. Romanovsky (Eds.), Architecting Dependable Systems IV. XIV, 435 pages. 2007.

Vol. 4613: F.P. Preparata, Q. Fang (Eds.), Frontiers in Algorithmics. XI, 348 pages. 2007.

Vol. 4612: I. Miguel, W. Ruml (Eds.), Abstraction, Reformulation, and Approximation. XI, 418 pages. 2007. (Sublibrary LNAI).

Vol. 4611: J. Indulska, J. Ma, L.T. Yang, T. Ungerer, J. Cao (Eds.), Ubiquitous Intelligence and Computing. XXIII, 1257 pages. 2007.

Vol. 4610: B. Xiao, L.T. Yang, J. Ma, C. Muller-Schloer, Y. Hua (Eds.), Autonomic and Trusted Computing. XVIII, 571 pages. 2007.

Vol. 4609: E. Ernst (Ed.), ECOOP 2007 – Object-Oriented Programming. XIII, 625 pages. 2007.

Vol. 4608: H.W. Schmidt, I. Crnkovic, G.T. Heineman, J.A. Stafford (Eds.), Component-Based Software Engineering. XII, 283 pages. 2007.

Vol. 4607: L. Baresi, P. Fraternali, G.-J. Houben (Eds.), Web Engineering. XVI, 576 pages. 2007.

Vol. 4606: A. Pras, M. van Sinderen (Eds.), Dependable and Adaptable Networks and Services. XIV, 149 pages. 2007.

Vol. 4605: D. Papadias, D. Zhang, G. Kollios (Eds.), Advances in Spatial and Temporal Databases. X, 479 pages. 2007.

Vol. 4604: U. Priss, S. Polovina, R. Hill (Eds.), Conceptual Structures: Knowledge Architectures for Smart Applications. XII, 514 pages. 2007. (Sublibrary LNAI).

Vol. 4603: F. Pfenning (Ed.), Automated Deduction – CADE-21. XII, 522 pages. 2007. (Sublibrary LNAI).

Vol. 4602: S. Barker, G.-J. Ahn (Eds.), Data and Applications Security XXI. X, 291 pages. 2007.

Vol. 4600: H. Comon-Lundh, C. Kirchner, H. Kirchner (Eds.), Rewriting, Computation and Proof. XVI, 273 pages. 2007.

Vol. 4599: S. Vassiliadis, M. Berekovic, T.D. Hämäläinen (Eds.), Embedded Computer Systems: Architectures, Modeling, and Simulation. XVIII, 466 pages. 2007.

Vol. 4598: G. Lin (Ed.), Computing and Combinatorics. XII, 570 pages. 2007.

Vol. 4597: P. Perner (Ed.), Advances in Data Mining. XI, 353 pages. 2007. (Sublibrary LNAI).

Vol. 4596: L. Arge, C. Cachin, T. Jurdziński, A. Tarlecki (Eds.), Automata, Languages and Programming. XVII, 953 pages. 2007.

Vol. 4595: D. Bošnački, S. Edelkamp (Eds.), Model Checking Software. X, 285 pages. 2007.

Vol. 4594: R. Bellazzi, A. Abu-Hanna, J. Hunter (Eds.), Artificial Intelligence in Medicine. XVI, 509 pages. 2007. (Sublibrary LNAI).

Vol. 4593: A. Biryukov (Ed.), Fast Software Encryption. XI, 467 pages. 2007.

Vol. 4592: Z. Kedad, N. Lammari, E. Métais, F. Meziane, Y. Rezgui (Eds.), Natural Language Processing and Information Systems. XIV, 442 pages. 2007.

Vol. 4591: J. Davies, J. Gibbons (Eds.), Integrated Formal Methods. IX, 660 pages. 2007.

Vol. 4590: W. Damm, H. Hermanns (Eds.), Computer Aided Verification. XV, 562 pages. 2007.

Vol. 4589: J. Münch, P. Abrahamsson (Eds.), Product-Focused Software Process Improvement. XII, 414 pages. 2007.

Vol. 4588: T. Harju, J. Karhumäki, A. Lepistö (Eds.), Developments in Language Theory. XI, 423 pages. 2007.

Vol. 4587: R. Cooper, J. Kennedy (Eds.), Data Management. XIII, 259 pages. 2007.

Vol. 4586: J. Pieprzyk, H. Ghodosi, E. Dawson (Eds.), Information Security and Privacy. XIV, 476 pages. 2007.

Vol. 4585: M. Kryszkiewicz, J.F. Peters, H. Rybinski, A. Skowron (Eds.), Rough Sets and Intelligent Systems Paradigms. XIX, 836 pages. 2007. (Sublibrary LNAI).

Vol. 4584: N. Karssemeijer, B. Lelieveldt (Eds.), Information Processing in Medical Imaging. XX, 777 pages. 2007.

Vol. 4583: S.R. Della Rocca (Ed.), Typed Lambda Calculi and Applications. X, 397 pages. 2007.

Vol. 4582: J. Lopez, P. Samarati, J.L. Ferrer (Eds.), Public Key Infrastructure. XI, 375 pages. 2007.

Vol. 4581: A. Petrenko, M. Veanes, J. Tretmans, W. Grieskamp (Eds.), Testing of Software and Communicating Systems. XII, 379 pages. 2007.

Vol. 4580: B. Ma, K. Zhang (Eds.), Combinatorial Pattern Matching. XII, 366 pages. 2007.

Vol. 4579: B. M. Hämmerli, R. Sommer (Eds.), Detection of Intrusions and Malware, and Vulnerability Assessment. X, 251 pages. 2007.

Vol. 4578: F. Masulli, S. Mitra, G. Pasi (Eds.), Applications of Fuzzy Sets Theory. XVIII, 693 pages. 2007. (Sublibrary LNAI).